Lecture Notes in Computer Science   11570

Commenced Publication in 1973
Founding and Former Series Editors:
Gerhard Goos, Juris Hartmanis, and Jan van Leeuwen

Sakae Yamamoto · Hirohiko Mori (Eds.)

Human Interface and the Management of Information

Information in Intelligent Systems

Thematic Area, HIMI 2019
Held as Part of the 21st HCI International Conference, HCII 2019
Orlando, FL, USA, July 26–31, 2019
Proceedings, Part II

 Springer

Editors
Sakae Yamamoto
Tokyo University of Science
Tokyo, Japan

Hirohiko Mori
Tokyo City University
Tokyo, Japan

ISSN 0302-9743   ISSN 1611-3349   (electronic)
Lecture Notes in Computer Science
ISBN 978-3-030-22648-0   ISBN 978-3-030-22649-7   (eBook)
https://doi.org/10.1007/978-3-030-22649-7

LNCS Sublibrary: SL3 – Information Systems and Applications, incl. Internet/Web, and HCI

This Springer imprint is published by the registered company Springer Nature Switzerland AG
The registered company address is: Gewerbestrasse 11, 6330 Cham, Switzerland

Foreword

The 21st International Conference on Human-Computer Interaction, HCI International 2019, was held in Orlando, FL, USA, during July 26–31, 2019. The event incorporated the 18 thematic areas and affiliated conferences listed on the following page.

A total of 5,029 individuals from academia, research institutes, industry, and governmental agencies from 73 countries submitted contributions, and 1,274 papers and 209 posters were included in the pre-conference proceedings. These contributions address the latest research and development efforts and highlight the human aspects of design and use of computing systems. The contributions thoroughly cover the entire field of human-computer interaction, addressing major advances in knowledge and effective use of computers in a variety of application areas. The volumes constituting the full set of the pre-conference proceedings are listed in the following pages.

This year the HCI International (HCII) conference introduced the new option of "late-breaking work." This applies both for papers and posters and the corresponding volume(s) of the proceedings will be published just after the conference. Full papers will be included in the *HCII 2019 Late-Breaking Work Papers Proceedings* volume of the proceedings to be published in the Springer LNCS series, while poster extended abstracts will be included as short papers in the HCII 2019 *Late-Breaking Work Poster Extended Abstracts* volume to be published in the Springer CCIS series.

I would like to thank the program board chairs and the members of the program boards of all thematic areas and affiliated conferences for their contribution to the highest scientific quality and the overall success of the HCI International 2019 conference.

This conference would not have been possible without the continuous and unwavering support and advice of the founder, Conference General Chair Emeritus and Conference Scientific Advisor Prof. Gavriel Salvendy. For his outstanding efforts, I would like to express my appreciation to the communications chair and editor of *HCI International News,* Dr. Abbas Moallem.

July 2019   Constantine Stephanidis

HCI International 2019 Thematic Areas and Affiliated Conferences

Thematic areas:

- HCI 2019: Human-Computer Interaction
- HIMI 2019: Human Interface and the Management of Information

Affiliated conferences:

- EPCE 2019: 16th International Conference on Engineering Psychology and Cognitive Ergonomics
- UAHCI 2019: 13th International Conference on Universal Access in Human-Computer Interaction
- VAMR 2019: 11th International Conference on Virtual, Augmented and Mixed Reality
- CCD 2019: 11th International Conference on Cross-Cultural Design
- SCSM 2019: 11th International Conference on Social Computing and Social Media
- AC 2019: 13th International Conference on Augmented Cognition
- DHM 2019: 10th International Conference on Digital Human Modeling and Applications in Health, Safety, Ergonomics and Risk Management
- DUXU 2019: 8th International Conference on Design, User Experience, and Usability
- DAPI 2019: 7th International Conference on Distributed, Ambient and Pervasive Interactions
- HCIBGO 2019: 6th International Conference on HCI in Business, Government and Organizations
- LCT 2019: 6th International Conference on Learning and Collaboration Technologies
- ITAP 2019: 5th International Conference on Human Aspects of IT for the Aged Population
- HCI-CPT 2019: First International Conference on HCI for Cybersecurity, Privacy and Trust
- HCI-Games 2019: First International Conference on HCI in Games
- MobiTAS 2019: First International Conference on HCI in Mobility, Transport, and Automotive Systems
- AIS 2019: First International Conference on Adaptive Instructional Systems

HCI International 2019 Thematic Areas
and Affiliated Conferences

Pre-conference Proceedings Volumes Full List

34. CCIS 1033, HCI International 2019 - Posters (Part II), edited by Constantine Stephanidis
35. CCIS 1034, HCI International 2019 - Posters (Part III), edited by Constantine Stephanidis

http://2019.hci.international/proceedings

Human Interface and the Management of Information (HIMI 2019)

Program Board Chair(s): **Sakae Yamamoto and Hirohiko Mori,** *Japan*

- Takako Akakura, Japan
- Yumi Asahi, Japan
- Linda Elliott, USA
- Shin'ichi Fukuzumi, Japan
- Tetsuya Harada, Japan
- Naotake Hirasawa, Japan
- Michitaka Hirose, Japan
- Yasushi Ikei, Japan
- Keiko Kasamatsu, Japan
- Daiji Kobayashi, Japan
- Kentaro Kotani, Japan
- Hiroyuki Miki, Japan
- Ryosuke Saga, Japan
- Katsunori Shimohara, Japan
- Takahito Tomoto, Japan
- Kim-Phuong L. Vu, USA
- Marcelo Wanderley, Canada
- Tomio Watanabe, Japan
- Takehiko Yamaguchi, Japan

The full list with the Program Board Chairs and the members of the Program Boards of all thematic areas and affiliated conferences is available online at:

http://www.hci.international/board-members-2019.php

HCI International 2020

The 22nd International Conference on Human-Computer Interaction, HCI International 2020, will be held jointly with the affiliated conferences in Copenhagen, Denmark, at the Bella Center Copenhagen, July 19–24, 2020. It will cover a broad spectrum of themes related to HCI, including theoretical issues, methods, tools, processes, and case studies in HCI design, as well as novel interaction techniques, interfaces, and applications. The proceedings will be published by Springer. More information will be available on the conference website: http://2020.hci.international/.

General Chair
Prof. Constantine Stephanidis
University of Crete and ICS-FORTH
Heraklion, Crete, Greece
E-mail: general_chair@hcii2020.org

http://2020.hci.international/

Contents – Part II

Haptic and Tactile Interaction

Information in Virtual and Augmented Reality

Machine Learning and Intelligent Systems

Human Motion and Expression Recognition and Tracking

Medicine, Healthcare and Quality of Life Applications

Contents – Part I

Data Visualization and Analytics

Information, Cognition and Learning

Information, Empathy and Persuasion

Knowledge Management and Sharing

Haptic and Tactile Interaction

Novel Display Using Percutaneous Electrical Stimulation for Virtual Reality

Kazuma Aoyama[1,2(✉)]

[1] Graduate School of Information Science and Technology,
The University of Tokyo, 7-3-1 Hongo, Bunkyo-ku, Tokyo 113-8656, Japan
`aoyama@vr.u-tokyo.ac.jp`
[2] Virtual Reality Educational Research Center,
The University of Tokyo, Tokyo, Japan

Abstract. Percutaneous electrical stimulation (PES) is a technology that induces various sensations by electrically stimulating sensory nerves and organs non-invasively. In the PES, the neural systems such as the sensory nerves, sensory organs, and brain nerves by applying the electrical current form the electrodes attached on the skin. PES induces various such as vestibular, visual, taste, and haptic sensations using small, lightweight devices with reasonable cost. Thus, this technology is expected to be used in sensory display systems in the fields of virtual reality and human computer interaction. The purpose of this paper is to introduce these technologies, methods, and applications with particular focus on vestibular sensation, visual sensation, and gustatory sensation; these PES methods are called galvanic vestibular stimulation, galvanic sight stimulation, and galvanic gustatory stimulation, respectively. Our research group developed a sensation display and applications using these technologies. This paper introduces our previous studies and applications, and the prospect of using these PES technologies for sensory displays in VR is discussed.

Keywords: Galvanic stimulation · Electrical stimulation ·
Percutaneous electrical stimulation · Virtual reality ·
Sensory display technology

1 Introduction

Sensory display technologies are one of the most important technologies in virtual reality (VR) and augmented reality (AR). Conventional sensory displays, including visual sensory displays, monitors, and head-mounted displays (HMDs), attempt to replicate physical phenomena. These visual displays include a light source and replicate physical phenomena such as optical waves. In another example, a motion platform is used for vestibular sensation in a 4D theater. This technology replicates physical phenomena such as acceleration and angular velocity by jerking, shunting, and rolling the chair and cabin ride.

Because human sensory systems such as vision, haptics, vestibular, taste, and others detect physical phenomena, these methods can induce natural sensation. However, there are problems in that devices that replicate various phenomena become large,

S. Yamamoto and H. Mori (Eds.): HCII 2019, LNCS 11570, pp. 3–14, 2019.
https://doi.org/10.1007/978-3-030-22649-7_1

heavy, and incur high costs. For example, a motion platform for vestibular display is extremely large, heavy, and incurs high costs, and while HMDs have become lighter, they are still heavy.

Percutaneous electrical stimulation (PES) may resolve these problems. PES is a technology for stimulating nerves and organs non-invasively. This technology only requires devices with light weight, small size, and reasonable electrical stimulation, and it could become a cost-efficient sensation display.

Recently, PES was used in neuro science and brain research. Three types of PES technologies, i.e., transcranial direct current stimulation (tDCS), transcranial alternate current stimulation (tACS), and transcranial random noise stimulation (tRNS), are used to modulate brain activity [1–3]. Different stimulation waveforms are used in these technologies. The waveforms used in tDCS, tACS, and tRNS are direct current, alternate current, and random current wave, respectively. Although these methods can modulate brain activities, these do not induce perceptible effects. Currently, these brain stimulation methods cannot be used with virtual reality (VR), where users perceive sensations and experience the world simultaneously.

In contrast, some kinds of PES methods can be used to stimulate sensory organs and nerves. These methods can induce various sensations such as vestibular, visual, and gustatory sensations. Because these PES methods can be used to stimulate the sensory nerves and organs non-invasively, these technologies have been conventionally used for medical checking.

Our research group expects that these technologies could be applied in sensory displays for VR. Three kinds of PES stimulation methods for inducing sensation, i.e., galvanic sight stimulation (GSS), galvanic vestibular stimulation (GVS), and galvanic gustatory stimulation (GGS), are introduced and discussed in this paper. GSS is a method used to induce visual sensation without a light source, GVS is used to induce vestibular sensation, including acceleration and angular velocity or virtual head motion, and GGS can be used to electrically modulate taste.

2 Galvanic Sight Stimulation

Many HMDs are commercially available. HMD is a device for displaying visual information with a visual display device placed on the head. An HMD is useful in applications such as VR, which provides an immersive experience in a virtual world, and in AR, which appends information to objects in the real world in the form of letters and figures. Of the HMDs suitable for VR, Oculus Rift and HTC Vive are popular. Of the HMDs suitable for AR, Google Glass and Microsoft HoloLens are well known.

There are three types of HMDs: non-see through HMD, video see through HMD, and optical see through HMD. Only see through HMDs are suitable for use in AR. HMDs for AR are eyeglasses or goggle-type devices that provide information by superimposing annotations and/or figures on the real world. These HMDs must have a wide viewing angle because the objects with added annotations must be within the display area. However, because HMDs are designed for wearable devices, their visual systems are small in order to reduce the weight of these devices, thus they can mostly display a narrow range of images. For example, the visual field range of Google Glass is 14° and that of Microsoft HoloLens is 40°. This is contrary to the 200° range of the human visual field [4]. Thus, an HMD user cannot obtain necessary annotation information at a high frequency because the object on which an annotation should be displayed does not exist within the visual field range of the HMD.

GSS may be ideal for use in lightweight HMDs with wide viewing angle. GSS can induce visual sensation with a flash of light, called a phosphene, by applying an electric current through the skin around the eyes.

Kanai et al. first reported the phenomenon that PES around the eye induces phosphene [5]. Although Kanai considered that phosphenes were caused by electric stimulation to the visual area of the brain, a series of subsequent studies revealed that electrical current was stimulating the peripheral nerve system such as the retina rather than the visual cortex [6]. We support the hypothesis that GSS stimulates the peripheral nerves.

However, the use of GSS rather than an HMD for visual display presents some problems. Conventional GSS cannot be used to display changes in the position, shape, and color of a phosphene. A method for changing the positions of phosphenes is introduced here. If we could present a phosphene at an arbitrary position and direction, it would be possible to indicate the position of a real object on which an annotation should be displayed.

In PES to the peripheral nerve, the position of the electrode and the spatial direction or intensity of the current dominantly determines the characteristic of the evoked sensation. According to these factors, GSS can also be used to selectively activate or deactivate nerves that accept vision by varying the current direction and current density distribution on the retina and visual nerves.

Photoreceptors are lined up on the surface of the retina. It is considered that the nerve in the region corresponding to the current density distribution formed on the retina and optic nerve ignites when an electric current is applied here. Therefore, it is expected that the position where the phosphene is created can be controlled by changing the position of the stimulation electrode around the eyes. We developed a novel method called multi-electrode GSS and show that it can be used to change the position of a phosphene.

2.1   Experiment and Results: Changing the Phosphene Position with Multi-electrode GSS

The relationship between the position of the electrodes and the position of the phosphene are investigated in this experiment. Five healthy adult males participated in this experiment. Informed consent was obtained from all subjects prior to performing the experiment. Seven electrodes (Clearode, Fukudadenshi, Inc.) were attached on the face of each subject. The experiment was conducted in a dark, quiet room. Subjects sat on a chair and their foreheads and chins were held fixed. Subjects measured the position of each electrode, left and right tail of the eyes, and nasion with a marker held in the hand. They closed their eyes and faced forward, and a stimulation current was applied. After stimulation, the subjects held the marker at the positions of where they perceived phosphenes, and we measured the position of each phosphene. When subjects perceived multiple phosphenes, they positioned the marker in order of high to low intensity of visual sensation. We measured the positions of electrodes, eye cones, and nasion with a three-dimensional motion capture system (Optitrack V120 Duo).

The 5.0 Hz alternating square wave stimulation current ranged from –0.30 to 0.30 mA with 4.0 s duration (Fig. 1-B). The electrodes were positioned in seven patterns: bilateral above the brows (E1–E7), bilateral under the eyes (E3–E5), bilateral outside of the eyes (E2–E6), outside the right eye and the nasion (E2–E4), outside the left eye and nasion (E4–E6), above the right brow and under the left eye (E1–E3), and above the left brow and under the left eye (E5–E7). These conditions allow stimulation of at least one eyeball along a straight line connecting the electrodes. Each arrangement was examined four times, yielding a total of 28 trials.

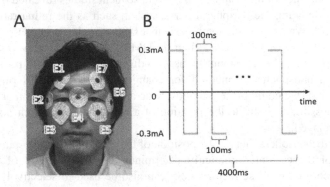

Fig. 1. The position of electrodes and stimulation current pattern [4].

Figure 2 shows the position of the phosphenes perceived for each stimulus condition in one subject from the front view and overhead view. The other subjects' results are available online. In these figures, the origin of the coordinate system is the gravity position (center position) of the right eye corner, left eye corner, and nasion. The horizontal axis is parallel to the line connecting eye corners and passing through the origin. The front/rear axis is parallel to the line connecting the origin and the nasion. The upper/lower line is vertical to the line connecting the origin and the nasion. The large gray ellipses in the figures show the positions of the subject's eyes. They are drawn as ellipses with a short side of 12 mm and a long side of 16 mm from the eye canes. The "x" markers indicate the position of the nasion. The small white ellipses indicate the electrode position, the small black ellipses indicate the electrode pair to which the stimulation current was applied, and the "*" markers indicate the position of the phosphenes perceived by the subject. Figure 2 shows the average position of each electrode, both eye corners, the nasion, and phosphenes perceived by each subject, while Fig. 3 shows the results from all subjects displayed on one set of plots. These figures indicate the subjects perceived phosphenes near the stimulation electrode, and this tendency was confirmed with patterns other than the E1–E7 stimulation pattern. Moreover, the average probability that each electrode was closest to the phosphenes in each case is shown in Fig. 4. This probability is the number of electrodes nearest to the phosphenes, divided by the total number of phosphenes perceived by each subject with each pattern. The "*" in Fig. 4 indicates a significant difference as determined from ANOVA ($p < 0.05$). Thus, the probability that the stimulated electrodes are the closest electrodes from the positions of the phosphenes is significantly higher.

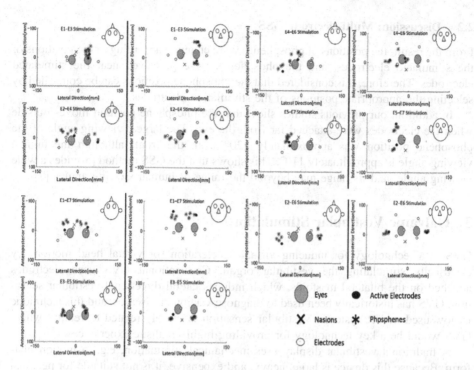

Fig. 2. Positions of phosphenes perceived by all subjects with E1–E7 stimulation patterns [4].

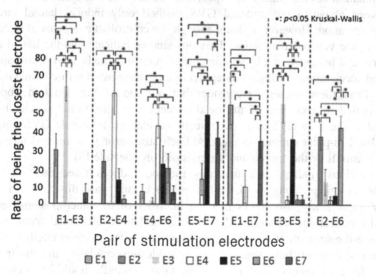

Fig. 3. Probability that each electrode is closest to the phosphenes [4].

2.2 Discussion: Multi-electrode GSS

From the result, the positions of phosphenes were changed according to the positions of the stimulated electrodes, and the phosphenes were perceived near the stimulated electrodes. Therefore, it is considered that the phosphene positions can be controlled by selecting the appropriate positions of the stimulation electrodes.

In addition, our previous studies show that the phosphene position moves outside when the electrodes were attached far from the eye. The largest viewing angle of the phosphene position was approximately 120° from the front; although the human viewing angle is approximately 110°. This shows that the GSS method provides a wide viewing angle, and its range may beyond the range of human viewing angles [7].

3 Galvanic Vestibular Stimulation

GVS is a technology for inducing virtual acceleration (or virtual head motion) by electrically stimulating the vestibular organ. Conventional GVS uses electrodes attached on the bilateral mastoids, which induces lateral directional vestibular sensation. GVS has historically been used to diagnose vestibular diseases, and this technique is now used in VR systems. Vestibular sensation is closely related to reality, where GVS would be a key technology for providing highly realistic experiences.

A traditional vestibular display uses mechanical stimulation, e.g., a motion platform. Because this device is large, heavy, and expensive, it is not suitable for personal use. On the other hand, GVS only requires a small, lightweight, and reasonable electrical stimulation device; thus, it is expected to be used in VR systems.

As noted above, a conventional GVS method only induces lateral directional vestibular sensation. However, it is not enough the controllable degrees of freedom for direction of the vestibular sensation. Previous studies indicate that the lateral acceleration is induced by applying a lateral directional current to the head and anteroposterior directional acceleration is induced by applying an anteroposterior directional current to the head. From these studies, we consider that an opposite directional anteroposterior current applied to each side of the head induces yaw directional acceleration. We developed a four-pole GVS to provide such stimulation. Four-pole GVS consists of three isolated bi-polar current stimulators. Each stimulator is connected to either the bilateral mastoids or the temple and the mastoid on one side [8].

Our previous studies show that this method induces three-directional virtual vestibular sensations along the lateral, front-back, and yaw directional directions. However, these study also shows that the intensity of the anteroposterior and yaw rotational accelerations are weaker than that of the lateral directional acceleration.

Because the strength of vestibular sensation correlates to the strength of the stimulation, the strong vestibular sensation is available by stimulating the strong current. However, from the aspect of safety, the stimulation strength should be limited. In our previous studies, the current strength should be limited to 3.0 mA [4, 7, 9]. We developed countercurrent stimulation (CCS) to induce stronger vestibular sensation using a current. CCS consists of two parts of stimulation, i.e., an opposite current part and forwarding current part. Here, forwarding current is the GVS current which induces the vestibular sensation directed to the intended direction and opposite current is that of inverted polarity. The vestibular sensation induced by the forward current is enhanced by the shift of electrical charges in the opposite current part. Our previous study shows that CCS evokes angular changes up to a factor 4 larger than those evoked under normal constant current stimulation [10]. We developed a demo that allows users to feel vestibular sensation while watching a VR movie.

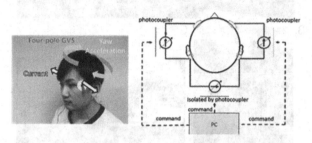

Fig. 4. Images for four-pole galvanic vestibular stimulation (left) and stimulation apparatus (right) [11].

3.1 Application: GVS RIDE: Multi-directional Vestibular Sensation Synchronized with a First Person Movie

We developed a demo using four-pole GVS and VR HMD, which we named "GVS RIDE." In the GVS RIDE, users watch a first person movie in which they are riding a roller coaster. Four-pole GVS is used to induce virtual vestibular sensation that mimics motion in the virtual world. Users perceive a higher sense of presence in the virtual world. We exhibited the demo at Computer Entertainment Developers Conference 2016, Tokyo Game Show 2016, Siggraph 2017, Laval Virtual 2017, and other exhibitions. Most users and visitors reported that this experience is closer to reality than a normal VR experience without vestibular sensation. However, some people reported a ticking sensation behind their ear [11, 12] (Fig. 5).

We developed the "Beaten by a Virtual Character" as another demo using HMD, GVS, and GSS. In this demo, users play a first person fighting game with a virtual character in a virtual world. When users were punched by the opposing character, users feel vestibular sensation and perceive a phosphene induced by GVS and GSS. Although it is difficult to have users experience damage effects in conventional fighting games, our novel demo allows users to perceive such effects.

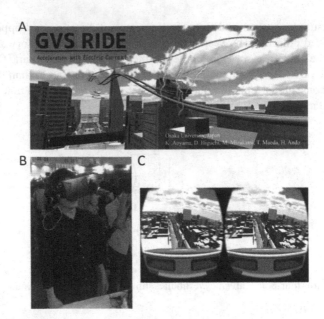

Fig. 5. Application of four-pole GVS. (A) Poster of GVS RIDE. (B) GVS RIDE demonstration. (C) First person movie seen by a user [11].

4 Galvanic Gustatory Stimulation

Galvanic gustatory stimulation (GGS) is a technology for modifying (induce, suppress, and enhance) taste sensation by applying electrical current stimulation to the mouth. Conventionally, electrical stimulation has been used for gustatory testing in the medical field. Recently, because GGS can be used to modify taste sensation, this technology was used for taste display in VR and human computer interaction in some previous studies [13, 14]. For example, a previous study conducted by Nakamura et al. (2013) proposed methods for applying electrical current to the mouth using a stimulation device whose electrode form is like folk and cup [13]. Ranasinghe et al. invented a method for inducing salty, sour, sweet, and bitter tastes by applying an electrical pulse through electrodes on the tongue [14]. Regarding the effect of inhibition and enhancement in GGS, we shows that GGS inhibits or enhances five basic tastes [15]. In this work, we investigated the inhibitory effects of GGS. We thought ionic migration in taste material water solution causes taste suppression. Then we tested whether or not GGS is effective with non-electrolyte (caffeine) and electrolyte ($MgCl_2$) water solutions as both materials are perceived as bitter. Taste suppression with GGS was only effective with an electrolyte water solution. This result supports the adequacy of ionic migration as the mechanism for taste suppression.

GGS may be a gustatory display that can be used to control taste sensation. It would help solve obesity and hypertension by supporting dieting. In particular, it could help people reduce their salt intake. In order to address such diseases, reducing salt intake requires modifying dietary habits.

However, GGS methods have two problems. One is that these require attaching electrodes or wires in the mouth. In terms of using GSS for supporting dietary habits, electrodes and wires should not be attached in a user's mouth because these disturb eating and drinking. Another problem is that the enhancement effect of GGS cannot continue after continuous eating and drinking. Our preliminary experiment shows that the enhancement effect of GGS persists for a few seconds. However, eating may take less than 5 s. Therefore, the effect of enhancing taste should persist for at least 5 s.

4.1   Continuous Square Current Stimulation and Galvanic Chin Stimulation

In our previous study [15], the mechanism of taste suppression via electrical stimulation can be described as follows: ionized materials, which trigger taste receptors, move away from the surface of the tongue due to electrical stimulation, as shown in Fig. 6. The decreased concentration of ions on the tongue results in taste suppression. On the other hand, the mechanism of taste enhancement is still not fully understood. Nevertheless, it seems that the suppression mechanism is associated with electrophoresis.

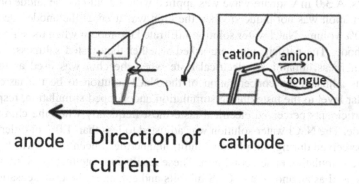

Fig. 6. Electrophoresis during cathode stimulation [16].

The enhancement duration is too short for this technology to support dieting. To solve these problems, we proposed using continuous square current stimulation. In the continuous square current stimulation, cathodes were attached near the mouth and anodes were attached on the back of neck, and a 10 to 15 Hz square wave was applied. Our previous work showed that this type of stimulation enhances taste with long duration [16] (Fig. 7).

In a previous work, stimulation was applied with a lead or a cathode attached on a straw. The anode was attached on the forehead or the back of the neck using a gel electrode. From the perspective of electrophoresis in the inner mouth, it is assumed that the cathode does not need to be attached in the mouth. It is generally known that attaching an anode in the mouth induces strong taste sensation, cathodal stimulation in the mouth does not induce a taste sensation. This phenomenon suggests that the gustatory nerve has selective response to the direction of electrical current. Thus, taste suppression or results if the electric potential of the tongue is lower than the electric

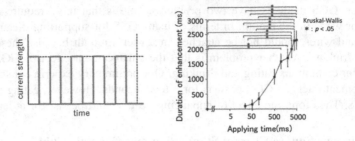

Fig. 7. Continuous square wave stimulation (left) and the duration of taste enhancement as a function of frequency (right) [16].

potential of food or solution. According to this hypothesis, we attached a cathode on the chin and anodal electrode attached on the back of neck. We called this stimulation method galvanic chin stimulation (GCS) [16]. Our previous study showed that GCS can be used to induce, suppress, and enhance taste sensation.

In the experiment, electrodes were attached on the chin and the back of the neck of participants. A 3.0 mA square wave was applied with the chin as the anode or cathode. A taste sensation was not induced when the chin was used as the anode. On the other hand, a 1.0% volume NaCl water solution infiltrated the mouth when the chin was used as the cathode. The participants were asked whether they tasted saltiness, sweetness, acidity, bitterness, umami, or electrical taste when the chin was used as the anode. Participants adjusted the concentration of the NaCl solution to be the taste strength were similar level to the taste during stimulation and stopped stimulation, respectively.

All participants perceived electrical taste most frequently when the chin was used as the anode. The NaCl water solution was adjusted to less than 1.0% in order to match the taste perceived during stimulation condition, and the concentration was higher than 1.0% in the stimulation ended condition. These results indicate that GCS induces when the chin is used as an anode, and GCS inhibits and enhances the taste sensation during stimulation and after stimulation [17] (Fig. 8).

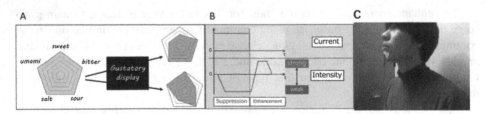

Fig. 8. (A) Galvanic chin stimulation, (B) continuous square wave stimulation, and (C) electrode attached to the inferior part of chin [16].

5   Conclusion and Future Work

PES can be used to induce various sensations using only small, lightweight electrical stimulation devices and could be used in a wearable sensory display device in the future. However, there are some problems in the PES technology. The most important problem is that a ticking sensation occurs at the skin under the surface electrode. PES current always passes through the skin and stimulates the tactile nerves and organs. This can induce pressure, vibration, and ticking sensations. This disturbs the perception of sensory information. The simplest solution is to reduce the current density on the interface between the skin and the electrodes. This requires cleaning the skin and using large electrodes. However, using large electrodes may activate unexpected nerves and organs. Therefore, the design of the electrodes used for PES should be optimized.

The use of the PES method for inducing and modifying the sensation is introduced in this paper. There are many kinds of PES methods, e.g., electrical muscle stimulation (EMS), electrical ulnar nerve stimulation, and electrical saliva stimulation. These stimulation methods could be used in a sensory display for VR and human computer interaction systems.

Acknowledgement. This work was supported by JSPS KAKENHI Grant-in-Aid for Young Scientist (A) Grant Number 17H04690.

References

1. Lang, N., Siebner, H.R., Ward, N.S., Lee, L., Nitsche, M.A., Paulus, W., et al.: How does transcranial DC stimulation of the primary motor cortex alter regional neuronal activity in the human brain? Eur. J. Neurosci. **22**, 495–504 (2005)
2. Vosskuhl, J., Huster, R.J., Herrmann, C.S.: BOLD signal effects of transcranial alternating current stimulation (tACS) in the alpha range: a concurrent tACS-fMRI study. NeuroImage **140**, 118–125 (2016)
3. Ambrus, G.G., Paulus, W., Antal, A.: Cutaneous perception thresholds of electrical stimulation methods: comparison of tDCS and tRNS. Clin. Neurophysiol. **121**, 1908–1914 (2010)
4. Higuchi, D., Aoyama, K., Kitao, T., Maeda, T., Ando, H.: Multi-electrods galvanic sight stimulation shifts position of phosphene. TVRSJ **21**(4), 613–616 (2016)
5. Kanai, R., Chaieb, L., Antal, A., Walsh, V., Paluus, W.: Frequency-dependent electrical stimulation of the visual cortex. Curr. Biol. **18**, 1839–1843 (2008)
6. Laakso, I., Hirata, A.: Computational analysis shows why transcranial alternating current stimulation induces retinal phosphenes. J. Neural Eng. **10** (2013)
7. Akiyama, H., Aoyama, K., Maeda, T., Ando, H.: Electrical stimulation method capable of presenting visual information outside the viewing angle. In: Proceedings of International Conference on Artificial Reality and Telexistence & Eurographics Symposium on Virtual Environments, Adelaide-Australia (2017)
8. George, R.J.S., Day, B.L., Fitzpatrick, R.C.: Adaptation of vestibular signals for self-motion perception. J. Physiol. **589**(4), 843–853 (2011)
9. Aoyama, K., Iizuka, H., Ando, H., Maeda, T.: Four-pole galvanic vestibular stimulation causes body sway about three axes. Sci. Rep. **5**, 10168 (2015)

10. Aoyama, K., Iizuka, H., Ando, H., Maeda, T.: Countercurrent enhances acceleration sensation in galvanic vestibular stimulation. In: Proceedings of International Conference on Augmented Tele-existence (2013)
11. Aoyama, K., Higuchi, D., Sakurai, K., Maeda, T., Ando, H.: GVS RIDE: giving the novel experience using head mounted display and four-pole galvanic vestibular stimulation. In: Proceeding of ACM SIGGRAPH (2017)
12. Nakayama, Y., Aoyama, K., Kitao, T., Maeda, T., Ando, H.: How to use galvanic vestibular stimulation. In: Virtual Reality, 20th Laval Virtual (ReVolution) (2018)
13. Nakamura, H., Miyashita, H.: Proposition of single-pole electric taste apparatuses for drink and food and evaluation of changing taste quality of polarity change. Inf. Process. Soc. Jpn. **54**(4), 1442–1449 (2013)
14. Ranasinghe, N., Cheok, A., Nakatsu, R., Do, E.Y.: Simulating the sensation of taste for immersive experiences. In: Proceedings of the 2013 ACM International Workshop on Immersive Media Experiences, ImmersiveMe 2013, pp. 29–34 (2013)
15. Aoyama, K., Sakurai, K., Sakurai, S., Mizukami, M., Maeda, T., Ando, H.: Galvanic tongue stimulation inhibits five basic tastes induced by aqueous electrolyte solution. Front. Psychol. **8**, 2112 (2017)
16. Aoyama, K., Sakurai, K., Morishima, A., Maeda, T., Ando, H.: Taste controller: galvanic chin stimulation enhances, inhibits, and creates tastes. In: ACM SIGGRAPH 2018 (2018)
17. Aoyama, K., Sakurai, K., Frukawa, M., Maeda, T., Ando, H.: New method for inducing, inhibiting, and enhancing taste using galvanic jaw stimulation. JVRSJ **22**(2), 137–143 (2017)

In-Vehicle Tactile Displays to Enhance Crew Situation Awareness and Understanding of Agents in a Simulated Driving Environment

David Chhan[✉], Timothy L. White, and Brandon S. Perelman

CCDC Army Research Laboratory, Aberdeen, USA
{david.chhan.civ,timothy.l.white1.civ,brandon.s.perelman.ctr}@mail.mil

Abstract. Chen et al. (2014) proposed the situation awareness-based agent transparency (SAT) model, which is a framework for improving human situation awareness and understanding of autonomous agents' actions, intentions, goals and reasoning. Research using the SAT model as a framework has traditionally focused on displaying transparency concept information in the visual modality. Presenting information in the visual modality exclusively can increase human operators' cognitive load. Multiple Resource Theory suggests that offloading information to other modalities can reduce cognitive load (Wickens 2002). One such modality that can potentially reduce workload is the tactile modality. Tactile displays, which use somatosensory stimulation, have been found to be useful in improving navigation performance with spatial information and providing alerts. One of the current Army Modernization Priorities is the development of Next Generation Combat Vehicles (NGCV), which conceptually includes both manned and unmanned vehicles. Here we present our work in implementing tactile displays to enhance crew situation awareness and improve the understanding of agents in this simulated environment. The operator, through a tactile belt, will be provided spatial information for navigation as well as information for notifications and alerts about the agent's status and actions. We hypothesize that the integration of tactile displays in the vehicle will improve crew situation awareness and their understanding of the agents for effective interaction and tasks performance.

Keywords: In-vehicle multimodal displays · Tactile display · Situation awareness · Human-agent Interaction · Crewstation

1   Introduction

In a typical and everyday driving task, a wealth of information is funneled to the driver's visual and auditory sensory channels. The driver is able to safely maneuver the car using the visual channel to steer, monitor the system for alerts,

S. Yamamoto and H. Mori (Eds.): HCII 2019, LNCS 11570, pp. 15–23, 2019.
https://doi.org/10.1007/978-3-030-22649-7_2

observe hazards (e.g., lane departures, objects in the road, pedestrians, unsafe driving distances) and observe road signs. The auditory channel of the driver can receive information which aids with safety such as horns, sirens, road noise (e.g. rumble strips), and vehicle noise. In addition, many drivers utilize the auditory channel for conversations and listening to the radio. Similarly, in military environments, Soldiers also receive a wealth of information via the visual and auditory channels. In addition to the driving task, hazard avoidance, and noises from the environment, they receive visual and auditory communications about their environment. With such an awesome amount of visual and auditory stimuli, critical, mission-related information can be easily missed. So in accordance with Multiple Resource Theory, information can be offloaded to another sensory channel to reduce cognitive workload (Wickens 2002). Such a channel must be salient (adequate signal to noise ratio) enough to draw the driver's attention. Research has indicated that tactile stimuli can be used to provide critical information to Soldiers in vehicles (Carlander and Eriksson 2006; Krausmann and White 2008).

Research and application of tactile displays in vehicles have been explored for many decades. One area of interest is the use of tactile displays for collision avoidance systems (e.g. forward collision warning, lane departure warning, lane change/merge warning and blind spot detection). Such a system employs tactors integrated into the seat, accelerator pedal and belt. Research on collision avoidance shows significant faster braking response and larger safety margins when tactile warning systems are used (Ho et al. 2006). When comparing tactile warnings to visual and auditory warnings, Scott and Gray (Scott and Gray 2008) also found significantly shorter response times. In another investigation, tactile warnings resulted in better localization of crash threats (Fitch et al. 2007). While the above research using simulated driving environment did not particularly address tactile signal saliency, the ability to detect tactile signal could be an issue in a real world driving with moving vehicle and road noises. As a result, Krausmann and White (Krausmann and White 2008) addressed this specific issue and showed that participants were able to detect tactile signals while on a ride motion simulator platform that simulates a Bradley Fighting Vehicle and High Mobility Multipurpose Wheeled Vehicle traversing a cross-country course or gravel road.

The development of Next Generation Combat Vehicles (NGCV) is one of the top modernization priorities of the Army. In support of this, Combat and Capabilities Development Command (CCDC) Army Research Laboratory (ARL) has created the Information for Mixed Squads (INFORMS) laboratory to study crew-agent interactions in a simulated environment. In this environment, up to 14 participants can control at least 6 manned and unmanned robotic vehicles. One of the roles of crew members is to manage robotic agents that aid in mission execution. The simulation environment allows experimenters to expose these manned vehicles and robotic agents to mobility hazards, traditional kinetic threats and electromagnetic spectrum threats. Crew members require the ability to be able to maintain situation awareness of the current status of robotic agents as well as potential hazards, in order to complete their missions. With such critical information, crew members are able to make decisions on assisting the robotic agents and guiding them to safety. The situation awareness-based agent transparency (SAT) model is a framework to improve the crew's situation awareness and understanding of the robotic agents (Chen et al. 2014). Prior research (Stowers et al. 2016) using SAT model-inspired interfaces has generally presented transparency information using visual displays. Because the visual channel is used heavily in vehicle crew stations, managing robotic agents based on information that is primarily visual can be problematic as the crew is easily overloaded by unimodal stimulation.

The Army has long been interested in using tactile displays to reduce cognitive workload and provide Soldiers the adequate situation awareness required to successfully execute their mission. Past ARL research have shown that tactile communication and multimodal displays are effective in land navigation and reducing cognitive workload for dismounted Soldiers (Coovert et al. 2007; Elliott et al. 2007, 2010; Pettitt et al. 2006; White 2010). In addition, tactile cueing was found to benefit operators performing military and robotics task in multi-tasking environment (Chen and Terrence 2008, 2009). Based on the the aforementioned research studies, it is hypothesized that tactile displays will effectively provide information that will improve crew situation awareness and understanding of robotic agents.

2 Methods

2.1 The INFORMS Laboratory

The INFORMS laboratory is one of the new CCDC ARL funded research facilities designed to house development of concepts and prototyping of the NGCV Warfighter Machine Interface (WMI). The objective is to be able to rapidly bring research concepts and best practices to our transition partners to improve the development of vehicle interfaces. Within the INFORMS laboratory, the WMI Manned-Unmanned Experimentation Laboratory, Simulation in the Loop (MEL-SIL) is being used as a testbed for research in human-autonomy teaming (see Fig. 1). The MEL-SIL is comprised of two 7-person NGCV crew station mockups. This setup allows ARL researchers to translate their relevant research into demonstrable products to showcase novel human-machine interfaces, interactions and teaming capabilities. We used the MEL-SIL of the INFORMS laboratory as the platform and experimentation setup to integrate tactile displays to enhance crew situation awareness and understanding of different components of the agent's actions and intents.

2.2 Tactile System

For tactile cuing, we integrated a system developed by Engineering Acoustics, Inc. (EAI) that consists of a tactile belt and a control unit. The belt, which is

Fig. 1. A picture of the MEL-SIL setup. Each crew station is equipped with a driving simulation with 3 touch-screen monitors. Each monitor screen provides different interfacing displays. The left screen contains high-level map information for coordination and route planning; the middle screen provides a live view of the manned or unmanned vehicle driving environment and status; the right screen shows a 360° view from sensors mounted on the vehicle. The interfaces are modular, allowing crew members to configure them dynamically to suit the current task requirements.

worn about the torso, contains 8 EAI-C2 tactors and is driven by the control unit (Fig. 2). The C-2 tactor is designed with a primary resonance in the 200–300 Hz range that coincides with peak sensitivity of the Pacinian corpuscle, the skin's mechanoreceptors that sense vibration. This 8-tactor torso arrangement was initially designed to provide spatial information for navigation purposes. The 8 tactors are arranged in the belt at 45° intervals, which can be associated with cardinal compass directions.

The tactile control unit is connected to the computer that is used to run the WMI via a USB interface. The WMI uses on-vehicle simulated sensors to gather information about the environment as well the status of the robotic vehicle (e.g. vehicle location, vehicle status, threat location, etc.). This information will be live streamed in using the Lab Streaming Layer (LSL) to initiate tactile stimuli. LSL is a system for the unified collection of measurement time series in research experiments that handles both the networking, time-synchronization and (near-) real-time data. The information obtained from the WMI will be sent to the tactor control unit via the LSL to activate specific tactile cues and messages.

2.3   Scenario and Tasks

The scenario used in the study involves a simulated reconnaissance mission in which the crew is tasked to operate a semi-autonomous robotic combat vehicle

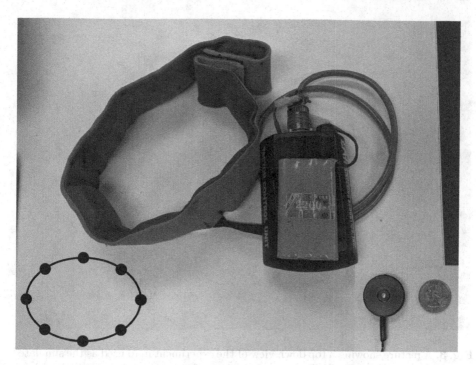

Fig. 2. A picture of the tactile belt and C2 tactor used in the study. A schematic depicting location of the tactors on the belt is also included.

(RCV) through an environment containing a gradient of complexity and urbanization while maintaining situation awareness. Along the RCV's route, the crew is also asked to mark targets by placing battle space objects (BSO) at the appropriate map location, communicate, and perform other tasks using the WMI. Different areas on the map are marked to indicate potential threats (kinetic threats, such as improvised explosive devices or IEDs, and electromagnetic threats such as signal jammers) (shown in Fig. 3). In addition, the crew is not operating the RCV in isolation. This is a team-based scenario in which other crew members within the team are working in the same environment, thus having the ability to communicate with each other. For instance, if crew member #2 places a BSO in the environment within the proximity of crew member #1, depending on the urgency of the information, an alert will be provided in the form of tactile signal.

In conveying information about the environment and alerts to the crew, we categorize tactile information into spatial and non-spatial. Spatial cues relate to directional information such as locations of the RCV relative to potential threats or information about next way point. Non-spatial information relates to notifications, alerts and warnings indicating when the RCV has encountered a mobility challenge, or when RCV is about to enter a dangerous area. For spatial information, a single tactor is activated in order to convey directional information that corresponds to the location of a target. For information that

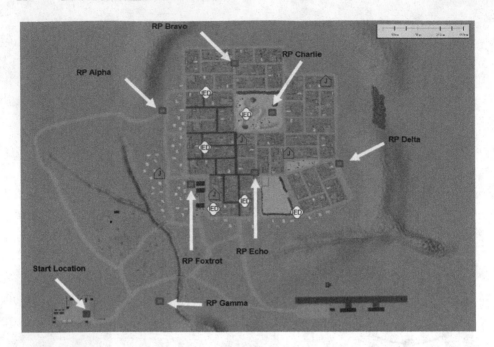

Fig. 3. A picture showing a top down view of the experiment map used as the simulated environment for the study. Yellow arrows point to different rally points along the driving route. Potential kinetic threats are marked as 'IED' and electromagnetic threats are marked as 'J' to indicate signal jammers. (Color figure online)

does not require a directional cue, a combination of tactors will be activated simultaneously or in sequence to form a tactile pattern or message. Non-spatial tactile information has been shown to be effective, intuitive, require little to no training to recognize and memorize the signals if the number of tactile messages are fewer than five (Fitch et al. 2011). Thus instead of designing tactile messages for every possible non-spatial event that could be communicated to the crew, we group the non-spatial information into three levels based on the attention required and the urgency of the information. Non-spatial information level 1 refers to the most critical warnings that require immediate attention (e.g. RCV encountering a severe mobility challenge, entering a different mission-relevant area, or entering close proximity to known threats in the environment); level 2 refers to intermediate level warnings that require crew situation awareness (e.g. RCV entering areas where threats are suspected); level 3 refers to general information that requires attention but is not an imminent threat to the mission or vehicle (e.g. RCV fuel low, incoming messages/communication, etc.). These three non-spatial tactile information will be comprised of vibration patterns that use stimuli of various duration, frequency, amplitude/intensity, inter-pulse interval, and numbers of tactors to be activated. These tactile signal parameters will be designed and crowd-source tested for effectiveness and intuitiveness before their implementation in the actual study.

The table below provides specific examples of the type of messages or cues to be displayed through tactile messages.

Information	Type
Direction	Spatial
RCV getting stuck	Non-spatial (L1)
RCV entering suspected IED area	Non-spatial (L2)
Incoming message	Non-spatial (L3)

2.4   Evaluation Metrics

Crew situation awareness and understanding of the RCV as well as task performance metrics will be evaluated both qualitatively and quantitatively. For qualitative measures, SAGAT (Endsley 1998) queries will be utilized to determine crew situation awareness and understanding of RCV actions, intentions, goals, and general reasoning during the experiment. SAGAT queries are questions like: is the RVC experimenting mobility problems? Is RCV near a danger zone? Where is the RCV next major turn? where and what is the next threat along the route? Participants will be queried both when completing the task with and without the tactile belt. Questionnaires related to tactile displays usability will also be included at the end of the experiment. Eye tracking data will be used to determine the crew's ability to maintain 360-degree situation awareness and security over the RCV using its sensors. Crew performance on target marking will be evaluated with quantitative measures of accuracy and response time. Crew performance on RCV mobility will be quantified using the time between arriving at rally points, total route completion time, and response time when RCV requires mobility assistance.

3   Summary

As part of the Army's modernization efforts, NGCV will be crewed by humans who are responsible for coordinating complex maneuvers between multiple manned and unmanned vehicles. Crew members must have situation awareness and an understanding of the robotic agents in order to successfully execute their mission. The present worked described in this paper is aimed at ensuring that crew members have such information via a tactile belt. Given the abundance of information provided to the visual and auditory channels of crew members, which can induce cognitive overload, the tactile channel is being explored as a potential means of communication. In order to investigate the potential advantages of tactile displays in NGCV, we will collect both quantitative and qualitative data. We hypothesize that the integration of tactile displays will enhance crew members ability to manage robotic agents by improving situation awareness and their understanding of those agents. Findings of this work will be transitioned to our partners within the Army to inform the design of the crew interface in Next Generation Combat Vehicles.

References

Carlander, O., Eriksson, L.: Uni- and biomodal threat cueing with vibrotactile and 3D audio technologies in a combat vehicle. Proc. Hum. Factors Ergon. Soc. Annu. Meet. **50**(16), 1552–1556 (2006). https://doi.org/10.1177/154193120605001608

Chen, J.Y., Boyce, M., Procci, K., Wright, J., Garcia, A., Barns, M.: Situation awareness-based agent transparency. ARL-TR-6905 (2014)

Chen, J.Y., Terrence, P.I.: Effects of tactile cueing on concurrent performance of military and robotics tasks in a simulated multi-tasking environment. Ergonomics **51**(8), 1137–1152 (2008). https://doi.org/10.1080/00140130802030706

Chen, J.Y., Terrence, P.I.: Effects of imperfect automation and individual di erences on concurrent performance of military and robotics tasks in a simulated multi-tasking environment. Ergonomics **52**(8), 907–920 (2009). https://doi.org/10.1080/00140130802680773

Coovert, M.D., Gray, A.A., Elliott, L.R., Redden, E.S.: Development of a framework for multimodal research: creation of a bibliographic database. ARL-TR-4068 (2007)

Elliott, L.R., Duistermaat, M., Redden, E.S., Van Erp, J.: Multi-modal guidance for land navigation. ARL-TR-4295 (2007)

Elliott, L.R., van Erp, J.B., Redden, E.S., Duistermaat, M.: Field-based validation of a tactile navigation device. IEEE Trans. Haptics **3**(2), 78–87 (2010). https://doi.org/10.1109/ToH.2010.3

Endsley, M.R.: Situation awareness global assessment technique (sagat). In: Proceedings of the IEEE 1988 National Aerospace and Electronics Conference, pp. 789–795 (1988)

Fitch, G.M., Hankey, J.M., Kleiner, B.M., Dingus, T.A.: Driver comprehension of multiple haptic seat alerts intended for use in an integrated collision avoidance system. Transp. Res. Part F **14**, 278–290 (2011). https://doi.org/10.1016/j.trf.2011.02.001

Fitch, G.M., Kiefer, R.J., Hankey, J.M., Kleiner, B.M.: Toward developing an approach for alerting drivers to the direction of a crash threat. Hum. Factors **49**(4), 710–720 (2007). https://doi.org/10.1518/001872007X215782

Ho, C., Reed, N., Spence, C.: Assesing the e ectiveness of "intuitive" vibrotactile warning signals in preventing front-to-rear-end collision in a driving simulator. Accid. Anal. Prev. **38**, 988–996 (2006). https://doi.org/10.1016/j.aap.2006.04.002

Krausmann, A.S., White, T.L.: Detection and localization of vibrotactile signals in moving vehicles. ARL-TR-4463 (2008)

Pettitt, R.A., Redden, E.S., Carstens, C.B.: Comparison of army hand and arm signals to a covert tactile communication system in a dynamic environment. ARL-TR-3838 (2006)

Scott, J., Gray, R.: A comparison of tactile, visual and auditory warnings for rear-end collision prevention in simulated driving. Hum. Factors **50**(2), 264–275 (2008). https://doi.org/10.1518/001872008X250674

Stowers, K., Kasdaglis, N., Newton, O., Lakhmani, S., Wohleber, R., Chen, J.: Intelligent agent trans- parency: The design and evaluation of an interface to facilitate human and intelligent agent collaboration. Proc. Hum. Factors Ergon. Soc. Annu. Meet. **60**, 1706–1710 (2016)

White, T.L.: Suitable body locations and vibrotactile cueing types for dismounted soldiers. ARL-TR-5186 (2010)

Wickens, C.D.: Multiple resources and performance prediction. Theor. Issues Ergon. Sci. **3**, 159–177 (2002)

Effect of Artificial Haptic Characteristics on Virtual Reality Performance

Daiji Kobayashi[1]([⊠]) [iD], Machika Ueda[1], Koki Hiraoka[1],
Hiroya Suzuki[2], Ryuki Tsukikawa[2], Takehiko Yamaguchi[3],
and Tetsuya Harada[2]

[1] Chitose Institute of Science and Technology, Chitose, Hokkaido, Japan
d-kobaya@photon.chitose.ac.jp
[2] Tokyo University of Science, Katsushika, Tokyo, Japan
[3] Suwa University of Science, Chino, Nagano, Japan

Abstract. In recent years, virtual reality (VR) systems, mainly applied to computer games, have become easily available and widely used by young people. Multipurpose haptic devices for the virtual environment, such as the SPIDAR system, have been developed for everyday training tasks. Therefore, the wide range of use contexts and user requirements should be considered to effectively design and evaluate the systems. However, the measurement of objective quality of VR systems from the user's experience has not been widely considered, although some questionnaires for evaluating the user's experience based on the sense of embodiment have been proposed. We investigate the measures relating to the user performance, especially with regard to the sense of embodiment. We find that the duration observed between an event and the root-mean-square electromyogram amplitude dropping to a local minimum, within two seconds, could be a measure for evaluating the quality of VR systems from the point of view of user performance.

Keywords: Virtual reality · Sense of embodiment · Haptics · Electromyogram

1 Introduction

In our previous study, we aimed to evaluate virtual reality (VR) performance from an ergonomics viewpoint and instigated the task for both the real and virtual environments to consider the requirements for developments in the virtual environment [1]. The difference between the performance of the real and virtual environments were considered from the perspective of the sense of agency (SoA). In particular, the VR performance was evaluated based on the two-step account of the agency model proposed by Synofzik et al. [2].

Meanwhile, the SoA and related concepts such as sense of embodiment (SoE), sense of body ownership (SoBO), and sense of self-location (SoSL) have been discussed in recent research in the field of VR. With respect to these concepts, Kilteni et al. considered SoE for understanding the artificial body and pointed out, based on review results, that the three concepts of SoBO, SoA, and SoSL were associated with the concept of embodiment [3].

© Springer Nature Switzerland AG 2019
S. Yamamoto and H. Mori (Eds.): HCII 2019, LNCS 11570, pp. 24–35, 2019.
https://doi.org/10.1007/978-3-030-22649-7_3

Recently, VR systems, mainly applied to computer games, have become easily available and widely used by young people. Meanwhile, multipurpose haptic devices for the virtual environment, such as the SPIDAR system, have been developed for everyday training tasks [4]. Therefore, the wide range of use contexts and user requirements should be considered to effectively design and evaluate the systems. However, the measurement of objective quality of VR systems from the user's experience has not been widely considered, although some questionnaires for evaluating the user's experience based on the SoE have been proposed [5]. This study aims to investigate the measures relating to the user performance for tasks such as erroneous behavior; in this regard, the relationships between the erroneous behavior and user experience are considered from the perspective of the SoE.

2   Method

To investigate the effect of VR systems on the user performance, we took the task that we designed in our previous study, the rod tracking task (RTT), and carried out experiments with participants undertaking the task both in reality and the virtual environment. Then we investigated and compared the participants' performances and experiences in the RTT. The experiment was between subject design and the procedures in the both conditions were almost the same.

2.1   Rod Tracking Task for Different Environments

To observe the user's SoE, we used the rod tracking task because the characteristics of the RTT, which was created in our previous study, are well understood [1].

When executing the RTT, the user is required to grasp a rod with their right hand and attempt to move the rod between the ends of a curved slit in a panel, without making contact with the sides of the slit. The panel is installed in front of the user and is rotated anticlockwise by 45° with respect to the user, as shown in Fig. 1.

Fig. 1. Experimental scene of a participant executing the RTT in reality. Two electrodes for the EMG are attached to the participants' lower arm and near the base of their fifth finger.

In the virtual environment, the user can be affected by various factors arising from the design of the VR, such as a sudden vibration of the rod on contact with the sides of the slit. Therefore, the performance in a normal situation refers to the performance in reality, and must be compared to the performance in the virtual environment. We set up a VR test for the RTT, as well as the apparatus for the same task to be executed in reality, as shown in Fig. 2. In addition, the experimental task should immerse the user, because the user's performance depends on their attention to their own behavior. Therefore, successful execution of the RTT requires a certain level of skill and the task must interest participants to some extent.

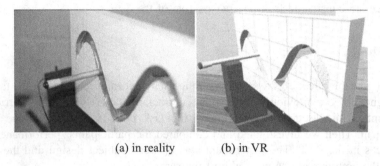

(a) in reality   (b) in VR

Fig. 2. The real slit panel and the rod for the RTT in reality (a) and its equivalent virtual scene in VR (b) [1].

The slit width, the size of the panel, and the rod's diameter of 10 mm were decided based on the required difficulty of the task (see Fig. 3). We concretely determined that the RTT needed to be difficult enough that an inexperienced participant was required to repeatedly practice around ten times before successfully executing the task in reality. The sine-curved slit and the direction of installation of the panel were also chosen from several patterns based on the required difficulty of the RTT. Furthermore, our previous study found that moving the rod in section B of the slit was the most difficult region for the participants and produced the greatest number of contacts, because it was difficult to see the gap between the rod and the slit as shown in Fig. 2. Therefore, in this study we have assumed that the user's SoE is lost or reduced in section B.

2.2   Experimental Equipment for Reality

To observe the participant's performance, we used the experimental equipment for the RTT composed of several devices, as shown in Fig. 4. To record the movement of the right hand, a motion sensor (Leap Motion) connected to a personal computer (DELL XPS 8700) was used. The movement was sampled and recorded as three-dimensional coordinates at 10 Hz. Meanwhile, to observe the participant's intentional and unintentional muscle tension while manipulating the rod, surface electromyograms (EMGs) on the muscle abductor digiti minimi (on the fifth finger) and muscle flexor carpi ulnaris (on the lower arm) were sampled and recorded at 100 Hz using a multi-telemeter (Nihon-Koden WEB-9500). Additionally, the signal recording contact

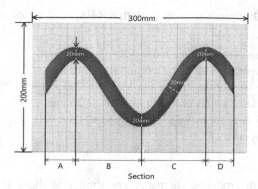

Fig. 3. Specification of the slit panel. The width of the slit panel is 20 mm and the track is divided into four sections (A–D) for convenience [1].

between the rod and the slit panel was sent to the PC via a USB I/O terminal (Contec AIO-160802AY-USB) and to a multi-telemeter, as well as illuminating a red LED indicator for the benefit of the participant.

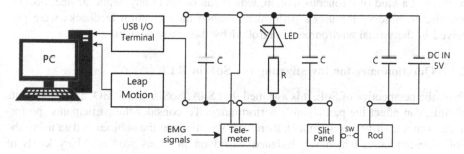

Fig. 4. Connection diagram of the devices recording the participant's performance in reality [1].

2.3 Experimental Equipment for the Virtual Environment

The new VR environment developed for this study for investigating human performance consisted of two user interfaces including a haptic interface (SPIDAR-HS2) and a head-mounted display (HTC VIVE PRO). SPIDAR-HS2, the human-sized haptic user interface for VR, controlled the rod's two endpoints. It consisted of the controllers and eight motor modules including a motor, a threaded pulley, and an encoder for reading the yarn winding of each pulley. The motor modules provided a sense of force, as well as detecting the positions and angle of the end effectors; in other words, they detected the rod movement. The other experimental conditions and the specifications of SPIDAR-HS2 are shown in Table 1, and further details of the specifications of SPIDAR can be found in reference [4].

In the case of the experiment in the virtual environment, the movement of the rod was recorded using SPIDAR-HS system and the surface EMGs on the same two body parts described above were also recorded using the multi-telemeter (Nihon Koden WEB-9500).

Table 1. Specifications of the SPIDER-HS2 used for the RTT.

Details	Specifications
Stick length (length of the rod in VR)	400 mm
Stick diameter (width of the rod in VR)	10 mm
Path size (size of the slit panel in VR)	200 × 300 × 20 mm
Path thickness (width of the slit in VR)	20 mm
Required force for moving vertical upward	Over 0.97 N
Positional error	1%

The physics of the rod and slit panel are similar to those of the real objects, especially visually, but are somewhat different in terms of the haptic sense, because of being in a virtual environment. For instance, the rod as the end effector of SPIDAR-HS2 did not fall owing to gravity during the task. Furthermore, SPIDAR-HS2 presented occasional vibrations to the user's kinesthetic sense when the rod came in contact with the sides of the slit, because the haptic interface could recreate a sensation closer to a real sense than the real kinesthetic and haptic sense. In this regard, we consider it a kind of erroneous motion, which can occur in any haptic device. Instead, we tried to observe the user's performance when the unnatural feedbacks were perceived in the virtual environment controlled by the many devices.

2.4 Questionnaire for Investigating the SoE in RTT

From the perspective of SoE, it is assumed that SoA, SoSL, and SoBO, as the elements of SoE, can affect the participant's performance. To consider the participants' performances in the virtual environment, therefore, we obtained the subjective data using the SoE questionnaire, which we designed based on previous studies. Many kinds of questionnaires for investigating SoE have been proposed in recent years. For instance, Mar and Tabitha proposed an embodiment questionnaire for investigating avatar embodiment in an immersive virtual environment [5]. The foci of the embodiment questionnaire were covered by six characteristics such as body ownership, agency and motor control, tactile sensations, location of the avatar's body, the avatar's external appearance, and response to external stimuli. For the RTT trials in a virtual environment, however, the participants looked at the movement of the rod which they controlled using SPIDAR-HS2. In other words, the participants could not look at their hand both in reality and on their avatar in the virtual environment while executing the RTT; therefore, we selected nine statements from the embodiment questionnaire for the RTT as executed in both reality and the virtual environment. In addition, to construct the questionnaire for assessing the SoE for the RTT, we arranged the relevant statements based on the characteristics of the RTT. The nine questionnaire statements were composed of three categories, SoBO, SoA, and SoSL; these are shown in Table 2.

The questionnaire was given to the participants at the end of the experiment. In this regard, Mar and Tabitha suggested that it should be clear that the questions are related to the participants' experience during the experiment; therefore, we instructed the participants to answer the questionnaire while recalling the situations described in each item using a seven-point Likert-scale. The Likert-scale ranged from strongly disagree (-3) to disagree (-2), somewhat disagree (-1), neither agree nor disagree (0), somewhat agree ($+1$), agree ($+2$), and strongly agree ($+3$).

In this study, the SoE score for the RTT was composed of the SoBO, SoA, and SoSL scores, which were estimated as follows:

SoBO score $= (-Q1 - Q2 - Q3)/3$
SoA score $= (Q4 + Q5 - Q6 - Q7)/4$
SoSL score $= (Q8 - Q9)/2$
SoE score $= (-Q1 - Q2 - Q3)/3 + (Q4 + Q5 - Q6 - Q7)/4 + (Q8 - Q9)/2$.

In other words, we assume the SoBO, SoA, and SoSL have equal impact on the SoE, ranging from -3 to $+3$, and the SoE score reflects the participants' experience.

Table 2. The ten questionnaire items for investigating the participant's subjective experience in RTT.

Category	Question
SoBO	1. It felt as if the real or the virtual rod I saw was moved by someone else
	2. It seemed as if I might have more than one hand
	3. I felt a sensation that I did not move my hand when I saw the rod moved, or I felt a sensation that I move my hand when I saw the rod stopped
SoA	4. It felt like I could control the real or the virtual rod as if it was my own rod
	5. The movements of the real or the virtual rod was caused by my behavior
	6. I felt as if the movements of real or the virtual rod was influencing my behavior
	7. I felt as if the real or the virtual rod was moving by itself
SoSL	8. I felt as if the rod in my hand was located where I saw the real or the virtual rod
	9. I felt as if the rod in my real hand were drifting toward the rod I see or as if the rod I see were drifting toward the rod in my real hand

2.5 Experimental Procedure in Reality

The 17 participants were male students ranging from 21 to 23 years of age and gave their informed consent for participation in advance. All participants were right handed and had no prior experience of the RTT.

A trial of the RTT in this experiment was to pull the rod from the far end of the slit to the end closest to the participant along the track. Subsequently, the participant had to push the rod from the close end to the far end and had to avoid contact of the rod with the sides of the slit except at both ends. The speed at which the participant moved the rod was chosen by the participant; as long as the participant held his/her head as steady as possible during the trial, as shown in Fig. 1.

Before the experiment, the participants were measured by the EMGs on the muscle abductor digiti minimi (on the fifth finger) and muscle flexor carpi ulnaris (on the lower arm) under a resting situation for ten seconds. After that, they repeated the trial for three days until they could avoid contact of the rod with the slit; however, the participants could take a rest and relax for a while if necessary and the trial was limited to fifteen times a day.

Using the experimental equipment, we recorded the movement of the participant's hand and the participant's surface EMGs. The contact signal, which was generated when the rod and slit panel came into contact, was recorded by both the PC and the multi-telemeter. The participants' opinions about most difficult section in the slit panel and the reason why the rod came into contact with the slit edges were recorded in an interview after every trial, if the participants could recall. At the end of the experiment, the participants reported their experiences and answered the aforementioned questionnaire.

2.6   Experimental Procedure in the Virtual Environment

We selected twelve male students ranging from 22 to 25 years of age as participants. The participants were different from those participating in the real-world experiment. The participants were right handed and had no prior experience doing the RTT in a real-world environment, but had executed other tasks in a virtual environment using the other SPIDAR system and a head-mounted display. In this regard, the participants were used to performing the RTT in virtual environments and we assumed they had accrued sufficient skill to perceive the virtual environment to some extent.

A trial of the RTT in this experiment was the same as in the real-world experiment; that is, they pulled the end effector like the rod from the far end of the slit to the near end along the track and then pushed the rod from the near end to the far end. During both parts of the task, they had to avoid contact of the rod with the slit edges except at both ends. The speed at which the participant moved the rod was decided by the participant; however, the participant was required to hold their head as steady as possible during the trial in the virtual environment.

Before the experiment, the respective participants were measured by the EMGs on the muscle abductor digiti minimi (on the fifth finger) and muscle flexor carpi ulnaris (on the lower arm) under a resting situation for ten seconds. After measuring the EMGs, the participants repeated the trial until their performance was improved up to a maximum of ten trials, and the participants could take a rest and relax as required.

Using the experimental equipment, we recorded the changing position and angle of the end effector as well as the participant's surface EMGs. The contact signal, which was generated by the PC when the rod and slit panel made contact, was also recorded by the multi-telemeter via USB I/O terminal. In addition, the participants' opinions, especially about the experience executing the RTT, were recorded in interviews and the participants answered the questionnaire at the end of experiment.

3   Results

3.1   Improvement of the Performance of the RTT in Reality

Our previous study showed that it was most difficult for the participants to move the rod without contact during section B of the slit because of the reason described before; however, it was not clear that the repetition of the RTT in real-world conditions resulted in the improvement of performance in section B. Thus, at first, we investigate the improvement of the performance within 3 days in the real-world for the RTT. Figure 5 shows that the number of instances of contact between the rod and the slit edges decreases day by day. The 95% confidence interval of the number of contact events in section B on the third day was 3.9 ± 2.0. However, the number of contact events in section B decreases insufficiently when compared to the other sections.

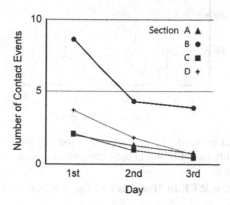

Fig. 5. Average number of contact events at the last trial for the RTT of each day in the real-world experiments (n = 17).

In the real-world experiment, only one of the seventeen participants could complete the RTT without contact in the first day; however, almost of the participants made contact between the rod and the slit edges. However, nine of the seventeen participants performed successfully in section B on the third day. That is, the nine participants made contact between the rod and the slit less than once a trial. In other words, in the real-world case, almost all of the participants were able to make progress controlling the rod in the RTT.

3.2   Number of Contacts in the Virtual Environment

The RTT in the virtual environment was more difficult for the other twelve participants and a greater number of contact events were observed in their last trial, excepting one participant. The number of contact events, therefore, can serve as a measure for evaluating the performance at each section of the slit panel for both environments of the RTT. This is shown in Fig. 6.

Figure 6 shows that it is significantly more difficult for participants to avoid contact in section B than any other section, regardless of the RTT's environment ($p < .05$). Furthermore, it can also be observed that the performance in the RTT in the virtual environment was unimproved by the last trial. Therefore, we infer that the factors existing in the virtual environment can affect performance and make the RTT more difficult in section B than it is in the real world.

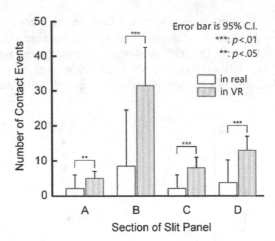

Fig. 6. Number of contact events during the last trial of the first day in each section of the slit panel, during trials in reality (n = 17) and in the virtual environment (n = 12).

3.3 Experiences of the RTT in Real and in the Virtual Environment

The participants' experiences, estimated using the questionnaire, were compared between the real and virtual environments. The 95% confidence interval of the SoE score in the virtual environment was 5.0 ± 0.9, whereas the SoE score in the real environment was 8.4 ± 0.4. The scores of each of the three components of SoE for the RTT are shown in the Fig. 7. Figure 7 also shows that the SoA score has a strong effect on the SoE score.

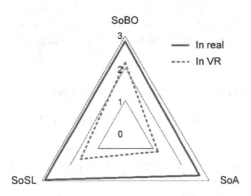

Fig. 7. Comparison of the average scores of the three components of SoE for the RTT trials in the two different environments.

3.4 Performance After Contact with Slit Edges

In our previous study, we measured the amplitudes of the EMGs at the surface of two body parts to evaluate the participants' skill in the RTT in both environments. The EMGs were calculated using the root-mean-square (RMS). The standard deviations of

RMS EMGs at the surface of the two body parts were also used to understand the SoA. We tried to determine the effect of the SoA on the performance in detail. The standardized RMS EMG waveforms of the participants' two body parts were obtained by dividing the RMS EMG signals during the RTT by the participant's averaged resting EMS EMG signals. The general trends of multiple participants' RMS EMG waveforms were obtained by averaging the standardized RMS EMG waveforms. Figure 8 shows two averaged standardized RMS EMG waveforms for two seconds after contact in section B of the slit; these wave forms are smoothed by the moving average method. The average standardized RMS EMG waveform in the real environment (a) was obtained by averaging forty samples from the first trials involving the seventeen real-world participants, and the average waveform in the virtual environment (b) was obtained by averaging eight samples from the first trials involving the twelve virtual-environment participants.

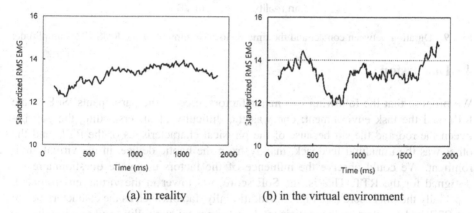

(a) in reality   (b) in the virtual environment

Fig. 8. Comparison of two trends of the RMS EMG waveforms over a period of two seconds after participants had made contact between the rod and the slit edges: in reality (a) and in the virtual environment (b).

Figure 8 indicates that the amplitude of the EMG decreases after contact is made, and the duration at local minimum differs between the real and virtual environments. Therefore, the times between contact and the amplitude of the RMS EMG dropping to a local minimum were measured, and the averages of the forty real-world samples and eight virtual-environment samples were compared. It was found that the average duration in the virtual environment case is statistically longer than in the real case. Figure 9 shows the results from the RMS EMG waveforms on the fifth finger, which represents the muscle tension for dexterous manipulation of the rod.

To explain the difference in these durations, we propose a kind of processing time for recognizing the situation, from when the contact was perceived to when the participant moves to the next action. From the viewpoint of motor readiness, the average of the duration in the real world could be valid, and could suggest that cognitive processes after contact progress smoothly in a short time. In other words, it is possible to say that the participants required more time for cognition in the virtual environment than in a similar real-world situation.

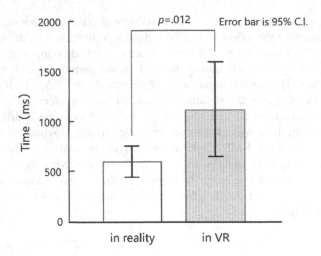

Fig. 9. Duration between contact and the time of local minimum of the RMS EMG amplitude.

4 Discussion

We propose that the following two major factors affected the participants' SoE in the RTT and the task environment: one was the difficulty of understanding the gap between the rod and the slit because of the physical characteristics of the RTT, and the other was the unnatural feedback, mainly from the haptic device, in the virtual environment. We could observe the influence of the factors using the questionnaire we designed for the RTT. That is, the SoE score was lower in the virtual environment, especially the SoA score (see Fig. 7). Additionally, factors such as the characteristics of the RTT had an effect on the participants' performance: controlling and moving the rod during section B produced more contact events than in the other sections, regardless of the task environment (see Fig. 6). The unnatural feedbacks in the virtual environment also caused more contact events; this is clear because the number of contact events in the virtual environment was significantly more than in the real world (see Fig. 6). With respect to this point, almost of the participants pointed out the unnatural feelings or feedbacks produced by the haptic devices; however, they acquired the skill of controlling the rod in the virtual environment, despite the difficulty of moving the rod through section B. In other words, they experienced the unnatural sensations such as the vibration of the rod by the haptic devices, but they learned to understand these sensations, and they improved at executing the RTT. In this sense, based on the two-step account of the agency model for explaining the mechanism of SoA [2], it is concluded that the participant's SoA could not make a successful perceptual representation in a feeling of agency, and the judgement of agency needed more time to achieve the propositional representation to understand the situation in the virtual environment. Therefore, in the virtual environment, the duration between contact and the RMS EMG amplitude dropping to a local minimum was longer in the virtual environment, as shown in Fig. 9. Moreover, the duration could be an objective measure for evaluating the RTT from the viewpoint of SoA.

Based on the above, we can say that in the virtual environment, especially the VR system we experimentally developed, unnatural or erroneous feedback from the VR system led the user's unsuccessful cognitive processes to decide what action is appropriate for the task in the situation.

5   Conclusion

In this study, we investigated the effect of the factors relating to the rod tracking task using a VR system on the user's performance from the perspective of SoE, especially SoA. We have successfully explained the waveforms of RMS EMGs in the period after the rod made contact with the slit edges, based on the two-step account of the agency model for SoA. Concretely, unnatural or erroneous feedback from the VR system decreased the user's situational awareness and required more time for decision-making. Furthermore, those undesirable feedbacks could make the user's subjective experience worse, such as decreasing the level of SoA then SoE in VR. Consequently, the effect of the artificial haptic characteristics on virtual reality performance could be revealed.

Based on the above, we propose that the waveforms of RMS EMGs could be useful as a measure of the duration required for awareness of situation and decision-making through this study; however, further research is required to confirm the validity of the measure.

References

1. Kobayashi, D., Shinya, Y.: Study of virtual reality performance based on sense of agency. In: Yamamoto, S., Mori, H. (eds.) HIMI 2018. LNCS, vol. 10904, pp. 381–394. Springer, Cham (2018). https://doi.org/10.1007/978-3-319-92043-6_32
2. Synofzik, M., Vosgerau, G., Newen, A.: Beyond the comparator model: a multifactorial two-step account of agency. Conscious. Cogn. 17(1), 219–239 (2008)
3. Kilteni, K., Groten, R., Slater, M.: The sense of embodiment in virtual reality. Presence 21(4), 373–387 (2012). Fall 2012
4. Tsukikawa, R., et al.: Construction of experimental system SPIDAR-HS for designing VR guidelines based on physiological behavior measurement. In: Chen, J.Y.C., Fragomeni, G. (eds.) VAMR 2018. LNCS, vol. 10909, pp. 245–256. Springer, Cham (2018). https://doi.org/10.1007/978-3-319-91581-4_18
5. Gonzalez-Franco, M., Peck, T.: Avatar embodiment. towards a standardized questionnaire. https://www.frontiersin.org/articles/10.3389/frobt.2018.00074/full. Accessed 10 Mar 2019

Rendering of Virtual Walking Sensation by a Vestibular Display

Koichi Shimizu[1], Vibol Yem[1], Kentaro Yamaoka[1], Gaku Sueta[1], Tomohiro Amemiya[2], Michiteru Kitazaki[3], and Yasushi Ikei[1(✉)]

[1] Tokyo Metropolitan University, Hachioji, Tokyo 191-0065, Japan
{shimizu,yem,yamaoka,sueta,ikei}@vr.sd.tmu.ac.jp
[2] NTT Communication Science Laboratory, Kyoto, Japan
tomohiro.amemiya@gmail.com
[3] Toyohashi University of Technology, Toyohashi, Japan
mich@tut.jp

Abstract. The current study describes a method for rendering the sensation of walking using a vestibular display (a motion seat) with three degrees of freedom. The sensations evoked by the vestibular display and real walking were investigated using a psychophysical method. The optimal motion of the vestibular display to induce the sensation of walking on a level surface and walking up/down stairs was obtained using the method of adjustment. The results revealed that an amplitude less than 10% of real motion was appropriate for the passive presentation of walking. A low level of asymmetry was observed in the speed and acceleration of the motion trajectory for the stair walking presentation. This finding suggested that a smaller amount of return motion compared with forward (first half) motion in a reciprocal motion for each step was appropriate for inducing the sensation of walking up/down stairs.

Keywords: Vestibular stimulus · Walking sensation · Level and stair walking

1 Introduction

Locomotion interfaces have been developed to create the bodily sensation of walking in a virtual space. These systems typically require a large physical space if voluntary walking motion of the user is allowed, and/or a device that cancels the user's physical movement, such as an omnidirectional treadmill [1]. Otherwise, the direction of active real walking can be changed or modified to keep the user within a limited area, as in the walk-in-place [2] and the redirect walking [3] methods.

An alternative approach for inducing the sensation of walking is to move parts of the user's body using mechanical devices. This is a form of passive body motion, in which the user does not move their body by themselves. The passive condition is appropriate when the user receives an experience of a particular virtual space that presents a first-person tour of a past real world scene, such as a multimodal movie. This may allow the user to share the body motion of another person who visited the place in the past. The simulated place may be a location of interest, such as a world heritage site, a high mountain, a beautiful beach, or a museum. Reproducing the experience of

© Springer Nature Switzerland AG 2019
S. Yamamoto and H. Mori (Eds.): HCII 2019, LNCS 11570, pp. 36–46, 2019.
https://doi.org/10.1007/978-3-030-22649-7_4

walking is a basic element of experience-sharing. We have developed a multisensory display for this purpose [4].

In the current study, we developed and tested a passive body-stimulation method to induce the sensation of walking up and down stairs, using a vestibular display (Fig. 1) while the user was sitting in real space. First, sensation scaling on the display motion was performed to show the characteristics of the stimuli presented by the display. The sensation of real walking was measured using nine factors as a reference for the design of the display. We tested participants walking on a flat floor and stairs, collecting data in each condition. Participants then adjusted the magnitude of motion on a vestibular display (a motion seat with three degrees of freedom) to create the sensation of walking on a level floor and up or down stairs. The selected magnitude of motion of the display was discussed.

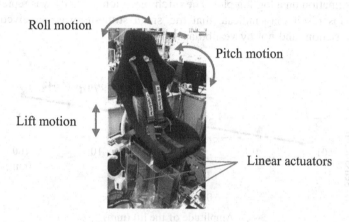

Roll motion

Pitch motion

Lift motion

Linear actuators

Fig. 1. A vestibular display (motion seat) with three degrees of freedom (lift, roll, pitch motions).

2 Sensation Scaling of Vestibular Display Stimulus

The psychological perception levels experienced by participants in response to the display motion were measured using sensory scaling in each degree of freedom (lift, roll, and pitch directions) separately.

2.1 Participants and Procedure

Participants in the experiment were five undergraduate and graduate students (average age: 22.8 years) for the lift stimulus, five students (average age: 22.4 years) for the roll stimulus, and six students (average age: 23.2 years) for the pitch stimulus.

Participants walked on a flat floor for 20 m with a walk period of 1.4 s (0.7 s each step) and remembered the sensations of the body motion of lifting, pitch and roll rotations during the walk. Participants then sat on the vestibular display and received one of the stimuli randomly selected from a set. They compared the stimulus with a standard stimulus and rated the sensation of each stimulus using a visual analogue scale (VAS). Participants closed their eyes and wore noise-emitting ear-phones during stimulation.

The standard stimulus was a 1.25 mm lift, a 0.68° roll rotation, and a 0.55° pitch rotation in a sinusoidal trajectory. The modulus was 10. The comparison stimuli of lift had seven levels of {0.02, 0.08, 0.33, 1.35, 5.50, 22.38, 91.20} mm with a lift speed of 100 mm/s rise and fall. The comparison stimuli of roll had 33 levels of degree {0.03, 0.06, 0.10, 0.19, 0.36, 0.68, 1.26, 2.34, 4.37, 8.13, 15.0} and deg/s {1.8, 4.5, 7.2}. The comparison stimuli for pitch had 36 levels of degree {0.03, 0.06, 0.13, 0.27, 0.55, 1.14, 2.34, 4.84, 10.0} and deg/s {0.7, 2.9, 5.0, 7.2}.

2.2 Result

The results (lift, roll, pitch) are shown in Figs. 2, 3, and 4. The non-linearity of sensation intensity was relatively large, with around 0.4 to 0.6 of the power index of the linear approximation on a log-log plot. The pitch sensation intensity was represented by two lines. This result may indicate that the small stimulus was perceived only by cutaneous sensation, and not by vestibular sensation.

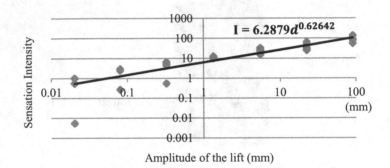

Amplitude of the lift (mm)

Fig. 2. Sensation scale of lift motion.

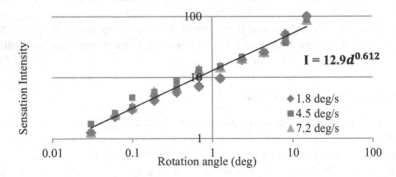

Fig. 3. Sensation scale of roll motion.

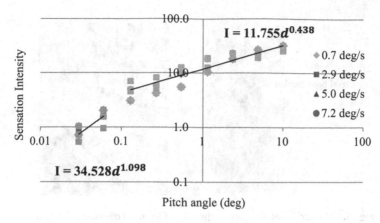

Fig. 4. Sensation scale of pitch motion.

3 Body Motion in Real Walking

Body motion trajectories during three real sessions of walking (walking on a level surface, walking up stairs, walking down stairs) were measured with an optical sensor (OptiTrak, V120), to be used as a reference for the motion of the vestibular display. Head motion was also measured with an acceleration sensor (TSND-121). Participants walked on a treadmill and up or down stairs (stair riser: 160 mm, tread width: 320 mm) with a walk period of 1.4 s, with markers attached at the head and the coxal bone (Fig. 5).

The body motion during real walking was as follows:

- Level walking: 30 to 40 mm lift, 5 to 6° roll rotation, and 1 to 2° pitch rotation, respectively. The vertical acceleration of the head was −1 to 5 m/s².
- Walking up stairs: 160 to 170 mm lift, 10 to 11° roll rotation, and 2 to 3° pitch rotation, respectively. The vertical acceleration of the head was −3 to 7 m/s².
- Walking down stairs: −160 to −180 mm lift, 3 to 4° roll rotation, and 1.5 to 3° pitch rotation, respectively. The vertical acceleration of the head was −3.5 to 7 m/s².

The amplitude of lift motion primarily depended on the step height of the stairs. Regarding the acceleration of the head, the range of acceleration was greater for stair walking compared with walking on a level surface. The amplitude of roll and pitch motions was greater during stair walking compared with level walking. The head roll while walking up stairs was greater than that when walking down stairs, as participants shifted their body weight to the support leg and lifted the body, creating a roll motion of the head. These characteristics were necessary to reproduce with the vestibular display.

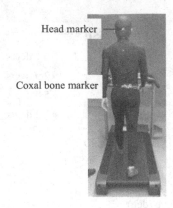

Head marker

Coxal bone marker

Fig. 5. Marker sites on the participant.

Fig. 6. The stairs the participant walked up and down.

4   Evaluation of Walking Sensation During Real Walking

The sensations of level walking, walking up stairs, and walking down stairs were first analyzed to compare them with the sensations generated by the vestibular display. The dimensions of the stairs were the same as those described in the previous section.

4.1   Participants and Procedure

Participants were 13 undergraduate and graduate students with an average age of 22.9 years. Participants walked on a flat floor and stairs while wearing visual information reduction glasses with a walk period of 1.4 s, and were instructed to remember the sensation of walking. Participants then evaluated the sensation of walking in terms of the nine factors listed in Table 1 using a VAS ranging from no sensation (0) to a very definite sensation (100).

Table 1. Factors of walking sensation.

Factors of walking sensation	Definition of factors (awareness)
Power (acceleration)	Sensation of applied force to make the body forward. Sensation of lifting the body at stairs
Walk velocity	Sensation of walking speed
Periodicity (repetitive motion)	Sensation of repetitiveness of the motion
Lateral alternation (lateral sway)	Sensation of the alternated contact motion of legs on the ground

(*continued*)

Table 1. (*continued*)

Factors of walking sensation	Definition of factors (awareness)
Muscle tension (perceived)	Sensation of muscular effort of lower extremity to support the weight of the body
Continuous body motion	Sensation of total amount of continuous motion of the body
Regularity of continuous body motion	Sensation of regular continuous motion of the body
Balance control (posture maintenance)	Sensation of maintaining/controlling posture to continue a balanced walking
Sole taction (tactile sensation) at the foot	Sensation of sole skin when the foot contacted to the ground

4.2   Result

The results are shown in Fig. 6. The sensation intensity of power (acceleration) was significantly higher during stair walking compared with level walking ($p < 0.01$). The sensation of walking velocity exhibited a moderate range for both level and stair walking. Periodicity and lateral alteration were clearly perceived in all walking conditions. During stair walking, muscle tension was strongly perceived in the lower limbs as the body was raised and lowered by its own muscles. Continuous body motion was perceived more clearly in stair walking compared with level walking, since the amount of total body motion was greater in stair walking. In contrast, the regularity of body motion was greater in level walking, because of the small amount of perturbation of the posture. A moderate level of balance control was perceived during level walking, whereas balance control was clearly perceived during stair walking. Foot sole taction (tactile sensation) was clearly perceived in both the level and stair walking, with a stronger sensation in stair walking than level walking when the body was lifted on one foot, or when body weight was supported during sole contact on the ground during stair walking.

Overall, the sensation intensity was lower during level walking compared with stair walking, except for the regularity of body motion. This finding may have been caused by difficulty perceiving level walking itself, as level walking is often a relatively automatic movement performed without conscious control of the body. In contrast, during stair walking, the participant focused on controlling their bodies to ensure they did not miss the step, requiring a considerable amount of attention to be directed to information about their own body, as well as the environment. This process would be likely to cause higher ratings of walking sensation (Fig. 7).

The intensity of the virtual walking sensation induced by the multisensory display would be expected to increase if the sensation levels obtained in this experiment are achieved.

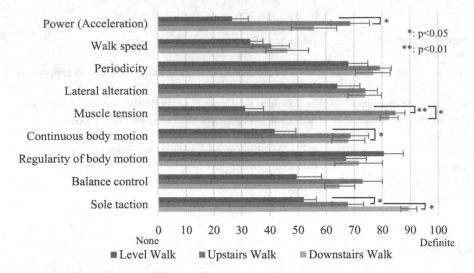

Fig. 7. Results of sensation ratings of level walking and stair walking.

5 Optimization of Motion Stimulus

Our preliminary experiment revealed that presenting the same amount of vestibular display motion (lift, roll, pitch) as that involved in real body motion was too intense to be perceived as the sensation of walking. Although the mechanisms underlying this effect are unclear, we considered that this difference in sensation may have been related to at least two inconsistencies between the real and virtual (passive) experience of walking. First, the motor command and its efference copy [5] are not produced in the case of passive experience, so processing of internal motion model (body schema) in the brain differs from that in active motion. The difference includes sensory inhibition which occurs in active motion to reduce the intensity of the sensation of body motion. The other inconsistency is related to posture; seated and standing postures create different joint motion profiles and muscle activities that would be expected to produce different motion sensations.

As adequate stimulus intensity was not obtained from an unknown body schema, the amount of stimulation, the amplitude of motion (lift, roll, pitch) for the walking sensation were experimentally tested, using the method of adjustment.

5.1 Participants and Procedure

Participants for the experimental measurement were 10 undergraduate and graduate students (average age: 23.1 years) for level walking, 10 students (average age: 23.5 years) for walking up stairs, and 10 students (average age: 23.8 years) for walking down stairs.

Participants walked on a flat floor and stairs with a walk period of 1.4 s, and were instructed to remember the sensations of body motion of lift, pitch and roll rotations during walking. Participants then sat on the vestibular display and adjusted the amplitude of the three degrees of freedom motion (lift, roll, pitch rotation) and the speed (rising and falling) to produce the optimal sensation of walking, where a regular trajectory was fixed to a sinusoidal curve. Participants kept their eyes closed and wore noise emitting earphones during the session. They were instructed to maintain a regular seated posture in which the backbone, thighbone and shin were at right angles to each other.

5.2   Results

The optimal (equivalent) trajectories are shown in Fig. 8. All the amplitudes were less than 1/10 of the body motion during real walking. The adjusted amplitude and speed are shown in Figs. 9 and 10. There was a significant difference between level walking and stair walking in the lift amplitude ($p < 0.0001$, Holm's multiple comparison). The amplitude of level walking was smaller than walking up stairs, and greater than walking down stairs. The speed and acceleration of first half of the trajectory when walking up and down stairs were greater than for level walking. A small amount of asymmetry was observed in speed and acceleration for stair walking (Fig. 10). We considered that this asymmetry represented the sensation of increasing load on the supporting leg and additional foot contact area during stair walking.

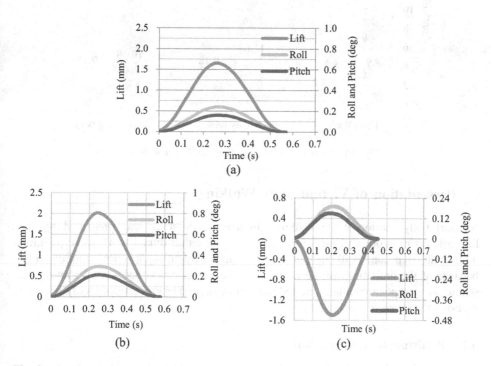

Fig. 8. Average trajectory for (a) level walking. (b) walking upstairs. (c) walking down stairs.

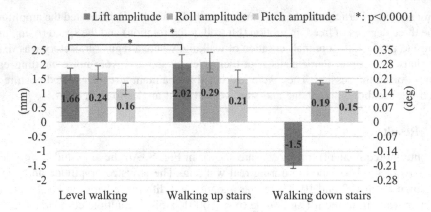

Fig. 9. Amplitude of level walking and stair walking.

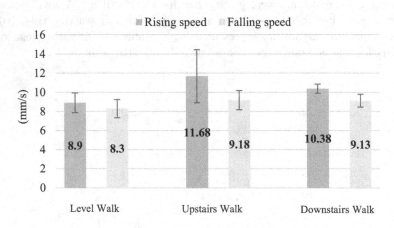

Fig. 10. Velocity of level walking and stair walking.

6 Presentation of Virtual Stair Walking

Vertical body motion while walking up and down stairs was presented by the lifting/lowering motion of the vestibular display in either direction. However, continuous multi-step stair walking cannot be achieved by lifting/lowering motion only, because of the limitations of the actuator stroke. Thus, it was necessary to return the seat to the start position after a limited number of steps. The characteristics of the return motion effect were investigated.

6.1 Participants and Procedure

Ten graduate and undergraduate students (average age: 23.5 years) participated in an evaluation experiment to compare four types of return motion. The second half (the return component) of the adjusted trajectory (Fig. 8) was changed in four ways;

reduced to 0 (the vestibular display continued lifted or lowered), 1/3 (return ratio 1/3), 2/3 (return ratio 2/3), 1 (complete return).

First, the participant walked on a flat floor and stairs with a walk period of 1.4 s, and made an effort to remember the sensation of the body motion. The participant then sat on the vestibular display with the backbone, thighbone and shin at right angles to each other. The stimuli were presented in a random order. The participant evaluated the walking sensation using a VAS ranging from no sensation (0) to the equivalent of real walking (100). The participant closed their eyes and wore headphones emitting noise during the session.

6.2   Results

Figure 11 shows the sensation of walking for the four return ratios. While walking up stairs, a return ratio of 2/3 was the strongest sensation, and showed a significant trend ($p = 0.06$) compared with return ratio 1. The sensation intensity for walking down stairs was significantly different among the return ratios ($p < 0.05$). These results indicate that the motion of walking both up and down stairs was required to present the sensation of walking up stairs, and for walking down stairs to a lesser extent.

This may reflect the profile of real stair walking. The head motion trajectory in real walking, measured in the previous experiment is shown in Figs. 11 and 12. These trajectories indicated that the head exhibited acceleration in both the up and down directions during each step when walking up or down stairs. There was downward motion of 7 mm while walking up stairs, and an upward motion of 10 mm while walking down stairs. Thus, the results suggested that motion with a return ratio of less than 1 is suitable for inducing the sensation of walking on stairs (Fig. 13).

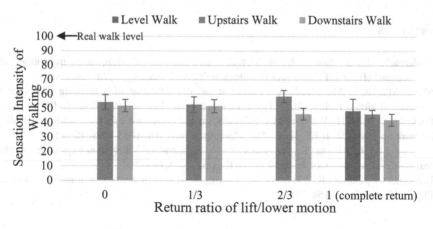

Fig. 11. Sensation of walking.

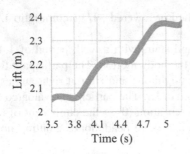

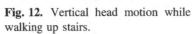

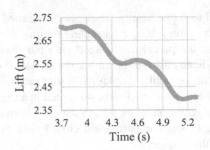

Fig. 12. Vertical head motion while walking up stairs.

Fig. 13. Vertical head motion while walking down stairs.

7   Conclusion

In the current study, we tested a method for inducing the sensation of walking using a vestibular display. The adjusted trajectory of the display motion to represent walking was less than 10% of real walking motion. Regarding the presentation of stair walking, the results suggested asymmetry in the motion trajectory. For walking up stairs, a return motion ratio of less than one was appropriate for increasing the sensation.

Future studies should examine the integration of the vestibular display with displays of other modalities. Moreover, it may be useful for future research to investigate the sensation of active control of the body (agency).

Acknowledgements. This work was partially supported by MIC/SCOPE #141203019, JSPS KAKENHI Grant Number JP26240029, 18H04118, and NICT #143u101 projects.

References

1. Hollerbach, J.M.: Handbook of Virtual Environments: Design, Implementation, and Applications (Human Factors and Ergonomics) (2002). Stanney, K.M. (ed.)
2. Slater, M., Usoh, M., Steed, A.: Taking steps: the influence of a walking technique on presence in virtual reality. ACM Trans. Comput.-Hum. Interact. **2**, 201–219 (1995)
3. Peck, T.C., Fuchs, H., Whitton, M.C.: The design and evaluation of a large-scale real-walking locomotion interface. IEEE Trans. Vis. Comput. Graph. **18**, 1053–1067 (2012)
4. Ikei, Y., Abe, K., Hirota, K., Amemiya, T.: A multisensory VR system exploring the ultra-reality. In: Proceedings of the VSMM 2012, pp. 71–78 (2012)
5. Rossignol, S., Dubuc, R., Gossard, J.-P.: Dynamic sensorimotor interactions in locomotion. Physiol. Rev. **86**, 89–154 (2006)

Implementation of Two-Point Control System in SPIDAR-HS for the Rod Tracking Task in Virtual Reality Environment

Hiroya Suzuki[1](✉), Ryuki Tsukikawa[1](✉), Daiji Kobayashi[2](✉),
Makoto Sato[3](✉), Takehiko Yamaguchi[4], and Tetsuya Harada[1](✉)

[1] Tokyo University of Science, 6-3-1 Niijuku, Katsushika-ku, Tokyo, Japan
`suzuki.hiroya.hrlb@gmail.com`, `8118530@ed.tus.ac.jp`,
`harada@te.noda.tus.ac.jp`
[2] Chitose Institute of Science and Technology,
758-65 Bibi, Chitose, Hokkaido, Japan
`daiji.kobayashi@dream.com`
[3] Tokyo Institute of Technology, 4259 Nagatsuta-cho,
Midori-ku, Yokohama, Kanagawa, Japan
`mkt.sato@gmail.com`
[4] Suwa University of Science, 5000-1 Toyohira, Chino, Nagano, Japan

Abstract. The purpose of this paper is to elucidate the contribution of haptic and visual sense to the sense of embodiment (SoE) in the virtual reality (VR) environment by physiological behavior measurement. To achieve the goal, we employed a rod tracking task which passes the rod held in hand in the sinusoidal path. However, there was some problem with the VR system. There is an unstable rotation of an end effector from its shape, as well as the misdirected force resulting from this rotation. In order to solve these problems, we implemented a two-point haptic system and constructed an application that efficiently performs the rod tracking task.

In the evaluation of the experimental environment, the device accuracy measurement in the workspace and the experimental environment evaluation via physiological behavior measurement was conducted. The experimental environment evaluation via physiological behavior measurement was conducted by measuring the myoelectric potential and subjective evaluation questionnaire in the rod tracking task. The evaluation results revealed that the device accuracy is not impressive in the workspace; the performance significantly decreased in the VR environment compared to the real environment.

In future research, we shall consider how to improve device accuracy, introduced a chroma key technology, development of a haptic model, to mention a few. Besides, we shall create an environment that can execute tasks for establishing SoE.

Keywords: VR · SPIDAR · SoE · Haptics

© Springer Nature Switzerland AG 2019
S. Yamamoto and H. Mori (Eds.): HCII 2019, LNCS 11570, pp. 47–57, 2019.
https://doi.org/10.1007/978-3-030-22649-7_5

1 Introduction

1.1 Background and Purpose

Based on "Virtual Reality Science" [1], virtual reality (VR) is a technology aimed at using an environment where a human is substantially equivalent to the real environment. It has self-projectability (SP), three-dimensional spatiality (TS), and real-time interactivity (RI). SP refers to the capacity to realize a consistent state between different human sensory modalities. Furthermore, TS and RI can be measured using objective values. However, it is challenging to evaluate SP because it is subjective to feelings. Gallagher [2] defined "a feeling that is causing a particular exercise or a feeling that it is oneself, not anyone else" as the sense of agency (SoA). SoA, or sense of embodiment (SoE) as a broader concept, is considered to be the same as the concept of SP. Moreover, it well-known that SoA is initially studied in the field of cognitive neuroscience. There are several ongoing types of research on the characteristics of SoE subjectivity even in the real environment. Among these researches, Hannah et al. [3] advocates the usefulness of applying the concept of SoA in the field of neuroscience to human-computer interaction (HCI). HCI is a field of research that is concerned with communication between humans and computers. In recent years, research that incorporates VR technology as a theme has been on the increase. Besides that, SoE is subjective to feeling; its evaluation can be quite challenging; moreover, an index for quantitative evaluation of SoE is unknown. Successful quantitative evaluation of SoE will undoubtedly lead to quantitative evaluation of all the three elements of virtual reality, which will significantly contribute to the development of VR technology.

This paper aims to elucidate the contribution of haptic and visual sense to SoE in a VR environment by physiological behavior measurement. To achieve the goal of this paper, we employed a rod tracking task which passes a rod held in hand along a sinusoidal path.

2 SPIDAR-HS

2.1 SPIDAR

SPIDAR is haptic devices configured by module(s) that uses a motor with a rotary encoder and a string. The module displays force sense on the end effector attached at the end of a string by the motor and measures its position by the encoder. Various kinds of haptics devices have been devised and constructed using the SPIDAR system. For example, SPIDAR-G is a 7-DOF haptic device; SPIDAR-I is a string built in a six-degree-of-freedom haptics device, and SPIDAR-S is for mobile devices using sound output. The SPIDAR system proposed in this paper which is extended to the human scale is named SPIDAR-HS. Moreover, we have improved this experimental environment. Figure 1 shows a SPIDAR-HS system. The green clothes are used for chroma keying.

2.2   System Configuration

Device

(a) *VIVE Pro HMD*

VIVE Pro HMD is used for immersive visual display, and the specifications are shown in Table 2.

VIVE Pro HMD can track 360° in a play area of at least 2×1.5 m up to 4.5×4.5 m. By using the front camera, user can check the surrounding situation while wearing the HMD. With this camera and the chroma key, user can project real hands and specific objects in the virtual world constructed by CG. The base stations, necessary for tracking HMD in the play area, are installed diagonally on the frame of SPIDAR-HS.

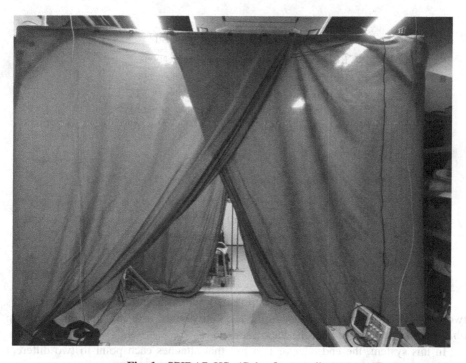

Fig. 1. SPIDAR-HS. (Color figure online)

(b) *SPIDAR-HS*

SPIDAR-HS has been improved to solve the problem in [5] which was found by the previous experiments. We applied two-point control to rod tracking task. The previous rod tracking task was performed using a 6DOF SPIDAR-GCC system. This system has a control method enabling the position measurement and force display with 3DOF position and 3DOF rotation on an end effector by the eight modules. In this control method, there was a problem of the rotation of the virtual end effector becoming unstable and the force sense presentation becoming inaccurate due to the shape of the end effector. Therefore, to avoid this problem, we adopted a two-point control system. This system consists of two 3DOF haptic points that use four modules each (Table 1).

Table 1. VIVE Pro HMD specifications [4]

VIVE Pro HMD specifications	
Screen	Dual AMOLED 3.5" diagonal
Resolution	1440 × 1600 pixels per eye
Refresh rate	90 Hz
Field of view	110°
Sensors	SteamVR Tracking, G-sensor, gyroscope, proximity, IPD sensor

Table 2. Motor specifications [6]

RE 25 maxon motor 118746 specifications	
Nominal voltage [V]	24
Starting current [A]	3.1
Maximum continuous torque [mN · m]	28
Pulley radius [m]	0.01

Table 3. Encoder specifications [7]

HEDS 5540 maxon motor 110511 specifications	
Count/rotation (resolution)	500
Maximum angular acceleration [rad/s^2]	250000
Maximum allowable speed [rpm]	12000

The benefit of this system is it controls two points. In instances where it attaches two points to an index finger and a thumb respectively, the user can pinch and move an object with one's finger with the haptic sense.

In this system, the end effector is a rod that attaches each point to two different positions on it. The SPIDAR-HS system can present 5DOF haptic sense and measure 5DOF position and posture, except for the role of the rod.

The end effector in the rod tracking task is a rod with 501 mm length and 10 mm diameter. The virtual end effector is an end effector that exists in the virtual environment and plays a role of reflecting the position and rotation of the actual end effector and visually presenting an appropriate end effector.

We also changed the motor and encoder. Tables 2 and 3 show the motor and encoder specifications, respectively. The string used is the fishing line of PE No. 6.

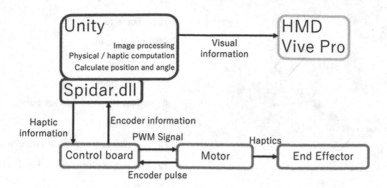

Fig. 2. The SPIDAR-HS system configuration diagram.

Software Configuration

(a) *Force feedback.*

Figure 2 shows the system configuration of the constructed device. The visual and haptic information is given by VIVE Pro HMD and SPIDAR-HS, respectively. Unity is a developing environment for 3D programs.

The flow of force sense presentation in this system is shown below.

1. The control unit reads the change in length of each string connected to the end effector.
2. The position on both ends of the end effector is notified to the unity via the Spidar.dll.
3. The force to be presented is calculated from the difference in position between the virtual and real end effector.
4. Passing the force to be presented to spidar.dll, the dll issues commands to some specific motors to wind up their strings.
5. The specified motors start winding up based on the commands, the end effector is drawn to the designated direction, and the force sense is presented to the user holding it.

The haptic update frequency is 50 Hz, and the minimum guaranteed frequency is 33 Hz.

Details of the haptic model in the rod tracking task are described below. Figure 3 shows a conceptual diagram of the haptic model, where $\vec{v}$ is the normal vector of the contact point calculated by Unity, and $\vec{N}$ is the force calculated by the spring-damper model.

Using the notations in Fig. 3, the force sense to be presented is given by Eqs. (1) and (2).

$$\vec{N} = K \cdot \left(\overrightarrow{P_R} - \overrightarrow{P_V} \right) + B \cdot \left(\dot{\overrightarrow{P_R}} - \dot{\overrightarrow{P_V}} \right); \tag{1}$$

$$\overrightarrow{N_V} = \frac{\vec{v}}{|v|} \cdot |\vec{N}|; \tag{2}$$

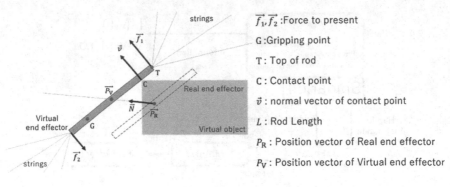

Fig. 3. A haptic model for rod tracking task.

$$\begin{cases} \vec{f_1} = \dfrac{L-\overline{GC}+\overline{GT}}{\overline{GC}} \cdot \vec{N_V}; \\ \vec{f_2} = \vec{N_V} - \vec{f_1}, \end{cases} \qquad (3)$$

where K and B are the spring and damper constants, respectively. The force shown in Eqs. (1) and (2) is based on the assumption that the contact point and the upper end of the rod are on the same side as seen from the gripping point. If this assumption is not satisfied, that is, if the collision point and the upper end of the rod are on different sides as seen from the gripping point, it is necessary to replace $\vec{f_1}$ with $\vec{f_2}$.

(b) *Chroma key*

Chroma key is a technique for transmitting a specific color component, thereby allowing a part of an image to pass through and combine with another image. By using the chroma key, a user's real body can be displayed in the VR environment. Projecting a real body in the VR environment is expected to raise the SE to a great extent. In the preparatory experiment, we ensured VIVE's front camera can be used as the chroma key camera. The image acquired by the camera is processed by the surface shader* based on the following algorithm below, it is displayed on the quad**, and synthesized in the VR environment.

We remark that the surface shader uses the following values: color to be transparent (KC), hue distance (N), saturation distance (SN), transparency gradient (G), and transparent hue distance (TN). The shader converts the image from the RGB color space to the HSV color space. The absolute value difference between the converted color and KC is calculated, and if the hue component difference is smaller than N and the saturation component is larger than SN, the pixel drawing of interest is discarded. Additionally, when the hue component difference is smaller than TN, and the saturation component is larger than SN, then the transparency of the pixel of interest is reduced based on the value of G. Figure 4 shows the appearance of the chroma key. One can see that the hand in the center of the screen is cut off from the wall of the upper screen side.

*Surface shader: Simplified description version of vertex shader and fragment shader.

**Quad: Unity primitive game object, rectangle mesh with four vertices.

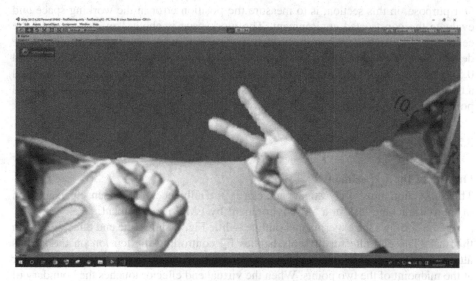

Fig. 4. Chroma key situation.

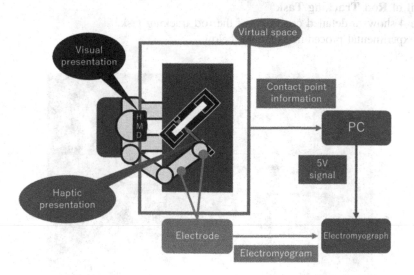

Fig. 5. Rod tracking task experimental outline diagram.

3   System Evaluation and Rod Tracking Task

3.1   Measurement of Position Error in the Working Space

Our purpose, in this section, is to measure the position error in the working space and evaluate the constructed environment. The workspace is about 1 m cube around the center of SPIDAR-HS. When the origin of the coordinates is set to the center of the device, the end effector is moved at a uniform speed for about 10 s at (−0.5, −0.5, and 0.5) corresponding to one of the vertices of the working space cube. Since we adopted a two-point control, the position coordinates of the two virtual end effectors point 1 and point 2 in the unity were recorded. This was repeated ten times.

3.2   Rod Tracking Task

Outline of the Experiment

This subsection aims to investigate and clarify the influence of force sense presentation of the rod tracking task in a VR environment by EMG measurement.

Figure 5 shows the experimental outline, while Fig. 6 shows the end effector used in this task. The end effector presents haptics by controlling the tension on the strings attached on both ends of the end effector. We set the position of the virtual end effector at the midpoint of the two points. When the virtual end effector touches the boundary of the path, myoelectric potential measurement is carried out.

Detail of Rod Tracking Task

Table 4 shows a detailed condition of the rod tracking task.
The experimental procedure is shown below.

Fig. 6. An end effector used in rod tracking task.

1. Leave the power of the right arm unplugged. At this time, the experimenter measures the myoelectric potential for 10 s as the myoelectric potential at rest.
2. Wear the HMD and grip the end effector.
3. Touch the virtual end effector at the starting point (the far end of the path), count from 1 to 5 orally for about 5 s, and move the rod along the path to the turning point (the near end of the path).
4. Touch and count again at the turning point and pass the rod along the path to the starting point.
5. When the participant returns to the starting point, count again.

In this task, the experimenter made the participant sit down so that his body will be parallel to the desk, and instructed to do tasks with only the arm without moving the head and body as much as possible. After conducting step 1 to 5, a subjective evaluation questionnaire was conducted. Under these conditions, the task was repeated until either the number of contacts between the rod and boundary of the path became less or equal to ten times, or the number of contacts increased.

Items on the subjective evaluation questionnaire include: "In which section did you touch the boundary of the path? (with reasons of contact)," "What did you do to avoid touching?", also, "Which section was the easiest? And which section was most challenging?" Twelve right-handed males in their twenties were used in this experiment.

4 Result and Discussion

4.1 Measurement of the Position Error of Working Space

Let one of the points of the two-point control be point 1, and another be point 2. In the rod tracking task, the position of the virtual end effector is the midpoint of the two points. Table 5 shows the relative error and coefficient of variation for each x, y, and z component of the virtual end effector of the conventional system, as well as the relative error of the virtual end effector.

Table 4. Detailed conditions of the task.

Experimental conditions	
Rod length [mm]	501
Rod diameter [mm]	10
Path size [mm]	$200 \times 300 \times 20$
Path width [mm]	20
Minimum required force* [N]	0.97
Myoelectric potential measurement location	Abductor digit minimal muscle

*The force to keep the string from loosening.

Table 5. Relative error and coefficient of variation of the virtual end effector.

	x component	y component	z component
Relative error [%]	−0.199	0.939	0.060
Relative error (previous) [%]	−0.38	−0.53	0.96

It is evident from Table 5 that the experimental result is not significantly different from the previous result obtained in [7]. Here, it is found that the relative error is less than the one in the previous research in [7]. The inaccurate force sense which was a problem in the research conducted in [7] was improved on by introducing, in this paper, the two-point control and the force which was not measured but felt as correct was displayed. Based on the experimental results, significant accuracy was ensured in the workspace.

5   Conclusions

The purpose of this paper is to construct an experimental environment for establishing quantitative evaluation index of SoE. To achieve this goal, we constructed a VR environment and conducted physiological behavior measurements during a task conducted therein.

In the rod tracking task, there was a problem with the force sense presentation in the previous environment. To solve this problem, we implemented the presentation of force by a two-point control technique. Besides, the lack of visual information such as shadows was improved.

Hence, in this paper, we achieved the following: First, the position accuracy of SPIDAR-HS proposed in this paper is considered to be good. Second, using the two-point control system, the force was presented at a more considerable level than the previous method.

From the above findings, we list the problems and prospects in this research. More accurate presentation of haptic information is required. In this research, haptics relies on the magnitude of force by spring-damper model. However, the rod tracking task requires more precise haptics. In such a case, it is considered necessary to devise a force presentation method by adopting a different force presentation model or multiple models. Finally, the visual presentation in this research has some problems such as the lack of the user's hand, and partially different from the real one in the appearance. This seems to be closely related to SoE. Therefore, it is a problem to be solved by introducing the chroma key technology mentioned in Sect. 2.2 Software Configuration (b). Moreover, it seems that it is crucial to clarify whether the haptic and visual improvements described above have any effect on the myoelectric potential, and also establish the SoE index.

Acknowledgement. We would like to thank all the research participants. And also we would like to thank Enago (www.enago.jp) for the English language review. This work was supported by JSPS KAKENHI Grant Number JP17H01782.

References

1. Tachi, S., Sato, M., Hirose, M.: Virtual Reality, 1st edn. The Virtual Reality Society of Japan, Tokyo (2011). (in Japanese)
2. Gallagher, S.: Philosophical conceptions of the self: implications for cognitive science. Trends Cogn. Sci. **4**(1), 14–21 (2000)
3. Limerick, H., Coyle, D., Moore, J.W.: The experience of agency in human computer interactions: a review. Front. Hum. Neurosci. **8**, 643 (2014)
4. HTC: VIVE Pro | The professional-grade VR headset. https://www.vive.com/us/product/vive-pro/. Accessed 10 Jan 2019
5. Tsukikawa, R., et al.: Construction of experimental system SPIDAR-HS for designing VR guidelines based on physiological behavior measurement. In: Chen, J., Fragomeni, G. (eds.) Virtual, Augmented and Mixed Reality: Interaction, Navigation, Visualization, Embodiment, and Simulation. LNCS, vol. 10909, pp. 245–256. Springer, Cham (2018). https://doi.org/10.1007/978-3-319-91581-4_18
6. maxon motor: RE 25. https://www.maxonmotorusa.com/maxon/view/product/motor/dcmotor/re/re25/118746. Accessed 01 Mar 2019
7. maxon motor: HEADS 5540. https://www.maxonmotorusa.com/maxon/view/product/sensor/encoder/Optische-Encoder/ENCODERHEDS5540/110511. Accessed 01 Mar 2019

Analysis of Differences in the Manner to Move Objects in a Real and Virtual Space

Yuki Tasaka[1]($\boxtimes$), Hikaru Ichimaru[1]($\boxtimes$), Sakae Yamamoto[1]($\boxtimes$),
Makoto Sato[2]($\boxtimes$), Takehiko Yamaguchi[3]($\boxtimes$), and Tetsuya Harada[1]($\boxtimes$)

[1] Tokyo University of Science, 6-3-1 Niijuku, Katsushika-ku, Tokyo, Japan
{8118528, 8115014}@ed.tus.ac.jp,
sakaeyam@jcom.home.ne.jp, harada@te.noda.tus.ac.jp
[2] Tokyo Institute of Technology, 4259 Nagatsuta-cho,
Midori-ku, Yokohama, Kanagawa, Japan
mkt.sato@gmail.com
[3] Suwa University of Science, 5000-1 Toyohira, Chino-city, Nagano, Japan
tk-ymgch@rs.sus.ac.jp

Abstract. One crucial property of virtual reality (VR) is "self-projection". This means that an avatar representing a user in a virtual space is the user itself with a higher level of reality. It can be referred to as a "sense of embodiment (SoE)". Using head-mounted display (HMD), a three-dimensional (3D) virtual space that is generated by a computer with visual sense can be recognized. Besides, if the user can touch objects in the virtual space and feel the haptic sense on one's hands using haptic devices, the SoE will undoubtedly increase. However, since the workspace of the user's hand in using the haptic device has limitations, the task performed in the virtual space differs from the task performed in the real space. Therefore, in this paper, we evaluate the degree of agreement between the performance of a task in a virtual space and real space through experiments consisting of the same task. As the haptic device for virtual space we used SPIDAR-GCC, which is a type of parallel wire haptic device. In the real space, we asked seven research participants to move a tennis ball and a cola-can placed on a desk to a prescribed position. With regard to the experiments in the virtual space, we developed two 3D spaces where a tennis ball or a cola-can are placed on a desk. Then, using HMD and SPIDAR-GCC, we asked the participants to move these objects to a prescribed position. We recorded these tasks in the form of videos and analyzed them. The result of the analyses revealed that there are significant differences in the manner in which these objects were moved.

Keywords: Haptic device · Force sense · Task analysis · SoE

1 Introduction

1.1 Background and Purpose

One crucial property of virtual reality (VR) is "self-projection". This means that an avatar representing a user in a virtual space is the user itself with a higher level of reality. It can be rephrased as "sense of embodiment (SoE)". By using a head-mounted

© Springer Nature Switzerland AG 2019
S. Yamamoto and H. Mori (Eds.): HCII 2019, LNCS 11570, pp. 58–69, 2019.
https://doi.org/10.1007/978-3-030-22649-7_6

display (HMD), it is possible to recognize a three-dimensional (3D) virtual space generated by a computer that has a visual sense. Also, if the user can touch objects in the virtual space and feel the haptic sense on one's own hands by using a haptic device, then the SoE will increase. Therefore, the feeling when touching the object in the virtual space must be realistically reproduced consistently. However, since the workspace of the user's hand using the haptic device has limitations, the task performed in the virtual space differs from the one performed in the real space. Therefore, in this paper, we focus on the examination of the degree of coincidence of human work in virtual and real spaces that are constructed to make the two as identical as possible. The final goal of this research is to evaluate the degree of the agreement between a task in the real and virtual space as well as to investigate the SoE. With regard to the task in the virtual space, we utilized SPIDAR-GCC, which is a haptic device that can present 6DOF force sense, and we also used HMD.

1.2   Outline of Research

In the real space, the research participants performed the task of moving the object a distance of 60 cm away, while in the virtual space, they moved the object a distance of 60 cm away using the haptic device SPIDAR-GCC and the HMD. Comparing the performances of the task performed in different kinds of spaces, we analyzed and evaluated the differences in distance and trajectory of the objects using captured videos.

2   Proposed Device and Application

2.1   SPIDAR-GCC

Sato et al. [1] developed a space interface device for artificial reality (SPIDAR) for presenting force sense using parallel wire scheme. Strings are tied to a force sense presentation part called end effector, and they are controlled by motors to generate tension. Owing to this tension, the user can feel force sense via the end effector. Besides, the position and orientation of the end effector can be obtained from the length of the strings. In this paper, we employed the SPIDAR-GCC shown in Fig. 1, which can present a force sense of 6DOF. The sphere grips serve as the end effector. Table 1 shows the specifications of SPIDAR-GCC. This specification is described in the source code "DeviceSpec.cpp" indicating the device specification of SPIDAR.

2.2   FOVE

We use an HMD, which a FOVE developed by FOVE Inc., to display the virtual space generated by the computer. Figure 2 shows the FOVE while Table 2 shows its specifications.

2.3   Developed Application

In this research, using SPIDAR-GCC and HMD, a task was conducted to grab and move objects in the virtual space. We developed virtual space using Unity [3] which is one of the developing environments for 3D programs. Figure 3 shows an example of a developed virtual space.

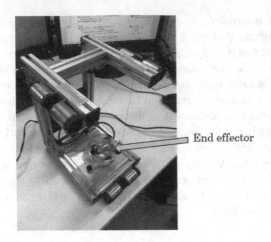
End effector

Fig. 1. SPIDAR-GCC.

Table 1. The specifications of SPIDAR-GCC.

Update rate [Hz]	500
Minimum tension [N]	0.45
Maximum tension [N]	2.0
Motor terminal voltage [V]	12
Motor terminal resistance [ohm]	7.84
Motor torque constant [Nm/A]	0.0092
Motor speed constant [rpm/V]	900
No load current [A]	0.06
Maximum duration of force presentation [s]	60
Grip radius [m]	0.0565
Connection	USB 2.0

When the end effector of SPIDAR-GCC is grasped and moved by hand, the virtual hand shown by the white sphere moves at a distance multiplication factor of 20. Also, while the user is pressing a button on the end effector with one's finger, an object can be grabbed. When the button is released, the object can be released; this makes it possible to grab, move, and release the object.

We chose a tennis ball and unopened cola-can. As reasons for choosing, both are well-recognized in terms of size and weight, and we thought that they are clues for the distance when objects are moving. In particular, the tennis ball is similar to the shape and size of the end effector of SPIDAR-GCC. Figures 4 and 5 show 3D models of tennis balls and cola-cans used in the virtual space. Also, the size and weight of tennis balls and cola-cans used in the virtual space were set to be the same as those used in real space; Table 3 shows their size and weight.

Fig. 2. FOVE.

Table 2. The specifications of FOVE [2].

Weight [g]		520
Resolution		2560 × 1440
Frame rate [fps]		70
Viewing angle [°]		up to 100
Connection		HDMI 1.4, USB 3.0, USB 2.0 (Power supply only)
Eye tracking sensor	System	Infrared eye tracking system × 2
	Accuracy	<1°
	Frame rate [fps]	120

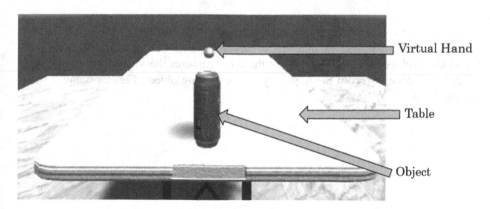

Fig. 3. Virtual space.

Fig. 4. 3D model of a tennis ball.

Fig. 5. 3D model of a cola-can.

Table 3. Size and weight of tennis ball and cola-can.

	Tennis ball	Cola-can
Diameter [cm]	6.54	5.2
Weight [g]	56	267
Height [cm]	——	13.3

To analyze the task of grasping and moving the object using videos, we set two cameras in the virtual space so that we can capture a video. One of the cameras captures the video displayed on the HMD, while the other captures the video from the left side of the workspace to record the trajectory of the moving object. Figures 6 and 7 show captured videos.

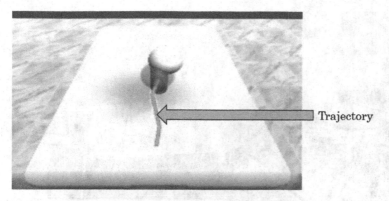

Fig. 6. Camera image displayed on HMD.

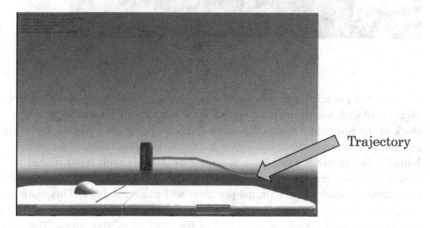

Fig. 7. Camera image from left side of the space

3   An Experiment of Motion Analysis

3.1   Experimental Method

Experiment in Real Space

In this experiment, the number of participants was seven. Figure 8 shows the real workspace. The procedure of the experiment is shown in (1) to (4) below.

(1) Three cameras A, B, and C were installed for the following purposes:
     Camera A: To record the eye movement of the research participant; it was placed left oblique in front of the research participant.
     Camera B: To record the movement of the object; it was placed on the left side of the workspace.
     Camera C: To record the movements of the participant's arms; it was placed left oblique behind of the research participant.

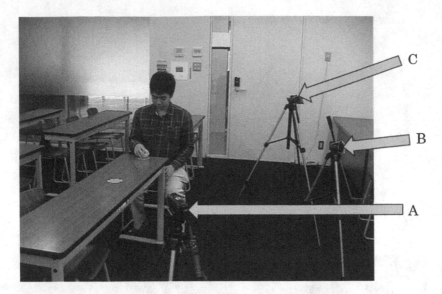

Fig. 8. Experimental setup in real space.

(2) The research participant moves the object from the initial position, i.e., where the object is placed, to another position that is 60 cm away. As the marker, a tape was stuck at the initial and terminal positions. The experimenter placed the object at the initial position.

(3) Initially, the research participant is sitting on a chair with hand placed on his knees. With our cue "Start" the research participant grabbed the object with his right hand, moved to the terminal position, and placed it there. This made them grasp the distance of 60 cm. As shown in Table 4, the research participant alternately moved the object linearly and freely in every five times. The experimenter decided the time of the task end as the point when the research participant placed the tennis ball on the desk and released his hand off it.

Table 4. Order of the manner to move.

	Linear	Freely
Order	1	2
	3	4
	5	6
	7	8
	9	10

(4) After the research participant had finished the task with the tennis ball, the experimenter changes the tennis ball to a cola-can, and the research participant repeats the steps mentioned in (3).

Experiment in Virtual Space

Figure 9 shows the state of the experiment in virtual space using SPIDAR-GCC and HMD. In the same manner, as the work in the real space, research participant moves each of the tennis ball and cola-can from the initial position to another position 60 cm away. Table 4 shows the manner of movement to be followed. In this case, since we allow the research participants to decide the distance of 60 cm, there were no markers on the initial and terminal positions. Initially, the research participant was sitting on a chair, wearing an HMD, and grasping the end effector of SPIDAR-GCC. With our cue "Start", the research participant pushed the button on the end effector, grasped the object, and moved to the terminal position. We regarded task end time as the instance when the research participant placed the object on the desk and released his hand from it by releasing the button.

Fig. 9. Experimental setup in virtual space.

3.2 Experimental Results and Discussion

Figures 10 and 11 demonstrate the movement distance of the tennis ball and cola-can in real and virtual spaces, respectively. Figure 12 shows the average of movement distance of objects obtained from observing seven participants. Besides, Figs. 13 and 14 show the lifting height of the objects, while Fig. 15 shows the average of maximum lifting height of objects obtained from observing seven participants.

First, we discuss Figs. 10 and 11. It was found that many of the research participants moved the object farther than 60 cm in the virtual space; we thought this could be owing to the sense of distance of 60 cm learned in the real space and the distance multiplication factor of 20 times in the virtual space.

Next, we discuss Figs. 13 and 14. It was found that all the research participants lifted the object higher in the virtual space than in the real world. As one of the causes, they were looking at the workspace in an overhead view, so it was challenging for them to grasp the lifting height of the object visually. Therefore, probably, the object being lifted higher in the virtual space is influenced by the distance multiplication factor.

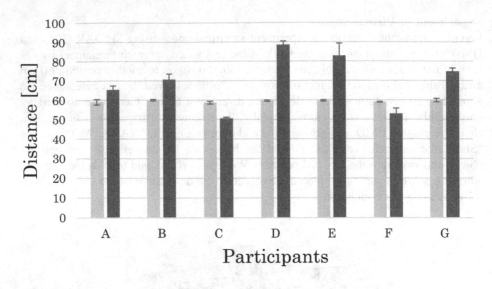

Fig. 10. The movement distance of tennis ball.

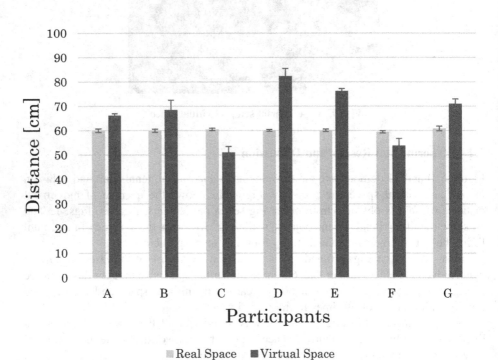

Fig. 11. The movement distance of cola-can.

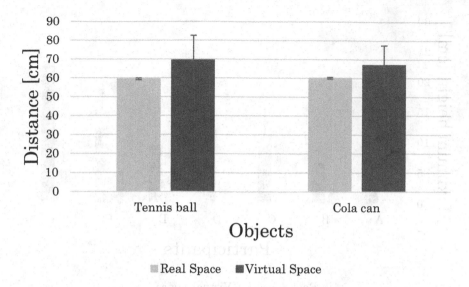

Fig. 12. The average of movement distance of objects obtained from observing seven participants.

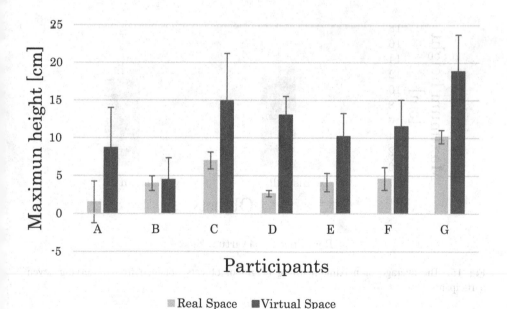

Fig. 13. Maximum lifting height of tennis ball.

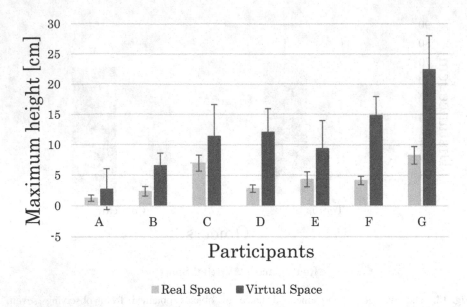

Fig. 14. The maximum lifting height of cola-can.

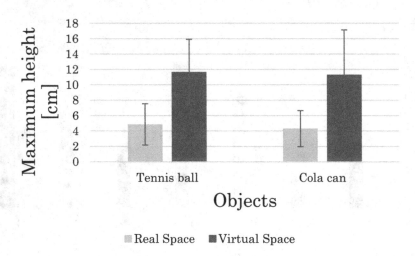

Fig. 15. The average of maximum lifting height of objects obtained from observing seven participants.

4   Conclusions and Future Work

In this paper, we analyzed the differences in the tasks in the real and virtual spaces using recorded videos. In the task performed in the virtual space, there was a tendency to move the object farther than 60 cm under the influence of the distance multiplication factor of the end effector of SPIDAR-GCC, and these are significant differences in the task in the real and virtual spaces. Furthermore, in our research, we set the multiplication factor to 20 times. The effect of this factor is evident in the difference in the task of moving objects. Therefore, in future research, we shall perform some experiments to adjust the distance multiplication factor for the task without conflicting feelings, and also explore the relationship between higher SoE and visual/haptic information. Also, it is considered that the space recognition in the virtual space is different from that in the real space; thus, the appearance of the object in the virtual space is different from its appearance in the real space. We shall also experimentally investigate this difference in our subsequent researches.

Acknowledgments. We would like to thank all the research participants. And also we would like to thank Enago (www.enago.jp) for the English language review. This work was supported by JSPS KAKENHI Grant Number JP17H01782.

References

1. Sato, M., Hirata, Y., Kawarada, H.: Space interface device for artificial reality–SPIDAR. EICE Trans. Fundam. Electron. Commun. Comput. Sci. D **J74-D**(7), 887–894 (1991)
2. Home - FOVE Eye Tracking Virtual Reality Headset. https://www.getfove.com/. Accessed 21 Feb 2019
3. Unity Technologies. https://unity3d.com/. Accessed 21 Feb 2019

The Design of the Body:Suit:Score, a Full-Body Vibrotactile Musical Score

Travis J. West[1,3,4]($\boxtimes$), Alexandra Bachmayer[2,3], Sandeep Bhagwati[3,4], Joanna Berzowska[2], and Marcelo M. Wanderley[1,4]

[1] Input Devices and Music Interaction Laboratory,
McGill University, Montreal, QC, Canada
`travis.west@mail.mcgill.ca`
[2] XSLabs, Concordia University, Montreal, QC, Canada
[3] matralab, Concordia University, Montreal, QC, Canada
[4] Center for Interdisciplinary Research in Music Media and Technology,
Montreal, QC, Canada

Abstract. We present the body:suit:score, a vibrotactile musical score that displays instructions and signals directly on musicians' bodies using an array of vibrating motors. Initially inspired by the third author's need for a new kind of score in his compositional practice, the body:suit:score facilitates the exploration of novel musical experiences and performer-audience relationships that are impossible or impractical without such a score, such as allowing the performers to freely move about the performance space amidst the audience. The body:suit:score has been designed through a close collaborative process between artists and technicians. A number of notable design elements and functionalities have emerged in response to this process, and in particular due to the strong requirements for usability and maintainability of the system.

Keywords: Vibrotactile display · Music notation · E-textiles

© Springer Nature Switzerland AG 2019
S. Yamamoto and H. Mori (Eds.): HCII 2019, LNCS 11570, pp. 70–89, 2019.
https://doi.org/10.1007/978-3-030-22649-7_7

1   Introduction

The impetus for the body:suit:score project arose from Bhagwati's research-creation into new forms of score for novel performance situations, in particular the scoring for and coordination of musicians moving through real space. Previous projects had included situational scores for musicians moving in three dimensions within a large stairwell ("Racines Éphémères" (Vienna 2008)) and isolated musicians moving through a cityscape, hearing each other solely via a constantly reconfiguring wireless audio network ("Nexus" (Montréal 2010)). All these projects, however, had required the musicians to memorize elaborate rule systems or to react intuitively to musical cue. These limitations seriously curtailed the kind of complex, situative coordination that we have come to rely on and expect in a stationary music performance with a score and a conductor. The initial motivation was thus to create a workable interface for moving musicians that could embody both the role of the score and that of the conductor.

After some initial tests with portable head-up displays (e.g. Google Glasses) it soon became clear that, for reasons of safety alone, such a score must be non-visual. Two sensory modalities were subsequently pursued in parallel at matralab: the elaborate audio score [1] and the vibrotactile body:suit:score. For the body:suit:score, several composers (Julian Klein, Adam Basanta, Csenge Koloszvari) were invited to accompany the development process, and it was decided early on–for research purposes and according to aesthetic preferences–that each would pursue the creative possibilities of a different approach to the system: its use to convey abstract symbols, continuous parametric changes, and as a replacement for the sense of hearing.

The system described here represents three years of development building on the earlier prototype body:suit:score presented in [2]. Since the beginning of the project, the implementation of the system has gone through two major iterations, with the second and current version designed in response to specific challenges presented by the original prototype, the demands of composers working with the system, and the pieces they envisioned using it for. We will discuss the particular design constraints and requirements of a vibrotactile musical score that have emerged from our collaborative research process, and describe the hardware and software and capabilities of the system that have resulted from these requirements and the various approaches taken by composers when using the body:suit:score.

2   Early Work

The earliest prototypes of the body:suit:score were based on hardware and software adapted from the Ilinx project [3], a multi-sensory installation where participants experienced full-body vibrotactile sensations together with light and sound. Our initial prototypes came to define many of the essential capabilities of the body:suit:score, and the structure of their implementation is strongly reflected in the current iteration (see Fig. 2). In the original version of the system, vibrating motors were activated by motor control boards distributed across

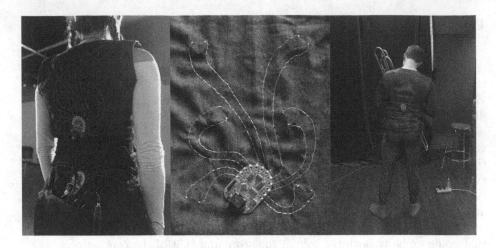

Fig. 1. The original body:suit:score as presented in [2]

the body. Each Arduino-compatible control board activated six motors[1]. The control boards were connected by Ethernet cables to a Beaglebone Black (BBB) single board computer (SBC). This central hub was responsible for receiving and parsing wireless Open Sound Control (OSC) based communication from a Max/MSP program dubbed the conductor program. Once parsed by the SBC, the messages were forwarded to the control boards in a more compact format using serial peripheral interface (SPI). The SPI stream along with power from a single central battery were carried over the Ethernet cables to each control board. The control boards and motors were sewn directly to the garments and electrically connected using silver low-resistance conductive thread with a polyester core (Fig. 1). The spacing of the motors on the suit was determined based on evaluations of the minimum distance at which two motors could be reliably discriminated: motors on the torso were spaced for maximum discrimination, whereas motors on the arms and legs were spaced closer together to allow sensations of continuous movement to be employed.

Several etudes were composed for these early body:suit:scores exploring a variety of approaches, documented in [2]. The work described in [4] was also carried out at this time, evaluating the ease with which different vibrotactile patterns can be recognized. A repertoire of these patterns were used in several pieces, beginning to form the basis of a tactile musical score language.

As well as these contributions, the early versions of the suit had important shortcomings and usability issues. The large SBC and central battery were

---

[1] VPM2 eccentric rotating mass (ERM) vibrating motors from Solarbotics have been used throughout the project, including the current version. These were selected for their availability, ease of use, and because their physical and perceptual characteristics had been characterized for use in musical notification systems during a previous study [5].

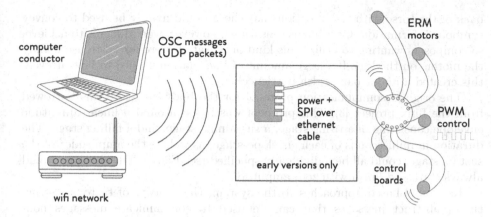

Fig. 2. The conceptual structure of the body:suit:score system from a technological perspective. The conductor program sends messages to control boards that activate vibrating motors.

identified as major sources of weight and bulk, and the use of Ethernet cables to connect these to the motor control boards meant that the suit could not be donned by musicians without assistance. The added bulk was also problematic during performance, as it impeded the wearers ability to move freely.

Difficulties were also encountered with the fit of the garments. A variety of fabrics were tested to try to improve the contact between the motors and the wearer's skin and provide good transmission of vibration from the suit to the body. More stretchy materials such as high-spandex knit fabrics were able to provide better contact with the motors by conforming to the wearer's body shape. In addition, early prototypes were tailored to the musicians who would wear them, providing an excellent fit. Unfortunately, these solutions resulted in other trade-offs. The conductive thread connecting the control boards to the motors had to be embroidered by hand when using these stretchy materials, introducing a significant cost in labour and reducing the repeatability of the manufacturing process. Tailoring the suits to individual musicians made each garment less versatile, providing a poorer fit when worn by other individuals.

As mentioned, the motors and control boards were initially sewn directly to the garments using conductive thread; while this provided an excellent and highly reliable mechanical and electrical connection, it also made the suits more difficult to maintain and wash. If electrical components failed for any reason, replacing them required sitches to be torn and re-sewn, causing significant wear on the garments in the process. While these issues were not immediately problematic, as repairs by hand and careful surface cleaning were still possible, our concern for the longevity of the garments motivated us to consider ways to improve the maintainability of the suits.

It was eventually found that the wide motor spacing on the torso was needlessly limiting. In part due to limitations on the number of motors that could be powered by the central battery, it was decided to widely space the motors on the back of the torso with the intention that these would mainly be used to convey symbolic information. Continuous sensations, however, were difficult to achieve, so composers wanting to utilize this kind of sensation were forced to use mainly the motors on the legs. If a large amount of information needed to be conveyed, this created a major bandwidth bottleneck.

The original communication protocol for the body:suit:score was borrowed from the Ilinx project [3]. This protocol was based around a linear amplitude envelope consisting of a rising stage, a sustaining stage, and a falling stage. The duration in milliseconds of each envelope stage, as well as the amplitude[2] of the sustain stage, could all be individually specified (see Fig. 6). The envelope would always start and finish with zero amplitude.

In symbol-based approaches to the system, the concept of tactons, "structured, abstract messages that can be used to communicate messages non-visually" [6], have provided an especially important framework for working with the suit. In our research we have developed a repertoire of tactons for the body:suit:score that can be used as symbols in a growing tactile language for conveying musical instructions. Using the original control protocol for the suit, a tacton could be displayed by sending several messages sequentially in order to engage and disengage a sequence of actuators in a certain pattern. Unfortunately, because a single tacton was composed of multiple separate messages sent at different times in distinct UDP packets, this introduced multiple opportunities for a tacton or other complex pattern being rendered on the suit to become corrupted by a lost UDP packet. This had the potential to seriously undermine performers' confidence in the system, as it introduced the possibility that at any time they might have to guess at the meaning of half of a tacton conveying a crucial musical instruction. We recognized this as a serious issue that had to be eliminated.

In addition to the amplitude envelope, the control messages also specified which motor to target. This was accomplished using an integer in the OSC address that referred to one of the control boards, and a real number between zero and one that referred to which of the six motors controlled by that board to target. The use of a real number was chosen to allow for the possibility that control boards in the future might include more than six motors. The numbering of the control boards and their motors was hard coded into the firmware of each control board so that the motors were ordered in a consistent manner from left-to-right and top-to-bottom. Unfortunately, when developing new iterations on the design, or if a control board had to be replaced, these hard coded variables were sometimes not properly updated, meaning that the numbering of the motors sometimes became messy and difficult to work with.

Finally, the aforementioned reliability issues also revealed a major challenge when working with the suits in rehearsal: in case there seemed to be a problem, it was very difficult to quickly troubleshoot the suits since the person operating

---

[2] Note that 'amplitude', throughout this paper, will generally refer to the PWM duty cycle from 0.0 to 1.0 inclusive. The duty cycle is considered out of convenience to roughly correspond to the amplitude of vibration of the motor under control.

the conductor program would have to communicate constantly with the musician wearing the suit to see if the messages being sent to the suit were having the expected effect. It was often difficult to explain to the musician exactly what to expect, as well as for the musician to explain exactly what they were feeling. There was clearly a need for more direct feedback from the suit that could be understood by people other than the wearer, such as a software status monitoring system or visual feedback. On the other hand, if visual feedback were added to the suit it was agreed that it should be possible to disable it, in case a composer would prefer a more neutral look during a performance.

Based on the successes and shortcomings of the original body:suit:score system, a set of requirements were developed for a new version:

- The suit must be lightweight and easy to put on and take off without expertise or assistance.
- Every suit must be adjustable to provide an excellent fit, as though tailored to the wearer, without requiring every wearer to have a custom made garment specific to their body shape.
- The suit must provide comfortable but firm contact between the wearer and the vibrating motors.
- The suit should allow total freedom of movement.
- All non-washable electronic components should be removable to facilitate maintenance and care of the garments.
- The spacing of the motors should permit sensations of continuous movement to be produced anywhere on the body.
- The communication protocol should allow complex tactons to be encoded in as few UDP packets as possible, to avoid their corruption by dropped packets.
- Every effort should be made to increase the reliability of the wireless communications.
- The communication protocol should be easy to compose and read, and the numbering of the motors should be adjustable on the fly in case a control board must be replaced.
- Direct feedback should be available from the suits to other people than the wearer to facilitate troubleshooting in rehearsal.
- Visual feedback should have the possibility of being disabled to allow composers some control over the appearance of the body:suit:score in performance.

3 Current Hardware

In response to the requirements that arose while working with the original version of the body:suit:score, the design of the system was revised. The most significant change was to eliminate the single board computer and central battery, opting instead for the motor control boards to have individual batteries and WiFi communication capabilities (Fig. 3). This decision resulted in a number of immediate design improvements: Ethernet cables were no longer necessary to connect each

Fig. 3. The current version of the body:suit:score with the LEDs removed

control board to a central hub, thus significantly reducing the bulkiness of the system, improving the freedom of movement of the wearer, and making it possible for musicians to put on and take off the suit without assistance; use of distributed power allowed additional control boards to be added to the system easily as long as there was a space to put them, whereas the central battery had previously imposed an upper limit on the number of control boards and motors that could be used on one suit; by distributing wireless communications directly to the control boards, several links in the chain of communication were removed, resulting in more reliable transmission of data all the way to the actuators, as well as somewhat simplified troubleshooting; and finally, the use of a more powerful 32-bit microcontroller (ESP8266) allowed for a less compact but much more readable communications protocol to be used all the way from the conductor program to the control boards, without any need for a more compact intermediate format.

To provide a balance between fit, motor contact, and manufacturability, the textile aspect of the garments was designed to combine the use of stretchy and non-stretch fabrics. The parts of the garments with motors were designed to use a medium weight linen, allowing the conductive thread to be layed automatically with a CNC embroidery machine. For other parts of the garments, such as the sides of the vests, stretchy high-spandex knit fabric was used to allow the garment to fit snugly. On the vests an adjustable fit was also achieved by using lace or ribbon on the sides of the vest to cinch down any slack in the fit of the garment (similar to the way a shoelace works). Using these enhancements, the current design of the garments allows them to fit a wide variety of body shapes while always providing very good contact with the motors.

To improve the maintainability of the garments, the motors and control boards were made to be removable from the suit. This was achieved using a variety of connectors (Fig. 4): the motors are now attached to the suit using custom-made conductive hook-and-loop tape connectors with two contacts separated by an insulating strip; the control boards are connected using non-coated nickel snap-on buttons. In both cases, the electronics are sewn with conductive thread onto an intermediary fabric patch. Matching connectors are sewn onto the patches and the suit, allowing any of the electronic components to be attached or removed at will. This allows the garments to be machine washed, as well as making replacement of faulty or damaged electronic components relatively trivial (as long as a replacement patch is available).

Using the same hook-and-loop connectors as the motors, LEDs were added to the suit to provide visual feedback coupled with the vibration intensity of the motors. The LEDs are simply placed in a parallel circuit with the PWM signal driving the motors to achieve this coupling. This has made troubleshooting the suits significantly easier, since it makes it easy to see when a motor is behaving as expected. The LEDs have also been used in several performances, and audiences have reported that this improved their understanding of how the suit works. Should a composer prefer a more neutral look, however, the LEDs can simply be removed from the suits.

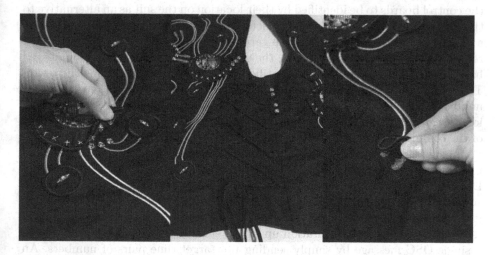

Fig. 4. (From left to right) Control boards are attached with metallic snap-on buttons. The fit of the vests can be adjusted by cinching down slack in the fit. Motors and LEDs are attached with conductive hook-and-loop tape. The small circular patches pictured here are LEDs, which coincide in position with the ERM motors that are on the opposite side of the garment (close to the wearer's body).

The number of control boards and motors on each suit was nearly doubled to provide for increased flexibility when designing vibrotactile patterns (Fig. 5). On the torso, more control boards were added, doubling the density of motors on the back and adding motors to the front of the torso with the same increased density[3]. Similarly, motors were added to the back of the legs where previously they had only covered the front of the legs. These increases in coverage and density were strongly motivated by the requirements for the piece *Tactile Topologies* envisioned by artist and composer Csenge Kolozsvari, particularly the requirement for continuous patterns of movement to be conveyed across the whole body including the torso. However, the changes to motor placement were also found to be advantageous for other approaches and uses of the system, such as allowing a wider variety of tactons to be developed for the torso.

The communications protocol was redesigned completely (see Fig. 6) to make it easier for programmers to work with and reduce the number of UDP packets that needed to be sent to achieve a complex pattern of vibration, as well as to improve the modularity of the control boards. Because each control board now had a separate and unique IP address (dynamically assigned by the DHCP server on the local area network), this was co-opted as a convenient identifier for each board. The indexing of the motors controlled by each board was designed to be dynamically assigned so that control boards would be effectively interchangeable, having no hard-coded constants related to their position on the suit. Finally, a simple mapping was implemented in the software library for working with the suit allowing the control boards to be identified by their location on the suit as an alternative to their IP address. This introduced the need for a simple setup procedure any time a control board was moved from one garment to another in order to set its current location; during this procedure, the motors were automatically re-numbered based on the location on the suit identified by the operator performing the setup. The combination of location-based addresses for the control boards and consistent numbering of the motors allowed a programmer working with the system to easily identify any individual motor from memory and greatly improved the readability of the communication protocol.

The linear envelope conceptual model of the original protocol was expanded to a more flexible model based on the line~object from Max/MSP and Pure Data. In this conceptual model, rather than a fixed number of rising and falling stages, a single pair of numbers represent one stage of the envelope, specifying it's target amplitude and the duration of the linear ramp toward that target (see Fig. 6). In our implementation up to ten envelope stages may be encoded in a single OSC message by simply sending ten target-time pairs of numbers. An optional preceding number can be used to specify where the envelope should start from; otherwise, the envelope will start from whatever the current amplitude value is when the message is received. The minimum message specifies at least one linear ramp in the form of a single target-time pair, or a single target value can be sent to request that the amplitude is immediately set to a new value. These minimum messages are especially useful when constantly updating the

---

[3] In fact, the density of motors on the back was originally tripled, but the motors in the very middle of the back were found not to add much benefit due to their very close proximity to the motors controlled by the two other boards. We found no use for them in any of the pieces we have developed so far, and they were ultimately removed from the design for future manufacturing runs.

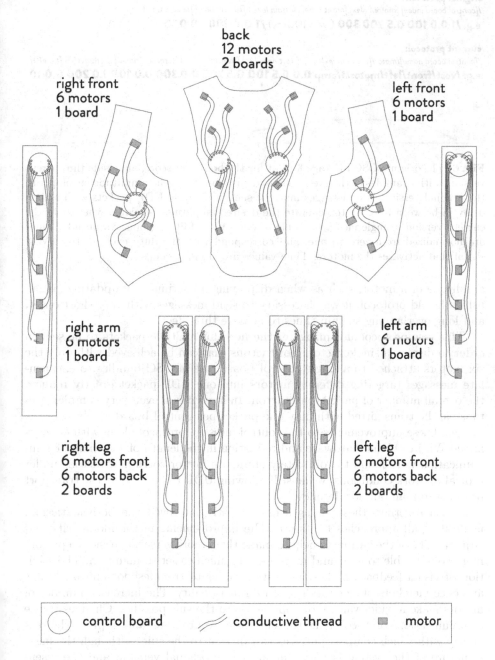

Fig. 5. The current motor layout, covering a greater area of the body and with a higher density of motors on the back of the torso than the original version.

original protocol:
/[control board index] [motor index] [onset time] [sustain level] [sustain time] [release time]
e.g. **/1 0.0 100 0.5 200 300** (wait 100ms) **/1 0.0 200 1.0 0 10**

current protocol:
/[control board name]/motor/[motor index]/amp [starting value] [target1] [time1] [target2] [time2] ... [target10] [time10]
e.g. **/vest/front/left/motor/1/amp 0.0 0.5 100 0.5 200 0.0 300 0.0 100 1.0 200 0.0 10**

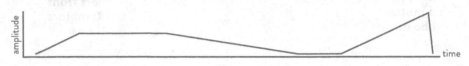

Fig. 6. The original OSC message format for the body:suit:score, alongside the current version, with examples of the messages used to create the same amplitude envelope. In the original version, two messages must be sent in separate UDP packets with a time delay in between in order to generate the desired amplitude envelope, whereas in the current version a single message is able to encode the full envelope. Amplitude values are normalized from zero to one, and correspond with the duty cycle of the PWM signal that activates the motors. Time values are in milliseconds.

amplitude of a motor, such as when displaying a continuously updating signal; using the old protocol, it was necessary to send messages with very short onset, and long overlapping sustain times to achieve this effect.

This new protocol also mitigates the need for multiple packets to be sent in order to display a single tacton. For tactons that can be achieved with only the six motors attached to a single control board, use of OSC bundles to encapsulate messages targeting different motors into one UDP packet greatly reduces the overall number of packets per tacton. In most cases, even very complex tactons can be transmitted with only one packet per control board involved in the tacton. These improvements to the control message protocol along with changes in the WiFi receiving hardware and reduction in the length of the chain of communication were found to completely eliminate lost or corrupted tactons under typical network conditions, while still allowing UDP to be used as the transport protocol to maintain low latency.

Taken together, these changes have greatly improved the body:suit:score, facilitating all approaches to its use. The improvements in the modularity and adjustability of the garments help to make them more versatile, easier to put on, more comfortable to wear and move in, and much easier to maintain. The addition of visual feedback makes the system easier to troubleshoot and facilitates audience members' understanding of its functionality. The increased number of motors make a wider variety of approaches to the suit possible. Changes to the communications protocol make the suit easier to program, and improve the reliability with which complex patterns can be sent to the suit. Although the basic structure of the system is very similar to the original version, and the essential capabilities were not drastically changed, the modifications to the design have made the system more maintainable, more reliable, and easier to use for musicians, programmers, and composers alike.

4   Tactile Metronome

In addition to the enhancements based on requirements discovered when using the original version of the body:suit:score, other technological developments have been motivated by the demands of composers working with the system. Early in the development of the second and current version of the body:suit:score, the suits were envisioned as individualized metronomes to be worn by several musicians: The system thus could improve on existing experiments with both individualized click tracks, (Bhagwati, "Iterations" (Berlin 2014)) which disrupt the musicians' listening, and visual conductors (either several human conductors, blinking lights, or video animations,) which musicians often find confusing and which impose severe spatial constraints on musician and audience placement and movement. In one movement of Bhagwati's large-scale work *Niemandsland-hymnen* (NLH, Montréal 2017), in which the musicians move within an equally mobile audience, each of the musicians improvises not only in a different tempo, but the constantly changing tempi perform a temporal choreography of pulsations from which a musical architecture emerges that would be impossible to conduct or to feel. The original goal of simply replacing the human conductor thus had been surpassed.

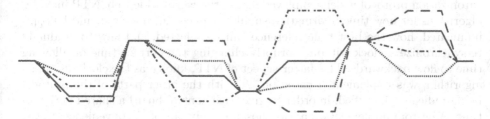

Fig. 7. A diagram of the tempo of each metronome over time as was employed in *Neimandslandhymnen*.

A clock synchronization scheme based on network time protocol [7] was implemented to achieve this effect, and a novel algorithm extending the work of [8] was designed that allows the body:suit:score to act as a highly accurate metronome, impervious to network delay, jitter, and dropped packets. The tempi of each body:suit:score acting as a metronome can be synchronized across garments while also allowing arbitrary phase and frequency modulations. Later, the metronome functionality was also found to be useful for composing cyclic or repeating tactons.

The most obvious way to deliver a metronomic pulse across multiple suits would be to simply send a message at the required rate to produce periodic pulses at the appropriate time; in this implementation, the conductor program would keep track of the time elapsed, and emit control messages to produce a pulse every so often according to the required tempo. However, this implementation can be problematic due to the latency and jitter inherent in wireless networked communications: although the pulse message for each suit might be *emitted* at roughly the same time, there is no way to guarantee that these messages will be *received* at the same time by each suit. As a consequence, the pulses felt on each suit would not be guaranteed to occur at the same time, thus failing to synchronize the musicians wearing the metronomes. Indeed, even with a single suit the rate of the metronome would be subject to network jitter, and should multiple control boards be used on the same suit, even these might not pulse in sync. All of this is not even considering the possibility that individual pulses could be entirely lost should a UDP packet be dropped. In practice, packets might not be dropped, and jitter might be relatively small, so this implementation is reasonable when only a single metronome is needed. However, when multiple metronomes are required, differences in the latency between the conductor program and the different devices becomes a serious issue.

In order to guarantee that the metronomic pulses felt on each suit would coincide as exactly as possible, it was necessary to use a different approach. We opted to allow the control boards to keep track of time instead of the conductor program, so that each control board would autonomously emit the metronome pulse at the correct time instead of waiting to receive a message from the conductor program. In order for this to work, each control board would have to agree on the present time. Network time protocol (NTP) is a ubiquitous time synchronization protocol widely employed across the world wide web. NTP includes algorithms for how time information should be encoded, how it should be communicated, how the best time reference can be selected, and how to gradually re-synchronize a clock without abruptly changing the current time or allowing time to flow backwards. This latter aspect of NTP, known as the clock discipline algorithm, was implemented based on [9], with the other parts of the protocol being radically simplified, in order to give each control board a shared notion of time. A custom implementation was chosen mainly out of to convenience; to the authors' knowledge, no NTP implementation was available for the MCU used in the control boards, and it was simpler to implement a subset of NTP rather than to fully comply with the protocol.

In our implementation, the conductor program is considered to be a stable and accurate source of the current time. The motor control modules periodically measure their offset and delay from the conductor according to the NTP method. Each control module individually disciplines its clock in order to gradually reduce the offset and improve the frequency of its clock so that it remains better in sync with the conductor. The UDP packet format defined by NTP was omitted in favor of a simplified OSC-based format, taking advantage of the existing communications implementation. NTP's extensive algorithms for selecting the best clock source were also omitted, since the conductor can be considered to be the only true source of time. Finally, rather than the 64-bit fixed point time format specified by NTP, a slightly modified format was chosen instead. We use 32- rather than 64-bit integers, since the microcontroller used on the control boards is able to process 32-bit integers with a single instruction, and the least significant bit was chosen to corresponds to one microsecond, since this is the smallest time increment that the motor control boards are able to measure. Using the clock synchronization algorithm, every motor control board is able to keep track of time and stay synchronized within a few milliseconds given typical network conditions.

Given this shared notion of time, the control boards can generate a metronomic pulse using the Global Metronome algorithm described by [8]. Using this algorithm, each control board is given an interval T between pulses (or equivalently, a frequency $f = 1/T$). The current phase $\phi(t)$ of the metronome is defined according to [8, eq. 4]

$$\phi(t) = \left[2\pi \left(\frac{t}{T} - \left\lfloor \frac{t}{T} \right\rfloor \right) + \theta \right] \mod 2\pi \tag{1}$$

Where θ is an optional local phase offset. The amplitude signal for the metronome $a(\phi)$ can then be determined as

$$a(\phi) = 1 \text{ if } \phi < d, \text{ else } 0 \tag{2}$$

Where d is a duty cycle parameter between 0 and 2π that determines how brief the metronome pulse is.

The Global Metronome algorithm guarantees that all metronome pulses across the different suits will coincide, because the phase of the metronome is determined by the shared time. However, for NLH it was also necessary to allow the metronomes to be deliberated brought in and out of sync by gradually modulating the frequency of each metronome to a different tempo, and then to a new shared tempo (see Fig. 7). This presented a challenge, because the frequency parameter of the global metronome cannot be smoothly modulated; any change to this parameter introduces significant immediate phase modulations that disrupt the consistent beat of the metronome. Although the local phase offset could be continuously modulated to achieve a change in frequency, we chose instead to introduce a separate mode for the metronome based on a phasor where $\phi(t)$ is derived from $\phi(t-1)$:

$$\phi(t) = (\phi(t-1) + 2\pi f * T_s) \mod 2\pi \tag{3}$$

Where T_s is the sampling period. Using this definition of phase, the frequency of a metronome could be smoothly modulated up or down. So to achieve the desired effect, the metronome on each suit would initially be set to the same tempo using the synchronized algorithm. Then, when it was desired to modulate the frequency, the metronome was switched to the modulation-tolerant algorithm. Later, when each metronome was modulated to a new shared tempo, the algorithm was once again switched to the synchronized version.

When switching from the synchronized metronome to the modulated metronome, it was not necessary to change the value of ϕ. The modulated metronome would simply pick up where the previous algorithm left off. Switching the other way around required the local phase offset θ to be set so that there would not be a jump in ϕ. This left one lingering issue, since θ would usually not be set to the same value for each metronome when the algorithm was switched to the synchronized version after having been modulated to different tempi. This was resolved by allowing θ to be modulated when using the synchronized algorithm. In this way, the metronomes could be brought back in sync by switching to the synchronized algorithm, and then gradually modulating each metronome's local phase offset toward zero. Both possible modulations (frequency while using the modulated metronome and phase while using the synchronized metronome) were implemented using the same linear envelope function as the amplitude envelopes, allowing complex frequency or phase modulation patterns to be specified in advance and sent in a single message from the conductor computer.

In later pieces, the metronome functionality was able to be repurposed for other effects. By setting the phase offset appropriately, repeating sweeping or circling sensations could be initiated very concisely compared to using amplitude envelopes to achieve the same effect. This was used to create rising and falling tactons for Bhagwati's piece *Silence Not Absence*. The periodic pulses could also be used for amplitude modulation, granting a limited ability to vary the frequency content of the vibrotactile signal generated by the ERM motors[4] used in the system. This allows 'rough' feeling vibratory textures to be rendered on the suit [10]. More in line with its use as a metronome, in *Tactile Topologies* (described in more detail below) the periodic pulsing was used as an analog to the periodic beating heard between two instruments playing slightly out of tune. If the musician wearing a suit was playing slightly higher than his or her partner, the motors on the back of his or her right leg would be pulsed at a rate equal to the beating frequency between his or her pitch and his or her partner's pitch. If the musician was playing slightly lower than his or her partner, the beating frequency would instead by displayed on his or her left leg. This mapping permitted the musicians to play precisely in tune with each other, even while unable to hear one another.

The clock synchronization functionality has yet to be utilized other than for the metronome, but at least one other use case has been identified. Specifically, in the future we will implement a forward synchronization policy using the synchronized clocks. By allowing the execution of a message to be deferred to a specific time in the future, concerns about network jitter or latency could be completely eliminated. Combined with using TCP/IP to send messages to the control boards rather than UDP, this would give a mechanism for the transmission of important messages to be guaranteed as long as they can be sent well enough in advance of the time when they need to be acted upon. This could benefit a wide range of applications, especially for symbolic approaches to the system.

---

[4] Due to the coupling between vibration amplitude and vibration frequency inherent in the design or ERM motors, it is normally impossible to independently vary the amplitude and frequency content of their vibrations.

5 Sound to Vibrotactile Translation

Another piece that lead to major technical developments is entitled *Tactile Topologies*. This piece, composed by interdisciplinary artist and composer Csenge Kolozsvari, explores the use of the body:suit:score as a sensory replacement. It considers how the sense of touch might facilitate new kinds of musical inter-relationships by inviting two musicians to perform a duet in which their only means of communication is through the body:suit:score. The musicians each wear industrial-grade ear plugs and ear muffs and play in separate rooms. The body:suit:score translates each performer's sound into choreographies of vibra-tion across the entire suit of the other performer.

In early experiments for *Tactile Topologies* we explored a variety of methods to attempt to convey as much sonic information through the body:suit:score as possible. We considered a large number of audio features [11], and mapping strategies ranging from machine learning to swarm algorithms. Ultimately, we chose to focus on representing the pitch and loudness of the sound alone. In traditional music notation, these features are given the most detailed attention, and musicians are expected to fill in the finer details of musical expression and interpretation. By focusing on pitch and amplitude, we were able to draw on this pre-existing skill.

The loudness feature was extracted using the pipo~Max/MSP extension by IRCAM [12], then scaled from zero to one based on the dynamic range observed during sound check before a performance. The mapping to the body:suit:score was designed to overcome the limited dynamic range of the ERM motors used on the suit by recruiting a large number of motors to increase the maximum possible intensity of vibration. 20 motors on the torso were partitioned into five groups, starting at the small of the back and radiating outward and upward to eventually wrap around the whole torso (see Fig. 8). The amplitude for each group a_g was then determined based on the loudness feature l using an ad-hoc exponential scaling that was found to give a good correspondence from the loudness feature to the sensation of vibration intensity:

$$a_g(l) = \frac{4 * 2^l}{g} \text{ subject to } 0 <= a_g(l) <= 1 \tag{4}$$

This has the effect that each group turns on one after the other as the loud-ness feature varies from zero to one, so that at maximum loudness nearly every motor on the torso is activated. The wrap around grouping of the motors was chosen because it was found by the musicians to provide a satisfying and intu-itive correspondence with loudness. By gradually increasing the overall area and number of actuators activated, we were able to convey a greater sense of intensity than if fewer motors had been used.

The pitch feature was estimated using a custom fundamental frequency esti-mator implemented in Max/MSP; a custom implementation was chosen rather than one of the available pitch estimators because we were able to achieve bet-ter accuracy by exploiting our prior knowledge about the range of pitches in the piece, and the spectral qualities of the instruments being performed (both musicians played french horn).

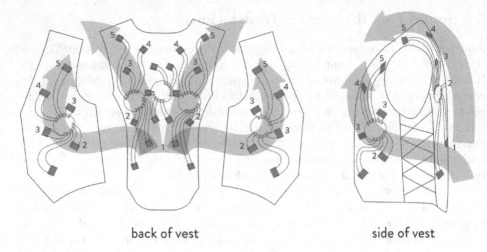

back of vest   side of vest

Fig. 8. The loudness-to-vibration mapping used in *Tactile Topologies*. As the loudness parameter increases, a greater and greater area of the torso is stimulated. This provides a wide dynamic range of intensity. The arrows indicate the direction in which the vibration seems to spread as the loudness of a sound increases. The numbers indicate the order in which the motors are activated as the loudness increases.

It initially seemed intuitive to try mapping pitch as a continuous line from one position on the body (e.g. the ankles) to another (e.g. the wrists), with each discrete pitch assigned to one motor. This approach was ultimately abandoned. The musicians were unable to reliably distinguish between adjacent motors (as was the intention in the design of the suit), and therefore the melodic patterns played in the piece did not produce recognizable patterns on the suit.

A more successful approach was found by separating the pitch mapping into two parts: pitch class, and octave. Two pitches an octave apart are perceived as having a close similarity due to the overlap of harmonic spectra that occurs between two periodic sounds an octave apart; sound perception can therefore be considered to have a spiral-like topology, in which pitches that are an octave apart fall into an equivalence class called the pitch class [13]. In eurological music it is most common to employ twelve pitch classes that make up the familiar chromatic scale. We were able to achieve a more effective pitch mapping for the body:suit:score by drawing on these phenomena. Each pitch class was mapped to a single motor, with the twelve pitch classes forming a circle up one arm and down the other. The octave was then separately mapped to the height of a vibration on the front of the legs. See Fig. 9 for more detail. Although it required slightly more analytic interpretation by the performers than e.g. the amplitude mapping, this pitch mapping was found to permit the musicians to roughly follow what the other was doing. It was also found to produce recognizable patterns across the arms when melodies were played.

In the end, *Tactile Topologies* also relied on the musician's pre-existing knowledge of the piece for its success. Because the musicians knew the overall plan

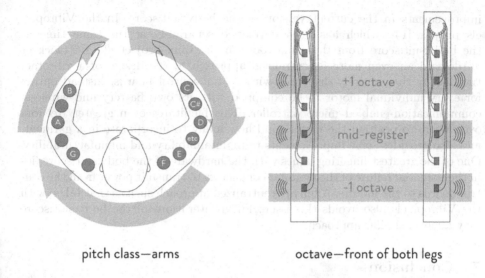

pitch class—arms   octave—front of both legs

Fig. 9. The pitch-to-vibration mapping used in *Tactile Topologies*. Pitch class is mapped in a circle around the arms, while octave is represented on the front of the legs. The arrows indicate the direction of motion felt when an ascending melodic pattern is played.

and structure of the piece in advance, they were able to use the signals from the body:suit:score as a close-enough approximation of the other performer's actions and fill in the details using their expectations and musical interpretation skills. Future experiments will consider the viability of the pitch and amplitude mappings devised for this piece as standalone music representations in absence of prior knowledge. This may include using the mappings to instruct musicians exactly what pitch and loudness to play next, or as an inspirational prompt for improvisation. These applications will allow the pitch and amplitude mappings to be employed as an additional score modality alongside tempo and symbol-based approaches employed in other pieces.

6   Future Work

The body:suit:score allows information and instructions to be transmitted to musicians in real-time. From the beginning of the project, we have also intended to incorporate motion and position sensing into the system in order to allow musicians actions, location, and spatial interrelationship to influence the direction and outcome of the musical system in a closed interactive loop. This remains as future work.

Although our design has improved significantly since its earliest prototypes, we continue to consider further refinements. Distributing the responsibility for power and communications across the suit lead to some of the most striking improvements in the current version of the body:suit:score. In the Vibropixels project [14], which has been developed separately at the same time as the body:suit:score from the same roots in the Ilinx project [3], Hattwick et al. devised an even more decentralized approach to the design of a vibrotactile display that entirely dispenses with motor control boards, instead opting for every individual motor to be equipped with its own battery and wireless-communication-enabled microcontroller. This facilitates even greater freedom over where to position the motors and how many to incorporate in a garment, and also provides some improvements to maintainability and manufacturability. One of the greatest lingering issues with the hardware of the body:suit:score lies in the potential failure of the modular connectors to transmit power from the control boards to the motors. A fully decentralized approach such as that taken with the Vibropixels also avoids this issue. Future iterations of the body:suit:score may adopt a similar approach.

7   Conclusion

By developing the body:suit:score to its current state, we've proposed one solution to the problem of making a vibrotactile musical score. We have striven to develop a robust implementation that is easily maintained and manufactured, and that is easy to use for programmers, musicians, and composers alike. Our system is capable of generating a wide range of sensations for its wearers, and we have explored a small portion of the many possibilities offered by the system. Through its use in numerous performances across North America and Europe, the reliability of the body:suit:score has been repeatedly validated.

Acknowledgements. This research has been funded by a grant from the Social Sciences and Humanities Research Council of Canada. The authors would like to acknowledge the work of all the musicians, composers, researchers, and collaborators who have participated in the project, and without whom this research would have been impossible.

References

1. Bhagwati, S.: Elaborate audio scores: concepts, affordances, and tools. In: Proceedings of the International Conference on Technologies for Music Notation and Representation, pp. 24–32 (2018)
2. Bhagwati, S., et al.: Musicking the body electric. In: Proceedings of the International Conference on Technologies for Music Notation and Representation (2016)
3. Giordano, M., et al.: Design and implementation of a whole-body haptic suit for "Ilinx, a Multisensory Art Installation." In: Proceedings of Sound and Music Computing (2015)
4. Giordano, M., Sullivan, J., Wanderley, M.M.: Design of vibrotactile feedback and stimulation for music performance. In: Papetti, S., Saitis, C. (eds.) Musical Haptics, pp. 193–214 (2018)

5. Frid, E., Giordano, M., Schumacher, M.M., Wanderley, M.M.: Physical and perceptual characterization of a tactile display for a live-electronics notification system. In: Proceedings of Sound and Music Computing (2014)
6. Brewster, S., Brown, L.M.: Tactons: structured tactile messages for non-visual information display. In: Proceedings of the Fifth Conference on Australasian User Interface, AUIC 2004, vol. 28, pp. 15–23. Australian Computer Society Inc., Darlinghurst (2004)
7. Mills, D.L.: Computer Network Time Synchronization: The Network Time Protocol on Earth and in Space, 2nd edn. (2010)
8. Oda, R., Fiebrink, R.: The global metronome: absolute tempo sync for networked musical performance (2016)
9. Mills, D., Martin, J.Ed. Burbank, J., Kasc, W.: Network Time Protocol Version 4: Protocol and Algorithms Specification. RFC 5905 (2010)
10. Rovan, J., Hayward, V.: Typology of tactile sounds and their synthesis in gesture-driven computer music performance. In: Wanderley, M.M., Battier, M. (eds.) Trends in Gestural Control of Music, pp. 1–15 (2000)
11. Peeters, G., Giordano, B.L., Susini, P., Misdariis, N., McAdams, S.: The timbre toolbox: extracting audio descriptors from musical signals. J. Acoust. Soc. Am. **130**(5), 2902–2916 (2011)
12. Schnell, N., Schwarz, D., Larralde, J., Borghesi, R.: PiPo, a plugin interface for afferent data stream processing modules. In: Proceedings of the International Symposium on Music Information Retrieval (2017)
13. Shepard, R.N.: Demonstrations of circular components of pitch. J. Audio Eng. Soc. **31**(9), 641 649 (1983)
14. Hattwick, I., Franco, I., Wanderley, M.M.: The vibropixels: a scalable wireless tactile display system. In: Yamamoto, S. (ed.) HIMI 2017. LNCS, vol. 10273, pp. 517–528. Springer, Cham (2017). https://doi.org/10.1007/978-3-319-58521-5_40

Proposal of Redirected Walking Using a Slope Parallel Component of the Slope Gravity

Takehiko Yamaguchi[1][(✉)], Shota Abe[1], Yukiko Watabe[2],
Sou Shiohara[1], Hiroya Suzuki[3], and Tetsuya Harada[3]

[1] Suwa University of Science, 5000-1, Toyohira, Chino-shi, Nagano, Japan
tk-ymgch@rs.sus.ac.jp
[2] Nagano Board of Education, 692-2, Nagano-shi, Nagano, Japan
[3] Tokyo University of Science, 6-3-1 Niijuku, Katsushika-ku, Tokyo, Japan

Abstract. In this research, we aimed to evaluate the effectiveness of a slope board by proposing visual tactile redirected walking using a parallel component of gravity on a slope to realize a new infinite linear walking experience. Specifically, when placing a plate with a diameter of approximately 1.2 m and an inclination of 0°, 5°, and 10° around the column and walking while placing a hand on the cylinder over the plate, the inclination is in a virtual space. Based on the results of the locus of locomotion measured during the experiment and the questionnaire answers of the walking sensation developed in this study, the straight walking sensation and walking balance sense were observed to be highest in the 10° inclination condition.

Keywords: Virtual reality · Redirected walking · Slope effect

1 Introduction

1.1 Recent Technology in Virtual Reality

Virtual reality (VR) is a technology that renders it possible to construct a completely three-dimensional (3D) computer generation environment where people can move around as if they are inside a virtual space [1]. It has made a tremendous progress in the last 20 years and shows a remarkable potential as a place of research in social, behavioral, and economic sciences and even in human-centered computer science [2]. VR allows a user to walk on a controllable computer generation environment to evaluate hypotheses that are difficult to systematically examine in real world [3].

Based on the recent VR technology, developing a realistic evocation environment with substantially immersive feeling is possible. That is, it is a head-mounted display (HMD)-based virtual environment. To further improve the immersion feeling, normal human actions must be naturally achieved. An example of these actions is walking, which is one of the most important interactions [5].

1.2   Locomotion Technologies in Virtual Reality

However, when adopting the actual walking, the size of VE is limited to the size of the tracking space in real world. Therefore, many alternative locomotion techniques have been proposed. Examples of these techniques are virtual movement techniques, such as teleportation [5] or hardware devices or motion platform [6], and walking in place [7]. However, these technologies require a special device, which reduces the immersion feeling.

1.3   Redirected Walking

Redirected Walking (RDW) is a collection of VR locomotion technology for an immersive virtual environment that enables humans to walk on a real-world path [8]. It is applied to a display scene through a redirection gain that forces a user to compensate by repositioning and/or redirecting himself to the user, mostly to maintain the intended walking direction within the VE [8].

RDW is a method that utilizes a minimal change of information that cannot be perceived by humans, and approaches related to the manipulation of visual information are mainstream. Apart from visual information, a method using audio information [9] or haptic sense [10] has been proposed.

In this research, we proposed a novel RDW method using visual tactile information and then evaluated its effectiveness.

2   Methods

2.1   Participants

A total of 14 students were recruited from Suwa University of Science. All of the participants were male whose mean age was 21 years (SD = 0.31). They have minimal or no experience with VR, as well as mixed reality, application.

2.2   Apparatus

Visual Display/Rendering. A Mirage Solo HMD was used for the experimental task. The headset covers a nominal field of view approximately $110°$ using two $2,560 \times 1,440$ pixel displays, which are updated at 75 Hz. As for the visual rendering, Unity3D was employed, rendering the graphics at 60 Hz.

3D Motion Tracker. The Mirage Solo has a motion tracker that can measure 3D position, as well as orientation, in real time.

Task Environment in Real Space. A customized experimental environment was developed for this study. This developed environment had a cylindrical column wall, which is 1.2 m across. Around the cylindrical column wall, several boards with different slopes were arranged, allowing the user to walk around the wall (Fig. 1).

Fig. 1. Task environment in real space.

Task Environment in VR Space. Figure 2 shows the VR space displayed through the HMD. The participant will see the straight aisle in the VR space, which is an unlimited aisle with 6 m width. The system captured data regarding trial time and the tracker position when the user's head location is in the x, y, and z coordinates.

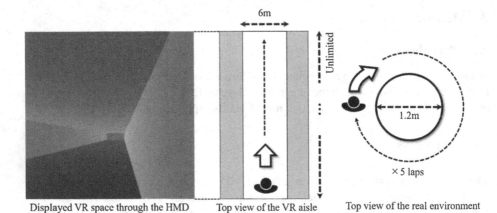

Fig. 2. VR environment and real environment of the experiment.

2.3 Experimental Task

The protocol for the experimental task was the same for all conditions. The participants must blindfold themselves when they enters the experimental room to ensure that they cannot recognize the task conditions, such as the degree of boards around the wall (i.e., 0°, 5°, 10°). After experimenter provided the instructions of the experiment, each of the participants was required to wear the HMD and earphones and then calibrate his position in a virtual environment that is displayed through the HMD. In the experimental task, they were required to walk five laps around the wall in real space while touching the wall using the right hand. The walking speed was controlled by metronome (60 bpm) heard from the earphones.

2.4 Experimental Design and Independent Variables

To examine the effect of the board slope around the wall in the customized task environments, a within-subjects factorial experiment design was used, resulting in three experimental tasks.

Slope Board Effect. The slope boards around the wall were designed for the following two purposes: (1) to control the participant's walking balance to ensure that he can walk accurately around the wall and (2) to support the participant' feeling of infinite straight-line walking on the VR aisle.

2.5 Dependent Variables

To systematically investigate the effect of slope board in the customized task environments, this study utilized several dependent measures, which can be categorized into two types of variables, The first one is task performance that includes the head trajectory of walking around the wall, area within the trajectory, displacement of the x and z directions, and standard deviation, which are extracted from the head trajectory of walking. The second one is subjective performance using the customized questionnaire that we developed for this study.

Task Performance. It includes the head trajectory of walking around the wall, area within the trajectory, displacement of the x and z directions of the walking, and its standard deviation. The head trajectory of walking is a sequence of x, y, and z positions, which are obtained from the 3D motion sensor on the HMD (Y-up system).

Subjective Performance. It includes a customized questionnaire that asked the participants' feeling of walking. Table 1 presents the detail of the questionnaire. All items used the Likert scale scoring (1–5).

2.6 Procedure

The participants were required to read and then signed an informed consent. After completion of the introduction paperwork, a short training was conducted to ensure that the participants become familiar when interacting in the customized experimental environment. Their goal was to walk through the wall while their hand is touching on the wall. Then, the experimental tasks began after the training session. Each participant completed three tasks in a randomized order, wherein each task consist of five laps. After completing each task, the participants were asked to answer the questionnaire.

Table 1. Questionnaire for the feeling of walking.

Questions
1. Did you feel that you are walking like circling around something?
2. Did you feel like walking straight in the VR space?
3. Did you feel like going to the left or right?
4. Did you feel uncomfortable compared to normal walking?
5. Did you feel a sense of fear?
6. Did you feel that your hand got away from the wall?
7. Did you feel as if you were losing your balance or being fluffy?
8. Did you feel the slope?
9. Did you feel as if you were approaching the wall?

2.7   Research Question

This study seeks to examine the effect of slope board on performance, as well as subjective performance, in three slope types, namely, 0°, 5°, and 10°. The research question can be formally stated as follows:

RQ (1) Do the participants feel that they are mostly walking linearly at the 10° condition?

RQ (2) Do the participants feel the most balanced feeling at the 10° condition?

3   Results

3.1   Task Performance

Head Trajectory of Walking. Figure 3 shows the x–z trajectory for each condition to confirm the trajectory difference among the three experimental conditions. In the figure, the x–z trajectory of Subject 1 is shown as an example.

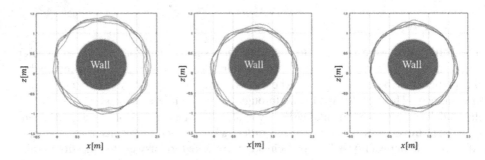

Fig. 3. Head trajectory of walking during an experimental task (Subject 1).

Area Within the Trajectory. The one-factor analysis of variance (ANOVA) with various slope board conditions (i.e., 0°, 5°, and 10°) as the within-subject factors exhibited the main effect, $F(2,26) = 4.94, p < .05, \eta^2 = .275$. A post hoc comparison (Bonferroni method, $\alpha = .05$) indicated a significant difference between the 0° condition ($M = 18.01, SD = 2.824$) and 10° condition ($M = 16.34, SD = 2.729$). In contrast, no significant difference was observed between the 0° and 5° conditions, as well as between the 5° and 10° conditions. Table 2 presents the results of the ANOVA for the trajectory area. Figure 4 shows the result of the average plot.

Table 2. Result of the ANOVA for the trajectory area.

	Sum of squares	df	Mean square	F	p	η^2
Degree	19.69	2	9.844	4.940	0.015	0.275
Residual	51.81	26	1.993			

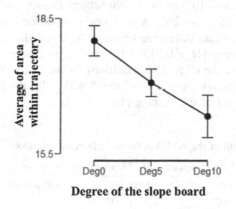

Degree of the slope board

Fig. 4. Average plot of the area within the trajectory.

Standard Deviation (SD) of the Trajectory (x direction). The one-factor ANOVA with various slope board conditions (i.e., 0°, 5°, and 10°) as the within-subject factors revealed the main effect, $F(2,26) = 5.769, p < .05, \eta^2 = .307$. A post hoc comparison (Bonferroni method, $\alpha = .05$) indicated a significant difference between the 0° condition ($M = 0.758, SD = 0.059$) and 10° condition ($M = 0.722, SD = 0.057$). In contrast, no significant difference was observed between the 0° and 5° conditions, as well as between the 5° and 10° conditions. Table 3 presents the results of the ANOVA for the SD of the trajectory (x direction). Figure 5 shows the result of the average plot.

Table 3. Result of the ANOVA for the SD of the trajectory (x direction).

	Sum of squares	df	Mean square	F	p	η^2
Degree	0.009	2	0.005	5.769	0.008	0.307
Residual	0.020	26	7.812e-4			

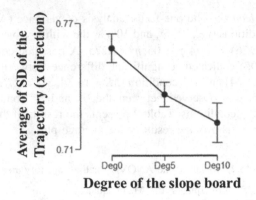

Fig. 5. Average plot of the SD of the trajectory (x direction).

SD of the Trajectory (z direction). The one-factor ANOVA with various slope board conditions (i.e., 0°, 5°, and 10°) as the within-subject factors revealed the main effect, $F(2, 26) = 4.754, p < .05, \eta^2 = .268$. A post hoc comparison (Bonferroni method, $\alpha = .05$) indicated a significant difference between the 0° condition ($M = 0.754, SD = 0.063$) and 10° condition ($M = 0.717, SD = 0.059$). In contrast, no significant difference existed between the 0° and 5° conditions, as well as between the 5° and 10° conditions. Table 4 presents the results of the ANOVA for the SD of the trajectory. Figure 6 shows the result of the average plot.

Table 4. Result of the ANOVA for the SD of the trajectory (z direction).

	Sum of squares	df	Mean square	F	p	η^2
Degree	0.010	2	0.005	4.754	0.017	0.268
Residual	0.026	26	0.001			

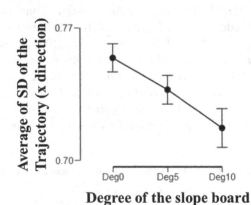

Fig. 6. Average plot of the SD of the trajectory (z direction).

3.2   Subjective Performance

Factor Analysis. Prior to the application of ANOVA on the questionnaire result, factor analysis was utilized on the result of the developed questionnaire to extract the main factors of the questionnaire. First, the mean and SD of the nine scale items of the original scale were calculated. Factor analysis (main factor method, promax rotation) was performed for the nine items. Based on Guttman's criteria and the interpretation possibility of the factor in the initial solution, the two-factor structure was determined to be valid and the factor number was fixed to 2. If the items were selected when the load amount on the factor was .40 or higher, then no double-load item was observed. Based on the result of the factor analysis, seven items remained.

In the item "1. Did you feel that you are walking like circling around something?" or "2. Did you feel like walking straight in the VR space?," a load amount of 55 or higher was observed. Considering that this factor seems to represent a strange feeling and a curved feeling of walking, which seems not to be walking linearly, this factor was referred to as the "Nonlinear walking feeling factor."." In the second factor, that is, "5. Did you feel a sense of fear?" and "9. Did you feel as if you were approaching the wall?," loading values of 56 or higher were noticed. Given that it represents the physical and psychological walking easiness against walking, it is referred to as "Balance feeling factor."." The number of items demonstrating a high loading amount for each factor was 4 for the Nonlinear walking feeling factors and 3 for the balance feeling factors. An average score of each factor item was calculated and used as a subscale score. When the correlation between factors was determined, a negative correlation ($r = -.36$, $p < .001$) was positively extracted between burden and acceptance.

Factor 1: Nonlinear Walking Feeling Factor. The one-factor ANOVA with various slope board conditions (i.e., $0°$, $5°$, and $10°$) as the within-subject factors revealed the main effect, $F(2, 16) = 5.445, p < .05, \eta^2 = .405$. A post hoc comparison (Bonferroni method, $\alpha = .05$) indicated a significant difference between the $0°$ condition ($M = 3.467, SD = 0.300$) and $10°$ condition ($M = 3.044, SD = 0.379$). In contrast, no significant difference was observed between the $0°$ and $5°$ conditions, as well as between the $5°$ and $10°$ conditions. Table 5 presents the results ANOVA for Factor 1. Figure 7 shows the result of the average plot.

Table 5. Result of the ANOVA for Factor 1: Nonlinear walking feeling factor.

	Sum of squares	df	Mean square	F	p	η^2
Degree	0.821	2	0.410	5.445	0.016	0.405
Residual	1.206	16	0.075			

Factor 2: Balance Feeling Factor. The one-factor ANOVA with various slope board conditions (i.e., $0°$, $5°$, and $10°$) as the within-subject factors revealed the main effect, $F(2, 16) = 11.59, p < .01, \eta^2 = .592$. A post hoc comparison (Bonferroni method,

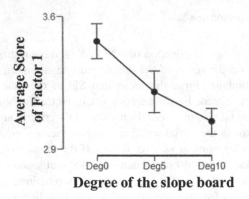

Fig. 7. Average score plot of Factor 1.

$\alpha = .01$) demonstrated a significant difference between the 0° condition ($M = 3.556$, $SD = 0.866$) and 10° condition ($M = 2.370, SD = 0.676$), as well as between the 0° condition ($M = 3.556, SD = 0.866$) and 5° condition ($M = 2.779$, $SD = 0.646$). In contrast, no significant difference was noticed between the 5° and 10° conditions. Table 6 presents the results of the ANOVA for Factor 2. Figure 8 shows the result of the average plot.

Table 6. Result of the ANOVA for Factor 2: Balance feeling factor.

	Sum of squares	df	Mean square	F	p	η^2
Degree	6.528	2	3.264	11.59	<.001	0.592
Residual	4.506	16	0.282			

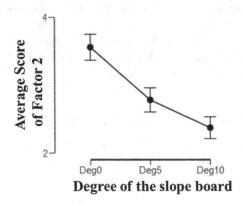

Fig. 8. Average score plot of Factor 2.

4 Discussion

4.1 Task Performance

By comparing the areas within the trajectory, a significant difference was observed between the 0° and 10° conditions, and the area was smallest in 10° condition. As the inclination angle of the board around the cylinder increases, the slope parallel component of the inclination gravity applied to the subject also increases. Therefore, the center of gravity of the subject was always inclined toward the center of the cylinder, and the distance of the subject's head from the cylinder was considered to be shorter than when no inclination was present. In the trajectory variation also, a significant difference was noticed under 0° and 10° condition, and the most unevenness was observed in 10° condition, suggesting that stable walking was possible. The reason is that similar to the area, given that the center of gravity of the subject was always inclined in the middle direction of the cylinder, we believe that maintaining a certain distance from the center of the cylinder contributed.

4.2 Subjective Performance

In the *Nonlinear walking feeling factor*, a significant difference was noticed between the 0° and 10° conditions, and the *Nonlinear walking feeling* was the lowest at the 10° condition. Hence, low value indicates that the *linear walking feeling* is high, suggesting that the *linear walking feeling* in the VR space was the highest under the 10° condition. Meanwhile, in the *Balance feeling factor*, significant difference was observed between the 0° and 10° conditions and between the 5° and 10° conditions. Moreover, the *Balance feeling factor* was also observed to be the lowest at the 10° condition. Thus, the lower the value is, the more stable the walking will be.

4.3 Answers to the Research Questions

Based on the results of the task performance and subjective performance, the answers to the Research Questions are as follows:

RQ (1) Do the participants feel that they are walking most linearly at the 10° condition? The subjective performance result suggested that we could walk on the VR space most linearly at the 10° condition.

RQ (2) Does the participants feel the most balanced feeling at the 10° condition? The results of task performance and subjective performance indicated that walking with the most balanced sense was possible under the 10° condition.

5 Conclusion

In this study, we examined the effect of the slope board to determine its effectiveness by proposing the visual tactile redirected walking using the slope parallel component of gravity on the slope to realize a new infinite linear walking experience. Based on the results of the locus of locomotion measured during the experiment and the question-naire answers for the walking sensation developed in this study, straight walking sensation and walking balance sense were observed to be highest under the 10° inclination condition.

As a future prospect, we will investigate the radius of different cylinders and the influence on infinite straight walking feeling when the cylinder is changed to another form.

Acknowledgments. This work was supported by the Grant-in-Aid for Scientific Research (B) from Ministry of Education, Japan, Grant Number: 17H01782.

References

1. Satava, R.M.: Virtual reality surgical simulator. Surg. Endosc. **7**, 203–205 (1993)
2. Bainbridge, W.S.: The scientific research potential of virtual worlds. Science **317**, 472–476 (2007)
3. Fink, P.W., Foo, P.S., Warren, W.H.: Catching fly balls in virtual reality: a critical test of the outfielder problem. J. Vis. **9**, 14 (2009)
4. Nilsson, N.C., et al.: 15 years of research on redirected walking in immersive virtual environments. IEEE Comput. Graph. Appl. **38**, 44–56 (2018)
5. Bozgeyikli, E., Raij, A., Katkoori, S., Dubey, R.: Point & teleport locomotion technique for virtual reality. In: Proceedings of the 2016 Annual Symposium on Computer-Human Interaction in Play - CHI PLAY 2016, pp. 205–216. ACM Press, Austin (2016)
6. Iwata, H., Yano, H., Tomioka, H.: Powered shoes. In: ACM SIGGRAPH 2006 Emerging Technologies (SIGGRAPH '06). ACM, New York (2006). Article 28
7. Langbehn, E., Eichler, T., Ghose, S., Bruder, G., Steinicke, F.: Evaluation of an omnidirectional walking-in-place user interface with virtual locomotion speed scaled by forward leaning angle. In: GI Workshop on Virtual and Augmented Reality (GIVR/AR), pp. 149–160 (2015)
8. Langbehn, E., Steinicke, F.: Redirected walking in virtual reality. In: Lee, N. (ed.) Encyclopedia of Computer Graphics and Games, pp. 1–11. Springer, Cham (2018). https://doi.org/10.1007/978-3-319-08234-9_253-1
9. Meyer, F., Nogalski, M., Fohl, W.: Detection thresholds in audio-visual redirected walking (2016)
10. Matsumoto, K., Ban, Y., Narumi, T., Yanase, Y., Tanikawa, T., Hirose, M.: Unlimited corridor: redirected walking techniques using visuo haptic interaction. In: ACM SIGGRAPH Emerging Technologies, p. 20 (2016)

A System of Tactile Transmission on the Fingertips with Electrical-Thermal and Vibration Stimulation

Vibol Yem[1](✉), Hiroyuki Kajimoto[2], Katsunari Sato[3], and Hidekazu Yoshihara[4]

[1] Tokyo Metropolitan University, Tokyo, Japan
yemvibol@tmu.ac.jp
[2] The University of Electro-Communications, Tokyo, Japan
kajimoto@kaji-lab.jp
[3] Nara Women's University, Nara, Japan
katsu-sato@cc.nara-wu.ac.jp
[4] Nippon Mektron, Ltd., Tokyo, Japan
hi_yoshihara@mektron.co.jp

Abstract. This paper introduces a system of tactile transmission on the fingertips in which there are two sides: tactile-sender and a tactile-receiver. For the tactile-sender side, we developed a tactile sensor array and attached it inside a glove. This tactile sensor can simultaneously measure the temperature and the pressure distribution by measuring the resistance changes of pressure-sensitive conductive layer and chip thermistors while a user grasps or touches an object. The preliminary experiment showed that the system can measure at up to 2.7 kHz sampling rate, which is fast enough to capture the collision phenomenon. This sensor covers three fingers, each finger comprises 5 by 10 pressure sensing points and 8 temperature sensing points. For the tactile-receiver side, we developed a tactile module that consists of 4 by 5 electrode array, a Peltier and a heater film, and a high fidelity vibration actuator for simultaneously presenting electrical, thermal and vibration stimulation. Each module was attached inside the thumb, index and middle fingers of a glove. A system evaluation was conducted to observe the ability of our proposed algorithm for the communication between tactile sensor and tactile display.

Keywords: Tactile transmission · Tactile-sender · Tactile sensor · Tactile-receiver · Three color tactile display · Telexistence

1 Introduction

Technological progress in network and mobile phone allows users to remotely share their voice or vision with high quality. Beside the voice and vision, sharing the sensation of touch is also important for a local user to explore the property of a remote material. Transmission of tactile sensation is widely study for tele-operation, tele-training or tele-touch communication [1, 2]. Such a tactile transmission is also required to immerse the sensation of being in a place other than where a person actually exists.

© Springer Nature Switzerland AG 2019
S. Yamamoto and H. Mori (Eds.): HCII 2019, LNCS 11570, pp. 101–113, 2019.
https://doi.org/10.1007/978-3-030-22649-7_9

This is called telexistence [3]. However, there are still challenges for the tactile transmission with realistic sensation of touch due to the lack of material information that measured by the tactile sensor and a small range of tactile feeling that reproduced by the tactile display.

Accelerometer, microphone or pressure sensor is commonly used for measuring the property of a material [4–6]. However, each of these sensors can measure in a limited range of spatial or temporal resolution. Temperature is also an important information for exploring the material property. Therefore, the tactile sensor is required to be able to simultaneously measure the vibration, pressure and temperature with high spatiotemporal resolution. Moreover, the sensor need to be lightweight and compact enough for mounting to the fingertip. On the other hand, tactile display is also required to be able to reproduce tactile sensation with rich information. In principle, we might be able to reproduce any tactile sensation if we could drive the skin with sufficient spatial (up to 1.5 mm at fingertip) and temporal (0 to 1 kHz) resolution, but as the skin has large mass and damper, it is still quite difficult to develop such versatile micro machine for tactile display.

In this study, we developed both tactile sensor and tactile display with high spatiotemporal resolution. The tactile sensor embedded inside a glove can simultaneously measure the temperature and the pressure distribution when a tactile sender wears the glove and touches the object with three fingers. The tactile display reproduces the touch sensation based on the data that measured and transmitted from the tactile sender (Fig. 1). Each module of tactile display consisted of electrotactile, vibrotactile and thermal tactile actuators, and was embedded inside a glove. With these three primary-tactile colors, our display can theoretically activate Merkel cells, Meissner corpuscles, Pacinian corpuscles and thermo-receptors, all of these are important for reproduce any tactile feeling.

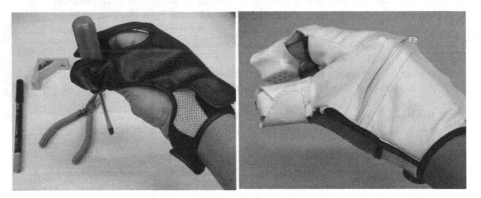

Fig. 1. The tactile-sender wears the sensor glove on the right hand and touches or grasps an object (left). The tactile-receiver perceives touch feedback sensation on the right hand when the tactile-sender touches the material.

2 Related Work

2.1 Wearable Tactile Sensor

Tactile sensors are widely used, including touch panels as input devices for information equipment, robot fingers for giving tactile abilities to the robots, pressure distribution for industrial applications and human behavior measurement [6–8]. In our study we focus on a wearable tactile sensor that can record various tactile sense in some tasks that use fingertips for operation. Such a wearable tactile sensor can be used for sharing tactile information of a remote user by combining with a tactile display.

It is desirable that the wearable tactile sensor does not hinder the original tactile sensation of the fingertip. For this reason, such a tactile sensor can be constructed by, for example, arranging a strain gauge on the side of the finger [9], measuring the color change of the nail [10] and the vibration on the nail [11, 12], which were designed not to cover the finger pad. However, with such a method, although it is possible to measure the force and vibration applied to the entire finger, it is not possible to measure the pressure distribution. Moreover, since the temperature perception is important when a person judges the material and surface quality of an object [13, 14], the measurement of the temperature distribution applied to the surface is also required.

Many glove-type tactile sensors have been developed, and many of which use pressure-sensitive conductive inks or sheets [15]. However, most of these did not evaluate the sensor's responsiveness, thus, it is difficult to directly compare with temporal and spatial resolution of human tactile perception. In recent years, for example, the High-Speed I-SCAN system developed by Nitta Co., Ltd. can measure at 720 Hz [16]. However, to the best of the author's knowledge, there were no wearable tactile sensor that combines the measurements of temperature distribution and pressure distribution together.

2.2 Tactile Feedback on the Fingertip

Many wearable tactile devices with different presentation methods have been proposed for fingertip interaction with virtual world. Vibration is commonly used for presenting texture sensation [17–19]. However, such a method can present a limited range of object properties due to its low spatial resolution. Several studies have developed a pin matrix to simulate shape sensation to users [20–22]. Though, the device can provide higher spatial resolution compare with vibrotactile system, the issues of low temporal resolution and large size still remain. Some wearable devices provide force feedback to the finger pads by presenting a pressure or skin deformation sensation [23–25]. These devices are mainly used for touch or surface exploration interactions in the virtual environment. Several other studies have focused on the illusion of softness or stickiness that can be induced by changing the contact area of the force applied to the skin [26, 27]. However, these devices can reproduce only some sort of tactile feeling.

Several studies have proposed using electrical stimulation to directly activate tactile receptors on the fingertip [28, 29]. Though this method achieves high responsiveness and small in size, reproducing realistic tactile sensation remains a challenge. In our previous study, we propose to combine electrical and mechanical stimulation to optimize the size and weight of a versatile tactile feedback device [30, 31]. Based on previous finding we considered that this method can selectively activate four kinds of mechanoreceptors. However, temperature presentation was not considered. Thermal tactile display has been widely studied [32], but a small-size tactile display that includes all of electrical, vibration and thermal tactile stimulation was not revealed. This paper also introduces our tactile display that can present all of the stimulation on the fingertip.

3   System

3.1   Tactile Sensor for the Sender

We developed a glove-type tactile sensor that is compatible with wearing on multiple fingers (Fig. 2). Figure 2 (left) shows the internal structure of the pressure and temperature distributions for three fingers. The pressure sensitive conductive sheet was used for pressure distribution sensing and the chip thermistor for temperature sensing. For each finger, the pressure distribution has 50 points (5×10) and the temperature distribution has 8 points as the measurement elements. The distance between the sensor elements is 2 mm. The flexible board meanders to correspond to the bending of the finger.

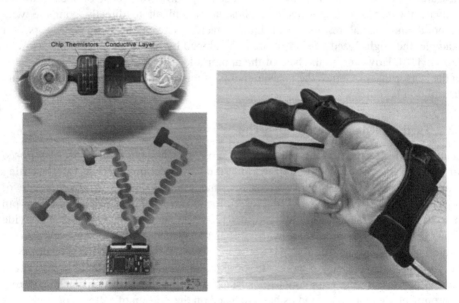

Fig. 2. Overview of the pressure and temperature distribution sensor (left) and the glove with the sensor inside (right) for three fingers.

Figure 3 (left) shows the structure of the sensor. The conductive layer has a pressure-sensitive property whose resistance value varies with pressure, and the change in resistance value is measured by two electrodes. The electrodes were formed on a flexible substrate; the chip thermistors (TDK, B 57232 V 5103 F 360) were arranged on the opposite side of this substrate. Figure 3 (right) shows the configuration of the data reading circuit. Both the pressure-sensitive film and the chip thermistor are the elements that change the resistance values. For this reason, we constructed a general resistance matrix detection circuit, which one row of the sensor matrix was selected by a digital output from a microprocessor (mbed NXP LPC 1768), and the voltage output divided by the fixed resistance was detected by a multi-channel AD converter (Texas Instruments, ADS 7953).

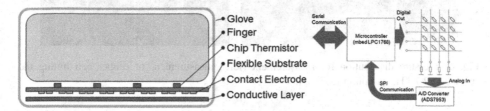

Fig. 3. Structure of the sensor and circuit diagram.

We used preliminary prototypes of pressure distribution (Fig. 4 (left)) for evaluation. The number of sensor elements is 256 points (16 × 16), and the sensor interval is 4 mm. Except for the influence of communication overhead with the PC, in order to obtain the upper limit value of the sensor reading speed, the measurement data was temporarily stored in the memory of the microprocessor. As a result, the pressure distribution of 16 × 16 could be measured 100 times (37 ms) at 2.7 kHz. This means that the time required for one measurement of 256 points was about 0.37 ms. Figure 4 (right) shows the time change of the pressure distribution when dropping the rubber ball onto the sensor. It can be observed how the pressure distribution spreads. Although the main measurement result does not indicate the physical responsiveness of the sensor element itself, since at least at the beginning and the end of the contact, a clear change is seen between consecutive frames (for example, frames 1 to 3, 13 to 15); which shows that it has high responsiveness.

3.2 Three Primary Color Tactile Display for the Receiver

Figure 5 shows the glove of tactile display for the receiver. The size of this glove can be adjusted to fit to any size of the fingertips. Three tactile modules and the module controller were embedded inside the glove.

Figure 6 shows a tactile module that consisted of an array of electrode for electrotactile, a vibration actuator for vibrotactile, and a Peltier and a heater for thermal tactile presentation. Three modules were used for tactile presenting to the thumb, index and middle finger. The vibration actuator, Peltier and heater, and module controllers were developed by one of joint group researches of Alps Alpine Co., Ltd. [33]. Though, Peltier can provide both coolness and hotness sensation, to efficiently reduce energy consumption we used it for cooling only and used heater made from a resistant instead for heating.

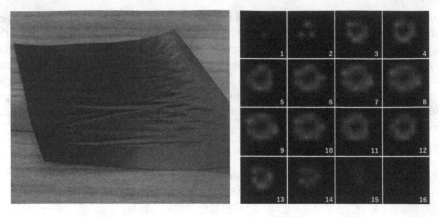

Fig. 4. Pressure distribution for measurement (left); measurement of rubber ball hitting the surface at 2.7 kHz sampling rate (right).

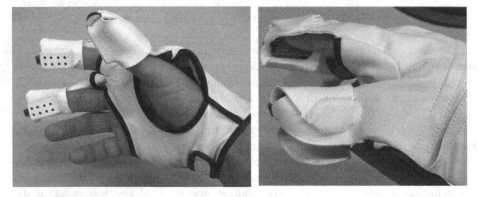

Fig. 5. The glove of tactile display (left). This glove can be adjusted to fit to any size of the fingertip (right).

3.3   Tactile Transmission System and Algorithm

As Fig. 1 shows, when a sender touches or grasps an object with the thumb, index or middle finger, the tactile sensor spatiotemporally measures the pressure and temperature of that object. Due to the tactile display cannot directly replay the measured data, algorithm of replay tactile sense is required (e.g. converting from pressure value to vibration density). Electrotactile stimulation can mainly present the movement of the pattern of a shape by changing the stimulation points of electrode array, vibrotactile stimulation for tapping or scrolling sensation, and thermal tactile stimulation for temperature sensation.

The data of pressure sensors were spatially filtered by using Eq. (1). We used Eq. (2) to convert spatiotemporal pressure values to the audio signal for vibration input. Though, there are many points of pressure distribution were contacted to the object, only maximum pressure value of each time frame were considered in this equation. For the electrical stimulation, the current intensity of each point was calculated with the Eq. (3).

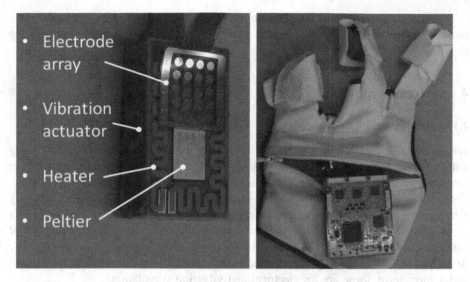

Fig. 6. A module of the tactile display (left) and controller (right).

$$p_{i,j} = \frac{p_{i,j} + p_{i+1,j} + p_{i,j+1} + p_{i+1,j+1}}{4} \tag{1}$$

$$A_t = k_1 \left(p_{max,t} - p_{max,t-1} \right) \tag{2}$$

$$I_{i,j} = I_{sense} + k_2 \times p_{i,j} \tag{3}$$

where p is pressure value, i and j are order number on the axis of width and height of the array. A_t and $p_{max,t}$ are vibration signal amplitude and maximum pressure at time t, $p_{max,t-1}$ is maximum pressure at previous time. I_{sense} is the sensation threshold of electrical intensity, k_1 and k_2 are constant.

To stabilize and to prevent pain sensation of electrical stimulation, we do not stimulate all points of electrode array even when all points of the pressure sensor were contacted to the object. As Fig. 7 shows, when the number of stimulation points becomes more than the maximum number (e.g. four), we keep stimulating the electrodes that correspond to the points of maximum pressure and its surrounding in which the total stimulated points are maximum number of the stimulation points.

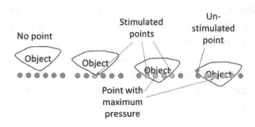

Fig. 7. Reducing the stimulated points of electrical stimulation.

For thermal tactile stimulation, we do not present the degree of the temperature the same as that of the object but the degree of the temperature difference after touching the object.

4   System Evaluation

4.1   Purpose and Conditions

We conducted a preliminary experiment to evaluate the ability of our system for tactile transmission. The main purpose of this experiment is to observe the ability of our proposed algorithm for converting the sensor values to the parameters of tactile display. Three performances operated by a tactile sender were used in this experiment: scrolling a hexagonal pencil, tapping between the thumb and the index finger, and holding a paper cup that one with hot water and other with cold water (Fig. 8). The purpose of using hot and cold water is to observe the speed of the temperature transmission. We developed a GUI to directly observe the pattern change of pressure distribution and audio wave form, these are for electrical and vibration stimulation.

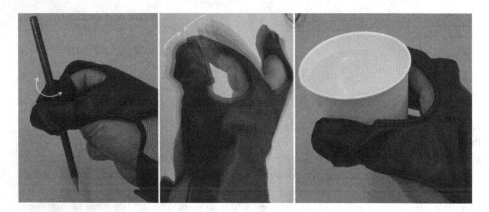

Fig. 8. Three performances operated by a tactile sender for system evaluation.

4.2   Result and Discussion

- Scrolling a hexagonal pencil

Figure 9 shows the pattern changing of the pressure distribution and audio wave-form while scrolling a hexagonal pencil. Each frame was captured at 10 Hz sampling rate. The scrolling patterns with three fingers can be observed. The patterns were transmitted and reproduced at the receiver side by the electrode array, and the receiver can perceive the movement of the shape. This result indicated that our algorithm can remain the scrolling shape even when the tactile sender strongly pressed the pencil and all points of pressure distribution detected.

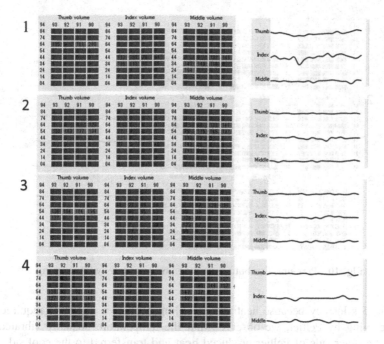

Fig. 9. Pressure distributions and audio waveforms while scrolling a pencil.

On the other hand, each audio waveform was observed to be a continuous vibration with a small amplitude. Due to the shape of the pencil is hexagon, we feel the vibration like discrete accordingly to the rotation of the pencil. In our algorithm, we focused on the temporally changing the maximum pressure. To create such discrete-like vibration, the spatially changing the contact area also should be considered.

- Tapping between the thumb and index finger

Figure 10 shows the pressure distribution and audio waveform while tapping between two fingers. Each frame was captured at 40 Hz sampling rate. The tapping patterns and vibration waveforms can be observed.

It is widely known that the vibration of tapping process can be modeled to be as damped sinusoidal waveform, and the frequency represents the hardness of the material. The waveforms by the proposed algorithm look like to impulse rather than sinusoidal waveform. Similar to scrolling performance, to reproduce tactile sensation with more realistic, the changing of contact area that is related to the object property should also be considered.

- Holding a paper cup with hot water and cold water

Figure 11 shows the temperature change of each finger at both sender and receiver sides in the process of grasping a paper cup of hot water, releasing, and grasping a paper cup of cold water. In our algorithm, we did not present the actual temperature of the object but the temperature different of the sender after touching the object. There

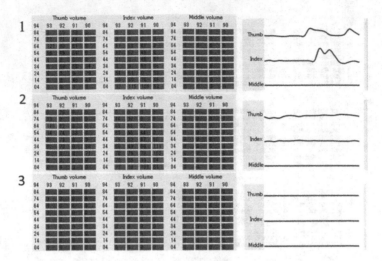

Fig. 10. Pressure distributions and audio waveforms while tapping.

was about 5 s latency because heating or cooling by heater or Peltier required time. During cooling by Peltier, we observed that the temperature unstably vibrated. It is because the other side of Peltier produced heat and transferred to the cool side.

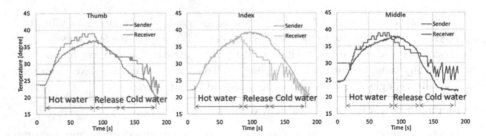

Fig. 11. Temperature transmission of each finger while holding a paper cup with hot water and cold water.

5   Conclusion

We developed a tactile transmission system that can transmit a tactile sense occurs while operating the object with three fingers: thumb, index and middle fingers. For tactile sender side, we developed a glove-type tactile sensor that can measure pressure distribution and temperature distribution simultaneously. For tactile receiver side, we developed a glove-type tactile display with three kinds of primary tactile color: electrical stimulation, thermal stimulation and vibration stimulation. We also developed the algorithm for reproducing tactile sense measured by tactile sensor (e.g. converting pressure distribution changing values to the parameters of vibration presentation).

We tested our system with three performances: scrolling a hexagonal pencil, tapping between the thumb and the index finger, and holding a paper cup that one with hot water and other with cold water. The results confirmed the ability of our system to transmit some sorts of tactile sense with rich information. In the future work we will redevelop more effective algorithm that can present the object property in wider range.

Acknowledgement. This research is supported by the JST-ACCEL Embodied and partly by JSPS KAKENHI Grant Number JP18H06481.

References

1. Cabibihan, J.-J., Zheng, L., Cher, C.K.T.: Affective tele-touch. In: Ge, S.S., Khatib, O., Cabibihan, J.-J., Simmons, R., Williams, M.-A. (eds.) ICSR 2012. LNCS (LNAI), vol. 7621, pp. 348–356. Springer, Heidelberg (2012). https://doi.org/10.1007/978-3-642-34103-8_35
2. Hirche, S., Buss, M.: Human-oriented control for haptic teleoperation. Proc. IEEE **100**(3), 623–647 (2012)
3. Fernando, C.L., Furukawa, M., Kurogi, T., Kamuro, S., Minamizawa, K., Tachi, S.: Design of TELESAR V for transferring bodily consciousness in telexistence. In: Proceedings IEEE Intelligent Robots and Systems (IROS) and IEEE/RSJ International Conference, pp. 5112–5118 (2012)
4. Culbertson, H., Romano, J., Castillo, P., Mintz, M., Kuchenbecker, K.J.: Refined methods for creating realistic haptic virtual textures from tool-mediated contact acceleration data. Departmental Papers (MEAM), 284 (2012)
5. Minamizawa, K., Kakehi, Y., Nakatani, M., Mihara, S., Tachi, S.: TECHTILE toolkit: a prototyping tool for design and education of haptic media. In: Proceedings of ACM Virtual Reality International Conference (VRIC) (2012)
6. Su, Z., et al.: Force estimation and slip detection/classification for grip control using a biomimetic tactile sensor. In: Proceedings of IEEE-RAS International Conference on Humanoid Robots, pp. 297–303 (2015)
7. Lin, C.H., Erickson, T.W., Fishel, J.A., Wettels, N., Loeb, G.E.: Signal processing and fabrication of a biomimetic tactile sensor array with thermal, force and microvibration modalities. In: Proceedings of International Conference on Robotics and Biomimetics, pp. 129–134 (2009)
8. Sato, K., Kamiyama, K., Kawakami, N., Tachi, S.: Finger-shaped GelForce: sensor for measuring surface traction fields for robotic hand. IEEE Trans. Haptics **3**(1), 37–47 (2010)
9. Nakatani, M., Kawasoe, T., Shiojima, K., Kinoshita, S., Wada, J.: Wearable contact force sensor system based on fingerpad deformation. In: Proceedings of IEEE World Haptics Conference, pp. 323–328 (2011)
10. Mascaro, S.A., Asada, H.: Photoplethysmograph fingernail sensors for measuring finger forces without haptic obstruction. IEEE Trans. Robot. Autom. **17**(5), 698–708 (2001)
11. Kurogi, T., et al.: Haptic transmission system to recognize differences in surface textures of objects for telexistence. In: Proceedings of IEEE Virtual Reality, pp. 137–138 (2013)
12. Maeda, T., Peiris, R., Nakatani, M., Tanaka, Y., Minamizawa, T.: Wearable haptic augmentation system using skin vibration sensor. In: Proceedings of International Conference and Exhibition on Virtual Technologies and Uses (2016)
13. Ho, N.H., Jones, L.A.: Contribution of thermal cues to material discrimination and localization. Percept. Psychophys. **68**(1), 118–128 (2006)

14. Yamamoto, A., Yamamoto, H., Cros, B., Hashimoto, H., Higuchi, T.: Thermal tactile presentation based on prediction of contact temperature. J. Robot. Mechatron. **18**(3), 226–234 (2006)
15. Wang, Z., Holledampf, J., Buss, M.: Design and performance of a haptic data acquisition glove. In: Proceedings of International Workshop on Presence, pp. 349–357 (2007)
16. NITTA Corporation: Surface pressure distribution measurement system, HIGH SPEED I-SCAN. https://www.nitta.co.jp/product/sensor/hi-speed_i-scan/. Accessed 2019
17. Martínez, J., García, A., Oliver, M., Molina, J.P., González, P.: Identifying virtual 3D geometric shapes with a vibrotactile glove. IEEE Comput. Graphics Appl. **36**(1), 42–51 (2016)
18. Muramatsu, Y., Niitsuma, M., Thomessen, T.: Perception of tactile sensation using vibrotactile glove interface. In: IEEE Cognitive Infocommunications (CogInfoCom), pp. 621–626 (2012)
19. Murray, A.M., Klatzky, R.L., Khosla, P.K.: Psychophysical characterization and testbed validation of a wearable vibrotactile glove for telemanipulation. Presence Teleoperators Virtual Environ. **12**(2), 156–182 (2003)
20. Wall, S.A., Brewster, S.: Sensory substitution using tactile pin arrays: human factors, technology and applications. J. Signal Process. **86**(12), 3674–3695 (2006)
21. Yang, T.-H., Kim, S.-Y., Kim, C.H., Kwon, D.-S., Book, W.J.: Development of a miniature pin-array tactile module using elastic and electromagnetic force for mobile devices. In: Proceedings of IEEE Eurohaptics Symposium on Haptic Interfaces Virtual Environment and Teleoperator Systems, pp. 13–17 (2009)
22. Kim, S.-C., et al.: Small and lightweight tactile display (SaLT) and its application. In: Proceedings of IEEE Eurohaptics Symposium on Haptic Interfaces Virtual Environment and Teleoperator Systems, pp. 69–74 (2009)
23. Leonardis, D., Solazzi, M., Bortone, I., Frisoli, A.: A wearable fingertip haptic device with 3 DoF asymmetric 3-RSR kinematics. In: Proceedings of IEEE World Haptics Conference, pp. 388–393 (2015)
24. Tsetserukou, D., Hosokawa, S., Terashima, K.: LinkTouch: a wearable haptic device with five-bar linkage mechanism for presentation of two-DOF force feedback at the fingerpad. In: Proceedings of IEEE Haptics Symposium, pp. 307–312 (2014)
25. Minamizawa, K., Fukamachi, S., Kajimoto, H., Kawakami, N., Tachi, S.: Gravity grabber: wearable haptic display to present virtual mass sensation. In: Proceedings of ACM SIGGRAPH Etech (2007)
26. Yamaoka, M., Yamamoto, A., Higuchi, T.: Basic analysis of stickiness sensation for tactile displays. In: Ferre, M. (ed.) EuroHaptics 2008. LNCS, vol. 5024, pp. 427–436. Springer, Heidelberg (2008). https://doi.org/10.1007/978-3-540-69057-3_56
27. Fujita, K., Ohmori, H.: A new softness display interface by dynamic fingertip contact area control. In: Proceedings of the World Multiconference on Systemics, Cybernetics and Informatics, pp. 78–82 (2001)
28. Kaczmarek, K.A., Tyler, M.E., Bach-y-Rita, P.: Electrotactile haptic display on the fingertips: preliminary results. In: Proceedings of IEEE Engineering in Medicine and Biology Society, vol. 2, pp. 940–941 (1994)
29. Kajimoto, H., Kawakami, N., Tachi, S.: Electro-tactile display with tactile primary color approach. In: Proceedings of the Intelligent Robots and Systems (2004)
30. Yem, V., Okazaki, R., Kajimoto, H.: FinGAR: combination of electrical and mechanical stimulation for high-fidelity tactile presentation. In: Proceedings of ACM SIGGRAPH Etech (2016)

31. Yem, V., Kajimo, H.: Wearable tactile device using mechanical and electrical stimulation for fingertip interaction with virtual world. In: Proceedings of IEEE Virtual Reality (VR), pp. 99–104 (2017)

32. Sato, K., Maeno, T.: Presentation of sudden temperature change using spatially divided warm and cool stimuli. In: Isokoski, P., Springare, J. (eds.) EuroHaptics 2012. LNCS, vol. 7282, pp. 457–468. Springer, Heidelberg (2012). https://doi.org/10.1007/978-3-642-31401-8_41

33. Nakatani, M., et al.: A novel multimodal tactile module that can provide vibro-thermal feedback. In: Hasegawa, S., Konyo, M., Kyung, K.-U., Nojima, T., Kajimoto, H. (eds.) AsiaHaptics 2016. LNEE, vol. 432, pp. 437–443. Springer, Singapore (2018). https://doi.org/10.1007/978-981-10-4157-0_73

Information in Virtual and Augmented Reality

User Experience and Map Design
for Wayfinding in a Virtual Environment

Meng-Xi Chen[✉] and Chien-Hsiung Chen

National Taiwan University of Science and Technology, Taipei 10607, Taiwan
cmxl2677@gmail.com

Abstract. Virtual environment (VE) has been developed rapidly in recent years. The level of complexity regarding the user interface in VEs has also increased. Users' performance in VEs can be affected by the field of vision, screen size, operation mode, individual difference, and other factors. While little research has been conducted on the effects of user experience and map design on wayfinding in VEs. The experiment is 2×2 between-subject design. Participants needed to complete three wayfinding tasks and fill out questionnaires regarding satisfaction, preference, and System Usability Scale (SUS). Forty participants were invited using convenient sampling method. The results are as follows: (1) In terms of the map design, participants performed significantly better by using the semi-transparent map than the opaque map in a difficult task. (2) In terms of the user experience, the results generated from the SUS questionnaire showed that experienced users had a significantly better subjective evaluation of interface usability than inexperienced users.

Keywords: Virtual environment · Wayfinding · Map design · User experience

1 Introduction

Virtual environment (VE) has been developed rapidly in recent years. The level of complexity regarding the user interface in VEs has also increased. Studies on wayfinding in VEs involve cognitive science, human factors, computer science and other fields. Machines are connected with humans by cognitive science, which inquire about the differences between humans and man-made objects in settling problems and the complicated inner workings [1]. Human factors are defined as a science field of creating a proper environment with safe and useful equipment for humans [2].

According to Darken and Sibert [3], VEs are classified by three attributes: size, density and activity. All the details of a large VE cannot be seen from a single viewpoint. There is a relatively large number of objects and cues in a dense VE, the objects obscure important cues and the positions of objects are not predictable. The positions and values of the objects with low activity do not change over time in a static environment. In our study, the controlled environment was a large and dense virtual exhibition with low activity. Users were immersed in the VE and allowed to explore the 3D scenes with input controller freely. Information visualization should be clear on wayfinding maps. Making use of transparency to represent layers of information seems to be an intuitive utilization. The frequency of using transparency on a wayfinding map

© Springer Nature Switzerland AG 2019
S. Yamamoto and H. Mori (Eds.): HCII 2019, LNCS 11570, pp. 117–126, 2019.
https://doi.org/10.1007/978-3-030-22649-7_10

is increasing, while studies on wayfinding map design only involved color, view, landmarks, level of detail and so on.

Users' performance in VEs can be affected by the field of vision, screen size, operation mode, individual difference, and other factors. There are two main types of perspective in VEs: the first-person perspective and the third-person perspective. Research conducted by Schuurink and Toet [4] indicated that adopting the third-person perspective can provide wider vision than the first-person perspective, but it also takes more time to find the target. Our study adopted the first-person perspective which is often used in virtual exhibitions, users pay more attention to the details of exhibits rather than the surrounding environment. Expect the environmental features, the interplay between individual abilities and environmental features can affect wayfinding performance [5]. Therefore, user experience should be considered as a prominent personal factor which could help wayfinding in VEs.

The goals of this research study are: (1) To explore the main issues of map design for wayfinding in a VE; (2) To investigate how map design affects wayfinding tasks in a VE; (3) To investigate how user experience affects their wayfinding behavior in a VE.

2 Map Design

Maps, which visualize spatial relationships with graphs, have been widely used to aid navigation in people's lives. On the aspect of carrier, maps are divided into electronic and paper maps. Electronic maps are not limited in size or display resolution. In terms of content, maps can be divided into general maps, thematic maps and pictorial maps. The main geographical features are reflected on general maps to emphasize the accuracy of spatial relationships. A thematic map usually adds an extra layer of concept upon the layer of general map. Instead of locations, the structure of a natural element or a social and economic issue is manifested in a thematic map. Pictorial maps, such as road maps and tourist maps, are not limited by the precise proportion of geographic locations. Pictorial maps could use various forms of expressions to suppress details and highlight the subject, conveying the theme. In direction, maps are divided into north-up and track-up maps. The environment is fixed on a north-up map, the icons representing users moves in the direction of users. Track-up mapstrack the direction of users' gaze and rotate with the users. In this study, the north-up maps are electronic and pictorial.

Map design, a combination of art and science, directly affects users' performance and feelings. Robinson [6] proposed principles of map design: (1) Letters and symbols are legible; (2) The contents of map have visual contrast to be discriminated; (3) The relationship between figure and background is handled well to make the main contents easy to be recognized; (4) The organization of map has hierarchy of features. Darken and Sibert [3] concluded that principles of map design in real world can be applied in VEs.

Basic graphic elements on maps, including point, line, plane and volume, are designed by changing the hue, brightness, saturation, transparency and other factors of the elements, which ensure the main content, headline, legend, illustration, scale and direction indicator are reasonable. The less target background similarity there is, the faster searching will be [7]. Using different degrees of transparency can display varying levels of importance. Opaque figures with clear borders improve the strength of visual stimulation to present important information. On the contrary, figures with a high degree of transparency present less critical information. But at the same time, figures which have light color could display more information to make best use of screen space. Effects of the transparency of maps on wayfinding performance and users' feelings in VEs are still to be confirmed.

3 User Experience

The experience of using smart devices is constantly changing in the face of new devices and functions. Forlizzi and Battarbee [8] clarified users' experience in interactive systems, the authors proposed three types of user-product interactions and three types of experience. Fluent interactions are automatic and practised, cognitive interactions focus on the product at hand and can result in correct knowledge or contrast; expressive interactions help users form relationships with products. The first type of experience is the continuous "self-talk" which occurs during the interactions. The second type of experience with a clearly defined start and end often makes changes in emotion and behavior. Co-experience, the third type of experience creates meaning and emotion through social interaction.

To understand the meaning of wayfinding maps in VEs, visual information is connected with the experience stored in memory, and then the process from perception to cognition is completed. Norman [9] suggested three types of human memories: sensory memory, long-term memory (LTM) and short-term memory (STM). The stimulus gets to the human sensors and is stored in the sensory memory for an extremely brief time. The stimulus is transmitted to the human brain and temporarily held in the STM [10]. Bailey [11] claimed that designers should try to know about the information stored in users' memories, and how to help users perform well through using new stimulus. If new information has a relationship with something in the LTM, it is easy to get into the LTM.

Users who know information technology devices well are more accurate and decisive in wayfinding [12]. Experienced users hold the usage of wayfinding aids in their LTM to help conduct wayfinding tasks in VEs. The operation and function of aids should be consistent with users' experience to meet their expectations.In this study, user experience referred to the usage of maps as wayfinding aids in VEs such as virtual museum, racing game and city navigation.

4 Methods

4.1 Participants

A total of 40 participants (20 men and 20 women) were invited to take part in a wayfinding experiment based on convenient sampling method. Half the participants have experience of using maps as wayfinding aids in VEs and the other half did not have user experience. 7 of the 20 experienced participants (35%) used maps in VEs more than 3 times a week. Participants who used maps in VEs once or twice a week, less than once a month, or one to three times a month were no more than 5 people (25%). Eighty percent of experienced participants have at least half a year of experience. 7 people have more than 3 years of experience (35%). 6 people have 1 to 3 years of experience (30%). People who have half to one year of experience, 1 to 3 months of experience, or 3 to 6 months of experience were less than 3 people (15%).

All of participants were university students aged from 18 to 30 years, 25 undergraduate students and 15 graduate students. 36 people used internet for an average of more than 2 h a day (90%). More than fifty percent of participants used internet for 2 to 6 h a day. Thus problems in basic operation during the experiment can be prevented. All participants finished tasks successfully.

4.2 Materials and Apparatus

A virtual exhibition area was created with 3D software, and the map of the exhibition was created with 2D software. The experiment operation was configured with 3D game engine. This experiment was conducted on an iPad Air 2. The 9.7-in. retina display was set to a resolution of 2048×1536 pixels. All experimental applications were run under the iOS 9.3 operating system.

4.3 Experimental Design

This experiment adopted a 2 (map design) $\times$ 2 (user experience) between-subjects design. According to the independent variables, participants were divided into four groups. There were two types of maps adopted in this study, i.e., an opaque map and a semi-transparent map. Previous studies have found that user experience is an important personal factor that makes a difference in the accuracy of wayfinding. Therefore, the experimental design included experienced users and inexperienced users.

The research hypotheses are as follows: (1) The operational efficiency of the opaque map may be significantly different from that of the semi-transparent map. (2) The subjective evaluation of the opaque map may be significantly different from that of the semi-transparent map. (3) User experience may cause significant difference in operational efficiency. (4) User experience may cause significant difference in subjective evaluation.

4.4 Procedure

Participants were asked to conduct three wayfinding tasks with increasing difficulty. The first task was the easiest task, which is to judge the farthest profile exhibition area. The second task was a more difficult task, which is to look for the Chinese calligraphy exhibition area and then count the number of calligraphy works. Compared with the first task, participants also needed to look over the details in the exhibition. The third task was the most difficult task, which is to look for all Chinese painting exhibition areas and then point out the longest Chinese painting. Participants needed to memorize and compare the contents in different exhibitions.

The data of operation performance were collected, such as the time required to find each target. After completing all the tasks, each participant was required to fill out a questionnaire regarding their overall satisfaction. The questionnaire was designed based on a 7-point Likert scale. After that, participants' preferences were investigated in the same way.

In addition, participants were also required to fill out the System Usability Scale (SUS) questionnaire in order to investigate their subjective evaluations. The questionnaire was designed based on a 5-point Likert scale anchored by 1: strongly disagree and 5: strongly agree. The higher the scores of SUS, the better usability of the map.

5 Results

5.1 Analysis of Task Operation Time

The data were analyzed using the statistical software SPSS. Table 1 presents the mean task operation time for each independent variable level, while Table 2 shows the ANOVA table from the analysis.

The first task was to find the farthest profile exhibition area. The result of ANOVA indicated that there was no significant effect of map design regarding the Task 1 operation time ($F = 3.658$, $p = 0.064 > 0.05$). The main effect of user experience on the Task 1 operation time was not significant ($F = 3.549$, $p = 0.068 > 0.05$). There existed no significant difference in the interaction effect between the variables of user experience and map design ($F = 0.041$, $p = 0.840 > 0.05$). It indicated that in the easiest task, user experience and the transparency of map did not significantly affect wayfinding performance.

The second task was to know the number of calligraphy works. According to the statistical analysis results acquired in Table 2, the main effect of map design on the Task 2 operation time was significant ($F = 4.533$, $p = 0.040 < 0.05$). The results suggested that the Task 2 operation time for the opaque map ($M = 9.647$, $Sd = 6.038$) was significantly longer than that for the semi-transparent map ($M = 6.386$, $Sd = 3.056$). One possible explanation for this result is that the opaque map covered the partial VE, thus participants cannot recognize their positions. As is shown in Table 2, the main effect of user experience on the Task 2 operation time was not significant ($F = 0.944$, $p = 0.338 > 0.05$). The interaction effect between the variables of user experience and map design were also not significant ($F = 0.145$, $p = 0.706 > 0.05$).

The third task was to look for the longest Chinese painting. Table 2 shows that there was no significant difference in the main effect of map design in terms of the Task 3 operation time ($F = 3.773$, $p = 0.060 > 0.05$). The main effect of user experience on the Task 3 operation time was not significant ($F = 0.304$, $p = 0.585 > 0.05$). It revealed that there existed no significant difference in the interaction effect between the variables of user experience and map design ($F = 2.739$, $p = 0.107 > 0.05$). Even though the last task was most difficult, user experience and the transparency of map did not significantly affect the process of memorizing and comparing information, as participants might already be familiar with the VE.

Table 1. Descriptive statistics of task operation time (s)

Variable		Task 1		Task 2		Task 3		N
		M	SD	M	SD	M	SD	
Map design	The opaque map	7.328	5.693	9.647	6.038	13.239	8.825	20
	The semi-transparent map	4.526	3.506	6.386	3.056	9.105	3.898	20
User experience	Inexperienced users	4.547	2.867	8.760	5.591	10.585	7.356	20
	Experienced users	7.307	6.050	7.272	4.355	11.759	6.872	20

Table 2. Two-way ANOVA of task operation time

Source		SS	df	MS	F	P
Task 1	Map design	78.484	1	78.484	3.658	.064
	User experience	76.148	1	76.148	3.549	.068
	Map design * User experience	.885	1	.885	.041	.840
Task 2	Map design	106.341	1	106.341	4.533	.040*
	User experience	22.141	1	22.141	.944	.338
	Map design * User experience	3.399	1	3.399	.145	.706
Task 3	Map design	170.900	1	170.900	3.773	.060
	User experience	13.783	1	13.783	.304	.585
	Map design * User experience	124.045	1	124.045	2.739	.107

$\alpha = 0.05$, *$p < 0.05$.

5.2 Analysis of Subjective Satisfaction

Participants selected their satisfaction levels for maps according to their subjective opinions on a 7-point scale, with the two end points labeled strong dissatisfaction and strong satisfaction. The descriptive statistics and two-way ANOVA of satisfaction are shown in Tables 3 and 4. The mean value of satisfaction in each group was more than 5, and the mean value of satisfaction (M = 6.250, Sd = 0.927) showed that participants were inclined to be satisfied.

Table 3. Descriptive statistics of subjective satisfaction

Variable		M	SD	N
Map design	The opaque map	6.100	.912	20
	The semi-transparent map	6.400	.940	20
User experience	Inexperienced users	6.000	.918	20
	Experienced users	6.500	.889	20

Table 4. Two-way ANOVA of subjective satisfaction

Source	SS	df	MS	F	P
Map design	0.900	1	0.900	1.174	.286
User experience	2.500	1	2.500	3.261	.079
Map design * User experience	2.500	1	2.500	3.261	.079

The ANOVA revealed no significant main effect for both map design (F = 1.174, p = 0.286 > 0.05) and user experience (F = 3.261, p = 0.079 > 0.05). There was also no significant interaction effect between the two factors (F = 3.261, p = 0.079 > 0.05). It is possible that user experience and the transparency of map did not relate to users' satisfaction.

5.3 Analysis of Subjective Preference

The data on subjective preference were analyzed to find out which map was most acceptable. The questionnaire was designed based on a 7-point scale, with the two end points labeled strongly dislike and strongly like. The descriptive statistics and two-way ANOVA of preference are shown in Tables 5 and 6. The mean value of preference in each group was more than 5, and the mean value of preference (M = 5.950, Sd = 0.986) showed that the maps were inclined to be acceptable.

Table 5. Descriptive statistics of subjective preference

Variable		M	SD	N
Map design	The opaque map	5.800	.951	20
	The semi-transparent map	6.100	1.021	20
User experience	Inexperienced users	5.800	.951	20
	Experienced users	6.100	1.021	20

Table 6. Two-way ANOVA of subjective preference

Source	SS	df	MS	F	P
Map design	.900	1	.900	.900	.349
User experience	.900	1	.900	.900	.349
Map design * User experience	.100	1	.100	.100	.754

The result showed that there was no significant difference in the main effect of both map design (F = 0.900, p = 0.349 > 0.05) and user experience (F = 0.900, p = 0.349 > 0.05). No significant interaction existed between map design and user experience (F = 0.100, p = 0.754 > 0.05). It showed that user experience and the transparency of map did not affect subjective preference.

5.4 Analysis of SUS

The descriptive statistics and two-way ANOVA of SUS are shown in Tables 7 and 8. The mean value of SUS in each group was above 75, and the mean value of SUS (M = 84.938, Sd = 13.052) showed that the maps have good usability. Participants have stated in the interviews that the interface is simple and easy to learn.

Table 7. Descriptive statistics of SUS

Variable		M	SD	N
Map design	The opaque map	83.625	14.315	20
	The semi-transparent map	86.250	11.879	20
User experience	Inexperienced users	80.750	14.870	20
	Experienced users	89.125	9.572	20

The result showed that there was no significant effect of map design ($F = 0.433$, $p = 0.514 > 0.05$). The main effect of user experience was significant ($F = 4.412$, $p = 0.043 < 0.05$). Experienced users ($M = 89.125$, $Sd = 9.572$) gave significantly higher SUS values than inexperienced users ($M = 80.750$, $Sd = 14.870$). The reason might be that the experience of using wayfinding maps in VEs was stored in users' LTM. Wayfinding maps were easier for experienced users to learn and use, therefore, experienced users gave a better evaluation than inexperienced users. The effect of interaction was not significant ($F = 0.945$, $p = 0.338 > 0.05$).

Table 8. Two-way ANOVA of SUS

Source	SS	df	MS	F	P
Map design	68.906	1	68.906	.433	.514
User experience	701.406	1	701.406	4.412	.043*
Map design * User experience	150.156	1	150.156	.945	.338

$\alpha = 0.05$, *$p < 0.05$.

6 Discussion

The results regarding operational efficiency revealed that participants performed significantly better by using the semi-transparent map than the opaque map only in the more difficult task which is to locate and review the information. The result confirmed our first hypothesis. The operational efficiency of the opaque map is significantly different from that of the semi-transparent map. The reason might be that the semi-transparent map increased information display and helped users perceive target objects and their positions in VEs. It is in accordance with previous studies which have proposed that the contrast between the main contents and background could make information on maps easier to be recognized in VEs [3, 6].

The statistical results revealed no significant difference between experienced users and inexperienced users in wayfinding performance. Contradicting the third hypothesis, operational efficiency was unaffected by user experience.

The results of this study showed that there existed no significant difference in the interaction effect among the variables of map design and user experience in terms of overall satisfaction and users' preferences. The results generated from the SUS questionnaire showed that experienced users had a significantly better subjective evaluation of interface usability than the inexperienced users. This result indicated that the fourth hypothesis is accepted. User experience causes significant difference in subjective evaluation. Using wayfinding maps in VEs is easier for experienced users. The reason might be that the operation and function of the wayfinding map was consistent with users' experience stored in LTM. The conclusion is in line with previous studies which have proposed that experienced users who know devices well may perform better and have less hesitation in wayfinding [12].

Based on the results generated in this study, there was no statistical significance between the SUS questionnaire results regarding the semi-transparent map and the opaque map. This also contradicted the second hypothesis. The subjective evaluation of the opaque map is similar to that of the semi-transparent map.

7 Conclusion

This study focused on the difference caused by user experience and map design in users' performance and feelings. Participants were satisfied with the maps, and the maps were inclined to be acceptable. Findings suggested that users with the semi-transparent map may conduct significantly better wayfinding performance in a VE than the opaque map. User experience did not significantly affect their wayfinding performance but affect subjective feelings.

Even though the experiment used a museum as the VE, the results obtained in the present study also can be applicable to all VEs, such as education games, virtual tourism and city navigation. Suggestions for further studies on wayfinding map design include a wider range of map element such as size, shape, and color.

References

1. McFarland, M.C., Parker, A.C., Camposano, R.: The high-level synthesis of digital systems. Proc. IEEE **78**(2), 301–318 (1990)
2. Huchingson, R.D.: New Horizons for Human Factors in Design. McGraw-Hill, New York (1981)
3. Darken, R.P., Sibert, J.L.: A toolset for navigation in virtual environments. In: Proceedings of the 6th Annual ACM Symposium on User Interface Software and Technology, pp. 157–165. ACM, Atlanta (1993)
4. Schuurink, L.E., Toet, A.: Effects of third person perspective on affective appraisal and engagement: findings from second life. Simul. Gaming **41**(5), 724–742 (2010)
5. Eaton, G.: Wayfinding in the library: book searches and route uncertainty. RQ **30**(4), 519–527 (1991)
6. Robinson, A.H., Morrison, J.L., Muehrcke, P.C., Kimerling, A.J., Guptill, S.C.: Elements of Cartography, 6th edn. Wiley, New York (1995)
7. Moraglia, G., Maloney, K.P., Fekete, E.M., Al-Basi, K.: Visual search along the colour dimension. Can. J. Psychol. **43**(1), 1–12 (1989)
8. Forlizzi, J., Battarbee, K.: Understanding experience in interactive systems. In: Proceedings of the 5th Conference on Designing Interactive Systems: Processes, Practices, Methods, and Techniques, pp. 261–268. ACM, Cambridge (2004)
9. Norman, D.A.: The Psychology of Everyday Things. Basic Books, New York (1988)

10. Newell, A., Simon, H.A.: Human Problem Solving. Prentice-Hall, Englewood Cliffs (1972)
11. Bailey, C.D.: Forgetting and the learning curve: a laboratory study. Manag. Sci. **35**(3), 340–352 (1989)
12. Lee, S., Kim, E.Y., Platosh, P.: Indoor wayfinding using interactive map. Int. J. Eng. Technol. **7**(1), 75–80 (2015)

AR Cooking: Comparing Display Methods for the Instructions of Cookwares on AR Goggles

Hiroki Hasada[✉], Junjian Zhang[✉], Kenta Yamamoto[✉],
Bektur Ryskeldiev[✉], and Yoichi Ochiai[✉]

Digital Nature Group, Pixie Dust Technologies Inc.,
University of Tsukuba, Tsukuba, Japan
{hirokihasada,tyookk,kenta.yam,bektour}@digitalnature.slis.tsukuba.ac.jp,
wizard@slis.tsukuba.ac.jp

Abstract. We explore effective display methods for instructions on complex tools on augmented reality (AR) goggles. We focused on three types of cookwares as complex tools in everyday life: avocado cutter, orange opener, and can opener. We implemented three AR applications for displaying the usage of three cookwares: images with text, videos, and three-dimensional (3D) animation. In this study, we investigated how each of these AR applications affects the understanding of complicated products and their applications. Using Microsoft HoloLens, we conducted user studies with the three aforementioned display methods. We measured the task completion time and investigated the psychological element. Based on the task completion time and whether the task could be completed, we found that the most efficient display method for the instruction of cookwares on AR goggles is 3D animation. We investigated how participants felt about cooking using AR goggles based on participant's comments. We believe that our contribution can be useful for the design of AR-based application.

Keywords: UX and usability ·
Qualitative and quantitative measurement and evaluation ·
User experience

1 Introduction

AR goggles are considered effective for various instructions such as cooking. In recent years, many cooking assistant technologies have been studied. Assistance cooking is an important research field for enriching human life. When people are cooking, one may encounter a cookware whose usage is not trivial by appearance. It is particularly typical in novelty products such as avocado cutter, orange opener, and can opener in Fig. 2(a)–(c). Currently, tutorials involving images with text and videos are typical as a method for presenting the usage of such products. In traditional cooking scenarios, people are used to learning cooking

© Springer Nature Switzerland AG 2019
S. Yamamoto and H. Mori (Eds.): HCII 2019, LNCS 11570, pp. 127–140, 2019.
https://doi.org/10.1007/978-3-030-22649-7_11

Table 1. Pros and cons of the three kinds of the media for instruction.

	Pros	Cons	Example
Paper manual	Almost all people are used to it as traditional media	More maintenance cost than digital data	Cook books Assembly manual
Tablet device	Rich contents can be achieved through Internet. Digital data is easily reserved	Hard to operate when hands are wet. Cannot operate without electric power	iPhone[a] iPad[b]
AR goggles	Understanding the needed information better by adding extra virtual information into real world	Current devices are heavy. The viewing angle is narrow. Cannot operate without electric power	Microsoft HoloLens[c] Magic Leap[d]

[a] https://www.apple.com/jp/iphone/ (Last accessed 2019-02-15)
[b] https://www.apple.com/jp/ipad/ (Last accessed 2019-02-15)
[c] https://www.microsoft.com/ja-jp/hololens (Last accessed 2019-02-15)
[d] https://www.magicleap.com/ (Last accessed 2019-02-15)

by reading the instructions through paper media or tablet devices. However, both hands may get wet or dirty during cooking, which can be a psychological barrier to touching paper or tablet devices directly. In addition, most tablet devices may be damaged when they are splashed with water. AR technologies are thought to be an effective approach to such problems in these traditional media. Table 1 shows the advantages and disadvantages of the three media. In this study, we focus on exploring an effective display method for cooking on Microsoft HoloLens, an AR goggles. We conducted experiments on cookwares as shown in Fig. 1(a). In this experiment, we displayed images with text, videos and 3D animation as shown in Fig. 1(b)–(d), on Microsoft HoloLens. Quantitative and qualitative results are presented from user surveys on 35 different participants.

The contributions of this research are as follows:

- We investigated how three display methods with Microsoft HoloLens affect users on the efficiency of cooking tasks.
- We discuss the evaluation results by quantitative and qualitative methods.
- We discuss the user experience from at free-description-type questionnaire.

2   Related Work

2.1   Instruction Method by AR Technology

Currently, many practical applications of AR technology are considered, e.g. medical and assembly work. Furthermore, research to compare AR goggles with

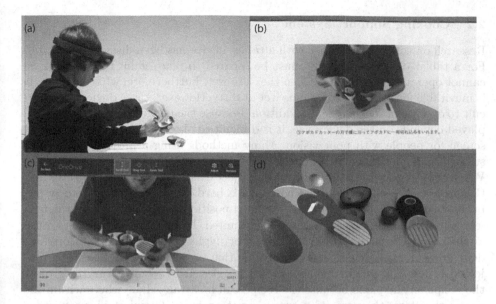

Fig. 1. Variety of cooking instructions. (a) the participants completed the task while watching the 3 instructions displayed on the AR goggles, (b) images with text, (c) the video, (d) the 3D animation.

Fig. 2. Variety of cookwares. (a) the avocado cutter, (b) the orange opener, (c) the can opener.

various display media have been conducted [1,3,4,8,11,13,15]. In 2017, Orsini et al. published a practical application using Microsoft HoloLens on cooking.[1] However, the relationship between cooking and display method was not explored. Furthermore, they did not explore what was effective for displaying on AR goggles. Cooking is a typical act performed in many families. Exploring the relationship between the display method and users is an important study related to the sense of use when making practical applications. Therefore, we attempted to explore the relationship between cooking and display methods on AR goggle and used it for future practical application designs.

---

[1] http://www.ece.rutgers.edu/sites/default/files/capstone/capstone2017/posters/ S17-35-poster.pdf (Last accessed 2019-02-15).

2.2   Cooking Support System

Research on cooking assistance with a tablet device has been discussed in [5,14]. For a tablet device, a location must be secured to place it in. In addition, we cannot operate tablet devices when they are wet. Furthermore, while cooking, it is inevitable for the hand to become wet or dirty. However, these devices are difficult to operate in such a case. In addition, because the image size that can be displayed depends on the device size, it is difficult to observe presbyopia or a small screen for people with poor vision. Many methods using a projector are being studied as a method that does not require touching by hand [2,6,7,9,10,12]. When projecting with a projector, if an object exists between the projector and the projection plane, a person who cooks is hard to see because a shadow has been generated. Depending on the installed position and orientation of the projector, the plane that can be displayed is limited. In addition, depending on the kitchen, a space for installing the projector might not be available. Moreover, depending on the kitchen, it is conceivable that an ideal plane that can be projected is non-existent. In the case of AR goggles, it is not necessary to project the recipe on the plane because the recipe can be arranged anywhere within the space; therefore, the projection space is not an issue. Orsini et al. proposed a system for displaying recipes using object recognition on AR goggles. In this system, three-dimensional (3D) animation was used to display, and when it becomes difficult to convey, the recipe of the animation can be viewed. However, they did not mention which display method was easier to convey. Various approaches have been reported for cooking-assistance systems. However, experiments focusing on display methods on AR goggles have not been conducted.

3   Design of Displaying Instructions on AR Goggles

Figure 3 shows overview of the experiment. Images with text and videos are displayed so that they are projected on a whiteboard about 1 m away from AR goggles. 3D animation was displayed in midair about 30 cm away from AR goggles. 3D animation can be seen simultaneously with the cooking area. However, images with text and videos cannot be seen simultaneously with the cooking area.

3.1   Images with Text

Figure 4 shows instruction of images with text of avocado cutter. Currently, the most popular instruction platform is the paper manual. Images with text are created by referencing the paper manual. Images were created by capturing screenshots from videos shown in Fig. 5. One should click on the right side of the screen to advance to the next page and click on the left side to return to the previous page. The image was fixed on a whiteboard at a distance of approximately 1 m and projected such that the entire image would fit in the viewing angle of Microsoft HoloLens to the participants. If we display the images

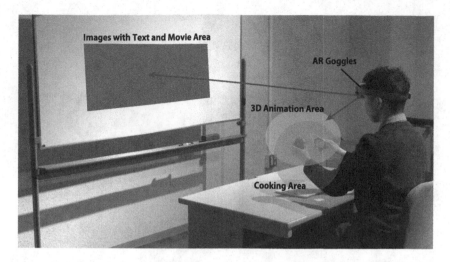

Fig. 3. Overview of experiment. Images with text and videos are displayed so that they were projected on a whiteboard about 1 m away from AR goggles. 3D animation was displayed in midair about 30 cm away from AR goggles.

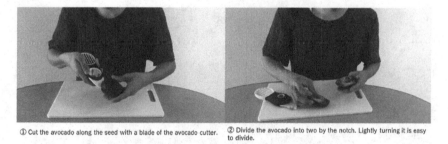

① Cut the avocado along the seed with a blade of the avocado cutter.   ② Divide the avocado into two by the notch. Lightly turning it is easy to divide.

Fig. 4. Images with text of the avocado cutter. Images were created by taking screenshots from videos in Fig. 5. Click on the right side of the screen to advance to the next page and click on the left side to return to the previous page.

in front of the participant, they can not see their hands. Therefore, we display the images on the whiteboard in front of the participants. We add text to each image because there is no visual movement information. This display method was considered to be inferior to the video and 3D animation in that there is no visual information of movement.

3.2 Video

Figure 5 shows instruction of the video of avocado cutter. The audio of the video was turned off. We can return to the video using the control bar, and we can stop the video with the play/pause button. The video was fixed on a whiteboard at a distance of approximately 1 m and projected such that the entire video would

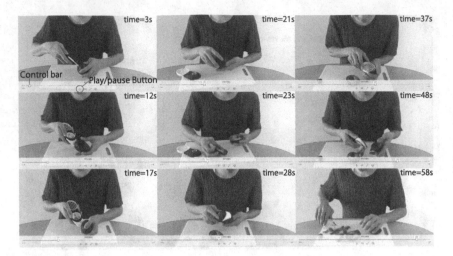

Fig. 5. The video of avocado cutter. We took the video of peeling avocado using avocado cutter from the front. We can return the video using the control bar, and we can stop the video with the play/pause button.

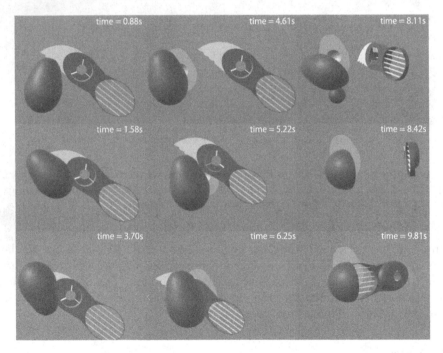

Fig. 6. 3D animation of avocado cutter. 3D animation was created to loop automatically.

fit in the viewing angle of Microsoft HoloLens to the participants. If we display the video in front of the participant, they can not see their hands. Therefore, we display on the whiteboard in front of the participant. We did not instruct by voice or subtitle. Therefore, we verified whether instructions are conveyed only with the video. We considered that this display method was superior to images with text because the visual movement information can be conveyed. However, we considered that this display method was inferior to 3D animation because 3D information cannot be conveyed and we cannot display at hand.

3.3   3D Animation

Figure 6 shows instruction of 3D animation of avocado cutter. The 3D animation instruction was implemented by Unity[2], and displayed at a distance of approximately 30 cm from the participant. The 3D animation was created to loop automatically. We display the 3D animation in front of the participants because their hands are not obscured by images or videos. We considered that participants prefer 3D animation to images with text and video because they could observe the three-dimensional information, as well as see both hands and instructions at the same time.

4   User Study

4.1   Methodology

Study Process. The independent variables ware the display method and cookwares. The dependent variables were seven-point Likert scale scores for measuring the efficiency and task completion times. Participants practised the hand gesture of Microsoft HoloLens before doing the task. They learned the air tap (corresponding to click on PC) and tap & hold (corresponding to drag & drop on PC). Task completion time was measured when each work was finished. The avocado-cutting task was deemed completed when the last slice was cut. The orange-opening task was deemed completed when the orange was completely peeled. The can-opening task was deemed completed when the participants emptied the can. We chose the task completion time as a quantitative evaluation. After the tasks ware completed, the participant was asked to complete posttest questionnaires: qualitative questionnaire, the demographic information and description formula.

Participants. Thirty-five participants (18 women and 17 men, with six left-handed participants) of ages from 18 to 24 participated (M = 20.8, SD = 1.4) in the experiments. Some of the participants performed multiple tasks using the two or three cookwares, and 68 trials were conducted. A previous questionnaire is conducted to ensure that all the participants have never use the cookware ever before and were not aware of the specific usage of the tool before the experiment.

---

[2] https://unity3d.com/jp (Last accessed 2019-02-15).

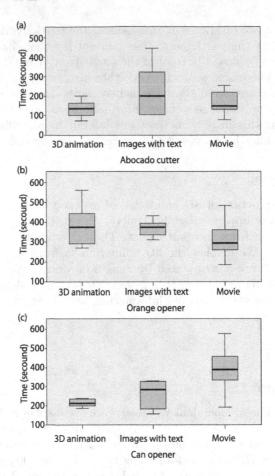

Fig. 7. Task Completion Times of three cookwares. (a) shows the result of the avocado cutter. (b) shows the result of the orange opener. (c) shows the result of the can opener.

It is noteworthy that all participants used the cookware for the first time in the experiment. It is necessary for each participant to not know the cookware usage presented to them. Therefore, cases exist where a few participants did not know the usage of one or two tools among the three tools. The number of people who did not know the usage of only one tool was 13; the number of people who did not know the usage of two tools was 11; and the number of people who did not know the usage of all three tools was 11.

4.2   Results

Task Completion Times. One participant quit the experiment for the task of images with text for a can opener. However, all other participants completed all the tasks. Figure 7(a)–(c) shows the task completion time result of each cookware. After removing the data points of participants who quit from the 68 data points, we excluded data that are over +3.0SD from the time required for each task as outliers. One data point was excluded from 67 data points. A one-way ANOVA was conducted to study the effect of the instructional method on the task completion times for each cookware. When the ANOVA indicated a significant difference between systems, pairwise comparisons were conducted using the Bonferroni correction. The effect was statistically significant, i.e., $F(2, 18) = 6.67$, $p = 0.036$. In the can-opening task, the ANOVA analysis indicates statistically significant effects between the video and 3D animation ($p = 0.036$). There is no significant effect between images with text and the video ($p = 1.000$), and between images with text and 3D animation ($p = 0.203$). However, no statistically significant difference is shown in any display method for the avocado cutter and orange opener.

Questionnaire Results from Participants. We conducted a questionnaire survey for five items for qualitative evaluation. The results of the questionnaire are reported in Fig. 8(a)–(e). The participants answered the questionnaires on items of efficiency, easiness, pleasantness, satisfaction, and hardship on a seven-point Likert scale and described the reasons for each of their responses. We conducted the ANOVA test on the questionnaire with the Likert scale. However, no significant difference was shown from any of the questionnaires. Therefore, we decided to explore why participants experienced efficiency or understandability from the description of the reasons for the five questionnaires. Sixty comments were obtained for each of the five questionnaires, except for no answers for 68 trials, and approximately 300 total descriptions were obtained.

5   Discussion

This section discusses the experimental findings based on the stated hypotheses. The implications of the results on the theoretical model are investigated, and further insights into the influence of AR in human performance and perception are provided.

5.1   Task Completion Times

From the results of the experiments on the cost time, the 3D animation approach was significantly faster than the video in the can-opening task. No significant difference is found in the avocado-cutting and orange-opening tasks. We consider that the effective display method depends on the task. However, depending on the task, it was shown that the task completion time by the display of 3D animation can be shorter than by the display of video. We consider that this result has been caused because the operation gesture is difficult for participants who are new to Microsoft HoloLens. In the display of the video, the participants must use the air tap gesture to play/pause a button and tap & hold of the control bar. On the other hand, the 3D animation is looped automatically by default. The control bar may be effective when watching a video on a smartphone or the

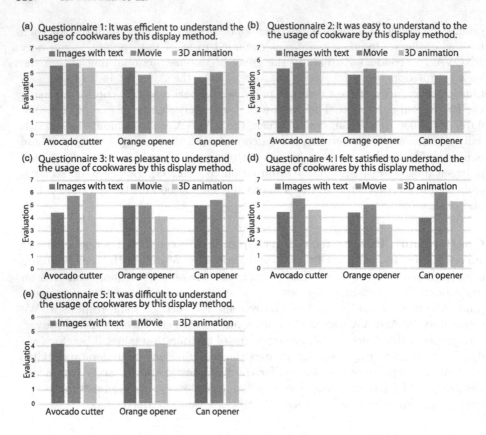

Fig. 8. Result of five Questionnaire. (a) Questionnaire 1: efficiency. (b) Questionnaire 2: easiness. (c) Questionnaire 3: pleasantness. (d) Questionnaire 4: satisfaction. (e) Questionnaire 5: hardship.

like. However, other operation methods may be better when watching a video on Microsoft HoloLens.

5.2   Participants' Comments

Sixty comments on each questionnaire were obtained except for no answer. We described the comments and their considerations in the following:

Questionnaire 1: Efficiency. Eleven people commented the following: "Microsoft HoloLens is usable even when I'm cooking with dirty hands." Therefore, we consider that it is effective for participants to cook with AR goggles. As for the display by 3D animation, a participant commented "It is stereoscopic and easy to understand." This indicates the possibility of 3D animation on AR goggles as for cooking. Meanwhile, 11 participants commented that there is little difference between AR goggles and other devices such as projectors, personal computers, displays, and tablet devices as the reason for not understanding efficiency. Two of them complied with the images with text, six of them complied with the video and three of them with 3D animation. Therefore, we consider that the video is harder to understand the merit of AR goggles than other display methods.

Questionnaire 2: Easiness. We did not observe many biased comments. However, some of the participants who saw the 3D animation commented that its understanding was difficult owing to the lack of a hand model. Whether a hand exists in 3D animation will be addressed in future work. A participant who performed the avocado-cutting task using 3D animation replied "It is easy because I could mimic the movement of the 3D animation." A load of work perception should decrease because it is sufficient to mimic the motion information. Furthermore, 3D animation can overlay on objects and ease objects observation, unlike the video. This is considered that the 3D animation is superior to the video as for the mimic of motion.

Questionnaire 3: Pleasantness. Eighteen participants commented "It was refreshing to understand how to cook on AR goggles." We considered that they felt pleasant cooking on AR goggles because almost all of them were not used to AR goggles. As for the display of the 3D animation, one participant that they tried the orange opening task commented "I am glad to see the backside of the task." The video can convey only information from the front. On the other hand, the 3D animation can convey the information on the backside. Currently, as for our 3D animation, we can see the backside by changing the viewpoint. It is a future work to make the direction of 3D animation changeable by voice and hand gesture.

Questionnaire 4: Satisfaction. Regardless of the display method is used, the participants were satisfied when the task is completed. One participant who watched the 3D animation answered, "I felt satisfied because it was interesting to overlay an avocado on 3D animation." It is difficult to overlay the avocado on the video or images with text. However, 3D animation can overlay the real object. Therefore, we consider that 3D animation is superior to the video and images with text. Further, one participant looking at the three types of display methods comments "Because the task difficulty level was not extremely high." A different result may be obtained if the task becomes more difficult such as making a dish from a recipe.

Questionnaire 5: Hardship. Further, 14 reasons were related to Microsoft HoloLens as an AR device, such as "heavy," "worrisome," "difficult to operate," "machine unfamiliarity." These improvements can be expected by improving the performance of the device. As for AR goggles, the development of devices is remarkable. Therefore, we consider that it is necessary to perform new experiments every time a new device is launched.

5.3   Participants Who Quit

As for the can-opening task, one participant that see images with text stopped doing before they have been completed. Unlike the video and 3D animation, it is considered that images with text have little information on the movement of the can opener. Therefore, it is difficult to understand how to move the can opener from the instruction of images with text. We consider that participants need motion information to understand how to use.

5.4   Experiment Design

We consider that increasing the number of tasks can be effective in verifying the effectiveness of display methods on AR goggles. From performing this experiment by many tasks in the future, it is important to classify tasks according to effective display method when an effective display method differs depending on tasks. Based on the results, it is considered that by examining the characteristics of the tasks, effective display methods can be predicted for tasks that have not yet been verified. In this study, we conducted experiments on cookwares. However, we would like to investigate other tasks in the future. Participants were supposed to live by themselves and assumed experiments with participants aged 18 to 24, assuming university students to start cooking. Further, experiments involving homemakers who are more likely to cook can be considered in the future.

6   Conclusion

From the following two points, we considered that it would be better to use 3D Animation because:

- Task completion time of can opener with the 3D animation was significantly shorter than with the video.
- In the display by images with text, a participant could not proceed because information regarding the move and direction are not conveyed.

Although no significant difference was observed from the qualitative questionnaire, many positive opinions were obtained on using the AR goggles for cooking from the participant's description. Therefore, we considered using AR goggles for cooking to be sufficiently useful. However, we discovered that the current device presented problems from the aspects of weight, fitting feeling, viewing angle, and operability. Freshness and device problems for AR goggles may be worth investigating to study how they change over time as the user's experience with this technology accumulates. We believe that our research contributes to the field of future AR instructions.

References

1. Blattgerste, J., Strenge, B., Renner, P., Pfeiffer, T., Essig, K.: Comparing conventional and augmented reality instructions for manual assembly tasks. In: Proceedings of the 10th International Conference on PErvasive Technologies Related to Assistive Environments, PETRA 2017, pp. 75–82. ACM, New York (2017). https://doi.org/10.1145/3056540.3056547
2. Bonanni, L., Lee, C.H., Selker, T.: Attention-based design of augmented reality interfaces. In: CHI 2005 Extended Abstracts on Human Factors in Computing Systems, CHI EA 2005, pp. 1228–1231. ACM, New York (2005). https://doi.org/10.1145/1056808.1056883
3. Boud, A.C., Haniff, D.J., Baber, C., Steiner, S.: Virtual reality and augmented reality as a training tool for assembly tasks. In: IV, p. 32. IEEE (1999)
4. Caudell, T.P., Mizell, D.W.: Augmented reality: an application of heads-up display technology to manual manufacturing processes. In: Proceedings of the Twenty-Fifth Hawaii International Conference on System Sciences, vol. 2, pp. 659–669. IEEE (1992)
5. Hamada, R., Okabe, J., Ide, I., Satoh, S., Sakai, S., Tanaka, H.: Cooking Navi: assistant for daily cooking in kitchen. In: Proceedings of the 13th Annual ACM International Conference on Multimedia, MULTIMEDIA 2005, pp. 371–374. ACM, New York (2005). https://doi.org/10.1145/1101149.1101228
6. Ju, W., Hurwitz, R., Judd, T., Lee, B.: Counteractive: an interactive cookbook for the kitchen counter. In: CHI 2001 Extended Abstracts on Human Factors in Computing Systems, CHI EA 2001, pp. 269–270. ACM, New York (2001). https://doi.org/10.1145/634067.634227
7. Lee, C.H.J., Bonanni, L., Espinosa, J.H., Lieberman, H., Selker, T.: Augmenting kitchen appliances with a shared context using knowledge about daily events. In: Proceedings of the 11th International Conference on Intelligent User Interfaces, IUI 2006, pp. 348–350. ACM, New York (2006). https://doi.org/10.1145/1111449.1111533
8. Nilsson, S., Johansson, B.: Acceptance of augmented reality instructions in a real work setting. In: CHI 2008 Extended Abstracts on Human Factors in Computing Systems, CHI EA 2008, pp. 2025–2032. ACM, New York (2008). https://doi.org/10.1145/1358628.1358633
9. Sato, A., Watanabe, K., Rekimoto, J.: Shadow cooking: situated guidance for a fluid cooking experience. In: Stephanidis, C., Antona, M. (eds.) UAHCI 2014. LNCS, vol. 8515, pp. 558–566. Springer, Cham (2014). https://doi.org/10.1007/978-3-319-07446-7_54
10. Scheible, J., et al.: SMARTKITCHEN media enhanced cooking environment. In: Proceedings of the 6th International Conference on the Internet of Things, IoT 2016, pp. 169–170. ACM, New York (2016). https://doi.org/10.1145/2991561.2998471
11. Schwald, B., De Laval, B., Optronique Sa, T., Guynemer, R.: An augmented reality system for training and assistance to maintenance in the industrial context. J. WSCG **11** (2003)
12. Suzuki, Y., Morioka, S., Ueda, H.: Cooking support with information projection onto ingredient. In: Proceedings of the 10th Asia Pacific Conference on Computer Human Interaction, APCHI 2012, pp. 193–198. ACM, New York (2012). https://doi.org/10.1145/2350046.2350084

13. Tang, A., Owen, C., Biocca, F., Mou, W.: Comparative effectiveness of augmented reality in object assembly. In: Proceedings of the SIGCHI Conference on Human Factors in Computing Systems, CHI 2003, pp. 73–80. ACM, New York (2003). https://doi.org/10.1145/642611.642626
14. Vildjiounaite, E., et al.: Designing socially acceptable multimodal interaction in cooking assistants. In: Proceedings of the 16th International Conference on Intelligent User Interfaces, IUI 2011, pp. 415–418. ACM, New York (2011). https://doi.org/10.1145/1943403.1943479
15. Webel, S., Bockholt, U., Engelke, T., Gavish, N., Olbrich, M., Preusche, C.: An augmented reality training platform for assembly and maintenance skills. Rob. Auton. Syst. **61**(4), 398–403 (2013)

Development of a System for Analyzing Hand-Raising Communication by Using a VR Headset to Synthesize Human-CG Character Interaction

Hayato Hirose[1]([✉]), Ken Minamide[1], Satoshi Fukumori[2],
Saizo Aoyagi[3], and Michiya Yamamoto[2]

[1] Graduate School of Science and Technology,
Kwansei Gakuin University, Sanda, Hyogo, Japan
H.H@kwansei.ac.jp
[2] School of Science and Technology,
Kwansei Gakuin University, Sanda, Hyogo, Japan
michiya.yamamoto@kwansei.ac.jp
[3] Faculty of Information Networking for Innovation and Design,
Toyo University, Kita-ku, Tokyo, Japan

Abstract. Embodied Body motions and actions play an important role in human communication. Hand raising is one of the typical body motions that people have been encouraged to performed since their childhoods, but almost no studies address it from the viewpoint of human–computer interaction. By focusing on its importance, the authors have been developed hand-raising robots and Computer Graphics characters to analyze the communication effect. In this study, we developed an analyzing system using a Virtual Reality (VR) headset that can enable users to immerse themselves into CG. We performed an evaluation experiment to analyze the effects of the number of CG characters who raised their hands and the height of the hand raising. The scene in which all CG characters raised their hands to a low point and the scene in which one-third of the CG characters raised their hands to a high point were rated equally. This means that the effect of the number of CG characters in VR was larger than in front of a large screen. As a result, the participants' impression of hand-raising communication changed.

Keywords: Embodied interaction · Hand-raising communication · VR headset

1 Introduction

In communication, humans use body motions and actions, such as nodding, body and hands gestures as well as spoken language [1]. Such motions and actions are referred to as nonverbal communication. Body motions play various roles and are classified as Emblems, Regulators, Illustrators, Affect Displays, and Adaptors. Hand raising is a typical body motion and indicates one's intention—such as wanting to say something, calling people, and greeting people. Especially, hand raising is used as a communication

S. Yamamoto and H. Mori (Eds.): HCII 2019, LNCS 11570, pp. 141–150, 2019.
https://doi.org/10.1007/978-3-030-22649-7_12

channel between teachers and students in classrooms, and it reflects active participation [2]. To actively participate in class, students must raise their hands [3]. Similar situations are observed outside classrooms as well because settings with group communication— such as meetings, group work, etc.—have many opportunities for raising hands. However, Japanese people tend not to their raise hands, even when they want to say something, because they feel ashamed.

Analyzing hand-raising communication and interaction is not easy because they involve so many factors. Fujiu performed one of a few systematic studies on this topic [4]. He analyzed the behavior mechanism of hand raising and showed that self-efficiency, outcome expectancy, and outcome value are the predicting factors. Sawabe et al. extended the study of hand-raising to students' cognitive factors, which the surrounding environment influences [5]. These studies are based on case studies in real classrooms. On the other hand, few people outside our research conduct engineering research about how the surrounding environment, such as embodied interaction affects these factors in hand raising. The authors have used a constructive approach. Kawabe et al. measured various instances of hand raising and classified them by height, angle, and speed [3]. It became clear that people's confidence affected the movements of their hands raising. Aoyagi et al. introduced the classified hand-raising motions into a hand-raising robot and clarified hand raising's effectiveness in active participation in classrooms [6]. However, these studies focused on single-person interactions.

To analyze hand raising in groups, Aoyagi evaluated participants' impressions of hand-raising actions by generating a Computer Graphics (CG) classroom with multiple CG characters [7]. In that case, a participant formed impressions and did not raise his/her hand in front of a large screen. In this study, we developed a system for analyzing hand-raising communication and interaction by using Virtual Reality (VR) headsets to synthesize human-CG character interaction.

2 Related Studies

2.1 Constructive Studies on Group Communication and Interaction

Robots and CG characters have been used in studies with a constructive approach because they can physically or visually express human embodiment. For example, Watanabe developed a speech-driven group-entrainment system called SAKURA by using five CG characters and focusing on nodding and its effect on entrainment [8] (Fig. 1). Fukushima et al. developed robots as "Flatterers" laugh-enhancer systems [9].

Takahashi et al. developed-hand clapping machines to transmit clapping remotely from the audience to the performer.

Such an approach is effective for analyzing interactions between talkers and listeners in group communication and interaction. Ishii and Watanabe synthesized CG listeners around a talker's video image and clarified their effectiveness as listeners [10]. Fukuda et al. developed a virtual classroom with multiple CG characters who perform various daily actions in classroom for teacher training [11].

In this study, we used a VR headset, which can express CG realistically. VR headsets are already used as tools for analyzing group interactions. For example,

Fig. 1. CG and Robot versions of Group-entrainment system SAKURA [9].

Tanaka developed an immersive presentation-experience system in which audience characters nod in response to lecturers' utterances [12].

2.2   Previous Studies on Group Hand-Raising Interactions

In previous studies, Kawabe et al. measured hand-raising motions by using a motion-capture system and extracted five typical motions with a cluster analysis. They converted the motions into CG characters from motion-captured data, as shown in Fig. 2 [3]. Here, Motions A and B were fast and went to high points. Motion B went the highest and fastest. Motions D and E were slow and went to low points. Motion C was in the middle position. The sensory evaluation of these motions revealed that the impressions of hand raising changed based on the motions' height and speed, and Motion B, which went the highest and fastest, was most positively rated [6].

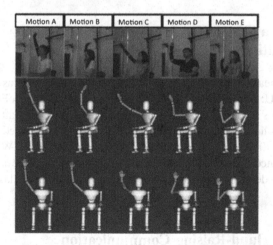

Fig. 2. Typical hand-raising motions of Japanese students [3].

Based on this, Aoyagi et al. developed a system for analyzing the impressions of group hand-raising. The CG classroom and characters that raised their hands are shown in Fig. 3. A projector projected this CG image on a large screen. Here, the authors introduced Motions B and E from Fig. 2 into the CG characters. All five CG characters raised their hands. The authors compared four scenes in to consider cases B or E and all five characters. The scene in which everyone raised their hands to a high point was rated as active and exciting, and the scene in which a small number raised their hands and only did so to a low point was given a low rating. By constructing interactions using CG, we could control the experimental conditions.

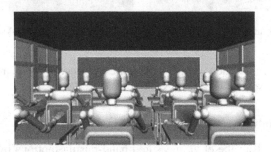

Fig. 3. Typical hand-raising motions of Japanese students.

However, this system could not subjectively evaluate the hand-raising communications that occurred in the same place. In this study, we developed a system that uses a VR headset that allows us to arrange the CG characters and users at the same place with the same group. By changing the behavior characteristics and the number of people that raise their hands, we analyzed the communication effect of hand-raising motions.

3   Developing a System for Analyzing Hand-Raising Communication

To develop a VR headset–based system, we configured the system as shown in Fig. 4. We used a PC (CPU: AMD, Ryzen 5 1600; video card: NVIDIA, GeForce GTX 1070), VR headset (Oculus VR, Oculus Rift), and two tracking sensors attached to the VR headset and controllers for both hands. For the analysis, we used a video camera (SONY, HDR-PJ790V) and a display (EIZO, FlexScan EV2450). While adapting the CGs to VR, we encountered some problems in terms of the size and reality of the objects, so we remodeled the virtual classroom to mimic the actual classroom's size and illumination.

4   Analysis of Hand-Raising Communication

4.1   Method

In the experiment, we showed the scene with a classroom and 20 CG characters in a VR headset. We explained to the participants that they were in a classroom with a

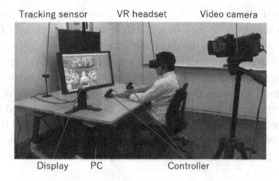

Fig. 4. System configuration.

presenter asking for opinions. We requested that they form impressions for each scene in five items described later. Four situations are constructed for evaluating the characteristics and the number of the hands raised and height of hand-raising as shown in Fig. 5: (a) a scene in which all CG characters raise their hands to a high point (high, all), (b) a scene in which all CG characters raise their hands to a low point (low, all), (c) a scene in which one-third of the CG characters raise their hands to a high point (high, one-third), and (d) a scene in which one-third of the CG characters raise their hands to a low point (low, one-third),

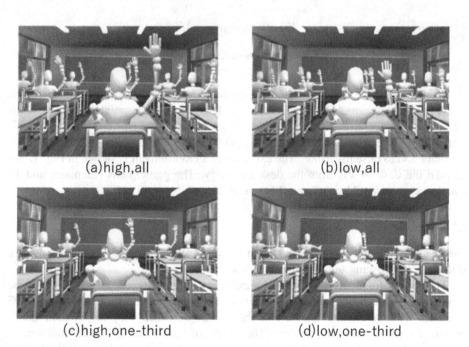

Fig. 5. Situations for evaluation of hand-raising motions in classroom situation.

In our previous studies in front of a screen, we randomly chose five CG characters, one-third of which would raise their hands. However, the number of CG characters in the VR field of view changed as the direction of user's face changed. To keep at least one-third of the CG characters in view at all times, we arranged the characters as shown in Fig. 6. Here, because the angle of the field of view was about 90°, the participant could see about nine CG characters at once. In the field of view, we divided the CG characters into a new group every 30° (Groups A to C), and raised the hand of one character in each group. To the sides of the field of view, we divided the CG characters into a new group every 45° (Groups D and E) and raised two characters' hands in each group. Seven CG characters raised their hands in total.

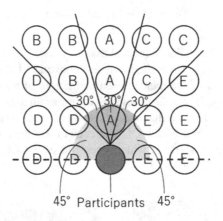

Fig. 6. Groups of CG characters

We instructed the participants to take the perspective of a member of the class and answer a questionnaire. They evaluated five items on a seven-point scale. The items were (1) "The scene gave me a positive impression", (2) "The classroom was animated", (3) "Everyone looked confident", (4) "Raising my hand felt easy", and (5) "I felt that I had to raise my hand". The experiment's environment is shown in Fig. 7. We adapted the desk in VR from the desk in reality. The participants (12 males and 12 females) comprised 24 people aged between 21 and 24 years old.

4.2   Results

The results of the questionnaire are shown in Fig. 8. We analyzed the results by using a Wilcoxon signed-rank test and Bonferroni's test.

The results for Items 1 and 2 had significant differences, except for those in the comparison between Situations B (low, all) and C (high, one-third). The number of CG character who raised their hands and the height to which they raised their hands affected the participants' impressions. The results of Item 3 had significant differences, except for those in the comparisons between Situations B (low, all) and C (high, one-third) and between Situations B (low, all) and D (low, one-third). In the scene in which many people raised their hands to a high point, everyone in the classroom looked

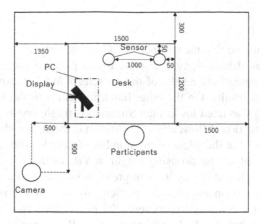

Fig. 7. Experimental environment.

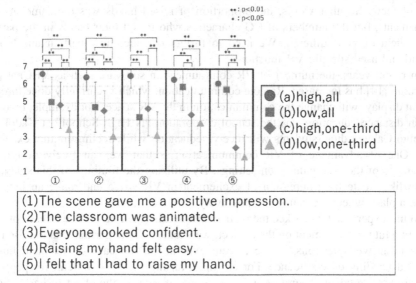

(1) The scene gave me a positive impression.
(2) The classroom was animated.
(3) Everyone looked confident.
(4) Raising my hand felt easy.
(5) I felt that I had to raise my hand.

Fig. 8. Results of Wilcoxon signed-rank test of impression evaluation of hand-raising motions.

confidence. The results of Items 4 and 5, which address the ease and necessity of raising one's hand, showed no significant differences in the comparison between the heights of the raised hands. However, the comparison between the numbers of CG characters who raised their hands showed significant differences. Only the number of CG characters who raised their hands affected the impressions regarding the ease and necessity of raising one's hand.

5   Discussion

This study clearly showed that the number of CG characters who raise their hands and the height of the raised hands gave the participants positive impressions in the VR space. When we compared the results of the on-screen and VR experiments, Items 1 and 2 had the similar results. On the other hand, in Item 3 in the screen experiment, Situation B (low, all) was rated lower than Situation C (high, one-third), and in Item 3 in the case of VR, Situation B (low, all) and Situation C (high, one-third) were rated the same. We determined that the effect of the number of people who raise their hands is larger than the effect of the hand-raising height in VR. In Items 4 and 5, Situation B (low, all) was rated higher than they were in previous studies. From this, we concluded that VR increases immersion and provides participants with an impression of the whole scene. In the case of the screen experiment, the participants saw five of the 15 CG characters who raised their hands. In this study with VR, the participants could see the same number of CG characters who raised their hands, regardless of which direction they turned. However, only three CG characters raised their hands in the participants' field of view. In other words, the proportion of raised hands was the same in both experiments, but the numbers of CG characters who raised their hands in the participants' field of view differed. We need to further consider how participants looked around and used specific VR functions.

In recent years, the number of VR communication software such as VRChat [13] and rumii [14] has increased. Remote communication, which is currently done through the flat display, will change the communication in the VR space. For example, by using VR in distance education—as the school corporation "N High School" at Kadokawa Dwango Gakuen did—students will receive education while feeling mutual existence [15]. One of advantage of VR communication is that we can freely design the appearance of the communication settings. By utilizing the findings of this study, we would like create the impression of excitement in VR space and make an index to create a place where we can speak positively.

In this experiment, we asked the participants to raise their hands to express opinions [16]. In a future experiment on the subject, we should ask the participants to raise their hands to answer questions. In the current experiment, the ease of the hand raising varied depending on confidence. For example, raising hands is difficult for people if they are not confident. Therefore, it is necessary to analyze the effect of hand-raising communication in various scenes to evaluate different levels of problems, change the situations, and conduct experiments that can change participants' motivations. In this study, one person evaluated the impressions of the classroom. By introducing communication functions and developing a system in which multiple people share the same VR space, we analyzed hand-raising communication among multiple people.

6   Summary

In this study, we developed a system for using a VR headset to analyze hand-raising communication. We developed a virtual classroom and CG characters who raised their hands, and made introducing the hand-raising motions measured in previous studies for a constructive analysis possible. Using our system, we performed an evaluation experiment with participants. The participants' impressions of the hand-raising communication changed as the heights of the raised hands and numbers of characters who raised their hands differed. In detail, the scene in which all CG characters raised their hands to a low point and the scene in which one-third of the CG characters raised their hands to a high point were rated equally. This means that the effect of the number of participants who raised their hands was larger in this study than it was when we projected CGs on a large screen. We think the reality of a VR headset caused this increase.

Acknowledgement. This research was partially supported by JSPS KAKENHI 16H03225, etc.

References

1. Richmond, V.P., McCroskey, J.C.: Nonverbal Behavior in Interpersonal Relations, 5th edn. Ally & Bacon, Boston (2003)
2. Fuse, M., Kodaira, H., Ando, F.: Positive class participation by elementary school pupils: motivation and differences in grade and gender. Jpn. J. Educ. Psychol. **54**(4), 534–545 (2006). (in Japanese)
3. Kawabe, R., Yamamoto, M., Aoyagi, S., Watanabe, T.: Measurement of hand raising actions to support students' active participation in class. In: Yamamoto, S. (ed.) HCI 2014. LNCS, vol. 8521, pp. 199–207. Springer, Cham (2014). https://doi.org/10.1007/978-3-319-07731-4_20
4. Fujiu, H.: A study on the relationships between kyosyu (hand raising), self-efficacy, outcome-expectancy and outcome value. Jpn. J. Educ. Psychol. **39**(1), 92–101 (1991). (in Japanese)
5. Sawabe, J., Okubo, T., Kishi, T., Nojima, E.: The influence of student's cognition of class on hand-raising behavior. Waseda J. Hum. Sci. **27**(2), 198–204 (2014) (in Japanese)
6. Aoyagi, S., Kawabe, R., Yamamoto, M., Watanabe, T.: Hand-raising robot for promoting active participation in classrooms. In: Yamamoto, S. (ed.) HCI 2015. LNCS, vol. 9173, pp. 275–284. Springer, Cham (2015). https://doi.org/10.1007/978-3-319-20618-9_27
7. Aoyagi, S., Yamamoto, M., Fukumori, S.: Analysis of hand raising actions for group interaction enhancement. In: Yamamoto, S. (ed.) HIMI 2016. LNCS, vol. 9734, pp. 321–328. Springer, Cham (2016). https://doi.org/10.1007/978-3-319-40349-6_30
8. Watanabe, T.: Entrainment and embodiment in embodied communication. Baby Sci. **2**, 11 p. (2002). Paper1. (in Japanese)
9. Fukushima, S., Hashimoto, Y., Nozawa, T., Kajimoto, H.: Laugh enhancer system: verification of laugh enhancement effect. Trans. Hum. Interface Soc. **12**(3), 199–207 (2010). (in Japanese)
10. Ishii, Y., Watanabe, T.: Evaluation of a video communication system with speech-driven embodied entrainment audience characters with partner's face. In: Proceeding of the Second International Conference on Human-Agent Interaction (HAI 2014), pp. 221–224 (2014)
11. Fukuda, M., Huang, H.H., Ohta, N., Kuwabara, K.: Proposal of a parameterized atmosphere generation model in a virtual classroom. In: Proceedings of the 5th International Conference on Human-Agent Interaction (HAI 2017), pp. 11–16 (2017)

12. Tanaka, K., Watanabe, T., Ishii, Y.: Development of immersive lecture experiencing system using voice driven type body attraction audience character. In: Human Interface 2018 DVD Proceedings, pp. 187–190 (2018). (in Japanese)
13. VRChat Inc. https://www.vrchat.net/. Accessed 22 Jan 2019
14. Doghead simulations. https://www.rumii.net/landing. Accessed 22 Jan 2019
15. School corporation Kadokawa Dwango Gakuen. https://nnn.ed.jp/. Accessed 22 Jan 2019
16. Hirose, H., Minamide, K., Aoyagi, S., Fukumori, S., Yamamoto, M.: A study on methods of system development for analyzing hand raising interaction by multiple persons. In: SICE SI, pp. 1254–1257 (2018). (in Japanese)

Immersive Virtual Reality Environment to Test Interface of Advanced Driver Assistance Systems for Elder Driver

Kenichiro Ito[1]([envelope])([ORCID]) and Michitaka Hirose[2]

[1] Institute of Gerontology, The University of Tokyo, 7-3-1 Hongo, Bunkyo-ku, Tokyo 113-8656, Japan
k.ito@iog.u-tokyo.ac.jp
[2] Graduate School of Information Science and Technology, The University of Tokyo, M7-3-1 Hongo, Bunkyo-ku, Tokyo 113-8656, Japan

Abstract. In Japan, the ratio and the number of elder driver have increased following with the number of traffic accidents which has become a social problem. The problem can easily be solved only if the elders does not need to drive by themselves, although, elders living in the country side or suburban areas still needs to drive for daily activities. Thus, supporting the mobility for the elders and preventing traffic accidents at the same time is very important. Self-driving cars are considered to become one of the solutions to solve this issue, though it is still one of the state-of-art technology still under challenging research. Therefore, this paper proposes a practical approach to test functions and interfaces of the self-driving car for elder drivers. In particular, this paper features use of an immersive virtual reality environment for a human-in-the-loop simulation test.

Keywords: Safety · Security and reliability · CAVE · Driving simulator · ADAS

1 Introduction

Self-driving cars is an emerging technology which is expected to give a huge impact in the transportation and mobility field. However, concerns regarding the various and complex riding situations require the self-driving technology to be highly accurate due to the serious consequences in case of any kind of errors. Hence, implementation of the state-of-art technology has started in a slow but a steady and reliable approach. Especially nowadays, assistive technologies are implemented to assist the driver in various ways which provide practical and convenient functions. On the other hand, technologies to provide autonomous functions are yet not practical enough, though some prototype tests or practical tests have recently started. These technologies are named as Advanced Driver Assistance Systems (ADAS) is under research and tests, although, on-road studies are highly limited to avoid serious accidents. Especially, tests to verify or

S. Yamamoto and H. Mori (Eds.): HCII 2019, LNCS 11570, pp. 151–163, 2019.
https://doi.org/10.1007/978-3-030-22649-7_13

validate under certain circumstances, such as testing with elder driver, needs to take care of extreme caution. Therefore, this paper proposes a practical approach to conduct safe and reliable tests for such circumstances. In particular, this paper proposes utilizing an affordable and highly customizable immersive virtual reality environment to conduct various human-in-the-loop simulation test.

2   Recent Approach for Advanced Driver Assistance System Tests

Recent developments ofnself-driving cars have reached to a level where an autonomous car can fairly drive through cities in normal traffic condition, though the system still needs special driver operations in case of difficult situations. In the field of self-driving cars, the action of moving the privilege from the driver to the system, or vise-versa, starts with an action named Take-Over-Request (TOR). While the design of TOR carefully respects the principle of Human-Machine Interface (HMI), it is normally done under simulated environment, typically using a driving simulator. Studies use reaction time [1] to measure the performance, though there are various studies using other indexes since there are various types of HMI display. Some studies of HMI display examples use visual display [2], auditory display [3], vibrotactical display [4] and the combination providing multimodal display [5,6]. It is also to be noted that the TOR occurs continuously while driving, depending on traffic situations or drivers will [7], and the performance of reaction to TOR may differs depending on various aspects like drowsiness [9], alcohol consumption [8] and distractions from non-driving related tasks [10] or related tasks [11]. Nonetheless, the driver's driving experience and habits are traditionally known to have meaningful relations with crash risks.

While the driver's characteristics and the crash risks tends to indicate some correlations [12], it typically is biased indicating other fundamental issues underlying [14]. For example, from the perspective of the aging society that Japan is facing, the increase of elder driver's crash risk is attributed to age-related and disease-related cognitive deficits rather than the term age itself. Therefore, the crash risk may be lowered if the driver focus on maintaining and strengthening situation awareness skills. Although one of the most effective act to strengthen the situation awareness skill is actual driving experience [15,16], driving on the road without having enough skill and experience is obviously dangerous. Hence, driving simulator is typically used for such kind of training which can expect certain amount of efficiency, even though there are limitations based on the configuration of the simulator [17].

Driving simulators can also be utilized as an environment to understand driving behaviour in general, critical use cases, or to test HMI prototypes. Due to various resource limitations, simulators typically have its resource weight to realize the main purpose of the simulator. Considering the fact that the actual proportion of how much visual information drivers rely to drive seems high as 80% or more [18], immersive virtual reality environments such as CAVE [19] are known to be effective in such simulators. Compared to Head-Mounted Display (HMD) environment, CAVE can easily integrate physical interfaces in the virtual reality environment where it can physically include a driving seat or a full-scale automobile. While CAVE has the ability to realize immersive virtual reality, the configuration scale becomes relatively large and complex which also has significant issues of the very high cost, whereas the original CAVE [20] and CAVE2 [21] are estimated to have cost $2,000,000 and $926,000 respectively. Therefore, the complexity and difficulty to control the simulation increases exponentially when making and deploying scenarios or actors within the driving simulator.

Recent research and commercial development has significantly reduced the cost to construct the CAVE, especially on the software. Low-cost CAVE has been introduced by using recent game technologies such as CryEngine [22] or Unity Engine [23,24]. There is also free low-level OpenGL library [25,26]. Low-level implementation has pros of capability with high customization and configuration, although, has cons of requirement of heavy programming when developing an application. Additionally, sensor integration for head tracking and bridging to the application uses many proprietary closed-source hardware and software which consumes high budget and human resource for configuration. Therefore, while trying to realize an immersive virtual reality environment, it is typical to configure the system for such main purpose. Also, it is not always easy to overcome the difficulties in financial and spatial resource to construct an immersive virtual reality environment. Therefore, the process of splitting the software development and usage of running the software within the virtual environment needs to be considered, composed by local software development and remote use.

Immersive virtual reality environment can be considered for use as a driving simulator with the aim to conduct safe and reliable tests of self-driving technology for elder drivers. Regarding that software development and running the application are not always capable in one physical location, systems engineering methods shall be adapted to keep the simulation entity and functions clear which is allocated to whichever software or hardware. Similar approach can be observed within the kinect-based KAVE [24]. However, this paper adopted a slightly different approach due to constraint of realizing a driving simulator application configured for elder driver. Considering the complexity of implementing ADAS functions, this paper utilized a proprietary physics-based simulation platform for driving simulator. In particular, we propose and demonstrate a practical method and approach to develop a CAVE driving simulator as an ADAS HMI test environment for elder driver.

3   Design of Human-in-the-Loop Simulation Using Immersive Virtual Reality Environmenmt

Human consideration in the process of engineering is important especially in human-centered domains [27]. It is commonly referred as human-in-the-loop simulation when a human can operate or interact within the simulation in real time.

The concept of using virtual reality environment for human-in-the-loop simulation can be observed in fields of system evaluation within the automobile field. For example, evaluation on steer-by-wire system [28], braking-based rollover prevention [29], and wheel loader [30]. The virtual reality environment can also act as an enabling system, in occasion when there is a different system of interest. This paper proposes the method to enable the virtual reality environment for both occasions with ease of switching in both directions to simulate within or without the system for testing.

3.1 Human-in-the-Loop Simulation for Advanced Driver Assistance System

In order to conduct practical simulation, it is important to understand the basic system architecture operated in the real world. Since this paper focuses on testing ADAS for elderly driver, therefore, understanding the system architecture of ADAS shall be the first step. Figure 1 illustrates the basic system structure of ADAS domain, based on HAVEit (Highly Automated Vehicle for Intelligent Transport) [31,32] perspectives. Described in a block definition diagram based on SysML (System Modeling Language) [33], the figure indicates that the domain of automobile ADAS is composed of ego vehicle driver, ego vehicle, ADAS, pedestrian, surround mobility, transport system, and physical environments. Since Fig. 1 only indicates the top level hierarchy, it is noted that some blocks shall be specified when necessary, for example, the *Surrounding Mobility* can be specified into *Rear Vehicle*, *Side Vehicle*, *Leading Vehicle*, and *Potential Vehicle*. Components such as roads and traffic signals, are also generalized as *Transport System*, and other objects are generalized as the *Physical Environment*.

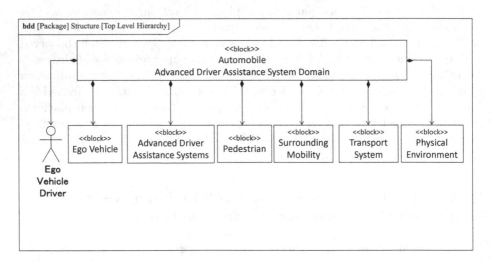

Fig. 1. Block definition diagram of automobile Advanced Driver Assistance System domain based on HAVEit.

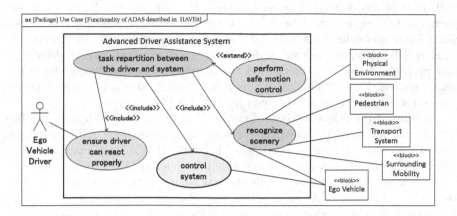

Fig. 2. Use case diagram of Advanced Driver Assistance System from HAVEit.

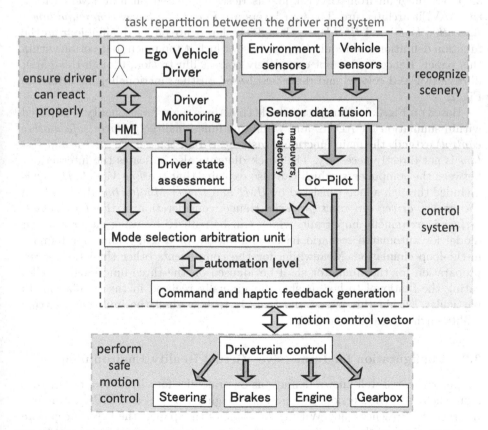

Fig. 3. Overall illustration with some basic physical components with indication what needs to be simulated to run a simulation.

Regarding the basic system architecture, HAVEit address 1 important key functional *task repartition between the driver and system*, which are described with 3 functional definitions included and 1 functional definition to extend. The 3 included functionals are *ensure driver can react properly*, *ensure driver can react properly*, *recognize scenery*, and the 1 extend functional as *perform safe motion control*. Figure 2 illustrates this functionality using a use case diagram, based on some early research analysis on HAVEit [34].

According to accident analysis done by HAVEit [32], it addresses the fact that 95% of all accidents are driver related and more than 22% are related especially to lack of driver's alertness. Therefore, HAVEit especially focus on including the driver as a key element when considering ADAS since there are occasions when ADAS cannot handle the situation and the driver needs to take over. Hence, following HAVEit's philosophy, the driver is considered included inside the system loop, which means the ADAS and the driver will both need to be included when performing research or development.

Overall, the approach of HAVEit can be illustrated as Fig. 3. Original overall block diagram from HAVEit [32] is described based on four layers within the HAVEit architecture. The four layers are *Perception layer*, *Command layer*, *Execution layer*, and *HMI layer*, though the layers are only explainable from the function definition and requirements phase, which it too much to describe within this paper. Hence, rather not completely correct illustration, though this paper illustrates Fig. 3 colored and described based on the functionality, described in Fig. 2.

Based on Fig. 3, it is understandable that three main functionality is required within simulation for ADAS, and while one functionality (*perform safe motion control*) extends the main functional *task repartition between the driver and system* is not directly necessary. The block diagram also indicates the interactions between the components, which can also explains that the *Ego Vehicle Driver* is included through a loop consisted by *HMI* and *Driver Monitoring*, derived from the *ensure driver can react properly*. Hence, consideration of the *Ego Vehicle Driver* is extremely important, which can be realized by using either a driver model for automated scenario based simulation, or a real human for human-in-the-loop simulation. Meanwhile, for the components other than the driver, preparation for the simulator shall be focused on the three functionality, allocating the funtional to how it shall be virtually realized in the simulation. In particular, within this paper, the issue is to how shall the immersive virtual reality environment can be utilized.

3.2 Configuration for Immersive Virtual Reality Environment

There are several well known definitions or principles for virtual reality environment such as I^3 (Immersion, Interaction, Imagination) [35] and AIP (Autonomy, Interaction, Presence) [36]. Within the topic of this paper, the key concept can be summarized as the following: iteraction in real-time, immersion in real-time, and environment in realistic 3D. Running the simulation based on human-in-the-loop simulation in real-time will basically provide the real-time-ness. Hence, the key aspects to consider for immersive virtual reality environment are on *interaction, immersion, realistic 3D environment*. In particular, an operative hardware or devices for *interaction*, big screens surrounding the driver's field of view for *immersion*, and a realistic vehicle model within a realistic simulation world for *realistic 3D environment*.

For *immersion*, if the costs are not a big issue, utilizing the CAVE [19] and enabling it as an immersive CAVE simulator shall be on technical approach to consider. This approach has been taken by previous research, for observation of drivers' behavior on narrow roads [37], and design of motorcycle head-up display [38]. Although both approach use real-time simulation and real driver realizing human-in-the-loop simulation, the loop does not consist ADAS.

For *interaction*, use of real controller or virtual (game-type) controller can be utilized within virtual reality environments. Although, when virtual reality environments are realized using a ead-mounted display, it normally uses dedicated controllers since the display is directly attached to the head, making the controllers physically non-visible. Therefore, again, CAVE type virtual reality environment has the advantage of capability of placing real or virtual controllers. Some CAVE type simulator, especially dedicated for driving simulator, have a full-scale real model of automobile or a driver seats are placed inside the screens. However, CAVE has many advantages as a virtual reality environment, it also has disadvantages of being a large system consuming both physical space and budget. Normally, trade-off decisions are made based on constraints and try to keep some minimum requirements based on the purpose of using the CAVE [24].

For *realistic 3D environment*, recent approach typically adapts use of game engines [22–24]. While building scenery of 3D environment can be relatively easy compared to making the full world from scratch, normally, the physical model of engine or calculation of the automobile is simplified [37]. In terms of realizing a *realistic 3D environment* for driving simulator, the precision of automobile model shall be virtually accurate as possible. Hence, this paper proposes to adopt a PLM software intended to test and design real automobiles. In particular, PreScan by Siemens which is a dedicated simulation software for ADAS and active safety was used to develop a realistic 3D environment [39]. PreScan uses Simulink, a well known component of Matlab to run the simulation model. Therefore, implementation of original software system and or hardware components are easily done through Simulink.

3.3   Considerations of Elder Drivers

There are many researches addressing the situations with elder drivers. Unless the individual lives in an urban city with sufficient public transportation, maintaining their mobility is important to support their quality of life [40]. However, it is clear that the spatial cognition ability declines with increase in age indicating that at some point the individual will become not capable to drive by themself. Furthermore, if there is no public transportation available, the loss of the ability to drive will also mean the connection loss of social activities, affecting the individuals' quality of life. To solve this issue, self-driving cars or automobiles with highly advanced ADAS are expected to contribute. Although, unless the self-driving car can drive on its own completely, issues regarding the Take-Over-Request (TOR) need to consider about the drivers' ability to drive upon the request. Therefore, understanding the characteristics with elder driver and their behaviours of interaction with the ADAS is important.

To understand the characteristics of elder driver, an approach of using a driving simulator is a typical approach since it is relatively safe. However, it is known that elders acceptance against the simulator is somewhat different with the young [41]. Early research about elder participation in virtual reality environments also argues with the decline of spatial cognition. Many clinical associated with clear evidence of decline in physical functions affecting negatively on general display recognition and 3D recognition [42–44]. It also has been reported with the sickness can occur even with simple driving simulators using only one CRT monitor [45, 46]. Although the are arguments that the driving performance can be unaffected [48], though some elderly feel extreme sickness which leads to dropout from the simulation [47]. Therefore, to minimize but ensuring the simulation environments, control of stereoscopic view and or fixing the head-tracking may be necessary in case of utilizing an immersive virtual environment.

4   Findings and Discussion

Based on the approach designed test ADAS interface for elder driver, the simulator to realize an immersive virtual reality environment was configured as follows. First, for designing the scenarios and use of simple virtual reality environment composed of three 65-inch LCD displays (Panasonic, TH-L65WT600), and a computer (Table 1). Using two GPU (Zotac, ZOTAC GAMING GeForce RTX 2080 Blower), the computer has full ability of rendering 60fps 4K for all three display using DisplayPort cables (DisplayPort 1.2a).

Table 1. Specification of the computer for simple virtual reality environment.

OS	Windows 10 Pro (64bit)
CPU	Intel Core i9–9820X CPU @ 3.3 GHz
RAM	32 GB (4 GB * 4)
GPU	Nvidia RTX 2080 * 2
GPU driver	418.81

Computer specification running the driving simulator software (Siemens, Prescan v8.5.0 and Mathworks, Matlab and Simulink R2017b).

While using a proprietary function within PreScan called *Remote Viewer plugin*, viewports can be easily placed within a vehicle's driver seat, or an actor sitting or standing in the virtual world (Fig. 4). While the GPU load relies heavily

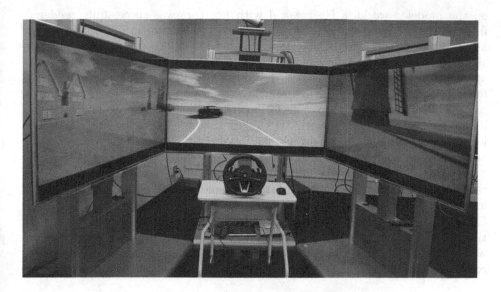

Fig. 4. Scenery of the virtual world built using PreScan.

Fig. 5. View from the top to see the whole virtual world built using PreScan.

on the modeled world, a basic world with few cars was successfully rendered in real-time. The top view of the modeled world is shown in Fig. 5, whereas it also indicates how easily the objects are realized including the lightings and the shadows. However, as observable in Fig. 4, the stereoscopic view has been disabled in this picture. Furthermore, in case of CAVE type display environment for immersive virtual reality environment, visual port can be placed on human models based near human eye-point for both left eye and right eye. Theoretically, if the display is compatible with 3D view, for example, side-by-side, rendering left eye and right eye on one display may realize a 3D view though it will need additional hardware or software configuration.

Head-tracking can also be integrated through Matlab and Simulink configuration, where it can directly specify the head movements within the simulation loop. While it can be implemented easily for head-mounted display, in case of CAVe type projection, it will need to consider and will need adjustment calculations. The calculation itself is nothing new considering it is already implemented with Uni-CAVE [23] and KAVE [24]. However, this implementation is theoretically possible, it has not yet been tested which shall be done as future work.

5   Conclusion

Regarding the background of the aging society and the upcoming technology of self-driving cars, this paper proposed the use and process of immersive virtual reality environment to test the Advanced Driver Assistance Systems (ADAS). Following the HAVEit system architecture, this paper proposes a simple driving simulator which can easily be adopted to CAVE type immersive virtual reality environment. Moreover, consideration of elderly was taken in within the configuration of the virtual reality environment. Controlling the immersiveness is difficult based on the elderly's acceptability against virtual reality environment, which will require an easy interface to activate and deactivate the stereoscopic view and head-tracking for comfort. Given the ease and the low requirement of setup for the simulation, extended use with CAVE type display environment, we expect that this paper address some solutions for approach in developing a safe and reliable ADAS system capable for elderly driver.

Acknowledgement. The research was partially supported from the Immediate, Ltd. Conflict of Interest: The authors confirm that there is no conflict of interest related to the content of this research.

References

1. Melcher, V., Rauh, S., Diederichs, F., Widlroither, H., Bauer, W.: Take-over requests for automated driving. In: 6th International Conference on Applied Human Factors and Ergonomics (AHFE 2015) and the Affiliated Conferences, Procedia Manufacturing, vol. 3, pp. 2867–2873 (2015)

2. You, F., Wang, Y., Wang, J., Zhu, X., Hansen, P.: Take-over requests analysis in conditional automated driving and driver visual research under encountering road hazard of highway. In: Nunes, I. (ed.) Advances in Human Factors and Systems Interaction. AHFE 2017, pp. 230–240. Springer, Cham (2017). https://doi.org/10. 1007/978-3-319-60366-7_22

3. Blattner, M.M., Sumikawa, D.A., Greenberg, R.M.: Earcons and icons: their structure and common design principles. Hum.-Comput. Interact. 4(1), 11–44 (1989)

4. Spence, C., Ho, C.: Tactile and multisensory spatial warning signals for drivers. IEEE Trans. Haptics 1(2), 121–129 (2008)

5. Lee, J.H., Spence, C.: Assessing the benefits of multimodal feedback on dual-task performance under demanding conditions. In: Proceedings of the 22nd British HCI Group Annual Conference on People and Computers: Culture, Creativity, Interaction, vol. 1, pp. 185–192. British Computer Society (2008)

6. Liu, Y.C.: Comparative study of the effects of auditory, visual and multimodality displays on drivers' performance in advanced traveller information systems. Ergonomics 44, 425–442 (2001)

7. Sebastiaan, P., Pavlo, B., Klaus, B., de Joost, W.: Take-over again: investigating multimodal and directional TORs to get the driver back into the loop. Appl. Ergon. 62, 204–215 (2017)

8. Katharina, W., Frederik, N., Johanna, W., Ramona, K.-M., Yvonne, K., Alexandra, N.: Effect of different alcohol levels on take-over performance in conditionally automated driving. Accid. Anal. Prev. 115, 89–97 (2018)

9. Frederik, N., Simon, H., Christian, P., Kathrin, Z.: From partial and high automation to manual driving: relationship between non-driving related tasks, drowsiness and take-over performance. Accid. Anal. Prev. 121, 28–42 (2018)

10. Klauer, S.G., Guo, F., Simons-Morton, B.G., Ouimet, M.C., Lee, S.E., Dingus, T.A.: Distracted driving and risk of road crashes among novice and experienced drivers. New Engl. J. Med. 370, 54–59 (2014)

11. Zeeb, K., Buchner, A., Schrauf, M.: Is take-over time all that matters? The impact of visual-cognitive load on driver take-over quality after conditionally automated driving. Accid. Anal. Prev. 92, 230–239 (2016)

12. Maltz, M., Shinar, D.: Eye movements of younger and older drivers. Hum. Factors 41(1), 15–25 (1999)

13. Mihal, W.L., Barrett, G.V.: Individual differences in perceptual information processing and their relation to automobile accident involvement. J. Appl. Psychol. 61, 229–233 (1976)

14. Scott-Parker, B., Regt, T.D., Jones, C., Caldwell, J.: The situation awareness of young drivers, middle-aged drivers, and older drivers: same but different?. Case Stud. Transp. Policy. https://doi.org/10.1016/j.cstp.2018.07.004

15. Crundall, D., Underwood, G., Chapman, P.: Driving experience and the functional field of view. Perception 28, 1075–1087 (1999)

16. Wu, J., Yan, X., Radwan, E.: Discrepancy analysis of driving performance of taxi drivers and non-professional drivers for red-light running violation and crash avoidance at intersection. Accid. Anal. Prev. 91, 1–9 (2016)

17. Upahita, D.P., Wong, Y.D., Lum, K.M.: Effect of driving inactivity on driver's lateral positioning control: a driving simulator study. Transp. Res. Part F Traffic Psychol. Behav. 58, 893–905 (2018)

18. Sivak, M.: The information that drivers use: is it indeed 90% visual? Perception 25, 1081–1089 (1996)

19. Cruz-Neira, C., Sandin, D.J., DeFanti, T.A., Kenyon, R.V., Hart, J.C.: The cave: audio visual experience automatic virtual environment. ACM Commun. **6**, 64–72 (1992)
20. Cruz-Neira, C., Sandin, D.J., DeFanti, T.A., Kenyon, R.V., Hart, J.C.: Surround-screen Projection-based virtual reality: the design and implementation of the CAVE. In: Proceedings of the 20th Annual Conference on Computer Graphics and Interactive Techniques, New York, pp. 135–142 (1993)
21. Febretti, A., et al.: CAVE2: a hybrid reality environment for immersive simulation and information analysis. In: The Engineering Reality of Virtual Reality 2013, Proceedings SPIE, vol. 8649, pp. 1–12 (2013)
22. Juarez, A., Schonenberg, W., Bartneck, C.: Implementing a low-cost CAVE system using the CryEngine2. Entertainment Comput. **1**, 157–164 (2010)
23. Tredinnick, R., Boettcher, B., Smith, S., Solovy, S., Ponto, K.: Uni-CAVE: a Unity3D plugin for non-head mounted VR display systems. In: 2017 IEEE Virtual Reality (VR), pp. 393–394 (2017)
24. Gonçalves, A., Bermúdez, S.: KAVE: building Kinect based CAVE automatic virtual environments, methods for surround-screen projection management, motion parallax and full-body interaction support. In: Proceedings of the ACM on Human-Computer Interaction, vol. 2, pp. 10:1–10:15 (2018)
25. Tateyama, Y., Oonuki, S., Sato, S., Ogi, T.: K-Cave demonstration: seismic information visualization system using the OpenCABIN library. In: 18th International Conference on Artificial Reality and Telexistence 2008, pp. 363–364 (2008)
26. Tateyama, Y., Ogi, T.: Development of applications for multi-node immersive display using opencabin library. In: ASIAGRAPH 2013 Forum in HAWAi'i, pp. 67–70 (2013)
27. Booher, R.H.: Handbook of Human Systems Integration. Wiley-Interscience, Hobken (2003)
28. Setlur, P., Wagner, J., Dawson, D., Powers, L.: A hardware-in-the-loop and virtual reality test environment for steer-by-wire system evaluations. In: Proceedings of the 2003 American Control Conference 2003, pp. 2584–2589 (2003)
29. Chen, B., Peng, H.: Differential-braking-based rollover prevention for sport utility vehicles with human-in-the-loop evaluations. Veh. Syst. Dyn. **4**, 359–389 (2001)
30. Fales, R., Spencer, E., Chipperfield, K., Wagner, F., Kelkar, A.: Modeling and control of a wheel loader with a human-in-the-loop assessment using virtual reality. J. Dyn. Syst. Measur. Control **3**, 415–423 (2005)
31. Hoeger, R., et al.: Highly automated vehicles for intelligent transport: HAVE-it approach. In: 15th World Congress on Intelligent Transport Systems and ITS America's 2008 Annual Meeting (2008)
32. HAVEit: The future of driving. Deliverable D61.1 Final Report, September 2011. http://www.haveit-eu.org/
33. Friedenthal, S., Moore, A., Steiner. R.: A Practical Guide to SYsML: The Systems Modeling Language, 3rd edn. Morgan Kaumann, imprint of Elsevier (2014)
34. Yun, S., Nishimura, H.: Automated driving system architecture to ensure safe delegation of driving authority. J. Phys. Conf. Ser. **744**, 012223 (2016)
35. Burdea, G.C., Coiffet, P.: Virtual Reality Technology. Wiley-Interscience, London (1994)
36. Zeltzer, D.: Autonomy, interaction, and presence. Presence Teleoperators Virtual Environ. **1**, 127–132 (1992)
37. Tateyama, Y., et al.: Observation of drivers' behavior at narrow roads using immersive car driving simulator. In: Proceedings of the 9th ACM SIGGRAPH Conference on Virtual-Reality Continuum and Its Applications in Industry, pp. 391–496 (2010)

38. Ito, K., Nishimura, H., Ogi, T.: Motorcycle HUD design of presenting information for navigation system. In: 2018 IEEE International Conference on Consumer Electronics (ICCE), pp. 67–70 (2013)
39. PreScan Homepage. https://tass.plm.automation.siemens.com/prescan/. Accessed 28 Feb 2019
40. Suen, S.L., Sen, L.: Mobility options for seniors. In: Transportation in an Aging Society: A Decade of Experience. Transportation Research Board, pp. 97–113 (2004)
41. McGee, J.S., et al.: Issues for the assessment of visuospatial skills in older adults using virtual environment technology. CyberPsychology Behav. 3, 469–482 (2000)
42. Kline, D.W.: Optimizing the visability of displays for older observers. Exp. Aging Res. 20, 11–23 (1994)
43. Cavanaugh, J.C.: Adult Development and Aging, 3rd edn. Brooks/Cole, Pacific Grove (1994)
44. Yetka, A.A., Pickwell, L.D., Jenkins, T.C.: Binocular vision: age and symptoms. Ophthalmic Physiol. Opt. 9, 115–120 (1998)
45. Lee, H.C.: The validity of driving simulator to measure on-road driving performance of older drivers. In: 24th Conference of Australian Institutes of Transport Research, pp. 1–14 (2002)
46. Mouloua, M., Rinalducci, E., Smither, J., Brill, J.C.: Effect of aging on driving performance. In: Proceedings of the Human Factors and Ergonomics Society 48th Annual Meeting, 48, pp. 253–257 (2004)
47. Park, G.D., Allen, R.W., Fiorentino, D., Rosenthal, T.J., Cook, M.L.: Simulator sickness scores according to symptom susceptibility, age, and gender for an older driver assessment study. In: Proceedings of the Human Factors and Ergonomics Society 50th Annual Meeting, vol. 50, pp. 2702–2706 (2006)
48. Allen, R.W., Park, G.D., Fiorentino, D., Rosenthal, T.J., Cook, L.M.: Analysis of simulator sickness as a function of age and gender. In: 9th Annual Driving Simulation Conference Europe (2006)

Performance Evaluation of Head Motion Input Used for AR-Based Communication Supporting System During Endoscopic Surgery

Takeru Kobayashi[1(✉)], Kentaro Kotani[1], Satoshi Suzuki[1],
Takafumi Asao[1], Kazutaka Obama[2], Atsuhiko Sumii[2],
and Tatsuto Nishigori[2]

[1] Department of Mechanical Engineering, Kansai University, Suita, Japan
{k749499,kotani,ssuzuki,asao}@kansai-u.ac.jp
[2] Department of Surgery, Kyoto University, Kyoto, Japan
{kobama,asmii,nsgr}@kuhp.kyoto-u.ac.jp

Abstract. During endoscopic surgery, communication between the operator and the assistant is an important problem to solve to prevent medical errors and to make the operation more efficient and precise. We have been developing an AR-based application for communication support in endoscopic surgery. This application has a function to enable line and shape drawings on the endoscopic images under the AR environment. The application enables the drawing of these images by head motions. To verify the effectiveness of this application, it was necessary to evaluate how much performance the drawing function by the head motion can provide the operator. In this paper, we investigated whether the drawing function by head motion offers effective performance for communication during endoscopic surgery by comparing the operation accuracy of the linear and circular drawings by direct hand motion and indirect mouse motion and modeled using the steering law. Results of the experiment demonstrated that the relationship between indices of difficulty and movement time was well modeled using steering law with more than 97% of coefficient of determination for all three input methods. In conclusion, the precision of drawing by head motion cannot exceed that of by hand and mouse when it is necessary to draw a circular object. It was suggested that the effectiveness of head motion drawing existed when the drawing lines were not precise, possibly for communication between typical practitioners and assistants, drawing straight lines or relatively rough shapes.

Keywords: Endoscopic surgery · Steering law · Usability

1 Introduction

Endoscopic surgery has been popular since the 1990s with number of successful cases and several researches have focused on its variety of cases and procedures [1]. Endoscopic surgery is performed using special forceps and endoscope inserting through small incisions to treat diseases. Owing to its low intrusiveness and dressing

© Springer Nature Switzerland AG 2019
S. Yamamoto and H. Mori (Eds.): HCII 2019, LNCS 11570, pp. 164–173, 2019.
https://doi.org/10.1007/978-3-030-22649-7_14

effect after the surgery compared with conventional open surgery, the demand of endoscopic surgery has significantly increased [2, 3].

The focus of the related research then shifted gradually to its safety and operability issues. According to Isaka [4], at a certain level of difficulty in the case of surgery, the intrusiveness for the endoscopic surgery exceeds that for open surgery. Difficult surgical procedures using endoscopy can be performed by a few skilled endoscopic surgeons and this problem related to technology transfer causes endoscopic surgery cases to be delayed to replace open surgery cases [4].

One of the causes for increasing the degree of difficulty in endoscopic surgery is that both hands of the operator and assistant have to be completely engaged in forceps throughout the operation because of security and maintenance of the surgical field once constructed. Consequently, when they communicate with each other discussing treatments such as which area of the body to resect, it is not possible to physically point at the image of the inside of the body projected on a monitor. Therefore, the operator and assistant have to share information associated with specific locations for treatment on endoscopic images projected on the monitor verbally. This problem means that accurate and effective communication is not fully achieved between the two, and, in the worst case, this may create the potential risk of a medical accident.

To avoid such miscommunication problems, we have developed an application for AR-based communication supporting system during endoscopic surgery. The application uses a see-through head mounted AR device, for visualization of graphical information superimposed with the monitor showing endoscopic images. The application allows the users to draw free lines and shapes on the projected endoscopic images using head motions additionally with the function of voice recognition. The drawn images are shared by both the operator and the assistant instantly; thus, the operator can provide instructions to the assistant on the surgical operation, such as the method of excising the affected area, without releasing his/her hand from the forceps.

When this system is practically employed in the surgical operation room environment, it is desirable to confirm an input accuracy that allows the lines and shapes to be drawn easily as intended by operators. In the field of HCI, quantitative evaluation for such input methods has been modeled using the steering law, a performance model for trajectory-based testing paradigms. Several studies have been conducted to compare existing input devices, such as mice and tablets, in the task of adjusting to activation using steering law, and it has been demonstrated that this law was useful as an indicator in comparing such performance [5]. As far as it is concerned, research regarding input device using head motions evaluated by steering law was, however, insufficient to apply the knowledge to our applications. Therefore, we conducted the experiment to compare and evaluate the input performance using the head motions with direct hand motions and indirect mouse input motions using steering law. The objective of this paper is to show the results of the experiment and discuss them, especially in terms of effectiveness of the communication supporting system during endoscopic surgery used for the operating room settings.

2   The Proposed System

We constructed the system using Microsoft HoloLens as a hardware platform for wearable AR and built a corresponding image drawing application, "Drawing" as well. As an application of Microsoft HoloLens in the medical field, position confirmation of blood vessels by superimposing and displaying a virtual model on a patient during operation [6], support of cancer removal surgery by near infrared light using AR technology [7], and practical training before surgery by holographicizing patient data and the surgical site in an operation room space [8].

Head motion and voice input were adopted as the operation methods of this application, thus the operators can perform hands-free communication with assistants, and they do not have to move their hands away from the surgical tool during communication. Using "Drawing", as shown in Fig. 1, it was possible to clearly convey the excision site from the in-vivo image on the monitor. In "Drawing", a line was drawn according to the motion of the cursor displayed on the object surface in a direction straight from the operator's head, and drawing was started and completed through speech input. In addition, the deletion of drawn lines, change of line thickness, and change of line color were also performed through voice input.

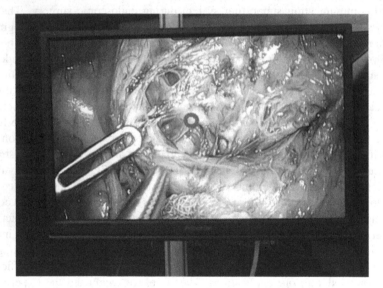

Fig. 1. The proposed system. Blue curved line at the center of the monitor was drawn by the operator for indicating to the assistant where and how to put a scalpel. The ring-shaped icon indicates where the operator is currently looking. (Color figure online)

3 Methods

3.1 Participants

Five male university students were recruited as participants for the experiment. Their ages ranged from 21 to 23 years. One of the participants had experience using head motion control devices.

3.2 Experimental Setup

The experimental setup and layout is as shown in Fig. 2. A test pattern for performing the steering task was projected on the screen. The distance from the participant to the screen was 1.5 [m], which was based on the distance from the operator to the monitor in the actual endoscopic surgery environment. The size of the projected image was 94.4 [cm] long and 53.2 [cm] wide. In the actual operating room environment, the operators perform surgery in a standing position, and they use not only head motions but also the whole body if they want to control cursors for drawing objects precisely on the screen. However, in the present experiment, we asked them to be seated to restrict them to only head motion so that we could compare the results with other types of motion such as hand and mouse motions.

Fig. 2. Experimental environment. Participant uses a laser pointer to move the light along with a test pattern. For head condition, the AR-head mounted device was equipped on the participant's head, instead.

In this experiment, we compared the quality of the drawing operation strategies under the three input conditions, i.e., direct head motion, direct hand motion, and indirect mouse motion. For the mouse condition, participants control the mouse by looking at an icon projected on the screen. For the hand condition, participants extended their arms, held the laser pointer, and operated the laser while looking at the projected screen (see Fig. 2). For the head condition, we used a head mounted device with a laser pointer attached as shown in Fig. 3. The switch of the laser pointer was maintained in the ON state, thus always emitting light. Wearing this device, the participant was able to operate the pointer according to the head motion. The cursor in this experiment was set to the same shape and size as the laser pointer.

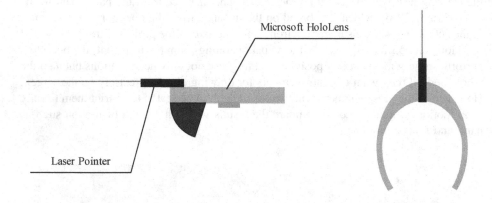

Fig. 3. Device used for the experiment

According to previous research [5, 9, 10], the steering task was performed using two types of objects, linear and circular as shown in Fig. 4. Indices of difficulty in the steering task with a linear object can be expressed by Eq. (1), and the Indices of difficulty in the steering task with a circular object can be expressed by Eq. (2).

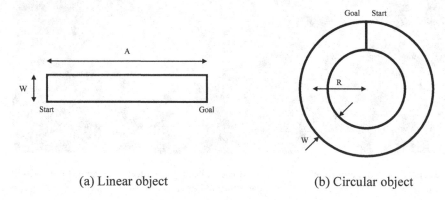

(a) Linear object   (b) Circular object

Fig. 4. Types of object for steering task

$$ID = \frac{A}{W} \tag{1}$$

$$ID = \frac{A}{W} = \frac{2\pi R}{W} \tag{2}$$

In these equations, A represents the length of the object, W represents the width of the object, and R represents the radius of the circular object. Table 1 summarizes the task conditions. Six levels of different IDs ranging from 5.7 to 26.7 were tested in this study.

Table 1. Test patterns with their features in the study.

Test pattern	Object	A [cm]	W [cm]	ID
1	Line	40	7	5.71
2	Line	40	5	8.00
3	Line	40	3	13.3
4	Line	80	7	11.4
5	Line	80	5	16.0
6	Line	80	3	26.7
7	Circle	40	7	5.71
8	Circle	40	5	8.00
9	Circle	40	3	13.3
10	Circle	80	7	11.4
11	Circle	80	5	16.0
12	Circle	80	3	26.7

3.3 Procedure

Participants were asked to be seated and were informed about the experiment before their informed consent was obtained. Subsequently, participants repeated the task patterns 6 and 12 ten times in a practice session to eliminate initial learning effect. This practice session was completed under each condition of mouse, hand, and head. After the practice session, the trial was started. The participant moved the pointer from the start position to the goal position as quickly and accurately as possible while preventing the trajectory from protruding to the test pattern projected on the screen. When the pointer reached the goal position, the next test pattern was displayed. When the test pattern was a line object, participants were asked to use a pointer to trace the object from left to right, and when the test pattern was a circular object, they were asked to trace it in a clockwise direction. In this manner, the participants repeated the trials until all test patterns were completed. If the pointer went out of the test pattern while the participant was in tracking operation, the trial was discarded and he had to try again from the starting position. The number of error trials was counted and error rates (i.e., number of error trials divided by total trials) were analyzed. Task patterns were displayed in a random order. The time elapsed as the pointer moved from the start position to the end position was recorded as *MT*. These series of operations were performed under the three conditions of mouse, finger, and head, for 144 trials of 12 trials (2 objects × 6 IDs), including each for four repetitions.

4   Results

Figures 5 and 6 show the relationship between *ID* and *MT* for linear and circular objects.

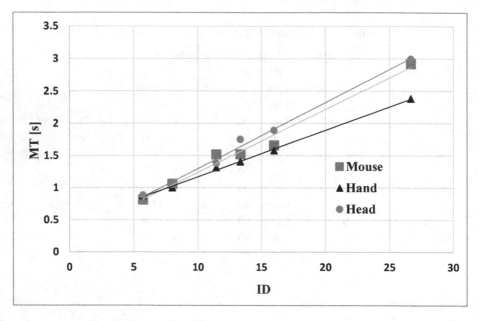

Fig. 5. The relationship between *ID* and *MT* for linear objects

Linear regression equations were obtained for each condition, and they are summarized in Table 2.

The coefficient of determination exceeded 0.97 even at the lowest task conditions, thus it was discovered that the task performances using the various input motions could be well described through the steering law. Table 3 shows *IPs* and error rates.

It was observed that the case of head condition demonstrated relatively lower performance than other cases according to the *IPs* and error rates.

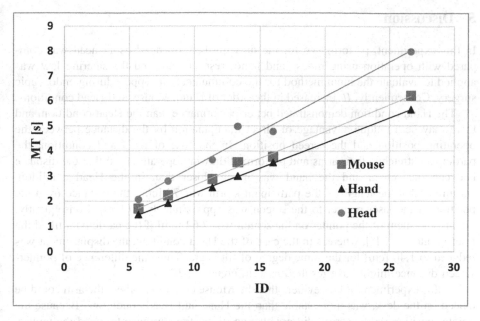

Fig. 6 The relationship between *ID* and *MT* for circular objects

Table 2. Linear regression equations and their coefficient of determination for each condition.

Motion condition	Object	Linear regression equations	Coefficient of determinations
Mouse	Line	$MT = 0.264 + 0.098 \times ID$	$R^2 = 0.980$
	Circle	$MT = 0.511 + 0.213 \times ID$	$R^2 = 0.995$
Hand	Line	$MT = 0.450 + 0.073 \times ID$	$R^2 = 0.998$
	Circle	$MT = 0.317 + 0.200 \times ID$	$R^2 = 0.999$
Head	Line	$MT = 0.276 + 0.102 \times ID$	$R^2 = 0.993$
	Circle	$MT = 0.602 + 0.279 \times ID$	$R^2 = 0.975$

Table 3. *IPs* and error rates for each condition.

Motion condition	Object	*IP* [s^{-1}]	Error rates [%]
Mouse	Line	10.20	0.833
	Circle	4.695	6.667
Hand	Line	13.69	3.333
	Circle	5.000	7.500
Head	Line	9.804	4.167
	Circle	3.584	19.17

5 Discussion

In this experiment, performance for the drawing task operated using head was compared with operation using mouse and hand, respectively, and the steering law was applied to evaluate the input method for the communication support during endoscopic surgery. Consequently, IP increased in the order of Hand, Mouse, and Head conditions.

The Hand condition demonstrated better performance than the Head condition, and there may be a unique advantage of direct manipulation by the distance between the operating position and the screen position. In the case of the Hand condition, the participant stretched their arms and performed drawing operations, so that the distance between the screen and the hand was much closer than in the Head condition. Assuming that the length of the participant's arm was 70 [cm], the distance from the position of the laser pointer to the screen was approximately 80 [cm]. Consequently, the displacement of the pointer on the screen was 2.62 [cm] if the participant tilted the laser pointer by 1 [°], whereas in the case of the Hand condition, the displacement was reduced to 1.40 [cm] for the same degree of tilt angle. Thus, the difference of pointer-screen distance might have resulted in a difference of IP.

In this experiment, it was evident that the Mouse condition, where the arm could be placed on the desk, was more stable than the Hand and Head conditions. Because the pointer position on the screen did not change unless the participant moved the mouse, the participant no longer needed to continuously control the position of the pointer. Because of the trade-off between speed and accuracy, a strategy that prioritizes speed under Hand conditions also appeared in the trend of error rates. It was inferred that the error rate at the Hand and Head conditions was higher than that at the mouse condition due to the difference in the operation strategy.

The error rate under the Mouse condition was 0.833% and 6.667% for a linear and circular object, respectively, whereas Accot and Zhai [5] reported that the error rate for Mouse condition was 9% and 14% for a linear and a circular object, respectively. The difference in error rate was unlikely to be owing to the difference in ID, because the range of IDs in this experiment was 5.7–26.7, which was fairly close to the range of IDs by Accot and Zhai [5], demonstrating 3.6–28.6. Therefore, although no distinct cause has been observed so far, it was speculated that differences in mouse precision may be affecting the difference in error rates.

The effectiveness of our application "Drawing" as an endoscopic surgery support system can be evaluated to a certain extent based on comments obtained from the endoscopic surgeons. According to them, it is desirable for the line to be drawn within ±1 [cm] of the assumed resection site projected on the screen. When this condition is applied to the steering task in this study, it corresponds to $W = 2$ [cm], for the steering task model. Under this condition, the ID is 10 when a quarter circle of 40 cm in circumference is drawn on the screen. From the regression line obtained in this experiment, it can be observed that there is a difference of approximately 1.5 [s] in movement time between head movement conditions and other conditions.

In this experiment, under the head condition, the operation control using the lower limb was not permitted. However, in practice, the operator is standing and predicts that the accuracy of the operation may be improved using additional control by lower limb motions. The disadvantage of the distance between the pointer and the screen at the time of the head condition also suggested that the operation at the head condition may not be as difficult as the difference in *IP* actually observed. Although stress may occur compared with the hand and mouse conditions, it is considered that this system has potential as an endoscopic surgery support system.

Acknowledgements. This research is partially supported by Strategic Core Technology Advancement Program (Supporting Industry Program), Ministry of Economy, Trade and Industry, JAPAN, 2019. The authors would like to thank Kazunori Okahisa for assistance with the initial stage of application development.

References

1. Yamakawa, T., Kimura, T., Matsuda, T., Konishi, F., Bandai, Y.: Endoscopic surgical skill qualification system (ESSQS) of the Japanese Society of endoscopic surgery. BH Surg. **3**, 6–8 (2013)
2. Kurita, Y., et al.: Force-based automatic identification and skill assessment of forceps manipulations. Trans. Jpn. Soc. Med. Biol. Eng. **50**(6), 581–590 (2012)
3. Tokushige, M., Suginami, H., Egawa, H.: Complications in laparoscopic surgery and its prevention. Jpn. J. Gynecol. Obstet. Endosc. **11**(1), 88–94 (1995)
4. Isaka, K.: Towards establishment of kinder and easier minimally invasive surgery. J. Tokyo Med. Univ. **75**(2), 177–186 (2017)
5. Accot, J., Zhai, S.: Performance evaluation of input devices in trajectory-based tasks: an application of the steering law. In: CHI 1999, pp. 15–20 (1999)
6. Katakura, A., Matsunaga, S., Sugahara, K., Odaka, D., Goto, T.: "Report by the jaw bone disease project" 3: new dental care with digital fabrication: FabLab TDC, bridge between basic research and the clinical field. J. Tokyo Dent. Coll. Soc. **118**(5), 369–376 (2018)
7. Cui, N., Kharel, P., Gruev, V.: Augmented reality with Microsoft HoloLens holograms for near infrared fluorescence based image guided surgery. In: SPIE, vol. 10049, pp. 1–6 (2017)
8. Microsoft Homepage. https://www.microsoft.com/ja-jp/business/hololens/showcase. Accessed 14 Mar 2019
9. Shimono, H., Yamanaka, S., Miyashita, H.: Evaluation of the user performance in steering tasks using tilt controlling. IPSJ SIG Tech. Rep. **172**(7), 1–6 (2017)
10. Naito, S., Kitamura, Y., Kishino, F.: A study on the steering law in a 2D spatially-coupled style. IEICE Trans. **87**(9), 1834–1841 (2004)

Demonstration Experiment of AR Exhibition System Inducing User Behavior with Visual Incompatibility

Isamu Ohashi[1]([✉]), Toshiyuki Numata[1], Hiroaki Yata[2], Shigeo Yoshida[3,4], Takuji Narumi[3,4], Tomohiro Tanikawa[3], and Michitaka Hirose[3]

[1] Graduate School of Interdisciplinary Information Studies, The University of Tokyo, 7-3-1 Hongo, Bunkyo-ku, Tokyo 113-8654, Japan
{isamu,numata}@cyber.t.u-tokyo.ac.jp

[2] Faculty of Engineering, The University of Tokyo, 7-3-1 Hongo, Bunkyo-ku, Tokyo 113-8654, Japan
yata@cyber.t.u-tokyo.ac.jp

[3] Graduate School of Information Technology and Science, The University of Tokyo, 7-3-1 Hongo, Bunkyo-ku, Tokyo 113-8654, Japan
{shigeodayo,narumi,tani,hirose}@cyber.t.u-tokyo.ac.jp

[4] JST PRESTO, The University of Tokyo, 7-3-1 Hongo, Bunkyo-ku, Tokyo 113-8654, Japan

Abstract. We propose an AR exhibition system inducing user behavior with visual incompatibility. The proposed method is to emphasize the edge of the image on the tablet screen and move its emphasized edge to a target direction. In addition, we implemented the AR exhibition system with the proposed induction method to validate the effectiveness of it, and conducted a demonstration experiment as an exhibition at a museum. Through our demonstration experiment, we confirmed that the proposed method induced participants to start looking around. The result of questionnaire suggested that our proposed method did not disturb audience's appreciation, and our proposed method would be applicable to the AR exhibition system. However, the method could not induce the participants to move to the target direction. In addition, the induction did not work while the participants were looking around.

Keywords: Digital museum · Behavior induction ·
Augmented reality · Edge emphasis

1 Introduction

Augmented reality (AR) has already become popular owning to the widespread of personal mobile devices with a camera. Museums have thus focused on the learning effectiveness of AR and have begun applying the technology to their exhibitions [1,2]. Through the use of AR, museums can show an audience not only an exhibition but also the relevant background information, such as the

S. Yamamoto and H. Mori (Eds.): HCII 2019, LNCS 11570, pp. 174–186, 2019.
https://doi.org/10.1007/978-3-030-22649-7_15

history of the exhibition. In addition, when audiences use an AR application, they often need to turn their body to find AR contents around them. This interaction fosters the audience's understanding of the background information of the exhibitions since they can learn spatial relationship between the real exhibition and AR contents [3]. Such interactive AR exhibitions are also applied outside of museums. "Crowd-Cloud Window to the past" is an example of an AR exhibition provided outside a museum [4]. This system is used for on-site AR exhibitions, and audiences can use an AR application along with their personal mobile device to view AR images of old photographs taken many decades ago. Audiences can understand the scenery better by comparing old scenery in AR contents to the present scenery. Meanwhile, spots where audiences can observe AR contents cover a widespread area, and it may be difficult for audiences to find other locations where they can observe another AR content in an efficient way after observing AR contents at a particular spot. In addition, the locations to experience AR almost always exist without explicit AR markers, and thus the audience needs to search for a location where the AR application can detect AR contents after reaching the AR spot. On the other hand, AR can also be used to induce an audience toward a certain behavior by showing explicit AR visual guidance such as arrow signs [5]. However, explicit AR instructions may disturb the audience's concentration toward the AR contents [6], thereby lowering the quality of audience experience. To solve this problem, AR induction should be implicit and intuitive. With such an AR induction, audiences can concentrate on the AR contents while observing them.

Therefore, in this study, we propose an implicit AR induction method without disturbing the audience's concentration while observing exhibitions, and validate the effectiveness of our proposed method through an experimental demonstration conducted in an actual museum exhibition.

2 Related Works

Many AR exhibition systems have been created for both inside and outside of museums. In addition, some AR exhibition systems include the induction of user behavior. Therefore, in this chapter, we first introduce AR exhibition systems without user behavior induction systems, and next introduce user behavior induction methods in AR exhibition systems.

2.1 AR Exhibition System Without User Behavior Induction

AR Exhibition Systems Inside Museum. Bimber et al. proposed a method for informing background information regarding paintings at museums [7]. In this system, using a projector, audiences can interact with a touch-panel in front of a painting, and can zoom in on it. As a result, the authors reported that using an AR application at a museum exhibition encourages the audience's understanding of a museum exhibition. AR exhibition systems have been applied to not only 2D exhibitions such as paintings but also to 3D exhibitions. Narumi et al. proposed

"Digital Diorama" to show how an exhibition was used in the past [3]. In this study, a display which an audience could view was set up in consideration of the position where a past image was taken, and the audience could view the past image overlapped with the current exhibition thorough the display. However, in these AR exhibition systems, projectors or displays were used and the physical constraints were strict.

AR Exhibition System Outside Museum. Personal mobile devices have become popular, and such portable devices have made it possible to create AR exhibition systems outside a museum. Some exhibitions have used a head mounted display (HMD) as a portable viewing device [1]. However, HMDs are not yet widespread, and audience are not used to their control, and their use in viewing exhibitions remains inappropriate. "Crowd-Cloud Window to the Past" by Osawa et al. [4] is an AR exhibition system applied outside a museums using mobile devices; in this system, audiences can also add the AR contents by themselves. Audiences can download this AR application onto their own mobile devices and visit a certain AR spot to observe the past scenery by superimposing an image over the present scenery. With this system, to show the past scenery, spherical images are used. With these spherical images, the audience members can interactively observe the past scenery depending on their position.

2.2 AR Exhibition System with User Behavior Induction

Guidance methods to guide users to pre-defined locations in the virtual and augmented environment have been proposed. One of these methods focused on steering users along a pre-defined path while at the same time allowing some extent of free exploring [8–10]. Another method uses an explicit arrow pointing at the target locations [11]. However, these methods are so intrusive that users cannot enjoy free exploration in the environment, and they hardly achieve a sense of accomplishment to find the target, which may decrease the quality of the experiment.

To inherently guide users to pre-defined locations in the virtual and augmented environment, while continuing to permit free explorations, Tanaka et al. proposed a method of inducing users to look at a pre-defined point in the spherical image by redirecting the virtual camera [12]. The users virtual camera direction is shifted to look at a point closer to a target point. Moreover, Tanaka et al. also proposed the guidance method "Guidance field" [13], which slightly alters users input for locomotion and rotation based on a potential field, which represents the drawing force to a target location. Iwasaki et al. also use this method to avoid showing low quality images in a virtual environment which is reconstructed with a lot of photographs and image-based rendering techniques [14]. They showed that these modifications successfully guided users to pre-defined locations and made users aware of the target objects in the virtual environment. However, this method did not extend the experience time of users. This result suggested that this method would enable us to draw users attention, but not enhance their interest to search virtual and augmented environments. In addition, the method have limitations when applied to augmented reality systems.

As an alternative approach, Narumi et al. focused on the shared attention, and developed a induction method which generated a joint attention by displaying the movement of the position and gaze direction of other concurrent/previous users in virtual and augmented environment [15]. This method also can work with the recorded others' activity in which other users experience the virtual and augmented reality contents. On the other hand, visualization of other user's action might disrupt user's attention to the exhibition.

As an AR exhibition system includes user behavior induction, Okada et al. proposed an audience gaze induction technique by changing the brightness of the area around the point of attention according to a specific pattern based on saliency-guided enhancement (SGE) [16,17]. However, this work focused on the induction of static actions such as audience gaze. Moreover, with the induction method used in this study, the brightness of the photographs was modified such that the scenery became different from its original state. Therefore, audiences may get the wrong impression of a scenery. Another AR exhibition system inducing dynamic actions was proposed by Arakawa et al. [18]. With this system, audiences can relive a video experience by imitating the rotational action of the videographer because an AR image showing a past photograph it is displayed depending on the direction the audience is facing, and the audience can observe the past scenery from eye of the videographer. However, this method is only available when the AR contents include a video exhibition. Therefore, in present study, we consider a user behavior induction method applicable to photographic contents.

3 Design of Proposed Exhibition System

3.1 Creation of AR Contents

Because interactive exhibitions enhance the audiences' understanding of the past situation, to create AR content we focused on panoramic photographs including wide-angle photographs and spherical photographs, which audience needs to look around for proper observation. In this paper, wide-angle photographs indicate traditional landscape-oriented photographs in which audience can only look right and left, whereas spherical photographs indicate 360-degree panoramic photographs in which audience can also look upward and downward. Because the exhibition through which we demonstrate our proposed AR exhibition system is set up inside, it is necessary to allow the audience to understand not only the past scenery but also the present scenery from panel exhibitions. In addition, because panel exhibitions need to be valuable on their own right as museum exhibitions, we used old photographs as the panel exhibitions, which are in black and white and were taken by a local photographer near the museum many decades earlier. Some old photographs were taken consecutively in terms of space and captured the landscape-oriented scenery; thus, we connected the spatially continuous photographs into a single wide-angle photograph. In addition, other old photographs captured consecutive events, e.g., an Olympic torch bearer running on the street, and thus we connected them into one wide-angle photograph, allowing audience to understand the temporal sequence. To compare the audience actions when observing panoramic photographs, wide-angle photographs or spherical photographs allowing them to look around fully, and normal photographs allowing them to observe all of the contents without looking around, were provided.

3.2   User Behavior Induction with Visual Incompatibility

In this section, we describes a user behavior induction method with visual incompatibility. According to previous related studies, many user behavior induction methods exist; however, some methods may disturb the audience's concentration on the exhibition, and others depend on the type of exhibition [16,18,19].

We focused on a projection technique used in "Deformation Lamps" [20]. In this study, a projection technique, adding luminance motion signals, was used to make static objects perceptually dynamic. However, such luminance motion signals are so related to the static target objects that generating luminance motion signals for all types of objects is difficult when there are many target objects present. Thus, with our proposal, we simplify the luminance motion signal, use the edge of the target object, and move the emphasized edge (Fig. 1).

Of course, adding an edge emphasizing filter to an entire image on a mobile device screen can be perceived as simply a visual incompatibility, and such incompatibility can lower the quality of the audiences appreciation. To solve this problem, we apply this method only to certain areas on the screen. More concretely, when the AR application is operating, the screen area of the mobile device is divided into two areas: an AR area and a raw area. The AR area indicates the area where the AR images appear, and the raw area is where the devices built-in camera image is rendered. In this case, the audience may not focus on the raw area when observing the AR exhibition. We then apply an edge emphasizing filter only to the raw area on the screen and move the emphasized edge slightly toward the direction we want the audience to rotate. This emphasizing edge is so slight that the audience concentrating on the AR area cannot perceive it consciously; however, as with the use of vection, we predict that their behavior would change unconsciously. Therefore, we added the edge emphasizing filter only to the raw area on the device screen.

Fig. 1. Comparison of images. Left: a normal image. Right: edge emphasized image.

4   Demonstration Experiments

In this section, we examine the effectiveness of user behavior induction based on visual incompatibility. Before that, however, we analyze the differences in user behavior among the contents through a demonstration experiment. In addition, we discuss a questionnaire regarding the demonstration experiment, which was shown when the participants pressed the finish button on the tablet used.

4.1   Overview of Exhibition

Our demonstration experiment was conducted in cooperation with the Museum of Contemporary Art Tokyo (MOT)[1], and we attended a 14-day exhibition called "MOT Satellite 2018 FALL - To Become a Narrative", which was held on Fridays, Saturdays, and Sundays between October 20 and November 18 of 2018. Regarding our exhibition area (Fig. 2), there were a total of 683 participating visitors. The number of participating visitors is calculated based on the collected log files from placed iPads. The number of log files is 1346, however some visitors might finish the system accidentally, thus we combined log files about same visitors. When the time lag between the start time of a certain log file and the end time of another log file is less than 10 s, we estimated that these log files were collected from the same visitor and combined them into one log file. In the exhibition, we placed six old photographs as panel exhibitions with their own value independent from our AR exhibition system. The six photographs selected were of locations that can currently be photographed (Fig. 3), and were taken by a local photographer many decades before. These exhibited photographs were used as AR markers allowing the audience to observe AR images by detecting these markers with an iPad placed near our exhibition area (Fig. 4).

We prepared three panoramic images and three non-panoramic images to make up the AR image. The panoramic images included two wide-angle images generated from old photographs (Fig. 5) and one spherical image, whereas the non-panoramic images included two normal images and one video image. In the video image, the viewpoint changes from a first-person viewpoint to a third-person viewpoint, allowing the participants to appreciate the location where the photographs were taken. Using Adobe Photoshop, we generated wide-angle images (Fig. 5) maintaining the spatial consistency. To validate the audience movement, we focused on the experience time and the angular distance, which we could obtain from the gyroscope sensor data of the iPad used by the participants. The experience time was measured as the AR marker was detected, and the angular distance was calculated as the sum of the absolute figure of angular variation per 0.5 s while the AR marker was detected.

Results. In Fig. 6 (left), the red bar shows the average experience time of the participants observing panoramic images and the blue bar shows the average experience time of the participants observing non-panoramic images. In Fig. 6

---

[1] http://www.mot-art-museum.jp/eng/.

(right), the red bar shows the average of their angular distance of the participants observing the panoramic images, and the blue bar shows the average of their angular distance of the participants observing the non-panoramic images. The error bars indicate the standard error. The audience viewed the panoramic images 615 times and the non-panoramic 600 times. The Mann-Whitney U test shows that there is significant difference in the experience time ($p = 2.74 \times 10^{-73}$). Additionally, the t-test also shows a significant difference in the angular distance ($p = 3.21 \times 10^{-124}$).

Fig. 2. Our exhibition area. Left: actual scenery of our exhibition area. Right: drawing of our exhibition area.

Fig. 3. Exhibited old photographs. Upper: photographs related to wide-angle or spherical AR images. Lower: photographs related to normal or video AR images.

Fig. 4. View from audiences using AR exhibition system.

Fig. 5. Panoramic images shown as AR images. Upper: the image capturing 270° scenery. Lower: the image capturing the temporal sequence of the Olympic torch bearer running on the street.

In terms of the average of experience time, audience observed panoramic images longer than non-panoramic images. Audience could observe whole part of non-panoramic images when they direct tablets toward panel exhibitions as AR markers, on the other hand, they needed to look around in order to observe whole part of panoramic images and looking around took more time. Regarding the average of angular distance, audience moved the tablet more when they observed panoramic images than when they observed non-panoramic images. They needed more time to move the tablet as they could observe whole part of panoramic images. Moreover, audience observing panoramic images moved more than 360°. Naturally the panoramic images cover less than 360° and we thought that audience observed same parts in panoramic images again, then audience could appreciate the exhibition by repeating observation. Therefore, we could conclude that using panoramic images fosters audience appreciation toward exhibitions as reported in previous related studies.

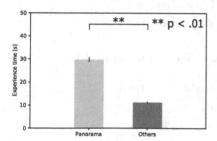
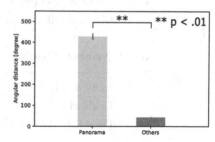

Fig. 6. Left: average of the experience time. Right: average of the angular distance. (Color figure online)

4.2 Results of Induction System

We assembled our proposed induction system into an AR exhibition, and then enabled the system for 9 days and disabled it for 5 days. The induction system was enabled only when the participants observed the upper wide-angle image shown in Fig. 5, and its emphasized edge moved toward the right inducing the participants to turn right.

Initial Motion. To evaluate the initial motion in the AR experience, we classified the participants based on the angle of their turning movement. The threshold between the moved and not moved was $\pm 31.5°$, because the horizontal angle of view of the camera on the tablet we used was $63°$. If an participant turned beyond this threshold, the participant was marked as having moved; otherwise, they were marked as not having moved (Table 1). A Chi-squared test showed that there was significant difference between the uses of the induction system ($DF = 1$, $\chi^2 = 6.75$, $p = 0.00935$). This result indicates that our proposed method increased the ratio of participants who had moved the tablet more than $63°$. It suggests that our proposed method provided some motivation for participants to start looking around.

Then we analyzed the direction of the participants who had moved over the threshold (Table 2). A Chi-squared test showed that there was no significant difference ($DF = 1$, $\chi^2 = 2.14$, $p = 0.143$). These results suggest that our proposed system could only allow participants to start moving, and it could not induct them to a certain direction. It seems that participants could perceive the moving emphasized edge, however they could not distinguish its direction. Then, after perceiving the moving edge, participants began to look around to find the reason of perception. Therefore, the number of participants who had moved and looked around increased with our proposed method, however the method could not control the direction which participants started to move to.

Table 1. Number of participants who moved or did not move the tablet

System	Moved	Not moved	Total
Enabled	239 (90.9%)	24 (9.13%)	263
Disabled	108 (81.2%)	25 (18.8%)	133

Table 2. Number of participants who moved to left or right

System	Left	Right	Total
Enabled	175 (73.2%)	64 (26.8%)	239
Disabled	70 (64.8%)	38 (35.2%)	108

Experience Time. We compared the experience time between the different uses of the induction system. Figure 7 shows the average length of the experience time per participant. The error bars indicate the standard error. The MannWhitney U test shows a tendency of significance ($p = 0.0596$). This result indicates that the experience time lengthened when the participants used our system. We think this is because the number of participants who never moved or looked around was decreased. Moreover, this supports the result of the evaluation of the initial motion.

Rotation Angle and Angular Velocity. To evaluate how the participants looked around, we measured the rotation angle and the angular velocity of the tablet during the viewing experience. Figure 8 shows the maximum rotation angle in the experience and the maximum angular velocity during the experience. The error bars indicates the standard deviation in Fig. 8. Regarding the maximum rotation angle, the t-test shows that there is no significant difference ($p = 0.4314$). About the maximum angular velocity, the t-test shows that there is no significant difference ($p = 0.7473$).

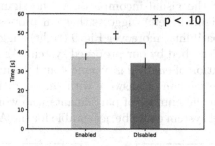

Fig. 7. Experience time

This result indicates that our system did not affect the participants while they were looking around. We thought the participants would be sensitive and be able to perceive the emphasized edge when they started to observe the AR images, and that they would tend to rotate the tablet while trying to find the reason of the emphasized edge. However, once they began to observe the AR contents, they focused on the AR area on the screen, and the participant's attention toward the raw area where the emphasized edge was moving was decreased. Therefore, our proposed system could not affect on the rotation angle and the angular velocity and participants paid attention only to the AR area after starting to observe the AR images.

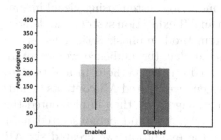 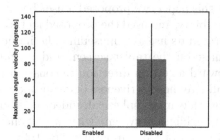

Fig. 8. Left: the maximum rotation during the experience. Right: the maximum angular velocity during the experience.

Questionnaire. The questionnaire regarding the demonstration experiment was shown when participants pushed finish button on the tablet. The questionnaire was evaluated on a 7-point Likert scale. It included the topic about visual compatibility, however answering the questionnaire was non-compulsory and only 20 participants did so. There were 15 answers when our induction system was enabled, there were 5 answers when our induction system was disabled. Then we analyzed answers with the MannWhitney U test. According to the question regarding an awakening of visual incompatibility, no significant difference was shown ($p = 0.3113$). In addition, for the question regarding the disturbance of the visual incompatibility, no significant difference was shown ($p = 0.4816$). Figure 9 (left) suggests that our proposed system might not give particular incompatibility, moreover Fig. 9 (right) suggests that the participants might not feel disturbed by our proposed system. As the upper quartile of answers with the condition of enabled is around 4 and the median of answers was 2, we thought that the median of answers with the condition of enabled would be at best 4 even when the number of participants who would answer increases. Therefore our proposed system could be acceptable for the AR exhibition system.

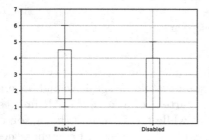 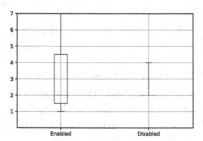

Fig. 9. The results of the questionnaire. Left: the awakening of visual incompatibility. Right: The disturbance of the visual incompatibility.

5   Conclusion

In this paper, we proposed a user behavior induction system using visual incompatibility, and used the proposed method in an AR exhibition system and demonstrated its use at a museum. The induction method emphasizes the edge of the image on the tablet screen, and we predicted that the audience would rotate toward a certain direction unconsciously based on the method. In addition, to validate the effectiveness of our proposed system, we created AR contents including wide-angle, spherical, video, and normal images. We then implemented the AR exhibition system with user behavior induction, and demonstrated it at Museum of Contemporary Art Tokyo. For the exhibition, we created six AR contents, namely, two wide-angle images, one spherical image, one video image, and two normal images, from old photographs taken by a local photographer. From the old photographs capturing a spatial or temporal sequence, we generated wide-angle images. Then, we applied the induction method to the AR exhibition system, we aimed that audience move to right by the induction, while audience viewed the wide-angle image showing also induction.

Through our demonstration experiment at the museum, we confirmed the effectiveness of wide-angle and spherical images in contrast to video or normal images, as related studies have reported. The experience time was longer, and the angular distance was greater, when using wide-angle or spherical images. Regarding the induction system, the initial movement of the audience was activated, however the system could not induce audience to the target direction. In addition, there were no significant difference about the rotation angle and the angular velocity. This demonstrates that the induction can attract an audience that is not apt to look around to start doing so; however, the induction did not work when the audience was looking around. The result of answers to the questionnaire suggests that our proposed induction system could be acceptable for AR exhibition.

Acknowledgement. The authors would like to thank T. Moriyama for advising us on the exhibit contents, and thank Y. Suzuki for offering old photographs as the exhibit contents. We also thank Museum of Contemporary Art Tokyo for giving us the chance of demonstration experiment. This work is partially supported by Dai Nippon Printing Co., Ltd. and Grant-in-Aid for Scientific Research (A) (16H01762).

References

1. Nakasugi, H., Yamauchi, Y.: Past viewer: development of wearable learning system for history education. In: Proceedings of the International Conference on Computers in Education, pp. 1311–1312. IEEE (2002)
2. Narumi, T., Kasai, T., Honda, T., Aoki, K., Tanikawa, T., Hirose, M.: Digital railway museum: an approach to introduction of digital exhibition systems at the railway museum. In: Yamamoto, S. (ed.) HIMI 2013. LNCS, vol. 8018, pp. 238–247. Springer, Heidelberg (2013). https://doi.org/10.1007/978-3-642-39226-9_27
3. Narumi, T., Hayashi, O., Kasada, K., Yamazaki, M., Tanikawa, T., Hirose, M.: Digital diorama: AR exhibition system to convey background information for museums. In: Shumaker, R. (ed.) VMR 2011. LNCS, vol. 6773, pp. 76–86. Springer, Heidelberg (2011). https://doi.org/10.1007/978-3-642-22021-0_10
4. Osawa, S., Tanaka, R., Narumi, T., Tanikawa, T., Hirose, M.: Crowd-cloud window to the past: constructing a photo database for on-site AR exhibitions by crowdsourcing. In: Yamamoto, S. (ed.) HIMI 2016. LNCS, vol. 9735, pp. 313–324. Springer, Cham (2016). https://doi.org/10.1007/978-3-319-40397-7_30
5. Suomela, R., Lehikoinen, J.: Context compass. In: The Fourth International Symposium on Wearable Computers, pp. 147–154. IEEE (2000)
6. McLean, K. M.: Planning for people in museum exhibitions (1993)
7. Bimber, O., Coriand, F., Kleppe, A., Bruns, E., Zollmann, S., Langlotz, T.: Superimposing pictorial artwork with projected imagery. In: ACM SIGGRAPH 2006 Courses, p. 10. ACM (2006)
8. Galyean, T.A.: Guided navigation of virtual environments. In: Proceedings of the 1995 Symposium on Interactive 3D Graphics, I3D 1995, p. 103-ff. ACM, New York, NY (1995)

9. Ropinski, T., Steinicke, F., Hinrichs, K.: A constrained road-based VR navigation technique for travelling in 3D city models. In: Proceedings of the 2005 International Conference on Augmented Tele-existence, ICAT 2005, pp. 228–235. ACM, New York (2005)

10. Abásolo, M.J., Della, J.M.: Magallanes: 3D navigation for everybody. In: Proceedings of the 5th International Conference on Computer Graphics and Interactive Techniques in Australia and Southeast Asia, GRAPHITE 2007, pp. 135–142. ACM, New York (2007)

11. Chittaro, L., Burigat, S.: 3D location-pointing as a navigation aid in virtual environments. In: Proceedings of the Working Conference on Advanced Visual Interfaces, AVI 2004, pp. 267–274. ACM, New York (2004)

12. Tanaka, R., Narumi, T., Tanikawa, T., Hirose, M.: Attracting user's attention in spherical image by angular shift of virtual camera direction. In: Proceedings of the 3rd ACM Symposium on Spatial User Interaction, SUI 2015, pp. 61–64. ACM, New York (2015)

13. Tanaka, R., Narumi, T., Tanikawa, T., Hirose, M.: Guidance field: vector field for implicit guidance in virtual environments. In: ACM SIGGRAPH 2016 Emerging Technologies, SIGGRAPH 2016, pp. 9:1–9:2. ACM, New York (2016)

14. Iwasaki, S., Narumi, T., Tanikawa, T., Hirose, M.: Guidance method to allow a user free exploration with a photorealistic view in 3D reconstructed virtual environments. In: Streitz, N., Markopoulos, P. (eds.) DAPI 2017. LNCS, vol. 10291, pp. 347–357. Springer, Cham (2017). https://doi.org/10.1007/978-3-319-58697-7_25

15. Narumi, T., Sakakibara, Y., Tanikawa, T., Hirose, M.: Attention sharing in a virtual environment attracts others. In: Yamamoto, S. (ed.) HIMI 2017. LNCS, vol. 10274, pp. 154–165. Springer, Cham (2017). https://doi.org/10.1007/978-3-319-58524-6_14

16. Okada, N., Imura, J., Narumi, T., Tanikawa, T., Hirose, M.: Manseibashi reminiscent window: on-site AR exhibition system using mobile devices. In: Streitz, N., Markopoulos, P. (eds.) DAPI 2015. LNCS, vol. 9189, pp. 349–361. Springer, Cham (2015). https://doi.org/10.1007/978-3-319-20804-6_32

17. Kim, Y., Varshney, A.: Saliency-guided enhancement for volume visualization. IEEE Trans. Vis. Comput. Graph. 12(5), 925–932 (2006)

18. Arakawa, T., Kasada, K., Narumi, T., Tanikawa, T., Hirose, M.: Reliving video experiences with mobile devices. In: 2012 18th International Conference on Virtual Systems and Multimedia (VSMM), pp. 581–584. IEEE (2012)

19. Nakano, J., Narumi, T., Tanikawa, T., Hirose, M.: Implementation of on-site virtual time machine for mobile devices. In: 2015 IEEE Virtual Reality (VR), pp. 245–246. IEEE (2015)

20. Kawabe, T., Fukiage, T., Sawayama, M., Nishida, S.: Deformation lamps: a projection technique to make static objects perceptually dynamic. ACM Trans. Appl. Percept. (TAP) 13(2), 10 (2016)

Sharing Augmented Reality Experience
Between HMD and Non-HMD User

Shihui Xu[1(✉)], Bo Yang[1], Boyang Liu[1], Kelvin Cheng[2],
Soh Masuko[2], and Jiro Tanaka[1]

[1] Waseda University, Fukuoka, Japan
shxu@toki.waseda.jp, kuroiiimizu@akane.waseda.jp,
waseda-liuboyang@moegi.waseda.jp, jiro@aoni.waseda.jp
[2] Rakuten Institute of Technology, Rakuten, Inc., Tokyo, Japan
{kelvin.cheng, so.masuko}@rakuten.com

Abstract. See-through type augmented reality (AR) head mounted displays (HMDs) allow for a highly immersive experience and are currently becoming widely used in e-commerce domains. Current AR systems mainly focus on improving the experience for the user who is wearing the HMD (HMD user), resulting in the exclusion of bystander without HMD (non-HMD user) from AR experience. We propose sharing the AR experience between the HMD user and non-HMD user by visualizing and synchronizing the virtual objects to a smartphone, thereby enabling non-HMD user to see and interact with the virtual objects on their smartphones directly. We also proposed a pre-experience system which provides users with a mobile AR based virtual product experience for enhancing online shopping. We share the experience between HMD user and non-HMD user to illustrate the concept of our approach, where the HMD user can interact with a virtual product when shopping online to get a better sense of the real product, and where the non-HMD user can have a similar AR experience through smartphones.

Keywords: Augmented reality · Sharing · Head mounted display

1 Introduction

Recently, see-through type head mounted augmented reality (AR) devices are developing rapidly, allowing users to see virtual objects embedded in the physical environment [1]. In fact, it has already been used in e-commerce domain such as the AR try on system, product recommendation based on the environment information, providing an immersive and interactable experience to users for online shopping [2]. In such cases, for user with see-through type head mounted display (HMD user), augmented information can be seen through their wearable device and they can have an immersive experience in AR.

Despite the fact that see-through type HMD allows for a highly immersive experience, bystander without HMD (non-HMD user) is excluded from having the same experience [3]. Currently, most AR systems still mainly focus on enhancing the experience of the HMD user, while non-HMD user cannot enjoy the AR experience to

© Springer Nature Switzerland AG 2019
S. Yamamoto and H. Mori (Eds.): HCII 2019, LNCS 11570, pp. 187–202, 2019.
https://doi.org/10.1007/978-3-030-22649-7_16

the same extent as HMD user. However, excluding non-HMD user can further lead to a complete isolation of the HMD user and could potentially lead to lowering the social acceptance of the technology [4]. Therefore, sharing experience between HMD user and non-HMD user is essential for improving the experience for both side, especially for non-HMD user.

The current paper focuses on sharing AR experience between HMD user and non-HMD user, in which they can share the view of the same virtual object [5]. But as the limitation of device, those without HMD cannot experience the same immersive augmented information as the HMD user, so it becomes difficult for HMD user to share AR experience and communicate with non-HMD user [6]. Thus, an approach is needed to solve the problem of asymmetric information and experience between HMD user and non-HMD user. Therefore, the focus of our work is on eliminating the gap between HMD user and non-HMD user, and enabling non-HMD user to participate in the AR experience that the HMD user already enjoys.

2   Goal and Approach

The goal of our research is to enable HMD user to share augmented reality information with non-HMD user and enable non-HMD user to interact with the same virtual objects.

We propose a system that enables the sharing of augmented reality experience, allowing the non-HMD user to have the same AR experience as the HMD user (Fig. 1).

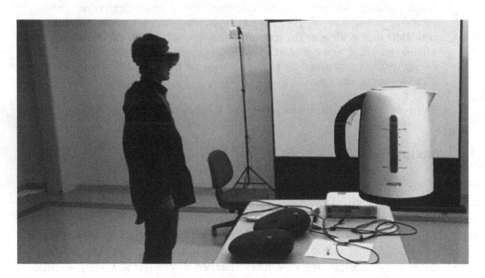

Fig. 1. Visualization for non-HMD user

We use smartphone to visualize the virtual objects for non-HMD user. By synchronizing HMD user's view to a smartphone, non-HMD user can experience holograms directly from their smartphones. In addition, non-HMD user can share AR experience to social media in the form of video rendered AR objects.

To increase the engagement and enjoyment of non-HMD user and the communications between HMD user and non-HMD user, we enable both of them to experience the same form of interaction with virtual objects in a co-located environment. Since users are not isolated from the real world, natural communication cues (e.g. speech, gestures and body position) can effectively be used during sharing activities between them [7]. Previous work showed that such kind of interaction - multiple users interacting with the same virtual elements embedded into the physical environment - has the potential to increase enjoyment and social behavior [8].

We also propose our Pre-experience system, which provides an AR experience of the product before purchasing online, to further explore the potential of our sharing system, showing the possibilities for shared AR shopping experience.

3 Sharing AR Information with Non-HMD User

3.1 General System Design

The main goal of this work was to investigate approaches for non-HMD user to have a similar augmented reality experience as the HMD user. In this design concept, there are two kinds of users: user who is using head mounted displays to view and interact with AR applications, and user, who does not have HMD. This is motivated by the fact that HMD is still quite expensive (for ones that have depth sensing), non-HMD user needs an alternate way to receive the same augmented information, and to communicate with HMD user and complete tasks together.

The augmented reality application will give HMD user appended information, and our research target is to also enable non-HMD user to get the augmented information with another device and receive the same information as that of the HMD user. Furthermore, we want to allow the non-HMD user to interact with the augmented reality objects in order to have a similar interactive experience. In this research, we focus on the communication between the HMD user and the non-HMD user using smartphones.

We designed two methods for sharing the augmented reality view, "view sharing" and "duplicate generation". View sharing means to share exactly the same view as the HMD user, while duplicate generation uses the smartphone to generate an interactive copy of the augmented reality object. The features of each methods are showed in the following Table 1.

Table 1. Features of view sharing and duplicate generation

Methods	View sharing	Duplicate generation
Interactivity	Non-interactive Viewing only	Interactive Each user can change the object by himself/herself
Object synchronization	Synchronous Share the same view and objects	Independent Each user has his/her own experience

3.2   View Sharing

In this method, we used the simple and efficient live streaming to achieve our goal. At first, the HMD user can see and interact with the augmented reality object. Meanwhile, the view of HMD user will be captured by the mixed reality capture function, render the situation to a live stream video, and share it with the smartphone through network. In this way, the non-HMD user can see exactly what is happening in the HMD user's view, so that they can receive the same augmented information and can communicate with each other.

One of the challenges of this method was to decide on the suitable size of view of HMD user for sharing. Fortunately, the field of view of HoloLens, the HMD we used, was relatively limited so that we can render the whole view of HMD user to the live stream video (Fig. 2).

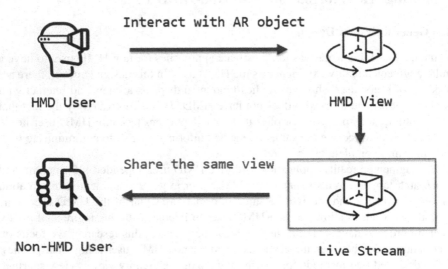

Fig. 2. Flowchart of view sharing

3.3   Duplicate Generation

In this second method, non-HMD user will receive a copy of the augmented reality objects which the HMD user is interacting with. Here, the smartphone acts as a window, that connect the non-HMD user to the augmented reality world. The non-HMD user can use their smartphone to initiate to receive a copy of the augmented world information from the HMD. This process need to be done in the same network environment. After that, the smartphone becomes an augmented reality device, and the target object would be generated independently in the smartphone's view. The duplicate of the object is independent to the one in HMD view.

The key point of this method is that non-HMD user can use the touch screen of smartphone to interact with the object using the click function. So that they can get the similar interaction experience with the HMD user. In order to enable the interaction on smartphone, we design the cursor function. The cursor of smartphone side is focused on the center of screen. With the help of the cursor, non-HMD user can click the object and get more information (Fig. 3).

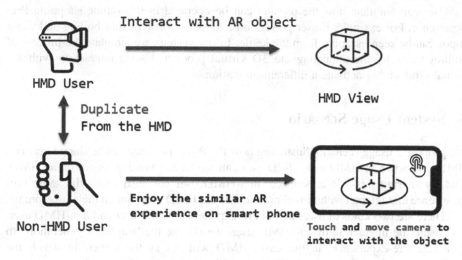

Fig. 3. Flowchart of duplicate generation

4   Pre-experience

Currently, e-commerce is developing rapidly. Consumers can easily browse the web-page full of merchandise and they can purchase merchandise without going to a physical shop. However, online shopping has the main drawback of users not knowing the actual physical experience of the merchandise. In contrast, when consumers go to a physical shop, samples of merchandise are available for consumers to know about the merchandise in details. Online consumers however, may risk purchasing items that are not ideal for them, due to the lack of physical samples, which may cause consumers disappointment and even lead to depression and complete withdrawal from e-commerce. To solve the problem that consumers cannot try out products when shopping online, we propose Pre-experience, which lets consumers get a sense of the real products before they make purchase when shopping online via Augmented Reality.

There are some previous work focusing on utilizing 3D models to represent the merchandises and let consumer have a broad understanding of real merchandise before purchase, such as *IKEA Place* [9] and *Houzz* [10]. But in these work, users can only place the 3D models or change the size of 3D models, which is not enough for users to know about merchandises when making purchases. That is because in most cases, consumer's consideration of the merchandise is more than just the appearance and size. There should be interactive behavior between consumers and virtual products, like interaction with products, seeing the operating status of electrical appliances, and others.

Pre-experience allows the HMD user to interact with the virtual 3D products, to get a sense of the real product before making purchases online. Pre-experience enables user to manipulate the virtual products similar to real world products and get the feedback from virtual products. We built a prototype of the Pre-experience on a see-through type AR HMD, since HMD can provide an immersive experience in AR so that users can have a relatively realistic feeling.

User can simulate how the product can be operated in this online shopping Pre-experience. For example, if user powers on a kettle, water will start boiling and water vapor can be seen escaping from the kettle. In our system, we simulate the process of boiling water by the animating the 3D virtual product. User's interaction with the virtual product can activate a different animation.

5   System Usage Scenario

We propose a usage scenario illustrating how the Pre-experience can be shared between HMD user and non-HMD user. HMD user can see an AR Pre-experience on an HMD. And by sharing this AR experience, non-HMD user can also enjoy the same Pre-experience and interact with virtual products as the HMD user, but on their smartphone.

There are two kinds of users in this Pre-experience: HMD user and non-HMD user. To ensure the interaction of non-HMD user, we choose the "duplicate generation" to share the Pre-experience. In our case, HMD will act as the server, in which the application is running on, so HMD user will get the augmented information independently, while non-HMD user need to get a duplicated augmented information from HMD user by connecting their smartphone to the HMD as a client.

5.1   Pre-experience of HMD Side

The Pre-experience of HMD side is an independent process, meaning that it can be accomplished without sharing to non-HMD user. The process of Pre-experience will be introduced in detail in the following sections.

Scanning Shopping Webpage with HMD. To start the Pre-experience, the HMD user needs to look at the shopping webpage with their HMD, as showed in Fig. 4. Since we use see-through type HMD in our system, HMD user can see AR information at the same time while shopping on a webpage through their HMD.

Recognizing Product Information. At the initial interface of our system, we added reminder texts to instruct user to start Pre-experience, as shown in Fig. 5. When HMD user is interested in a product and wants to click into the product's webpage to see the details of it, our system will recognize product's information by its photo. HMD user needs to make sure the camera of HMD is pointed to the photo of the product. The process of recognition may take a few seconds, after that, our system can then recognize which product the user is looking at, and make further response.

Getting 3D Virtual Products. After recognizing successfully, the reminder text will disappear. Then our system will scan around the environment to combine the virtual world coordinate with the real-world coordinate. At this stage, the surface of the physical environment will be recognized and visualized as white wireframes for later

Fig. 4. Scanning shopping webpage with HMD

Fig. 5. Initial interface in HMD

use. Then a 3D virtual product that correspond to the product on the webpage will then pop up in front of HMD user's view. The virtual product has the same appearance and size as the real physical product, as the Fig. 6 shows. The small white point in the center is the cursor of HMD.

Interacting with Virtual Products. We provide several ways of interaction when using the Pre-experience. As we have already built the connection between virtual world and real world, HMD user can place the virtual product on the real world's surface that we have detected in the previous stage. Besides, every time when making a placement of virtual products, our system will detect surface once again and update the virtual space, so that the placement of virtual product matches the environment of real world.

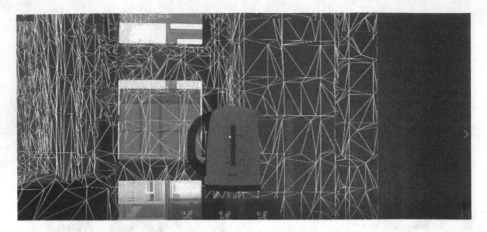

Fig. 6. 3D virtual product in HMD

User can simulate how product can be operated in this online shopping Pre-experience. Even without trying out the real physical product, user can understand how the product works (Fig. 7).

Fig. 7. Interaction with virtual product

5.2   Sharing Pre-experience to Non-HMD User

In conjunction with our sharing system, non-HMD user can also experience this Pre-experience on their smartphones.

Synchronizing HMD and Smartphone. The first step to sharing the Pre-experience is to synchronize HMD and smartphone. Below is the procedure of building synchronization between HMD and smartphone.

- Ensure that both HMD and smartphone are on the same network.
- Start the application on both HMD and smartphone. The process of starting the application on the smartphone should trigger the HMD camera to turn on and begin taking photos.
- As soon as the application starts smartphone, it will look for surfaces, such as floors or tables. When surfaces are found, a marker will be shown on the screen of smartphone. Non-HMD user will need to show this marker to the HMD user, and HMDwill establish connection with the smartphone according to this marker.
- Once established, the marker will disappear and both devices should be connected and spatially synchronized, which means that information of the AR Pre-experience, including the virtual products, location information of virtual products and status of virtual products, that runs on HMD should be synchronized to the smartphone (Fig. 8).

Fig. 8. Synchronized virtual object showed in smartphone (captured by HMD)

Pre-experience of Non-HMD user. After synchronizing with the HMD, as the HMD user has already received the 3D virtual products, non-HMD user do not need to scan shopping webpage anyone. Instead, non-HMD user can see the same 3D virtual product directly on their smartphone, and the position and status of the virtual product is the same as in the HMD. In addition, non-HMD user has the same authority as HMD user when interacting with virtual product and the interaction with virtual product is independent to HMD user's action. That is to say, non-HMD user's interaction with virtual product is not influenced by HMD user. Non-HMD user can interact with 3D virtual product by manipulatingsmartphone. With this kind of sharing system, non-HMD user can get the equivalent AR Pre-experience as HMD user.

Sharing Pre-experience to Social Media. We also provide a method for non-HMD user to share their Pre-experience to social media. Non-HMD user can record the interaction by recording the screen of smartphone and share the recording to social media.

6 Implementation

The implementation of our work consists of development environment, implementation of view sharing, implementation of duplicate generation and implementation of Pre-experience.

6.1 Development Environment

The hardware used for development of the sharing application include an HMD, a Computer with Unity, and a smartphone.

We choose Microsoft HoloLens as the see-through type Head Mounted Display for mixed reality experience. The HoloLens features an inertial measurement unit (IMU) (which includes an accelerometer, gyroscope, and a magnetometer) four "environment understanding" sensors, an energy-efficient depth camera with a 120° × 120° angle of view, a 2.4-megapixel photographic video camera, a four-microphone array, and an ambient light sensor [11]. The operating system of HoloLens is Windows 10, which can run the universal windows platform applications (Fig. 9).

Fig. 9. iPhone X and HoloLens

The smartphone we used in this work is iPhone X. The ARkit, provided by Apple, combines device motion tracking, camera scene capture, advanced scene processing, and display conveniences to simplify the task of building an AR experience [12].

We choose Unity 3D, a cross-platform game engine, as the development IDE of our project because it offers a method to solve the multi-platform network communication between HMD and smartphone. We use the ARkit tool SDK on Unity to support the development of AR application with iPhone X. We also referenced the mixed reality tool examples which is offered by Microsoft.

6.2 Implementation of View Sharing

In our system, we aim to extract the augmented information in the HMD view and send it to the smartphone in the form of a live streaming video. In order to get the view with augmented reality information, we need to record the angle of camera and render the view of virtual object with real-world video.

This time, we use the Microsoft mixed reality capture to capture the HMD view. Mixed reality capture (MRC) let's us capture the experience as either a photograph or a video. It in turns allows us to share the experience with others, by allowing others to see the same holograms of virtual information as seen by the HMD. These videos and photos are from a first-person point of view [13].

We chose the Mixed Remote View Compositor from the SDK for implementing the live streaming of HMD view. Mixed Remote View Compositor provides the ability for developers to incorporate near real-time viewing of HoloLens experiences from within a viewing application. This is achieved through low level Media Foundation components that use a lightweight network layer to transmit the data from the device to a remote viewing application [14].

6.3 Implementation of Duplicate Generation

In this method, the goal of our system is to generate the interactive virtual object for smartphone user. To achieve this, we need to acquire the location information of the object, by synchronizing the smartphone with HMD. We used Spectator View Preview, provided by Microsoft, to synchronize between HoloLens and smartphone [14].

We used Unity as the engine because Unity enable one application to run on different platforms. On the HoloLens side, we use Mixed Reality Toolkit to help us develop the contents. The Mixed Reality Toolkit is a collection of scripts and components intended to accelerate development of applications targeting Microsoft HoloLens and Windows Mixed Reality headsets.

On the smartphone side, we use Unity-ARKit-Plugin to provide the augmented reality experience. This is a native Unity plugin that exposes the functionality of Apple's ARKit SDK to our Unity projects for compatible iOS devices. Includes ARKit features such as world tracking, pass-through camera rendering, horizontal and vertical plane detection and update to Unity developers for their AR projects. The process of synchronization help us get the transform data of virtual object, which is used to locate the object in smartphone. As for interaction on the smartphone, a cursor is created at the center of the touch screen. Non-HMD user can move the smartphone to align the cursor onto the place they want to interact, and touch directly on the screen to activate the click function. As the objects are independent from the ones in HMD user's view, non-HMD user can operate them by himself or herself and have a similar experience as the HMD user has.

6.4 Implementation of Pre-experience

The application, Pre-experience, consists of the recognition of products' webpages and interaction with virtual products.

We use Vuforia Engine [15] for recognizing the product's information. Our goal is to recognize specific product by its image directly. Vuforia Engine brings an important capability to connect AR experiences to specific images and objects in the environment. We set the photo of the product as image target, which is used for target recognition and tracking in Vuforia. One photo correspond to one 3D virtual products. In this way, we can build the association between image of product and virtual product.

For interaction with virtual products, we need to combine the real world and virtual world together to make sense to the Pre-experience. We use Spatial Mapping, provided by Microsoft, enabling a detailed representation of real world surfaces in the environment around the HMD. By merging the real world with the virtual world, the virtual products can seem real so that user can make real-world behaviors and interactions [16]. We use gaze and gesture as the input methods for HMD user and touch as the input method of non-HMD user. To achieve the simulation of operating status of product, we use Animator Controller to control the transition of virtual product [17]. Animator Controller allows to arrange and maintain a set of animation clips and associated animation transitions for a character or object. The simulation of operating status of product has multiple animations and switches between these animations. By using Animator Controller, the transition of virtual product could be more fluent.

7   Related Works

Our work is strongly influenced by the fields of *Shared/Collaborative Augmented Reality* and *Sharing Virtual Experience Between Asymmetric Devices*.

7.1   Shared/Collaborative Augmented Reality

Shared AR was first defined by Rekimoto [5] in 1996 as an environment that allows several users to share the same view of virtual objects and any modifications of the objects, in which the virtual objects are embedded in the real physical world. He presented a shared AR system called TransVision which augments real table-top with the virtual objects. Multiple users hold a palmtop size see-through display and look at the same virtual and real world through it.

In 2002, Billinghurst and Kato [18] extended this concept by defining collaborative AR, which enables interaction and collaboration among several users. They presented a system that contains variety of interfaces blending reality and virtuality, allowing communication behaviors in a co-located environment.

These two terms are quite similar, while collaborative AR emphasize the asymmetric visualization and input capabilities of different users. In this paper, we use the latter term. Since we have HMD user and non-HMD user, whose input capabilities and visualization of virtual objects are different, caused by the differences of devices.

7.2 Sharing Virtual Experience Between Asymmetric Devices

ShareVR [3], proposed by Gugenheimer et al. follows an asymmetric interaction approach by offering individual interaction and visualization concepts for users without an HMD in a co-located collaboration. ShareVR uses floor projection and mobile displays in combination with positional tracking to visualize the virtual world for non-HMD user, enabling them to interact with HMD user and become part of the VR experience. In this work, non-HMD user cannot acquire the same information as the HMD user, and non-HMD user is at a less engagement level with AR experience than HMD user.

FaceDisplay [6] is a concept proposed by Gugenheimer et al. for a mobile VR HMD that is designed to have the HMD user within the environment with all other people. FaceDisplay consists of three displays arranged around the back side of the HMD to function as a visualization for the non-HMD user. They also attached a Leap Motion facing outwards to allow for gestural interaction. In this work, the devices used for enhancing the interaction of non-HMD user are all mounted on the HMD, which may be unhygienic to HMD user. In addition, non-HMD users need to touch the screen mounted on HMD user's face. However, gamedesigns including heavy movements can results in too strongly perceived touch impacts on the HMD User. Having an unpredictably moving user could also result in safety hazards for thenon-HMD user.

Stafford et al. [4] presented "god-like interactions", an approach to enable asymmetric interaction between a user with an AR HMD and a user with a tablet. "God-like interaction" is a metaphor for improved communication of situational and navigational information between AR HMD users equipped with mobile augmented reality systems, and non-HMD users equipped with tabletop projector display systems. Physical objects are captured by a series of cameras viewing a table surface, the data is sent over a wireless network, and is then reconstructed at a real-world location for AR HMD users.

Compared with the aforementioned system, our work has several advantages. First, our system is meant to reduce the gap between HMD user and non-HMD user in the condition of asymmetry caused by differences of devices. Even though the asymmetry of devices exists, non-HMD user can get the same AR information as HMD user. Second, once receiving the shared AR information from HMD user, non-HMD user can interact with virtual objects independently, instead of being under the control of the HMD user.

8 Conclusion

In this paper we present two ways for sharing the Augmented Reality Experience between HMD and Non-HMD User, in order to improve the communication between the two kinds of users when the information is not equal. We also design a scenario, a Pre-experience based online shopping system that demonstrate the utility of these techniques between HMD user and non-HMD user and describe how the system works to improve the communication.

The first method of our sharing system, is to share the live stream view of HMD user with non-HMD user. It means that non-HMD user can view all of the information and process during the interaction, as well as the operations made by HMD user. However, in this method, the virtual object is fully under the HMD user's control so that the listener of the live stream may be confused about the changing view. This passive way of receiving information may cause confusion and anxiety to users during sharing.

The second method of our sharing system focuses on the smartphone AR. After synchronizing with the HMD user, the smartphone can generate the same augmented reality object, at the same physical location. The virtual object in the smartphone AR is independent and interactable. It means that, the object on the smartphone is a separate copy of that in the HMD. In this way of sharing, the non-HMD user can enjoy the augmented information proactively and receives the complete information. Of course, this method also has its disadvantage. Both HMD and non-HMD users cannot know the condition of the object in the opponents' view, which may cause some communication problem when they would like to talk about the objects in real time.

9   Discussion and Future Work

In this paper, we present two ways for sharing the Augmented Reality Experience between HMD and Non-HMD User. Both methods have some disadvantages on the process of sharing the augmented reality information.

For the first method, the sharing view, we intend to share the augmented reality experience through sharing the live stream video of HMD user's view. The most significant shortcoming of this method, is that the non-HMD user cannot do any interaction within the scene. They are forced to understand the augmented video passively, which may make the contents difficult to understand.

In order to solve this problem, we are considering adding some function to enhance the communication between the users. Such as sending stamps or enabling voice chat so that the users can communicate and react to the content being shared.

For the second method, the duplicate generation, the augmented reality experience is shared by creating the same situation for non-HMD user, using their smartphone. Non-HMD user can get the similar experience and information through the process of interacting with the duplicate object independently.

In order to enable an approximate experience and avoid the conflict operation, the virtual object has its own status when it is created in the smartphone. However, as the status of the object is not shared between the two devices, it is difficult for the non-HMD user to know what is happening in the HMD user's view. They need to share the status by talking or sending messages currently. As future work, we can add a switch for non-HMD user to choose if we should synchronize the status of object or not. The users can choose one side of the client to control over the object. Alternatively, nonconflicting interaction method for the AR contents can be designed, so that they can interact with the same object at the same time.

Another problem of the second method is that the two kinds of users must be at the same place to do synchronization, as the use case of the application is designed for augmented reality application. The environment data is necessary to simulate the HMD's view. It would also be interesting to consider a virtual reality situation and the remote experience sharing solution.

As the field of view of augmented reality HMD increases in the coming years, and at the same time the screen size of smartphone's touch screen remains limited, the sharing field of view for the non-HMD user could become an important challenge for us to solve in the near future [19, 20]. The core problem could be in finding the most important content that is shown in the HMD view and only share those important content, which may improve the experience for the non-HMD user.

References

1. Billinghurst, M., Clark, A., Lee, G.: A survey of augmented reality. Found. Trends Hum.-Comput. Interact. **8**(2–3), 73–272 (2015)
2. Benko, H., Ishak, E., Feiner, S.: Collaborative mixed reality visualization of an archaeological excavation. In: 3rd IEEE and ACM International Symposium on Mixed and Augmented Reality, pp. 132–140. IEEE, Arlington (2004)
3. Gugenheimer, J., Stemasov, E., Frommel, J., Rukzio, E.: ShareVR: enabling co-located experiences for virtual reality between HMD and non-HMD users. In: Proceedings of the 2017 CHI Conference on Human Factors in Computing Systems, pp. 4021–4033. ACM, Denver (2017)
4. Stafford, A., Piekarski, W., Thomas, B.: Implementation of god-like interaction techniques for supporting collaboration between outdoor AR and indoor tabletop users. In: Proceedings of the 5th IEEE and ACM International Symposium on Mixed and Augmented Reality, pp. 165–172. IEEE, Washington (2006)
5. Rekimoto, J.: Transvision: a hand-held augmented reality system for collaborative design. In: Proceedings of Virtual Systems and Multi-Media, pp. 18–20. IEEE, Gifu (1996)
6. Gugenheimer, J., Stemasov, E., Sareen, H., Rukzio, E.: FaceDisplay: towards asymmetric multi-user interaction for nomadic virtual reality. In: Proceedings of the 2018 CHI Conference on Human Factors in Computing Systems, no. 54. ACM, Montreal (2018)
7. Kiyokawa, K., Billinghurst, M., Hayes, S., Gupta, A., Sannohe, Y., Kato, H.: Communication behaviors of co-located users in collaborative AR interfaces. In: International Symposium on Mixed and Augmented Reality, pp. 139–148. ACM, Darmstadt (2002)
8. Lindley, S., Couteur, J., Berthouze, N.: Stirring up experience through movement in game play: effects on engagement and social behaviour. In: Proceedings of the SIGCHI Conference on Human Factors in Computing Systems, pp. 511–514. ACM, Florence (2008)
9. IKEA Applications. https://www.ikea.com/ms/ja_JP/customer-service/about-shopping/download-ikea-apps/#app_place. Accessed 25 Jan 2019
10. Houzz. https://www.houzz.jp/?m_refid=olm_google_171700067_9563462027_aud-31292 3979530:kwd-361607895357&pos=1t1&device=c&nw=g&matchtype=e&gclid=CjwKCAi AyrXiBRAjEiwATI95mRJF4bjmQJ82mE18PgHhbZwrJM8U29FNzWkZ9KZf7spG7aO ou-SkwxoCQEMQAvD_BwE. Accessed 27 Jan 2019

11. Microsoft HoloLens. https://en.wikipedia.org/wiki/Microsoft_HoloLens. Accessed 25 Jan 2019
12. ARKit. https://developer.apple.com/documentation/arkit. Accessed 25 Jan 2019
13. Mixed reality capture. https://docs.microsoft.com/en-us/windows/mixed-reality/mixed-reality-capture. Accessed 25 Jan 2019
14. MixedRealityCompanionKit. https://github.com/Microsoft/MixedRealityCompanionKit/tree/master/MixedRemoteViewCompositor. Accessed 25 Jan 2019
15. Developing Vuforia Engine Apps for HoloLens. https://library.vuforia.com/articles/Training/Developing-Vuforia-Apps-for-HoloLens. Accessed 25 Jan 2019
16. Spatial Mapping. https://docs.microsoft.com/en-us/windows/mixed-reality/spatial-mapping. Accessed 25 Jan 2019
17. Animator Controller. https://docs.unity3d.com/2018.1/Documentation/Manual/class-AnimatorController.html. Accessed 25 Jan 2019
18. Billinghurst, M., Kato, H.: Collaborative augmented reality. Commun. ACM **45**(7), 64–70 (2002)
19. The human eye diopter. https://baike.baidu.com/item/%E4%BA%BA%E7%9C%BC%E8%A7%86%E5%BA%A6/5997035?fr=aladdin. Accessed 25 Jan 2019
20. Field of view. https://en.wikipedia.org/wiki/Field_of_view. Accessed 25 Jan 2019

Machine Learning and Intelligent Systems

Show Something: Intelligent Shopping Assistant Supporting Quick Scene Understanding and Immersive Preview

Hao Dou[1]([⊠]), Zhinan Li[1], Minghao Cai[1], Kelvin Cheng[2],
Soh Masuko[2], and Jiro Tanaka[1]

[1] Waseda University, Kitakyushu, Japan
{douhao, lizhinan}@fuji.waseda.jp,
mhcai@toki.waseda.jp, jiro@aoni.waseda.jp
[2] Rakuten Institute of Technology, Rakuten, Inc., Tokyo, Japan
{kelvin.cheng, so.masuko}@rakuten.com

Abstract. In this paper, we introduce an intelligent shopping assistant system supported by quick scene understanding and augmented-reality 3D preview. By understanding the scene that users are looking at, and using the detected scene information, our system recommends related products that are not in the current scene and which could potentially interest users. With the help of existing speech recognition techniques, our system extracts users' voice command and keywords, and provides responses in real-time, which allows users to search and filter specific products just by using voice. After finding the potential target products, our system provides users with an augmented-reality preview experience. It automatically brings products to the suitable space in front of the users by using life-size three-dimensional virtual products and spatial understanding. Users can also use two-hand gestural manipulation to operate the virtual products. Through our system, users can obtain products that are strongly related to the current environment, and intuitively preview the products in the current scene by automatic placement and two-hand manipulation to make shopping decisions.

Keywords: Immersive shopping · Intelligent system · Context awareness

1 Introduction

Online shopping systems have developed rapidly due to its flexibility and its ability to connect to large information networks, enabling users to purchase products whenever and wherever they want [1]. However, current online shopping systems are still limited. The recommendation functions of these shopping systems are usually limited to purchase history or search history. Image-based searches typically focus on methods on finding the same class of products given an image of the scene. The dominant objects from the image are extracted, and identical or similar products are returned from an e-commerce platform. However, users do not necessarily want to purchase the exact same item as in the scene. For example, when a user looks at a sink in the kitchen, the user may want to purchase detergent, cutlery, and other kitchen items instead of buying another sink.

© Springer Nature Switzerland AG 2019
S. Yamamoto and H. Mori (Eds.): HCII 2019, LNCS 11570, pp. 205–218, 2019.
https://doi.org/10.1007/978-3-030-22649-7_17

In addition, current web shopping systems are mostly limited to showing 2D information and usually cannot let users see a digital preview of items in the physical world instantly. Recently, evolving technologies that make use of Augmented-Reality (AR) and computer vision techniques seek to automate tasks that enhance the human visual system can bring new opportunities for intelligent shopping environments.

This work aims to realize an intelligent shopping assistant system supported by quick scene understanding. Combining voice control, automatic placement and two-hand manipulation, this system can also provide users with an immersive augmented-reality preview experience. Using our system, users can get high-quality product recommendations based on the current scene and make quick shopping decisions through products filtering and previewing.

2 Goal and Approach

Our work aims to present an intelligent shopping assistant system which supports quick scene understanding to recommend the user scene-related products which users do not own themselves, and help users make shopping decision quickly. Our system also supports intelligent voice control, an immersive augmented-reality preview experience, as well as providing support for two-hand manipulation with automatic placement.

The quick scene understanding is aimed to recommend products intelligently according to the current scene of the users. Users only need to look at the current scene, and the system will capture and analyze the current scene rapidly and provide result precisely. This can be realized by using scene recognition method. With this method, the picture received from the camera can be analyzed, and objects in the picture are recognized, and finally the possible scene is inferred.

Voice control is used to integrate the intelligent shopping experience for the users. It allows users to say exactly what they want by using voice commands, allowing the use of multiple keywords in one sentence, and filtering out products by using adjectives. We realized this by using text analysis [2] method. It can extract more than one keyword from a sentence accurately. Adjectives can also be extracted to search more precisely, such as "blue shirt" or "big table". It should also allow the users to filter the products, such as "I want to buy a pair of shoes.", "Filter, I prefer Nike." The system will search for all the shoes first and then search for Nike shoes.

Two-hand manipulation will allow users to interact with the preview of the products in augmented-reality. The search results should contain 3D virtual objects that can be dragged into the real world. Users can use two-hand manipulation [3] to move and rotate the virtual objects.

The system should automatically place the virtual objects according to the space availability in the physical world. After scanning the scene, the system will find enough space to place the object and place them automatically. If there is not enough space, the products which do not fit in the space well will not be placed.

3   Intelligent Shopping Assistant

3.1   Scene Understanding

Current systems that search through images typically focus on methods that search for products that are identical to products within the image. They extract specific objects from the image and try to search the exact same item in the e-commerce platforms. However, sometimes users do not necessarily want to buy the same item as in the scene. In an image, the ambiance of the users' environment can also be treated as a source of rich contextual information [4]. When people visit various places throughout the day, many of the impulses that drive shopping are generated by objects in the environment. For example, when users see a sink in the kitchen, they may want to buy some detergent, cutlery, and other kitchen items instead of buying another sink.

In this system, we introduce a way to search for products within the scene. By understanding the scene that users are currently looking at, and using the detected scene information, our system recommends related products which could potentially interest users (see Fig. 1).

Fig. 1. The system recommends relevant products to the user according to the current scene in the user's environment. Scene recognition results: a kitchen with a sink and a mirror.

A scene is a view of a real-world environment where users are physically located, and which contains multiples surfaces and objects, organized in a meaningful way. With the help of computer vision techniques [5], the scene can be understood quickly, after generating an overall description of the scene (e.g. kitchen, or restroom), dominate objects that the system is able to recognize (e.g. desktop computer, or desk) from the ambient environment is included. We use the keyword of the current scene (e.g. kitchen) to search the products in the e-commerce platform that have the related categories as the dominate objects in the scene (instead of the dominate objects themselves). In this way, we recommend users with products that are strongly associated with the current scene.

For example, a user scans the current environment through our system and expects to receive product recommendations. Our system scans to find out that the current environment is a kitchen, and the current environment has a dominate object, a microwave oven. The system first obtains the search keyword: "kitchen". Next, the e-commerce platform searches for the category relationship of the dominant objects. For example, the category of the microwave oven is: "microwave oven", it has a parent category "appliances." We will use the keyword "kitchen" to search for the category "appliances" and exclude the category "microwave oven" from the search results. Users will get search results for kitchen appliances such as coffee machines, bread machines, and electronic ovens. If there are multiple dominant objects, we will use each dominant object and repeat the above search process. The search results will be combined and return to the users. In this way, we recommend users products that are closely related to the current scenario that users may not already own.

Figure 2 shows the process of searching products by scene: (a) The user issues the voice command "show something", the system then takes a photo, and the photo is sent to the scene recognition server. (b) The scene recognition server analyzes the keyword "kitchen" in the current scene and the dominant object "microwave oven" in the scene and sends the dominant object "microwave oven" to our e-commerce category API. (c) The directory API searches for the category and parent category of the "microwave oven" (d) The system searches for the current scene keyword "kitchen" in the parent category "appliances" and exclude the category "microwave oven" and returns the recommended products to the user.

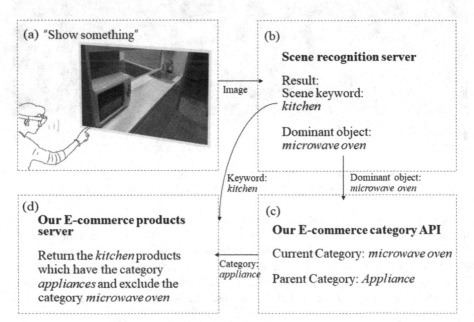

Fig. 2. The process of searching products by scene:

These recommended items are displayed in augmented-reality in a virtual panel that floats in the real world. Users can visually see the links between recommended products and the real world, and view the details of the recommended items, or directly filter the recommended items by voice command and quickly find the products they are interested in.

3.2 Voice Command

To be able to get specific products, a method of interaction is required. In this section, we introduce an intelligent voice interaction approach.

Previous intelligent voice control is quite simple. Many intelligent speech recognition systems can only recognize simple sentences and cannot understand the meaning of the user's voice instructions through context [6]. Users can only ask the system to search specific products instead of searching detail information. If users are not satisfied with the search result, users can not add more filter conditions to filter the searching result. Instead of using this kind of voice control, users prefer using a keyboard to type the searching conditions through the keyboard.

To improve on the existing voice control methods, we propose an intelligent voice control approach, which allows users to use voice command to search products with different attributes and filter the products by voice command.

Table 1. Nouns extracted from example instructions

Instructions	Keyword
"I want to buy a book."	book
"I would like a bag."	bag
"A table is what I need."	table
"Would you please show me a chair?"	chair
"Show a lamp."	lamp

In order to search products through voice command, we need to analyze users' voice instruction and extract the core content of the instruction. We used text analysis method to get the users' keywords from the sentence. This method first analyzes the user's voice instruction and classify the words by their part-of-speech. We extract the nouns as the keywords of the instruction (Table 1).

To search products in a more precise way, we allow users to search with multiple nouns. In this case, more than one noun can be extracted. The nouns can be used as the qualifiers or other keywords (Table 2).

Table 2. Multiple nouns extracted from example instructions

Instructions	Keyword
"I want to buy a children book."	children book
"Show a lady backpack."	lady backpack
"I would like a floor lamp."	floor lamp
"I want a notebook and a pencil."	notebook, pencil

We also made the adjectives qualifiers, so that the users can search the products with different attributes (Table 3).

Table 3. Nouns (Modified by adjectives) extracted from example instructions

Instructions	Keyword
"I want to buy a blue chair."	*blue chair*
"I want a big table."	*big table*
"Show the latest laptop."	*latest laptop*
"I'd like a lotion for dry skin."	*lotion, dry skin*
"I am sensitive skin and I want to buy a sunscreen."	*sensitive skin, sunscreen*

In addition, users can say multiple sentences to filter the products. Users can first say a sentence to search a product, they can then add more filter conditions to narrow down the search results. The more filter conditions users add, the more accurate the results are (Table 4). Users can also say "Go back" to recall their filter operation.

Table 4. Nouns (Filtered by conditions) extracted from example instructions

Instructions	Keyword
"I want to buy a pair of sneakers.", "Filter, I love Adidas."	*Adidas sneakers*
"I want a table.", "Filter, I want cheaper ones."	*cheaper table*

With the above search methods, users are able to perform accurate products searching (see Fig. 3).

Fig. 3. Users can filter the sneakers by saying "I love adidas."

3.3   Immersive Preview

Our system offers two ways of providing users with immersive shopping experience in augmented reality: automatic placement of virtual products, and manipulation of virtual products with two hands.

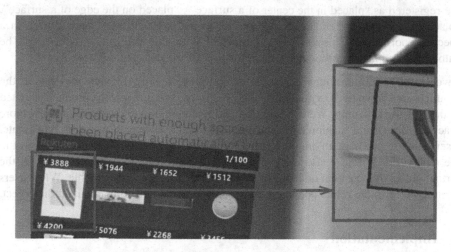

Fig. 4. The system automatically found a place to put the wall painting on the wall

Automatic Placement. In order to let users visually see whether the recommended products are suitable for the current environment, we designed a way to automatically place virtual products into the real world (see Fig. 4).

Before getting the recommended products, we have taken the current scene to extract the dominate objects in the real environment. By recording the location of these key objects, we can place the recommended items in a physical location nearby. Different products have their own placement rules. For example, decorative paintings and racks are usually hung on the wall. The vases are usually placed on a table or other flat surface, and chandeliers are usually hung from the ceiling. In order for the virtual object to automatically follow the placement rules for placement, we needed a higher level of understanding about the user's environment.

We solved this problem by introducing the spatial mapping function. Using this, we can analyze the basic structure of the user's current environment and identify surfaces such as walls, ceilings, and floors. We set up a voice command "place". When users invoke this voice command, the system will tell them to walk around, while collecting the surfaces information of their environment by using HoloLens' depth camera and environment-aware cameras. When enough data is collected, the system will notify users to stop scanning, and the spatial understanding component in the Microsoft Mixed Reality Toolkit [7] will analyze the scanned data. Through this analysis, we can get the orientation (vertical or horizontal), position and size of the corresponding surface in 3D space.

The virtual products are pre-registered with features corresponding to the plane attributes. Products can be pre-registered with one of four attributes: "placed on a wall", "placed on a floor", "placed on a ceiling", or "placed on a platform". We search the environment in which the users are located to see if there is a corresponding surface. Then decide whether to place the products.

In addition to the surface placement rules, different items also have different layout-related placement habits. We designed another set of placement rule. Products can be pre-registered as "placed in the center of a surface ", "placed on the edge of a surface", "placed away from other virtual objects that in the same surface", and "placed in a specific coordinate (Close to a real object)". With this rule, the products can be automatically placed in the appropriate position of the detected surface.

Two-Hand Manipulation. To provide an augmented-reality preview experience, the products are shown as 3D virtual objects. It helps users to preview the products situated in the real-world setting. We use the two-hand manipulation to make the preview more practical. Two-hand manipulation includes two kinds of operations: drag and rotate. Users can use one hand to drag the virtual objects as if they were grasping an object in the real world. We have also implemented the spatial mapping, so users can drag the virtual object to a position on a physical surface, such as the floor or table. When users want to perform the rotate operation, they can use two hands to manipulate the object.

4   Implementation

Figure 5 shows the overview of our system. We divided this system into two parts: HMD client and server.

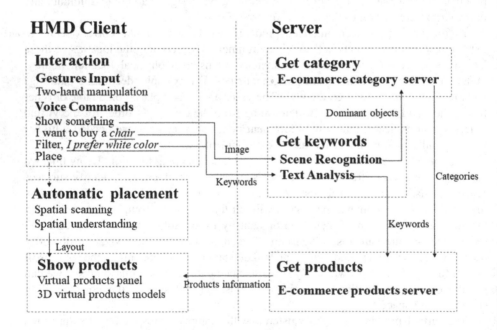

Fig. 5. System overview

On the client side, we used Microsoft HoloLens as the user's terminal. It blends cutting-edge optics and depth sensors to deliver 3D holograms pinned to the real world around the user. Built-in microphones and speakers are used to capture the user's voice and provide audio feedback. When the user makes a voice command, we use the HoloLens dictation system to convert the user's voice commands into text.

4.1 Get Virtual Products

Get Recommended Items Through the Current Scene. When the voice command "show something" is issued, the HoloLens' camera is used to capture the current scene and send the captured photos to the server's Microsoft Azure computer vision server [8]. A description of the current scene and the dominant objects of the scene will be extracted. The current scene-dominant objects are selected, and their related categories are obtained from an e-commerce platform [9]. Then, product search is performed by a fusion of categories and scene description keyword [10] to obtain products recommendations with strong relevance.

Search and Filter Specific Products with Voice Commands. When voice command is used to search a product directly, the microphone will capture the user's voice command, the voice command will first be classified, and is then sent to the cloud analysis platform [11, 12]. The sentence will be analyzed, and keywords extracted. If users issue additional voice command to further refine their filter conditions, additional keywords will be extracted from the command. These keywords will be sent to the e-commerce platform, and products information will be returned. If the user says "filter", we will send the current keyword and the filter condition together to the e-commerce platform. In this way, users' searching results will be more and more precise.

4.2 Automatically Place Virtual Products

When the voice command "place" is issued, spatial understanding will begin. The system prompts users to walk around and start scanning the surrounding physical environment. Within the Microsoft HoloLens, the cameras group in front of the device are used to perceive the surface information in the surrounding environment. MRTK's spatial understanding component [8] is used to analyze the metadata captured by the cameras group to identify specific ceilings, floors, walls, and other flat information. Combined with the preset information for the virtual item placement feature, we calculate the location that is suitable for placing the virtual products and automatically place them.

4.3 Interact with Virtual Products

We built a 3D virtual object library to store the 3D models. Each product in our system has its own 3D virtual object. So that when the products result is returned, the 3D virtual objects can also be shown.

We pre-processed the virtual models to make sure that they can be operated successfully. Using MRTK [8], bounding box around the virtual objects is used to help users judge the size of the objects. By adding two-hand manipulation scripts in MRTK, users can use their hands to drag and rotate the virtual objects [13].

5   Evaluation

In this section, we introduce our user research and results analysis. We asked participants to accomplish their shopping tasks in a traditional online shopping mobile application which supports searching for items using text and filtering items by price, sales, and shelf date [14] and our intelligent shopping assistant system (they have the same product library). The main purpose of this study was to test whether our system can provide users with high-quality product recommendations that could interest them and whether our system can help them make shopping decisions in a specific situation. We will also discuss the received feedback from a questionnaire.

5.1   Participants

We invited 12 participants (4 females and 8 males), ranging from 19 to 25 years of age. All participants have basic computer skills. Two of them had experience with head-mounted displays. They were divided into two groups evenly.

5.2   Task and Procedure

Before each study, we introduced the basic operations of Microsoft HoloLens to the participants. After the participants became familiar with the device, we asked them to search for products of interest that are related the current environment in three different scenes (kitchen, student office and one corner of the room). For each scene, group 1 was asked to first use the traditional mobile shopping system for 30 min, and then use our intelligent shopping assistant system to shop for another 30 min (see Fig. 6).

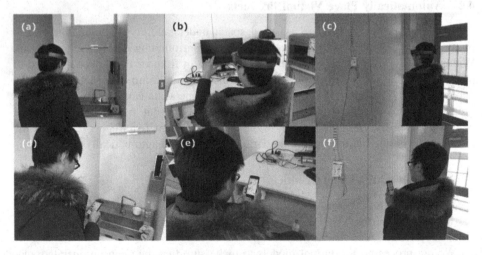

Fig. 6. Evaluation: (a) Using our system in the kitchen. (b) Using our system in the student office. (c) Using our system in one corner of the room. (d) Using current mobile shopping system in the kitchen. (e) Using current mobile shopping system in the student office. (f) Using current mobile shopping system in one corner of the room.

Group 2 was asked the opposite and used our system first. We asked all 12 participants to record the number of products they are interested in when using the shopping system. After the participant completed the whole study, we asked them to fill out a questionnaire with 5 questions to obtain qualitative feedback. Participants rated each question from 1 to 5 (1 = very negative, 5 = very positive).

5.3   Result and Discussion

At the end of the experiment, we collected 36 sets of data from 12 participants using two systems with three scenarios. We calculated the average number of products that participants were interested in (see Table 5).

Table 5. The average number of products that participants interested in thirty minutes.

Scene	Group1		Group2	
	Current system	Our system	Current system	Our system
1 Kitchen	2.3	4.3	3.0	4.5
2 Student office	1.5	3.3	3.2	5.3
3 One corner of the room	1.0	2.5	2.3	4.8

As shown in Table 5, in the three different scenarios, participants of both groups using our system found more products that were of interest compared to using the traditional mobile e-commerce system. In other words, our system recommends more related items for the current scene for the participants. One participant mentioned that using our shopping system has brought him more shopping inspiration. *"When I use the mobile shopping app in the corner of the room, I don't have any shopping ideas. When I scanned the environment with your system, I realized that I could buy some paintings to decorate the walls."*

Table 6 shows the results of our questionnaire. We also divided the results into two parts – using current mobile e-commerce app and using our system. We calculated the average score of each question.

Table 6. Questionnaire.

Question	Current system	Our system
1 I could get high-quality product recommendation	2.8	4.6
2 I could fully understand the product information	3.8	4.5
3 I felt the system operation was easy enough	4.0	4.0
4 I could easily filter out the products I want	3.0	4.3
5 I could make shopping decisions quickly	2.6	4.7

Question 1 is used to judge whether our system can recommend high-quality products to users. From the result, we can see that participants are not satisfied with the recommendation mechanism of the traditional mobile shopping system under scene-based shopping. This may be because the traditional recommendation mechanism cannot judge what items are missing in the current scene, so it recommends to users many duplicate items. By using search for products by scene feature of our system, users can get recommended products that are strongly related to the current scene, thereby improving the quality of recommended products.

Question 2 is used to compare traditional mobile shopping application with our system for product information display. As can be seen from the results, participants thought that using our system can better understand products information than traditional mobile shopping systems. Traditional mobile shopping systems typically use limited 2D images and captions to describe the specifics of the product, and users may not be able to get more specific information from these descriptions. Our system allows users to understand the product more fully by visually displaying a rotatable virtual 3D product with descriptive information.

Question 3 is used to test the ease of use and usability of the system. Participants gave us the same rating as the traditional mobile shopping system. The result show that even though users are not familiar with the operation of the head-mounted display, our voice-based system is still easy to use.

Questions 4 and 5 are used to determine whether our system can help users filter out the products they want and help them make purchasing decisions. Our ratings are higher than the traditional mobile shopping system. When using the traditional mobile shopping system, users often need to constantly view the descriptions of the products to make shopping decisions. In our system, by using voice commands, users can easily narrow down the search range and filter out items of interest. With the automatic placement feature, users can check whether a virtual item has a suitable location to be placed and visually compare different virtual items in the environment. This in turn can make shopping decisions faster.

In general, all participants rated our system higher than the traditional system. This may signify that our system is designed to be reasonable and practical. It demonstrates that our system can build a new way of shopping, allowing users to intuitively get high-quality recommended products based on the current scene and make quick shopping decisions.

6 Related Works

One of the related works is a smart assistant toward product-awareness shopping [15]. This research employs sensor techniques in developing a smart assistant for home furniture shopping. In their work, it helps consumers to locate the product easily. Their recommendation method eliminated duplicated products display. The assistant can help to avoid the unnecessary crashing of huge shopping carts in a crowded situation. Their work has integrated the consumer, retailer and the warehouse sides. It is a new shopping pattern.

Another related work isMR-Shoppingu [16]. This research realized an MR shopping system which combines physical and digital information spaces to make digital content accessible directly on physical objects. In this research, they also used Microsoft HoloLens as the see-through type head-mounted display. When the user sees products through the head-mounted display, he can see the products as well as the digital information of the products which includes pricing information, customer reviews or product video.

Their research provides users a natural way of interacting with the real world without any special input. The combination of the real world and the digital world can provide a more entertaining shopping experience for consumers. This work has inspired our design of virtual user interface to help us build an immersive feeling to the user.

7 Conclusion and Future Work

In this paper, we presented an intelligent shopping assistant which support quick scene understanding and immersive preview. By integrating cloud services, the system can smartly recommend products which are related to the current scene. Users can search for products with natural language using voice command and invoke multiple modification conditions and filter search results. After receiving the results, the system can help users place the virtual objects automatically in their scene and enabling users to manipulate virtual products with hand gestures.

We received feedback from the users by conducting a user study. Overall, we received positive feedback and our system is practical that the users are willing to use it.

In future work, we will continue to improve the system. Since the system is in a demonstration stage, the system is not fully completed. The number of 3D virtual models is very limited. Only some of the objects have 3D virtual objects, so in the future work, it is necessary to expand the library of 3D virtual products.

References

1. Luo, P., Yan, S., Liu, Z.Q., Shen, Z.Y., Yang, S.W., He, Q.: From online behaviors to offline retailing. In: Proceedings of the 22nd ACM SIGKDD International Conference on Knowledge Discovery and Data Mining 2016, pp. 175–184 (2016)
2. Westus.dev.cognitive.microsoft.com: Microsoft Cognitive Services Text Analytics API (v2.0) (2018). https://westus.dev.cognitive.microsoft.com/docs/services/TextAnalytics.V2.0/operations/56f30ceeeda5650db055a3c6. Accessed 10 Jan. 2019
3. Docs.microsoft.com: Gestures - Mixed Reality (2018). https://docs.microsoft.com/en-us/windows/mixed-reality/gestures. Accessed 9 Jan 2019
4. O'Hara, K., Perry, M.: Shopping anytime anywhere, extended abstracts. In: Proceedings of the ACM CHI 2001 Conference on Human Factors in Computing Systems, pp. 345–346 (2001)
5. Li, L.-J., Li, F.-F.: What, where and who? classifying events by scene and object recognition. In: 2007 IEEE 11th International Conference on Computer Vision, pp. 1–8 (2007)
6. Wang, Y.Y., Yu, D., Ju, Y.C., et al.: An introduction to voice search. IEEE Signal Process. Mag **25**(3), 28–38 (2008)
7. Docs.microsoft.com: Describing images - Computer Vision - Azure Cognitive Services (2018). https://docs.microsoft.com/en-us/azure/cognitive-services/computer-vision/concept-describing-images. Accessed 13 Jan 2019

8. Microsoft 2018b: MixedRealityToolkit-Unity, 29 March 2018. https://github.com/Microsoft/MixedRealityToolkit-Unity. Accessed 12 Jan 2019
9. Webservice.rakuten.co.jp: Rakuten Web Service: Ichiba Genre Search API (version:2012-07-23)|API (2019). https://webservice.rakuten.co.jp/api/ichibagenresearch. Accessed 12 Jan 2019
10. Webservice.rakuten.co.jp: Rakuten Web Service: Ichiba Item Search API (version:2017-07-06)|API (2019). https://webservice.rakuten.co.jp/api/ichibaitemsearch/. Accessed 12 Jan 2019
11. Docs.microsoft.com: Voice design - Mixed Reality (2018). https://docs.microsoft.com/en-us/windows/mixed-reality/voice-design. Accessed 15 Jan 2019
12. Docs.microsoft.com: Voice input - Mixed Reality (2019). https://docs.microsoft.com/en-us/windows/mixed-reality/voice-input. Accessed 17 Jan 2019
13. Chaconas, N., Hollerer, T.: An evaluation of bimanual gestures on the microsoft hololens. In: 2018 IEEE Conference on Virtual Reality and 3D User Interfaces (VR), pp. 33–40 (2018)
14. Mobile APP|Rakuten.com (2019). https://www.rakuten.com/info/mobile-app/. Accessed 15 Jan 2019
15. Chen, C.C., Huang, T.C., Park, J.J., et al.: A smart assistant toward product-awareness shopping. Pers. Ubiquit. Comput. 18(2), 339–349 (2014)
16. Cheng, K., Nakazawa, M., Masuko, S.: MR-Shoppingu: physical interaction with augmented retail products using continuous context awareness. In: Munekata, N., Kunita, I., Hoshino, J. (eds.) ICEC 2017. LNCS, vol. 10507, pp. 452–455. Springer, Cham (2017). https://doi.org/10.1007/978-3-319-66715-7_61

Initial Investigation of a Notification System for Indoor Alarm Sounds Using a Neural Network

Takeru Kadokura[1], Kohei Watanabe[1], Yoshikaze Yanagiya[1],
Elisa Sihombing[2], Syauqan Wafiqi[2], Yasuhiro Sudo[1],
and Hiroshi Tanaka[1(✉)]

[1] Kanagawa Institute of Technology,
1030 Shimo-ogino, Atsugi-shi, Kanagawa, Japan
{s1885004,s1521053,s1621092}@cce.kanagawa-it.ac.jp,
{sudo,h_tanaka}@ic.kanagawa-it.ac.jp
[2] Electronic Engineering Polytechnic Institute of Surabaya,
JL. Raya ITS – Kampas PENS Sukolilo, Surabaya 60111, Indonesia
elisasihombingspc@gmail.com, siconfix@gmail.com

Abstract. Many devices can inform the user of everything from a visitor's arrival at the door to a dangerous gas leak detection. For hearing-impaired people, there are some devices that can notify using light, etc., rather than by sound. However, these are individual devices and are relatively expensive due to their limited production volume. In this paper, a neural network was used as a method to classify alarm sounds of eight types of equipment. Two feature elements such as power spectrum and Mel Frequency Cepstrum Coefficients (MFCC) are taken as feature quantities to enter in this network, and its performance was evaluated. We implemented a neural network learned model on a Raspberry Pi and constructed a system that transmits classification results to a smartphone via Bluetooth. We generated 8 types of alarm sounds, plus indoor environmental sounds and speech sounds, for a total of ten kinds of sounds in the actual use environment of the classification experiment. This produced classification rates of 83.0% and 82.0% in experiments using learned models generated by power spectrum and MFCC. For the 8 alarm sounds, the classification rate was 87.5% by power spectrum and 77.5% by MFCC. It was confirmed that good performance could be obtained if power spectrum is used to determine feature elements in alarm sound classification.

Keywords: Alarm sound · Classification · Neural network · Feature element · Smart phone

1 Introduction

Quite a lot of equipment is available for use in the home to inform the owner of important events, ranging from visitors at the door to gas leaks, all of which require immediate attention, though with quite different responses and different urgency levels. Though the usual notification is a special sound signal, for hearing-impaired persons

S. Yamamoto and H. Mori (Eds.): HCII 2019, LNCS 11570, pp. 219–231, 2019.
https://doi.org/10.1007/978-3-030-22649-7_18

and those too distant to hear such signals, many products communicate by methods other than sound. However, remote warning devices are specialized in ways that make them much more expensive than ordinary devices [1, 2]. It would be useful to have a single system to recognize all these various alarm signals and communicate their messages through a single channel to their intended recipients, whether disabled, distant, or simply distracted.

Machine learning techniques have already been widely applied in fields such as image recognition, speech recognition [3] and automatic translation [4], so it seems reasonable to apply them to the classification of various alarm sounds, whether smoke alarms or kitchen trimers. Although there are studies aimed at detecting alarm sounds [5–7], it is two divisions of alarm sounds and non-alarm sounds, and a plurality of various alarm sounds are not classified. In addition, it is an examination of the element technology, and no investigation has been done on a system for communicating the occurrence of alarm sound to the user.

In this paper, we propose a system that recognizes various alarm sounds using machine learning, and transmits the notifications to the smartphone of an individual user. Here we describe the results of the primary prototyping of such a system.

2   Alarm Sound Classification

An image of the application of the proposed system is shown in Fig. 1. We propose a system which classifies various alarm sounds by machine learning and notifies the user by vibration of the user's smartphone and displays the sound source on its screen. Although there are special devices that notify of an abnormality by other than sound, such as light, for users with hearing disabilities, they are all individual devices. As in the proposal shown in Fig. 1, it is thought that a useful system can be realized at low cost by detecting the sounds of all the alarms, identifying them and informing the user of the classification via smartphone, by means of vibration, etc.

Sound notification system for deaf persons and those faraway

Fig. 1. Service image of proposed system

2.1   Feature Data Creation of Each Sound

Eight kinds of equipment, including a door alarm, two smoke alarms, a gas alarm, entrance bell, kettle alarm, and two timer alarms were selected as indoor alarm-sound producers in this investigation. The appearance of each alarm equipment and their spectrograms are shown in Fig. 2. The x-axis of the spectrogram graph is time (0 to 60 s), the y-axis is frequency (0 to 8000 Hz), and the sound level is −40 to 40 dB.

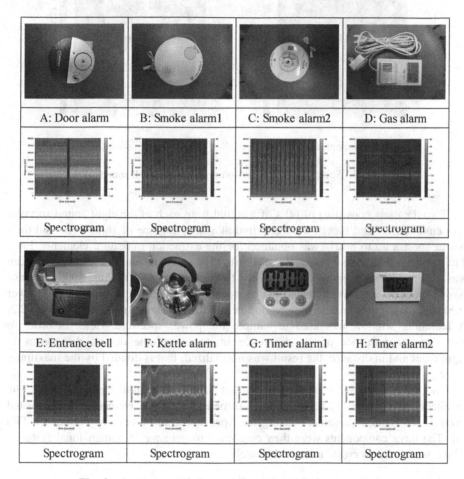

Fig. 2. Appearance of alarm equipment and their spectrograms

Here, it is necessary to consider the environment of any classification. That is, the classifier output produced even in the absence of an alarm sound. We selected two indoor sound environments: one in which air conditioners etc. are operating, but without conversation, i.e. just environmental sounds, and the other with normal speech sounds. These two sound backgrounds will be included for classification. The spectrograms of these two sound environments are shown in Fig. 3. It was confirmed that the spectrograms of each sound source (10 kinds of sound) were different and classification could be conducted by appropriate methods. To classify these sound sources, it was then necessary to select distinctive feature elements for each. In this investigation, we decided to use power spectrum and the Mel-Frequency Cepstrum Coefficients (MFCC) used in speech recognition as the feature elements for classification.

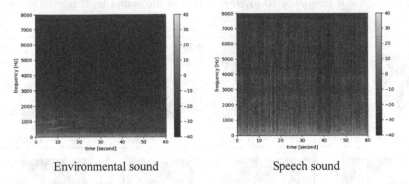

Environmental sound   Speech sound

Fig. 3. Spectrograms of environmental and speech sounds

Two data sets consisting of 60 s of a signal from each of the eight sound sources, plus environment and speech were acquired at a sampling rate of 16,000 Hz, and their power spectra up to 8 kHz was obtained for the extraction of feature elements. Each data set was divided into segments of 32 ms (512 samples), and the power spectrum was obtained by overlapping the bits every 10 ms (160 samples). Thus, 6000 pieces of power spectrum data were created for each data sample, for a total of 12,000 power spectrum data sets for use in the creation of the learned model described in Sect. 2.2. A hamming window was used to sample the power spectrum. Here, in order to eliminate the influence of the difference in sound volume due to differences in equipment and in distance, the result was normalized, that is divided by the maximum value.

The same data sets were used to extract MFCC as feature elements. Here, the number of Mel filter banks was 30, and 13-dimensional MFCC elements were extracted from 32 ms frame data samples using the Speech Signal Processing Toolkit (SPTK) [8]. The three components were then combined to generate 39 dimensional features, which were used to create a learned model.

2.2 Creation of Learned Model

The configuration of the neural network for learning is shown in Fig. 4. Each of the feature elements of the power spectrum and MFCC were used for training, both using the same neural network model, and a learned model was created. The intermediate layer is composed of two layers. A dropout configuration with 50% probability was introduced in the intermediate layer in order to avoid over-fitting.

Learning processes for the power spectrum and MFCC feature elements are shown in Fig. 5. The cross entropy error is used for the loss function, and the size of the mini

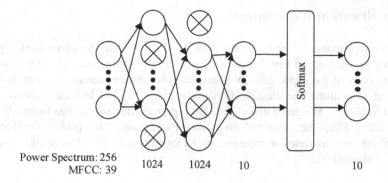

Power Spectrum: 256
MFCC: 39   1024   1024   10   10

Fig. 4. Neural network configuration

batch is set to 20. We confirmed convergence of accuracy for the mini batch and loss obtained from the error function. For creation of a valid learned model, the number of epochs was set to 1000 to reach a stable status via this process. From the viewpoint of learning performance using feature data of 60 s, slightly better results were obtained when MFCC was used rather than power spectrum.

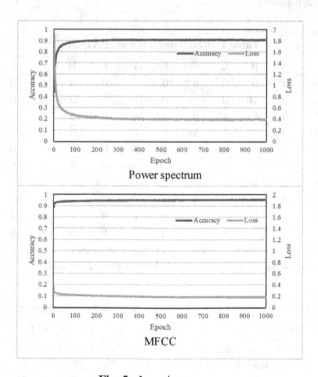

Fig. 5. Learning process

3   Classification Experiment

Giving the importance of early detection of an alarm sound, the classification performance for the data of the first 5 s of the alarm sounds was evaluated. Five seconds of
data from each of the eight different alarm sounds, environmental and speech sounds
were used to evaluate the classification performance by the learned network model
obtained in Sect. 2. We generated sounds from prerecorded sound data from a Wav file
and a speaker. Here, the mean and the standard deviation of the probability that is the
output of the softmax function were examined together with the classification result for
quality of classification.

3.1   Results by Power Spectrum

The classification performance when the power spectrum was used is shown in Table 1
as a confusion matrix. The overall accuracy was 96.0% (4 misjudgments among 100).
Tables 2 and 3 show the average and the standard deviation of the output values of
each classification target of the softmax function. Here, those whose value exceeds 0.1
are bolded. It can be understood from this average and standard deviation that misclassification occurred between the door alarm and kettle sounds as well as environmental and speech sounds.

Table 1. Result using power spectrum

	A	B	C	D	E	F	G	H	I	J
A	9	0	0	0	0	1	0	0	0	0
B	0	10	0	0	0	0	0	0	0	0
C	0	0	10	0	0	0	0	0	0	0
D	0	0	0	10	0	0	0	0	0	0
E	0	0	0	0	10	0	0	0	0	0
F	0	0	0	0	0	10	0	0	0	0
G	0	0	0	0	0	0	10	0	0	0
H	0	0	0	0	0	0	0	10	0	0
I	0	0	0	0	0	0	0	0	8	2
J	0	0	0	0	0	0	0	0	1	9

A: Door B: Smokel C: Smoke2 D: Gas E: Entrance
F: Kettle G: Timerl H: Timer2 I: Environment J: Speech

Table 2. Average values of softmax function for power spectrum

	A	B	C	D	E	F	G	H	I	J
A	**0.82**	0.02	0.02	0.00	0.00	**0.11**	0.01	0.01	0.00	0.00
B	0.01	**0.56**	**0.19**	0.05	0.00	0.00	0.01	**0.17**	0.00	0.00
C	0.01	0.04	**0.82**	0.02	0.00	0.01	0.01	0.07	0.00	0.01

(continued)

Table 2. (*continued*)

	A	B	C	D	E	F	G	H	I	J
D	0.01	0.02	**0.11**	**0.76**	0.00	0.00	0.01	0.09	0.00	0.00
E	0.00	0.00	0.00	0.00	**0.75**	0.00	**0.13**	0.00	0.03	0.09
F	0.00	0.00	0.09	0.00	0.01	**0.80**	0.04	0.00	0.04	0.03
G	0.00	0.01	0.01	0.00	0.02	0.02	**0.82**	0.01	0.01	**0.10**
H	0.00	0.08	**0.21**	0.03	0.00	0.00	0.01	**0.67**	0.00	0.01
I	0.00	0.00	0.00	0.00	0.01	0.00	0.02	0.00	**0.73**	**0.23**
J	0.00	0.01	0.01	0.00	0.10	0.01	**0.13**	0.00	**0.24**	**0.51**

A: Door B: Smoke1 C: Smoke2 D: Gas E: Entrance
F: Kettle G: Timer1 H: Timer2 I: Environment J: Speech

Table 3. Standard deviation of softmax function for power spectrum

	A	B	C	D	E	F	G	H	I	J
A	**0.20**	0.04	0.02	0.00	0.00	**0.13**	0.02	0.01	0.00	0.00
B	0.00	0.03	0.03	0.01	0.00	0.00	0.01	0.04	0.00	0.00
C	0.00	0.01	0.03	0.01	0.00	0.01	0.01	0.01	0.00	0.01
D	0.00	0.02	0.06	**0.15**	0.00	0.01	0.02	0.08	0.00	0.01
E	0.00	0.00	0.00	0.00	**0.12**	0.00	0.08	0.00	0.03	0.05
F	0.00	0.00	0.07	0.00	0.01	**0.18**	0.04	0.00	0.05	0.03
G	0.00	0.01	0.01	0.00	0.01	0.02	0.06	0.01	0.01	0.03
H	0.00	0.07	0.03	0.01	0.00	0.00	0.01	0.07	0.00	0.01
I	0.00	0.00	0.00	0.00	0.01	0.00	0.02	0.00	**0.34**	**0.31**
J	0.00	0.01	0.01	0.00	0.04	0.01	0.08	0.00	**0.13**	**0.12**

A: Door B: Smoke1 C: Smoke2 D: Gas E: Entrance
F: Kettle G: Timer1 H: Timer2 I: Environment J: Speech

3.2 Result by MFCC

Classification performance when MFCC is used is shown in Table 4. The overall recognition accuracy was 87.0% (13 misjudgments among 100). The erroneous classification of the environmental sound and the speech sound is similar to the result when using power spectrum, but erroneous classification also occurred for timer 1 and timer 2. The spectrogram in Fig. 2, shows that the very same sound is produced by each in the first time span. This is a very different result from the power spectrum case.

Tables 5 and 6 show the average value and the standard deviation of the output values of each classification target of the softmax function output, which are the same as in the power spectrum. In addition to environmental sound and speech sound, of course erroneous classifications of timer 1 and 2 occur.

Table 4. Result using MFCC

	A	B	C	D	E	F	G	H	I	J
A	9	0	0	0	0	1	0	0	0	0
B	0	10	0	0	0	0	0	0	0	0
C	0	0	10	0	0	0	0	0	0	0
D	0	0	0	10	0	0	0	0	0	0
E	0	0	0	0	10	0	0	0	0	0
F	0	0	0	0	0	10	0	0	0	0
G	0	0	0	0	0	0	10	0	0	0
H	0	0	0	0	0	0	10	0	0	0
I	0	0	0	0	0	0	0	0	8	2
J	0	0	0	0	0	0	0	0	0	10

A: Door B: Smoke1 C: Smoke2 D: Gas E: Entrance
F: Kettle G: Timer1 H: Timer2 I: Environment J: Speech

Table 5. Average values of softmax function for MFCC

	A	B	C	D	E	F	G	H	I	J
A	**0.75**	0.00	0.09	0.03	0.00	0.10	0.00	0.02	0.00	0.01
B	0.00	**0.81**	0.05	0.01	0.01	0.00	0.08	0.03	0.00	0.00
C	0.00	0.02	**0.85**	0.03	0.01	0.01	0.01	0.05	0.00	0.00
D	0.00	0.04	0.04	**0.85**	0.00	0.00	0.05	0.02	0.00	0.00
E	0.00	0.02	0.02	0.01	**0.76**	0.00	**0.15**	0.00	0.00	0.04
F	0.00	0.00	0.02	0.00	0.00	**0.95**	0.01	0.00	0.00	0.02
G	0.00	0.09	0.05	0.04	0.01	0.00	**0.73**	0.03	0.00	0.04
H	0.00	0.08	0.00	0.03	0.07	0.00	**0.65**	**0.16**	0.00	0.00
I	0.00	0.01	0.00	0.01	0.00	0.00	0.00	0.00	**0.59**	**0.39**
J	0.00	0.03	0.00	0.02	0.02	0.00	0.01	0.00	0.05	**0.87**

A: Door B: Smoke1 C: Smoke2 D: Gas E: Entrance
F: Kettle G: Timer1 H: Timer2 I: Environment J: Speech

4   Development of Alarm Sound Notification System

4.1   System Requirements and Configuration

Based on the results in Sect. 3, we judged that a learned model capable of classifying each alarm sound had been created, and designed and developed an alarm sound notification system using this learned model. We constructed a system to notify a target user terminal such as a smartphone of an alarm and its source, as shown in Fig. 6. Vibration of the user terminal notifies the user of the occurrence of an alarm, and its display shows the source.

Since the classifier must always be in the power ON state, it is important for the classifier to have a low power consumption, so a Raspberry Pi with Bluetooth was used

Table 6. Standard deviation of softmax function for MFCC

	A	B	C	D	E	F	G	H	I	J
A	**0.20**	0.04	0.02	0.00	0.00	**0.13**	0.02	0.01	0.00	0.00
B	0.00	0.03	0.03	0.01	0.00	0.00	0.01	0.04	0.00	0.00
C	0.00	0.01	0.03	0.01	0.00	0.01	0.01	0.01	0.00	0.01
D	0.00	0.02	0.06	**0.15**	0.00	0.01	0.02	0.08	0.00	0.01
E	0.00	0.00	0.00	0.00	**0.12**	0.00	0.08	0.00	0.03	0.05
F	0.00	0.00	0.07	0.00	0.01	**0.18**	0.04	0.00	0.05	0.03
G	0.00	0.01	0.01	0.00	0.01	0.02	0.06	0.01	0.01	0.03
H	0.00	0.07	0.03	0.01	0.00	0.00	0.01	0.07	0.00	0.01
I	0.00	0.00	0.00	0.00	0.01	0.00	0.02	0.00	**0.34**	**0.31**
J	0.00	0.01	0.01	0.00	0.04	0.01	0.08	0.00	**0.13**	**0.12**

A: Door B: Smoke1 C: Smoke2 D: Gas E: Entrance
F: Kettle G: Timer1 H: Timer2 I: Environment J: Speech

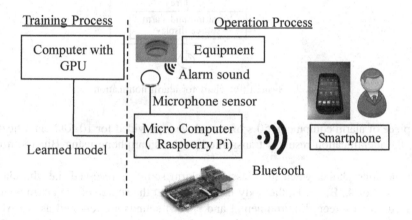

Fig. 6. Alarm notification system configuration

in this first prototype system. The learned model created in Sect. 3 was set up in the Raspberry Pi, which connects the microphone, and a smartphone was selected as the user terminal. The microphone is omnidirectional, and can be connected to the Raspberry Pi via USB, and is the same one used for data acquisition for the learning process.

4.2 System Design and Implementation

The system flowchart for activating the alarm sound is shown in Fig. 7. When an abnormality is detected, the alarm from the device continues to sound. It is necessary for the system to detect it and to notify the user as soon as possible. Therefore, in this prototype system, data acquired every 5 s was used, and the classification data was overlapped into 10 ms (duration 32 ms), that is, 500 pieces. Thus, 500 classification results are obtained, and the final result is determined by their majority decision. For

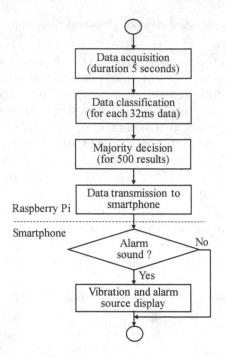

Fig. 7. System flowchart for alarm notification

each piece of alarm equipment, 50 s of sound were provided for 10-fold classification. Here, the identification result is transmitted to the smartphone using Bluetooth each time.

In the smartphone, when the classified alarm sound is received, i.e. the classification result of A, B, …, H, the body is vibrated and the source of the alarm sound is displayed on its screen. Environmental and speech sounds are reported as No Alarm.

The function of the smartphone that receives the classification result from Raspberry Pi by Bluetooth, makes its body vibrate, and displays the result, was implemented using MIT App Inventor 2 [8]. This development software provides functions to be implemented in a smartphone by dragging and dropping a visual representation of each instruction and function by using a graphical interface.

5   Initial System Evaluation

Initial evaluation of the alarm notification system composed in Sect. 4 was carried out. In this evaluation, the distance between the microphone sensor and each alarm sound source was 1 m, and the alarm sound to be classified was emitted continuously. Each 5 s of sound data from 8 types of alarm, and environmental and speech sounds were classified for evaluation.

An overview of the equipment used in the system is shown in Fig. 8. There are several of the sound-producing alarms, a microphone sensor, a Raspberry Pi, and a

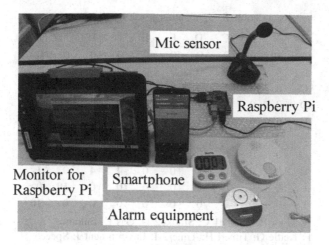

Fig. 8. Overview of components of alarm notification system

smartphone. The other device is a monitor for checking the output of the Raspberry Pi. As shown in this photo, very inexpensive equipment will suffice, so if a satisfactory level of classification performance can be secured there is a high possibility that a useful system can be realized for people with impaired hearing.

The classification experiments were carried out by implementing the learned model created by using power spectrum and MFCC in a Raspberry Pi. Results are shown in Tables 7 and 8 as a confusion matrix. There is little difference between the classification rates of 83.0% and 82.0%. In both cases, erroneous classification of timers 1 and 2 occurred. However, when MFCC was used, there was also misclassification of smoke 1 and the gas-alarm sound of smoke 2's alarm sound, while in power spectrum there was no additional error. For the 8 alarm sounds, the classification rate was 87.5% by power spectrum and 77.5% by MFCC. Although there were misclassification in

Table 7. Evaluation result by power spectrum

	A	B	C	D	E	F	G	H	I	J
A	**0.20**	0.04	0.02	0.00	0.00	**0.13**	0.02	0.01	0.00	0.00
B	0.00	0.03	0.03	0.01	0.00	0.00	0.01	0.04	0.00	0.00
C	0.00	0.01	0.03	0.01	0.00	0.01	0.01	0.01	0.00	0.01
D	0.00	0.02	0.06	**0.15**	0.00	0.01	0.02	0.08	0.00	0.01
E	0.00	0.00	0.00	0.00	**0.12**	0.00	0.08	0.00	0.03	0.05
F	0.00	0.00	0.07	0.00	0.01	**0.18**	0.04	0.00	0.05	0.03
G	0.00	0.01	0.01	0.00	0.01	0.02	0.06	0.01	0.01	0.03
H	0.00	0.07	0.03	0.01	0.00	0.00	0.01	0.07	0.00	0.01
I	0.00	0.00	0.00	0.00	0.01	0.00	0.02	0.00	**0.34**	**0.31**
J	0.00	0.01	0.01	0.00	0.04	0.01	0.08	0.00	**0.13**	**0.12**

A: Door B: Smoke1 C: Smoke2 D: Gas E: Entrance
F: Kettle G: Timer1 H: Timer2 I: Environment J: Speech

Table 8. Evaluation result by MFCC

	A	B	C	D	E	F	G	H	I	J
A	**10**	0	0	0	0	0	0	0	0	0
B	0	**10**	0	0	0	0	0	0	0	0
C	0	4	1	4	0	0	1	0	0	0
D	0	0	0	**10**	0	0	0	0	0	0
E	0	0	0	1	9	0	0	0	0	0
F	0	0	0	0	0	8	0	0	0	2
G	0	0	0	0	0	0	**10**	0	0	0
H	0	0	0	1	0	0	4	4	0	1
I	0	0	0	0	0	0	0	0	**10**	0
J	0	0	0	0	0	0	0	0	0	**10**

A: Door B: Smoke1 C: Smoke2 D: Gas E: Entrance
F: Kettle G: Timer1 H: Timer2 I: Environment J: Speech

Fig. 9. Example of alarm display of smartphone

environmental and speech sounds when using power spectrum, this error is not a problem in terms of the required functions of the proposed system. From this result, it can be said that better performance can be obtained by using power spectrum when these particular alarm sounds are to be discriminated.

An example of the alarm display of the smartphone is shown in Fig. 9. Although there was classification error, it was confirmed that there was no problem in the operation of the system.

6 Conclusion

In this paper, we described a method for classifying various alarm sound sources and evaluated their classification performance using eight kinds of alarm sounds as well as conversational voice and environmental sounds. Then we proposed an alarm sound notification system using the created learned model, actually constructed the system as a prototype, and confirmed its basic functionality. We will conduct detailed evaluations and examine methods for enhancing accuracy in noisier environments. This time, the distance between the sound source and the microphone sensor was 1 m, and only two kinds of sound were involved: normal room sounds and speech sounds as the peripheral sound environment at the time of classification. In an actual life space, there will also be noises due to music, home appliance operation, etc. Improvement of classification performance and examination of evaluation methods considering various kinds of noises are future tasks.

References

1. Hearing Impairment Supplies Guide. https://moo-haya.ssl-lolipop.jp/nancho/kasai.html. Accessed 2 Jan 2019. (in Japanese)
2. "Warning light" informing people with hearing disorder. https://www.tbsradio.jp/13060. Accessed 26 Jan 2019. (in Japanese)
3. Graves, A., Mohamed, A., Hinton, G.: Speech recognition with deep recurrent neural networks. In: IEEE International Conference on Acoustics, Speech and Signal Processing, 5 p. (2013)
4. Bahdanau, D., Cho, K., Bengio, Y.: Neural machine translation by jointly learning to align and translate. In: The International Conference on Learning Representations, pp. 1–15 (2015)
5. Carmel, D., Yeshurun, A., Moshe, Y.: Detection of alarm sounds in noisy environments. In: 25th European Signal Processing Conference (EUSIPCO), 5 p. (2017)
6. Raboshchuk, G., Nadeu, C., Jancovic, P., Lilja, A.: A knowledge-based approach to automatic detection of equipment alarm sounds in a neonatal intensive care unit environment. IEEE J. Transl. Eng. Health Med. 6, 10 (2018)
7. Speech Signal Processing Toolkit (SPTK). http://sp-tk.sourceforge.net/. Accessed 26 Jan 2019
8. MIT App Inventor | Explore MIT App Inventor. http://appinventor.mit.edu/explore/. Accessed 26 Jan 2019

High Sensitivity Layer Feature Analysis in Food Market

Yoshio Matsuyama[✉] and Yumi Asahi

School of Information and Telecommunication Engineering,
Department of Management System Engineering,
Tokai University, Shibuya, Japan
6bjm2110@mail.u-tokai.ac.jp, asahi@tsc.u-tokai.ac.jp

Abstract. It is not uncommon to conduct test marketing for the purpose of market research when dropping new products to the market. However, if you actually drop it you will need a lot of money. This study, we pay attention to innovation theory. In Japan, the study reported a long sales period. However, the study didn't report a short sales period. Therefore, we report of a short sales period, especially food. This study, we call "High Sensitivity Layer" the innovators and the early adopters in innovation theory in term of to be interested in the innovation of products, sensitive to trends and constantly collecting new information by themselves and to have greater influence on other consumers. We think that those that collect a lot of empathy in the "High Sensitivity Layer" are diffusive in the innovators and the early adopters, and grab the characteristics of highly sensitive consumers who gather many empathies. I think that it may be able to fulfill the purpose of test marketing by seeing the response of new products of food to this consumer. We prepare a generalized model with a deep learning model and report features of highly sensitive consumers, visually and numerically clearly, using decision tree analysis from that model. From the analysis results, attached more images, and the older, the better it got a report that empathizes with sensitive consumers. When conducting test marketing, it is predicted that high-sensitivity consumers will be able to obtain preferable results by targeting people with this characteristic. Also, it was found that gender and emotion are not related to the characteristics of the person who writes the report sympathized with the consumer. In the future, I would like to further accurate classification by text mining of posted characters and analysis of posted images.

Keywords: Innovation theory · Test marketing · High sensitivity layer · Deep learning · Decision tree analysis · Foods marketing

1 Introduction

In this study, we analyze characteristics of highly sensitive consumers who write reports diffusive in the food market. You will be wondering why this analysis was done. We focused on innovation theory. In the first place, innovation theory was proposed by Professor Rogers in 1962. This theory has been successful in a wide range of fields including communication, agriculture, public health, criminal justice, and marketing. In Japan, Morio (2012) has reported that "the appropriateness of companies

© Springer Nature Switzerland AG 2019
S. Yamamoto and H. Mori (Eds.): HCII 2019, LNCS 11570, pp. 232–243, 2019.
https://doi.org/10.1007/978-3-030-22649-7_19

in introducing new kinds of unique vegetables" is researched. In this study, long sales periods are assumed. Therefore, we target foods that can develop short ones. From innovation theory, if it can be disseminated to Innovators and Early Adopters, it is known that leading to Early Majority and Late Majority (Fig. 1), the market share will rise significantly (Fig. 2).

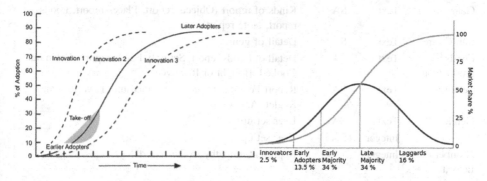

Fig. 1. Diffusion process   **Fig. 2.** Category classification

The characteristics of the Innovator and Early Adopter are that they are interested in product innovation and are sensitive to trends and constantly collect new information themselves and have a great influence on other consumers. In this study, these two layers are called "High Sensitivity Layer". We think that "High Sensitivity Layer" with keeping them eyes open, and products that them sympathize will diffusion from the innovation theory to the Early and Late Majority and the market share is expanded to expand. We think that those that collect a lot of empathy in the "High Sensitivity Layer" are diffusive in the innovators and the early adopters, and grab the characteristics of highly sensitive consumers who gather many empathies. I think that it may be able to fulfill the purpose of test marketing by seeing the response of new products of food to this consumer. In this study, we report characteristics of highly sensitive consumers.

2   Data Summary

In this study, we used "Minrepo Data" from INTAGE Inc. distributed by IDR Dataset Service of National Institute of Informatics. We analyzed the report posted on the living post & enterprise co-creation SNS (Social Networking Service) application "Minrepo". In this analysis, the data shown in Table 1 was mainly used among the data included in the report. In this study, 6,367 reports with genre "Foods report" and type "Bought or Received" were targeted. The used data period is from January 1, 2016 to June 30, 2016. The Minrepo official website says (2018), "High quality word of mouth contributions gather, which expresses products more attractive with high sensitivity consumers from photos and comments", "real life actuality data". That is, the Minrepo is an SNS where realistic living conditions data of high sensitivity consumers gather. The

Table 1. Mainly used variables

Variables name	Data type1	Data type2	Details
Image file1	Text	FA	Name of image file
Image file2	Text	FA	Name of image file
Image file3	Text	FA	Name of image file
Genre	Text	SA	Kinds of report (Objects report, Places report, Foods report, Note report)
Sub Genre	Text	SA	Detail of genre
Foods report type	Text	SA	Detail of Foods report. Set only Foods report. (Eaten out, Cooked, Bought or Received)
Feelings	Text	SA	Report Feelings (Excitement, Pleasure, Favorite, Puzzle, Reglet, Angry)
Gender	Text	SA	User set up
Age	Integer	SA	User set up
Number of favorite	Integer	–	Represent empathy to the report
Number of wish	Integer	–	Number entered in other user's wish list
Number of activity	Integer	–	Number tapped by people who did similar actions

high sensitivity sensitive consumer's post "Reports" of "Minrepo users" will receive responses from the same highly sensitive consumers.

The posting of this SNS resemble Tweet of the famous Twitter post, and it is posted when there is something the submitter is interested in or what he/she wishes to teach. The point different from Twitter is that there is no limit on the number of characters, and emotion at posting can be added. Figure 3 shows the number of characters for each report. From this Fig. 3, even if there is no limit on the number of characters, it is understood that about 50% of people contribute with the number of characters of 100 characters or less. Of the remaining people, about 45% of the people have posted within 300 characters, and as a whole, about 95% of people can confirm that they post within 300 characters. Figure 4 shows the gender of each report. From this Fig. 4, it is found that posting about food is about 20%, more women than men. Figure 5 shows the age group for each posted report. While SNS such as Twitter and Instagram has many young people, this Minrepo accounts for about 75% at the age of 35 to 50, and about 15% at 15 to 30 years old shows that there are few young people. Figure 6 shows the percentage of emotions when posting a report. It is understood that the report which posted about food just like a soliloquy without emotion accounted for about a quarter. Looking at the proportion of the remaining emotions, we can see that positive emotions account for about 70% of the total. Conversely, only 3% of the negative emotions are present, and when you come up with something happy, you can confirm that the report is very often posted.

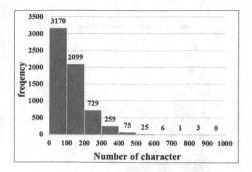

Fig. 3. Number of characters

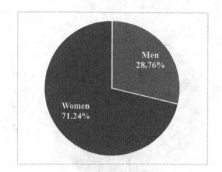

Fig. 4. Gender proportion

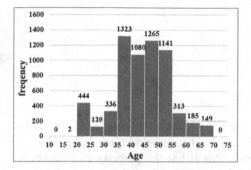

Fig. 5. Age distribution

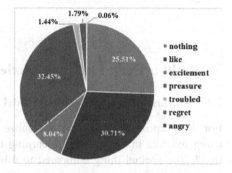

Fig. 6. Feelings proportion

The data used in this study included image files, but we created a variable (Number of images) simply counting the number of attached images. Figure 7 shows the ratio of the number of attached images in all reports. There are almost no reports with 0 attached images, and only one report accounts for about 55%. About 22% each report attached 2, 3 images, it turned out that many people attached multiple images.

On the popularity tab of Minrepo, reports posted within 3 days are sorted in descending order of "favorites" and introduced. Reports that are loaded at one time occupy more than 10 favorites. Figure 8 shows the distribution of Number of favorites in the overall report. It is worth noting here that the number of favorites shown in Fig. 8 is the total value since posting. The size of that number has no meaning. It is important that Number of favorites exceeds 10 within 3 days. In this study, we define "empathy report" for favorite number of 10 or more, and "non-empathetic report" for less than 10 favorites.

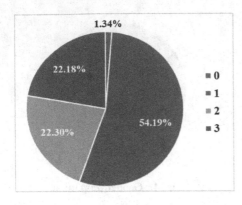

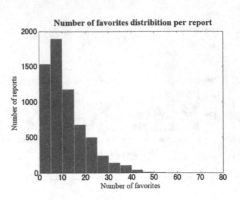

Fig. 7. Proportion of the number of attached images

Fig. 8. Gender proportion

3 Build a Deep Learning Model

3.1 Outline of Deep Learning Model

For the purpose of creating a generalized model, we prepare a deep learning model using the data in Sect. 2. Deep learning is "a type of parametric function approximation". The special thing compared to others is that it has the property that "arbitrary functions can be approximated with arbitrary precision by using a large parameter set". This property is a property not found in the linear model. Learning is conducted with the "empathy report" and "non-empathy report" defined in Sect. 2 as objective variables. The deep learning model built in this study is a classified model of binary categories in supervised learning. From the data we handle, we use a network structure called Multi-layer perceptron (Fig. 9) to construct a deep learning model. The perceptron was developed by Rosenblatt (1958). For the explanatory variable, select "number of images", "emotion", "gender", "age".

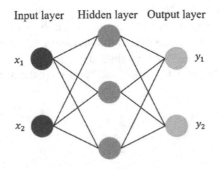

Fig. 9. Architecture of multi-layer perceptron

The purpose of this research is to predict the probability (1) of which category from the binary classification by logistic regression.

$$P(\hat{y}^{(i)} = \{0,1\}|x^{(i)}) = \textbf{softmax}(Wx^{(i)} + b)\#$$ (1)

At this time, $x^{(i)}$ is the input, the parenthesized superscript is the data number, $\hat{y}^{(i)}$ is the output. Also, the coupling weight W is a (C, D) matrix and the bias term b is a C dimensional vector (C: number of categories, D: dimension of each data point). The accuracy of the deep learning model is improved by adjusting the parameter $\{W, b\}$ to be close to supervised data. The softmax function is a function that returns d probability values with the d-dimensional vector as an argument, and is represented by (2).

$$\text{softmax}(v)_i = \frac{\exp(v_i)}{\sum_{i=1}^{d} \exp(v_i)}\#$$ (2)

The probability value thus obtained and the observation value of the actual category $\{c^{(i)}\}_{i=1}^{N_{data}}$ are measured by the smallness of the cross entropy loss function (3), and adjusts parameters. We aim to minimize loss function by stochastic gradient descent method.

$$L = -\sum_{i=1}^{N_{data}} \log(P(\hat{y}^{(i)} = \{0,1\}|x^{(i)}))\#$$ (3)

In the logistic regression described above, there was only one pair of coupling weight W and bias term b for performing linear transformation as a parameter. In a multilayer perceptron with k hidden layers, there are $(k+1)$ combining weights and biases, and they convert the input $h^0 = x$ to (4).

$$h^1 = \text{activate}_1(W^1 h^0 + b^1)(h^0 = x)$$
$$h^2 = \text{activate}_2(W^2 h^1 + b^2)$$
$$\vdots$$
$$h^k = \text{activate}_k(W^k h^{k-1} + b^k)$$
$$h = Wh^k + b$$

(4)

h^0 is the input layer, h^k is the hidden layer k, h is the output layer.

There are "wish count" and "number of activities" as responses to the report, but these two are attached to the "favorite" report and are not explanatory variables. One of the things to keep in mind when asking explanatory variables is the problem of multiple collinearity. This is a problem especially in multiple regression analysis. However, according to Yoshida (1987), multicollinearity is said to be an essential problem that the correlation matrix is not regular when there is a correlation between explanatory variables, so that the solution cannot be obtained or is unstable. In this study, regularization by Dropout is carried out, prevention of over learning and prevention of multiple collinearity are also done Srivastava et al. (2014) has shown the prevention of over-learning by regularization..

As a precaution, look at the relationship between explanatory variables here. From the scale of explanatory variable (Table 2), use Spearman's rank correlation coefficient for ordinal scale and ratio scale, correlation ratio on nominal scale, ordinal scale nominal scale, ratio scale, and Cramer's coefficient of association for nominal scale. The results are shown in Table 3.

Table 2. Scale chart

Explanatory variable	Scale
Number of images	Ordinal scale
Feelings	Nominal scale
Gender	Nominal scale
Age	Ratio scale

Table 3. Relationship between explanatory variables

variable 1	variable 2	Rank correlation coefficient
images	age	0.15

variable 1	variable 2	Coefficient of association
feelings	gender	0.07

variable 1	variable 2	Correlation ratio
feelings	images	0.04
feelings	age	0.06
gender	images	0.00
gender	age	0.13

3.2   Hyper Parameter Setting

In order to create a deep learning model, it is necessary to set a large number of hyperparameters. First of all, for learning of this model, 80% (5,094 cases) of the total 6,367 reports were used for learning and the remaining 20% (1,237 cases) were used for verification.

Next, we set the number of hidden layers in a multi-layer perceptron. According to Asakawa (2014), if there is only one hidden layer, we can solve only linearly identifiable problems, so we know that at least two or more hidden layers are needed. Also, according to Nielsen (2014), as the number of hidden layers increases, the stochastic gradient descent method is said to cause gradient disappearance problem/instability of gradient, so increase the number of hidden layers too much. For these reasons, we set two hidden layers in this model.

In each hidden layer, it is necessary to set three hyperparameters of "output dimension number", "activation function", and "dropout ratio". In this model, three parameters are set by Bayesian optimization for Accuracy in confusion matrix.

Finally, set up learning. In the multi-layer perceptron, it is necessary to set parameters for proceeding learning of "optimization function", "learning rate", "epochs" and "mini-batch size".

We compare accuracy with representative "Adam", "SimpleSGD", "AdaDelta", "AdaGrad", "RMSprop". This is because the optimum optimization function differs depending on the data to be used. The optimization function selects an optimization function with a high rate of accuracy (Needless to say, the other parameters are the same). From Table 4, the optimization function of this model sets "AdaDelta".

According to Taguchi (1998), if the learning rate is increased, the convergence of the error becomes faster, but it becomes unstable. When it is decreased, the stability of error increases but it is said that it takes time to converge. However, in this model, since "AdaDelta" was set as the optimization function, it became unnecessary to set the initial value learning rate. The details are described in detail by developer Zeiler (2012). In fact, even if the learning rate was greatly changed and compared, the change in the correct answer rate was not recognized (Table 5). In order to do learning it is necessary to set the learning rate, so the default value of 0.0001 is set in this model.

Regarding the mini-batch size, it is preferable to divide it into 2^n for memory access efficiency. The smaller the size is, the higher the accuracy rate increases, but the overfitting becomes more likely to occur.In this model, we change the value from 128 to 64, 64 to 32 with the default value of 64 as a reference, and set 64 which was high effect (Table 6).

The epochsis the number that learns one training data repeatedly. In deep learning, parameters are learned by learning training data repeatedly, so it is necessary to take many epochs to the extent that over learning does not occur. Santos (2007) reports on the error caused by taking too many epoch numbers. Therefore, we set epochs using Early stopping method. Early stopping is a method proposed by Prechelt (1998). Early Stopping is to stop learning when errors begin to converge. This makes it possible to stop learning so as not to overfitting. In this model, we set 100 which the error began converging to the epochs.

In this model, we made the above setting and finally got a model that gains 73.3% accuracy.

Table 4. Accuracy for each optimization function

Optimization function	Adam	Simple SGD	AdaDelta	AdaGrad	RMSprop
Accracy		0.72536	0.68	0.73263	0.64	0.72

Table 5. Accuracy for each learning rate

Learning rate	0.001	0.0001	0.00001
Accuracy	0.73263	0.73263	0.73263

Table 6. Accuracy for each mini-batch size

Mini-batch size	32	64	128
Accuracy	0.73380	0.73263	0.72556

4 Decision Tree Analysis

In Sect. 3, a deep learning model was created. In this section, we report features of highly sensitive consumers, visually and numerically clearly, using decision tree analysis from that model. A positive feature of decision tree analysis is that it is easy to interpret the output result, it is possible to handle various scales for explanatory variable/objective variable. The primary reason for using decision tree analysis is that the classification process can be visualized in an easy-to-understand manner. Of course, there are not only good things but also negative features. The analysis is likely to over-adapt and the generalization performance may be lowered. Overfitting refers to excessive learning of the observed data, which also sensitively reacts to noise, which means that the fitness to unknown data worsens. As mentioned earlier, since it is top priority to visualize the classification process in an easy-to-understand manner, we will make efforts to minimize excessive adaptation. The reason for creating a deep learning model is also to make observation data closer to true category and to improve generalization performance.

The explanatory variables used in this model have values as shown in Table 7. Apply this model created as a generalized model, predict which "empathy report" or "Non-empathetic report" will be written and analyze the binary features predicted by decision tree analysis. Table 8 shows the settings used for the decision tree analysis. After creating the decision tree model, we pruned for the purpose of improving generalization performance.

Table 7. Value to be taken by explanatory variable

Images	Feelings	Gender	Age
0	Nothing	Men	16
1	Like	Women	17
2	Excitement		·
3	Preasure		·
	Troubled		·
	Regret		68
	Angry		69

Table 8. Setting of decision tree analysis.

Explanatory variable	Max buranch	Parameter	Contents
Number of images	5	Objective variable	Empathy or non-empathetic
Feelings	Unlimited	Branching method	Gini coefficient
Gender	Unlimited	Min number of data	0.80%
Age	5	Max branch (common)	5
		Node impurity	0.01
		Height limit	Unlimited
		Weighting	Nothing

The Gini coefficient of the branching method is defined by (5).

$$\text{Gini coefficient} = 1 - \sum_{i-1}^{c} p_i^2 \# \tag{5}$$

Figure 10 shows the results of the decision tree analysis. In this model, it is important to see the state of branching and the proportion of each class. For example, when the number of attached images is 1 or less, it is found that the ratio of Non-empathetic report is 92.7% and if the number of attached images is 1 or less, it is almost written a Non-empathetic report. In the other hand, when the number of attached

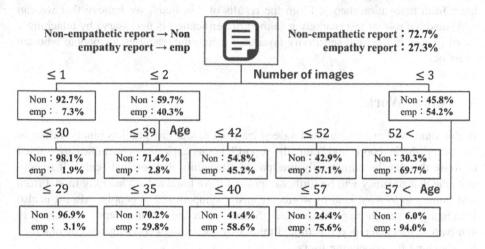

Fig. 10. Result of decision tree analysis

images is 3, and when the age exceeds 57 years old, you can find that you write almost empathy report.

5 Discussion

Based on the results of the decision tree analysis, it is found that the report is more likely to be empathized as the number of images is larger. Reports that only 0 and 1 images are attached are classified as non-empathetic reports by 92.7%. Therefore, 2 or more images are necessary as the first condition of the empathy report. It is understood that visual information has more information amount than simple text data, and it is easy to acquire empathy.

Next, in the group with a large proportion of "empathy report", the report attached with 2 images shows that the age is 43 years old or more, and the report attached with 3 images shows that the age is 36 years old or over. Under the condition that there are two or more attached images, it turns out that people who are years old can acquire empathy more easily. Also, from the result of the decision tree analysis, it is understood that the more the age, the more the proportion of the empathy report is increasing.

Conversely, 97% or more is classified as non-empathic report at the age of 30 or under even if the number of images is 2 or 3. If the number of images is 2 and 39 years old, if the number of images is 3, 70% or more are classified as non-empathy report even under 35 years old. Therefore, writing an easy-to-empathy report is understood from the "Arafor" (Arafor: Referring to people, aged around 40).

In addition, the explanatory variable contains emotion and gender in addition to the number of images and age. Emotions and gender were not recognized as such important conditions from the model created in this study.

When developing a new product of food, it is necessary to care about the sensitive layer from innovation theory. From the results of this study, we believe that we can withstand the role of test marketing (although verification is necessary) by attaching a lot of images in the high sensitivity layer and seeing the reactions for people who are years old.

6   Future Work

In this time, we have constructed a deep learning model that predicts binary values of "non-empathetic report" and "empathy report", but its explanatory variables are limited to those that can be numerically interpreted (including the nominal scale). It is conceivable that accuracy will be further improved if we build a deep learning model from text mining as to what kind of words are easily sympathized to people. Also, it is also interesting to search empathize words. Since I searched whether reports are easy to sympathize for each report this time, I think that interesting knowledge can be obtained by searching by associating users.

In addition, this time data included image files. Since the importance of the image is indicated also from the result of the decision tree analysis, I want to verify what type of image is easily sympathized by carrying out image tagging with AI or the like and performing text mining.

Finally, we decided to use the decision tree analysis with the highest priority for ease of interpretation. There is a logistic regression analysis as a binary classification model, so I would like to verify this as well.

References

Rogers, E.M.: Diffusion of Innovations, 3rd edn. Macmillan Publishers, London (1962)

Morio, A.: Suitability of companies when introducing distinctive new vegetables varieties-a case study of new varieties of sweet potato. Bull. Naro Agric. Res. Center (17), 39–48 (2012)

INTAGE Inc. Minrepo Campaign. https://www.intage.co.jp/solution/process/product-development/minrepocp. Accessed 20 Oct 2018

INTAGE Inc. Minrepo SNS analysis. https://www.intage.co.jp/solution/process/market/minreposns. Accessed 20 Oct 2018

Rosenblatt, F.: The perceptron: a probabilistic model for information storage and organization in the brain. Psychol. Rev. **65**(6), 386–408 (1958)

Yoshida, M.: Multicollinearity and ridge regression in regression analysis. Fac. Hum. Sci. Bull. **13**, 227–242 (1987)

Srivastava, N., Hinton, G., Krizhevsky, A., Sutskever, I., Salakhutdinov, R.: Dropout: a simple way to prevent neural networks from overfitting. J. Mach. Learn. Res. **15**, 1929–1958 (2014)

Asakawa, S.: Deep learning and the meanings of hidden layer. In: The 12th Annual Convention of the Japanese Society for Cognitive Psychology Bibliography, p. 28 (2014)

Nielsen, M.A.: Neural Networks and Deep Learning. Determination Press (2014)

Taguchi, I.: The convergence condition and learning acceleration in the backpropagation neural network. Keiai Univ. Int. Res. (2), 77–109 (1998)

Zeiler, M.D.: Ada delta-an adaptive learning rate method. Cornell University (2012)

Prechelt, L.: Early Stopping – but when? Fakultät für Informatik; Universität Karlsruhe, pp 55–69 (1998)

Santos, J.M.: Data classification with neural networks and entropic criteria. Universidade da Beira Interior Tese de doutoramento (2007)

Construction of a Prediction Model for Pharmaceutical Patentability Using Nonlinear SVM

Kei Miyaoka[1](✉) and Takako Akakura[2]

[1] Graduate School of Engineering, Tokyo University of Science, 6-3-1 Niijuku, Katsushika-ku, Tokyo 125-8585, Japan
4415089@ed.tus.ac.jp
[2] Faculty of Engineering, Tokyo University of Science, 6-3-1 Niijuku, Katsushika-ku, Tokyo 125-8585, Japan
akakura@rs.tus.ac.jp

Abstract. The Japanese Patent Act follows a first-to-file principle, so it is crucial that important patent applications must be filed earlier than those by other inventors. However, inventors will not be awarded a patent if the description of the invention in the application is insufficient. Regarding this problem, a previous study investigated use of logistic regression in a prediction model for patentability (probability of acquiring patent rights). However, that model used linear discrimination, so the discrimination accuracy was not high. To increase prediction accuracy, this study instead uses a nonlinear support vector machine (SVM) in the predictive model for patentability. Evaluation experiments using the SVM model show that the prediction accuracy of the SVM-based model is better than that of the model used in the previous research. These results suggested that a nonlinear SVM model is effective for constructing a prediction model for pharmaceutical patentability.

Keywords: Patentability · SVM · Nonlinear

1 Introduction

Our civilization is supported by various devices, and patent rights protect rights related to the invention of those devices. Patent rights assign exclusive rights for the implementation of inventions to their inventors as a reward for their contribution to the development of industry. It is therefore important to obtain patent rights for use of one's inventions. Patent rights are particularly important for companies focused on technology development. According to a survey of patent applications filed with the Japanese Patent Office in FY2017, the number of patent applications is increasing in 11 of 18 industries [1]. These figures suggest the high importance of patent rights.

The pharmaceutical industry has a special relationship with patent rights in two ways. First, the fundamental research and clinical studies for drug development require about 9–17 years, with research and development investments of

S. Yamamoto and H. Mori (Eds.): HCII 2019, LNCS 11570, pp. 244–253, 2019.
https://doi.org/10.1007/978-3-030-22649-7_20

20 to 50 billion yen and success probabilities as low as 1 in 20,000 [2]. However, successful development of a new drug can result in huge profits. According to a 2017 IQVIA survey, the ten best-selling domestic drugs had sales of over 60 billion yen per year [3]. Each pharmaceutical patent is therefore extremely important.

Second, pharmaceutical patents require special systems and examinations. Because pharmaceutical inventions require long periods for experiments, manufacturing, and marketing approval, there is a possibility that patent rights cannot be implemented during the twenty-year duration of an awarded patent. Patent durations can therefore be extended by up to five years. The Japanese Patent Office establishes patent examination guidelines for medical fields [4]. In general, it is difficult to determine from the structure and name of a pharmaceutical invention what it does and how to use it. A description of the results of pharmacological experiments must therefore be provided, following the examination guidelines.

Despite the pharmaceutical industry's special relationship with patent rights, problems can arise when filing a patent. The Japanese Patent Act follows a first-to-file principle, so important patent applications must be filed earlier than other inventors. However, inventors will not be awarded a patent if the description of the invention in the application is insufficient. In the pharmaceutical industry in particular, the time and money required for R&D and pharmaceutical preparations call for early patent applications. An evaluation index for descriptions of the invention in a patent application is necessary to solve this problem.

We propose construction of a prediction model for pharmaceutical patentability using a nonlinear support vector machine (SVM) to improve prediction accuracy over that of a model proposed in previous research, described below. Specifically, we extract description features and correct labels from the Japanese Unexamined Patent Application Publication (2006) for pharmaceutical preparations, and input them into the SVM.

2   Previous Research

2.1   Patentability

It is difficult to immediately judge whether applicant descriptions meet criteria for novelty, progress, and so on. Therefore, Hido et al. [5] introduced "patentability" as an evaluation criterion for patents. Patentability describes the likelihood of a patent being awarded, with higher scores suggesting increased likelihood that patent description requirements are met.

2.2   Target Data

To construct their patentability prediction model, Hido et al. created correctly labeled data from the Japanese Unexamined Patent Application Publication. These data were extracted from about 300,000 patent applications filed between

1989 and 1998. These data show whether a patent was actually granted or denied for each application. In this study, we constructed a prediction model from data with correct labels by using the statistical characteristics of the description, word age, syntactic complexity, and term frequency–inverse document frequency (TF–IDF). These features are calculated for each description, and the resulting values are input to the model as an explanatory variable vector. Figure 1 shows an overview of model construction. For each description, Hido et al. prepared correct labels and feature sets for patentability to construct their prediction model. In contrast, we prepared a prediction model in which explanatory variables are varied, and conducted accuracy evaluation experiments. The following four prediction models were prepared.

- Model 1: Statistical characteristics of the description
- Model 2: Statistical characteristics of the description + word age
- Model 3: Statistical characteristics of the description + word age + syntax complexity
- Model 4: Statistical characteristics of the description + word age + syntax complexity + TF–IDF

Experiments were carried out by ten-fold cross validation using the area under the curve (AUC) value as the model evaluation value. In these experiments, the evaluation value for model 1 was 0.594. The highest accuracy was obtained from model 4 with all features added, which produced an evaluation value of 0.607.

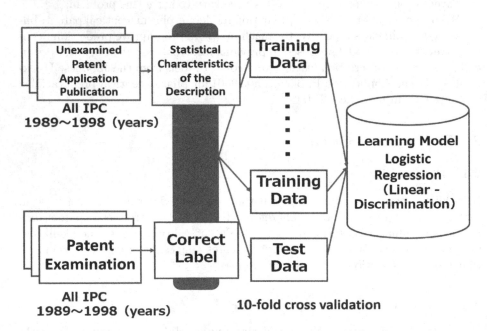

Fig. 1. Model 1 (previous research)

2.3   Limitations of the Previous Research

Hido et al.'s research established a patentability prediction model using logistic regression for all patents from 1989 to 1998. The previous research had two problems.

First was an inability to construct a patentability prediction model applicable to all patents. Models were divided into eight types A–H according to the International Patent Classification (IPC) item in the description. The word information, word age, and effective statistical characteristics in the description varied greatly for each IPC, so target data had to be limited.

The second problem is that their patentability prediction model used a logistic model regression that is weak to separate nonlinear problems. Since this logistic regression model makes it difficult to nonlinearly discriminate features, prediction accuracy tends to decrease. The present research aims at solving these two problems.

3   Proposed Model

3.1   Features

We constructed a prediction model for pharmaceutical patentability using statistical characteristics of the description, which is an explanatory variable derived from structure and sentences in the description. We used the explanatory variable set used by Hido et al. and Nagata et al., along with the number of examples of pharmacological examinations related to the examination guidelines for medical fields. Table 1 shows the features used in this study.

Table 1. Statistical characteristics for the description

Number of characters in description	Number of claims
Number of characters in all claims	Number of characters in claim 1
Number of figures and tables	Number of IPC combinations
Number of characters in Detailed Description of the Invention	Number of inventors
Number of cited references	Number of "Examples of Pharmacological Examination"
Number of "Domestic Priorities"	Number of "Priorities under the Paris Convention"

3.2   Correct Label

We extracted patentability from patent examination data in the description of pharmaceutical patents. Table 2 shows correct patentability labels. When applied to the logistic regression model, 1 indicates an awarded patent, and 0 a declined patent. When applied to SVM, 1 indicates an awarded patent, and −1 a declined patent.

3.3   Scaling

Features are scaled to mean 0 and standard deviation 1. This scaling makes it possible to prevent information loss in the inner product of the kernel function features.

Table 2. Correct label

Examination status for patent applications				
Application	Request for exam	Examination decision	Request for appeal	Trail
Submitted	Requested	Approved		
		Rejected	Requested	Approved before trial
				Approved
				Rejected
				In progress
				Withdrawn
			Pending	
			Rejection confirmed	
		In progress		
		Withdrawn		
	Pending		Patentability: Available	
	Expired		Patentability: Not available	

3.4   Under-Sampling

Under-sampling was applied because there was bias in the obtained data for correct answer labels. Under-sampling is a method of randomly extracting from majority data to match numbers of minority data. In this study, we extracted 1,834 data for awarded patents from among 3,492 data, in accordance with the no-patent-awarded data, and treated the total as 3,668 data.

3.5   Overview of SVM

We constructed the prediction model using SVM. SVM is a method of constructing a two-class pattern classifier that learns parameters from margin maximization in a training sample. Margin maximization determines the hyperplane in which the Euclidean distance is maximal with respect to the one closest to the other class (a support vector) in the learning data. The target Euclidean distance is called the "margin," represented as $|w|^{-1}$. Maximizing the margin allows minimization of the discrimination error for the undersampling data. To find the optimal hyperplane with the largest margin, we calculate the parameter that minimizes a cost function (here, Eq. (1)) under a constraint condition (Eq. (2)). In this study, we used a soft margin and the kernel trick as SVM methods. We describe each below.

$$\min : \frac{1}{2}\|w\|^2 \tag{1}$$

$$\text{sub.to} : t_i(w^T x_i + b) \geq 1 \tag{2}$$

3.6   Soft Margin

Soft-margin SVM is a method for relaxing constraints to allow some error. Relaxing constraint conditions allows for acceptable results even when the margin is not maximal. Therefore, it can be applied even when separation fails. To find the optimal soft-margin hyperplane, we calculate the parameter value that minimizes the cost function (Eq. (3)) under a constraint condition (Eq. (4)).

$$\min : \frac{1}{2}||w||^2 + C\sum_{i=1}^{N} \xi_i \tag{3}$$

$$\text{sub.to} : t_i(w^T x_i + b) \geq 1 - \xi_i, \xi_i \geq 0 \tag{4}$$

Parameter C is a constant that determines the balance between the magnitude of the margin and the degree of protrusion.

3.7   Kernel Trick

The kernel trick is a method of linearly discriminating feature vectors after nonlinear transformation to deal with nonlinearity problems. In ordinary SVM, it is not always possible to construct a classifier with high performance in intrinsically nonlinear, complex discrimination problems. With the kernel trick, however, it is possible to construct an optimum discrimination function using kernel calculations only, by mapping to a higher dimension. To find the optimal discrimination function, we maximize a cost function (Eq. (5)) under a constraint condition (Eq. (6)).

$$\max : \sum_{i=1}^{N} \alpha_i - \frac{1}{2}\sum_{i,j=1}^{N} \alpha_i \alpha_j y_i y_j K(x_i, x_j) \tag{5}$$

$$\text{sub.to} : 0 \leq \alpha_i \leq C, \sum_{i=1}^{N} y_i \alpha_i = 0 \tag{6}$$

The K in the second term is called the "kernel." In this study, we used the radial basis function (RBF) kernel (Eq. (7)).

$$K(x_i, x_j) = \exp(-\gamma||x_i - x_j||^2) \tag{7}$$

3.8   Study Model

Figure 2 shows an overview of the model construction. We divide statistical characteristics for the description and the correct labels into training data and test data, and input these into the SVM. Furthermore, we adjusted the C and γ parameters in Eqs. (6) and (7) to construct the optimal hyperplane. This resulted in a prediction model for pharmaceutical patentability that allowed for nonlinear discrimination.

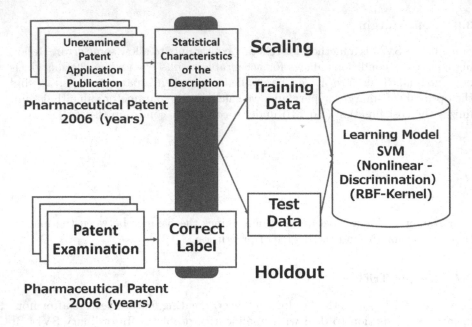

Fig. 2. Study model

4   Overview of the Experiment

4.1   Target Data

In this study, we collected 14 types of patents related to pharmaceutical preparations. We used 5,326 Unexamined Patent Application Publications published
between January 1 and December 31, 2006, along with data describing whether
these applications resulted in an awarded patent. By under-sampling, it was possible to acquire 3,668 Unexamined Patent Application Publications from these
data. We used 2006 data because the eighth edition of the IPC used in Japan
was issued in 2006, and data associated with that edition are most numerous.

4.2   Evaluation

We used AUC to evaluate accuracy. AUC is defined as the area between the
vertical and horizontal axes of the receiver operating characteristic (ROC) curve
plotting the true positive rate (TPR) and the false positive rate (FPR). This
value ranges from 0 to 1, with proximity to 1 indicating increased accuracy.
Where classification is impossible, the value is defined as 0.5. TPR is the ratio
of values judged as positive when the true class is positive. FPR is the ratio of
values incorrectly judged as positive despite the true class being negative.

5   Results and Discussion

5.1   Search for Parameters

To find the optimum parameters, we searched parameter C at 0.1 intervals in the range $1 \leq C \leq 10$ and parameter γ in the range $1 \leq \gamma \leq 10$ at 0.01 intervals. Table 3 and Fig. 3 show the experimental results. Table 3 shows that we construct the best hyperplane when $C = 2.0$ and $\gamma = 7.6$. Figure 3 shows that smaller values of C are more likely to be affected by γ, and it can be discriminated by using appropriate support vectors.

5.2   Comparison of Prediction Models

Table 4 and Fig. 4 show the experimental results when using SVM. As the figure shows, the AUC value for logistic regression was 0.566, and the AUC value with SVM was 0.701. The SVM model thus improved accuracy by 0.107 compared with the 0.594 result by Hido et al. The AUC value improved because the logistic regression model linearly discriminates the feature space as it is, whereas the SVM model is linearly separated by mapping to a higher-dimensional feature space by nonlinear transformation. Therefore, an SVM capable of nonlinear

Table 3. Best parameters and AUC

Model	C	γ	AUC
SVM	2	7.6	0.701

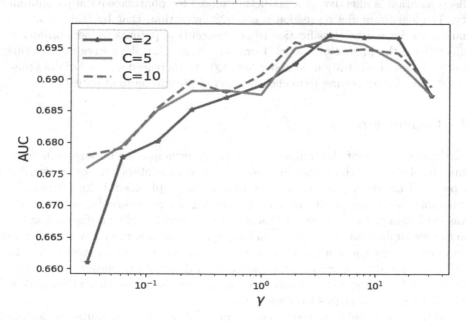

Fig. 3. Parameters

Table 4. AUC

Model	AUC
SVM	0.701
Logistic regression	0.566
Hido [5]	0.594

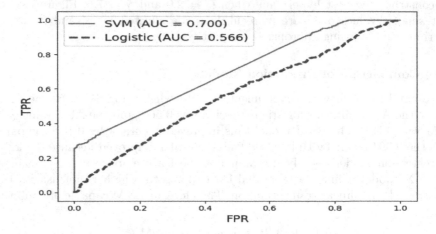

Fig. 4. ROC curve for SVM and logistic regression

discrimination is effective in a prediction model for pharmaceutical patentability. The logistic model regression was 0.028 lower than that by Hido et al., so narrowing down data classification to pharmaceutical patents cannot considered effective for the prediction model. However, while 5,326 data were used in this study, the previous study used about 300,000. An increased amount of data may be effective for narrowing data classification of pharmaceutical patents.

6   Conclusion

The Japanese Patent Act follows a first-to-file principle, so important patents must be filed earlier than other inventors. However, inventors will not be awarded a patent if the description of the invention in the application is insufficient. To solve this problem, a prediction model using logistic regression for patentability was studied in previous research. However, that model used linear discrimination, so the discrimination accuracy was not high. In this study, to increase prediction accuracy, we used a nonlinear SVM in a predictive model of patentability. In SVM model evaluation experiments, we confirmed the effectiveness of a nonlinear SVM model for constructing a prediction model for pharmaceutical patentability. The following summarizes the experiments.

In the experiments, we used a nonlinear SVM and logistic regression to construct the prediction model for pharmaceutical patentability. The experiments showed that the SVM model was more effective than the linear model. From the experimental results, the AUC of the SVM model using a RBF kernel was 0.701, and AUC increased to 0.107 more than that for the linear model in the previous study. A nonlinear SVM model is thus more effective for prediction of pharmaceutical patentability than is the logistic regression model.

As a future issue, in order to improve accuracy, it is necessary to increase the number of data, add features, and verify the model.

References

1. Japan Patent Office: Intellectual Property Activity Survey H 29. https://www.jpo.go.jp/shiryou/toukei/files/h29_tizai_katsudou/kekka.pdf. Accessed 16 Jan 2019. [in Japanese]
2. Touma, H.: About patents related to pharmaceutical patents and generic medicine, Takashima International Patent Office. http://www.phs.osaka-u.ac.jp/homepage/yaku/sotugo/pdf/h22_04_0.pdf. Accessed 16 Jan 2019. [in Japanese]
3. IQVIA: Pharmaceutical market statistics sales data period: January–December 2017. https://www.iqvia.com/-/media/iqvia/pdfs/ap-location-site/japan/thought-leadership/top-line-market-data/2017/toplinedata_fy_2017.pdfla=ja-jp&hash=AD8 242E8E82DDEFC1B2E11F9B7BEE3D79A13FA64&_=1546662689338. Accessed 16 Jan 2019. [in Japanese]
4. Japan Patent Office: Patents, utility model examination handbook Annex B Chapter 3 Pharmaceutical inventions Patents. https://www.jpo.go.jp/shiryou/kijun/kijun2/pdf/handbook_shinsa_h27/app_b3.pdf. Accessed 16 Jan 2019.[in Japanese]
5. Hido, S., Suzuki, S., Nishiyama, R., et al.: Modeling patent quality: a system for large-scale patentability analysis using text mining. J. Inf. Process. **20**(3), 1180–1191 (2012)
6. Hayashi, D., Akakura, T.: Sequential writing authentication method using SVM in e-Testing. Technical report of IEICE, vol. 118, no. 294, pp. 43–46 (2018). [in Japanese]

A Proposal of Video Evaluation Method Using Facial Expression for Video Recommendation System

Masashi Okubo$^{(\boxtimes)}$ and Shun Tamura

Doshisha University, 1-3 Tatara-Miyakodani,
Kyotanabe, Kyoto 610-0321, Japan
mokubo@mail.doshisha.ac.jp, shun.tamura@outlook.com

Abstract. Recently, video sharing services and video on demand services like YouTube, Netflix and Amazon Prime Video have come to prominence world-wide. These services try to get the users' evaluation of videos for the better recommendation. For example, some of them prepare the thumbs-up/down buttons and star buttons in their interface to get users' explicit evaluation. However, the effect of this method is doubts. The reason is these method needs user's conscious operation. Therefore, we need efficient method for getting users' implicit evaluation of videos. In this study, we focus on facial expressions especially smile of users watching videos. In this paper, we have developed the system that can get user's expression of users watching videos by some APIs, and investigated the relation between evaluation of videos by scoring and facial expression by using the proposed system. As a result of the experiment, positive correlations between the ranking by the user's scoring and the ranking based on the amount of smile of users watching videos are shown in 22 of the 28 participants. In addition, strong positive correlations were found among 13 of them. This result suggests possibility of using the implicit evaluation like smiling as well as the explicit evaluation like a scoring. So, it is suggested that recommendation method based on facial expression is effective.

Keywords: Facial expression · Recommendation method · Video on demand

1 Introduction

In recent years, video-on-demand websites like Netflix, Amazon Prime Video, and even user-submitted video sites like YouTube have taken the world by storm. These websites utilize a keyword search engine to better help users find videos they are looking for without having to manually navigate the massive video libraries these sites offer. These search engines pull information from a video's title or synopsis that matches the input keyword. However, in websites where the synopsis can be freely edited by the up loader, there are many times where the information provided does not match the video's content. This can understandably prevent users from finding the video they are looking for. It is also common for searches to produce a vast number of pages of results, so finding a video that piques the interest of the user may be a bit daunting. In order to solve this dilemma, many websites offer a video recommendation

© Springer Nature Switzerland AG 2019
S. Yamamoto and H. Mori (Eds.): HCII 2019, LNCS 11570, pp. 254–268, 2019.
https://doi.org/10.1007/978-3-030-22649-7_21

system which can be fine-tuned to suggest videos the user may be interested in. Netflix, one of the world's biggest video-on-demand retailers, shows us just how valuable this recommendation system is since nearly 80% of the videos watched are the result of recommendations [1].

The standard method in which videos are recommended is through collaborative filtering. The degree of similarity is calculated between users who vote on a video, and videos are recommended to other users that fall into that degree of similarity whenever a user with similar tastes approves of a video. Recently as well, recommendation systems that utilize machine learning have come into the spotlight. YouTube, for example, has created a neural network for its recommendation system which is built up of tens of billions of points of training data stemming from nearly a billion parameters [2]. Likewise, the act of user input in the form of voting on videos is an integral part of this method as well. A user's video evaluation index is expanded whenever the user performs explicit acts like pressing the "thumbs up" button on the webpage or subscribing to a content creator. Acts the user may not even know about add information to this index like watching a video to the end or watching the same video multiple times.

However, explicit actions like actively rating a video may be troublesome for the user, and so there is reason to believe that not many users do this. Further, even if a user were to watch a video to the end, it still does not necessarily mean they think highly of it, and so may not reflect exactly how the user feels. It is believed to be for these reasons that there is a need for an implicit rating system which can accurately reflect how the user feels about a video.

2 Video Recommendation System from Facial Expressions

2.1 Research Regarding Implicit Video Rating

In reference to the dilemma stated earlier, M. Suganuma and associates devised a method which utilized retinal information and brain waves [3]. During their experiments, it was suggested that reaction patterns from the participants in regards to video stimulation could be sorted into types. Conversely, D. Natsume and associates proposed an alternative video recommendation method based on tracking eye movement during a video. There, a user's video recommendation would be built up upon other similar data points taken from other users [4]. In their experiment, 20 participants were made to watch a multitude of videos while having their eye movement tracked. At the same time, participants were required to rate each video on a 1–4 scale which would create a degree of interest. A recommendation rank would then be defined through the recommendation target user and other user's similar points of interest. After calculating the rank correlation created from actual participant input degrees of interest, it turned out that it had a correlation average of 0.61.

Regardless of the method, it is indeed true that special instruments would be needed to analyze brain waves and eye movement. Furthermore, equipping users with such instruments would be no easy feat. Therefore, there is much reason to believe that a more natural and easy to use system is necessary.

2.2 Video Recommendation System from Facial Expressions

The main objective of this research is to obtain an index which can appropriately reflect a user's implicit evaluation of a video. Moreover, this method is meant to be utilized for standard video scenes, and ideally the use of special equipment should not be necessary. Essentially, this research deals with facial expressions, as facial expressions play an essential role in a person's emotional expression [5]. However, with recent advancements in facial expression recognition technology, facial expressions taken from a portrait photo can be recognized easily even if taken from a standard camera. Therefore, it is suggested that by filming a user's face while they watch a video, it is possible for a method to read their implicit evaluation of the video based solely on their facial expressions. Additionally, this research aims to develop a video recommendation system which utilizes a user's facial features to find videos they may find interesting. An outline of the proposed system can be found in Fig. 1.

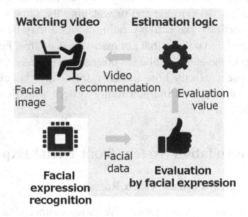

Fig. 1. Outline of proposed system

3 Relationship Between Facial Expressions During a Video and Its Evaluation

3.1 Outline

An experiment was carried out with 8 participants at Doshisha University with the aim of verifying the relationship between facial features made by a viewer during a video and video evaluation.

3.2 Test System

Since the goal of this research is to track the facial expressions of a viewer during a video while at the same time not putting too much of a physical burden on them, I developed a system which would record the facial expressions analyzed through a web camera loaded with a facial expression recognition API and which would then list them chronologically. The proposed system outline can be found in Fig. 2.

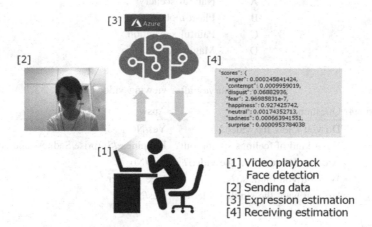

[1] Video playback
    Face detection
[2] Sending data
[3] Expression estimation
[4] Receiving estimation

Fig. 2. Outline of test system

There are 4 videos within this test system. The web camera automatically begins photographing the user's face as soon as they press the video's play button. The web camera continues to take a photo of the user's face every three seconds. After the video is finished, the photos are sent to an outside web API. The facial expression recognition results are then sent from the web API and are stored inside the system.

Emotion API, which is a web API part of the Cognitive Services API pack developed though Microsoft's machine learning, was used in recognizing the facial expressions during this experiment [6]. Emotion API analyzes the received images of a person's face, and then performs facial expression recognition and emotion estimations. The feelings it can detect are 7 in total. These are anger, contempt, disgust, fear, happiness, sadness, and surprise. If it cannot ascertain a feeling from the image, then it analyzes it as a neutral feeling. The API's emotion estimation results appear as a confidence, where each feeling can receive a max confidence score of 1.

3.3   Experiment Method

A participant is directed into a room and is instructed to watch 4 different videos, as required in the test system. The content of the videos is explained in Table 1. After the first video is finished, the participant is then asked to answer a survey where they will state how they felt after it finished and to what degree of interest they are currently at. Survey questions can be found in Table 2. All the participants watched the videos in the order of A, B, C, and then D. After all the videos were finished, the Emotion API was sent the photographed facial expressions where they were then assigned an estimated emotion value. It was hypothesized that there are not many users who actively watch videos which cause them to feel feelings like anger, fear, and contempt, so only feelings like neutral, happiness, sadness, and surprise were given an estimated emotion value.

Table 1. Video contents

Video#	Contents
A	Natural scenery
B	Flash mob
C	Painful separation
D	Magic show

Table 2. Survey after viewing video

Question#	Question	Answer
Q1	Do you know the video?	Yes/No
Q2	What kind of feelings sprang out?	Happiness/Surprise/Sadness/and so on
Q3	Are you interested in the video?	Yes/No
Q4	Why do you think so?	Free answer
Q5	Do you want the similar video?	Yes/No

3.4   Experiment Results

Figure 3 features an example result taken from participant 1. It displays the time scale of the emotion "happiness" which was analyzed during video D viewing. From this data we can see that happiness hits the confidence threshold multiple times. The participant stated they felt a mix of happiness and shock, and that they ranked the video a 5 on the degree of interest scale.

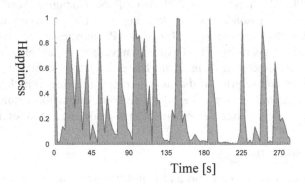

Fig. 3. Transition of happiness scores for participant 1 (video D)

Throughout the experiment, participant 1 changed facial expressions many times according to which videos they found high on their degree of interest scale. The other 4 participants also showed a similar reaction to a couple videos as well. However, it was not possible to attain a video evaluation reading based on the changing facial expressions of 3 different participants. Further, since "happiness" was the emotion which had the most changes in terms of confidence across all participants, there is reason to believe that it easy for the algorithm to recognize.

4 Relationship Between a Viewer's Smile and Video Evaluation

4.1 Outline

From the experiment mentioned in Sect. 3, the smiles made during the videos allowed the algorithm to better recognize them, so one could then assume that there is indeed a relation between video evaluation and facial features. Doshisha University conducted another experiment for even further testing. This time the target facial expression was restricted to smiles only, and 28 students were observed to see if there was a relation between smiling during a comedy video and video evaluation.

4.2 Test System

This test works in the same way as the experiment in Sect. 3. Participants' facial expressions were tracked during a video while at the same time not putting too much of a physical burden on them. The system I developed would record the facial expressions through a web camera and send the images to the facial expression recognition component. The difference between this test and the one mentioned in Sect. 3 is the facial expression recognition component. On the assumption that real-time analysis would be integral to an actual recommendation system, I incorporated an SDK into the system which will help alleviate possible network lag issues due to the web based API. More on the SDK will be explained below. The system can be accessed through a web interface, where the 9 comedy videos to be used will be hosted. On the starting screen, buttons will be displayed in random order. Each button linked to a video and its survey. Once the play button is pressed on the video page, the web camera will automatically begin taking photos of the face. Photos of the face during the video will be sent to the facial expression recognition component, where facial expression recognition protocols will be carried out until the video ends. After the video is over, the facial expression recognition results will then be stored on the PC. An overview of this system is shown in Fig. 4.

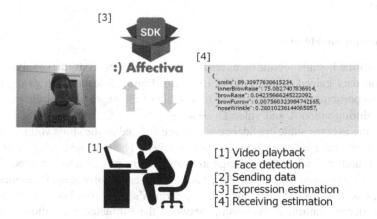

[1] Video playback
    Face detection
[2] Sending data
[3] Expression estimation
[4] Receiving estimation

Fig. 4. Overview of the test system

Affectiva's Affectiva Emotion SDK is being used as the built-in type facial expression recognition SDK. When images are input into the Affectiva Emotion SDK, it starts by extracting the facial boundaries from each image. Then it extracts and confirms features that make up the face, like eyes, eyebrows, and lips. By utilizing Affectiva's own model, it can determine if parts on the face like eyes are open or if one's eyebrows are raised. After that, those conditions are compared with the Facial Action Coding System's (FACS) Action Units (AU), where then facial expression recognition and an estimation of emotion begins [7].

FACS is an analysis tool part of Ekman and their associates' proposed facial expression theory [8]. FACS takes anatomical knowledge about the face and applies it to classify relationships between the movement of mimetic muscles and how those muscles express emotion. AU is a term used to classify one codified way of moving for a mimetic muscle, and facial expressions are built upon numerous AU components working together. For example, combining AU6's "raises cheeks" with AU12's "raises corners of mouth" creates a smile, which is generally understood as signifying happiness or joy. The Affectiva Emotion SDK evaluates the submitted facial photos combined with AU data, allowing facial expression recognition and emotion estimations to take place. The results are then split into two separate JSON files: one for expressions and one for emotions. Expressions contains information on physical indicators like smiles or frowns, while emotions contains data on expressed emotion like joy or anger. There, both expressions and emotions are scaled 0 to 100 in terms of confidence.

4.3 Experiment Method

The process is carried out according to the above-mentioned test system. A participant is ushered into a room and is shown 9 4-min comedy videos. After watching a video, the participant must then evaluate what he/she saw by grading it 1–100, and if it is something he found to be particularly interesting, then he is free to give his thoughts on it. The videos are shown to the participant randomly, but in order to establish a base for evaluation across all participants, each participant begins by watching the same video (video A).

4.4 Evaluation Method

First, confirmed smile confidence results are extracted from the analyzed facial expression data gained through the test system. Figure 5 features an example result taken from participant 3. It displays the time scale of the expression "smile" which was analyzed during video A and video D viewing.

Next, the average smile confidence scores are defined as the smile volume, which is calculated into each video each participant watched. These volumes, big or small, are compared, and the videos the participants watched are placed into a ranked list. Furthermore, results from the survey data taken from each participant is applied and a ranked list is also created from this data. Spearman's rank correlation coefficient was used in order to confirm a relationship between the estimated evaluation based on a participant's facial features during a video and the explicitly evaluated data they

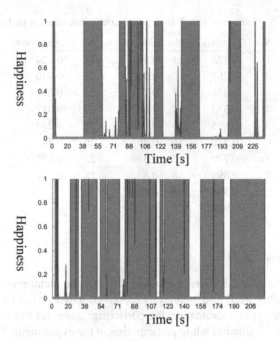

Fig. 5. Participant 3's time scale on smile confidence scores during video A (upper) and video D (lower) viewing

submitted when grading a video [9]. Spearman's rank correlation coefficient takes two variables converted through rank and finds their correlation by defining them through the following Eq. (1). A rank correlation coefficient of +1 or −1 occurs when each of the variables is a perfect monotone function of the other.

$$r_s = 1 - \frac{6\sum_{i=1}^{n} d_i^2}{n(n^2 - 1)} \tag{1}$$

n: number of videos, d_i: difference between the two ranks.

4.5   Evaluation Results

Table 3 features the calculated results after running both evaluation ranks (participants' graded video scores and the volume of smiles per video) through Spearman's rank correlation coefficient.

A strong rank correlation coefficient is considered to be $0.7 \leq |r_s|$, while a weak correlation coefficient would be $0.3 \leq |r_s| < 0.7$. Out of the 28 participants in this study, 13 expressed what is considered a strong positive rank correlation coefficient. Furthermore, 9 participants expressed a weak positive rank correlation coefficient. However, 1 participant expressed a strong negative rank correlation coefficient.

Table 3. Spearman's rank correlation coefficient of each participant

No.	Correlation	No.	Correlation	No.	Correlation
1	0.535	11	0.851	21	−0.824
2	−0.067	12	0.863	22	0.940
3	0.834	13	0.717	23	0.872
4	0.373	14	0.661	24	−0.017
5	0.895	15	0.638	25	0.274
6	0.370	16	0.262	26	0.740
7	0.770	17	0.559	27	0.655
8	0.899	18	0.832	28	0.891
9	0.538	19	0.586		
10	0.929	20	0.119		

4.6 Observations

In the case of participant 21, there is a possibility that the facial recognition algorithm misunderstood his/her smile and incorrectly identified it as a crying face. There is also a possibility that the explicit evaluation the participant gave did not match the implicit (facial expressions) evaluation while participating in the experiment. Therefore, there is reason to believe that either the written evaluation or the user's own smile fails to accurately reflect the user's true evaluation of the video.

Conversely, since the other 22 participants showed a positive correlation in regards to their smiles during the videos, there is reason to believe that implicit smile-based video evaluation is indeed possible. By digitizing the evaluation data, it seems further possible that it can be applied to currently available recommendation systems like collaborative filtering. Essentially, this means that recommendation feedback loops, like users being able to discover recommended videos from other users with the same interests, all without having to perform explicit evaluation tasks like pressing a thumbs up button, will be possible.

5 Video Recommendation via a Viewer's Smile

5.1 Outline

As the experiment in Sect. 4 has shown, smiling during a video and that video's evaluation seem to be related to each other. In this chapter, recommendations based on the data gained through Sect. 4's experiment will be used, and the possibility of the implementation of a recommendation system attained through smiling during a video will be explored.

5.2 Recommendation Method

The method in this video recommendation experiment is based off the ideas concerning collaborative filtering. Collaborative filtering is a method that seeks to find a degree of similarity between users and then, based on that similarity, suggests recommended videos that a user has yet to see based on similar tastes in previously evaluated videos. This experiment will pre-process the obtained data and calculate a degree of similarity. A ranking of the recommended videos will then be determined after passing the results through the 3 processes of prediction value evaluation.

First, pre-processing of the previously obtained data in order to create a model is to be carried out. It is understood that users currently using such services watch videos that pertain to their interests. There, recommendations will be taken from the user's top 3 rated, previously watched, received recommendations. An outline of the pre-processing for participant 18 is explained in Fig. 6.

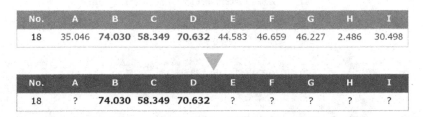

No.	A	B	C	D	E	F	G	H	I
18	35.046	**74.030**	**58.349**	**70.632**	44.583	46.659	46.227	2.486	30.498

No.	A	B	C	D	E	F	G	H	I
18	?	**74.030**	**58.349**	**70.632**	?	?	?	?	?

Fig. 6. Pre-processing for participant 18

Next, a calculation will be run from the 3 videos in order to find a degree of similarity between the former recipient and another participant. The method used to find the degree of similarity is the Pearson's correlation coefficient. The values are participants i and j, as well as the degree of similarity similarity(i, j). This is then put into the formula (2) and becomes $-1 \leq similarity(i, j) \leq 1$.

A sample of participant 18's results through this method is shown in Fig. 7. A degree of similarity was calculated from the extracted videos B, C, and D during pre-processing and the amount of smiling other participants did during said videos. For example, participant 1's degree of similarity was similarity(18,1) = 0.3666, and participant 14's degree of similarity was similarity(18,14) = 0.9999. By extracting the top 4 participants that shared a positive correlation, the prediction value evaluation for participant 18 resulted in the 4 participants being participant 14, 17, 23, and 27.

$$similarity(i,j) = \frac{\sum_{p \in P} \left(r_{ip} - \overline{r_i} \right) \left(r_{jp} - \overline{r_j} \right)}{\sqrt{\sum_{p \in P} \left(r_{ip} - \overline{r_i} \right)^2} \sqrt{\sum_{p \in P} \left(r_{jp} - \overline{r_j} \right)^2}} \tag{2}$$

i: Recommended participant, j: Participants excluding the recommended participant,

r_{ip}: Evaluation of video(p) by participant(i),

$\overline{r_i}$: Average evaluation of participant(i),

r_{jp}: Evaluation of video(p) by participant(j),

$\overline{r_j}$: Average evaluation of participant(j),

P: Top 3 videos evaluated by i, p: video.

Object participant

No.	B	C	D	correlation
18	74.030	58.349	70.632	-

&   Top 4 participants

No.	B	C	D	correlation
1	96.914	96.740	96.645	0.3666
⋮				⋮
14	22.416	0.009	17.586	0.9999
⋮				⋮
17	69.886	9.379	61.997	0.9961
⋮				⋮
24	6.893	2.715	5.618	0.9955
⋮				⋮
27	53.332	13.175	48.506	0.9952
28	51.761	33.075	34.661	0.7226

Fig. 7. Degree of similarity calculated from participant 18

Next, an estimation of the number of smiles an unwatched video recommended through the prediction value evaluation based on the degree of similarity will get will be determined. This prediction formula is displayed in formula (3). The estimation takes the values from the top 4 participants based on their degree of similarity but excludes any participants who have a negative correlation coefficient. The recommendation rank of videos will be listed by rank from the highest predicted evaluation value.

$$predict(i,p) = \bar{r}_i + \frac{\sum_{j \in N} similarity(i,j)(r_{jp} - \bar{r}_j)}{\sum_{j \in N} |similarity(i,j)|} \tag{3}$$

i: Recommended participant, j: (i) and participants that have a high degree of similarity (Max 4),

p: Predicted videos,

$\bar{r}_i$: Evaluation average of participant(i),

$\bar{r}_j$: Evaluation average of participants(j),

r_{jp}: Participants'(j) evaluation of videos(p),

N: i and users with a high degree of similarity.

The process used for participant 18 is shown in Fig. 8. Since participant 18's top 4 similar users were participants 14, 17, 24, and 27, the number of smiles for participant 18 and the previously mentioned users for each video were used to find a degree of similarity. Then, based off this data, a prediction regarding the number of smiles for unseen videos was made. For example, the calculated estimation value for video A is 72.246 and the value for video D is 58.706.

No.	A	B	C	D	E	F	G	H	I
14	7.257	22.416	0.009	17.586	5.574	5.952	4.243	8.312	2.426
17	36.032	69.886	9.379	61.997	9.692	85.243	82.425	0.922	58.621
24	12.971	6.893	2.715	5.618	2.474	5.888	10.155	1.837	7.384
27	58.263	53.332	13.175	48.506	42.577	37.465	24.787	6.373	37.241

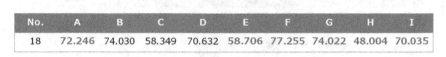

No.	A	B	C	D	E	F	G	H	I
18	72.246	74.030	58.349	70.632	58.706	77.255	74.022	48.004	70.035

Fig. 8. Participant 18's prediction value evaluation

Extrapolating from the recommendation method explained above, we can conclude that recommendations through grading videos work in the same way even by replacing explicit participant grading with the volume of implicit smiles made during the video.

5.3 Evaluation Method

Spearman's rank correlation coefficient was used in order to evaluate the calculated recommendation rank taken from the previous paragraph's recommendation method [9]. Specifically, it seeks out the rank correlation coefficient between two variables. The first is the rank which is created from videos based on smile volume. The second is the evaluation rank based on smile volume the user receiving the recommendation made which was measured by the system in regards to the same videos. Further, it seeks out the rank correlation coefficient between the displayed rank of recommendations based on marked results and the evaluated rank based on actual markings.

Participant 18's example can be found in Fig. 9. Regarding pre-processing, the ranks for the 6 unwatched videos A, E, F, G, H, I were based on the measured smile volumes and the predicted smile volumes the system made. A strong positive correlation of 0.829 was found when seeking out Spearman's rank correlation coefficient based on the ranks.

5.4 Evaluation Results

Upon calculating the rank correlation coefficient of each participant based on each of the methods, we find that, in terms of recommendations based on smile volume, 5 participants showed a strong positive correlation, 3 participants showed a weak positive correlation, and 1 participant showed a strong negative correlation. However, for videos that were graded or marked, 2 participants showed a strong positive correlation, 13 participants showed a weak positive correlation, and 1 participant showed a weak negative correlation.

Measured smile value

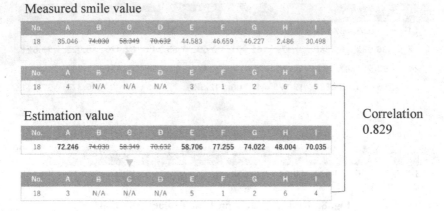

Estimation value   Correlation
                                                                                    0.829

Fig. 9. Evaluation of participant 18's recommended video results

5.5   Observations

From the results, the data showed that participants had both rank correlation coefficients (the rank correlation coefficient between graded recommendation ranks and evaluated ranks and the rank correlation coefficient between recommendation ranks based on smiles and evaluated ranks) that showed strong positive correlations greater than 0.7. This data is shown in Table 4.

Table 4. Rank correlation coefficient of participants ranging 0.7+

No.	Correlation between ranking by evaluation and	
	Ranking based on score	Ranking based on smile
1	-0.293	1.000
3	N/A	0.714
5	-0.131	0.714
9	0.667	0.771
10	0.841	-0.029
16	0.736	0.143
18	0.493	0.829

From the table, we can see there were no participants who showed a strong positive correlation between recommendations created through both grading and smiles. Therefore, it is possible to assume that the recommendations based on the recommendation index varies from person to person.

6 Conclusion

To recap, the aim of this paper's research was to propose a method which could be used to obtain implicit video evaluation based on a user's facial features while they watched a video. Additionally, the relationship between facial features and video evaluation was explored by photographing the face of a user while they watch a video and developing a system which utilizes facial expression recognition APIs and SDKs. Development on the recommendation method was carried out in part due to the facial features data obtained through the experiment.

It was found, through the results from investigating the relationship between the facial features appearing on the viewer while watching a video and video evaluation, that there seemed to be a relationship between graded videos by users deemed by the system to have clear facial expressions and the volume at which facial features changed during the viewing of a video. Additionally, it was found that facial features changed often when viewing videos that made people smile. Therefore, if a smile is made during a video, and that smile is easily recognized by the system, then there is a possibility that a relationship between video evaluation and changes in facial features exists.

Next, concerning the results obtained after investigating the relationship between smiles during a video and video evaluation, it was found that of the 28 tested participants, 22 showed a positive correlation between how they evaluated the videos by grading and how they were evaluated by smile volume. Of those 22 participants, 13 showed a strong positive correlation. This showed that facial features could be used as an implicit index much in the same way grading works as an explicit index, which means that it is possible for videos to be evaluated by an index of smiles while the video is being watched.

Furthermore, the possibility of creating a video recommendation index through the volume of smiles expressed during a video was investigated, in which similar recommendations were based off the data set obtained through the prior experiment.

From the results of the experiment, it was found that no participants expressed a strong positive rank correlation between both recommendations made from an explicit graded index and recommendations made from an implicit smile volume index. This meant that it was possible for applicable video recommendation indexes to differ depending on the person.

However, though recommendation results based on smile volumes of specially selected participants seems to be effective, the rank correlation coefficient average was found to be lower than recommendation results based on grading. Throughout the experiment, a simple index for recommendations was made by taking the average of smile confidence scores during a video. However, there is a possibility that this index may not have been appropriate. There is still much to be investigated in terms of just how far a model created through smile confidence data will go when used in recommendations.

Additionally, the target of this report was restricted to smiles. However, there exist many videos which depict drama or horror which in turn can bring about a plethora of varying facial expressions. The evaluation index of these emotions is a worthwhile topic for further study.

Acknowledgements. This work was supported by JSPS KAKENHI Grant Number 18K11414.

References

1. Gomez-Uribe, C.A., Hunt, N.: The netflix recommender system: algorithms, business value, and innovation. ACM Trans. Manag. Inf. Syst. **6**(4), 1–19 (2016). 13
2. Covington, P., Adams, J., Sargin, E.: Deep neural networks for YouTube recommendations. In: Proceedings of the 10th ACM Conference on Recommender Systems, pp. 191–198 (2016)
3. Suganuma, M., Kawamura, E., Kameyama, W.: Preliminary study on estimating degree of interest for audiovisual information using user's bio signals. In: The Institute of Image Information and Television Engineers Winter Annual Convention 2011, pp. 7–4 (2011)
4. Natsume, D., Iribe, Y., Katsurada, K., Nitta, T.: Proposal of video recommendation method using eye mark. In: Information Processing Society National Conference Proceedings, pp. 857–858 (2008)
5. Ekman, P., Friesen, W.V.: Unmasking the Face: A Guide to Recognizing Emotions from Facial Clues. Malor Books, 202 p. (2003)
6. Microsoft Corp.: Emotion API–Emotion detection. https://azure.microsoft.com/services/cognitive-services/emotion. Accessed 26 Jan 2018
7. Senechal, T., Mcduff, D., Kaliouby, R.: Facial action unit detection using active learning and an efficient non-linear kernel approximation. In: Proceedings of the IEEE International Conference on Computer Vision Workshops, pp. 10–18 (2015)
8. Ekman, P., Friesen, W.V.: Measuring facial movement. Environ. Psychol. Nonverbal Behav. **1**(1), 56–75 (1976)
9. Kendall, M.G.: Rank Correlation Methods. Hodder Arnold, 272 p. (1948)

Sentiment Analysis of Images with Tensor Factorization

Ayumu Sakaguchi and Ryosuke Saga(✉)

Osaka Prefecture University, Sakai-shi, Nakaku, Gakuen-cho, 1-1, Osaka, Japan
sxa01106@edu.osakafu-u.ac.jp, saga@cs.osakafu-u.ac.jp

Abstract. In recent years, large amounts of information have been transmitted through SNSs. Mainstream SNSs focus mainly on images. Given that many individuals use SNSs to express their sentiments, understanding the individual feelings of such users can be useful for helping identify potential demand in the society. Sentiment analysis of images in SNSs has thus attracted research attention. However, many existing studies have utilized a supervised learning approach with a high cost for labeling. By contrast, Wang et al., who used unsupervised learning, have acquired the sentiment of images through matrix decomposition from text information and visual information. However, text and visual information are not sufficient to acquire the desired result. In addition, sentiment polarity of the image is greatly influenced by text information. Therefore, this work will conduct a sentiment analysis of images by using tensor decomposition with an unsupervised learning approach. By considering the sentiment polarity of both text and visual features, this work aims to avoid being influenced only by text information.

Keywords: Sentiment analysis of images · Unsupervised learning · Tensor factorization

1 Introduction

We are currently living in an era of information overload, wherein abundant information is being sent through SNSs. In recent years in particular, mainstream SNSs have centered on images. For example, as of October 2018 and June 2018, the total number of Twitter users and Instagram users reached 326 million and 1 billion, respectively. Compared to the total number of Twitter and Instagram users as of October 2014 and December 2014, at 284 million and 300 million, respectively, these figures indicate how popular the platforms have become. Given that SNSs are used by people to express their opinions and emotions, analyzing SNSs can lead to discoveries on the potential opinions, emotions, and demand of the society as a whole. Consequently, research on the sentiment analysis of images has attracted increasing attention.

Although attention to the sentiment analysis of images has increased, the majority of existing research has applied an approach based on supervised learning. For example, some approaches are based on local features [2, 3], some on mid-level features [4, 5], and others on deep learning [6]. These approaches are difficult to label even with enough training and are thus inefficient because of the labor and time

© Springer Nature Switzerland AG 2019
S. Yamamoto and H. Mori (Eds.): HCII 2019, LNCS 11570, pp. 269–285, 2019.
https://doi.org/10.1007/978-3-030-22649-7_22

required. Therefore, the current study analyzes the sentiment of images through an approach based on unsupervised learning.

Wang conducts research on the sentiment analysis of images using unsupervised learning [1]. He shows that the frequency of appearance of each image in the text is text information and the mid-level feature of each image is visual information. Then he proposes the unsupervised sentiment analysis (USEA) framework, which acquires the sentiment polarity of the image through the matrix decomposition of text information and visual information.

In Wang's [1] research, the sentiment of images is obtained through matrix decomposition from text information representing the text features of each image and from visual information representing the visual features of each image. However, in this model, only 2-D information can be handled because it can be solved by matrix decomposition. Thus, the sentiment polarity of the image composed of text information and visual information cannot be directly obtained. The sentiment polarities of the image obtained from the text information and from visual information are calculated respectively, and the difference of the sentiment polarities of the image obtained from both types of information are made to be as small as possible. In addition, the sentiment polarity of text features is pre-assigned, whereas that of visual features is not. Hence, the results are largely affected by text features.

On the bases of the above discussion, this work analyzes the sentiment of images directly from both types of information by using a constrained tensor decomposition that includes text and visual features. Furthermore, by imparting sentiment polarity to both text and visual features, we avoid being affected only by text information. CP decomposition is conducted as a solution to tensor decomposition. The alternating least squares (ALS) method is popular as CP decomposition in ordinary tensor, but because the proposed method has constraint conditions, the ConCMTF-ALS method proposed by Bahargam [7] is used instead. In the present study, we obtain the sentiment polarity of the image by solving the proposed model using the ConCMTF-ALS method with two constraints.

2   Related Work

Siersdorfer et al. [8] describe the sentiment of images represented by metadata and the relevance of their visual features. To consider both the color distribution of the image and the textual representation of visual features, we estimate the sentiment of the image by using the SentiWordNet thesaurus for extracting numerical values on sentiment from accompanying text metadata and by performing discriminant analysis of the visual features with SVM. Fersini et al. [9] use a model of ensemble learning to reduce noise related to linguistic ambiguity and estimate a more accurate sentiment polarity. The ensemble learning of this study is based on Bayesian model averaging, where the uncertainty and reliability of each single model are taken into account. Cao et al. [10] propose a visual sentiment topic model (VSTM) to obtain the sentiment polarity contained in the blog image. They first acquire the characteristics of visual sentiment using visual sentiment ontology and then build the VSTM by using all the images in the same topic. Finally, according to the distribution of visual sentiment features within the topic, better visual sentiment features are selected. Xu et al. [11] propose a new visual sentiment prediction framework that understands images via deep convolutional neural network (CNN). They conducting metastatic learning from CNN using millions of pre-trained parameters for large-scale data on object recognition. Nguyen et al. [12] aim to construct a model for predicting stock price fluctuations by using sentiment of social media. In the model, the sentiment of a topic of a company is incorporated into the inventory forecasting model. Sentiments related to topics are automatically extracted from the text on the message board through existing topic models and sug- gested models. Katsurai et al. [13] propose an approach that exploits the potential correlation of visual view, text view, and SentiWordNet. Their proposed method finds a potential embedding space where the correlation between three views is maximized. The features projected into latent space are used to train sentiment classifiers that consider supplemental information from different views. Mahalakshmi [14] uses three sentiment dictionaries, namely, SenticNet, SentiWordNet, and SentislangNet, to esti- mate the polarity of sentiment on Twitter. Gelli et al. [15] use three new context features of object features, features extracted from tags, and features extracted from content to predict the number of "nice" social images and propose the visual sentiment features. Vadicamo et al. [16] propose a cross-media approach that trains visual sen- timent classification by using textual sentiment polarity from large datasets generated but not labeled by users. In their study, the text associated with each image is often noisy and has little correlation with image content but is beneficial for training CNN. Wang et al. [17] propose an approach for the visual sentiment analysis of deep neural networks of adjectives and nouns. First, they learn mid-level sentiment expressions by learning the deep neural networks of both adjectives and nouns to reduce large variance within the class. The prediction network is further optimized based on the learned sentiment expression to deal with the slight differences that often exist in fine image categories. Finally, when adjective and noun labels are not available, the training of mutual monitoring of learned adjective and noun networks is generalized with the Rectified Kullback–Leibler loss.

3 Problem Statement

In this paper, scalars are denoted by lower-case letters (a, b, ...; α, β, ...), vectors by lower-case bold letters (a, b, ...), and matrices by boldface uppercase letters (A, B, ...). n is the number of images, m_v is the visual feature of an image, and m_t represents the text feature. $X_v \in \mathbb{R}^{n*m_v}$ is the visual information for each image, and $X_t \in \mathbb{R}^{n*m_t}$ is the text feature for each image.

$X \in \mathbb{R}^{n \times m_t \times m_v}$ of the proposed model equation shows the tensor with the text and visual features for each image. $U \in \mathbb{R}^{n \times R}$ is the sentiment polarity for each image, $T \in \mathbb{R}^{m_t \times R}$ is the sentiment polarity of the text feature, $V \in \mathbb{R}^{m_v \times R}$ is the sentiment polarity of the visual feature, $T_0 \in \mathbb{R}^{m_t \times R}$ is the sentiment polarity of the previously learned text feature, $V_0 \in \mathbb{R}^{m_v \times R}$ is the sentiment polarity of the visual feature given in advance, and $D \in \mathbb{R}^{R \times R}$ and $E \in \mathbb{R}^{R \times R}$ adjust the sentiment polarities of the text feature and visual feature, respectively, $R = 2$ (positive, negative).

4   USEA Framework

Wang et al. [1] propose the USEA framework that analyzes the sentiment of images through an approach based on unsupervised learning. In the case of supervised learning, sentiment labels are attached to visual features and the sentiment polarity of images is obtained by training these features. However, the unsupervised learning Wang et al. propose carries out the sentiment analysis of images to generate the model by learning from visual and text features. To utilize text information, the authors describe how to incorporate text information into visual information and model sentiment polarity in text information. In their study, sentiment polarity k has three value namely, positive, negative, and neutral.

Wang et al. assume that both visual and text information are related to the same image file. Hence, we assume that both types of information share the same sentiment polarity, and the sentiment polarity of the image matches the sentiment polarity of the text information associated with it. Specifically, the sentiment polarity U_0 is $U_0(i,j) = 1$ when the ith image data belong to the image label c_j, and $U_0(i,j) = 0$ otherwise. Equation (1) is an expression that integrates visual information and text information on the basis of non-negative matrix decomposition. The diagram representing Eq. (1) is shown in Fig. 1.

Fig. 1. Sentiment analysis for images of USEA framework.

$$min_{UV}||X_v - U_vV_v^T||_F^2 + \alpha||X_t - U_tV_t^T||_F^2 + \beta(||U_v - U_0||_F^2 + U_t - U_0||_F^2)$$
$$\text{s.t. } U_v \geq 0, U_t \geq 0, ||U_0(i,:)||_0 = l \, i \in \{1,\ldots,n\}, U_0(i,j) \in \{0,1\} j \in \{1,\ldots,k\}$$

$$(1)$$

$U_0 \in \mathbb{R}^{n \times k}$ is the sentiment polarity for each image; $U_v \in \mathbb{R}^{n \times k}$ and $U_t \in \mathbb{R}^{n \times k}$ are the sentiment polarities learned from visual information and text information, respectively; and $V_v \in \mathbb{R}^{m_v \times k}$ and $V_t \in \mathbb{R}^{m_t \times k}$ represent the sentiment polarities of visual features and text features, respectively. Moreover, α adjusts the degree of influence of text information on the model, and $|| \cdot ||_0$ is the number of nonzero elements in the vector. The term $\beta(||U_v - U_0||_F^2 + ||U_t - U_0||_F^2)$ guarantees that both types of information share U_0.

Next, to make $V_{t0} \in \mathbb{R}^{m_t \times k}$ the sentiment polarity of the text feature, let $V_{t0}(i,j) = 1$ if the ith word belongs to c_j; otherwise, set $V_{t0}(i,j) = 0$. Equation (2) is an expression that gives sentiment polarity to the text features:

$$min||V_t - V_{t0}||_{2,1} \tag{2}$$

$||X||_{2,1}$ allows the sparsity of matrix $\mathbf{X}$. By using Eqs. (1) and (2), Wang et al. propose a USEA sentiment analysis model. The proposed expression of their model is shown in Eq. (3). The parameter γ controls the sparseness of the regularization term.

$$min_{UV}||X_v - V_v^T||_F^2 + \alpha||X_t - U_t V_t^T||_F^2 + \beta(||U_v - U_0||_F^2 + ||U_t - U_0||_F^2) + \gamma||V_t - V_{t0}||_{2,1} \tag{3}$$
$$\text{s.t. } U_v \geq 0, U_t \geq 0, U_0^T U_0 = \mathbf{I}, U_0 \geq 0$$

5 Proposed Model

In the USEA framework shown in Sect. 4, the sentiment polarities learned from visual information and from text information share the sentiment polarity of images according to the term $\beta(||U_v - U_0||_F^2 + ||U_t - U_0||_F^2)$. However, each sentiment polarity does not completely match, and a possibility exists that the sentiment polarities may be biased toward either the result of visual information or of text information. Therefore, it cannot be said that the sentiment polarities are results that were learned sufficiently from both visual and text information. It uses matrix decomposition, which depends on the fact that it can handle only 2-D information. This problem can be solved by extending it to a tensor that can handle multi-dimensional information.

To obtain the sentiment polarity of the image that has both text and visual information, the objective function of the tensor with both text and visual feature in the mode is solved through CP decomposition. The equation to calculate the sentiment polarity of images is shown below:

$$min_{U,T,V}||X - \sum_{r=1}^{R} u_{\cdot r} \circ t_{\cdot r} \circ v_{\cdot r}||_F^2 \tag{4}$$

U, T, and V obtained from (4) are the sentiment polarity of images, sentiment polarity of text features and sentiment polarity of visual feature learned from the text and visual information of a certain image file, respectively. Given that $R = 1$ is positive and $R = 2$ is negative, $u_{\cdot 1}$ is an image showing a positive polarity and $u_{\cdot 2}$ is an image showing a negative polarity. Therefore, if $u_{\cdot 1}$ shows a larger value than does $u_{\cdot 2}$, then the image has a positive polarity; conversely if $u_{\cdot 2}$ is larger, then the image has a negative polarity.

The text feature can thus be indicated as having abundant sentiment information. For example, "happy" has a positive meaning and "disappointed" has a negative meaning. The MPQA dictionary [18] is used in the present research because the sentiment polarity of a word can be obtained through a public sentiment dictionary. An expression obtained by adding the sentiment polarity of text features obtained from this MPQA dictionary to Eq. (4) is shown in Eq. (5).

$$min||T_0 - TD^T||_F^2 \tag{5}$$

Equation (5) adjusts the value of D because the predicted sentiment polarity of the text feature has a value as close as possible to the sentiment polarity of the true text feature.

Furthermore, in the USEA framework, the sentiment polarity of the text feature is assumed to be equal to the sentiment polarity of the image. However, in texts, even though they are positively speaking at first glance, images may be posted with negative meanings. For example, suppose a user uploaded 0 point image in the text and posted "I am a genius!" In this case, the document has a positive meaning, but the image posted has a negative meaning. Therefore, the sentiment polarity of the image cannot be said to be equal to the sentiment polarity of the text information. Hence, the visual feature is assumed to have sentiment polarity as well, and the sentiment polarity of the image is thought to be learned from the sentiment polarities of both text feature and visual feature. Here, Eq. (6) is shown to be an expression that gives the sentiment polarity of the visual feature in advance.

$$min||V_0 - VE^T||_F^2 \tag{6}$$

In Eq. (6), as with the text feature, the visual feature has a value as close as possible to its sentiment polarity, and so it is adjusted by the value of E.

From the above, we propose a model that includes Eqs. (5) and (6) as a model of image sentiment analysis (7). Figure 2 shows the proposed model.

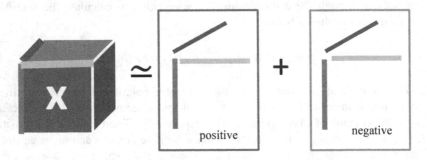

Fig. 2. Sentiment analysis of images using CP decomposition.

$$min_{U,T,V}||X - \sum_{r=1}^{R} u_{:r} \circ t_{:r} \circ v_{:r}||_F^2 + ||T_0 - TD^T||_F^2 + ||V_0 - VE^T||_F^2$$
$$\text{s.t. } U \geq 0, T \geq 0, V \geq 0, D \geq 0, E \geq 0, T_0 \geq 0, V_0 \geq 0,$$
$$\forall i \; ||U_i||_1 \leq \varepsilon_U, ||T_i||_1 \leq \varepsilon_T, ||V_i||_1 \leq \varepsilon_V, ||D_i||_1 \leq \varepsilon_D, ||E_i||_1 \leq \varepsilon_E, \tag{7}$$
$$\forall i,j \; U_i^T U_j \leq \varepsilon_U, T_i^T T_j \leq \varepsilon_T, V_i^T V_j \leq \varepsilon_V, D_i^T D_j \leq \varepsilon_D, E_i^T E_j \leq \varepsilon_E i \neq j$$

6 Feature Extraction

This section will explain the tensor mode, text feature, and visual feature that are constraints. First, with respect to the visual feature, we will extract local features from the image and make the result fuzzy C-means to obtain the cluster. Then the visual information is the degree of belonging to each cluster which can be obtained from the clustering result. Meanwhile, words with sentiment polarity obtained from the MPQA dictionary are taken as text features. For text information, at first, keywords are extracted from the comments for each image. Next, stemming processing and deletion of the stop word are performed as preprocessing. Word2Vec [19] is then used to find the similarity between the text feature and the keywords. The obtained similarity is defined as text information.

6.1 Gist Descriptor

Gist Descriptor [20] is a low-dimensional global feature describing a scene and can be obtained by applying a Gabor filter to the image. The 2-D Gabor filter is a simple model type in the primary visual cortex of a human being, and it uses a Gaussian envelope and a sinusoidal carrier wave for filtering. The Gabor filter is a feature that extracts local direction and spatial frequency.

6.2 Hog Feature

Hog feature [21] is a histogram of the gradient direction of the local region's luminance. To extract this feature, the intensity and direction of the luminance gradient are first calculated in each pixel in the local region. The calculation formula is shown below:

$$m(x,y) = \sqrt{L_x^2(x,y) + L_y^2(x,y)}, \theta(x,y) = tan^{-1}\frac{L_y(x,y)}{L_x(x,y)} \tag{8}$$

Equation (8) uses the image L(x, y) on which the smoothing filter is applied, and where the luminance gradients in the x and y directions are $L_x(x,y)$ and $L_y(x,y)$, respectively. Next, a pixel of $N_p \times N_p$ is regarded as one region and a luminance gradient histogram is calculated among them. In the Hog feature, we do not consider the direction signs and consider the degrees from 0 to 180° by 20°, resulting in the number of bins $N_\theta = 9$. Finally, the feature is normalized and the adjacent 3×3 cells are assumed to be one block.

6.3 Fuzzy C-Means Clustering

Fuzzy C-means [22] is a soft clustering technique. It is a parameter of the degree of membership to each cluster, making it possible to find how close a membership is to each cluster. Fuzzy clustering allows K-means uniquely determined by a cluster to belong to more than one cluster.

6.4   Word2Vec

Word2vec is a distributed expression of words using a neural network published by Mikolov et al. [19] in 2013. Initially, a word prediction task is set that predicts each word in the text from surrounding words. Next, this task is learned from a large amount of text in a neural network, and the weight of each word in the middle layer is extracted to acquire a concept vector for a word. The learning model of word2Vec has a continuous bag-of-word (CBOW) model and a skip-gram model. The CBOW model fixes input words and predicts words co-occurring next to one another. The skip-gram model learns what kind of word group appears when a certain word is input. In the optimization model, hierarchical softmax, the output vector is expressed in a binary tree with all vocabularies as leaves and uses only a part for calculation and updating. A negative sampling also exists which does not update all output vectors in each iteration to reduce the calculation amount by sampling the wrong word accordingly.

6.5   MPQA Dictionary

We use the MPQA dictionary proposed by Wiebe et al. [18] as text with sentiment polarity. The MPQA dictionary contains words frequently and regularly used by people. It has 2006 positive words and 4783 negative words.

7   Tensor Factorization

In relational data learning, the binary relation can be expressed as a matrix, while the set of polynomial relations is represented as a multidimensional array, which is expressed as a tensor. A method for compressing the tensor to a lower dimension is called tensor decomposition, which was first introduced by Hitchcock in 1927 [23]. Tensor decomposition minimizes the difference between the tensor and the Frobenius norm of the model. It is expressed as follows:

$$min_{u,v,w} \left\| X - \sum_{r,s,t} u_r \circ v_s \circ w_t \right\|_F^2 \tag{9}$$

Tensor decomposition mainly includes Tucker decomposition and CP (COMP/PARAFAC) decomposition. Tucker decomposition is used when the order of each mode is different and the core tensor becomes dense. The formula for Tucker decomposition is shown below.

$$x_{ijk} \simeq \sum_{r=1}^{R} \sum_{s=1}^{S} \sum_{t=1}^{T} C_{rst} u_{ir} v_{js} w_{kt} \tag{10}$$

CP decomposition is a special system of Tucker decomposition, which is a natural extension of singular value decomposition where the core tensor is diagonal. The formula for CP decomposition is shown below.

$$x_{ijk} \simeq \sum_{r=1}^{R} u_{ir} v_{jr} w_{kr} \tag{11}$$

In Tucker decomposition, if the dimensions of each mode are equal and the core tensor is a unit tensor, then Tucker decomposition is equivalent to CP factorization. This study decomposes the mode into a binary of positive and negative, and so the dimension of the mode of all latent factor matrices is fixed as $R = 2$. In addition, because the core tensor is an identity matrix, a solution will be obtained by CP factorization.

7.1 Constrained Tensor Factorization

In normal tensor factorization, the latent factor matrix is unknown, no constraints are allowed, and the input is only the value of the tensor. However, in this research, the latent factor matrix of the text and visual features needs to be the sentiment polarity in order to guarantee that the latent factor matrix of the image file is the sentiment polarity of the image file. Consequently, each mode is completely unknown to give sentiment polarity in advance to both text and visual features, which are modes. Specifically, both tensor (image files, text feature, visual feature) and matrices (text feature, sentiment polarity/visual feature, sentiment polarity) are required and each mode has constraints. The CP factorization of the tensor with the constraint condition can be expressed by Formula (12), as proposed by Bahargam et al,

$$min_{u,v,w} \left\| X - \sum_r u_r \circ v_r \circ w_r \right\|_F^2 + \left\| Y - \sum_r u_r d_r^T \right\|_F^2 \tag{12}$$

Here, the latent factor matrix of tensor factorization, including matrix factorization, must be a matrix that does not take negative values. Many real world tensors do not have negative values, and factor elements can have physical meanings only when they are not negative. Thus, it is very important that latent factor matrices become non-negative values. Non-negativity improves the possibility of interpretation, but such improvement is not enough to understand data. When the purpose of tensor decomposition is to find potential topics of tensors and matrices, each latent factor matrix should have a structure that does not overlap. The fact that each latent factor matrix does not overlap means that the potential topic is concise and interpretable. To control duplication in the latent factor matrix, it is important to impose orthogonality constraints on each latent factor matrix. Therefore, given that U, which is a latent factor matrix, has orthogonality constraints, we set $U_i^T U_j \leq \epsilon_U$ i $\neq$ j. When is ϵ_U 0, the latent factor matrix is perfectly orthogonal. On the other hand, when the value is larger than 0, the latent factor matrix means that duplication is permitted.

Sparseness will encourage the idea that the least possible hypothesis should be made when describing or theorizing a certain event and that generating a model that is simpler and easier to interpret is possible. Sparsity constraints can be imposed on all latent factor matrices and core tensors.

Sparseness will encourage the idea that the least possible hypothesis should be made when describing or theoreticalizing a certain event, and it is possible to generate a simpler and easier to interpret model. Sparsity constraints can be imposed on all latent factor matrices and core tensors.

7.2   ALS Estimation Method

Tensor decomposition is an NP-hard problem, but the method most often used to solve it and make it converge locally is the ALS estimation method [24]. ALS estimation is used to fix two latent factor matrices, estimate one latent factor matrix by the least squares method, and update the matrix by replacing it. At first, the cost function is defined as follows:

$$L = \frac{1}{2} \sum_{i,j,k} \left(x_{ijk} - u_i^T (v_j^\circ w_k) \right)^2 \tag{13}$$

To find U, which minimizes the expression of Eq. (13), it is differentiated from u_i as follows:

$$\frac{\partial L}{\partial u_i} = -\sum_{jk} x_{ijk} \left(v_j \circ w_k \right) + (V^T V \circ W^T W) u_i \tag{14}$$

Equation (15) can be obtained by defining the expression as $\bar{x}_i^{vw} = \sum_{jk} x_{ijk} (v_j \circ w_k)$ and solving it as 0 in Eq. (14).

$$U = \overline{X}^{vw} (V^T V \circ W^T W)^{-1} \tag{15}$$

Similarly, V, W can be obtained.

7.3   ConCMTF-ALS Estimation Method

Bahargam et al. [7] propose the ConCMTF-ALS method because the ALS estimation method shown above cannot solve the tensor decomposition that includes the constraint condition. ConCMTF-ALS method imposes non-negativity, sparsity, and orthogonality by setting constraints, such as $U \geq 0, \forall i \ \|U_i\|_1 \leq \varepsilon_U, \forall i,$ and $j U_i^T U_j \leq \varepsilon_U i \neq j$. Furthermore, unlike the ALS method, which is executed alternately to solve each element, this method is solved separately for each column of each element. Compared to ALS, this algorithm is faster because it solves independently for each column of each matrix.

7.4   Estimation Method of Proposed Model Using ConCMTF-ALS

The proposed model of Eq. (7) with two constraints is solved using the ConCMTF-ALS estimation method. The algorithm used in this research is as follows.

Estimation algorithms of proposed model using ConCMTF-ALS

Input: $X \in \mathbb{R}^{n \times m_t \times m_v}$, $T_0 \in \mathbb{R}^{m_t \times R}$, $V_0 \in \mathbb{R}^{m_v \times R}$

Output: $U \in \mathbb{R}^{n \times R}$, $T \in \mathbb{R}^{m_t \times R}$, $V \in \mathbb{R}^{m_v \times R}$, $D \in \mathbb{R}^{R \times R}$, $E \in \mathbb{R}^{R \times R}$

1. Initialization $U \in \mathbb{R}^{n \times R}$, $T \in \mathbb{R}^{m_t \times R}$, $V \in \mathbb{R}^{m_v \times R}$, $D \in \mathbb{R}^{R \times R}$, $E \in \mathbb{R}^{R \times R}$

2. **while** convergence criterion is not met do

3. $U = min_U \|X_U - U(T \otimes V)^T\|_F$

4.   s.t. $U \geq 0$, $\forall i \, \|U_i\|_1 \leq \epsilon_U$, $\forall i,j \, U_i^T U_j \leq \epsilon_U \, i \neq j$

5.   Normalize the columns of U

6. $T = min_T \|[X_T \, T_o] - T[(V \otimes U)^T \, D^T]\|_F$

7.   s.t. $T \geq 0$, $\forall i \, \|T_i\|_1 \leq \epsilon_T$, $\forall i,j \, T_i^T T_j \leq \epsilon_T \, i \neq j$

8.   Normalize the columns of T

9. $V = min_v \|[X_V \, V_o] - V[(U \otimes T)^T \, E^T]\|_F$

10.   s.t. $V \geq 0$, $\forall i \, \|V_i\|_1 \leq \epsilon_V$, $\forall i,j \, V_i^T V_j \leq \epsilon_V \, i \neq j$

11.   Normalize the columns of V

12. $D = min_D \|T_o - TD^T\|_F$

13.   s.t. $D \geq 0$, $\forall i \, \|D_i\|_1 \leq \epsilon_D$, $\forall i,j \, D_i^T D_j \leq \epsilon_D \, i \neq j$

14.   Normalize the columns of D

15. $E = min_E \|V_o - VE^T\|_F$

16.   s.t. $E \geq 0$, $\forall i \, \|E_i\|_1 \leq \epsilon_E$, $\forall i,j \, E_i^T E_j \leq \epsilon_E \, i \neq j$

17.   Normalize the columns of E

18.   return U, T, V, D, E

---

8 Experiment

8.1 Dataset

This research will use Twitter's dataset from Yang et al. [3]. This dataset has a total of 409 images with text. Given that this experiment is unsupervised learning, labeling in the experiment is unnecessary, but sentiment labels are used for verification of the result. The dataset has 321 positive images and 88 negative images. In this experiment, the text used as text consists of the context (including the tag) in the tweet and the reply to that tweet.

8.2 Experimental Result

Let the input value of the tensor be the product of visual information and text information. The text features comprise 2006 positive words and 4783 negative words on the MPQA dictionary. Visual features are the number of clusters of clustering results by the fuzzy C-means method.

Accuracy, precision, recall, and specificity are used as evaluation indices. These indices consist of true positive (TP), false positive (FP), false negative (FN), and true negative (TN). TP is the number when both the predicted result and the label for verification are positive. FP is the number when the predicted result is positive while the label for verification is negative. FN is the number when the predicted result is negative while the label for verification is positive. TN is the number when both the predicted result and the label for verification are negative. Accuracy is (TP + TN)/ (TP + FP + TN + FN), precision is TP/(TP + FP), recall is TP/(TP + FN), and specificity is TN/(FP + TN).

Experiment 1

Experiment 1 examines the change in each cluster when sentiment analysis is performed using all data. Table 1 shows the results when 5–30 clusters are increased by 5 at a time. The experimental results reveal that the accuracy is 0.73 when the number of clusters is 25, which is the best accuracy. With accuracy close to 70% even in the case of 10 and 15 clusters, it does not necessarily improve as the number of clusters increases. However, because accuracy is poor when the number of clusters is 5, the number of clusters is thus necessary for a certain number or more.

Table 1. Result for each cluster of all data

	5	10	15	20	25	30
Accuracy	0.5	0.69	0.69	0.57	0.73	0.57
Precision	0.8	0.8	0.79	0.77	0.79	0.78
Recall	0.49	0.8	0.81	0.88	0.88	0.63
Specificity	0.57	0.26	0.24	0.15	0.15	0.34

Consider the case of cluster 25, where both precision and recall show high accuracy. This finding indicates that the prediction result becomes positive when the true result is positive in many data. The fact that recall is higher than precision means that most of the incorrect answers are positive results of prediction. The fact that specificity has a very low result also shows that most prediction results are positive. Based on the above result, the reason the predicted result is more than 70% is attributed to the fact the true sentiment polarity of all the data is more positive than the ones with negative polarity, and many of the results had positive polarity.

Experiment 2

In experiment 2, the numbers of positive and negative data are equalized in order to investigate whether the result of Experiment 1 estimates uneven sentiment polarity in any case. The results are shown in the Table 2. The numbers of clusters are 10, 15, and 25, all of which show high accuracy in Experiment 1.

The results in Table 2 show that the best accuracy is obtained for cluster 15. However, the accuracy is 0.56, which is considerably poor compared to the experiment at the time of all data. This result is considered to be caused by the small amount of data; that is, the accuracy of the specificity is better than the experiment when all the data are employed in the total number of clusters. The fact that accuracy and specificity both exceed 50% means that the bias of the sentiment polarity of the prediction result

Table 2. Result for each cluster after data reduction

	10	15	25
Accuracy	0.54	0.56	0.54
Precision	0.52	0.55	0.54
Recall	0.73	0.6	0.44
Specificity	0.35	0.52	0.64

of Experiment 1 affects the data. Specifically, only when bias occurs in the sentiment polarity of the data will the data of the estimation result be biased. Therefore, the result of Experiment 1 is valid, and the results of Experiments 1 and 2 indicate that accuracy is better when the number of data is larger.

Experiment 3

In Experiment 2, given that the validity of the result of Experiment 1 is proved, the experiment is carried out in comparison with the USEA framework when the numbers of clusters are 10, 15, and 25, wherein the accuracy is better in Experiment 1. Table 3 shows the accuracies of the proposed model, the USEA model, and the proposed model. In the USEA model for α, β, and γ, we used 0.7, 0.7, and 0.6, respectively, as proposed by Wang et al. to show the best accuracy within this study.

Table 3. Comparison between proposed model and USEA model

	10	15	25
Proposed model	0.69	0.69	0.73
USEA model	0.69	0.66	0.63

In this experimental result, when the number of clusters is 25, which is the number of clusters showing the best accuracy in the proposed model, the proposed model is 10% higher than the USEA model. In all clusters, the proposed model shows better accuracy than the USEA model. From the above results, (1) direct sentiment polarity is obtained from both textual information and visual information using tensor factorization, and (2) sentiment polarity is given to both text and visual features. Thus, the proposed model suggests higher precision than the USEA model.

Experiment 4

In experiment 4, we investigate changes in the values of ϵ_U, ϵ_T, ϵ_V, ϵ_D, ϵ_E, which are constraints of ConCMTF-ALS. Figures 3 and 4 show the orthogonality when the sparse

In experiment 4, we investigate changes in the values of ϵ_U, ϵ_T, ϵ_V, ϵ_D, and ϵ_E, all of which are constraints of ConCMTF-ALS. Figures 3 and 4 show the orthogonality when the sparse degree is fixed and the sparsity when the orthogonality is fixed, respectively. Data are a combination of positive and negative data numbers, and the number of clusters is 15.

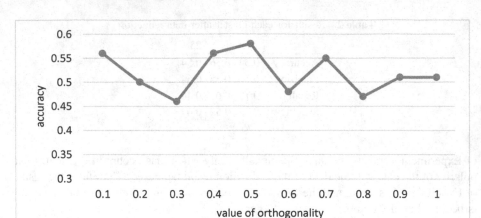

Fig. 3. Accuracy for each orthogonality

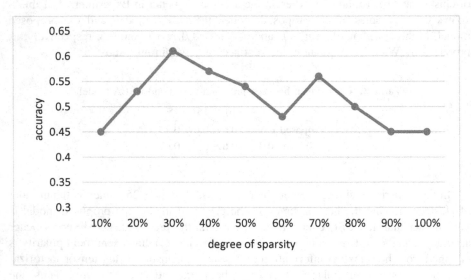

Fig. 4. Accuracy for each sparsity

Figure 3 shows the accuracy when the degree of orthogonality is varied between 0.1 and 1.0 by 0.1 when the sparsity is fixed as $\{\epsilon_U = 20, \epsilon_T = 40, \epsilon_V = 10, \epsilon_D = 4, \epsilon_E = 4\}$. The X axis represents orthogonality, and the Y axis represents accuracy. From the experimental results, when the orthogonality is 0.5, the accuracy is 0.58, which is the best result. This outcome indicates that the best accuracy is obtained when some overlap is allowed.

Figure 4 shows the change in sparsity when the orthogonality is fixed at 0.5. The sparse degree is the accuracy when changing the ratio of the latent factor matrix to the number of data by 10% within 0 to 100%. The X axis represents sparsity, and the Y axis represents accuracy. Experimental results show that the accuracy is 0.61 when the sparseness degree is 30%, which shows the best result. As can be seen from Fig. 4, a sparseness degree between 30% and 40% achieves better results when the sparseness is lower, but poor results when the degree is lower than 10%. Additionally, when the degree of sparsity exceeds 80%, very poor results are obtained.

The results of Experiment 4 reveal that when orthogonality is 0.4–0.5, the best accuracy is obtained when the overlap of the latent factor matrix is permitted to some extent. Sparseness also achieves the best accuracy when the sparseness degree is relatively low at about 30%.

9 Discussion

This research proposed a tensor composed from both text information and visual information and from the direct solution of sentiment polarity using the sentiment polarity of both text and visual features. First, we examined how the results change by changing the number of clusters and the number of data. The number of clusters with the best accuracy is 25 clusters when using all the data, while the best accuracy is achieved when 15 clusters are used when reducing the data. A total of 407 data are used, and 176 data reductions are made in accordance with 88 negative data with a small number of data. This finding suggests that the number of clusters has the best accuracy when it is 5%–10% of the data. In other words, visual features are considered to have sentiment polarity that differs by approximately 1/10 in the dataset.

In addition, the number of data is greatly affected by the result because the accuracy is better when experiments are performed with all the data than when performed with a small amount of data. In other words, a tensor composed of text information and visual information can be said to have correct sentiment polarity when the number of data is larger.

We likewise examined how orthogonality and sparsity affect the results. Given that orthogonality has good accuracy when it is between 0.4 and 0.5, the accuracy increases when the latent factor matrix allows overlapping to some extent. This is not the case where the latent topic is completely concise and interpretable but consists of text information and visual information when allowing about 50% overlap. Here, image information is classified as the correct sentiment polarity.

Finally, when the degree of sparsity is relatively low, on the order of 30%, the accuracy is considered to be better when it is classified as a complex latent factor that requires a somewhat complicated interpretation. Thus, the degree has a correct sentiment polarity.

10 Conclusion

In this paper, we conducted sentiment analysis of images on the basis of unsupervised learning approach through constrained tensor factorization without using sentiment labels. By using tensor factorization, we could obtain the sentiment polarity of an image from the image information having both text and visual information.

This approach made it possible to fully utilize the two types of information. Moreover, by giving sentiment polarity to visual features, situations could be avoided where the sentiment polarities of the text feature and of the image certainly coincide. This visual feature also has sentiment polarity, and the proposed model, which is a tensor where the sentiment polarity of the image does not necessarily coincide with the sentiment polarity of the text, was shown to be better than existing models.

In future work, trial experiments with larger datasets and 4-D tensor models with user information will be taken into account.

Acknowledgement. This work was supported in part by JSPS KAKENHI Grant Number 16K01250.

References

1. Wang, Y., Wang, S., Tang, J., Liu, H., Baoxin, L.: Unsupervised sentiment analysis for social media images. In: 24th International Joint Conference on Artificial Intelligence, pp. 2378–2379 (2015)
2. Jia, J., Wu, S., Wang, X., Hu, P., Cai, L., Tang, J.: Can we understand van Gogh's Mood? Learning to infer affects from images in social networks. In: The 20th ACM International Conference on Multimedia, pp. 857–860 (2012)
3. Yang, Y., Jia, J., Zhang, S., Wu, B., Li, L., Tang, J.: How do your friends on social media disclose your emotions? In: The 28th AAAI Conference on Artificial Intelligence, vol. 14, pp. 1–7 (2014)
4. Borth, D., Ji, R., Chen, T., Breuel, T., Chang, S.: Large-scale visual sentiment ontology and detectors using adjective noun pairs. In: The 21th ACM International Conference on Multimedia, pp. 223–232 (2013)
5. Yuan, J., Mcdonough, S., You, Q., Luo, J.: Sentribute: image sentiment analysis from a mid-level perspective. In: The 2nd International Workshop on Issues of Sentiment Discovery and Opinion Mining, p. 10 (2013)
6. You, Q., Luo, J., Jin, H., Yang, J.: Robust image sentiment analysis using progressively trained and domain transferred deep network. In: 29th AAAI Conference on Artificial Intelligence, pp. 381–388 (2015)
7. Bahargam, S., Papalexakis, E..: Constrained coupled matrix-tensor factorization and its application in pattern and topic detection. In: IEEE/ACM International Conference on Advances in Social Networks Analysis and Mining, pp. 91–94. IEEE (2018)
8. Siersdorfer, S., Hare, J.: Analyzing and predicting sentiment of images on the social web. In: The 18th ACM International Conference on Multimedia, pp. 715–718 (2010)
9. Fersini, E., Messina, J., Pozzi, F.A.: Sentiment analysis: Bayesian ensemble learning. Decis. Support Syst. **68**, 26–38 (2015)
10. Cao, D., Ji, R., Lin, D., Li, S.: Visual sentiment topic model based microblog image sentiment analysis. Multimed. Tools Appl. **75**(15), 8955–8968 (2016)
11. Xu, C., Cetintas, S., Lee, K., Li, L.: Visual sentiment prediction with deep convolutional neural networks. arXiv preprint, pp. 1411–5731 (2014)
12. Nguyen, T., Shirai, K., Velcin, J.: Sentiment analysis on social media for stock movement prediction. Expert Syst. Appl. **42**, 9603–9611 (2015)

13. Katsurai, M., Satoh, S.: Image sentiment analysis using latent correlations among visual, textual and sentiment views. In: IEEE International Conference on Acoustics, Speech and Signal Processing (ICASSP), vol. 7, pp. 2837–2841 (2016)
14. Pandarachalil, R., Sendhikumar, S., Mahalakshmi, G.S.: Twitter sentiment analysis for large-scale data: an unsupervised approach. Cogn. Comput. **7**(2), 254–262 (2015)
15. Gelli, F., Uricchio, T., Bertini, M., Bimbo, A., Chang, S.: Image popularity prediction in social media using sentiment and context features. In: Proceedings of the 23rd ACM International Conference on Multimedia, pp. 907–910 (2015)
16. Vadicamo, L., et al.: Cross-media learning for image sentiment analysis in the wild. In: Proceedings of the IEEE International Conference on Computer Vision, pp. 308–317 (2017)
17. Wang, J., Fu, J., Xu, Y., Mei, T.: Beyond object recognition: visual sentiment analysis with deep coupled adjective and noun neural networks. In: Proceedings of the IJCAI, pp. 3484–3490 (2016)
18. Wiebe, J., Wilson, T., Cardie, C.: Annotating expressions of opinions and emotions in language. Lang. Resour. Eval. **39**(2–3), 165–210 (2005)
19. Mikolov, T., Sutskerver, I., Chen, K., Corrado, G., Dean, J.: Distributed representations of words and phrases and their compositionality. In: Advances in Neural Information Processing Systems, pp. 3111–3119 (2013)
20. Oliva, A., Torralba, A.: Modeling the shape of the scene: a holistic representation of the spatial envelope. Int. J. Comput. Vision **42**(3), 145–175 (2001)
21. Dalal, N., Triggs, B.: Histogram of oriented gradients for human detection. Comput. Vision Pattern Recogn. **1**, 886–893 (2005)
22. Bezdek, J., Ehrlich, R., Full, W.: FCM: the fuzzy c-means clustering algorithm. Comput. Geosci. **10**(2–3), 191–203 (1984)
23. Hitchcook, F.: The expression of a tensor or a polyadic as a sum of products. J. Math. Phys. **6**(1–4), 164–189 (1927)
24. Carroll, D., Chang, J.: Analysis of individual differences in multidimensional scaling via an n-way generalization of 'Eckart-Young' decomposition. Psychometrika **35**(3), 283–319 (1970)

Ant Colony Optimization to Reduce Schedule Acceleration in Crowdsourcing Software Development

Razieh Saremi[✉], Ye Yang, and Abdullah Khanfor

Stevens Institute of Technology, Hoboken, NJ 070390, USA
{rlotfali,yyang4,akhanfor}@stevens.edu

Abstract. The complexity of software tasks and the variety of developer skill sets requires to accomplish the tasks, provides a challenge in the planning process for software project managers. Uncertainty based on crowd workers' different time zone and first language adds a layer of complexity to the CSD task scheduling. Therefore, accessing a scheduling model which can ease task allocation to improve task success and decrease project duration is essential. Existing models are either focused on the task allocation based on workers quality, or task availability in the crowdsourced platform. To create a flexible and effective model in CSD, we present an Ant Colony Optimization algorithm. The proposed approach shows a plan based on a list of available tasks in the platform and available workers based on their performance and rating metrics. The presented model is composed of four components: task fitness, workers' attraction, task-worker availability, and task scheduler. Experimental results on 408 projects demonstrate that the proposed method reduced project duration on average 74 days.

Keywords: Crowdsourced software development · Ant Colony Optimization · Task fitness · Task similarity · Workers' availability · Topcoder

1 Introduction

There is an emergent trend in software development projects that mini-tasks can be crowdsourced to achieve accelerated development and delivery. The characteristics of crowdsourcing tasks, in general, are short, simple, repetitive, requires little time and effort, while in crowdsourced software development (CSD) tasks are more complex, independent and requires a significant amount of time, effort, and expertise to achieve the task requirements [1]. For task owners, requesting a crowdsourcing service is more challenging due to the uncertainty of the similarity among available tasks in the CSD platform and the new arrival tasks, [2, 3], as well as, crowd workers' skill sets and performance history [4, 5] in the platform. These factors raise the issue of fitness of the assigned worker to the suitable task, since crowd workers may be interested in multiple tasks from different requestors among a pool of open tasks based on their individual goals and preference which provides resource inconsistency. It is reported that workers are more interested in working on tasks with similar concepts, monetary prize, technologies, complexities, priorities, and durations [3, 5–7]. Attracting workers to a group

© Springer Nature Switzerland AG 2019
S. Yamamoto and H. Mori (Eds.): HCII 2019, LNCS 11570, pp. 286–300, 2019.
https://doi.org/10.1007/978-3-030-22649-7_23

of similar tasks may cause zero registration, zero submissions, or unqualified sub-missions for some tasks due to lack of time from workers [2, 8, 9]. Therefore, it is beneficial to make efficient project plans to be able to assure the availability of crowd to work on the arrival CSD tasks and to submit them on time. To receive qualified submission as a task outcome in CSD, a good understanding of task characteristics, and crowd workers sensitivity to arrival tasks is required. To address that, we presented a task scheduling approach in CSD based on ant colony optimization (ACO) algorithm [41]. The proposed method represents a plan by a task list and a planned crowd allocation matric based on the workflow of Topcoder [10], one of the primary software crowdsourcing platforms.

The paper is organized as follows: Sect. 2 introduces the background and related work; Sect. 3 presents the research design and methodology; Sect. 4 reports the experimental design of the proposed model. Section 5 Limitation and Treats to Validity; and finally, Sect. 6 gives a Conclusion and outlook to future work.

2 Background and Related Work

2.1 Task Scheduling in Software Engineering

In the traditional software development process, task scheduling is the next step occurs after defining requirement development and deciding on task decomposition [11], which takes place based on specific groups of requirements [12]. There is a limitation on literature addressing scheduling in software development even though 80% of the software projects suffering from lack of schedule planning [13]. In practice, more than half of software requirements are interdependent, and only a few of them are inde-pendent, which notably impacts scheduling complexity [12].

To overcome the scheduling challenge different traditional scheduling techniques such as program evaluation and review technique (PERT), the critical path method (CPM) [39], and the resource-constrained project scheduling problem (RCPSP) [40] model have been used in software engineering. However, due to nature of software projects that is a people-intensive activity [13], task dependencies make available human resources awaiting completion of pre-requisites. Traditional scheduling techniques do not consider human resource allocation in scheduling, or if they do, they do not cover the resources with various skills. Since human is the main resource in software projects, scheduling can be more flexible in comparison with other industries [14]. One of the approaches to address this need can be search based optimization problem.

Recently, project managers have been using global software development tech-niques to reduce cost and shorten release time although, different time zone and resource location may add to the scheduling challenges [15, 16]. In which, team members are distributed into different zones and countries. It seems the best practice to optimize task scheduling in this approach is following the sun [17]. Follow the sun happens when software development is distributed over a twenty-four-hour working day. In this method, tasks are distributed among workers with different time zone, and all the team members work on the same phase and tasks of the project in their own day hours.

2.2 Task Scheduling in CSD

Due to the different characteristics of the machine and human behavior, delays can occur in product release and lack of systematic processes to balance the appropriate delivery of features with the available resources [18]. Therefore, improper scheduling would result in task starvation [6]. Parallelism in scheduling is a great method to create the chance of utilizing a greater pool of workers [19, 42] as this method encourages workers to specialize and complete the task in shorter period and promote solutions in which benefits the requestor to clearly understand how workers decide to compete on a task and analyze the crowd workers performance [6]. Shorter schedule planning can be one of the most notable advantages of using CSD for managers [20].

Complex crowdsourced projects cannot be performed based on simple available parallel approaches. Complex projects have more dependencies and multiple occurrences of changing requirements [21]; they require different workers with diverse levels of expertise. Therefore, this is one of the main challenges in applying an effective method to schedule decomposed projects in crowdsourcing [22]. Since coordinating workers is difficult among a distributed global crowd, in most cases, organizational coordination techniques such as programming and feedback as general coordination methods can be applied to crowd work as well [23, 24].

Batching tasks is another effective method to reduce the complexity of tasks, and it will dramatically reduce cost [25]. Batching crowdsourcing tasks would lead to a faster result than approaches, which keep workers separate and is also quicker than the average of the fastest individual worker [26]. There is a theoretical minimum batch size for every project as one of the principles of product development flow [27]. To some extent, the success of software crowdsourcing is associated with reduced batch size in small tasks.

Besides, the delay scheduling method [5] was specially designed for crowdsourced projects to maximize the probability of a worker receiving tasks from the same batch of tasks they were performing. Extension of this idea introduced a new method called "fair sharing schedule" [28]. In this method, various resources would be shared among all tasks with different demands, which ensures that all tasks would receive the same amount of resources to be fair. For example, this method was used in Hadoop Yarn. Later, Weighted Fair Sharing (WFS) [3] was presented as a method to schedule batches based on their priority. Tasks with higher priority are introduced first. Another proposed crowd scheduling method is based on quality of service (QOS) [9], a skill-based scheduling method with the purpose of minimizing scheduling while maximizing quality by assigning the task to the most available qualified worker. This scheme was created by extending standards of Web Service Level Agreement (WSLA) [29]. The third available method would be a game with a purpose [30], in which a task will not be started unless a certain number of workers registered for it. The most recent method is HIT-Bundle [3] a batch container which schedules heterogeneous tasks into the platform from different batches. This method makes for a higher outcome by applying different scheduling strategies at the same time.

2.3   Workers' Motivation

The diversity of software workers in crowdsourcing, makes motivational factors be typically divided into two categories: intrinsic factors and extrinsic factors. First, intrinsic clusters comprise enjoyment factors and community values that are associated with age, location, personal career, society and even task identity [31]. In addition, participation motivation categories [32] such as learning, and self-marketing are considered as some of the main intrinsic factors for workers which are mentioned in the concept of "activation enabling". Second, Extrinsic clusters include financial and social aspects, which are the direct effect of the educational background, household income, and task award or payment [31]. It is reported that [32], motivations such as organizer appreciation, prizes, and knowledge experts are the highest ranked among workers. Another high-ranking motivation factor is the presence of requesters with a prestige brand name, such as Google, or NASA, which attracts software workers to apply for tasks, as it can potentially be used to strengthen resumes and affect software workers ratings either indirectly or directly [33].

Different studies on motivation patterns of crowdsourcing workers reported that monetary prize is one of the top motivating factors to attract and involve potential workers in task competition in crowdsourcing market [1, 6, 34]. The monetary prize typically correlates with the degree of task complexity and required competition levels as well as task priority in the project development [6, 34]. The second motivation factor which affects monetary prize is the worker's skill level [31]. Higher skilled level workers generally have higher motivation level of winning a prize and gaining communal identification while the top motivational factors of occasional workers are typically a pas-time human capital investment and skill variety. Therefore, task requesters usually struggle to distribute awards for the tasks with a good scheduling plan in the hope of getting the best possible task submissions in terms of the tasks' type based on workers historical activities and submissions [6].

2.4   Challenges in CSD

Considering the highest rate for task completion and accepting submissions, software managers will be more concerned about the risks of adopting crowdsourcing. Therefore, there is a need for better decision-making system to analyze and control the risk of insufficient competition and poor submissions due to the attraction of untrustworthy workers. A traditional method of addressing this problem in the software industry is task scheduling. Scheduling is helpful in prioritizing access to the resources. It can help managers to optimize task execution in the platform to attract the most reliable and trustworthy workers. Normally, in traditional methods, task requirements and phases are fixed, while cost and time are flexible. In a time-boxed system, time and cost are fixed, while, task requirements and phases are flexible [17]. However, in CSD all three variables are flexible. This factor creates a huge advantage in crowdsourcing software projects.

Generally, improper scheduling could lead to task starvation [6], since workers with high abilities tend to compete with low skilled workers [34]. Hence, users are more likely to choose tasks with fewer competitors [33]. Also, workers intentionally choosing less popular tasks to participate could potentially enhance winning proba-bilities, even if workers share similar expertise. It brings some severe problems in the CSD trust system and causes a lot of dropped and none- completed tasks. Moreover, tasks with relatively lower monetary prizes have a high probability to be chosen and be solved, which results in only 30% of problems in platform being solved [24]. This may attract higher numbers of workers to compete and consequently makes the higher chance of starvation for more expensive tasks and project failure. The above issues indicate the importance of task scheduling in the platform in order to attract the right amount of trustable and expert workers as well as shorten the release time.

3   Research Design and Methodology

To solve the scheduling problem, we present an ant colony optimization approach. We extend the model proposed in [35] to be adopted to CSD domain. A scheduling approach with an event-based scheduler and an ant colony optimization algorithm is introduced in [35]. In each colony, ants provide some pheromone (chemical tracking) to react to workers and tasks history as the pheromone (workers and tasks history) to present a better scheduling method. The presented approach represents a task list and a planned worker allocation matrix. To create the final task scheduler, it is essential to understand required pheromones in the model. This model contains three heuristic pheromones of time box, task scheduling batching, and worker availability.

3.1   Time Box

A project manager is creating an ordered list of decomposed tasks per project. In CSD planning, each task can be associated with multiple workers, the minimum slack time (MINSK) process [36] per task is used to create the time pheromone. This heuristic is usually used for sequential task scheduling adoption. The task with smaller MINSK implies that it is either more urgent or simpler to perform. The MINSK for a task can be estimated as follow:

Definition 1: MINSK is the amount of time a task may be delayed from its posting date without delaying the submission due date is total slack of task (i),TST_i:

$$TST_i = LED_i - EED_i \; or \; TST(i) = LST_i - EST_i \tag{1}$$

In which:

> EST_i, the task registration date in the platform,
> LST_i, latest task registration date in the platform,
> EED_i, the task submissions date in the platform,
> LED_i, the worker submissions date in the platform.

Definition 2: Amount of time a task can be delayed from its earliest starting time without delaying the starting time of any of its immediate sequential tasks is called free slack of task (i), FST_i:

$$FST_i = Min\,(EED_i - ESD_i) \tag{2}$$

Definition 3: Task with minimum slack are bottlenecks. Bottleneck task (i), BNT_i, calculates as diverse ratio of minimum slack time per task (TST_i). The smaller the BNT_i, is the more urgent the task is, in terms of schedule as early as possible.

$$BNT_i = \frac{1}{TST_i} \tag{3}$$

To build a feasible list of tasks by workers, each worker creates an eligible list of tasks that satisfy their skillset. The list maker includes the following steps:

Step a: add the task that the worker is interested in the eligible list of tasks.
Step b: for k = 1 to n:
Step b-1: select a task from eligible list and put it in the kth position of the task list following random number (v).

Definition 4: The probability of task T_i is chosen to be registered by workers based on time box pheromone is:

$$TBTR_i = \frac{T_i * BNT_i}{n}, \ where\ n\ is\ total\ number\ of\ task\ per\ project \tag{4}$$

This means that the task has a probability of being taken with the maximum pheromone value, so the algorithm can strongly exploit the past search of tasks.

Step b-2: update the eligible list by removing the selected task from the eligible list and adding a new feasible task that satisfy the workers' skillset.

After step b-1 and b-2 repeated n times a feasible task list is built.

3.2   Task Similarity Batching

Task Similarity Analysis
To analyze task similarity in the platform there is a need to understand the tasks' local distance from each other and task similarity factor based on it.

Definition 5: Task local distance (Dis_j) it is a tuple of all tasks' attributes in the data set. In respect to introduce variables in Table 1, task local distance is:

$$Disi = (Award,\ Registration\ date,\ Submission\ Date,\ Task\ type,\ Technology,\ Task\ requirement) \tag{5}$$

Table 1. Description of top 50% of task type in CSD platform [10]

Task type	Description
First2Finish	The first person to submit passing entry wins
Assembly competition	Assemble previous tasks
Bug hunt	Find and fix available bugs
Code	Programming specific task
UI prototype	User Interface prototyping is an analysis technique in which users are actively involved in the mocking-up of the UI for a system
Architecture	This contest asks competitors to define the technical approach to implement the requirements. The output is a technical architecture document and finalized a plan for assembly contests
Test suit	Competitors produce automated test cases to validate the quality, accuracy, and performance of applications. The output is a suite of automated test cases

Definition 6: Task Similarity Factor (TSi,j) is dot product and magnitude of local distance of two tasks:

$$TSi,j = \frac{\sum_{i,j=0}^{n} Disi(Tj, Ti)}{\sum_{i=0}^{n} \sqrt{Disi(Ti)} * \sum_{j=0}^{n} \sqrt{Djsj(Tj)}} \tag{6}$$

Task Similarity Pheromone

The similarity matrix specifies the causal similarity among tasks. Before creating the heuristics, it is important to understand the fitness of task (i), FT_i, in the platform.

Definition 7: the fitness of task (i), FT_i, in the platform to receive registration ix:

$$FTi = \frac{\sum_{i=1}^{n} (TSi * MaxRi * TDi)}{\sum_{i=1}^{n} TDi} \tag{7}$$

Now, to create the pheromone, we assumed there is a minimum number of registrations for tasks, which helps a task get a higher chance of being successfully complete. If a task leaves the pool of open tasks and enter the pool of registered tasks, there will be minimum 1 registration associated with the task. This is called the initial task registration (ITR).

Definition 8: Probability of task (i) from similarity batch (j) is registered by a worker is:

$$TR(i,j) = FTi * ((1 - TSi) * N + TSi * ITR) \tag{8}$$

While N is the total available task in the platform in the same timeframe.

This heuristic helps project managers to choose the best so far task in their list and have a higher chance for receiving a qualified submission.

3.3 Workers Availability

Last heuristics is helping to make a suitable pheromone for worker availability. The heuristic of worker (j) attraction on registering for task (i) is define as Worker Attraction (i, j), AW_{ij}:

$$WA_{ij} = \begin{cases} MinRej + AveRej * WERTj & WRDj = TPDi \\ MinRej + AveRej * WERTj + (WRDij - TDi) * MaxRej & TPDi < WRDj \le TSDi \end{cases} \quad (9)$$

In which:

Definition 9: Minimum reliability of worker (j), $MinRe_j$, represent the lowest reliability associate to worker j before taking the task (i) and after taking the task (i).

$$MinRe_j = Min\left\{OldReliability_j, NewReliability_j\right\} \quad (10)$$

Definition 10: Average reliability of worker (j), $AveRe_j$, represent the average reliability associate to worker j before taking the task (i) and after taking the task (i).

$$AveRe_j = \frac{OldReliability_j + NewReliability_j}{2} \quad (11)$$

Definition 11: Maximum reliability of worker (j), $MaxRej$, represent the highest reliability associate to worker j before taking the task (i) and after taking the task (i).

$$MaxRe_j = Max\left\{OldReliability_j, NewReliability_j\right\} \quad (12)$$

Definition 12: Worker (j) earliest registration time, $WERTj$, represent the minimum worker task registration time, $WTRTj$ associate to worker j in worker's task registration history.

$$WERTj = Min\{WTRT1, WTRT2, \ldots, WTRTj\} \quad (13)$$

Definition 13: Registration date of worker (j) for task (i), $WRDij$, is the date worker j registered for task i.

Definition 14: The pheromone heuristic of worker availability is the probability that worker (k) will submit the taken task (i):

$$TS(i,k) = WAij * Prob(WRi) * PLSi * M \quad (14)$$

While M is total registered task in the platform in the same time frame.

The upper bound estimation of workers' availability is 1. This means that all the workers in the platform have required skillset for performing the arrival task.

The scheduling problem in CSD is tracible as both task list and the workers' allocation have to be optimally decided. However, there are heuristics that can help us to build the task list and select workers' allocation, it is difficult to create an effective heuristic that can predict the exact workers who registers for the task. Therefore, we coupled the presented AOC model with a search-based procedure.

Table 2. Workers availability in CSD platform [38]

Workers' belt	Rating range (X)	% workers
Gray	X < 900	90.02%
Green	900 < X < 1200	2.88%
Blue	1200 < X < 1500	5.39%
Yellow	1500 < X < 2200	1.54%
Red	X > 2200	0.16%

4   Experimental Studies

4.1   Data Set

The gathered dataset contains 403 individual projects including 4907 component development tasks and 8108 workers from Jan 2014 to Feb 2015, extracted from Topcoder website [10]. After removing workers who never registered or submitted any task in their membership history, the number of active workers reduced to 5062 workers.

In the experiment phase we test the proposed method on 408 projects and 4900 decomposed tasks performed by 5700 workers.

Based on the Topcoder definition we clustered tasks under 14 task type [37], however we have considered 7 highest common task type in this research. Table 1 summarized the description of the considered task types per project decomposed tasks.

Also, Topcoder categorized workers under 5 group belts based on workers rating [38]. Table 2 summaries worker distribution respectively.

4.2   Experimental Setting

The main objective in this research is to minimize the project duration and maximizing the task success rate. Therefore, we need to update the set up the experiment based on workers' arrival in the platform to schedule the task arrival. The parameters of the proposed ACO are set as follows:

The start number of arrival ants follows the average of competition level per tasks and equal to 18 [7] and the minimum number of workers registering per task is 1. The umber of task arrival in the platform follows the task arrival schedule based on the actual data gathered from Topcoder. Moreover, the assigned random number in choosing the eligible list of tasks is used as the degree of aggressiveness in the algorithm. The larger the random number is, the stronger the algorithm exploits the past search experience and exhibits a fast converging manner.

4.3 Results and Analysis

Task Attraction

According to the result, tasks with duration of 3 weeks or less provides higher level of average attraction for workers to perform and make a submission. Interestingly tasks with 27–29 days duration provide the highest level of attraction for workers with degree of attraction of 99%. Figure 1 illustrates the overall result of task attraction after applying ACO model.

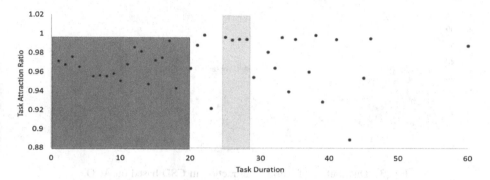

Fig. 1. Task attraction in the CSD based on ACO

Task Fitness

Deeper investigation of task fitness in the platform shows that tasks with duration less than 10 days and similarity degree of 60% and above would provide the average task fitness of 17%. Task with duration between 10 and 20 days reduce the task fitness to 10%. And interestingly task with duration more than 20 days dropped the task fitness dramatically. Figure 2 shows the details of task fitness based on different task duration and similarity degree of 60% and above.

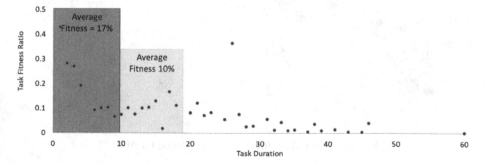

Fig. 2. Task fitness in CSD based on ACO

Workers' Attraction

Applying worker reliability pheromone provides the result that tasks with duration less than 10 days can attract on average 13 workers to perform them. And tasks wit duration between 25–35 days can attract on average 9 workers to perform them. While tasks with duration between 10–25 days and more than 35 days can attract less than 8 workers to perform them. Figure 3 presents the distribution of workers' attraction and task duration based on worker availability pheromone.

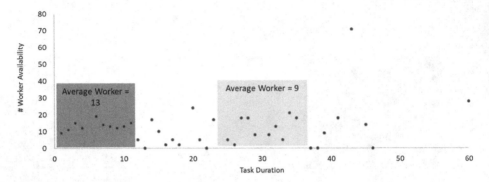

Fig. 3. Distribution of workers' attraction in CSD based on ACO

Task-Worker Attraction

Applying all the 3 pheromones to the dataset provides the task-worker attraction metrics. As it is shown in Fig. 4, 20 new arrival task per week in the platform results in to attracting on average 90 workers to perform the tasks, while 20–40 task arrival will lead to attracting on average 168 active worker. 40–60 tasks provide on average 200 available worker and 80 tasks brings 348 available workers in the platform.

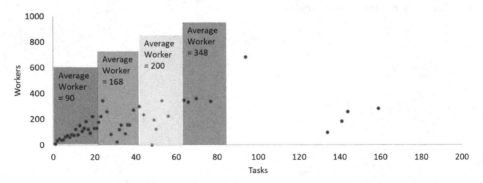

Fig. 4. Task-worker attraction in CSD based on ACO

Schedule Acceleration

Applying overall ACO scheduling model reduced the project duration to on average 74 days. As it is presented in Fig. 5, projects with decomposed number of 50 tasks can be done with in 4 weeks. Projects that are decomposed between 50–100 tasks need 6 weeks duration to be complete. Projects with number of tasks between 100–150 require 9 weeks of schedule duration. And all the projects with more than 150 tasks can be completed with on average of 12 weeks duration. 83% of the projects can be scheduled to be complete with in 10 weeks or less.

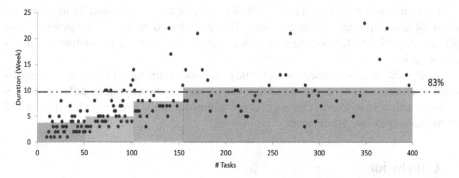

Fig. 5. Schedule acceleration in CSD based on ACO

Table 3 summarized the overall status of the projects in our dataset. As it is presents, the suggested ACO scheduling method decreased the task failure ratio for average of 2%, increased the Workers reliability in making a submission for 1.5% and Workers trust-ability in not only making a submission but make a valid submission on average 12%.

Table 3. Summary of project level task scheduling in CSD

Number of task per project	Number of project	Duration (Week)		Failure ratio		Worker reliability		Worker trust-ability	
		Original	Suggested	Original	Suggested	Original	Suggested	Original	Suggested
50	194	10	4	16%	15%	13%	13%	69%	72%
100	68	11	5	17%	16%	14%	14%	68%	81%
150	36	12	5	18%	16%	13%	15%	72%	85%
200	12	11	4	20%	20%	13%	14%	67%	83%
250	11	9	4	23%	16%	13%	14%	73%	85%
300	10	19	6	18%	16%	14%	15%	44%	69%
350	6	12	5	22%	19%	12%	12%	57%	79%
400	4	30	10	17%	15%	10%	12%	57%	73%
450	1	1	1	18%	14%	13%	22%	80%	85%
500	7	30	9	18%	13%	13%	15%	51%	70%
550	1	9	2	20%	16%	12%	16%	84%	95%
600	0	0	0	0%	0%	0%	0%	0%	0%
650	1	22	9	25%	17%	12%	14%	85%	89%
700	5	4	1	18%	17%	14%	15%	66%	79%
750	1	2	2	15%	14%	12%	13%	53%	77%
800	0	0	0	0%	0%	0%	0%	0%	0%

5   Limitation and Threats to Validity

There are several threats to validity. First the presented model is based on the data gathered during Jan 2014–Feb 2015. There is a chance that data set from different time line may lead to slightly different result.

Second, the proposed method does not consider worker's multi-tasking factors, i.e., how many tasks can a worker take, at maximum, during the same period of time. Though this is one of the important factors influencing software project scheduling decisions, we don't see there is a pattern in the upper bound limits for worker's multi-tasking.

Third, the data preparation and similarity analysis are complicated by the temporal nature of task attributes and descriptions. However, based on the utility factor of each individual workers, different sets of task attribute can be used to analyze similarity among tasks.

Lastly, the data sets used in this study for both training and testing are mostly unbalanced data sets in terms of the number of samples belonging to different classes for both tasks and workers. The issue is not addressed in the presented model and will be considered in our future work.

6   Conclusion

CSD provides software organizations access to infinite worker resource supply from the Internet. Assigning tasks to a pool of unknown workers from all over the glob is challenging. A traditional approach to solve such challenge is scheduling. Generally, dependencies among tasks and workers make task scheduling an NP-hard problem. Improper task scheduling in CSD may cause to zero task registration, zero task submissions or low qualified submissions due to uncertain workers behavior. This research addressed a new scheduling model for solving the CSD planning problem has been developed. The proposed model adopted ant colony heuristics to solve the complicated planning problem via CSD. The experimental experience lead to reducing project duration for average of 74 days (i.e. 2.5 months) and provide a more stable workload assignment to available workers in the platform.

In the future research we will focus on the trust network among available workers and apply the proposed scheduling model based on the recognized trust network in the platform, to understand the impact of assigned workers to the same task on workers' decision making and consequently task failure ratio.

References

1. Stol, K.-J., Fitzgerald, B.: Two's company, three's a crowd: a case study of crowdsourcing software development. In: The 36th International Conference on Software Engineering (2014)
2. Saremi, R.: A hybrid simulation model for crowdsourced software development. In: Proceedings of the 5th International Workshop on Crowd Sourcing in Software Engineering (2018)

3. Difallah, D.E., Demartini, G., Cudré-Mauroux, P.: Scheduling human intelligence tasks in multi-tenant crowd-powered systems. ACM (2016)
4. Yang, Y., Karim, M.R., Saremi, R., Ruhe, G.: Who Should take this task? – Dynamic decision support for crowd workers. In: Proceedings of ESEM (2016)
5. Gordon, G.: A general purpose systems simulation program. In: EJCC, Washington D.C. (1961)
6. Faradani, S., Hartmann, B., Ipeirotis, P.G.: What's the right price? Pricing tasks for finishing on time. In: Proceedings of the Human Computation (2011)
7. Yang, Y., Saremi, R.L.: Award vs. worker behaviors in competitive crowdsourcing tasks. In: ESEM, Benjin, Chaina, Imperical Software Engineering and Measures (2015)
8. Khanfor, A., Yang, Y., Vesonder, G., Ruhe, G.: Failure prediction in crowdsourced software development. In: 24th Asia-Pacific Software Engineering Conference (2017)
9. Khazankin, R., Psaier, H., Schall, D., Dustdar, S.: QoS-based task scheduling in crowdsourcing environments. In: Kappel, G., Maamar, Z., Motahari-Nezhad, H.R. (eds.) ICSOC 2011. LNCS, vol. 7084, pp. 297–311. Springer, Heidelberg (2011). https://doi.org/10.1007/978-3-642-25535-9_20
10. Topcoder Website. http://www.Topcoder.com
11. Mao, K., Capra, L., Harman, M., Jia, Y.: A survey of the use of crowdsourcing in software engineering. Technical report RN/15/01, Department of Computer Science, University College London (2013)
12. Ma, C.: The Business of Software. Free Press, New York (2004)
13. Regnell, B., Brinkkemper, S.: Market-driven requirements engineering for software products. In: Aurum, A., Wohlin, C. (eds.) Engineering and Managing Software Requirements. Springer, Heidelberg (2005). https://doi.org/10.1007/3-540-28244-0_13
14. Carlshamre, P., Sandahl, K., Lindvall, M., Regnell, B., Nattoch Dag, J.: An industrial survey of requirements interdependencies in software product release planning. In: RE 2010. IEEE Computer Society (2001)
15. Vathsavayi, S., Sievi-Korte, O., Koskimies, K., Systä, K.: Planning global software development projects using genetic algorithms. In: Ruhe, G., Zhang, Y. (eds.) SSBSE 2013. LNCS, vol. 8084, pp. 269–274. Springer, Heidelberg (2013). https://doi.org/10.1007/978-3-642-39742-4_23
16. Gao, C., Zhang, H., Jiang, S.: Constructing hybrid software process simulation models. In: 11th International Conference on Software and Systems Process (ICSSP) (2015)
17. Cooper, R.: Agile–stage-gate hybrids. In: Research-Technology Management (2016)
18. Saliu, M.O., Ruhe, G.: The art and science of software release planning. In: IEEE Software (2005)
19. Ngo-The, A., Ruhe, G.: Optimized resource allocation for software release planning. Trans. Softw. Eng. (2009)
20. Lakhani, K.R., Jeppesen, L.B., Lohse, P.A., Panetta, J.A.: The value of openness in scientific problem solving. HBS Working Paper Number: 07-050, Harvard Business School (2007)
21. Kittur, A., et al.: The future of crowd work. In: CSCW (2013)
22. LaToza, T.D., Ben Towne, W., van der Hoek, A., Herbsleb, J.D.: Crowd development. In: The 6th International Workshop on Cooperative and Human Aspects of Software Engineering (2013)
23. March, J.G., Simon, H.A.: Organizations. Wiley, New York (1958)
24. Ross, J., Irani, L., Silberman, M.S., Zaldivar, A., Tomlinson, B.: Who are the crowdworkers? Shifting demographics in Amazon mechanical turk. ACM (2010)
25. Marcus, A., Wu, E., Karger, D., Madden, S., Miller, R.: Human-powered sorts and joins. VLDB Endow. (2009)

26. Bernstein, M., Brandt, J., Miller, R.C., Karger, D.R.: Crowds in two seconds: enabling realtime crowd-powered interfaces. In: The 24th Annual ACM Symposium on User Interface Software and Technology (2011)
27. Reinertsen, D.G.: The Principle Product Development Flow, Second Generation Lean Product Development. Celeritas Publishing, Redondo Beach (2009)
28. Ghodsi, A., Zaharia, M., Hindman, B., Konwinski, A., Shenker, S., Stoica, I.: Dominant resource fairness: fair allocation of multiple resource types. USENIX Association (2011)
29. IBM. http://www.research.ibm.com/wsla/
30. Zaharia, M., Borthakur, D., Sen Sarma, J., Elmeleegy, K., Shenker, S., Stoica, I.: Delay scheduling: a simple technique for achieving locality and fairness in cluster scheduling. ACM (2010)
31. Kaufmann, N., Schulze, T., Veit, D.: More than fun and money: worker Motivation in crowdsourcing - a study on mechanical turk. In: 17th AMCIS (2011)
32. Krcmar, H., Bretschneider, U., Huber, M., Leimeister, J.M.: Leveraging crowdsourcing: activation-supporting components for IT-based ideas competition. J. Manag. Inf. Syst. **26**, 197–224 (2009)
33. Yang, J., Adamic, L.A., Ackerman, M.S.: Crowdsourcing and knowledge sharing: strategic user behaviour on Taskcn. In: 9th ACM Conference on Electronic Commerce (2008)
34. Archak, N.: Money, glory and cheap talk: analyzing strategic behavior of contestants in simultaneous crowdsourcing contests on Topcoder.com. In: 19th International Conference on World Wideweb (2010)
35. Chen, W.-N., Zhang, J.: Ant colony optimization for software project scheduling and staffing with an event-based scheduler. IEEE Trans. Softw. Eng. **39**(1), 1–17 (2013)
36. Ozdamar, L.: A genetic algorithm approach to a general category project scheduling problem. IEEE Trans. Syst. Man Cybern. Part C Appl. Rev. **29**(1), 44–59 (1999)
37. Saremi, R., Yang, Y.: Empirical analysis on parallel tasks in crowdsourcing software development. In: 30th IEEE/ACM International Conference on Automated Software Engineering Workshop (ASEW) (2015)
38. Saremi, R., Yang, Y., Ruhe, G., Messinger, D.: Leveraging crowdsourcing for team elasticity: an empirical evaluation at Topcoder. In: ICSE-SEIP (2017)
39. Shtub, A., Bard, J.F., Globerson, S.: Project Management: Processes, Methodologies, and Economics, 2nd edn. Prentice Hall, Upper Saddle River (2005)
40. Brucker, P., Drexl, A., Mohring, R., Neumann, K., Pesch, E.: Resource-constrained project scheduling: notation, classification, models and methods. Eur. J. Oper. Res. **112**, 3–41 (1999)
41. Dorigo, M., Maniezzo, V., Colorni, A.: Ant system: optimization by a colony of cooperating agents. IEEE Trans. Syst. Man Cybern. Part B Cybern. **26**(1), 29–41 (1996)
42. Saremi, R.L., Yang, Y.: Empirical analysis on parallel tasks in crowdsourcing software development. In: 30th IEEE/ACM International Conference on Automated Software Engineering Workshop (ASEW), pp. 28–34, November 2015

Distributed Constraint Satisfaction Among Android Devices

Konatsu Tagawa and Suguru Ueda$^{(\boxtimes)}$

Saga University, Saga 840-8502, Japan
sgrueda@cc.saga-u.ac.jp

Abstract. The constraint satisfaction problem (CSP) has been widely studied in the AI literature, where the aim of this problem is to find an assignment of values to variables that satisfies all constraints. A distributed CSP (DisCSP) is a CSP where variables and constraints are distributed among agents. Various application problems in multi-agent systems can be formalized as DisCSPs. The asynchronous backtracking (ABT) algorithm has been developed for solving DisCSPs in a distributed manner. In this paper, we implement the ABT algorithm as an Android application, which we call ABT on Androids. We evaluate our application by solving the 2-queens problem.

Keywords: DisCSP · Multi-agent system · Android

1 Introduction

Multi-agent systems (MASs) have been one of the major research topics in artificial intelligence [3]. The focus of an MAS is to develop a (social) system where multiple agents work together. An agent is a computational entity, such as an AI software program or an intelligent robot, which can act autonomously to achieve the system's objective. If these agents are cooperative, we can develop the system to achieve a common objective. Otherwise, agents are designed to compete with each other for their individual goals to achieve a social outcome in the end. Both theoretical and experimental research has been conducted.

Cooperative settings include distributed problem solving, where a problem to solve is distributed among agents and they solve the problem in cooperation [4]. There are two distributed problem-solving models: distributed constraint satisfaction problems (DisCSPs) [5] and distributed constraint optimization problems (DCOPs) [2]. These models are based on a constraint reasoning model, and they have become a fundamental problem in distributed problem solving.

A DisCSP is a prominent model of distributed problem solving. In a constraint satisfaction problem (CSP) [1], variables and constraints exist among these variables. The goal of the CSP is to find a consistent assignment of values to variables. A DisCSP is a CSP where variables and constraints are distributed among agents in an MAS. Various real-world applications can be formalized as

© Springer Nature Switzerland AG 2019
S. Yamamoto and H. Mori (Eds.): HCII 2019, LNCS 11570, pp. 301–310, 2019.
https://doi.org/10.1007/978-3-030-22649-7_24

DisCSPs considering that each variable represents an action of a corresponding agent. We can find a consistent combination of agent actions applying a distributed algorithm for solving DisCSPs in such applications.

Let us illustrate a motivating example of an emergency camera drone system. Imagine the period immediately following enormous natural disasters, such as earthquakes, violent storms, or volcanic eruptions and suppose that sending unmanned aerial vehicles, commonly known as drones, with a camera to damaged areas without overlapping. Drones are autonomous agents in this MAS, and the possible actions of each drone include determining which damaged areas the drone is going to be sent to take photos to determin how extensively the area is damaged. Constraints among actions are designed to avoid redundant actions. A distributed algorithm solves this problem, having drones communicate with each other without a central control.

One can argue that, in principle, this problem can be solved in a centralized manner. For example, a central server collects all the information and solves the problem. Then, the server sends the assignment to the drones. However, an important drawback in this centralized manner is that preparing the server would be difficult in this case. Furthermore, we may lose electric power to run the server. For example, in southern Hokkaido, Japan, on 6 September 2018, an earthquake cut all power. Therefore, a distributed manner would be more robust than a centralized manner from this viewpoint.

As far as the authors are aware, few research studies applied the DisCSP (or DCOP) to a real-world problem, though many theoretical results have been provided. With advancing technological progress in the microcomputers used in mobile phones, tablet devices, and drones, the possibilities of such research have been widened.

In this paper, we aim to apply techniques and algorithms obtained in DisCSP research to the emergency camera drone system described above. As the first step of our research, we implement the asynchronous backtracking (ABT) algorithm, which was first introduced to solve a DisCSP, as an Android application, which we call ABT on Androids. We suppose that each drone is controlled via a corresponding Android device, and these Android devices communicate with each other. We evaluate our application by solving a representative problem: the n-queens problem.

The rest of the paper is organized as follows. In Sect. 2, we introduce the problem definition of a DisCSP and the ABT algorithm. Then, we briefly explain Android devices and possible communication protocols among Android devices in Sect. 3. In Sects. 4 and 5, we develop ABT on Androids and we evaluate it. Finally, in Sect. 6, we conclude the paper.

2   Distributed Constraint Satisfaction Problems

In this section, we introduce formal definitions, which are the base of our Android application. We first introduce the definitions of CSPs with the n-queens problem (Sect. 2.1). Then we extend it to the definitions of DisCSPs (Sect. 2.2). Lastly, we

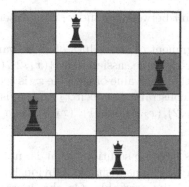

Fig. 1. Example of a CSP: 4-Queens problem

describe the ABT algorithm for solving DisCSPs by having agents communicate with each other (Sect. 2.3).

2.1 Constraint Satisfaction Problem

CSPs are defined by a tuple $\langle X, D, P \rangle$ as follows:

- $X = \{x_1, x_2, \ldots, x_n\}$ is a finite set of variables.
- $D = \{D_1, D_2, \ldots D_n\}$ is a finite set of domains, where D_i is the finite set of possible values for variable x_i.
- $P = \{p_1, p_2, \ldots\}$ is a finite set of constraints.

For simplicity, we assume that all constraints are binary constraints in which only two variables are involved. Thus, each constraint $p_k(x_i, x_j) \in P$ is a binary constraint between x_i and x_j that is defined on the Cartesian product $D_i \times D_j$. If the value assignment of these variables satisfies this constraint, the constraint returns a Boolean value of satisfied (= true). Otherwise, the constraint returns unsatisfied (= false). Solving a CSP involves finding an assignment of values to all variables such that all constraints are satisfied.

Let us describe how we formalize a problem as a CSP in the following example of a n-queens problem.

Example 1 (n-queens problem). The n-queens problem is a famous puzzle, where the objective is to place n chess queens on a board with $n \times n$ squares so that these queens do not threaten each other. Figure 1 illustrates a n-queens problem where $n = 4$ (4-queens problem).

Let us formalize the 4-queens problem as a CSP. There are four variables $X = \{x_1, x_2, x_3, x_4\}$, each of which corresponds to the position of a queen. Because it is obvious that only one queen can be placed in each row, each queen is associated with its own row. The domain of a variable is $\{1, 2, 3, 4\}$. To describe the constraint such that the queens do not threaten each other, for each pair of variables x_i and x_j, a constraint between x_i and x_j can be represented as follows:

$$x_i \neq x_j \wedge |i - j| \neq |x_i - x_j|$$

For example, the constraint between x_2 and x_4 is represented as $x_2 \neq x_4 \wedge |x_2 - x_4| \neq 2$.

A solution is an assignment of the values of these variables so that all constraints are satisfied. For example, assignment $\{(x_1, 2), (x_2, 4), (x_3, 1), (x_4, 4)\}$, where (x_i, d_i) represents that the value of variable x_i is set to d_i, is not a solution to this CSP because the constraint between x_2 and x_4 is unsatisfied ($x_2 = x_4$). Another assignment $\{(x_1, 2), (x_2, 4), (x_3, 1), (x_4, 3)\}$ is a solution to a 4-queens problem.

Note that some CSPs have no solutions, that is, no assignment satisfies all constraints. We call such CSPs unsatisfiable. Obviously, the CSP formalization of the 2-queens problem is unsatisfiable. On the contrary, we call CSPs that have at least one solution satisfiable. As shown in the above example, the CSP formalization of the 4-queens problem is satisfiable.

2.2 Distributed Constraint Satisfaction Problems

A DisCSP is a CSP where the variables and the constraints are distributed among autonomous agents. DisCSPs are defined by a tuple $\langle A, X, D, P, \alpha \rangle$ as follows:

- X, D, P are a set of variables, domains, and constraints, respectively, as in CSPs.
- $A = \{a_1, a_2, \ldots\}$ is a finite set of agents.
- $\alpha : X \to A$ is a function that maps each variable to an agent that owns it.

In this paper, we assume that each agent owns exactly one variable. Thus, we will use the term variables and agents interchangeably. In addition, we assume the following communication model:

- Agents communicate by sending messages.
- The delay in delivering a message is finite, though random.
- Message are received in the order in which they were sent.

2.3 Asynchronous Backtracking Algorithm

The ABT algorithm is a distributed, asynchronous version of a well-known backtracking (BT) algorithm. Similar to BT, ABT assigns values to variables in a depth-first manner and backtracks when a constraint is violated. The key difference between ABT and BT is that procedures of value assignment and backtracking searches are done in a distributed and asynchronous manner.

Algorithm 1. When received $(\mathbf{ok?}, (x_j, d_j))$

1: revise *agent_view*;
2: **check_agent_view** (Algorithm 3);

Algorithm 2. When received $(\mathbf{nogood}, x_i, V)$

1: record V as a new constraint;
2: *old_value* $\leftarrow$ *current_value*
3: **check_agent_view** (Algorithm 3);
4: **if** *old_value* = *current_value* **then**
5:     send $(\mathbf{ok?}, (x_j, current_value))$ to x_j;
6: **end if**

A DisCSP (also a CSP) can be visualized as a graph, where nodes are agents and edges are constraints. Note that, in this paper, all constraints are assumed binary. Then, from this graph, we construct a depth-first search tree, which defines the priority order between any pairs of agents.

Let us briefly describe ABT. In ABT, agents send two types of messages, a *ok?* message and a *nogood* message. As described above, the priority order of variables/agents is determined. An agent sends a *ok?* message to its children to communicate the current value of that agent. In more detail, a *ok?* message is of the form $(\mathbf{ok?}, (x_i, d_i))$, which agent x_j sends to its children to communicate that a value of x_i is set to d_i. On the contrary an agent sends a *nogood* message to its parent to communicate that the current assignment violates some constraints and to generate a new constraint to prohibit the assignment. More formally, a *nogood* message is of the form $(\mathbf{nogood}, x_i, V)$, which agent x_j sends to its parent to communicate a new constraint V is generated. Here, V, called *nogood*, is a partial value assignment that violates some constraints. Sending a *ok?* message corresponds to assigning a value to a variable in BT, while sending a *nogood* message corresponds to backtracking in BT.

Each agent has the current value assignment of its parent, called *agent_view*. If an agent received a *ok?* message from its parent, the agent records that parent's assignment in *agent_view* (Algorithm 1). Then, the agent checks whether its current assignment and *agent_view* are consistent (Algorithm 3). If its current assignment and *agent_view* are consistent, that is, no constraint is violated thus far, the agent does nothing and waits until another message. Otherwise, the agent has to change its value. If the agent can choose a new value that violates no constraint, the agent will change its value to the new value and send a *ok?* message to its children. Unfortunately, if the agent cannot choose any value as a new value, that is, all value assignment violate some constraints, the backtrack procedure has to be initiated (Algorithm 4). The agent generates a new constraint *nogood* V from *agent_view* and sends a *nogood* message to its parent so the parent can change its value. The procedure when an agent receives a *nogood* message is described in Algorithm 2.

Algorithm 3. check_agent_view

1: **if** *agent_view* and *current_value* are not consistent **then**
2:     **if** no value in D_i is consistent with *agent_view* **then**
3:         **backtrack** (Algorithm 4);
4:     **else**
5:         selects $d \in D_i$, where *agent_view* and d are consistent
6:         *current_value* $\leftarrow d$;
7:         sends (**ok?**, (x_i, d)) to children;
8:     **end if**
9: **end if**

Algorithm 4. backtrack

1: generates a *nogood* V
2: **if** V is an empty *nogood* **then**
3:     broadcasts to other agents that there is no solution, terminates this algorithm;
4: **end if**
5: selects (x_j, d_j) where x_j has the lowest priority in a *nogood*;
6: sends (**nogood**, x_j, V) to x_j;
7: removes (x_j, d_j) from *agent_view*;
8: **check_agent_view** (Algorithm 3);

This process continues until either all agents are assigned values and no *nogood* messages are sent, at which point ABT has found a solution, or some agent generates an empty *nogood*, at which point ABT has found there is no solution.

3 Android Devices

Android is an operating system for mobile devices developed by Google. The current version is "9.0 Pie", which was released on 6 August 2018. Google provides the Android software development kit (SDK) which enables us to make our own application with Kotolin, Java, and C++ languages.

In this section, we briefly explain communication protocols among Android devices that we can utilize Sect. 3.1.

3.1 Communication Protocols

We can use the following three protocols to communicate among Android devices:

Wi-Fi. Android devices can connect to the Internet via Wireless LAN connection and they can communicate each other by TCP/IP.

Bluetooth. A Bluetooth API has been introduced at API Level 5. Thus, a Bluetooth connection is available.

Wi-Fi Peer-to-Peer. A Wi-Fi peer-to-peer API has been introduced from Android 4.0 (API Level 14).

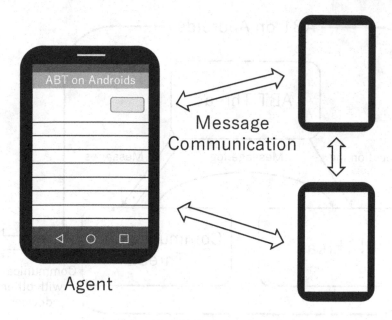

Fig. 2. Overview

4   ABT on Androids

In this section, we implement the ABT algorithm as an Android application, which we call ABT on Androids. ABT on Androids is developed using Android Studio 3.2.1, and it is written in Java.

An overview of ABT on Androids is shown in Fig. 2. Each Android device corresponds to each agent. ABT is executed among multiple Android devices by sending messages to each other.

4.1   Application Design

Let us explain ABT on Androids in more detail. ABT on Androids consists of the following three threads (Fig. 3):

UI Thread. The UI thread is the main thread of the application. This thread controls all UI elements and the screen display.

Communication Thread. The communication thread takes charge of sending and receiving messages. In an Android application, we must separate the network operation from the UI thread. If this is violated, a NetworkOn-MainThreadException is thrown and the application terminates.

ABT Thread. ABT thread executes ABT algorithm. This thread receives messages from other agents via the communication thread, and it also sends messages to other agents via the communication thread.

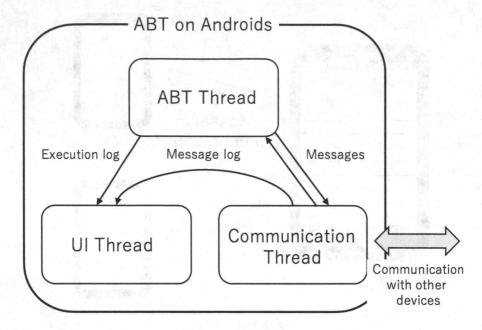

Fig. 3. Application design

4.2   Communiation with Wi-Fi

In ABT on Androids, we suppose that all Android devices are connected on a private network via Wi-Fi connection. We use TCP/IP and assume that each Android device knows all information the device needs, that is, the IP addresses of the parent and children agents (and also port number).

5   Evaluation

We evaluate our application using two Android devices. We attempt to solve the 2-queens problem.

Let us introduce the formal definitions of the 2-queens problem:

variable x_1, x_2
domain $D_1 = D_2 = \{1, 2\}$

In addition, we have two constraints:

- $x_1 \neq x_2$
- $|x_1 - x_2| \neq 1$

From the above constraints, it is obvious that there is no solution. For example, assignment $\{(x_1, 1), (x_2, 1)\}$ violates the first constraint. Furthermore, assignment $\{(x_1, 2), (x_2, 1)\}$ violates the second constraints. Thus, we can confirm that our implementation works correctly if ABT on Androids generates an empty **nogood** and then terminates.

Fig. 4. Execution result: x_1 **Fig. 5.** Execution result: x_2

In this evaluation, we used the following devices:

– Agent x_1
  Model JCI VA-10J
  Android Version 5.0.2
– Agent x_2
  Model Nexus 5X
  Android Version 7.1.1

The execution results of agents x_1 and x_2 are shown in Figs. 4 and 5. Let us confirm these execution results systematically. Note that the message logs shown in these results would be slightly different from the notations we defined earlier.

First x_1 assigns 1 to its variable and then sends $(\mathbf{ok}?, (x_1, 1))$ to x_2. After x_2 receives this *ok?* message, x_2 searches possible value assignments by procedure **check_agent_view** (Algorithm 3). However, assigning neither 1 nor 2 to x_2 violates constraints. Then, procedure **backtrack** (Algorithm 4) is called and x_2 sends $(\mathbf{nogood}, x_1, (x_1, 1))$ to x_1.

Second, because x_1 received the above *nogood* message, x_1 assigns 2 to its variable and again sends $(\mathbf{ok}?, (x_1, 2))$ to x_2 Similar to the above, x_2 searches possible value assignments by procedure **check_agent_view**. Because all value assignments violates constraints, x_2 sends $(\mathbf{nogood}, x_1, (x_1, 2))$ to x_1. After x_1 receives this *nogood* message, x_1 tries to assign a value by procedure **backtrack**. However, because assigning neither 1 nor 2 to x_1 violates recorded *nogoods*, x_1 cannot assign any value to its variable. Thus, an empty *nogood* is generated and x_1 confirms this problem is unsatisfiable, that is, there is no solution.

Finally, x_1 sends a *nosolution* message to x_2, which is a special message to communicate that there is no solution. Then x_1 terminates. Similarly, after x_2 receives the *nosolution* message from x_1, x_2 terminates. Thus, we confirmed that ABT on Androids can detect unsatisfiable DisCSPs.

6   Conclusion

In this paper, we implement ABT algorithm as an Android application, which we call ABT on Androids. Then, we evaluated our application by solving the 2-queens problem with two Android devices.

Future work will evaluate ABT on Androids on more than three Android devices. In addition, we will develop an application that enables an Android device to control a drone, and we will merge this application and ABT on Androids. After formalizing the emergency camera drone system that is illustrated in the Introduction as a DisCSP, we will develop the system by utilizing the developed applications.

Acknowledgements. Suguru Ueda is supported by the Adaptable and Seamless Technology Transfer Program (A-STEP, project number: J180600012) We wish to thank Koichi Nakayama and Chika Oshima for their assistance and comments.

References

1. Mackworth, A.K.: Constraint satisfaction. In: Shapiro, S.C. (ed.) Encyclopedia of Artificial Intelligence, pp. 285–293. Wiley (1992)
2. Modi, P.J., Shen, W., Tambe, M., Yokoo, M.: Adopt: asynchronous distributed constraint optimization with quality guarantees. Artif. Intell. **161**(1–2), 149–180 (2005)
3. Weiss, G.: Multiagent Systems. The MIT Press, Cambridge (2013)
4. Yeoh, W., Yokoo, M.: Distributed problem solving. AI Mag. **33**(3), 53–65 (2012)
5. Yokoo, M., Durfee, E.H., Ishida, T., Kuwabara, K.: The distributed constraint satisfaction problem: formalization and algorithms. IEEE Trans. Knowl. Data Eng. **10**(5), 673–685 (1998)

Model-Based Multi-objective Reinforcement Learning with Unknown Weights

Tomohiro Yamaguchi[1(⊠)], Shota Nagahama[1,2P],
Yoshihiro Ichikawa[1], and Keiki Takadama[3]

[1] National Institute of Technology, Nara College, Nara, Japan
{yamaguch, ichikawa}@info.nara-k.ac.jp,
[2] Nara Institute of Science and Technology, Nara, Japan
nagahama.shota.nll@is.naist.jp
[3] The University of Electro-Communications, Tokyo, Japan
keiki@inf.uec.ac.jp

Abstract. This paper describes solving multi-objective reinforcement learning problems where there are multiple conflicting objectives with unknown weights. Reinforcement learning (RL) is a popular algorithm for automatically solving sequential decision problems and most of them are focused on single-objective settings to decide a single solution. In multi-objective reinforcement learning (MORL), the reward function emits a reward vector instead of a scalar reward. A scalarization function with a vector of n weights (weight vector) is a commonly used to decide a single solution. The simple scalarization function is linear scalarization such as weighted sum. The main problem of previous MORL methods is a huge learning cost required to collect all Pareto optimal policies. Hence, it is hard to learn the high dimensional Pareto optimal policies. To solve this, this paper proposes the novel model-based MORL method by reward occurrence probability (ROP) with unknown weights. There are two main features. The first feature is that the average reward of a policy is defined by inner product of the ROP vector and the weight vector. The second feature is that it learns ROP in each policy instead of Q-values. Pareto optimal deterministic policies directly form the vertices of a convex hull in the ROP vector space. Therefore, Pareto optimal policies are calculated independently with weights and just once. The experimental results show that our proposed method collected all optimal policies under four dimensional Pareto optimal policies, and it takes a small computation time though previous MORL methods learn at most two or three dimensions.

Keywords: Multi-objective reinforcement learning · Model-based ·
Average reward · Reward occurrence probability · Reward vector

1 Introduction

This paper describes solving multi-objective reinforcement learning problems where there are multiple conflicting objectives with unknown weights. Reinforcement learning (RL) is a popular algorithm for automatically solving sequential decision problems which is commonly modeled as Markov decision processes (MDPs). Despite numerous

© Springer Nature Switzerland AG 2019
S. Yamamoto and H. Mori (Eds.): HCII 2019, LNCS 11570, pp. 311–321, 2019.
https://doi.org/10.1007/978-3-030-22649-7_25

reinforcement learning methods, most of them focused on single objective settings where the goal of an agent decides a single solution by the optimality criterion. This reinforcement learning methods are classified according to the learning algorithm and the optimality criterion. The former, there are two kinds of learning algorithms whether directly estimating the MDP model or not, one is the *model-based* approach such as real-time dynamic programming (RTDP) [1] and H-Learning [16] which takes a small time complexity but a large space complexity, and another one is the *model-free* approach [18] such as Q-learning. The *model-based* approach starts with directly estimating the MDP model statistically, then calculates the value of each state as V(s) or the quality of each state action pair: (s, a) (is called a rule) Q(s, a) using the estimated MDP to search the optimal solution that maximizes V(s) of each state. In contrast, the *model-free* approach directly learns V(s) or Q(s, a) without estimating the MDP model.

The latter, there are two kinds of optimality criteria whether using a discount factor or not, one is maximizing the sum of the *discounted rewards*, and another one is maximizing the *average reward* without any discount factor [2, 8, 16, 18]. Most previous RL methods are model-free approach with a discount factor since the model-based approach takes the large space complexity.

A multi-objective MDP (MOMDP) is an MDP in which the reward function emits a reward vector instead of a scalar reward. A scalarization function with a vector of n weights (weight vector) is a commonly used to decide a single solution. The simple scalarization function is linear scalarization such as weighted sum. In this paper, we mainly target the weighted sum function for the scalarization function. However, our method can be applied to other scalarization function such as Tchebycheff norm method.

Multi-objective reinforcement learning (MORL) [6, 11, 13, 14] has several methods which can be divided into two main approaches, the scalar combination and Pareto optimization [3]. In the former case, the scalar combination is to find a single policy that optimizes a combination of the rewards. MOMDP and known weights are input to the learning algorithm, then it output a single solution. In the latter case, Pareto optimization is to find multiple policies that cover the Pareto front, which requires collective search for sampling the Pareto set [10].

MOMDP is input to the learning algorithm, then it output a solution set. Note that there are two ways to select a single solution in the set, one is the scalarization with known weight, another one is a user selection.

Most of the state-of-the-art MORL are model-free value-based reinforcement learning algorithms [4, 7, 9, 13] with a main problem that is MORL previous methods incorporate a huge learning cost to collect all Pareto optimal policies. First, they need a sufficient number of executions for each state-action pair (rule) to collect all Pareto optimal policies since they are model-free methods. Secondly, Pareto optimal set is calculated for each V (state) or Q (state, action) since these methods are value-based. Thirdly, when updating V-values or Q-values, Pareto candidates are added or updated as V/Q-value vector, it must keep a large number of candidates until each Pareto optimal set is converged. Therefore, previous MORL methods take large number of calculations to collect Pareto optimal set for each V/Q-value vector. In contrast, model-based MORL can reduce such a calculation cost [19] than model-free MORLs. However, second and third problems as described above are still remained, and this method is for only deterministic environments. Thus, it is hard to learn high dimensional Pareto optimal policies by previous methods.

To solve these problems, this paper proposes the novel model-based MORL method by reward occurrence probability with unknown weights. Our approach is based on the average reward model-based reinforcement learning [8] and there are two main features to it. The first feature is that the average reward of a policy is defined by inner product of the ROP vector and the weight vector. The second feature is that it learns ROP in each policy instead of Q-values. Pareto optimal deterministic policies directly form the vertices of a convex hull in the ROP vector space. Therefore, Pareto optimalpolicies are calculated independently with weights and just one time.

The key points of our approach are as follows:

(1) Each objective is defined by a reward rule and its unknown weight.
(2) Multi-objective is defined by the fixed reward rule set and the unknown weight vector.
(3) Each policy is assigned to the reward occurrence probability (ROP) vector where n^{th} value is the occurrence probability of nth reward rule of the policy.
(4) In the ROP vector space (rectangular coordinate system), any stationary policy is mapped to a point where coordinates are indicated by its ROP vector.
(5) Optimal deterministic stationary policies with unknown weights form the vertex of convex hull in the ROP vector space.
(6) Average reward of a policy is defined by the inner product of the ROP vector of the policy and the weight vector.
(7) The range of the weight vector of each optimal deterministic stationary policy can be calculated geometrically.
(8) The stochastic learning environment can be learned by standard MDP model identification method and our proposed search method collects all Pareto optimal policies.

The experimental results show that our proposed method collect all optimal policies under four rewards (four dimensional Pareto optimal policies), and it takes a small computation time though previous MORL methods learn at most two or three dimensions.

2   Model-Based Reinforcement Learning

This chapter describes the framework of model-based RL methods that estimate a model of the environment while interacting with it and search for the best policy of its current estimated model under some optimality criterion. Some comparisons have shown model-based RL are much more effective than model-free methods such as Q-learning [1]. Figure 1 shows an overview of the model-based reinforcement learning system. Note that s is an observed state, a is an executed action, and Rw is an acquired reward. At each time step, the learner is in some state s, and the learner may choose any action that is available in state s. At the next time step, the environment responds by randomly moving into a new state s', giving the learner a corresponding reward $R(s, a)$. In Fig. 1 the learning agent consists of three blocks which are model identification block, optimality of policies block and policy search block. The details of these blocks are described in following section. The novelty of our method lies in policy search block which collects all *reward acquisition policies* on an identified mode according to average reward optimality. The detail of this block is described in Sects. 2.4 and 3.3.

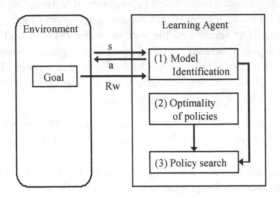

Fig. 1. Framework of model-based reinforcement learning

2.1   MDP Model and Markov Chains

A *Markov decision process* (MDP) [12] in this paper is a discrete time and a discrete state space stochastic control process. It provides a mathematical framework for modeling decision making in situations where outcomes are partly random and partly under the control of a decision maker. Note that for a decision maker, actions are the allowing choice, and rewards are giving motivation. A MDP model is defined by of following four elements;

1. Set of states: $S = \{s_0, s_1, s_2, ..., s_n\}$
2. Set of actions: $A = \{a_0, a_1, a_2, ..., a_n\}$
3. State transition probabilities $P(s'|s, a)$: a probability of occurring state s' when execute action a at state s
4. Reward function $R(s, a)$: an acquired reward when execute action a at state s

State action pair (s, a) is called a *rule*. $R(s, a)$ means that a reward is assigned to a rule (s, a). A *stochastic policy* π is a probability distribution over actions for every possible state. A *deterministic policy* is defined by a function that selects an action for every possible state. This paper mainly deals with *deterministic policies*. $P(s'|s, a)$ means that the probability that the process moves into its new state s' is influenced by the chosen action. Thus, the next state s' depends on the executed rule, that is the current state s and the decision maker's action a, and is independent of all previous executed rules. It is called *Markov property*.

A *Markov chain* is a stochastic model describing a sequence of possible states in which the probability of each state depends only on the previous state. It's an intension of Markov decision processes, the difference is that there is neigher actions nor rewards in a *Markov chain*. This paper focuses on the property that a *policy* of a MDP forms a *Markov chain* of the MDP, it is described later in Sect. 3.4.

We assume MDP model is *ergodic* where the model satisfies these conditions as follows;

1. *irreducible*: All states can be reached from all others.
2. *aperiodic*: Each state is visited without any systematic period.
3. *finite states*: The number of states is finite.

2.2 Model Identification

In model identification block, the state transition probabilities $P(s'|s, a)$ and reward function $R(s, a)$ are estimated incrementally by observing a sequence of (s, a, r). This estimated model is generally assumed by MDP.

Model-based RL methods learn the transition and reward models of the environment by making use of counters that are used in a Maximum-Likelihood Estimation (MLE) to compute approximate transition probabilities and average rewards [19].

Note that the MLE probability is same as the occurrence based probability. Each time the agent selects rule (s, a) and makes a transition to state s', the transition model's counter values $C(s, a)$ and $C(s, a, s')$ are increased by one. In a similar fashion, the obtained reward r is added to the value $R_t (s, a)$ which computes the sum of all rewards obtained by selecting rule (s, a). Finally, the maximum likelihood model of the MDP is computed as Eq. (1).

$$P(s'|s, a) = C(s, a, s')/C(s, a) \text{ and } R(s, a) = R_t(s, a)/C(s, a) \tag{1}$$

2.3 Average Reward Optimality Criterion

Optimality of policies block defines the optimality criterion of the learning policy. In this research, a policy which maximizes average reward is defined as an optimal policy. There are two kinds of optimality criteria on average reward RL, one is gain-optimal which considers acquired rewards only in a stationary cycle, the other is bias-optimal which considers acquired rewards both on a temporally path and the stationary cycle [8]. Equation (2) shows the definition of gain optimal average reward.

$$g^\pi(s) \equiv \lim_{N \to \infty} E\left(\frac{1}{N} \sum_{t=0}^{N-1} r_t^\pi(s)\right) \tag{2}$$

where N is the number of step, $r_t^\pi(s)$ is the expected value of reward that an agent acquired at step t where policy is π and initial state is s and $E()$ denotes the expected value.

2.4 LC-Learning

This section summarizes LC-Learning [5, 15] which is our basic method of policies search. LC-Learning is one of the average reward model-based reinforcement learning methods. It collects all reward acquisition *deterministic* policies under *unichain* condition. The *unichain* condition requires that every policy in an MDP result in a single *ergodic* class, and guarantees that the optimal average cost is independent of the initial state [17]. The features of LC-Learning are following; (1) Breadth search of an optimal policy started by each reward rule. (2) Calculating average reward using reward acquisition cycle of each policy.

3   Model-Based MORL by Reward Occurrence Probability

3.1   Weighted Reward Vector

To represent multi objective, the reward is divided into d reward types one for each objective, and a weight which represents the importance or preference of that reward is associated with each reward type [4, 10]. In this paper, the reward function is defined by a vector of d rewards (reward vector) $\vec{r} = (r_0, r_1, \ldots, r_{d-1})$ where each r_i represents a position of reward rule and the weight vector $\vec{w} = (w_0, w_1, \ldots, w_{d-1})$ which represents a trade-off among multi objective. A scalarization function with a weight vector is called a *weighted sum of rewards*. Equation (3) shows a weighted sum of rewards defined by inner product of the reward vector $\vec{r} = (r_0, r_1, \ldots, r_{d-1})$ and the weight vector $\vec{w} = (w_0, w_1, \ldots, w_{d-1})$.

$$r(\vec{w}) = \sum_{i=0}^{d-1} w_i r_i = \vec{w} \cdot \vec{r} \tag{3}$$

3.2   Average Reward by Reward Acquisition Probability

Average reward is the expected received rewards per step when an agent performs state transitions routinely according to a policy. A step is a time cost to execute an action. Under an unichain policy π and reward vector $\vec{r} = (r_0, r_1, \ldots, r_{d-1})$, *Reward Acquisition Probability* (ROP) vector $\vec{P}_\pi$ is defined as shown in Eq. (4). In that, P_i is the expected occurrence probability per step for reward r_i.

$$\vec{P}_\pi \equiv (P_0, P_1, \ldots, P_{d-1}) \tag{4}$$

Average reward ρ_π under a policy π is defined by the inner product of the ROP vector $\vec{P}_\pi$ and the weight vector $\vec{w}$ as shown in Eq. (5).

$$\rho_\pi(\vec{w}) = \sum_{i=0}^{d-1} w_i P_i = \vec{w} \cdot 2 \tag{5}$$

3.3   Collecting All Reward Acquisition Policies [15]

Our searching method for reward acquisition policies is based on LC-learning as we described in Sect. 2.4. Deterministic policies which acquire some rewards are searched by converting a MDP into the tree structures where reward acquisition rules are root rule. Figures 2, 3 and 4 shows an illustrated example. The MDP shown in Fig. 2 which consists of four states, six rules and two rewards is converted into the two tree structures shown in Fig. 3. In a tree structure, the path from the root node to the state that is same state to the initial node is the policy. In stochastic environment, some of the rule is deliquesce stochastically. In such case, path from parent node of stochastic rule to the state that is already extracted is part of a policy that contains the stochastic rule. Figure 4 shows all reward acquisition policies in Fig. 2.

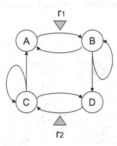

Fig. 2. An example of MDP model

After collecting all reward acquiring policies, for each policy, the state transition probability matrix P_π of the policy π is prepared as *Markov chain* by estimated **by** MDP model as we described in Sect. 2.2.

3.4   Calculating ROP Vector for Each Reward Acquisition Policy

When the occurrence probability of state i is α_i, it is equivalent to the occurrence probability of the reward rule (i, a) under a deterministic policy π. Calculating method of each ROP vector $\vec{P}_\pi$ for each reward acquisition policy π associated with P_π. From the reward acquisition policy set is as follows;

step 1: Set up simultaneous linear equations for each P_π.
Under a deterministic policy π, the occurrence probability vector for all states $\vec{\alpha}_\pi$ defined as Eq. (6) is the solution of simultaneous linear equations Eq. (7).

$$\vec{\alpha}_\pi \equiv \left(\alpha_0, \alpha_1, \ldots, \alpha_{|S|-1}\right) \tag{6}$$

$$\vec{\alpha}_\pi P_\pi = \vec{\alpha}_\pi \tag{7}$$

step 2: For each P_π, solve Eq. (7) by Gaussian elimination.
step 3: For each $\vec{\alpha}_\pi$ derived at step 2, forms ROP vector $\vec{P}_\pi$ by picking up the occurrence probability of each reward rule.

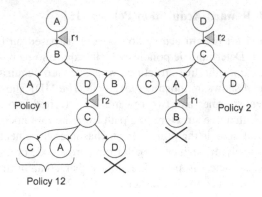

Fig. 3. Searching reward acquiring policies

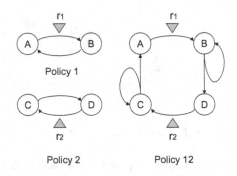

Fig. 4. Three kind of reward acquiring policies

step 4: Make a ROP vector set from the ROP vectors derived at step 3.

step 5: Make a mapping from the reward acquisition policy set to the ROP vector set.

Note that in Eq. (6), α_i is the occurrence probability of state i, the sum of all α_i is 1. In Eq. (7), P_π is the state transition probability matrix of the policy π since the occurrence probability of each state under a policy forms the *Markov chain* as we described in Sect. 2.1.

3.5   Calculating a Convex Hull from a ROP Vector Set

After collecting all ROP vectors as a set, each ROP vector is located at a point in the reward occurrence probability (ROP) vector space. Figure 5 shows an illustrated example of 2 dimension ROP vector space. In Fig. 5, there are two axis, where the horizontal axis is ROP P_0, and the vertical axis is ROP P_1. For example, the ROP vector of $\vec{P}_{\pi 2}$ is (0.33, 0.33). There are four ROP vectors which are the vertices of the convex hull. We use n dimension convex hull algorithm of free Python library. Note that $\vec{P}_{\pi 1,3}$ is associated with two policies π_1 and π_3.

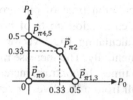

Fig. 5. An illustrated example of 2D ROP vector space with four ROP vectors

The advantage of the proposed method is that Pareto optimal deterministic policies directly form the vertices of a convex hull in the ROP vector space. Therefore, Pareto optimal policies are calculated independently with weights and just one time. Besides, our method can be easily applied to other scalarization function such as Tchebycheff norm method in the ROP vector space.

4 Experiments

4.1 Experimental Setup

We conduct the experiment to analyze the bottle neck of our proposed method by evaluating the computation cost of our major processes described in Sect. 3.3 to 3.5.

Experimental conditions on stochastic MDP model as the learning environment are as follows;

(1) The number of states is four cases, 7, 8, 9, and 10 states.
(2) The number of actions is three.
(3) The number of rewards is four.
(4) The transition probability or each rule is setup randomly under the condition that the number of branches of transitions is randomly setup between 1, 2 or 3.

Experimental results are averaged one hundred experiments. Measurement items are Calculation time for each process from Sect. 3.3 to 3.5 as follows;

(1) Section 3.3: Collecting All Reward Acquisition Policies
(2) Section 3.4: Calculating ROP vector for each Reward Acquisition Policy
(3) Section 3.5: Calculating a Convex Hull from a ROP vector set

4.2 Experimental Results

We conducted the learning experiment for one hundred times and each measurement item is an averaged calculation time, its unit is second. In stochastic and ergodic environment, our proposed method successfully collected all reward acquisition deterministic policies including all Pareto optimal policies under a weighted sum scalarization function where weights are unknown. Note that the numbers of stationary cycles of the reward acquisition policies are from 600 (7 states) to 6000 (10 states), the numbers of vertices of the convex hull are from 31 (7 states) to 46 (10 states). Table 1 shows the calculation time for each process of Sects. 3.3 to 3.5 as we described before section.

Table 1 shows that the calculation time of our proposed method is much small under ten states. However, the calculation costs of both (1) Collecting All Reward Acquisition Policies and (2) Calculating ROP vector for each Reward Acquisition Policy seem to be increase exponentially. The increase rate of item (1) is about 10 times and that of item (3) is about 100 times. In contrast, increase rate of the calculation costs of (3) Calculating a Convex Hull from a ROP vector set is about 3 times and is much smaller than (1) and (2).

Table 1. Calculation time for each process of Sects. 3.3 to 3.5

The number of states	(1) Sect. 3.3 [sec]	(2) Sect. 3.4 [sec]	(3) Sect. 3.5 [sec]
7	0.180	0.900	0.00219
8	0.468	4.93	0.00187
9	1.09	32.5	0.00375
10	2.82	207	0.00606

5 Conclusions

This paper proposed the novel model-based MORL method by reward occurrence probability (ROP) with unknown weights and reported our work under the stochastic learning environment with up to ten states, three actions and three or four reward rules. There are two main features. First one is that average reward of a policy is defined by inner product of the ROP vector and the weight vector. Second feature is that it learns ROP in each policy instead of Q-values. Pareto optimal deterministic policies directly form the vertices of a convex hull in the ROP vector space. Therefore, Pareto optimal policies are calculated independently with weights and just once. The experimental results show that our proposed method collected all optimal policies under four dimensional Pareto optimal policies, and it takes a small computation time though previous MORL methods learn at most two or three dimensions.

Future works is to reduce calculation cost for collecting Pareto optimalpolicies. We are planning two ways, one is pruning in the policy search on collecting all reward acquisition policies by estimating the length of the reward acquisition cycle. Another approach is applying parallel computing techniques, multi processing by Multi-core CPU for policy search, and GPGPU for calculating ROP vector.

Achnowledgement. The authors would like to thank Prof. Shimohara and Prof. Habib for offering a good opportunity to present this research. This work was supported by JSPS KAKENHI (Grant-in-Aid for Scientific Research ©) Grant Number 16K00317.

References

1. Barto, A.G., Steven, J., Bradtke, S.J., Singh, S.P.: Learning to act using real-time dynamic programming. Artif. Intell. **72**(1–2), 81–138 (1995)

2. Gao, Y.: Research on Average Reward. Reinforcement Learning. Algorithms, National Laboratory for Novel Software Technology, Nanjing University, 5 November 2006. http://lamda.nju.edu.cn/conf/MLA06/files/Gao.Y.pdf

3. Herrmann, M.: RL 16: Model-based RL and Multi-Objective Reinforcement Learning, University of Edinburgh, School of Informatics (2015). http://www.inf.ed.ac.uk/teaching/courses/rl/slides15/rl16.pdf

4. Hiraoka, K., Yoshida, M., Mishima, T.: Parallel reinforcement learning for weighted multi-criteria model with adaptive margin. Cogn. Neurodyn. **3**, 17–24 (2009)

5. Konda, T., Tensyo, S., Yamaguchi, T.: LC-learning: phased method for average reward reinforcement learning—preliminary results—. In: Ishizuka, M., Sattar, A. (eds.) PRICAI 2002. LNCS (LNAI), vol. 2417, pp. 208–217. Springer, Heidelberg (2002). https://doi.org/10.1007/3-540-45683-X_24

6. Liu, C., Xu, X., Hu, D.: Multiobjective reinforcement learning: a comprehensive overview. IEEE Trans. Syst. Man Cybern. Syst. **45**(3), 385–398 (2015)

7. Lizotte, D.J., Bowling, M., Murphy, S.A.: Linear fitted-Q iteration with multiple reward functions. J. Mach. Learn. Res. **13**, 3253–3295 (2012)

8. Mahadevan, S.: Average reward reinforcement learning: foundations, algorithms, and empirical results. Mach. Learn. **22**, 159–196 (1996)

9. Van Moffaert, K., Nowe, A.: Multi-objective reinforcement learning using sets of pareto dominating policies. J. Mach. Learn. Res. **15**, 3663–3692 (2014)

10. Natarajan, S., Tadepalli, P.: Dynamic preferences in multi-criteria reinforcement learning. In: Proceedings of International Conference on Machine Learning (ICML-2005), pp. 601–60 (2005)

11. Pinder, J.M.: Multi-objective reinforcement learning framework for unknown stochastic & uncertain environments. Ph.D. Thesis (2016)

12. Puterman, M.L.: Markov Decision Processes: Discrete Stochastic Dynamic Programming, pp. 385–388. Wiley, New York (1994)

13. Roijers, D.M., Vamplew, P., Whiteson, S., Dazeley, R.: A survey of multi-objective sequential decision-making. J. Artif. Intell. Res. **48**, 67–113 (2013)

14. Roijers, D.M., Whiteson, S., Vamplew, P., Dazeley, R.: Why multi-objective reinforcement learning? In: European Workshop on Reinforcement Learning, pp. 1–2 (2015)

15. Satoh, K., Yamaguchi, T.: Preparing various policies for interactive reinforcement learning. In: SICE-ICASE International Joint Conference 2006 (2006)

16. Tadepalli, P., Ok, D.: Model-based average reward reinforcement learning. Artif. Intell. **100**, 177–224 (1998)

17. Tsitsiklis, J.N.: NP-hardness of checking the unichain condition in average cost MDPs. Oper. Res. Lett. **35**, 319–323 (2007)

18. Yang, S. Gao, Y., Bo, A., Wang, H., Chen, X.: Efficient average reward reinforcement learning using constant shifting values. In: Proceedings of the Thirtieth AAAI Conference on Artificial Intelligence (AAAI-16), pp. 2258–2264 (2016)

19. Wiering, M.A., Withagen, M., Drugan, M.M.: Model-based multiobjective reinforcement learning, In: ADPRL 2014: Proceedings of the IEEE Symposium on Adaptive Dynamic Programming and Reinforcement Learning, pp. 1–6 (2014)

Estimating Timing of Head Movements Based on the Volume and Pitch of Speech

Haruka Yanagi, Chika Oshima$^{(\boxtimes)}$, and Koichi Nakayama

Saga University, Saga 840-8502, Japan
karin27@sa3.so-net.ne.jp, knakayama@is.saga-u.ac.jp

Abstract. Our research aims to create two friendly communication robots to talk with elderly people in nursing facilities. If the robots synchronize their head movements in response to the elderly person, the elderly person may react favorably to the robot. Then, the elderly person can enjoy talking with these two robots. In this paper, we investigated whether the volume and pitch of the speech are useful data for estimating the timing of head movements. Because the robots need to move their heads in real time, when one of the robots or the person is talking, we focus on the volume and pitch of the speech, not the content. Moreover, it was cleared which machine learning method creates suitable classifier models for estimating the timing of head movements. The experimental results showed that Random Forest classifier was the most suitable method.

Keywords: Machine learning · Scikit-learn · Communication robot

1 Introduction

We have developed a communication robot, "CATARO" for elderly people in nursing facilities [1]. The robot can move its head, although it cannot move its hands or legs. We plan to adopt two robots that can talk with the elderly person according to a prescheduled conversation [2], because the conversation ends when the elderly person stops speaking. Our aim is for the elderly person to enjoy the conversation and feel familiarity with the robots. Chartrand and Bargh found that subjects whose movements were mirrored by a confidant liked that partner more (chameleon effect [3]). Therefore, we presume that if the robot's head movements synchronize with the elderly person, then the elderly person will react favorably towards the robot.

Generally, people move their heads without premeditated thought during a conversation. They may also intentionally move their heads to match their partners' position [4]. We think that the timing of head movements is quasi-different between people. One person does not move his/her head until the other finishes speech, and another person moves his/her head as often as the other's speech breaks off. Therefore, an individual model of the head movement is required so that the robot can move its head in synchronization with each person.

Busso et al. aimed to quantify differences in the head motion patterns displayed under expressive utterances. They used "hidden Markov model (HMM)" to estimate the discrete representation of head poses from prosodic features [5]. Munhall et al. studied

© Springer Nature Switzerland AG 2019
S. Yamamoto and H. Mori (Eds.): HCII 2019, LNCS 11570, pp. 322–332, 2019.
https://doi.org/10.1007/978-3-030-22649-7_26

the impact on speech perception of a talker's head movement. The head movement was correlated with the fundamental frequency and amplitude of the voice during speech [6].

In our research, the robot moves its head in real time in response to the speech of the other robot or the person. Therefore, we employ volume and pitch data from the speech of the person or the robot to estimate the appropriate timing of head movements.

In this paper, we investigate which method is appropriate to create a learning model that estimates the timing of head movements in response to speech. We collect the volume and the pitch data of a radio program by examining when each subject (human) moves their head. Then, we apply three kinds of classifier models for each subject through three kinds of machine learning, support vector machine (SVM) [7, 8], K-neighbors classifier [9, 10], and Random Forest classifier [11] using scikit-learn [12] which is an open-source library used for machine learning.

In the next section, we introduce a communication robot, "CATARO". Section 3 shows an experiment to construct a classifier model estimating the head motion timing. We discuss which machine learning method creates suitable classifier models for estimating the timing of head movements in Sect. 4, and we conclude our research in Sect. 5.

2 CATARO

Figure 1 shows "CATARO [1]" (Care and Therapy Assistant RObot), a communication robot. The main body is 391 mm in height, 283 mm in width, and 200 mm in depth. A smartphone is attached to CATARO's eyes. Its facial expressions are displayed through the screen of the smartphone. CATARO can learn and recognize the faces of patients through the mounted smartphone. Further, the direction of the robot's face is automatically adjustable (180 degrees in the horizontal and vertical) [1].

In nursing facilities for the elderly people (care receivers), caregivers are very busy caring about the care receivers: toileting, eating, bathing or dressing. Generally, the caregivers cannot have long conversation with the care receivers. On the other hand, some care receivers want to talk with someone about their old days, their family, today's weather, and so on. The other care receivers cannot talk so for a long time because they often run out of topics and are tired. However, the care receivers feel lonely when nobody talks to them.

Therefore, as shown in Fig. 2, we plan to adopt two CATAROs that can talk with the elderly person according to a pre-scheduled conversation [2]. Even if the elderly person runs out of topics and stops speaking, because the CATAROs keep talking, he/she does not feel lonely. Moreover, our aim is for the elderly person to enjoy the conversation and feel familiarity with the CATAROs. It is one of solutions that the CATARO's head movements synchronize with the elderly person. The elderly person may feel that he/she and the CATARO share the same values. Then, his/her closeness to the CATARO may increase.

Fig. 1. Framework (left side) and CATARO covered with a cloth (right side).

Fig. 2. Two CATAROs talk with an elderly person.

3 Experiment

3.1 Aim

We conducted an experiment to construct a classifier model estimating the head motion timing of a nod, based on the volume and pitch of speech. We employed three methods of machine learning: support vector machine (SVM) [7, 8], K-neighbors classifier [9, 10], and Random Forest classifier [11]. Then, an appropriate model contribution was made by comparing these three methods.

3.2   Method

In the experiment, we employed about 10 min of speech by a male radio personality. Because the radio personality spoke alone, speech recognition accuracy was relatively high. Each of the nine university students (S1–S9) listened to the speech, pushing a button on an application whenever they moved their head in response.

3.3   Volume and Pitch Data

Figure 3 shows a processing flow for creating a classifier model from the speech data. First, audio data was inputted into a speech conversion software corresponding to Audio Stream Input/Output (ASIO) through Quad Capture Interface (Roland). Then, the software calculates the volume and pitch of the audio data by Fourier transformation. About 200 values of each volume and pitch were acquired per second. The data was then continuously outputted to comma separated value (CSV) format files. Then, classifier models were built using three kinds of machine learning models.

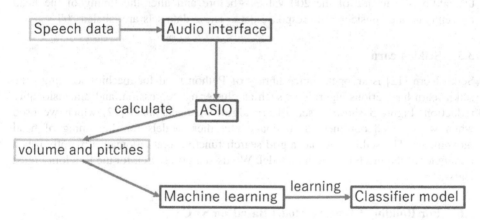

Fig. 3. Processing flow for making a classifier model from the speech data.

3.4   Data Set

Figure 4 shows how to calculate a data set per head movement (response). The volume and pitch data were written in 200 lines per second, respectively. 400 lines (400 volume data and 400 pitch data) were considered one data set. Then, two kinds of array are prepared for one data set. One of them is to store the volume data. The other is to store the pitch data. The yellow part in Fig. 4 shows that these arrays ("volume array" and "pitch array") are shifted one by one between zero to three seconds before the head movement. The volume and pitch data are stored in each array every shift. Finally, we obtained 200 data sets per one response. These data sets are labeled "1".

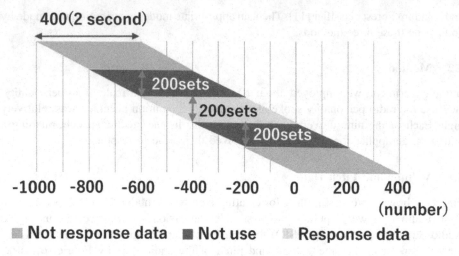

Fig. 4. The way of collecting data for learning model.

On the other hand, the 400 kinds of volume and pitch data from the beginning of the audio file outside of the 200 values—before and after the timing of the head movement—are considered no-response data. These data sets are labeled "0".

3.5   Scikit-Learn

Scikit-learn [12] is an open-source library of Python used for machine learning. The scikit-learn has various algorithms, such as clustering, regression, and dimensionality reduction. Figure 5 shows a scikit-learn algorithm cheat-sheet [12] which we used when we selected our methods to make classifier models for the timing of head movements. The scikit-learn has a grid search function that automatically optimizes a parameter of the machine learning model. We used a grid search for the Random Forest classifier.

3.6   For Building Classifier Model Based on SVC

Support vector machine classification (SVC) means support vector machine (SVM) [7, 8] in the scikit-learn. SVC is one of the supervised learning techniques used for regression, classification and outlier detection. SVC detects the boundary line between label 0 and label 1 using training data and predicts the label of sample data. The scikit-learn has two kinds of SVC, kernel and linear, to set parameters. In this experiment, we only used linear.

3.7   For Building Classifier Model Based on K-Neighbors Classifier

K-neighbors classifier [9, 10] determines the label of sample data through a majority decision. Then, the K-neighbors classifier uses k training data near the sample data. In the K-neighbors classifier by scikit-learn, we can set two parameters: weight and

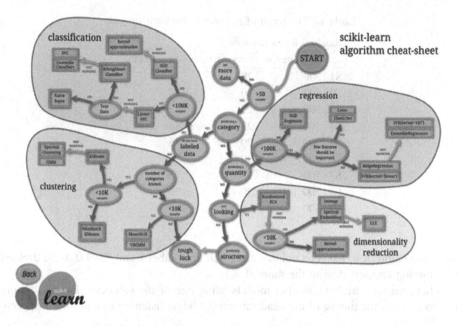

Fig. 5. Scikit-learn algorithm cheat-sheet [12]

n_neighbors. We selected distance at the weight. In this case, closer neighbors of a query point carry more weight than distant neighbors. The n_neighbors can set a number of neighbors to use. If a number of the n_neighbors is too small or too large, the learning model will not be able to correctly predict the label of the sample data. Therefore, we selected "5", which is a default number.

3.8 For Building Classifier Model Based on Random Forest Classifier

Random Forest classifier [11] is a kind of ensemble classifier in scikit-learn. The learning model predicts the label of the sample data using multiple Random Forest classifiers. Each Random Forest is built from training data with a bootstrap sample. The bootstrap sample is a resampling technique which samples a dataset with replacement. Three parameters, n_estimators, max_features, and max_depth were set using grid search, which is one of the functions of the scikit-learn. The grid search automatically sets parameters for machine learning to optimum values. The parameter, class_weight, was set as "balanced". The n_estimators was set at 7 values: 5, 10, 20, 30, 50, 100, and 300. The max_features were set at 5 values: 3, 5, 10, 15, and 20. The max_depth was set at 10 values: 3, 5, 10, 15, 20, 25, 30, 40, 50, and 100. Table 1 shows the results of the parameters for each subject by the grid search.

3.9 Analysis

The classifier models generated by the three kinds of methods are evaluated per each subject based on accuracy, precision, recall, and F-score, and calculated using k-fold

Table 1. The result of parameters for each subject.

	Random forest classifier		
	n_estimators	max_features	max_depth
S1	300	20	15
S2	300	20	20
S3	300	20	15
S4	300	20	40
S5	300	20	15
S6	300	20	15
S7	100	15	15
S8	300	20	20
S9	300	5	20

cross-validation (k = 10). The volume and pitch data, label 1 and label 0, were divided into training and test data in the ratio of 9:1.

Then, we recreate the classifier models using one of the subject's data as training data to confirm the timing of the head movement while listening to a partner's speech.

Table 2. The results of classifier models using Linear SVC.

Subject	Condition	Linear SVC			
		Precision ratio	Recall ratio	F-score	Accuracy rate
S1	0	0.63	0.78	0.70	0.58
	1	0.39	0.23	0.29	
S2	0	0.98	0.06	0.11	0.31
	1	0.28	1.00	0.44	
S3	0	0.97	1.00	0.98	0.97
	1	0.24	0.01	0.02	
S4	0	0.92	0.05	0.09	0.45
	1	0.44	0.99	0.61	
S5	0	0.86	0.33	0.47	0.40
	1	0.19	0.75	0.30	
S6	0	0.89	1.00	0.94	0.89
	1	0.00	0.00	0.00	
S7	0	0.91	1.00	0.95	0.91
	1	0.00	0.00	0.00	
S8	0	0.96	1.00	0.93	0.86
	1	0.00	0.00	0.00	
S9	0	1.00	0.03	0.06	0.08
	1	0.05	1.00	0.10	
Average		0.54	0.51	0.39	0.61

3.10   Result

Tables 2, 3 and 4 shows the results of the recall and precision ratios, F-score, and accuracy rates of the three kinds of classifier models built by linear SVC, K-neighbors classifier, and Random Forest classifier in each subject. The average accuracy rates were 0.61, 0.81, and 0.95 at the classifier models, respectively. The averages of F-score were 0.39, 0.65, and 0.86 at the classifier models, respectively. These results show that Random Forest classifier is the most suitable method to model for head movement in response.

Table 5 shows the average precision ration, recall ration, F-score, and accuracy rate in each classifier model, using one of the subject's data as training data by Random Forest classifier. The average F-scores are from 0.45 to 0.57, the accuracy rates are from 0.64 to 0.82, and the individual classifier models are 0.86 and 0.95, respectively (See Table 4).

Table 3. The result of classifier models using K-neighbors classifier

Subject	Condition	K neighbors classifier			
		Precision ratio	Recall ratio	F-score	Accuracy rate
S1	0	0.74	0.77	0.76	0.69
	1	0.59	0.55	0.57	
S2	0	0.82	0.57	0.67	0.60
	1	0.37	0.67	0.47	
S3	0	0.98	1.00	0.99	0.97
	1	0.80	0.19	0.31	
S4	0	0.79	0.98	0.87	0.84
	1	0.95	0.65	0.77	
S5	0	0.87	0.69	0.77	0.66
	1	0.26	0.51	0.34	
S6	0	0.91	1.00	0.95	0.91
	1	0.96	0.24	0.38	
S7	0	0.95	0.77	0.85	0.75
	1	0.18	0.54	0.27	
S8	0	0.90	0.99	0.94	0.90
	1	0.88	0.43	0.43	
S9	0	0.96	1.00	0.98	0.97
	1	0.97	0.31	0.46	
Average		0.77	0.66	0.65	0.81

Table 4. The result of classifier models using Random Forest classifier.

Subject	Condition	Random Forest classifier			
		Precision ratio	Recall ratio	F-score	Accuracy rate
S1	0	0.94	0.97	0.96	0.97
	1	0.95	0.93	0.90	
S2	0	0.96	0.99	0.97	0.96
	1	0.96	0.88	0.92	
S3	0	0.99	1.00	0.99	0.98
	1	0.80	0.52	0.63	
S4	0	0.97	0.97	0.97	0.97
	1	0.96	0.97	0.96	
S5	0	0.97	0.97	0.97	0.95
	1	0.85	0.87	0.86	
S6	0	0.98	0.99	0.98	0.97
	1	0.88	0.80	0.84	
S7	0	0.98	0.99	0.98	0.97
	1	0.89	0.76	0.82	
S8	0	0.97	0.97	0.97	0.94
	1	0.79	0.79	0.79	
S9	0	0.83	0.98	0.90	0.81
	1	0.20	0.02	0.04	
Average		0.88	0.85	0.86	0.95

Table 5. The result that one of the subject's data was a training data for creating the classifier models using Random Forest classifier.

Training data	Classifier model	Average			
		Precision ratio	Recall ratio	F-score	Accuracy rate
S1	Other than S1	0.57	0.60	0.55	0.70
S2	Other than S2	0.55	0.56	0.54	0.75
S3	Other than S3	0.55	0.50	0.48	0.77
S4	Other than S4	0.55	0.62	0.54	0.64
S5	Other than S5	0.60	0.59	0.57	0.78
S6	Other than S6	0.56	0.51	0.49	0.80
S7	Other than S7	0.56	0.52	0.50	0.79
S8	Other than S8	0.61	0.58	0.57	0.79
S9	Other than S9	0.49	0.50	0.45	0.82

4 Discussion

Even if the robot cannot reply to the elderly person appropriately, the elderly person is not discouraged when two robots continue to talk in front of them [2]. Moreover, if the robot synchronizes its head in response to the elderly person, they may consider the robot friendly. The results of the experiment demonstrated that the volume and the pitches of the speech are useful data for estimating the timing of head movements if the classifier model was based on an individual. The results also showed that the timing of head movements is different among the subjects.

In this experiment, Random Forest classifier was the most appropriate method of the three for creating the classifier model. The Random Forest algorithm is based on ensemble learning. First, random forests create various decision trees on randomly selected data samples. Finally, appropriate classifiers are decided according to the shared proportion. Namely, the precision of the classifier becomes higher. If an individual classifier model for head movement is to be built, we suggest Random Forest classifier.

5 Conclusion

In this paper, we investigated whether the timing of head movements can be estimated based on the volume and the pitch of a speech, and which of the three learning model methods (SVM, K-neighbors classifier, and Random Forest classifier) are most useful for a classifier model to estimate the timing of head movements. In the experiment, each of the nine university students listened to the speech which was about 10 min of speech by a male radio personality. They pushed a button on an application whenever they moved their head in response. The experimental results showed that the volume and the pitch were useful for estimating the timing of head movements, and that Random Forest classifier is the most effective method of the individual classifier model.

In the future work, we will construct two robots which will move their heads in synchronization with an elderly person, based on the individual classifier model.

Acknowledgment. This work was supported by JSPS KAKENHI Grant Number 17K20011.

References

1. Hock, P., Oshima, C., Nakayama, K.: CATARO: a robot that tells caregivers a patient's current non-critical condition indirectly. In: Proceedings of the Genetic and Evolutionary Computation Conference, GECCO 2018, pp. 1841–1844. ACM (2018)
2. Iio, T., Yoshikawa, Y., Ishiguro, H.: Pre-scheduled turn-taking between robots to make conversation coherent. In: Proceedings of the Fourth International Conference on Human Agent Interaction, pp. 19–25. ACM (2016)
3. Chartrand, T.L., Bargh, J.A.: The chameleon effect: the perception–behavior link and social interaction. J. Pers. Soc. Psychol. **76**(6), 893 (1999)

4. Stamenov, M., Gallese, V. (eds.): Mirror Neurons and the Evolution of Brain and Language, vol. 42. John Benjamins Publishing, Amsterdam (2002)
5. Busso, C., Deng, Z., Neumann, U., Narayanan, S.: Learning expressive human-like head motion sequences from speech. In: Deng, Z., Neumann, U. (eds.) Data-Driven 3D Facial Animation, pp. 113–131. Springer, London (2008). https://doi.org/10.1007/978-1-84628-907-1_6
6. Munhall, K.G., Jones, J.A., Callan, D.E., Kuratate, T., Vatikiotis-Bateson, E.: Visual prosody and speech intelligibility: head movement improves auditory speech perception. Psychol. Sci. **15**(2), 133–137 (2004)
7. Cortes, C., Vapnik, V.: Support-vector networks. Mach. Learn. **20**(3), 273–297 (1995)
8. Burges, C.J.: A tutorial on support vector machines for pattern recognition. Data Min. Knowl. Disc. **2**(2), 121–167 (1998)
9. Weill, P.: The relationship between investment in information technology and firm performance: a study of the valve manufacturing sector. Inform. Syst. Res. **3**(4), 307–333 (1992)
10. Suguna, N., Thanushkodi, K.: An improved k-nearest neighbor classification using genetic algorithm. Int. J. Comput. Sci. Issues **7**(2), 18–21 (2010)
11. Breiman, L.: Random forests. Mach. Learn. **45**(1), 5–32 (2001)
12. scikit-learn. https://scikit-learn.org/stable/index.html

Human Motion and Expression
Recognition and Tracking

The Qualitative Analysis in Eye Tracking Studies: Including Subjective Data Collection in an Experimental Protocol

Tiffany Andry[(✉)]

Université Catholique de Louvain, Louvain-la-Neuve, Belgium
tiffany.andry@uclouvain.be

Abstract. When conducting eye tracking studies, the benefits of collecting qualitative data are significant. In this paper, we propose to take qualitative data collection even further by exploring participants' emotions and habitus during a semi-directive interview guided by the user himself. This method is part of a research on data visualization: how does the user make sense of data visualization and what is the influence of visualizations embellishment on this sense making? Since sense making can be stimulated as much by the human perceptual system as by personal experience and opinions, the methodological challenge of this research is to design an experimental protocol that considers these two dimensions. It is of great interest to combine an eye tracking study with qualitative data collection, which is intended to be both complementary and expanding. The challenge is to find the right method for collecting qualitative data when studying subjective elements. We then propose a semi-directive post-experimental interview method that will integrate all these aspects into the research.

Keywords: Eye tracking · Qualitative method · Data visualization

1 Introduction

Nowadays, eye tracking methods are widely used in many disciplines such as computer interaction, UX or marketing. Eye tracking is a tool aimed at capturing the eye movements on mobile or static systems. During our research, we used a static eye tracker arranged under a screen. According to Just and Carpenter eye-cognition hypothesis [1], what the individual is looking at indicates that he is thinking about this element, without there being any gap between this fixation point and his cognitive task. From this point of view, eye tracking covers many potentialities. However, as Hyökki says, the metrics that can be studied through eye tracking make it possible to know what the individual is looking at, as well as other factual elements without answering the question we are in fact asking more often: "the question why" [2]. To obtain answers to this question, qualitative methodologies have improved. The eye tracking retrospective think aloud is one of the best-known qualitative methods in the field. While the method has proven its worth in studies on digital objects usability, it has weaknesses that lead to participant's distraction or silence, which is not conducive to the exploitation of personal characteristics, experience or habitus. However, as far as

© Springer Nature Switzerland AG 2019
S. Yamamoto and H. Mori (Eds.): HCII 2019, LNCS 11570, pp. 335–346, 2019.
https://doi.org/10.1007/978-3-030-22649-7_27

our study is concerned, this "why question" focuses on the individual and on his habitus, personal characteristics and emotions. It is also close to a "how question". Thus, the purpose of this paper is to present the methodology used in our research on data visualization, and to particularly focus on the qualitative step developed during the eye tracking tests conducted exclusively for this study.

Our research consists in studying how people make sense about data visualization, while evaluating what is the influence of data visualizations embellishment on this sense making. This study will serve as the backdrop to this paper: we will focus more on the method used than on the results. Thus, we will explain how individual and self-reported appreciations collected during the eye tracking test can help the researcher in a semi-directive interview. We propose a method that provides more structure to this qualitative phase, being initiated by the participant and perfectly controlled by the researcher. It applies exclusively to eye tracking studies that address participants' habitus regarding the appropriation of the studied object.

First, we will briefly present the research and its context. We will then discuss the methodology used by describing the different steps of the experimental protocol followed. Finally, we will discuss the added value of including a qualitative method in the experimental protocol before concluding.

2 Research Context

Our research therefore concerns the sense making performed by data visualizations users. Beyond that, we wonder about the influence of data visualization embellishment on sense making. After finding that different studies on embellished data visualizations [3–6] did not give a clear definition of "embellishment", we chose to define the term, based on these studies and our own observations. Embellishment appears in a context of media and technological evolution. The increasing use of infographics in the media, as well as the expression of visualized information, is in full upsurge. Embellishment is an aesthetic contribution to a standard form of data visualization (that some call "raw chart" [5]). This contribution can consist of a pictorial, metaphorical or metamorphic contribution of the pixels (or "ink") relating to the data on the graph. It is undoubtedly part of the design process, without necessarily being a separate step. Thus, data visualization embellishment would become a visualization technique, without us deciding on its utility, its advantages or its defects. It would seem, then, that embellishment covers aesthetic criteria that can evoke emotion.

The concept of embellishment obviously does not correspond to the design principles of data visualizations advocated by the great theorists of information visualization, Bertin and Tufte. The concept of effectiveness, identically described by the two authors[1] under somewhat different words is quite functional and requires the fastest possible understanding, in a small space and using the least "ink" (pixels) possible [7, 8]. Their recommendations are of minimalist style: a chart, to be as efficient and understandable as possible, must be very simple from an aesthetic point of view. Many of their

---

[1] Effectiveness for Bertin [6], graphical excellence for Tufte [7].

principles converge on this simplicity in style, which is meaningful according to them [7–10]. Several authors question this. For example, Inbar, Hill and their colleagues question the principle of "data-ink ratio maximization" according to which the ink dedicated to the data on a graph must be maximized in a non-redundant way [11, 12]. Indeed, the words of Bertin and Tufte make sense, but are mainly based on the human perceptual system. Nevertheless, the sense making do not only happen thanks to the perceptual system: we could extend the notion of efficiency to the users' habitus.

Thus, a person's sense making at the time of reading a data visualization can cover multiple aspects. We study two in particular.

1. The person can make sense and understand a visual representation through his cognitive activity and through his perceptual system. Moreover, the whole point of data visualization is to lighten cognitive work [11]. Does the arrangement of visual elements thus promote visual and perceptual appropriation of information?
2. From a constructivist and cognitivist perspective, information is understood and interpreted from the point of view of the individual, where each one depicts its own reality [12]. The sense making is then a process resulting from the knowledge and other subjective characteristics of people, such as their experiences, environment, opinions, etc. [13]. We can call this "the habitus". Looking at this, how does a person make sense of information?

These two aspects are reminiscent of Dervin's definition of sense making, for which it is an internal behavior, namely cognitive, and external, where the person will act in space and time according to his/her experience, which makes sense making a communicative process. In addition, in relation to the second aspect, Kennedy and her colleagues distinguished two groups of factors that interfere with a person's engagement to a visualization: (1) human, social, and visualization-specific factors; (2) the emotions generated by the visualizations in the person's mind [14, 15].

In relation to all these elements, our research question is: "How do we make sense of data visualization and which influence does data visualization embellishment have on it?". To answer this question, it is therefore crucial to develop a methodology that takes into account the different aspects of sense making. Regarding visual and cognitive reception, the design of an eye tracking experiment is relevant, and in this case went hand-in-hand with the study of the participants' habitus influence on data visualizations appropriation. We thus integrated a qualitative analysis step into the experiments.

3 Methodology Development and Experimental Protocol Design

3.1 Preliminary Choices in Experimental Design

Laboratory Conditions

Above all, it is good to know that we conducted the experiments under laboratory conditions. We invited each participant to the multi-room usability lab[2]. Thus, the

---

[2] Social Media Lab, UCLouvain, the lab of social network analysis in a professional context.

experimentation computer was controlled from the management room. The researcher and the participant were therefore not in the same room at the time of the eye tracking test. In the same way, a third room reserved for brainstorming or debriefing activities was ready to conduct interviews. This is an advantage, allowing participants to clearly move to the second stage of the experience. Our study, consisting of evaluating the influence of data visualizations embellishment on the users' sense making, did not need to be conducted in context. Indeed, we wanted to present to the participants different data visualizations whose different constitutive variables were under control (more on this later). This also allowed the participants to present a significant number of data visualizations.

The Choice of Participants Sample

The study was conducted on a sample of 40 people working in the field of digital communication, or in a related field. Our approach being qualitative, we carried out a reasoned sampling [15]. We did not take into consideration the age and demographics, believing that, by their profession, the people in our sample occasionally see data visualizations during their free time or professional activity. The results of this study ultimately only apply to digital communication professionals.

3.2   The Eye Tracking Test

Technology Used

We used the device Tobii Pro X3-120. This eye tracker is a wide bar that easily attaches to the bottom edge of the screen, making it non-intrusive. The tool allows launching tests in a controlled environment, with a computer processing completely dedicated to the collection of gaze data. The sampling frequency is 120 Hz, which makes scientifically reliable data collection.

The Choice of Test Corpus

For a few weeks, we looked for static data visualizations that did not respect design principles on the web, in the media, blogs, and so on. It was not difficult to find such images. Indeed, we chose rather than creating ourselves prototypes of embellished visualization from real cases. We have subsequently created "correct" data visualizations regarding design principles, based on the same data and the same subject. In short, for an original and embellished image, we created the standard visualization, tending towards what Bertin and Tufte advocate. In addition, we chose to stick to the bar chart for it is the data visualization most easily perceptible. The bar chart requires a perceptual task of a basic level [17]. Choosing it allowed us to focus on one particular element, but also to create standard visuals that are accessible to our entire sample. The most important variable of the corpus focuses on charts embellishment. Thus, the standard visualizations made by ourselves are only bar charts.

We did not present dynamic or interactive visualizations to participants but only static data visualizations. Anyway, the human and emotional factors discovered by Kennedy and her colleagues have influenced the visualizations choice but also some minor transformations we brought (delete the source, translate into the mother tongue of the participants, etc.). The entire corpus is composed of 40 images: 20 embellished visualizations from the media and 20 corresponding standard visualizations, created by us.

Conduct of the Experiments

Once the participant had completed the calibration phase of the device, necessary in any eye tracking study [18], we presented to him 20 data visualizations. We asked him to read them one by one before moving on to the next one. Then, the participant had to give five self-reported appreciations on Likert scales, about each visualization – from "strongly disagree" to "strongly agree": beauty, clarity, interest, understanding, and appreciation. No other directive was given: we considered that a visualization in itself must give sufficient reading keys for a certain understanding, if we refer to the recommendation of Bertin and Tufte to proceed at a clear and complete labeling [7, 8]. Moreover, "the task given to users affects their gaze paths even without any need task" [1]. We therefore did not wish to add other more complicated tasks. Thus, apart from the intention to evaluate the differences in gaze patterns between standard static data visualization and embellished data visualization, we did not wish to formulate hypotheses at this stage. We will then explain it: the semi-directive interviews will allow us to develop them further. Nevertheless, we are here rather in a diagnostic situation in order to evaluate the "objective and quantitative evidence on user's visual and attentional processes" [2].

Not all participants have seen the same static data visualizations. They observed as many standard visualizations as embellished visualizations. People who saw an embellished visualization could not observe the standard version built on the same data, in order to avoid the learning effects specific to the data and the topic addressed by visualization. Since time is an important factor in receiving a visualization [14, 15], they had the time they wanted to look at each image. They should then pass to the next image through a command. The eye tracking tests lasted between 12 and 15 min on average. Then, it was therefore equally important to control threats to the internal validity of our experience [16], to ensure the reliability of the experimental protocol [19]. To control various threats, sequence effects and other undesirable effects [19] we chose the randomization method by *latin square*, which allows to control at least two sources of harm to the internal validity of the experiment simultaneously [20]. By presenting 20 visualizations per person, this method allows to obtain an order of visualizations presentation of such that (1) each participant visualizes the images in a different order and (2) each participant visualizes 10 standard images, created by us, and 10 embellished images, from real cases. Once the eye tracking test was completed, the participant was ready to move in the brainstorming room for the second phase: the semi-directive interview.

3.3   Post-experimentation Interviews

Theoretical and Methodological Considerations

The purpose of the semi-directive interviews that directly followed the eye tracking test was to awaken the participants' words about how they read and understood the visualization, taking into account their characteristics and listening to their own interpretation. We were not just trying to find out why a person had produced such a fixation point or saccade during the experiment. The interest was then to evoke the personal sense making, thus giving importance to the expression of the person's emotions and habitus. Therefore, what type of interview could we have chosen and what process could we have implement?

Different theoretical sources have been an inspiration for our own interview model design. First, we could have thought of a think aloud method where the participant is asked to say as much as possible what he thinks during the experience. Most of our thoughts do not take verbal form. Putting words in them does not reveal all the substance of their meaning, but makes it possible to obtain very complete and interesting data [21]. The benefit is to capture thoughts that otherwise would have disappeared almost instantly. Nonetheless, tasks that require high cognitive load may interfere with verbalization [21]. Asking someone to think aloud during a complicated task can simply confuse his thoughts as well as gaze data captured by the eye tracker. To overcome this, many researchers practice the retrospective think aloud (RTA), especially regarding eye tracking studies. The principle remains the same but, as its name suggests, the verbal production takes place after the experiment. The gaze replay is then shown to participants who must therefore say what they thought during their gaze path. While this method is very effective in some cases, different studies have revealed weaknesses. If in some UX studies it increases the detection of usability problems, seeing the gaze replay is actually a distraction for the participant who sees it for the first time [22]. This makes the interview longer. In other cases, adding the replay gaze to the exercise does not change the verbalization and weighs it down [23]. The interaction between the researcher and the participant is more difficult. It could not match with our study: we needed the participants to be able to address their thoughts and emotions as freely as possible. We also wanted their words not to be subject to various distractions.

Finally, in order to avoid these distracting effects, and also because RTAs are more suitable for detecting usability problems than for exploring the role of the habitus in the appropriation of a digital object, we chose a semi-directive interview while using an unconventional interview guide. The self-reported appreciations selected by the participants during the experiment formed the interview guide.

The Self-reported Appreciations as an Interview Guide

In relation to all this, we chose to show to participants data visualizations they viewed during the experiment. The gaze replay was available: after explaining the principle of this video to the participant, we gave them the opportunity to ask us to show it to him if he felt it necessary. To conduct this interview, we had prepared questions in advance. They consisted of making the interviewee talk about himself, about the visualizations they preferred, hated, and so on. Thus, open questions left flexibility to the interviewee who, far from feeling "questioned", could speak freely. Questions about the emotions and factors of Kennedy and her colleagues were also planned [14, 15]. Nevertheless, the real interview guide was the self-reported appreciation that we had on a tablet. As a reminder, participants gave ratings after each viewing on Likert scales about visualizations: how much they liked, understood, found clear, beautiful, etc. After spending a few minutes in the management room reading these reviews, we were ready to exploit them during the interview. In the same way, we had these appreciations under our eyes on a tablet. It allowed us to go back to a data visualization with the participant and take stock with him:

T: *This one: you found it beautiful (4/5), but not super clear (2/5) and well understood (3/5). Explain to me.*

E: *It is pretty too, but less clear ... I understood right away but you have to read everywhere, look at lots of spheres to understand ... Not understand but ... get the information.*

T: *Is it less intuitive?*

E: *Yes it is. The comparison is not straightforward even though for the bubbles, the size corresponds to the number of days.*

T: *And about aesthetics?*

E: *I do not know ... if I look at it in detail ... If the message goes. The aspect does not bother me. But would I have an interest to read bubble by bubble? And the little drawing helps.*

Conduct of Interview

Thus, after participating in the eye tracking test, participants went to the brainstorming room in which was located a large screen. The interview always opened with the same question: "What visualization did you notice the most? Why?". Following his/her answer, the interviewee could choose a second, then a third visualization that had retained his attention. This question concerned as much the positive or negative feelings mentioned by the participants. Then, taking control thanks to the self-reported appreciations, we guided the participants on the most interesting reactions regarding our research question. Silences were infrequent, and the interviewees always had something to say. In fact, they justified their answers, harvested very quickly after reading the visualization. Returning to their actions and thoughts allowed them to express how they felt about the reception of visual elements placed on the visualizations.

N: It's not nice. I have a phobia of mathematics and numbers and there are plenty of them, so it did not help. I did not take anything away from this information. And it takes time to understand it ... it bothers me and it would have been clearer with a small image.

Depending on the participants, these interviews lasted from 40 min to one hour. At first glance in our research, it seemed to us that simply analyzing gaze paths without having participants return to the visualizations could mislead us. For example, if the participant gives the reading up, eye tracking could not explain the reason for this abandonment, especially if the reason is related to personal and emotional elements and not a bad design. It was essential to hear the participant speak about how he felt or how he thought he had acted, beyond a simple explanation of gaze replay.

4 The Wealth of Data: What We Learned About It

Through this method, we were able to collect data relating to two equally interesting and essential aspects of data visualization: (1) visual and spontaneous reading, "the first impression" [2] and (2) each person's reception and interpretation of data visualization, which are two aspects of sense making as we see it. We are thus in possession of data which give us an indication of the behavioral and physiological progress of the reading of a data visualization. These are the gaze data, which will undergo a statistical treatment. We will be able to identify through different hypotheses the influence of embellishment in relation to a data visualization reading tending towards minimalism. We are therefore in the case of a spontaneous reading. Moreover, as we indicated, studying only visual perception is not enough since human and emotional factors are taken into account in a person's engagement to visualization. The qualitative data analysis allows to understand the extent to which the data visualization embellishment is important for individual sense making. Thus, we can greatly improve the hypotheses to develop in the context of statistical analysis by the first conclusions to draw from the qualitative analysis.

Indeed, the qualitative analysis carried out on the transcript of 30 h of recorded video will be a real asset to raise the level of the hypotheses to be tested. The textual data, resulting from the semi-directive interviews, underwent a content analysis by thematic coding. This type of qualitative analysis makes it possible to interpret the content and to penetrate it in depth to comment on its meaning [24]. In order to carry out the work of interpretation, it is necessary to classify the opinions present in the recorded dialogues [25]. After identifying the main ideas of these data, it is therefore necessary to proceed to a precise thematic coding. "The thematic analysis aims at identifying fundamental semantic elements by grouping them within categories. Themes are basic semantic units". [25] The thematic analysis allowed us to evaluate the convergences and differences of participants' opinions. There have been many comments on the visuals themselves that is visualization as implied by Kennedy and his colleagues in their emotional factors [14, 15]. The conclusions are prominent. They also provide guidance for the hypotheses that will be tested in the quantitative data statistical analysis. The purpose of our paper is to show the contribution of qualitative data to quantitative analysis, so we will not go through all of the conclusions. However, it is relevant to show a type of conclusion that highlights the possible extension of qualitative exploration after an eye tracking test. We are referring here to the research extension, not to a complementary contribution. We will also show a second example that can lead to the enrichment of the production of hypotheses to be tested in the quantitative analysis. As a reminder, the qualitative analysis is almost completed, while we are about to start the gaze data statistical analysis.

Thus, as a first example, we can mention that the majority of participants were not disturbed by an effort to be made when reading the data visualization, as long as it was accompanied by a pleasant feeling when reading. Thus, participants said they would like to focus on an embellished visualization if it seemed attractive and enjoyable to them. This pleasant feeling motivated them to read and understand data visualization. Other communication professionals who have not completed their school careers in the field of communication (IT, management, etc.) have proved to be less sensitive to this aspect of visualization. This type of conclusion does not really complement the analysis of gaze even if, for our study, such an observation is valuable and revealing with regard to personal sense making linked to the habitus.

As a second example, we can highlight the allusive aspect of data visualizations embellishments. Thus, many participants felt that embellishment could contribute to maintaining the universe addressed by the subject of visualization. Some believe that it is not necessary to reread the title to remember the data visualization subject. For others, this can only work if embellishment is a very simple addition to data visualization: a pictogram with simple colours, a drawing without too many details and so on. An aesthetic effort with too many details would thus bring confusion by preventing the allusion capacity that embellishment can bring. In this case, this conclusion may lead us to test new hypotheses as part of the quantitative analysis, or to pay attention to new areas of interest when analyzing gaze data. For example, we could check the number of jerks between the chart and the title for a standard visualization and an embellished visualization. We could also check if, indeed, the more aesthetically charged visualization are subject to more jerks, without returning to the title. We are therefore at this stage in this research: the analysis of gaze paths and the pattern search is of course planned for gaze data. However, beyond the analysis, we will be able to realize hypotheses that will be in phase with the conclusions resulting from the thematic analysis, and therefore with the thoughts and feelings evoked by the sample. Indeed, the data collected are very numerous: we have 800 gaze plots, i.e. 800 diagrams representing the eye path of the individual on a data visualization of data. The hypotheses could be just as numerous and varied. Precisely, the qualitative analysis from which cases similar to our example will be derived will allow us to formulate relevant and refined hypotheses regarding our test population. This is one of its main contributions.

Through the quantitative and qualitative data analysis, we wanted to discover which elements are influential in the sense making, on the one hand perceptual and on the other hand related to perceptual characteristics while taking into account the data visualization embellishment. The contribution of qualitative analysis in this study allows to largely cover one of the two aspects of sense making while feeding the former by allowing to elaborate logical hypotheses regarding the participants' comments. The data collections were carried out at two different times, but not independently of each other: the Likert scales, collected during the eye tracking test and mobilized during the semi-directive interview, bring consistency and stability to the study. The participants were able to comment and justify their answers, thus bringing new elements to the research. Acting this way consists in developing a qualitative strategy that allows to structure the interview process based on the participant's opinions through the self-reported appreciations. The participant initiates the structure of the interview, but the researcher control sit. This facilitates the study of subjective properties during appropriation of the objects studied by an eye tracking method. This is true at least if we consider that this object appropriation can diverge depending on the participants' habitus. This concerns many fields. Through this paper, we wish to show that such an interview is an opportunity not only to collect explanatory and complementary elements to the gaze data, but also to identify deeper, more individual-specific qualitative elements related to the habitus, which is often highlighted in social sciences. It is therefore a question of going beyond the simple complementary and anecdotal contribution of information by completely extending the results of one's own research.

5 Conclusion

While eye tracking studies are increasing, we wanted to share our experience developed as part of our research about the reader's sense making of data visualizations, especially when these visualizations are embellished. Forty digital communication professionals came to our laboratory to take part in an experiment for which we designed the entire experimental protocol. The implementation of this protocol has sometimes required creativity. Indeed, combining theoretical and methodological ambitions could seem challenging for us. The production and analysis of qualitative data is often seen as an explanatory contribution to the statistical conclusions to which gaze data analysis leads. However, our qualitative analysis consisted in the production of a thematic coding to be interpreted. It can provide much more than conclusion justifications about gaze paths produced by the eye tracker. The real opportunity is to extend one's research to other horizons while saving effort. It is not easy to gather so many people for a laboratory experiment. For us, considering to go beyond the simple interpretation of gaze path from a qualitative point of view perfectly corresponds to our theoretical ambitions that find the elements that generate or influence the sense making in the experience and habitus of each one. It is not an effortless process and can sometimes give the researcher the felling of being a "tinkerer" who must be inventive to give coherence to his experimental system. In this way, the conduct of an eye tracking test and a qualitative exploration that directly follows it is not to be considered as a sequenced way but rather as the integration of all dimensions within a single experience. In our case, the use of Likert scales filled in during the eye tracking test was crucial and constituted the interview guide necessary to conduct the qualitative phase. The interview model is therefore designed in an integrated way, in conjunction with the design of the experimental protocol developed as part of the eye tracking test. All this made it possible to better structure the semi-directive interviews that lie at the heart of the participant's feelings. Subjective or habitus elements were easily highlighted regarding to data visualization sense making. At this time, with our research in full swing, we have not yet interpreted all the data nor drawn all the conclusions that it can offer. However, it appears that the interpretation of qualitative data leads to many conclusions, while the analysis of gaze paths and other visual data provides many clues as to the correct arrangement of visual elements on a data visualization. The real benefit of a method that gives full credit to qualitative exploration in an experimental model is to obtain real potentialities for research and the creation of consistent hypotheses, which bring coherence and strength to the said research. This is the opportunity to exploit the research to its full potential by going beyond the factual aspect that sometimes appears in eye tracking studies. Obviously, this has limits. The analysis of all these different data types takes a lot of time because of their diversity. Similarly, such a method would probably not be applicable if the researcher's intention was to generalize his results to the entire population. In our case, this will only be possible for Belgian digital communication professionals. Its main asset remains the data quality and the results depth.

Acknowledgement. This research is supported by the European Regional Development Fund (ERDF).

References

1. Just, M.A., Carpenter, P.A. Using eye fixations to study reading comprehension. In: New Methods in Reading Comprehension Research, pp. 151–182 (1984)
2. Hyökki, S.: Eye tracking in user research. Interdisc. Stud. J. 1(4), 65 (2012)
3. Bateman, S., Mandryk, R.L., Gutwin, C., et al.: Useful junk?: the effects of visual embellishment on comprehension and memorability of charts. In: Proceedings of the Sigchi Conference on Human Factors in Computing Systems, pp. 2573–2582. ACM (2010)
4. Borgo, R., Abdul-Rahman, A., Mohamed, F., et al.: An empirical study on using visual embellishments in visualization. IEEE Trans. Vis. Comput. Graph. 1, 2759–2768 (2012)
5. Skau, D., Harrison, L., Kosara, R. An evaluation of the impact of visual embellishments in bar charts. In: Computer Graphics Forum, pp. 221–230. Wiley Online Library (2015)
6. Moere, A.V., Tomitsch, M., Wimmer, C., Christoph, B., Grechenig, T.: Evaluating the effect of style in information visualization. IEEE Trans. Vis. Comput. Graph. 18, 2739–2748 (2012)
7. Bertin, J.: Sémiologie Graphique. Mouton, Paris (1967)
8. Tufte, E.: The Visual Display of Quantitative Information. Graphics Press, Cheshire (1983)
9. Tufte, E.: Envisioning Information. Graphics Press, Cheshire (1991)
10. Tufte, E.: Visual Explanations: Images and Quantities, Evidence and Narrative. Graphics Press, Cheshire (1997)
11. Kirsh, D.: Thinking with external representations. AI Soc. 25(4), 441–454 (2010)
12. Maurel, D.: Sense-making : un modèle de construction de la réalité et d'appréhension de l'information par les individus et les groupes. In :Études de communication. Langages, information, médiations, pp. 31–46 (2010)
13. Savolainen, R.: The sense-making theory: reviewing the interests of a user-centered approach to information seeking and use. Inf. Process. Manage. 29, 13–28 (1993)
14. Kennedy, H., Hill, R.L.: The feeling of numbers: emotions in everyday engagements with data and their visualisation. Sociology 52(4), 830–848 (2018)
15. Kennedy, H., Hill, R.L., Aiello, G., Allen, W.: The work that visualisation conventions do. Inform. Commun. Soc. 19(6), 715–735 (2016)
16. Bertacchini, Y.: Petit Guide à l'usage de l'Apprenti-Chercheur en Sciences Humaines & Sociales. In: Coll les ETIC. Presses Technologiques, Toulon (2009)
17. Cleveland, W.S., McGill, R.: Graphical perception: theory, experimentation, and application to the development of graphical methods. J. Am. Stat. Assoc. 79(387), 531–554 (1984)
18. Duchowski, A.T.: Eye Tracking Methodology: Theory and Practice, 2nd edn. Springer, London (2007). https://doi.org/10.1007/978-1-84628-609-4
19. Campbell, D.T., Stanley, J.C.: Experimental and Quasi-Experimental Designs for Research. Houghton Mifflin Comp., Boston (1967). (2. print)
20. Saville, D.J., Wood, G.R.: Latin square design. In: Saville, D.J., Wood, G.R. (eds.) Statistical Methods: The Geometric Approach, pp. 340–353. Springer, New York (1991). https://doi.org/10.1007/978-1-4612-0971-3_13
21. Charters, E.: The use of think-aloud methods in qualitative research an introduction to think-aloud methods. Brock Educ. J. 12(2) (2003). Proceedings of Visualization, pp. 74–81. IEEE
22. Elbabour, F., Alhadreti, O., Mayhew, P.: Eye tracking in retrospective think-aloud usability testing: is there added value? J. Usabil. Stud. 12(3), 95–110 (2017)
23. Elling, S., Lentz, L., de Jong, M.: Retrospective think-aloud method: using eye movements as an extra cue for participants' verbalizations. In: Proceedings of the Sigchi Conference on Human Factors in Computing Systems, pp. 1161–1170. ACM (2011)

24. Fallery, B., Rodhain, F.: Quatre approches pour l'analyse de données textuelles: lexicale, linguistique, cognitive, thématique. In: XVI ème Conférence de l'Association Internationale de Management Stratégique, Montréal, Canada, pp. 1–16 (2007)
25. Negura, L.: L'analyse de contenu dans l'étude des représentations sociales, SociologieS [En ligne], Théories et recherches, mis en ligne le 22 octobre 2006, consulté le 08 juin 2019. http://journals.openedition.org/sociologies/993

Combination of Local Interaction with Remote Interaction in ARM-COMS Communication

Teruaki Ito[1]([⊠]), Hiroki Kimachi[2], and Tomio Watanabe[3]

[1] Faculty of Computer Science and Systems Engineering,
Okayama Prefectural University, 111 Kuboki,
Soja-shi, Okayama 719-1197, Japan
tito@ss.oka-pu.ac.jp
[2] Graduate School of Advanced Technology and Science,
Tokushima University, 2-1 Minami-Josanjima, Tokushima 770-8506, Japan
c501732024@tokushima-u.ac.jp
[3] Faculty of Computer Science and System Engineering,
Okayama Prefectural University, 111 Tsuboki, Souja, Okayama 719-1197, Japan
watanabe@cse.oka-pu.ac.jp

Abstract. ARM-COMS detects the orientation of a human subject face by the face-detection tool based on an image processing technique, and mimics the head motion of a remote partner during video conversation in an effective manner to enhance entrainment as reported before. However, ARM-COMS does not make any appropriate reactions if a communication partner speaks without move in video communication. Therefore, audio signal from the human subject is another option to use as a driving force of ARM-COMS to enhance the physical entrainment. In this study, a configuration of voice signal-based local interaction subsystem was implemented. Using this subsystem, handing of two types of individual input signals were studied: one is from the head-motion image of a remote partner, and the other one is from the combination of voice signals of a local user and its remote partner. This paper presents how the combination of remote interaction and local interaction was implemented in ARM-COMS communication, and discusses the feaibility of this approach.

Keywords: Embodied communication ·
Augmented tele-presence robotic arm · Face detection · Audio interaction ·
Combination of remote and local interaction

1 Introduction

A smartphone-based video communication tool is now one of the convenient popular tools freely available to many people. Supported by ICT (Information and Communication Technology) technologies, further enhancement of better quality in communication is being expected. In the meantime, this tool addresses the two types of critical issues, which are the lack of tele-presence feeling and the lack of relationship feeling in remote video communication as opposed to a typical face-to-face communication.

Several ideas of robot-based remote communication systems have been proposed as one of the solutions to the former issue; these robots include physical telepresence

© Springer Nature Switzerland AG 2019
S. Yamamoto and H. Mori (Eds.): HCII 2019, LNCS 11570, pp. 347–356, 2019.
https://doi.org/10.1007/978-3-030-22649-7_28

robots. Anthropomorphization is another new idea to show the telepresence of a remote person in communication system. Remote communication can be basically supported by the primitive functions of physical tele-presence robots, such as a face image display of the operator, as well as tele-operation function such as remote-drivability to move around, or tele-manipulation. However, there are still an open issue to be studied to narrow the gap between robot-based video communication and face-to-face one.

The second issue in the lack of relationship-type feeling in remote video communication is another big challenge. Recently, an idea of robotic arm-type systems draws researchers' attention. For example, Kubi, which is a non-mobile arm type robot, allows the remote user to "look around" during video communication by way of commanding Kubi where to aim the tablet with an intuitive remote control over the net. Furthermore, an idea of enhanced motion display has also been reported to show its feasibility over the conventional display. However, the usage of the human body movement of a remote person as a non-verbal message is still an open issue.

This research proposes an idea of motion-enhanced display that utilizes the display itself as the communication media, which mimics the motion of human head to enhance presence in remote communication. The idea has been implemented as an augmented tele-presence system called ARM-COMS (ARm-supported eMbodied COmmunication Monitor System). ARM-COMS is a solution to this second issue [3].

In order to mimic the head motion using the display, ARM-COMS detects the orientation of a face by face-detection tool based on an image processing technique. Even though ARM-COMS mimics the head motion of a remote partner, a reaction delay was recognized in communication experiments. Furthermore, ARM-COMS does not make appropriate reactions if a communication partner speaks without move in video communication, which has been often recognized during communication experiments. In order to solve these problems, this study proposes a voice signal during the video conversation as the driving force of local interaction and/or remote interaction. Therefore, the combination of local interaction activated by voice signal of a local user with the remote interaction activated by head motion of a remote user is the challenge of this study.

First, this paper overviews ARM-COMS, including its basic concept, basic functions, and experimental results conducted so far. Then, the paper focuses on the issue of communication without move, which has been recognized by the use of ARM-COMS. Configuration of voice signal-based local interaction prototype system will be presented to show its implementation. Handing of two types of individual input signals, one is from the head-motion of a remote partner, and the other one is from the combination of voice signals of a local user and a remote user, will also be shown to implement the combination of remote interaction and local interaction in ARM-COMS communication. Concluding remarks with some discussions will be given in the final part of this paper.

2 System Overview and Network Configuration of ARM-COMS (ARm-Supported eMbodied COmmunication Monitor System)

2.1 Basic System Overview of ARM-COMS

ARM-COMS (ARm-supported eMbodied COmmunication Monitor System) is composed of a tabletPC and a desktop robotic arm. The table PC in ARM-COMS is a typical ICT (Information and Communication Technology) device and the desktop robotic arm works as a manipulator of the tablet, of which position and movements are autonomously manipulated based on the behavior of a human user who communicates with remote person through ACM-COMS. This autonomous manipulation of ARM-COMS is controlled by the head movement, which can be recognized by a general USB camera.

Considering the two issues mentioned in the introduction section, this paper focuses on the nodding motion as a non-verbal message contents in remote communication using ARM-COMS. Figure 1 shows the system overview of ARM-COM for the experiment in this study. Face detection procedure of a prototype of ARM-COMS is based on the algorithm of FaceNet [6], which includes image processing library OpenCV 3.1.0, machine learning library dlib 18.18, and face detection tool OpenFace which were installed on a control PC with Ubuntu 14.04 as shown in Fig. 1. Using the input image data from USB camera, landmark detection is processed.

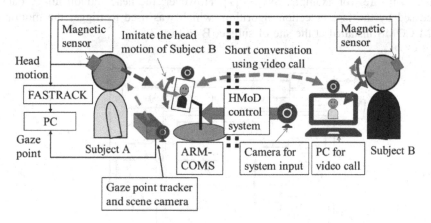

Fig. 1. Basic system configuration for ARM-COMS experiments

2.2 Network Configuration Overview of ARM-COMS

ARM-COMS is configured to implement network communication. The system is composed of various sensors to collect data, MQTT broker server, calculation server, database server, web server, client PC and application PC.

MQTT communication [5] is based on the combinaiton of publisher, MQTT server, and subscriber. Publisher defines each message as a topic and delivers it to the MQTT broker, and then is transfered to the subscriber, which is illustraed in Fig. 2. The subscriber selects a message based on its topic and receives only the message which mathes the selected topic. Eash message is specified as three types of QoS (Quality of Service). QoS0 is not guaranteed to be delivered. QoS1 is to be sent at least one time, which is quick to be delivered if it works fine but its delivery would be without gurantee. QoS2 is guranteed to be delibered.

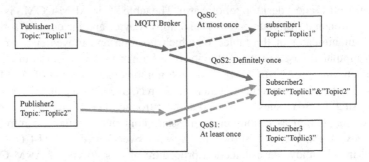

Fig. 2. MQTT communication process

Head motion of Subject A is used as a non-verbal communication to ARM-COMS which interact with Subject B. Video commminication itself was performed by a typical software (for example, Skype) [1]. However, the head motion image data is processed by the face detection algorithm, which was used to trigger the motion of ARM-COMS installed at the site of subject B in Fig. 3.

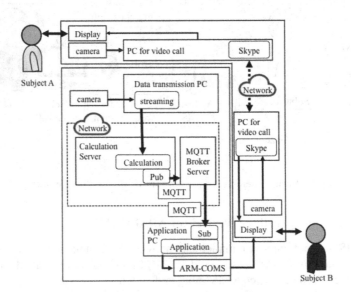

Fig. 3. Network-based configuration of ARM-COMS communication

3 Experimental Configurations of ARM-COMS System

3.1 Image-Based Interaction Subsystem

Using BGR image of human subject face collected from a USB video camera, the orientation of the subject face is calculated by OpenFace tool, which uses Contrrained Local Network Field (CLNF) composed of point distribution mode, patch expert, and fitting. In order to use this tool, the following data processing algorithm is conducted. First, a video image of Mjpeg-streamer from the USB video camera is streamed in and converted it from color image to black-and-white image by OpenCV tool. Haar Cascade method is used to detect the face area, from which feature point of 68 landmarks are extracted using dlib library tool as shown in Fig. 4.

Fig. 4. Image-based processing to determine the face orientation

Now, an image analysis for face detection is conducted by Haar Cascade face detector, which uses difference in brightness using a variety size of rectangles as shown in Fig. 5. Then 68 landmarks are defined using dlib library, and orientation of subject head is estimated by OpenFace tool. Using this orientation data, ARM-COMS can be controlled as head-up as shown in Fig. 5 and head-down shown in Fig. 6.

Fig. 5. Head-up detection for ARM-COMS control

Figure 7 shows the overview of ARM-COMS, which mimics the head motion of a human subject using the robotic arm of ARM-COMS in the image-based interaction subsystem.

When Fig. 8 shows the time delay comparison between standalone and network configurations, which was measured by the experimental setup illustrated in Fig. 1. This graph shows no significant difference between the two difference environment, which means that the experimental setup was appropriately configured.

Fig. 6. Head-down detection for ARM-COMS control

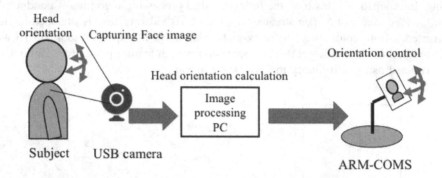

Fig. 7. ARM-COMS control to mimic head motion

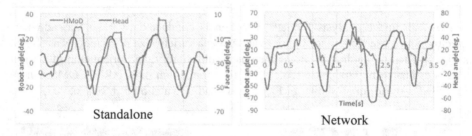

Fig. 8. Time delay comparison between standalone and network configurations for ARM-COMS

3.2 Combination of Audio and Video Interaction Subsystem

Combination of audio from local interaction and video from remote interaction was preliminaly implemented by the simple addition of the two signals as shown in Fig. 9. Pan angle and title angle generated from video signales are defined as *Mimicp(c)* and *Tiltct(c)*. Then the output nodding angle of ARM-COMS will be given as scheme (**1**). Figure 9 also shows the combined signals to be used to control ARM-COMS.

$$\begin{cases} Pan(t) = Mimic_p + Nod(t) \\ \quad Tilt(t) = Mimic_t(t) \end{cases} \tag{1}$$

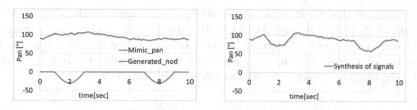

Fig. 9. Synthesis of nodding signals based on the combination of local and remote signals

3.3 Experimental Configuration for the Combination of Remote and Local Interaction

Based on the system configuration combined with image-based interaction and audio-based interaction, a new experimental environment was setup as shown in Fig. 10. Since image-based interaction was already implemented and tested so far, this configuration was based on audio signals only. A local user talks over the network with its remote partner using a video communication software, or Skype. ARM-COMS is setup in a local site only. When a local user talks, ARM-COMS detects the interval of the voice and makes nodding using the image-based interaction subsystem, which is supposed to enhance physical entrainment [7]. During that interaction, its remote user says "Yes" to interject the talk, which overrides the nodding of ARM-COMS.

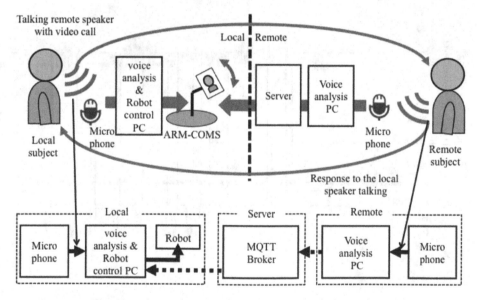

Fig. 10. Experimental setup for remote and local interaction

Figure 11 shows the experiment scene where audio signals and robot motion were recorded as shown in Fig. 12. In this example, nodding angle in local interaction is smaller than the nodding angle in remote interaction, which can be seen from the graph.

The scenario of this experiment was as follow: (a) Subject A (local) read 1 min. manuscript to Subject B through ACM-COMS, which makes local interaction based on the voice signals given by Subject A. Subject B listen to the talk of Subject A on a remote site, and says "Yes" to show that Subject B is listening to Subject A, which initiates the remote interaction in ARM-COMS with Subject A.

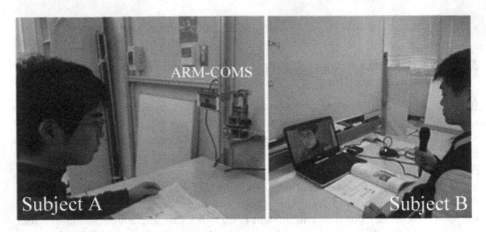

Fig. 11. Experiment scene under local and remote interactions

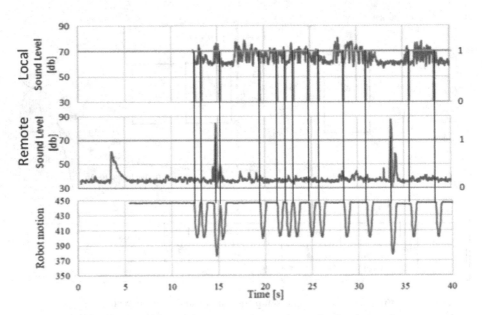

Fig. 12. Local interaction, remote interaction and robot interaction

3.4   Results and Discussion

ARM-COMS mimics the head motion of a remote subject during video conversation. Image-based interaction subsystem was implemented and evaluated [4] by the motion sensors [2] to calculate the time delay. The delay was ave. 120 [ms] for standalone environment and 210 [ms] for network environment. The delay in standalone environment was due to the process time of 100 [ms] in 10 [frames/sec] and physical motion delay in operation. The delay was ave. 209 [ms] in network environment, which is due to the streaming delay and MQTT communication delay.

Audio-based interaction subsystem was also implemented and tested to see if it works appropriately. Audio signals could be given by a local user or by a remote user. In either case, audio-based interaction worked fine to promote physical entrainment with ARM-COMS.

Combination of local and remote interaction was implemented using a two types of input signals, one of which comes from the local user and the other one of which comes from the remote user. The nodding angles could be the same or different. According to some preliminary experiments, it was recognized that the different angle was better to distinguish the local interaction from that of the remote partner. However, further studies and experiments are required to make accurate analysis.

4   Concluding Remarks

ARM-COMS detects the orientation of a subject face by the face-detection tool based on an image processing technique, and mimics the head motion of a remote partner in an effective manager as reported before. However, ARM-COMS does not make any appropriate reactions if a communication partner speaks without move in video communication. Therefore, audio signal is another option to use as a driving force of ARM-COMS. Configuration of voice signal-based local interaction subsystem was presented to show how it was implemented. Using this subsystem, handling of two types of individual input signals, one is from the head-motion image of a remote partner, and the other one is from the combination of voice signals of a local user and the remote partner, was presented to show how the combination of remote interaction and local interaction was implemented in ARM-COMS communication. This papers mainly focuses on the system implementation and only a small number of user experiments. For future work, this research will evaluate the effectiveness of the idea to find appropriate system parameters.

Acknowledgement. This work was supported by JSPS KAKENHI Grant Numbers JP16K00 274. The author would like to acknowledge all members of Collaborative Engineering Labs at Tokushima University, and Center for Technical Support of Tokushima University, for their cooperation to conduct the experiments.

References

1. Bertrand, C., Bourdeau, L.: Research interviews by Skype: a new data collection method. In: Esteves, J. (ed.) Research Methods, pp. 70–79. IE Business School, Spain (2010)
2. FASTRK. http://polhemus.com/motion-tracking/all-trackers/fastrak
3. Ito, T., Watanabe, T.: Motion control algorithm of ARM-COMS for entrainment enhancement. In: Yamamoto, S. (ed.) Human Interface and the Management of Information: Information, Design and Interaction. LNCS, vol. 9734, pp. 339–346. Springer, Cham (2016). https://doi.org/10.1007/978-3-319-40349-6_32
4. Krafka, K., et al.: Eye Tracking for everyone. In: IEEE Conference on Computer Vision and Pattern Recognition (CVPR) (2016)
5. Light, R.: Mosquitto: server and client implementation of the MQTT protocol. J. Open Source Softw. **2**(13), 265 (2017). https://doi.org/10.21105/joss
6. Schoff F., Kalenichenko, D., Philbin, J.: FaceNet: a unified embedding for face recognition and clustering. In: IEEE Conference on CVPR 2015, pp. 815–823 (2015)
7. Watanabe, T.: Human-entrained embodied interaction and communication technology. In: Fukuda, S. (ed.) Emotional Engineering, pp. 161–177. Springer, London (2011). https://doi.org/10.1007/978-1-84996-423-4_9

Postural Movement when Persons Feel Uncomfortable Interpersonal Distance

Yosuke Kinoe(✉), Yuna Akimori, and Akane Sakiyama

Faculty of Intercultural Communication, Hosei University,
2-17-1, Fujimi, Chiyoda City, Tokyo 102-8160, Japan
kinoe@hosei.ac.jp

Abstract. This paper described our experimental study which shed light on individuals' small but meaningful physical motions while they are approached by other person. The experiment aimed to capture the presence of this movement and investigated when, where and how it happened in individual's body. We employed the combination of motion capture system and the stop-distance method.

Six university students participated. Each participant was asked to say "stop" orally when she/he felt uncomfortable about the closeness. The results revealed the presence of the characteristic movements which occurred at the moment when each participant said "stop" or immediately after then (all 6 participants). More interestingly, the results suggested that a kind of precursor of that characteristic movement occurred prior to the moment of "stop" at least some of focal musculoskeletal systems including shoulder and trunk (6 participants), head/neck and upper- and fore- arm (5 participants). To establish a robust criterion for distinguishing between natural postural sway and them, further studies will be needed.

This basic research is also expected to develop a methodology based on non-verbal behavior, which will be helpful for us to analyze undiscovered phenomena which relate to the invasion to personal space of person with difficulties of linguistic behavior, or of older elderlies.

Keywords: Peri-personal space · Postural sway · Motion analysis · Biomechanics

1 Introduction

1.1 Intrusion to Peri-personal Space

People often experience discomfort when other individual infringes upon a self-established psychological boundary of preferred interpersonal distance. This phenomenon is related to the concept of (peri-)personal space [9]. It is well-known that the intrusion to personal space sometimes results in a physically explicit behavior such as an unpleasant facial expression and a withdrawal [11]. However, few study discussed how individuals behave while being approached by other person before they express an explicit behavior. The present study emphasized this segment of time.

© Springer Nature Switzerland AG 2019
S. Yamamoto and H. Mori (Eds.): HCII 2019, LNCS 11570, pp. 357–371, 2019.
https://doi.org/10.1007/978-3-030-22649-7_29

1.2   Previous Works

Methodology for Determining Uncomfortable Interpersonal Distance. The stop-distance method is the most widely used method as a feasible and reliable technique for measuring an interpersonal distance [4]. In this method, an assistant experimenter initially stands apart from an evaluator, then slowly approaches an evaluator until an evaluator begins to feel uncomfortable about the closeness. By saying "stop", an assistant experimenter's approach halts. The remaining distance between them is measured. This method is effective for detecting the psychological boundary of personal space.

On the other hand, our focal interest is what happens to an evaluator before and when an evaluator expresses an oral cue of "stop". To capture an evaluator's nonverbal behavior can be considered as one of useful approaches for investigating such phenomena. Therefore, we emphasized bodily movements.

Capturing Postural Movements. The upright human body is an inherently unstable system. The whole body center of mass is typically maintained at a variable but short distance in front of the ankle joints. Gravity acts on the body to topple the person forwards. Posture maintenance and control are fully dynamic and complicated process [7]. Recently, evaluation method of postural sway has become one of the important issue, especially, it is expected as a foundation for assessing fall risks of elderly adults (*e.g.*[1, 2, 10]). In previous conventional studies, CoM (center of mass) based sway analysis had been widely adopted as the index for evaluating the static stability (see Fig. 4-b) (*e.g.* [3]). It provides with a practical method that indirectly analyzes sway in the projection of the barycenter of whole body on a supporting plane, by using a force plate. However, its sensitivity and the temporal/spatial resolution of the motion analysis depends on the material characteristics of current force sensors.

By applying body pressure mapping, Kinoe and Tatsuka attempted to detect postural sway which relates to the invasion to preferred personal space [6]. The study suggested that some kind of postural sway occurred during the approach by other person but it was a very small movement and disappeared in short period. In order to directly capture a small postural movement, a 3D motion capture technology (MoCap) was adopted in the present study. The use of MoCap is growing in various areas including sport, entertainment and rehabilitation. The combination of MoCap and the conventional stop-distance method will be discussed below.

Analyzing Motion Based on Kinesiology. In order to precisely analyze human postural movement, the underlying biomechanics needed to be considered. The motion analysis was enhanced based on kinesiological framework [8] of the human musculoskeletal system of an upper body including head, neck, trunk, shoulder, and upper- and fore-arm, which provides form, support, stability, and movement to the body.

1.3   Objectives and Our Approach

We hypothesized that *people would make a kind of physical motion when other person invades to their personal boundaries of their comfortable interpersonal distances, prior to their escapes from the circumstance.* Based on the hypothesis, the objectives of the present study were to investigate the following research questions:

Q1. When a participant of the study is approached by the other person, is there a movement identified in the body of a participant, other than natural postural sways?

Q2. When does that body movement happen? That is, at the moment when a participant begins feeling uncomfortable with the closeness of interpersonal distance to the approacher? Or after the moment or before that?

Q3. In which part of a participant's body does that body movement happen?

Q4. How does a participant's body move? (*e.g.* its amplitude, speed and duration).

In order to investigate the above questions, we adopted the following approach that had fourfold: (a) the emphasis on a process prior to the moment of a participant's oral cue of "stop", (b) a methodology which combines a conventional verbalization-based and non-verbalization based methods, (c) a kinesiological framework for analyzing physical motions of a participant's individual body part, and (d) measurement of interpersonal distance according to the "center-center" model. Figure 1 describes a set of anatomical landmarks chosen for a kinesiological analysis of postural movement of an upper body. Figure 2 describes the "center-center" model [5], which is considered useful to capture interpersonal distance in case people would make sways.

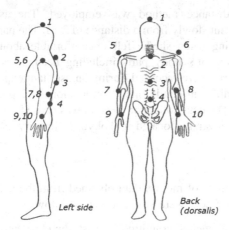

Fig. 1. The anatomical landmarks of an upper body and markers set for MoCap. (1) Vertex, (2) C7 (Cervical Vertebra VII), (3) Th8 (Thoracic Vertebra VIII), (4) L4 (Lumbar Vertebra IV), (5, 6) Greater tubercle (Humeral Greater tubercle, L/R), (7, 8) Olecranon (L/R), and (9, 10) Pisiform (medial wrist joint, L/R).

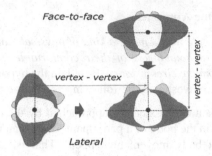

Fig. 2. The Center-Center model. In each bodily orientation, an interpersonal distance is measured by the remaining distance between their vertexes.

2 Preliminary Experiment

The purpose of the preliminary experiment was to examine whether people make any movement when other person approaches the boundary of personal space. The applicability of the adopted methodology that combined the conventional stop-distance method and MoCap was also examined.

2.1 Method

Participants. Three healthy university students (1 male and 2 females) participated.

Procedure. The stop-distance method was employed. The assistant experimenter approached the participant slowly from a distance of 3 M. The participant was asked to say stop without moving when she/he felt uncomfortable about the closeness. The movements of a participant's body parts including head, neck (C7), lumbus (L4), shoulder, elbow and wrist were recorded during an assistant experimenter's approach.

Motion data under different conditions (2 orientations × 2 postures) were obtained from each participant. The data collection session was carried out during daytime, in a quiet class room of a university located in Tokyo, in January 2018.

2.2 Results

Figure 3 shows an example of motion data obtained from the participants. The results of the preliminary experiment were summarized as follows:

1. Under a certain experimental condition at least, the characteristic position changes were observed in 3D motion data, which showed a quick and bigger amplitude than other natural postural sways. In this experiment, the characteristic movements were observed in several body parts including a neck (C7) and a lumbus (L4) (Fig. 3-a, b, c).
2. However, we could not identify what kind of body movements those position changes were caused by.
3. The methodology that combined the stop-distance method and MoCap was workable but several enhancements were needed in data collection and motion analysis.

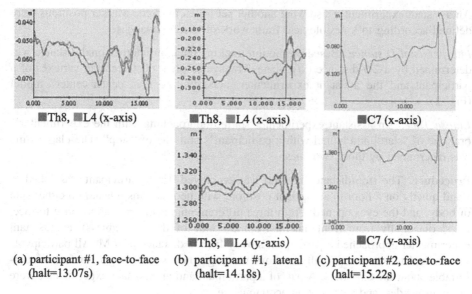

(a) participant #1, face-to-face   (b) participant #1, lateral   (c) participant #2, face-to-face
(halt=13.07s)   (halt=14.18s)   (halt=15.22s)

Fig. 3. Motion tracking data of neck (C7) and lumbus (L4).

3 Experiment

The objectives of the experiment were to examine the following four research questions: (Q1) When a participant is approached by the other person, does a participant's body make any kind of movement? (Q2) When does that movement happen (e.g. at a moment when a participant says "stop", or before or after that)? (Q3) In which part of a participant's body does that movement happen? (Q4) How does a participant's body move? (e.g. its speed, amplitude, duration, etc.). In order to achieve this, based on anatomy and kinesiological framework of human musculoskeletal system, several methodological enhancements were made to improve the quality and the accuracy of motion capture and motion analysis.

In the experimental design, there were two factors. The within-subject factors were "posture" (2 levels: standing vs. chair-sitting) and "angle of orientation" (3 levels: face-to-face vs. diagonal-67.5° vs. lateral). In the lateral condition, a participant was approached from the side of the handedness.

3.1 Method

Participants. Six healthy university students (3 males and 3 females; age range: 20–23 years) took part in the experiment. The participants were informed that the study dealt with spatial preferences. They gave their informed consent before the participation.

Measurements

Motion Data. 3D movements of the featured body parts were captured by using the Simi Motion system with a set of ten markers attached to a participant (Fig. 1).

An assistant experimenter also wore another set of ten markers. Marker positions were defined according to kinesiological framework of motion analysis.

Interpersonal Distance. Based on motion tracking data, an interpersonal distance was determined by a 2D distance (x/y plane, Transverse plane) between the vertexes of a participant and the assistant experimenter, according to the "center-center" model (Fig. 2).

Elapse Time. An assistant experimenter started approaching with the experimenter's oral cue of "start" and halted with a participant's oral cue of "stop". The elapse time was determined by those two cues.

Procedure. The stop-distance method was employed. Each participant was asked to stand quietly on a floor in an upright position, with her/his arms relaxed on either side of body, and the eyes opened. From three different angles of orientation (face-to-face, 67.5° diagonally from front, lateral from the side of the handedness), an assistant experimenter approached a participant slowly from a distance of 3 M. All participants were asked to say "stop"orally without moving when she/he began to feel uncomfortable about the closeness. A pair of a participant and an assistant experimenter were different gender, and were not an acquaintance.

The data collection was carried out during daytime, in a quiet class room of a university which locates in Tokyo. The brightness was appropriately maintained with an indoor lighting. It took approximately half an hour per participant. The data collection was performed between December 2018 and January 2019.

3.2   Analysis

Model. Based on the consideration of the underlying biomechanics, we adopted a kinesiological model for the analysis of detailed postural movement (Fig. 4-a) instead of a CoM-based model.

Analysis Stages. At first, the following analysis viewpoints were established: (a) a global view of 3D positions of each body part according to the absolute coordinate system), (b) understanding of local movement of individual body part based on the consideration of the underlying biomechanics, according to a relative coordinate system, (c) temporal change of 3D position, velocity, acceleration, angle of individual body parts and (d) frequency spectrum (FFT) of motion data. Thus, both the absolute coordinate system and a relative coordinate system were employed in the analysis. By using the positions of the anatomical landmarks (Fig. 1) and the joint centers, a relative coordinate system is determined for each body part which is origin of the proximal joint center of the respective segment. For instance, a relative coordinate system for calculating the angle of left arm can be defined by 3D positions of Greater-tubercle L, Olecranon L and Pisiform L.

By using the viewpoints, the analysis process was divided into five stages. According to analysis procedure, at first, we (1) created a chart of 3D position tracking of each body part according to the absolute coordinate system by using motion data, (2) created a set of charts that described local movements of individual body part according to a relative coordinate system, (3) in order to extract candidates of time-

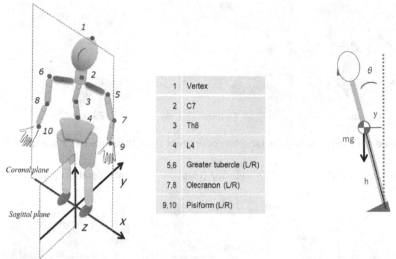

1	Vertex
2	C7
3	Th8
4	L4
5,6	Greater tubercle (L/R)
7,8	Olecranon (L/R)
9,10	Pisiform (L/R)

(a) Kinesiological model for motion analysis.   (b) CoM (center of mass) based model for postural sway analysis.

Fig. 4. Model for the analysis of postural movement.

frames that required more attention in the further analysis, created frequency spectrum charts by using the results of 1 and 2, (4) as for each time-frame candidate, analyzed postural movement of each body part in more detail, by using a set of charts previously described, and finally (5) significant characteristic movements that appeared on a participant's body were summarized.

4   Results

4.1   Analysis Results I: Creating Basic Charts

According to the experimental design of the study, six motion data under different conditions (3 orientations × 2 postures) were obtained from each participant. In the present paper, we first focused on a condition of "stand-up face-to-face". Standard deviation of motion tracking error with calibrations was 0.89 mm. Fig. 5 shows an example of 3D motion tracking data obtained from participant #1 under the condition of face-to-face.

3D Position Tracking of the Featured Body Parts (Absolute Coordinate System). In the first stage of the analysis, 3D position tracking chart was created according to the absolute coordinate system as for each body part. Figure 6(a)–(c) show examples of the charts of 3D position tracking, the velocity and the acceleration of movement, which were calculated based on the motion data of the participant #1 (face-to-face).

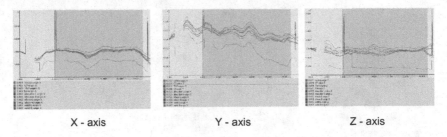

X - axis   Y - axis   Z - axis

Fig. 5. Motion data of upper body parts (absolute coordinate sys.): Participant #1 (face-to-face).

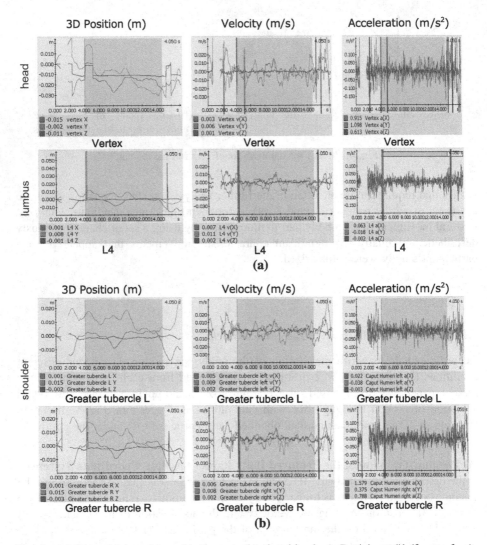

Fig. 6. (a) 3D position tracking of body parts (head and lumbus): Participant #1 (face-to-face). (b) 3D position tracking of body parts (shoulder): participant #1 (face-to-face). (c) 3D position tracking of body parts (upper-, fore-arm): participant #1 (face-to-face).

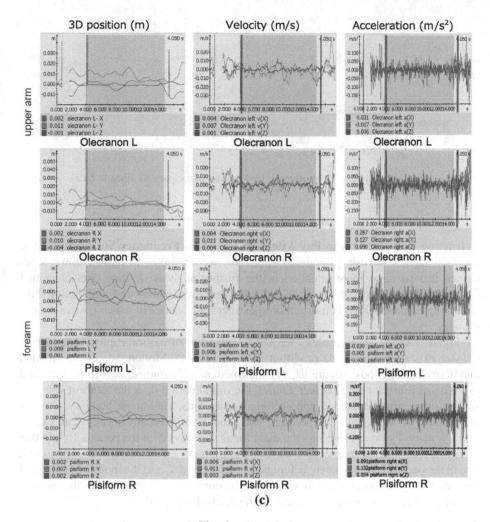

Fig. 6. (*continued*)

Local Movement of Body Parts (Relative Coordinate System). In the analysis stage 2, a set of charts that described local movements of individual body part was created according to a relative coordinate system. Figure 7 shows an example of the analysis of local movements of the featured body parts of the participant #1 (face-to-face).

Figure 8 shows an example of the analyses of the angles that body parts formed, its angular velocity, and its angular acceleration, based on the motion data of the participant #1 (face-to-face).

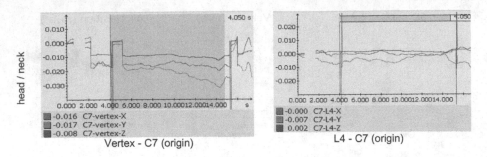

Fig. 7. Local movement of upper-body parts: participant #1 (face-to-face).

4.2   Analysis Results II: Movement Analysis

Extracting Time-Frames to Pay Attention Based on Frequency Spectrum. In the analysis stage 3, by using frequency spectrum, we attempted to narrow down time-frames that required more attention in the further analysis. Motion data contained various types of waves that consisted of different frequencies and amplitudes. Frequency spectrum analysis is useful tool to extract time-frames in which a wave pattern changes.

Figure 9 shows an example of frequency spectrum of motion capture data of participant #1's vertex under the condition of "face-to-face". Motion data can be divided into four short periods: (0) initial, (1) intermediate, (2) immediate before halt, and (3) halt and immediately after halt. During the initial period 0, at the moment when an assistant experimenter started approaching participants, significant body movements were observed. Then after few seconds, body movements became steady state except for their natural sways. Therefore, the main focus was placed on the periods 1–3. In this example, based on the frequency spectrum, three time-frames were chosen, i.e. around 9 s. in the period 1, immediately before halt in the period 2, and the moment of halt and immediately after halt. They were chosen as the candidates of time-frames that needed further detailed analyses of movement in the analysis stage 4 and 5.

Analysis of Characteristic Movements. In the analysis stage 4, as for each focal time-frame, we evaluated the occurrence of the characteristic movements of individual body part by using the charts of 3D position tracking (Fig. 6) and the charts of local movements of the featured musculoskeletal systems (Figs. 7 and 8). In addition to 3D position tracking, the charts of velocity, acceleration and angle of movement were useful for identifying characteristic postural movements. An analysis example is explained below.

Period 3 (Moment of Halt and Immediately After Halt). Based on Fig. 6, the significant changes of 3D positions of the featured body parts including Vertex, L4, Greater-tubercles and Pisiforms were identified in the period 3. Also, based on Figs. 7 and 8, the characteristic local movements of some of the featured musculoskeletal systems including head, trunk, shoulder, upper arm and forearm were identified in the period 3.

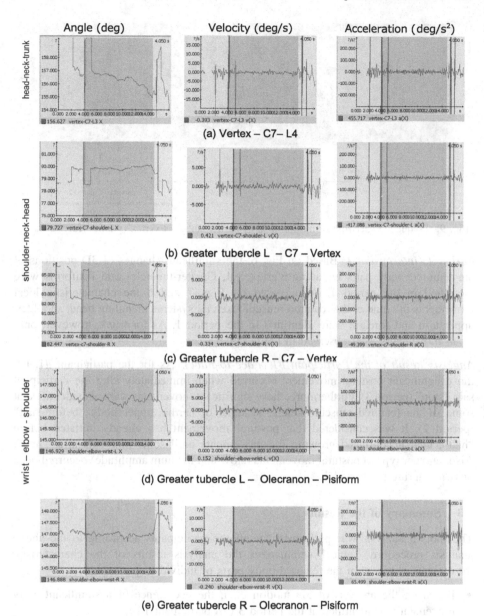

Fig. 8. Angle that body parts formed, its angular velocity, and its angular acceleration (head-trunk, shoulders, upper-/forearm): participant #1 (face-to-face).

Period 2 (Immediately Before Halt). Based on Fig. 6, the significant changes of 3D positions of the featured body parts including Vertex, L4, Greater-tubercles and Pisiforms were identified in the period 2. Also, based on Figs. 7 and 8, the characteristic local movements of some of the featured musculoskeletal systems including head, trunk, shoulder, upper arm and forearm were identified in the period 2.

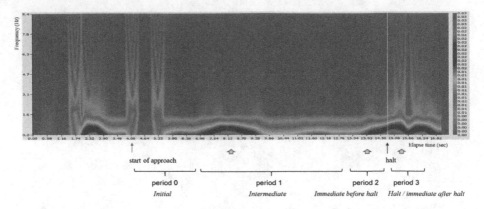

Fig. 9. Frequency spectrum of motion data of participant #1's vertex (y-axis) (face-to-face).

Period 1 (Intermediate). Based on Fig. 6, the significant changes of 3D positions of the featured body parts including Vertex, L4, Greater-tubercles and Pisiforms were identified in the period 1. Also, based on Figs. 7 and 8 the characteristic local movements of some of the featured musculoskeletal systems including head, shoulder, upper arm and forearm were identified in the period 1. As for trunk, however, only small movements were observed in the period 1.

Analysis Result of the Participant #1 (Face-to-Face). As for the participant #1, the most significant postural movement occurred when immediately after the participant said "stop" (period 3). Furthermore, those significant movements were also identified at some of the featured musculoskeletal systems of her/his upper body "before halt" (period 2). It was considered that postural movement had already initiated before "halt", then it continued growing the movements until some moments after "halt". Also, another type of postural movements (slow and medium amplitude) occurred once or twice during the period 1.

4.3 Summary of the Results

The motion analysis was performed for all the participants according to the above analysis procedure. Table 1 summarizes the analysis results of the characteristic movements observed in the featured body parts of individual participant.

- Based on the analysis of 3D motion data, the occurrence of a significant body movement was identified at the period 3 (all participants).
- Interestingly, a precursory movement of that significant body movement had already appeared at least at the plural parts of musculoskeletal systems immediately before a participant said "stop" (period 2).
- The locations of the characteristic movements of focus musculoskeletal systems at period 2 were not the consistent among the participants. Most popular musculoskeletal systems in which those characteristic movements occurred were: trunk and shoulder (all 6 participants), and head/neck, upper-arm and forearm (5 participants).

Table 1. Summary of the characteristic movements in the periods 1, 2 and 3 (all participants).

Absolute or Relative	Parts of upper body	- period 1 - Intermediate						- period 2 - immediately before halt						- period 3 - halt					
		participant						participant						participant					
		1	2	3	4	5	6	1	2	3	4	5	6	1	2	3	4	5	6
Absolute 3D coordinates	Vertex	x	-	x	x	x	x	x	-	-	x	-	x	x	x	x	x	x	x
	Lumbus L4	x	-	x	x	x	x	x	x	x	-	-	x	x	x	x	x	x	x
	Greater Tubercle (L/R)	x	x	x	x	x	x	x	x	x	x	-	x	x	x	x	x	x	x
	Pisiform (L/R)	x	-	x	x	x	x	x	x	x	-	x	x	x	x	x	x	x	x
Local movements of skeletal systems	Head & Neck (Vertex-C7)	x	-	-	-	x	-	x	x	x	x	-	x	x	x	x	x	x	x
	Trunk (C7-L4)	-	-	-	-	x	x	x	x	x	x	x	x	x	x	x	-	x	-	x
	Shoulder (Greater tubercle–C7) (L/R)	x	-	x	x	x	x	x	x	x	x	x	x	x	x	x	x	x	x
	Upper arm (Olecranon–G.turbercle) (L/R)	x	-	x	x	x	x	x	-	x	x	x	x	x	x	x	x	-	x
	Forearm (Pisiform-Olecranon) (L/R)	x	-	x	x	x	x	x	-	x	x	x	x	x	x	x	x	-	x

- Another type of postural movements (slow and medium amplitude) appeared once or more times at least at the plural parts of musculoskeletal systems during the period 1(5 participants except for #2).
- The locations of that type of postural movements during the period 1 were not the consistent among the participants. The most popular musculoskeletal systems in which that type of postural movements occurred were: shoulder, upper-arm and forearm (5 participants). Particularly during the period 1, a type of a quick postural movement appeared rhythmically in some of the participants (3 participants).
- In order to distinguish between natural postural sway and the characteristic movements previously described, further empirical studies will be needed to establish a robust criterion.

5 Discussion

This research can be considered as an experimental study that investigated the relationship between a psychological process of feeling uncomfortable with the interpersonal distance and a biomechanical process of postural movement during quiet standing. In our research project, the succeeding empirical study in which elderly persons participate is underway.

On the other hand, postural sway can be influenced by various internal self-generated factors. Recent studies reported the difference in postural sway in the context of fall risks of elderly persons [10]. Other recent study discussed a classification of sway patterns between healthy adults and patients with PD (Parkinson's disease) [12].

Recent discoveries in related areas are expected to provide with a useful foundation for our further studies. To evaluate phenomena of human postural sway as a consequence of multiple factors and a complex of multiple underlying mechanisms including central nervous system is gaining its importance.

6 Concluding Remarks

The present paper described our experimental study which shed light on individuals' small but meaningful physical motions while they are approached by other person. Such a small physical movement mostly be unaware or probably be hidden among our everyday activities. Our experiment aimed to capture the presence of this movement and investigate when, where and how it happens in individual's body.

The results revealed the presence of the characteristic movements which occurred at the moment when each participant said "stop" or immediately after then (all 6 participants). More importantly, the results indicated that a kind of precursor of that characteristic movement occurred prior to the moment of "stop" at least some of focal musculoskeletal systems including shoulder and trunk (all 6 participants), head/neck and upper- and fore- arm (5 of 6 participants).

It is essential to establish a more well-defined and robust criterion for distinguishing between the characteristic movements and natural postural sways of quiet standing. Further empirical studies are needed.

Our methodology based on non-verbal behavior will be helpful for us to analyze undiscovered phenomena which relate to the invasion to peripersonal space of person with difficulties of linguistic behavior, or of older elderlies.

Acknowledgements. We thank all the study participants and our lab. members 2018. We thank Y. Kuwahara, M. Kojima, N. Honda, A. Suga, and Y. Ikeya who devotedly supported for conducting our experiments.

References

1. Accornero, N., Capozza, M., Rinalduzzi, S., Manfredi, G.W.: Clinical multisegmental posturography: agerelated changes in stance control. Electroencephalogr. Clin. Neurophysiol. **105**, 213–219 (1997)
2. Berg, K., Maki, B.E., Williams, J.I., Holliday, P.J., Wood-Dauphinee, S.L.: Clinical and laboratory measure of postural balance in an elderly population. Arch. Phys. Med. Rehabil. **73**(11), 1073–1080 (1992)
3. Bottaro, A., Casadio, M., Morasso, P., Sanguineti, V.: Body sway during quiet standing: is it the residual chattering of an intermittent stabilization process? Hum. Mov. Sci. **24**, 588–615 (2005)
4. Hayduk, L.A.: Personal space: where we now stand. Psychol. Bull. **94**(2), 293–335 (1983)
5. Kinoe, Y., Mizuno, N.: Dynamic characteristics of the transformation of interpersonal distance in cooperation. In: Zhou, J., Salvendy, G. (eds.) Human Aspects of IT for the Aged Population. Healthy and Active Aging. LNCS, vol. 9755, pp. 26–34. Springer, Heidelberg (2016). https://doi.org/10.1007/978-3-319-39949-2_3

6. Kinoe, Y., Tatsuka, S.: Effect on postural sway of the invasion to preferable interpersonal distance. In: Yamamoto, S. (ed.) Human Interface and the Management of Information: Information, Knowledge and Interaction Design. LNCS, vol. 10273, pp. 539–553. Springer, Heidelberg (2017). https://doi.org/10.1007/978-3-319-58521-5_42
7. Loram, I.D., Maganaris, C.N., Lakie, M.: Paradoxical muscle movement in human standing. J. Physiol. **556**(3), 683–689 (2004)
8. Neumann, D.A.: Kinesiology of the Musculoskeletal System, 3rd edn. Elsevier, Amsterdam (2017)
9. Schienle, A., Wabnegger, A., Schöngaßner, F., Leutgeb, V.: Effects of personal space intrusion in affective contexts: an fMRI investigation with women suffering from borderline personality disorder. Soc. Cogn. Affect. Neurosci. **10**(10), 1424–1428 (2015)
10. Sieńko-Awierianów, E., Lubkowska, A., Kolano, P., Chudecka, M.: Postural stability and risk of falls per decade of adult life – a pilot study. Anthropol. Rev. **81**(1), 102–109 (2018)
11. Sommer, R.: Personal Space: The Behavioral Basis of Design. Bosko Books, Bristol (2008). Updated Edition
12. Yamamoto, T., et al.: A classification of postural sway patterns during upright stance in healthy adults and patients with Parkinson's disease. J. Adv. Comput. Intell. Intell. Inform. **15**(8), 997–1010 (2011)

A Facial Authentication Method Robust to Postural Changes in e-Testing

Masashi Komatsu[1(✉)] and Takako Akakura[2]

[1] Graduate School of Engineering, Tokyo University of Science,
6-3-1 Niijuku, Katsushika-ku, Tokyo 125-8585, Japan
4415040@ed.tus.ac.jp
[2] Faculty of Engineering, Tokyo University of Science,
6-3-1 Niijuku, Katsushika-ku, Tokyo 125-8585, Japan
akakura@rs.tus.ac.jp

Abstract. Examinee posture changes during e-Testing, making it difficult to perform facial authentication throughout the duration of the exam. We propose two methods for addressing this. The first method is to combine facial detection and tracking of facial information during the test. The second method is to pre-register facial information at various postures for authentication by computing the most similar image at the time of authentication. We conducted certification experiments using 21 examinees. The results showed authentication accuracy of 82.8%, an improvement of 16.8% over previous research, thus demonstrating the effectiveness of the proposed method.

Keywords: e-Testing · Biometrics · Facial authentication

1 Introduction

e-Learning is becoming increasingly more popular at universities [1]. Web-based e-Learning overcomes temporal and geographical restrictions, allowing broader segments of students to take classes. e-Learning also has advantages not found in traditional classroom instruction. For example, by sequentially storing learning-history data, students can be provided with adaptive feedback and lectures can be viewed at their own pace.

However, few universities give credits for e-Learning courses, or require test-taking at examination sites, thereby negating e-Learning's inherent advantages. There is thus a need for mitigating testing constraints and e-Testing is one such effective method because it has various advantages over conventional paper tests:

- Evaluation of remote examinees
- Adaptive testing that can estimate examinee abilities at any time and tailor questions to examinee abilities
- Automatic scoring and instant feedback
- Data acquisition that cannot be measured in paper testing, such as time required for answering and revision

© Springer Nature Switzerland AG 2019
S. Yamamoto and H. Mori (Eds.): HCII 2019, LNCS 11570, pp. 372–384, 2019.
https://doi.org/10.1007/978-3-030-22649-7_30

The above-mentioned advantages are found in e-Testing. However, most current e-Testing performs identity authentication using an ID and password at the start of the examination, making fraudulent acts during the examination easy to perform. There is thus a need for continual authentication during testing. It is inappropriate to ask examinees to perform frequent authentication operations during testing, because doing so would interfere with the examination. Methods for continual authentication must therefore operate without active examinee input.

2   Related Research

Methods for authentication based on facial recognition during testing have been proposed in studies on fraud prevention in e-Testing.

Tanaka et al. [2] authenticated individuals using examinee handwriting information from pen tablet input and facial information from a camera attached to the top of a PC display. One limitation in their method was that consistent facial detection was unreliable due to changes in examinee posture, such as when the examinee looked away from the screen or leaned on their hand while thinking. Thus it was impossible to maintaining facial authentication throughout the entire examination.

Kawamata et al. [3] searched for the nose when the examinee's face could not be detected, and derived facial information based on the detected nose position. As a result, they succeeded in acquiring 61% of facial information over the whole examination time, but authentication accuracy was only 65%.

As Fig. 1 shows, these studies are limited in that authentication cannot be performed during the entire examination time.

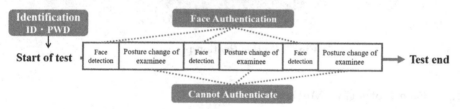

Fig. 1. Face authentication in existing e-Testing.

3   Purpose of This Study

In this study, based on the task in our previous research, we aimed to make individual authentication possible at all times when e-Testing was conducted with a camera attached on top of the display. The focus of this study was to simultaneously apply facial recognition and tracking method. Specifically, when the examinee's face cannot be detected due to a posture change, the area surrounding the nose is tracked from the next successful face detection point. Individual authentication is performed from the resulting face images throughout the examination time.

4   Proposed Method

4.1   Overview of Face Authentication

Facial authentication calculates the distance between a preregistered facial image and facial images captured during testing. Figure 2 shows the examinee authentication flow assumed in this study. Kawamata et al. [3] authenticated examinees from a single registered image. However, because examinees' facial expressions and posture change, it is difficult to perform authentication from a single registered image. We therefore propose "PreTest" for the registration process, a method that acquires information of various postures by applying facial detection with tracking. During e-Testing, the distance to the image having the nearest facial orientation as acquired by PreTest is calculated for examinee authentication.

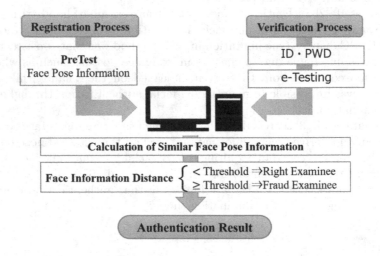

Fig. 2. Authentication process

4.2   Face Detection Method

Face detection is a process for automatically determining regions in an input image containing a face. Face detection uses a method proposed by Viola et al. [5]. This method is capable of high-speed face detection by using a combination of specific rectangular features in the input image (Fig. 3). Rectangular features are described using properties such as differences in luminance under the eyes and between the nose and nose ridge. The figure shows an example of its use.

Fig. 3. Face detection

4.3   Face Tracking Method

For face tracking, we use the
MeanShift method proposed by
Comaniciu et al. [6]. MeanShift
is a method for tracking the
region with the highest distance between color histograms.
Tracking is performed when face
detection cannot be performed
due to attitude variation of the
examinee, and the face area is
tracked from the very next successful face detection point. Per-

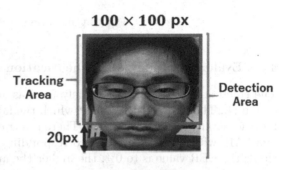

Fig. 4. Tracking area

sonal authentication is performed throughout the examination from the resulting
face information. Based on the results of Kawamata et al., we use a facial area
that is difficult to hide during tracking as shown in Fig. 4. Specifically, the region
within 20 pixels of the position where the coordinate value is lowest within the
face detection part is set as the tracking part. The authentication method combining face detection and tracking proposed in this study is called the "hybrid
method."

4.4   Numerization of Facial Images

To perform face authentication, it is necessary to quantify similarity between
facial images acquired by face detection and tracking. In this study, we use a
method proposed by Ojala et al. [7]. In this method, an image is first divided into
arbitrary rectangular regions, neighboring pixels are binarized with the central
pixel as a threshold in each region, and that region is represented as a binary
number. After that, a local binary pattern histogram (LBPH) is created using
a local binary pattern (LBP) value obtained by converting the binary number
obtained for each area to a decimal number. An image distance between the
registered image and the verification image is calculated using the histogram It
is a method to compare similar images. LBPH in this study is calculated by the
following procedure (Fig. 5):

(1) LBP is calculated by comparing the pixel value of the target pixel and the pixel value of 8 neighborhood.
(2) A LBP histogram is created for each area when the image is divided into 64 sections.
(3) Concatenate the LBP histograms of the whole area.

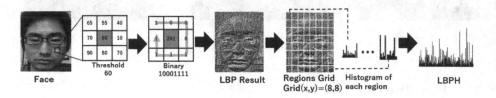

Face   Threshold 60   Binary 10001111   LBP Result   Regions Grid Grid(x,y)=(8,8)   Histogram of each region   LBPH

Fig. 5. Calculation of LBPH

4.5 Evaluation Index of Authentication Accuracy

The equal error rate (EER) is widely used as an evaluation index for authentication [4]. The EER is the value at which the false rejection rate (FRR) and the false acceptance rate (FAR) agree. There is a trade-off relationship between FRR and FAR, with a decrease in one corresponding to an increase in the other. The closer the EER value is to 0%, the higher the authentication accuracy (Fig. 6).

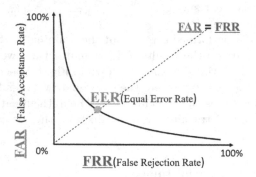

Fig. 6. Error rate curve

5 Evaluation Experiment

5.1 e-Testing System

We developed an e-Testing system to achieve the objectives of this study. Figure 7 shows the system. One feature of this system is that taking exams requires only mouse operations. The screen display includes a calculator and memo space and displays the remaining time.

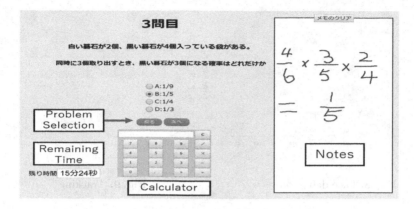

Fig. 7. e-Testing system

5.2   Experiment Contents

To achieve the objectives of this study, we conducted an experiment involving 21 college students. Table 1 shows the questions and the test duration. The evaluation method is compared with the authentication accuracy in Kawamata et al. [3], which was EER = 35.0%. We used the results from Kawamata et al. It was set as the target value because the authentication time was 61% and the authentication time was long. The camera used in this experiment captured images at 30 fps. PreTest acquires all frames and performs authentication every 30 frames. In other words, authentication is performed every second. Face detection, tracking, and LBPH calculations were performed using the open source software package OpenCV.

Table 1. Question Contents

	PreTest	e-Testing
Test Time	Within 10 min	Within 25 min
Contents	Inference	Long text
	Probability	Inference
	Special calculation	Probability
		Special calculation

6   Experimental Result and Discussion

Through these experiments, we obtained 155,656 registered images with PreTest and 23,765 verification images with e-Testing. Figures 8, 9, and 10 show the error rate curves for the authentication results using face detection, tracking, and the hybrid method.

Figure 11 summarizes the results in Figs. 8, 9 and 10. Table 2 shows authentication times and authentication accuracy. In Fig. 9, the vertical axis shows FAR

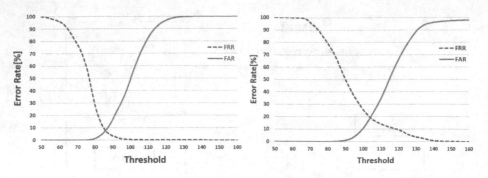

Fig. 8. Face detection   **Fig. 9.** Tracking

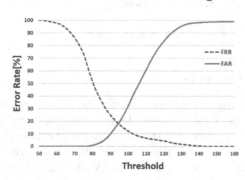

Fig. 10. Hybrid

and the horizontal axis shows FRR. EER is the value where FAR = FRR. The authentication accuracy is considered based on the results shown in Fig. 11.

The following describes the results from face detection, tracking, and the hybrid method shown in Fig. 11 and Table 2.

Face detection had an EER of 7.4%. The authentication accuracy is highest because face detection is performed when the examinee is facing forward.

Tracking had an EER value of 19.3%. Authentication is performed correctly when PreTest and e-Testing detect the same changes in posture, but authentication could not be performed when posture differed from PreTest.

Table 2. Authentication results

	Acquisition time	EER
Previous research [3]	61%	35.0%
Face detection	53%	7.4%
Tracking	47%	19.3%
Hybrid	100%	18.2%

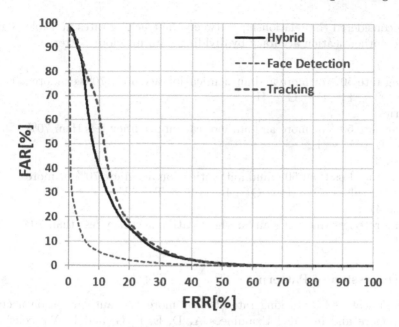

Fig. 11. ROC curve of error rate

The hybrid method resulted in an EER of 18.2%. This is a 16.8% improvement in authentication accuracy over Kawamata's EER of 35.0%. Therefore we believe that the result of the hybrid method is effective. Tables 3 and 4 summarize the authentication accuracy for examinees in order of highest tracking rate. We consider results from the hybrid method shown in Tables 3 and 4.

Table 3. Tracking rate of 21 examinees in descending order (1/2)

Examinee	A	B	C	D	E	F	G	H	I	J
Face detection rate [%]	0.9	1.4	2.4	5.0	11.4	12.3	19.4	24.9	27.6	41.3
Tracking rate [%]	99.1	98.6	97.6	95.0	88.6	87.7	80.6	75.1	72.4	58.7
Authentication accuracy [%] (EER = 18.2%)	74.0	3.6	14.8	94.7	96.1	92.0	78.2	86.6	51.5	61.6

Table 4. Tracking rate of 21 examinees in descending order (2/2)

Examinee	K	L	M	N	O	P	Q	R	S	T	U
Face detection rate [%]	51.8	55.6	60.8	91.2	92.8	96.4	97.3	98.5	99.5	99.7	99.8
Tracking rate [%]	48.2	44.4	39.2	8.8	7.2	3.6	2.7	1.5	0.5	0.3	0.2
Authentication accuracy [%] (EER = 18.2%)	88.6	86.6	59.1	98.0	96.9	96.4	98.7	97.6	99.6	97.3	99.8

We considered the relationship between the tracking rates in Tables 3 and 4 and the authentication accuracy by dividing data into four patterns.

(Pattern 1)
Tracking rate 50% or more and authentication accuracy 70% or more
⇒ A · D · E · F · G · H
(Pattern 2)
Tracking rate 50% or more and authentication accuracy less than 70%
⇒ B · C · I · J
(Pattern 3)
Tracking rate less than 50% and authentication accuracy 70% or more
⇒ K · L · N · O · P · Q · R · S · T · U
(Pattern 4)
Tracking rate less than 50% and authentication accuracy less than 70%
⇒ M

6.1 Discussion of Pattern 1

Pattern 1 featured a tracking rate 50% or more and authentication accuracy 70% or more and included Examinees A, D, E, F, G, and H. We considered Examinee E, who had high authentication accuracy, and Examinee A, who had low authentication accuracy. Time series data for examinees A and E are shown in Figs. 12 and 13.

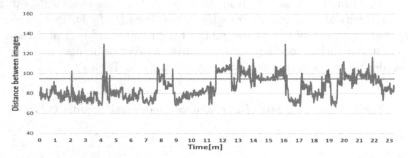

Fig. 12. Results of examinee A

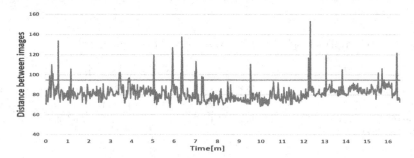

Fig. 13. Results of examinee E

For Examinee A, there was a tendency for erroneous detection of the right eye as a face area. Authentication accuracy possibly decreased due to tracking of an erroneously detected face area.

Authentication accuracy for Examinee E is thought to be lowered due to blurring of the image resulting from a low camera frame rate. To reduce blurring, a camera with a higher frame rate should be used.

6.2   Discussion of Pattern 2

Pattern 2 featured a tracking rate of 50% and authentication accuracy less than 70%, and included Examinees B, C, I, and J. We consider the results for Examinee B, who had extremely poor authentication accuracy, and Examinee I, whose certification accuracy was 50%.

From Fig. 14, Examinee B did not succeed in authentication except when face detection succeeded. During e-Testing, authentication likely failed because the face area was not accurately tracked due to the examinee looking at the bottom of the screen throughout the duration of the exam.

From Fig. 15, authentication accuracy was lower for Examinee I because there was no posture change that took the hands during PreTest and because a misdetected face region was tracked in the latter half of the test.

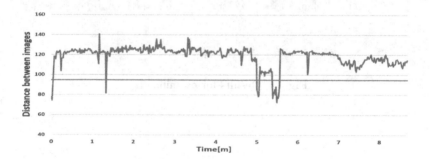

Fig. 14. Results for examinee B

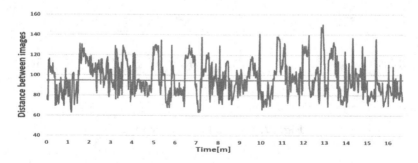

Fig. 15. Results for examinee I

6.3   Discussion of Pattern 3

Pattern 3 featured a tracking rate less than 50% and authentication accuracy of 70% or more, and included Examinees K, L, N, O, P, Q, R, S, T, and U.

Pattern 3 had overall high authentication accuracy. We consider Examinee L, who had the lowest authentication accuracy in this pattern, and Examinee U, who had the highest.

Figure 16 shows that Examinee L failed authentication when repositioning eyeglasses and when yawning. The action of correcting for changes in eyeglass positioning may be possible if authentication is during during registration at PreTest.

Figure 17 shows that authentication for Examinee U was successful except when he turned his neck. Authentication accuracy was likely high because the examinee did not have obscuring objects such as eyeglasses or long hair covering the facial area.

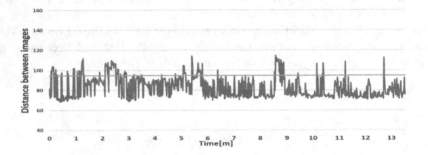

Fig. 16. Results for examinee L

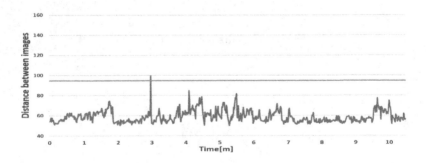

Fig. 17. Results for examinee U

6.4   Discussion of Pattern 4

Pattern 4 featured a tracking rate less than 50% and authentication accuracy less than 70%, and included only Examinee M.

From Table 4, the accuracy of authentication for Examinee M was almost the same as the face detection rate. From Fig. 18, Examinee M had a high face detection rate but low authentication accuracy. The low authentication accuracy was likely due to tracking.

Figure 19 shows the face tracking area for Examinee M. Figure 2 shows that Examinee M wore a hooded sweatshirt that was included in the tracking area. Tracking likely followed this clothing instead of the examinee's face, lowering authentication accuracy.

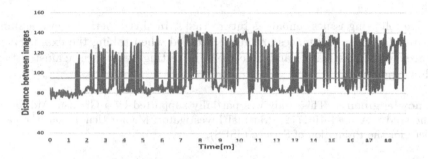

Fig. 18. Results for examinee M

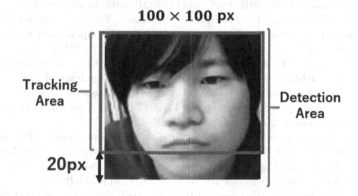

Fig. 19. Face tracking area of examinee M

7   Conclusion

We proposed two methods for authentication throughout the duration of an examination.

The first method was to register various facial orientations of examinees using PreTest, calculating the closest distance between images registered during e-Testing, and performing facial authentication even when the examinee posture changed.

We also proposed an authentication method that performs face authentication for throughout the exam by tracking the face area when face detection was not possible.

The results suggested that the authentication accuracy was 16.8% higher than in previous study, and that the proposed method is robust against posture changes.

The following issues remain as future tasks. In this experiment, we assumed that regular exam examinees are authenticated when taking the exam. Future research will investigate fraud detection by testing resistance against attacks such as spoofing.

Acknowledgments. This study was partially supported by a Grant-in-Aid for Scientific study (A) (#15H01772; Principal Investigator: Maomi Ueno) from the Japan Society for the Promotion of Science (JSPS).

References

1. University ICT Promotion Council: Survey study survey report on ICT utilization in higher education institutions (2016). http://www.mext.go.jp/a_menu/koutou/itaku/__icsFiles/afieldfile/2016/06/02/1371459_01.pdf. (in Japanese)
2. Tanaka, Y., Yoshimura, Y., Tomoto, T., Akakura, T.: Examinee authentication method using face image in e-Testing toward preventing impersonation. D Abstracts IEICE Trans. Inf. Syst. (Japan. Ed.) **J98–D**(1), 174–177 (2016)
3. Kawamata, T., Ishii, T., Akakura, T.: A study on robust face authentication method for examinees' attitude variation in e-Testing. In: Proceedings of the 2010 IEICE General Conference Papers, Information and Systems Society Special Project Student Poster Session Proceedings, p. 214 (2017). http://www.ieice.org/~iss/jpn/Publications/issposter_2017/data/pdf/ISS-SP-214.pdf
4. Hangai, S.: Biometric textbook From principle to programming, The Institute of Image Information and Telecommunications, Corona Company, Tokyo (2012)
5. Viola, P., Jones, M.: Rapid object detection using a boosted cascade of simple features. Proc. Comput. Vision Pattern Recogn. **1**, 511–518 (2001)
6. Comaniciu, D., Ramesh, V., Meer, P.: Real-time tracking of non-rigid objects using mean shift, vol. 2, pp. 142–149 (2000)
7. Ojala, T., Pietikänen, M., Harwood, D.: A comparative study of texture measures with classification based on featured distributions. Pattern Recogn. **29**, 51–59 (1996)

Corneal-Reflection-Based Wide Range Gaze Tracking for a Car

Takashi Nagamatsu[1]([envelope]), Mamoru Hiroe[1], and Gerhard Rigoll[2]

[1] Kobe University, 5-1-1 Fukae-minami, Higashi-nada, Kobe, Japan
nagamatu@kobe-u.ac.jp, 173w107w@stu.kobe-u.ac.jp
[2] Technical University of Munich, Munich, Germany
rigoll@tum.de

Abstract. When an eye tracking system is used in a car, user-calibration-free system is suitable because a driver can sometimes change. In addition, we usually look at the mirrors while driving a car, and so the system should track the driver's gaze in a wide range. In this study, we proposed a new method that calculates the gaze directions in a wide range by improving a user-calibration-free gaze tracking method. Our new method changes the calculation method based on the detected number of feature points of the eye. We installed cameras and LEDs in a car simulator that used a real car in a laboratory based on a simulator for developing a gaze sensitive environment. The evaluation results of a developed system for one participant showed that the system could track gazes when the participant looked mirrors.

Keywords: Gaze tracking · Car · Corneal reflection · Calibration free

1 Introduction

Most of accurate gaze tracking systems use a corneal-reflection-based method [1]. The system flushes the infrared light to the user and the system calculates the gaze from the relation between the corneal reflection and the pupil center.

Gaze tracking systems are beneficial for the safety of a car. For example, by checking the gaze of a driver, the system can alert the driver when the driver is not looking at the pedestrian who is crossing the road. If such an accident were to unfortunately occur, the driver's behavior while driving can be checked; it is useful to investigate the cause of the accident.

The corneal reflection-based gaze trackers are often used for gaze tracking in a car [2,3]. Many gaze tracking systems can measure the gaze as long as the driver is looking straight ahead. However, it is difficult to measure peripheral gaze directions. One way to achieve wide range gaze tracking is adding cameras [4]. It raises the cost of a gaze tracking system.

On the other hand, in the case where an eye tracking system is used in a car, a user-calibration-free system is suitable because a driver can sometimes change.

© Springer Nature Switzerland AG 2019
S. Yamamoto and H. Mori (Eds.): HCII 2019, LNCS 11570, pp. 385–400, 2019.
https://doi.org/10.1007/978-3-030-22649-7_31

In this paper, we describe a wide range gaze tracking system that encompasses a calibration-free function. Our work is similar to the Model's work [5], which only shows the case in computer displays. Our approach is more flexible than theirs because of the application of the simulator for developing gaze sensitive environment proposed by Nagamatsu et al. [6].

The contributions of our work are as follows:

- to propose a new calculation method for corneal-reflection based gaze tracking system when some of the feature points of the eye images are not detected.
- to show the feasibility of the gaze calculation method for mirror-looking scenario for a car.

2   Related Works

The method of the reconstruction of the optical axis of the eye differs depending on the system configuration (i.e. number of cameras and light sources). General theory of remote gaze estimation is described in detail in Gustrin's work [7]. On the basis of their work, if at least two cameras and two light sources are used, the reconstruction of the optical axis of the eye can be achieved without a user-specific calibration procedure. If one camera and multiple light sources are used, the reconstruction of the optical axis of the eye can be achieved when some of the user-specific parameters (i.e., radius of the cornea R, distant between centers of the cornea and pupil K) are known. If one camera and one light source are used, the reconstruction of the optical axis of the eye can be achieved when the distance between the camera and the eye is known in addition to R and K. Therefore, the system with two cameras and two light sources are suitable from the aspect of the user calibration procedure and user's head movement.

On the other hand, the measurable range of a system using two cameras is smaller than that of a system using one camera. Model et al. proposed a method to extend a tracking range of two-camera system by switching two-camera system to one-camera systems after determine the user-specific parameters [5].

Nagamatsu et al. proposed the mathematical model to calculate the gaze measurable range [8]. The range is represented as overlapping area of cones that is called *gaze cone*. The gaze cone is formed by the relation between eye, camera, and light source. Based on the gaze cone, they proposed a simulator for developing gaze sensitive environment [6].

3   User-Calibration Free Gaze Tracking Method

This section describes an existing method of calibration-free gaze estimation, which helps to understand our proposed method. Here, bold faces indicate 3D vector.

3.1   Eye Model

Figure 1 shows a typical model of an eye that is used in the model-based approach [7,9–11]. The model contains a mixture of large and small spheres. The cornea is modeled as a small sphere. There are two important axes: one is the optical axis, which is the line passing through the geometric center of the eye, and the other is the visual axis, which is the line of sight connecting the fovea and the point of gaze (POG). It is approximated that the two axes of the eye intersect at the center of the corneal curvature. The difference between the optical and visual axes is called angle κ.

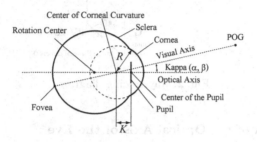

Fig. 1. Eye model

There are five user-specific parameters $(R, K, \alpha, \beta, \text{and } n_2)$, where R is the radius of the corneal curvature, K is the distance between the centers of the cornea and the pupil, α is the horizontal component of the angle κ, β is the vertical component of the angle κ, and n_2 is the effective refractive index of the cornea; in this paper, we assume n_2 is constant.

3.2   Estimation of the Position of the Corneal Center [12]

Figure 2 shows a ray tracing diagram for the estimation of the optical axis of the eye. $\mathbf{L}_i$ is the position of the light source i $(i = 0, 1)$ and $\mathbf{O}_j$ is the nodal point of camera j $(j = 0, 1)$. The value of $\mathbf{L}_i$ is measured and $\mathbf{O}_j$ is determined by the camera calibration beforehand. A ray from $\mathbf{L}_i$ is reflected on the corneal surface such that it passes through $\mathbf{O}_j$ and intersects the camera image plane at a point $\mathbf{G}'_{ji}$ (glint: reflection on the outer surface of the cornea). The plane including $\mathbf{O}_j$, $\mathbf{L}_i$, and $\mathbf{G}'_{ji}$ is expressed as

$$\{(\mathbf{G}'_{ji} - \mathbf{O}_j) \times (\mathbf{L}_i - \mathbf{O}_j)\} \cdot (\mathbf{X} - \mathbf{O}_j) = 0, \tag{1}$$

where $\mathbf{X} = (x, y, z)^{\mathrm{T}}$ is a point on the plane. When a ray is reflected on a spherical corneal surface, the plane passing through the incident and reflection vectors includes the center of the sphere $\mathbf{C}$; i.e. the plane expressed by Eq. 1 includes $\mathbf{C}$. There exist four planes represented by the Eq. 1. $\mathbf{C}$ is determined by the intersection of these planes.

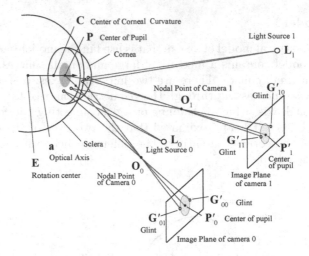

Fig. 2. Ray tracing diagram

3.3 Estimation of the Optical Axis of the Eye

The optical axis **a** is obtained by the equation as follows:

$$\mathbf{a} = \frac{((\mathbf{O}_0 - \mathbf{P}'_0) \times (\mathbf{C} - \mathbf{O}_0)) \times ((\mathbf{O}_1 - \mathbf{P}'_1) \times (\mathbf{C} - \mathbf{O}_1))}{||((\mathbf{O}_0 - \mathbf{P}'_0) \times (\mathbf{C} - \mathbf{O}_0)) \times ((\mathbf{O}_1 - \mathbf{P}'_1) \times (\mathbf{C} - \mathbf{O}_1))||}, \tag{2}$$

where $\mathbf{P}'_0$ and $\mathbf{P}'_1$ are the pupil center positions on the image sensor of camera 0 and 1, respectively.

3.4 Estimation of the Visual Axis of the Eye

There are several approaches to estimate the angle κ [13,14]. In this stage of this study, we adopted the method by Nagamatsu et al. [13], which estimates the angle κ by averaging both of the optical axes of the eyes. After the angle κ is obtained, we can calculate the visual axis of the eye when the eye rotates.

4 Applying to a Car Simulator

4.1 Simulation for Developing a Gaze-Sensitive Environment in a Car

We used a simulator for developing a gaze sensitive environment for a car proposed by Nagamatsu et al. [6]. The simulator is based on the mathematical model proposed by Nagamatsu et al. [8], which is a common model for corneal reflection-based gaze trackers. According to the model, the measuring range of gaze direction forms a cone, which is called gaze cone (Fig. 3).

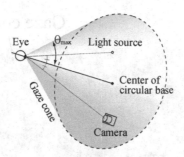

Fig. 3. Gaze cone; the range of the gaze direction in which the light reflected on corneal surface

Eye LED   Cameras LED   Gaze cone

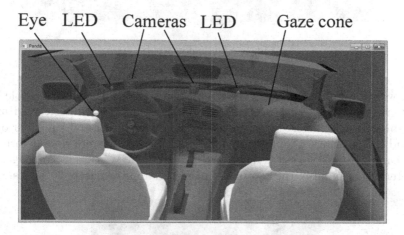

Fig. 4. Simulator for developing a gaze-sensitive environment in a car (Color figure online)

Figure 4 shows the screen image of the simulator. In Fig. 4, four gaze cones for the right eye (transparent blue), two cameras (blue), and two LEDs (yellow) are shown. We can move the positions of the cameras, eyes, and LEDs.

We used a calibration-free gaze tracking method described in Sect. 3. The method requires the overlapping area of at least three gaze cones, so that the intersection of Eq. 1 makes a point.

By using this simulator, we adjusted the position of the cameras and LEDs, so that three gaze cones have overlapping areas in the front direction and at least one gaze cone contains each side mirror. Figure 5 shows the simulation result.

4.2   Installing Gaze Tracker in a Car Simulator

After deciding the positions of cameras and LEDs, we installed them in a car simulator (Fig. 6) as shown in Fig. 7. This system consisted of two monochrome GigE digital cameras (HXG20NIR, Baumer GmbH), projector, and a laptop Windows-based PC (Windows 7). Each camera was equipped with a 2/3″ CMOS image

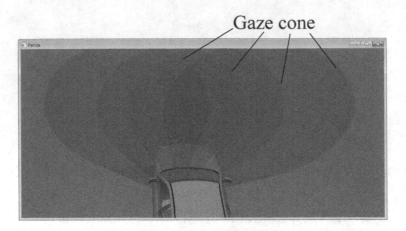

Fig. 5. Simulation result

sensor with a resolution of 2048 × 1088 pixels. A 16-mm lens and a visible light cut filter were attached to each camera. These cameras were positioned under the display. IR-LEDs were attached to the rear view mirror and left pillar of the car, and the positions were measured. The camera parameters were determined beforehand. The software was developed using OpenCV in C++ language. The diameter of the pupil in the captured image was approximately 30 pixels.

Fig. 6. Car simulator in laboratory

4.3 CG Software for Displaying Gazes

The point of gaze can be displayed on the front screen by the projector. However, the gazes for when the driver looked at the mirrors were not shown on the screen because the screen size was not wide enough. Therefore, we developed CG software that displays the gaze as shown in Fig. 8. The visual axes of the right and left eyes are expressed in green and red, respectively.

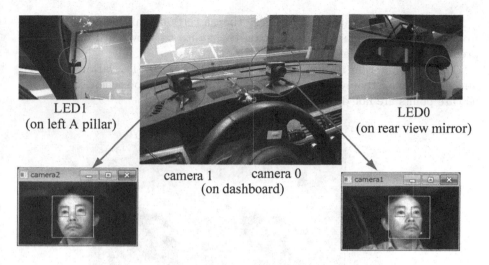

Fig. 7. Installation of cameras and LEDs

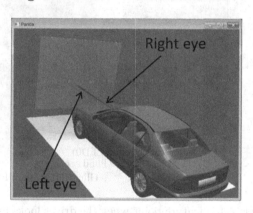

Fig. 8. CG software for displaying gazes (Color figure online)

5   New Gaze Calculation Method to Achieve Wide Range Gaze Tracking

5.1   Problem when Eye Rotates Largely

When a driver looked forward in the car simulator, the gaze tracking system based on the method described in Sect. 3 detected the feature points of the eye (glints and pupil centers) as shown in Fig. 9, and estimated the visual axes of both the eyes as shown in Fig. 8. However, when the eyes rotate largely, e.g. the user looked at the mirrors, the system could not estimate the visual axis of the eye.

When the user rotates the eye more than a certain limit, some of the light from the LEDs become not to reflect on the cornea as shown in Fig. 10; it was predicted by the simulation.

Therefore, in order to measure the wide range of gaze (i.e. various positions and directions of the eye), we propose a calculation method when some of the feature points are not detected.

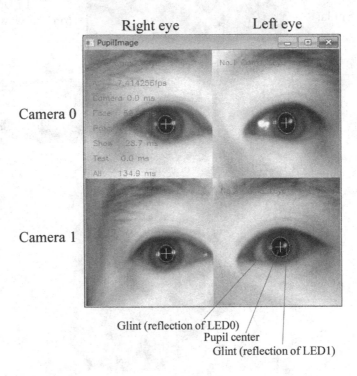

Fig. 9. Detected feature point when the driver looks forward

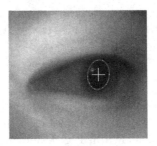

Fig. 10. Eye image when the eye rotate largely. Only one of two glints is detected

5.2 Classification of Cases of Detected Feature Points

We considered calculation methods when some of the glints are not detected or one of the pupils is not detected. We divided the situations into three cases. Figure 11 shows cases according to the detected feature points. These cases were classified by the number of detected glints (cyan) and pupil center (red). It is to be noted that 0 and 1 (regarding the camera number) can be replaced.

The following sections describes calculation methods for each case.

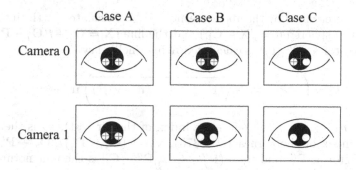

Fig. 11. Cases according to the detected points (Color figure online)

5.3 Calculation Method for Case A

In this case, all feature points are detected and the optical axis is calculated based on the existing method described in Sect. 3. We estimate that most of driving falls under this case because the driver looks forward most of the time.

In addition to the optical axis, here, we calculate R, K, the vector between glints, and the angle κ, which are used for the calculation of other cases.

Calculating R. Figure 12 shows a plane that includes, $\mathbf{L}_i$, $\mathbf{O}_j$, and $\mathbf{C}$. The estimation procedure of R is as follows.

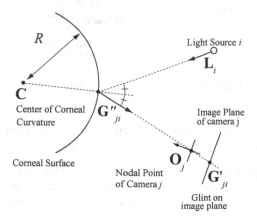

Fig. 12. Plane of reflection.

After setting the initial R, $\mathbf{G}''_{ji}$ is calculated by the intersection of the corneal sphere ($R = ||\mathbf{X} - \mathbf{C}||$) and the line ($\mathbf{X} = \mathbf{O}_j + t(\mathbf{O}_j - \mathbf{G}'_{ji})$). Then, the normal vector of the corneal sphere at $\mathbf{G}''_{ji}$ ($\mathbf{G}''_{ji} - \mathbf{C}$), the incident vector ($\mathbf{G}''_{ji} - \mathbf{L}_i$), and the reflection vectors ($\mathbf{O}_j - \mathbf{G}''_{ji}$) are calculated. Then, R is determined so that the incident angle is equal to the reflection angle. R can be found between about 6–9 mm (the average of the radius of the cornea is about 7.8 mm).

Calculating K. Figure 13 shows a plane that contains $\mathbf{C}$, $\mathbf{P}$ (pupil center), and $\mathbf{O}_j$.

As R is determined by the above method, $\mathbf{P}''_j$ is calculated by the intersection of the corneal sphere ($R = ||\mathbf{X} - \mathbf{C}||$) and the line ($\mathbf{X} = \mathbf{O}_j + t(\mathbf{O}_j - \mathbf{P}'_j)$). The refracted vector at $\mathbf{P}''_j$ ($\mathbf{t}_j$) is calculated using Snell's law as,

$$\mathbf{t}_j = \left(-\rho \mathbf{n}_j \cdot \mathbf{v}_j - \sqrt{1 - \rho^2 \left(1 - (\mathbf{n}_j \cdot \mathbf{v}_j)^2\right)} \right) \mathbf{n}_j + \rho \mathbf{v}_j, \qquad (3)$$

where $\rho = n_1/n_2$, n_1 is the refractive index of the air (≈ 1), n_2 is the effective refractive index of the cornea (≈ 1.3375), $\mathbf{v}_j = (\mathbf{O}_j - \mathbf{P}'_j)/||\mathbf{O}_j - \mathbf{P}'_j||$ is the incident vector at $\mathbf{P}''_j$, and $\mathbf{n}_j = (\mathbf{P}''_j - \mathbf{C})/||\mathbf{P}''_j - \mathbf{C}||$ is the unit normal vector at $\mathbf{P}''_j$.

The center of the pupil $\mathbf{P}$ is calculated by the intersection between the two lines $\mathbf{X} = \mathbf{P}''_0 + tt_0$ and $\mathbf{X} = \mathbf{P}''_1 + st_1$, where t, s are parameters. Thus, K is calculated as $K = ||\mathbf{P} - \mathbf{C}||$.

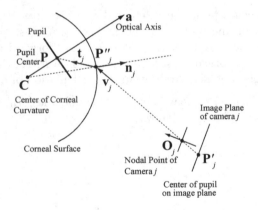

Fig. 13. Plane including the optical axis

Calculating the Vector Between Glints. The vector between glints is saved in case A, which is used for the calculation of case C.

Calculating Angle $\kappa(\alpha, \beta)$. When the results of detection of the feature points of both the eyes are classified to the case A, we calculate the angle κ (α, β) by Nagamatsu's method [13]. α and β are used in case B or case C to calculate the optical axis of the eye.

5.4 Calculation Method for Case B

In this case, two glints and a pupil center are detected using camera 0, and no glint and no pupil center are detected using camera 1. This situation may happen when the driver looks at mirrors. The following method is effective after R and K are estimated.

The center of the corneal curvature should be on the intersection line made by the two planes: $((\mathbf{G}'_{00} - \mathbf{O}_0) \times (\mathbf{L}_0 - \mathbf{O}_0)) \cdot (\mathbf{X} - \mathbf{O}_0) = 0$ and $((\mathbf{G}'_{01} - \mathbf{O}_0) \times (\mathbf{L}_1 - \mathbf{O}_0)) \cdot (\mathbf{X} - \mathbf{O}_0) = 0$. The unit direction vector of the intersection line is as follows.

$$\mathbf{l} = \frac{((\mathbf{G}'_{00} - \mathbf{O}_0) \times (\mathbf{L}_0 - \mathbf{O}_0)) \times ((\mathbf{G}'_{01} - \mathbf{O}_0) \times (\mathbf{L}_1 - \mathbf{O}_0))}{||((\mathbf{G}'_{00} - \mathbf{O}_0) \times (\mathbf{L}_0 - \mathbf{O}_0)) \times ((\mathbf{G}'_{01} - \mathbf{O}_0) \times (\mathbf{L}_1 - \mathbf{O}_0))||}, \tag{4}$$

Then, $\mathbf{C}$ is expressed using $\mathbf{l}$ as $\mathbf{C} = \mathbf{O}_0 + u\mathbf{l}$, where u is a parameter. u is calculated as follows.

When the initial value of u is set, $\mathbf{C}$ is calculated. $\mathbf{G}''_{0i}$ is calculated by the intersection of the corneal sphere ($R = ||\mathbf{X} - \mathbf{C}||$) and the line ($\mathbf{X} = \mathbf{O}_0 + t(\mathbf{O}_0 - \mathbf{G}''_{0i})$). Then, u is determined so that the incident angle is equal to the reflection angle at $\mathbf{G}''_{0i}$. Since u is a distance between the camera and the eye, it can be found between about 300–900 mm. Thus, we can estimate the position of the center of the corneal curvature $\mathbf{C}$.

The corneal sphere is determined by $R = ||\mathbf{X} - \mathbf{C}||$. The refraction vector $\mathbf{t}_0$ is described as Eq. 3. Therefore, the position of the pupil center $\mathbf{P}$ is expressed as $\mathbf{X} = \mathbf{P}'_0 + v\mathbf{t}_0$. v is determined to satisfy $K = ||\mathbf{P} - \mathbf{C}||$. v is smaller than the radius of the cornea. It is enough to search v in the range of 0–9 mm.

5.5 Calculation Method for Case C

In this case, one glint and a pupil center are detected using camera 0, and no glint and no pupil center are detected using camera 1. When the eyeball rotates greater than a certain limit, the light cannot reflect on the cornea. The number of reflections on the cornea decreases to one.

In a car, the driver is sitting, so the driver's movement is limited. Therefore, we estimates that the distance between the camera and the eye is almost constant.

We add a virtual glint on the eye image using the vector between glints saved in case A, so that the relative position between the two glints are the same as that when the driver looks forward.

Then, we can use the calculation method in case B.

6 Evaluation

6.1 Method

For evaluation, we made a scenario as shown in Fig. 14. In this scenario, the driver looked in the order as follows.

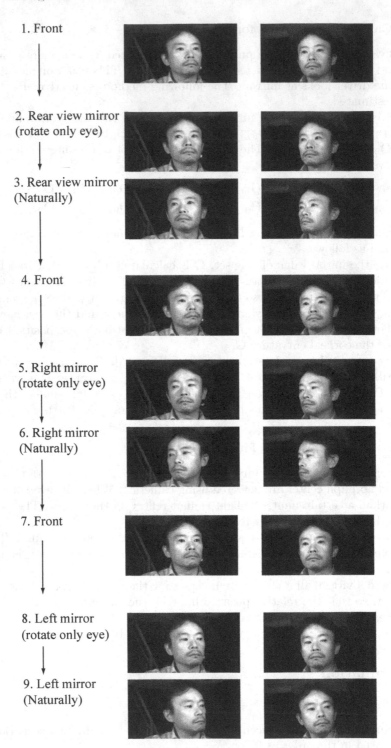

1. Front

2. Rear view mirror
(rotate only eye)

3. Rear view mirror
(Naturally)

4. Front

5. Right mirror
(rotate only eye)

6. Right mirror
(Naturally)

7. Front

8. Left mirror
(rotate only eye)

9. Left mirror
(Naturally)

Fig. 14. Scenario

1. The driver looked forward.
2. The driver looked at the rear view mirror intending to move only his eyes.
3. The driver looked at the rear view mirror naturally.
4. The driver looked forward.
5. The driver looked at the right mirror intending to move only his eyes.
6. The driver looked at the right mirror naturally.
7. The driver looked forward.
8. The driver looked at the left mirror intending to move only his eyes.
9. The driver looked at the left mirror naturally.

The reason why the driver looked at the front and the mirrors alternately was that the calculations of cases B and C need to be calculated after case A (the driver sees the front).

We captured images of camera 0 and 1 when a driver looking at four directions: forward, the rear view mirror, the right mirror, and the left mirror. For each direction, two sets of images of camera 0 and 1 were saved. Using saved eight sets of images, we calculated gazes and thier accuracies.

6.2   Results

Figure 15 shows the eye images and the visual axes of both eyes in CG based on the scenario.

Figure 15(a) and (b) show the case where the driver looked forward. In this case, all the feature points were detected, so the calculation is conducted by the calculation method in case A. Figure 15(c) and (d) show the cases where the driver looked at the rear view mirror. The visual axes of the right and left eyes were calculated by the methods in case C and case B, respectively. Figure 15(e) shows the case where the driver looked at the right mirror rotating only his eyes. The visual axes of the right and left eyes were calculated by the method in case C. Figure 15(f) shows the case where the driver looked at the right mirror naturally. The visual axis of the right eye were not detected, and the visual axes of the left eye were calculated by the method in case C. Figure 15(g) and (h) show the cases where the driver looked at the left mirror. The visual axes of the right and left eyes were calculated by the methods in case C. Thus, the system could track gazes when the driver looked mirrors.

Table 1 shows the accuracy in degree when the driver looked at the mirrors. The first row shows the mirror that the driver looked at. The second row shows left (L) or right (R) eye. The third row is the results when the driver looked at the mirrors intending to rotate only his eyes. The fourth row is the results when the driver looked at the mirrors naturally.

6.3   Discussion

We proposed a novel method to achieve wide range gaze tracking, and evaluated it for one participant; it worked well. However, evaluation of this method is insufficient, so we will increase the number of participants.

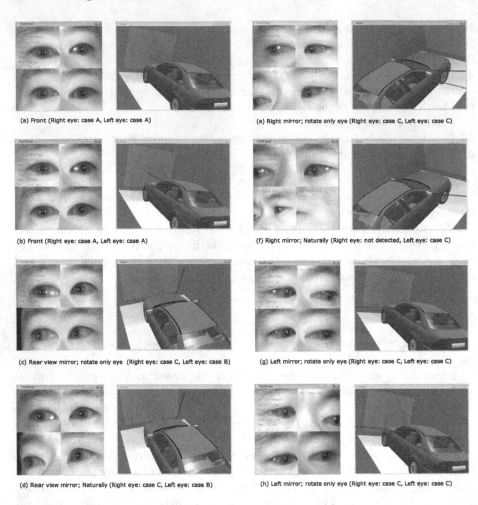

(a) Front (Right eye: case A, Left eye: case A)

(b) Front (Right eye: case A, Left eye: case A)

(c) Rear view mirror; rotate only eye (Right eye: case C, Left eye: case B)

(d) Rear view mirror; Naturally (Right eye: case C, Left eye: case B)

(e) Right mirror; rotate only eye (Right eye: case C, Left eye: case C)

(f) Right mirror; Naturally (Right eye: not detected, Left eye: case C)

(g) Left mirror; rotate only eye (Right eye: case C, Left eye: case C)

(h) Left mirror; rotate only eye (Right eye: case C, Left eye: case C)

Fig. 15. Eye images and visual axes of both eyes in CG

Although we applied the proposed method described in Sect. 5 to a car simulator, this method can be generally applied to all the situations when the corneal reflection is partially not detected. For example, the situations happen when the resolution of the camera is low, when the eyeball rotates largely, when the hand blocks the camera or the light source, or when the user blinks.

Table 1. Accuracy (degree).

Mirror	Rear-view		Right		Left	
Eye	L	R	L	R	L	R
Looked intending to rotate only his eyes	14.9	3.4	7.4	13.0	7.4	1.7
Looked naturally	14.3	1.2	7.1	–	0.4	3.4

7   Conclusion

We proposed a novel calculation method of a gaze tracker for a car when the driver rotates their eyes largely. At that time, some of the feature points of the eye images are not detected. Our proposed method changes the calculation method based on the detected feature points of the eye. We implemented the method and installed it in a car simulator in a laboratory. The evaluation results for one participant showed that the system could track gazes when the participant looked mirrors. The accuracy was 0.4–14.9°.

Acknowledgement. This work was supported by JSPS KAKENHI Grant Numbers 23300047, 16H02860.

References

1. Hansen, D.W., Ji, Q.: In the eye of the beholder: a survey of models for eyes and gaze. IEEE Trans. Pattern Anal. Mach. Intell. **32**(3), 478–500 (2010)
2. Trosterer, S., Meschtscherjakov, A., Wilfinger, D., Tscheligi, M.: Eye tracking in the car: challenges in a dual-task scenario on a test track. In: Adjunct Proceedings of the 6th International Conference on Automotive User Interfaces and Interactive Vehicular Applications, pp. 1–6. ACM (2014)
3. Fletcher, L., Zelinsky, A.: Driver inattention detection based on eye gaze-road event correlation. Int. J. Robot. Res. **28**(6), 774–801 (2009)
4. SmartEye. http://smarteye.se/research-instruments/se-pro/
5. Model, D., Eizenman, M.: A general framework for extension of a tracking range of user-calibration-free remote eye-gaze tracking systems. In: Proceedings of the Symposium on Eye Tracking Research and Applications, pp. 253–256. ACM (2012)
6. Nagamatsu, T., Yamamoto, M., Rigoll, G.: Simulator for developing gaze sensitive environment using corneal reflection-based remote gaze tracker. In: Proceedings of the 2nd ACM Symposium on Spatial User Interaction, p. 142. ACM (2014)
7. Guestrin, E.D., Eizenman, M.: General theory of remote gaze estimation using the pupil center and corneal reflections. IEEE Trans. Biomed. Eng. **53**(6), 1124–1133 (2006)
8. Nagamatsu, T., Yamamoto, M., Sugano, R., Kamahara, J.: Mathematical model for wide range gaze tracking system based on corneal reflections and pupil using stereo cameras. In: Proceedings of the Symposium on Eye Tracking Research and Applications, pp. 257–260. ACM (2012)
9. Shih, S.W., Liu, J.: A novel approach to 3-D gaze tracking using stereo cameras. IEEE Trans. Syst. Man Cybern. B **34**(1), 234–245 (2004)
10. Nagamatsu, T., Kamahara, J., Iko, T., Tanaka, N.: One-point calibration gaze tracking based on eyeball kinematics using stereo cameras. In: Proceedings of the 2008 Symposium on Eye Tracking Research & Applications, pp. 95–98 (2008)
11. Villanueva, A., Cabeza, R.: A novel gaze estimation system with one calibration point. IEEE Trans. Syst. Man Cybern. B **38**(4), 1123–1138 (2008)
12. Nagamatsu, T., Kamahara, J., Tanaka, N.: Calibration-free gaze tracking using a binocular 3D eye model. In: Proceedings of the 27th International Conference Extended Abstracts on Human Factors in Computing Systems, pp. 3613–3618. ACM (2009)

13. Nagamatsu, T., Sugano, R., Iwamoto, Y., Kamahara, J., Tanaka, N.: User-calibration-free gaze estimation method using a binocular 3D eye model. IEICE Trans. Inf. Syst. **E94–D**(9), 1817–1829 (2011)
14. Model, D., Eizenman, M.: User-calibration-free remote gaze estimation system. In: Proceedings of the 2010 Symposium on Eye-Tracking Research & Applications, pp. 29–36. ACM (2010)

rapoptosis: Renatusu via Apoptosis - Prototyping Using Clothes

Young ah Seong[1($\boxtimes$)], Tomoko Hashida[2], and Ryoko Ueoka[3]

[1] The University of Tokyo, 7-3-1 Hongo, Bunkyo-ku, Tokyo, Japan
yabird@gmail.com
[2] Waseda University, 3-4-1 Okubo, Shinjuku-ku, Tokyo, Japan
hashida@waseda.jp
[3] Kyushu University, 4-9-1 Shiobaru, Minami-ku, Fukuoka, Japan
r-ueoka@design.kyushu-u.ac.jp

Abstract. To redefine the way artifacts are inexhaustively produced, consumed, and discarded, the authors define a new form of death for "things" and propose a system in which artifacts circulate and transform themselves in our society. This system is inspired by the characteristics of organisms, such as self-death and regeneration, in nature. We redefine the death of artifacts as the time when their intrinsic existence value ceases to exist in the relationship between the object and the user, rather than when it ceases to function (self-death: apoptosis), and we propose a method to allow artifacts to judge their intrinsic existence value themselves and survive by having them change users autonomously (rebirth: renatusu). We propose to call this system "rapoptosis" (renatusu via apoptosis). In this paper, we report the results of the rapoptosis prototyping using clothes and investigate the current general methods, timing, and potential requirements of methods to dispose of clothes.

Keywords: Self-death · Apoptosis · Artifacts · Sustainability · Intrinsic existence value

1 Introduction

Artificial objects have been inexhaustively produced, consumed, and discarded throughout history. Thus, when developing items in this context, the manner of retiring the item, or its "death," has received little consideration. Meanwhile, infrastructure development on the Internet that enables easy trading and sharing between individuals has progressed recently. Thus, not only when an item is no longer usable, but also when it is no longer being used, options other than disposal are being considered increasingly. However, the entity that decides the timing and method of releasing things remains a person.

On the other hand, in nature, not only life but also the manner of death is programmed carefully. For example, apoptosis is the self-death of programmed cells in multicellular organisms. Even though the cell still functions, it purposefully self-destructs for the greater good of the entire life form. We were impressed

© Springer Nature Switzerland AG 2019
S. Yamamoto and H. Mori (Eds.): HCII 2019, LNCS 11570, pp. 401–411, 2019.
https://doi.org/10.1007/978-3-030-22649-7_32

with the autonomous and altruistic nature of death in the apoptosis process and wished to extend appropriately to the existence of items, specifically, the timing of the death of these items when their existence ceases to have value to the user. Additionally, we define the method of death as movement to other users in society, in much the same manner in which cells that have killed themselves via apoptosis are absorbed by the surrounding cells and regenerated within the individual. In summary, if an object judges that its existence ceases to have value to its user, it can leave on its own (apoptosis) after its estimation of value is confirmed by the user. Then, they arrange their transfer to another place/user, effectively being regenerated in the society (renatusu). We define autonomous and sustainable regeneration as a new form of the death of things, which we term "rapoptosis" (renatusu via apoptosis, Fig. 1).

Fig. 1. The concept of rapoptosis.

The literature commonly recognizes artifacts as having their value determined when they are produced; however, based on recent share economies and blockchain technologies, the value of things changes constantly depending on the user and context. From these contexts, the mechanism by which things themselves change their own places and owners to increase their value in society is similar to biological phenomena, such as metamorphosis. Metamorphosis occurs when organisms change greatly to achieve an optimum form, lifestyle, and/or place for survival in their development process. Although rapoptosis does not change the shape of the object itself, it acts to actively increase its inherent value. In other words, rapoptosis is an example of applying the mechanism of circulation and transformation of an ecosystem consisting of self-death and regeneration of life. It also can be positioned as a new artificial life system that can be integrated into daily life by utilizing the recent social/information infrastructure.

2   Design Guideline of rapoptosis

rapoptosis shows the way that objects themselves are autonomous and sustainable. Figure 2 schematically shows the process required for this prototyping system. Specifically, the system operates by progressing through the following steps.

1. The item judges its existential value in relation to its user.
2. The item checks its existential value with its user.
3. If this value has ceased to exist, the item removes itself from the user in the real world.
4. The item performs the action of seeking new users on social networking or internet services (SNS/WEB).
5. The item performs the action of moving to a new place in the real world.

In this way, rapoptosis is thought to be realized as a mechanism that spans both the real and information worlds. Because the potential existence value of things is decided within the relationship with the user, it is desirable to finally calculate from plural parameters. By using the existing SNS/WEB platform, one can communicate in a natural and easy-to-see manner in a more natural way by displaying the intention to users and searching for new users. On the other hand, as the objects perform the real-world removal and direct the movement, we expect that the objects themselves will convey their intention to leave to the user intelligibly. In this paper, as a first prototype to embody rapoptosis, we focused on clothes.

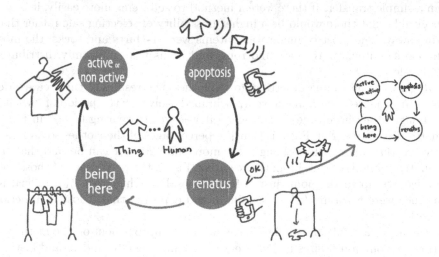

Fig. 2. The process of rapoptosis.

3   User Research on How to Let Go of Clothes

Prior to prototyping rapoptosis for clothes, we surveyed the method and timing of releasing clothes and the present situation on clothing possession by a
questionnaire to investigate the potential needs for rapoptosis.

3.1   Method and Time to Let Go of Clothes

To concretely consider the death of the defined object, we used a web questionnaire to survey the methods by which people dispose of clothes. The questions
covered the most common method used by each individual (disposal, sell face
to face, sell on the internet, give away, or other), the reason for choosing that
method, items that sell usually, and estimated timing to let go (i.e., the duration
between when the item was purchased and when it was let go). There were 67
subjects (47 males, 20 females) aged from 10 to 30 years old.

For the most common method, in multiple responses, 88.1% answered "disposal," 43.3% of people said "give to an acquaintance," and 13.5% said "sell
on the internet or face-to-face" (5 people said internet and 4 said face-to-face
sales). As a result, about half of the subjects had an experience of giving clothes
to acquaintances. The reason provided for this transfer was that the clothes were
good and could still be used, so there were many responses indicating that the
users wanted the clothing to be reused. Despite being a method that can be
reused as well, there are still few people who sold clothes online or face-to-face.
This is thought to be a hurdle as a system because a sale is more labor-intensive
than a simple transfer. If there were a method to sell items more easily, it is also
conceivable that there would be a higher possibility of selecting sale rather than
giving away. The most common waste items were T-shirts and socks, the most
common sale items were coats and tops, and items were uniformly distributed
for transfer.

Regarding the timing of letting go of clothes, the results of three categories
(one year or more, less than one year, or immediately) for the period of "when it
was bought (purchase time)" and "when it was worn (wearing time)" in Fig. 3.
What is distinctive from Fig. 3 is that the percentages of the clothes sold or gave
away less than on year from bought are more than 20%. It can be said that the
circulation period is brief. From the results in Fig. 4, the percentage of those who
wore clothes up to the point just before disposal was high (29.3%), indicating
that they were worn until the last minute and expected that it lost its function
as cloth.

Finally, as a result of listening to the need for improvement on the method of
letting go, common desires included easy recycling, easy-to-understand instructions, a single-step process and instructions as to what to discard. There was
an opinion about extra value that "I want to preserve my memories," and there
was a need for a delicate design for the value that emphasizes the rapoptosis
system's construction.

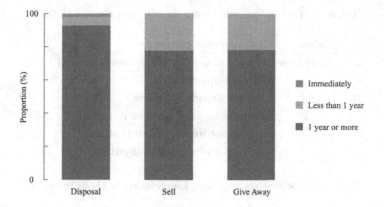

Fig. 3. The length of time from purchase to letting go.

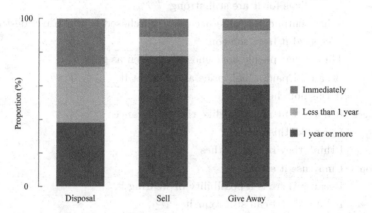

Fig. 4. The length of time from wearing to letting go.

3.2   Amount of Clothes Owned

In order to clarify the overall picture of the possession of clothes, we asked to count the total number of clothes they have and the number of clothes they had not worn for more than one year for the three categories of representative tops, bottoms, and coats. We also asked respondents to explain, in a free-response section of the questionnaire, why they do not dispose of infrequently used clothes, despite not wearing them for more than a year.

There were 68 subjects (45 males, 23 females) aged from 10 to 30 years old. As for the total number of clothes, the proportion of clothes not worn more than one year is defined as the percentage of idle assets, and the proportion was examined. As a result, the percentages of the idle assets in each categories were tops (26.0%), bottoms (25.4%), and coats (18.3%). In the case of a coat with a relatively high price for the tops and bottoms, the proportion of idle assets was small.

Table 1. The reasons why users do not wear certain clothes.

Value	Questionnaire answers
Body type	The clothing does not fit my body well
	The clothing is small
Trend	It is not trendy anymore
	There is no place to wear it
	It does not match my current style
	My preferences have changed

Table 2. The reasons why user keep clothes without wearing.

Value	Questionnaire answers
Memories	My feelings for it are still strong
	It has sentimental value because I purchased it at a travel destination
	I received it from someone
	Things that people have chosen or given as gifts.
Prices	Because I paid a high price and bought it
	It was not cheap.
Preferences	It doesn't fit me, but I like the appearance
	I just like this pattern
	I think they're nice clothes.
Indecision	I may use it someday
	Because there is a possibility of wearing it
	I think that I can still wear it

Tables 1 and 2 show free descriptions obtained of answers about why they are not wearing certain clothes and why they do not want to let them go. We also categorised and defined the inherent values. As shown in Table 1, there are many opinions that changes in body type, social trends, and personal preference are important factors, and these value standards have the main influence on the frequency of use. In Table 2, factors such as "memories," "prices," "preferences," and "indecision due to sensitivity" are seen as reasons not to let go, in addition to the items'original functions as clothes. This indicates how individuals ascribe personal value to their clothes in addition to their original functional value. We defined this as the intrinsic existence value. These intrinsic existence values suggest that the period that one wants to keep the clothing can change, even if the clothing is not worn, because of the intrinsic existence value. In other words, when designing autonomous apoptosis timing, it is necessary to consider these value criteria for each individual. Furthermore, even in the way that things determine their autonomous death, if the intrinsic existence value can be considered, there is a possibility that more efficient and effective separation methods can be produced.

4 Prototyping with Clothes

4.1 System

Although it is desirable to take multiple parameters, for the purposes of the prototype, we considered only the period of unused for designing the time of death. And the condition is set that clothes are always hung on the same hanger. A sensor in each hanger detects whether the clothing is used or not. Eliminating the clothes is realized by actuators in each hanger. The specific structure of the system consists of a hanger-type device (Fig. 5) with shoulders movable by gear control, Arduino Yun Mini for Wi-Fi connection, a power supply, a PC, an external SNS platform (Twitter API), and a smartphone.

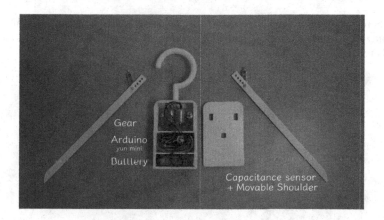

Fig. 5. Overview of hanger device.

The process flow is as follows.

1. The hanger detects when the user tries to put on clothes with a switch and counts the presence, absence, and frequency of use for a certain period.
2. If a clothing item is not used for a certain period, it expresses its intention to leave to the user through Twitter's mention function (Fig. 6).
3. The user reconsiders the existence value of the item and gives or denies permission for the proposed movement (Yes/No) to the hanger, using the reply function.
4. When the user agrees to the movement of the item, the hanger's arms are closed and the item falls to simulate the act of eliminating the clothing item in the real world (Fig. 7).
5. Simultaneously, detailed information associated with that clothing item is released on Twitter along with a hashtag "#forsale" (Fig. 8).
6. When the next user is found, the clothing item is moved to the entrance of the home in an addressed cardboard box (easy to imagine as a new function of a robot vacuum cleaner in home) and is collected by a courier (like a reverse use of the Amazon delivery service).

Fig. 6. Screenshot of a cloth's message to the user (written on screen: the cloth is mentioning the owner, @Sarang_914 and talking "I have not been worn since 15th September 2015. I will go to the next person soon.").

Fig. 7. Physical interface ceasing to exist.

4.2   Demonstration and Feedback

In this prototype, we implemented each of steps 1, 2, 4 and part of 6 ((Fig. 9). We exhibited our system at a conference and received high praise for the effectiveness and necessity of the concept from the participants and committee [1, 2]. They pointed out that this is an opportunity to rethink the relationships between people and things. Furthermore, the method of allowing things to communicate by SNS offered the possibility that people can see things as being alive, which helped to clarify the judgment of existence value. The participants' opinions indicated that it would be more effective to change the method of separation and to consider a variety of intrinsic existence values that things may have.

Fig. 8. Screenshot searching for a new owner (written on screen: "Please buy me #for-sale, Brand name: please wardrobe, Category: no sleeve tops, Size: M, Color: White, Status: Good, Number of Uses: 8 times, Date of purchase: 2014/1/1, Price: 4000 yen.").

5   Related Works

5.1   Robot Considered with Death

In the field of artificial objects, such as the pet robot AIBO, the method and timing for determining death is well discussed in the literature. Users felt emotional connections with artifacts [5] and acknowledged their death in the form of a funeral [3,4]. Experiences with a pet AIBO showed that the artifact value for the object transforms into affection over time, consequently changing the definition of death of the artifact for those people. This should not apply to the types of artifacts for which rapoptosis is proposed, as it is intended for commoditized, utilitarian daily life products, such as clothes, that exist in a different context from pet robots. Based on the feedback from the questionnaires, if rapoptosis could autonomously detect intrinsic existence values, such as "emotional memories" and "personal preference," the system could teach itself and apply those values as parameters in the object-death determination. We believe that this would hold the possibility to defining new relationships between artifacts and people in the future.

5.2   IoT Device for Context-Aware Consumption

In the field of human interface, context-awareness research, such as providing adequate information or changing environmental conditions by sensing a user's conditions, are studied [6]. Ubiquitous computing and internet of things (IoT) research based on context awareness are focusing on service related works, such as tracking a user's SNS or purchase history and trajectory history log to estimate a user's preferences and provide information that is closer to the user's needs. Our proposed system, rapoptosis, can be considered a next generation context-awareness system, as it will change the definition of ownership when

Fig. 9. Exhibited rapoptosis at the conference [1].

an artifact itself automatically behaves adequately while actively considering the relations between the user and itself. Recently, Amazon [7] and Google [8] proposed the ideas of promoting a purchasing system based on a user's life-long patterns. Although automatization and customization of the service will be penetrated in the future by using AI technology, systems like rapoptosis, which connects the timing of releasing objects and the social cycle as a comprehensive system, will provide us a novel way to engage with artifacts.

6   Discussion and Conclusion

In this paper, we proposed the concept and method of rapoptosis, in which items themselves judge their intrinsic existence values in relation to their users, and leave them autonomously, changing users and thereby surviving and extending their lifespan. As a result of prototyping, we were able to confirm the support and potential requirements for the concept of rapoptosis. Future tasks include determining parameters to measure the intrinsic existence value of things in relationship to users and calculating this value. Depending on the type of intrinsic existence value, we would like to further study how to design a method of breaking relationships with users, performing apoptosis, and the implementation of movement in the real world for renatusu.

Acknowledgement. This work was supported by the Okawa Foundation for Information and Telecommunications, Japan.

References

1. Seong, Y., Hashida, T., Ueoka, R.: rapoptosis: Renatusu via Apoptosis Prototyping using Clothes. Information Processing Society of Japan Interaction 2018, 3B24, pp. 958–962 (2018). (Japanese)
2. rapoptosis movie. https://youtu.be/nJXNER5eZaE. Accessed 11 Feb 2019
3. In Japan, a Buddhist Funeral Service for Robot Dogs, National Geographic article. https://www.nationalgeographic.com/travel/destinations/asia/japan/in-japan-a-buddhist-funeral-service-for-robot-dogs/. Accessed 11 Feb 2019
4. There is one man, and only one man, who can still repair your robot dog, Motherboard article. https://motherboard.vice.com/en_us/article/8qxk3g/there-is-one-man-and-only-one-man-who-can-still-repair-your-robot-dog. Accessed 11 Feb 2019
5. Friedman, B., Kahn Jr., P.H., Hagman, J.: Hardware companions?: What online AIBO discussion forums reveal about the human robotic relationship. In: CHI 03 Proceedings of the SIGCHI Conference on Human Factors in Computing Systems, pp. 273–280. (2003)
6. Perera, C., Zaslavsky, A., Christen, P., Georgakopoulos, D.: Context aware computing for the internet of things: a survey. IEEE Commun. Surv. Tutorials **16**(1), 414–454 (2014)
7. Amazon is going to let your gadgets order groceries automatically, Wired. https://www.wired.com/2015/03/amazon-dash-2/. Accessed 11 Feb 2019
8. How predictive AI will change shopping, Harvard Business Review. https://hbr.org/2016/11/how-predictive-ai-will-change-shopping. Accessed 11 Feb 2019

User Stress Measurement of Remote Operation Supporting System with Hand Gesture Transmission Function

Yusuke Suzuki[✉] and Shunsuke Ichihara

OKI Electric Industry Co., Ltd.,
1-16-8 Chuou, Warabi-shi, Saitama 335-8510, Japan
suzuki543@oki.com

Abstract. In this paper, we report the experimental results that try to measure user stress when the user communicates with a remote operation supporting system that applies a wearable camera and a wearable display. The remote operation supporting system refers to an audiovisual communication system that enables communication between a worker in real fields and a director in a remote site with sharing eyesight of the worker with wearable devices and mobile communication network. Various systems have been proposed such as early research by Kuzuoka [1] and a more recent project by Kasahara [2]. Some of these systems are commercialized, however, have not been widely used yet. Our developing system has a feature that enables experts (matured workers) send their hand movements and shapes to guide workers (non-matured workers) by using a gesture sensor in addition to conventional audiovisual communication systems. As the evaluation criteria of the effect of introducing worker support systems, the task completion time reduced by the system has been generally used. Reducing work completion time is an important measurement; however, that is not necessarily beneficial for the system users. Only applying this explicit measuring index could hinder finding further development of the system and popularizing of the system. In this report, we focus on stress as the evaluation measurement of the system users' situation. We expect that the feature of our system that enables the expert's natural hands movements as a directional method would reduce users' stress. To verify the effect, we conducted experiments that measure users (experts and operators) physiological index data, i.e. the heart rate of users with wearable devices, while they are operating tasks using the proposing remote operating support system. Through that experiment, we report that physiological effect of hand gestures transmission function instead of task completion time. Moreover, we discuss the required functions or a development process to the remote operation supporting system to be used widely.

Keywords: Remote collaboration · Wearable device · User centered design · Evaluation

© Springer Nature Switzerland AG 2019
S. Yamamoto and H. Mori (Eds.): HCII 2019, LNCS 11570, pp. 412–425, 2019.
https://doi.org/10.1007/978-3-030-22649-7_33

1 Introduction

These days, first-line workers or on-site practitioners who work in fields such as maintenance and manufacturing industries are facing problems for aging society including lack of labor force especially declining number of matured workers and difficulty of quality control of jobs. Because the number of matured workers is limited, the time required to arrange the matured worker for the job directly decides response time when sending the workers to the workplace are necessary. To shorten the response time, Non-mature workers would be sent to the field. That sometimes could sacrifices quality of works due to lack of experience of the workers.

At the same time, hardware improvement of wearable cameras and head-mounted displays and the development of a mobile communication network enable a remote operation supporting system to use in real fields, not in research laboratories.

In this paper, the remote operation supporting system refers to an audiovisual communication system that enables communication between a worker in real fields and a director in a remote site with sharing eyesight of the worker with wearable devices and mobile communication network.

Figure 1 shows the typical structure of the system. The worker(s) in the field wears a camera, a display, and an audio headset. The camera captures image and video of the environment where the worker is conducting their jobs. The image and the video are sent to the computer of the expert(s) who are staying in the dedicated office. Then experts superimposed guidance on the image or video then send back the guidance to the remote worker. The worker can watch the guidance on their wearing display. Of course, voice communication like that of mobile phones is also available throughout the operation.

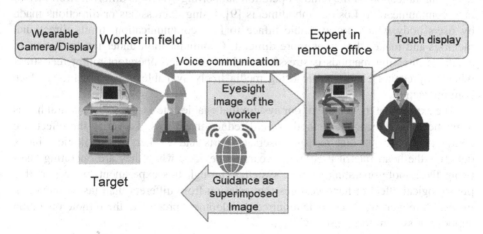

Fig. 1. Overview of remote operation supporting system.

These systems could solve the problem mentioned above. Matured workers (from now on, experts) would stay a dedicated center and can support non-matured workers (from now on, workers) work at the remote field with the system. That would save time for the expert to visit the field because they always stay at the center and workers who located on the closest site can be sent regardless of their experiences. Moreover, the system guarantees the quality of work by providing proper guidance and checks to the non-experienced worker from that center.

Many support systems have been proposed, and some of them are commercialized. They, however, have not been widely used yet.

Our developing system has a feature that enables experts to send their hand movements and shapes to guide workers by using a gesture sensor called Leap Motion in addition to conventional audiovisual communication systems [5]. That features provides merits including;

1. The experts can reflect their natural hand movements to directions for the operators.
2. The experts can send real-time continuous directions without interruption by taking a snapshot or a still image.

After we developed a conceptual model of the system, we iteratively have conducted trial tests with real field workers and have improved the system to reflect opinions from the users (User-Centered development). The examples of functions reflecting the users' opinions include the system should be "easy to wear," and the camera on the head-mounted display should be detachable to make the system useful for workers.

In general, the evaluation criteria of these systems focus on the task completion time reduced by using the system. Reducing work completion time is an important measurement; however, it is not necessarily beneficial for system users. Only applying these explicit measuring indexes might hinder finding further development of the system and popularizing of the system. So, in this paper, we focus on stress as the measurement of the system user's situation.

Communication on the remote operation supporting system is different from face to face communication. Losing embodiments [9], losing expressions or directions made by users body which are available inface to face communication, limits directional methods and makes directions more difficult. Communication under the limitation of available directing methods is stressful. Both experts and operators might feel stress when they cannot communicate using media freely available in case of face to face communication.

We expect that the feature of our system that enables the expert to use natural hands movements as directional methods would reduce that stress. To verify the effect, we conduct experiments that measure users (experts and workers) physiological index data, i.e. the heart rate of users with wearable devices, while they are operating tasks using the remote operating support system. Through this experiment, we report that physiological effect of hand gestures transmission from different than task completion index. Moreover, we discuss the required development process to the remote operation supporting system to be used widely.

2 Related Research

Remote operation supporting system has a relatively long history, and various researches have been consecutively proposed since the 1990s. One of the pioneering researches "Shared-View System" has been proposed by Kuzuoka [1]. More recently, Kasahara et al. [2] proposed a "JackIn" system that redefined a remote operation supporting system from the concept of Human Augmentation approach. Ou et al. [3] showed that superimposing computer graphics lines on the captured image of remote site enabled a variety of guidance in the remote operation supporting system for a robot assembling task as an instance case.

Various remote operation supporting systems place importance on hands-free operation: enabling workers to receive or watch the visual information without holding a display by their hands and keeping their hands open and free for dedicating for their jobs. To provide this hands-free working environment to the worker, such system commonly uses head-mounted display (HMD); however, Kurata et al. [4] proposed the WACL system that applies shoulder worn display system to achieve the same goal.

Whereas, Microsoft developed a Hololens system that is all-in-one type Mixed Reality (MR) device: self-supporting operation is available without additional computing devices. Chen et al. [5] also provided a remote supporting system as a Skype application.

As we can see various systems have been proposed in accordance with the development of hardware, and some of these research results have been commercialized.

3 Feature of Our Proposing System

In this section, we describe the detail of our developing remote support operating system. Our system has a base on typical audiovisual communication. Using a WebRTC technology, peer to peer media (audio and video) data communication is enabled between browsers working on one site terminal and remote site wearable devices respectively.

3.1 Gesture Transmission Function

Adding to that basic function, our system has a gesture transmission function. The function enables the remote experts to send hand shapes and movements information that he/she behaves in front of a terminal of remove site using a gesture sensor. Present system applies a gesture sensor called Leap Motion. The gesture sensor captures the shapes and movements of the expert's hand and sends captured data over the WebRTC data transmission.

We expect our feature: gesture sending function could provide two additional merits to the system such as;

1. The experts can reflect their natural hand movements to a direction for the operators. Pointing important part on the image as if the expert were pointing the real object in the actual field, Sending hand shapes to tell how to grab a target object are example usage of hand gesture.

2. The experts can send real-time directions without interruption by taking a snapshot. Taking snapshots and drawing directions on them are widely used directing method in many remote support systems [5].

Figure 2 shows an overview of our proposed system. The gesture recognition device is added on the expert's side, and synthesized computer graphics hand images are superimposed on the captured image of the worker wearing a camera. Fig. 3 shows actual image of an expert's side setup (left) and captured superimposed image (right).

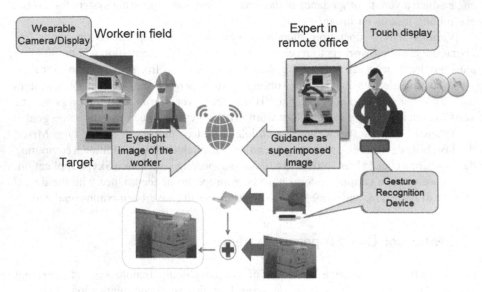

Fig. 2. Overview of our proposed system.

3.2   Other Functions

Like as the prior proposed system [3], our system also provides a drawing transmission function. The expert can draw lines on the captured image with the touch screen, and the worker can watch that image simultaneously on his wearable display. The expert can record and store what he draws and resend them as guidance. These data transmissions are also over the WebRTC [6].

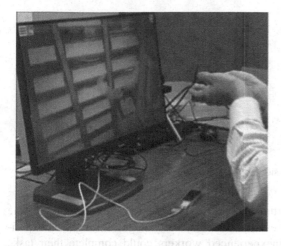

Fig. 3. Setup of the expert site (left), an image superimposed on the remote workers' eye-sight (right).

Fig. 4. Worker side appliances (Early stage of development).

4   User-Centered Development

After we have developed our primary concept model system, we iteratively improved the system iteratively under the principle of User-Centered design; we have been working with on-site workers and ask them to use our system and reflect their compliments and opinions to improve the system.

Figure 4 shows an early stage of the prototype of our proposed system. At this stage, a wearable display and a wearable camera were not light enough (approx. 160 g), and the worker must wear the helmet to sustain the weight of the wearable device (Fig. 4 left). Moreover, the required computational performance and a form factor of the notebook computer for the worker side forced the worker to wear the backpack contained notebook computer (Fig. 4 right).

Fig. 5. Worker side appliances (Present system).

We believe that the fact is worthy of mention that we were able to confirm the effectiveness of the system worked even at this very early stage; Through the experiment, we could observe that the inexperienced workers could complete their tasks (assembling the electronics system and test of the system) under the guidance of the remote expert. Through the experiments with this prototype, requirements for introducing our proposing system into the real field were clarified as the areas for improvement including;

1. The wearable device of the system for the worker should be "easy to wear."
2. The wearable camera should be "detachable."

4.1   Ease of Wearing

The reasons '"ease of wearing" of the system matters' include the following points;

- A remote operating support system will be used for quickening response to the problem occurred, and therefore, if the device system is too bulky and difficult to put on by workers themselves, the system cannot satisfy the basic needs.
- If the device is difficult to wear, the psychological barrier to use that system hinder workers/users to use the system, and they could choose a conventional method of communication such as mobile phones.

Recently, hardware advancement has been faster, and through the developing process, we were able to replace the hardware components to better and lighter ones. The wearable display and camera became smaller and lighter, then wearing helmet became unnecessary. Now the worker wears the headband type wearable display and camera on his/her work cap. Figure 5 left shows the appearance of the present system. The display is AirScouter MD-300A by Brother, Inc. and the camera is HX-A1H by Panasonic, Inc. Now the system utilizes a small computer dynaedge DE-100, by Toshiba, Inc., the whole system became so small that can be stored in a small fanny pack (Fig. 5 right).

With the improvements of the system mentioned above, the present system requires the users to take just two actionsto use the system; wearing the display and the camera over the cap and fastening the belt of the pack around their waist.

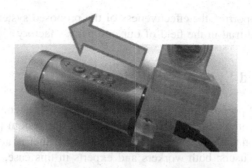

Fig. 6. Detachable wearable camera system.

4.2 Detachable Camera System

The "detachable" camera system is a mechanism that is for a wearable camera fixed on a headband should be used as a temporary hand carry camera. Figure 6 shows that image. Workers can slide the camera forward and release the camera from the attachment of the headband. The attachment part has a magnet inside and holds parts when workers put the camera part back to the attachment part.

This function is required in such cases when the worker works in a dedicated server room and maintains network facilities. In such cases, more than one similar facility: possible working targets for the worker should exist in the same room. The workers, therefore, sometimes has to capture a detailed image of labels that show machine's names or ID's to ask the remote expert confirm the workers is working on a proper facility. The labels could be put on the inner part of the machine the other side of the ceiling of that. If the wearable camera is fixed on the head part, the worker has to crouch, bend down deeply and poke his/her head into the narrow place. These movements or postures could be stressful for the worker. With the detachable camera, the worker, instead, detach and hold the camera and poke it to take a closer look at the labels.

Digital or analog zooming might be another possible solution to the problem, however, to apply that solution, we have to develop another user interface for controlling zooming of the fixed wearable camera and ask the worker to get used to it. We think the "detachable" mechanism is a reasonable solution in these points.

1. That is easy to understand and easy to control the captured image.
2. The worker is not required to train themselves for a new interface.

We have been reporting the effectiveness of the proposed system for toy problems in the laboratory and trial in the field of our company's factory [7].

5   User-Centered System Evaluation

Evaluation criteria of proposed remote operation supporting systems generally focus on efficiency: the task completion time reduced by using the system [8]. Reducing work completion time is an important measurement; however, that is not necessarily beneficial for the system users: both workers and experts in this case. Only applying that explicit measuring index might hinder finding further improvement or development of the system. Also, we think that the lack of this kind of perspective might be a one of the reasons why this remote operation supporting system not widely accepted in the real fields. In this paper, as a first step for setting up new "user-centered" criteria to understand the user, we focus on stress as a measurement of the system users' situation.

Communication over the remote operation supporting system is different from face to face communication (from now on, F2F) in various aspects. Losing embodiments [9], losing expressions or directions made by users body parts and their movements available in case of F2F (such as pointing by the finger and showing proper hand shape and movements how to grab the handle of the machine) restrict directional methods and make the guidance more difficult. Communication under these limitations could be stressful. Both workers and experts feel stress when they cannot communicate using media freely available in case of F2F.

We expect that the main feature of our system that enables the expert's natural hands movements as a directional method could reduce that stress, because, at least the expert can behave and communicate similarly as in the F2F situation.

To verify the effect, we conduct experiments that measure users (experts and workers) physiological index data, concretely, the heart rate of users with wearable devices while they are operating tasks over communication with the proposed remote operation support system. Through this experiment, we report that physiological influence of hand gestures transmission function instead of task completion index.

5.1   Stress Measurement with Bio-Medical Measurement

Stress measurement and stress evaluation with biomedical measurement has widely been studied, and various are practically and clinically used. Measuring heart ratio, electrodermal activity (EDA), and skin temperature are examples that require wearable or fixed monitors. Besides, measuring eye movement with a particular eye tracking camera and collecting users' saliva to check the amount of cortisol are also used.

We applied the heart rate monitor for our research because we find that method is well balanced between ease of measurement and validity and it can obtain continuous data. We also highly evaluated that because that method provides a lower load during the work operation.

To estimate user stress from the heart rate signal, the LF (Low Frequency)/HF (High Frequency) ratio is commonly used after Pagani's research [11]. The LF is power spectral density of the low frequency bands and the HF is that of high frequency bands.

The LF suggests activities the sympathetic nerve systems and the HF reflects that of the parasympathetic nerve system. Therefore, the value ratio is commonly used to estimate the extent's of user stress. We applied that LF ratio as a measurement of the experiment.

To measure heart rate, we adopted a chest-worn heart rate monitor (my Beat WHS-1 and chest strap with electrodes by Union tool Corp. Figure 7 shows the appearance.). The monitor works on a coin cell (CR2032) and can store the measured data on an inner memory.

Fig. 7. Chest strap type heart rate monitor

RRI (R-R interval) of workers and an expert were measured. The sampling rate for Electrocardiogram (ECG) measurement was 1000 Hz. After measurement, data was processed for further analysis. Autocorrelations were used to obtain frequency components and squared power of each frequency was obtained. Moreover, the LF/HF ratios were calculated. In the experiments, LF was defined as ranges from 0.04 Hz to 0.02 Hz and HF from 0.15 to 0.4 Hz. These parameters are commonly used after the research by Malki et al. [10].

6   Experiment

The experiment reported in this paper is a preliminary study for a small group. The number of experiment participants is three. Two are for workers, and one is for the expert. All of them are male and the ages of them range from their forties to fifties.

The expert and the worker are arranged on different rooms (Fig. 8 shows the environment of the experiment). Under the guidance of the expert, the worker assembles a communication apparatus. The worker wears the wearable devices, and audio communication headset and all the communication between the worker and the expert is conducted over the proposed remote support system.

In addition to that, both the expert and the worker wear a heart rate monitor and heart rate is recorded throughout the operation (providing guidance and assembling an apparatus respectively).

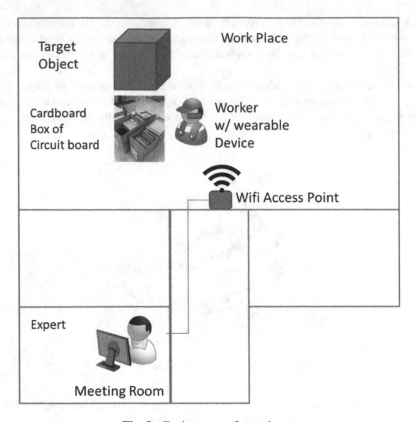

Fig. 8. Environment of experiment.

Video images are also recorded for further analysis. The expert stands still and does not walk around; therefore, two fixed cameras on tripods are used. Whereas the worker walks around the space to conduct a task; therefore, one camera is fixed, and an experimenter holds one portable camera, and behavior of the worker are captured.

The worker's target objecti.e., the communication apparatus is a kind of shelf in the form of a cuboid, and the size is approximately 1500*800*600 mm. Electronics circuit boards (from now on, ECBs) that should be inserted to that shelf are packed inside cardboard boxes and are arranged nearby thatapparatus.

The worker follows guidance by the experts and conduct process following,

1. Move around and find the cardboard box contains required ECB.
2. Open the box with a cutter.
3. Unwrap the ECB.
4. Confirm the ECB is the required one.
5. Insert the ECB to the proper position in the right direction.

These processes repeated several times until its completion. One set of experiment is a work for one shelf each. Two sets of the experiment are conducted by each worker and expert pair. One experiment is conducted on the remote operation supporting system with gesture transmission function, and the other is conducted without that function. In each experimental set, the order of the function's availability has changed. One set of experiments requires about 20 min. In total 40 min are required for one participant's group (an expert and a worker).

We analyze the psychological effect of the difference in available communication media. We also do a brief structured interview and ask the participants to answer the 5 point Likert scales questionnaires.

7 Results and Discussion

Because the experiment is a preliminary study, we have not applied detailed statistical analysis for the data. Instead, we observe the LF Ratio data. Figure 9 shows the graphs of the experimental result on. Upper charts show the results of first group. The left is the first trial's result. The right isthe second. The gesture transmission is available on the second trial (right one). Lower charts show result of the second group (the same expert and the other worker). The gesture is available on the first (left).

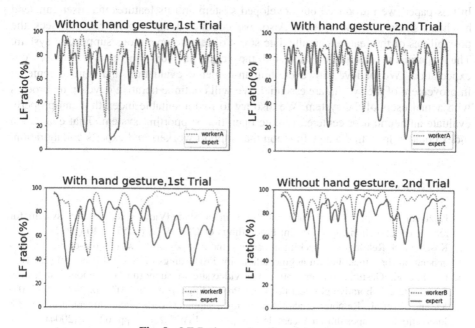

Fig. 9. LF Ratio graphs of participants.

In each graph, vertical axis shows percentage of the LF ratio over the HF. That shows stress level of the users. Horizontal axis shows time and note that that does not apply same scale for each case.

The expert and the first worker's result did not show clear differences between conditions. The second worker's stress levels, however, are higher than the first worker we can observe from the chart. Also, his mean LF ratio increased for the second trial: the case that gesture transmission is not available. The worker B's Mean LF ratio for the first trial was 83.60% (S.D. was 16.44) and that for the second trial was 90.29% (S.D. was 7.03).

Through the whole experiments the expert seemed to be relaxed and his answer for the questionaries' and the interview result showed the consistent tendency. Availability of situation awareness that means the user of the system can obtain the environmental information of the remote place and contextual information of the user, the expert might feel less stress even with very basic function of the remote operation supporting system.

Second worker's LF ratio result suggests the hypothesis that our proposed method might influence the stress of the users might be supported. We still cannot negate the order effect because the number of experience is limited. Further analysis and investigation are required.

8 Conclusion

In this paper, we introduced our developed system and its features that user can send his hand shape and movements. Also, we conducted the experiment that seek the possibilities of the feature can alleviate stress of remote operations supporting system. The experiment was preliminary and the result still did not clearly support our expectation. We believe, however, human-centered evaluation and human-centered improvement of the system are essential. We will continue iterative developing process with actual users of the system. We also try to find a suitable index that can properly evaluate authentic user-centered remote operation supporting system. That evaluation index could help to find a new function that support workers and experts collaboration.

References

1. Kuzuoka, H.: Spatial workspace collaboration: a SharedView video support system for remote collaboration capability. In: Proceedings of CHI 1992, pp 533–540 (1992)
2. Kasahara, S. Rekimoto, J.: JackIn: integrating the first-person view with out-of-body vision generation for human-human augmentation. In: Proceedings of AH 2014, no. 46 (2014)
3. Ou, J., et al.: Gestural communication over video stream: supporting multimodal interaction for remote collaborative physical tasks. In: Proceedings of ICMI 2003, pp. 242–249 (2003)
4. Kurata, T., et al.: Remote collaboration using a shoulder-worn active camera/laser. In: 8th International Symposium on Wearable Computers (ISWC 2004), pp. 62–69 (2004)
5. Chen, H., et al.: 3D collaboration method over HoloLens™ and Skype™ end points. In: ImmersiveME ACM Multimedia (2015)
6. Ichihara, S., Suzuki, Y.: An effect study of remote support system using hand gesture and drawing line. In: Proceedings of IPSJ Interaction 2016 (2016). (in Japanese)
7. Suzuki, Y., et al.: Remote work support system-field trials at ICT systems NUMAZU plant. OKI Tech. Rev. 81(1), 16–19 (2018). 231. (in Japanese)

8. Abraham, M., Annunziata, M.: Augmented reality is already improving worker performance. Harvard Bus. Rev. (2017). https://hbr.org/2017/03/augmented-reality-is-already-improving-worker-performance
9. Heath, C., Luff, P: Disembodied conduct: communication through video in a multi-media office environment. In: Proceedings of CHI 1991, pp. 99–103 (1991)
10. Malik, M., et al.: Heart rate variability: Standards of measurement, physiological interpretation, and clinical use. Eur. Heart J. **17**, 354–381 (1996)
11. Pagani, M., et al.: Power spectral analysis of heart rate and arterial pressure variabilities as a marker of sympatho-vagal interaction in man and conscious dog. Circ. Res. **1986**(59), 178–193 (1986)

Laugh Log: E-Textile Bellyband Interface for Laugh Detection and Logging

Ryoko Ueoka[✉]

Faculty of Design, Kyushu University,
4-9-1 Shiobaru, Minami ku, Fukuoka City, Japan
r-ueoka@design.kyushu-u.ac.jp

Abstract. Laughter is said to be linked to satisfactory human relationships and to have a positive impact on health, hence it is often related to perceived improvements in the quality of life. In this paper, we focused on the stomach to detect natural laughter resulting from funniness, which is positive even in laughter. Consequently, by measuring the pressure change in the abdomen using a textile sensor we can build a wearable laugh log system capable of detecting and recording laughter.

In our pilot experiment, we conducted experiments that induce laughter under environmental settings and examined a deep learning method to detect laughter in a period within the measured log. Results demonstrated the possibility of detection of laughter in a controlled environment. We then simulated daily scenes that were likely to trigger laughter, and then we measured and examined the detection of laughter through deep learning.

Keywords: Life log · Laugh · Laugh log · Deep learning · E-textile

1 Introduction

Laughter is said to be linked to satisfactory human relationships and to have a positive impact on health, hence it is often related to perceived improvements in the quality of life (QOL) [1].

For this reason, research on laughter has gathered momentum in the human interface area, for instance to design a system that promotes smiles [2–5]. In addition, the impact of "laughter yoga" that triggers laugh spontaneously has drawn attention as a way to maintain daily health [6]. However, specific indicators linking the effects on people, the frequency of laughing episodes in a day, and the type of laugh that is desirable, are lacking.

In addition, in recent years, wearable devices have had the capability to obtain various life logs, but a method has yet to be established to record quantifiable indicators related to feelings and laughter. If it was possible to obtain a quantitative laughter life log from our daily life, the relationship between long-term laughter and health and well-being could be clarified, and it would be conceivable for laughter to be used as a quantitative index of QOL.

© Springer Nature Switzerland AG 2019
S. Yamamoto and H. Mori (Eds.): HCII 2019, LNCS 11570, pp. 426–439, 2019.
https://doi.org/10.1007/978-3-030-22649-7_34

In this paper, we focused on the stomach to detect natural laughter resulting from funniness, which is positive even in laughter. Consequently, by measuring the pressure change in the abdomen using a textile sensor we can build a wearable laugh log system capable of detecting and recording laughter.

In our pilot experiment, we conducted experiments that induce laughter under environmental settings and examined a deep learning method to detect laughter in a period within the measured log. Results demonstrated the possibility of detection of laughter in a controlled environment. We then simulated daily scenes that were likely to trigger laughter, and then we measured and examined the detection of laughter through deep learning.

2   Related Work

Although laughter has been studied as an effective way to improve health and promote positive human relationships, quantification requires a large number of samples.

The ILHAIRE project, which produces a conversational agent using natural appearance and laughter, presents databases with large samples of laughter [7]. They categorize three types of laughter: natural expression, induced reaction, and made-up feeling, in connection with laughs measured. Natural expressions are caused by natural emotions as measured in the real world, but this measurement is difficult. By contrast, induced reactions were collected by presenting content such as comedy videos to encourage laughter. In addition, made-up emotions occur when one is directed to laugh; they are most readily measurable, but are not linked to a natural laugh.

This research aims to measure laughter by natural expression. However, the work presented in the above database points to difficulties in using the data collected in a natural environment [8]. Therefore, in this study, we first collect data by measuring laughter induced by external stimuli, such as viewing content that encourages laughter. We then establish a detection method and finally measure and detect laughter in daily scenes.

As a method to log laughs, the usage of face, voice, and skin surface potential in the vicinity of the diaphragm has been proposed. Laugh detection identifies smiling faces by extracting a quantified feature of the face from a camera image, and this functionality is increasingly mounted on cameras that are on the market such as Omron's smile scan [9].

In addition, with the loud smile meter that measures vocal cord vibration data via a pharyngeal microphone, occurrences of laughter are logged over time from daily life.

With the diaphragm type laughter measuring instrument, the skin surface potential in the vicinity of the diaphragm is monitored by tracking the myoelectric potential reaction of the xiphoid process upper surface muscle at the time of laughter using a surface myoelectric potential measuring device, which measures amount, length, and timing of laughter [10].

Ikeda et al. used the two laugh measurements of a laughing counter and a diaphragm type laughter simultaneously, to classify laughter using the face, throat, and stomach. Reportedly, detection occurs even with smoldering in the face and throat measurement [11]. However, stomach measurements did not display signs of smoldering laughter and instead were only sensitive to true laughter. This suggested that laughter related to natural emotions can only be detected using a diaphragm type measurement device on the stomach. However, with the diaphragm type laughter measuring device, there were complaints from subjects that resting the electrode directly on the skin was annoying. In addition, a diaphragm type laughter measuring method that requires a large electromyograph is not suitable for long term measurement. Therefore, in this research, we aim to develop a stomach type wearable laughter measurement system that can measure true laughter.

3   Pilot Experiment of Laugh Detection

The textile sensor used in this study was woven with yarns that comprised of a chemical thread twisted with conductive material. The sensor has a two-layer structure: in the first layer, a yarn containing a conductive material is woven in the longitudinal direction, and in the second layer, it is woven in the transverse direction. When pressure is applied, a conductive yarn in a section where the vertical and horizontal conductive materials cross each other leads to capacitance changes as the distance changes. The change in electrostatic capacity is used as pressure value. The pressure can be measured in a 6×14 matrix, and the measurement value is communicated wirelessly using Bluetooth. In this study, we designed a PC and android application with an accuracy of 10 Hz. The system created is displayed in Fig. 1 below, and the way it is worn is shown in Fig. 2.

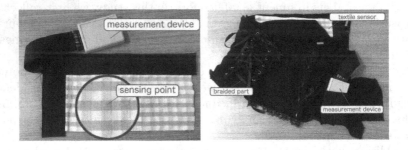

Fig. 1. Textile sensor (left) and wearable laugh log system (right)

To investigate the capabilities of the prototype system in laughter detection, we conducted a measurement experiment by setting two conditions: "watch a movie" and "talk with a friend". Two males and eight females, with a mean age of 21.5 years old, participated in the experiment. After measuring the resting state of the subjects for one minute, we measured the abdomean pressure under two conditions for five minutes each, under two postures consisting of sitting

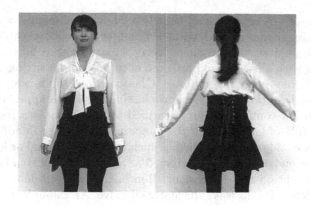

Fig. 2. A person wearing a laugh log

and standing, respectively. During the experiment, we recorded the state of the subject and extracted the timing of laughers from the log data. An overview of experimental conditions is shown in Fig. 3.

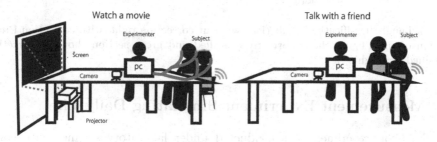

Fig. 3. Experimental conditions

3.1 Analysis Using Deep Learning

Analysis of measurement results was performed by normalizing the average value of the pressure distribution. From previous research [12], we observed that the pressure suddenly decreased when laughter occurred. However, the measurement value and its variation vary greatly among individuals, and it was difficult to detect laughter using a threshold value. Therefore, we had to study the detection of laughter using deep learning while observing the characteristics of pressure change. Learning is performed using a fifty-dimensional vector taken out by shifting a five-second portion every 0.1 s from the five-minute data during the experiment as one sample. The neural network used for learning is a classification model that considers time series data, known as long short term memory (LSTM). The same number of correct answers (with the center of the vector included in the laugh section) and incorrect answers (without the laughter in the vector) were randomly extracted and learned. The accuracy was 86%, and the recall rate was 88%. A new subject, namely a 24-year-old female, was monitored using the learning model created, and the laughter detection capabilities of deep learning were evaluated. Measurement freely set situations conducive to laugher such as talking with a friend and measured each position in sitting and standing postures three times every five minutes. Classification results were corrected to become one laugh section when sections classified as laugh appeared frequently and those with low confidence were identified as incorrect. As a result, we were able to detect 75% of laughs out of 102 in six measurements. In addition, half of the laughs that could not be classified as such lasted one second or less, and even laughs of one second or more were detected at a position close to a laugh without overlapping, except on three occasions. Hence, this method demonstrated that the ability to detect laughs was sufficiently effective. An example of the corrected classification result is shown in the Fig. 4 below.

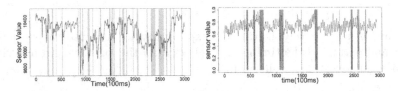

Fig. 4. Laugh classification result (left: without correction right: with correction Pink section of right figure shows correctly classified and green section shows incorrectly classified as laughing).

4   Measurement Experiment Simulating Daily Life

As the pilot experiment was conducted under laboratory settings with constrained behavior, it was necessary to also identify laughter from measurement data related to various behaviors in everyday life. Therefore, it was necessary to measure laughter with various behaviors and prepare learning data, although laughter is accidental, and it is difficult to measure while performing a specific action. Hence, we set some scenes conducive to laughter under daily scenarios and conducted a logging experiment. As it is expected that signals from various behaviors will be included, we revised the laugh log system to reduce noise.

4.1   Revision of Laugh Log System

We performed actions such as gait, step up and down, and having a meal. In a preliminary measurement in this experiment, it appeared that noise was created as the measurement device was being shaken in the pocket installed in the lower part of the bellyband interface. Therefore, a belt type pocket was designed with a stretchable cloth, and the measuring device was fixed by winding the belt around the waist. We also improved the ability of the application to estimate the behavior under measurement. Acceleration and geomagnetic sensors built in android were used to calculate the acceleration along three axes and the inclination of the android device so that they could be measured. A pocket was attached to the back of the belly band so that the android device could be stored and the inclination of the upper body could be estimated by the inclination of the android device. An overview of the improved system is displayed in Fig. 5. In addition, as this experiment was conducted in the winter, when wearing the system from a thick knit, the pressure was absorbed by clothes, and the pressure could not be measured accurately. Therefore, during measurement, after wearing the laugh log on top of a thin long-sleeved T-shirt, it was layered with the sweater.

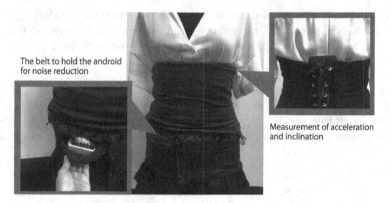

Fig. 5. Improved laugh log system

4.2 Experiment Settings

One subject, a 24 years old female, was monitored in each of six types of daily scenes conducive to laughter for ten periods of twenty minutes. The experiment was divided into several days, and the measurement was performed a plurality of times, consecutively, each day. Measurements were made in places such as laboratories, facilities within the university, and nearby stores. During measurement, a pin microphone was installed on the chest and voice was recorded. The timing of laughs was extracted from the recorded voice for analysis. Based on the assumption that multiple people typically talk while laughing, we set the following six scenes, expected to include complex movements such as standing up, walking, walking ahead, and shouting aloud. Considering the characteristics of the textile sensor whose humidity influences measured values, scenarios that may lead to sweating such as those related to sports were not included this time. To measure natural laughter, we instructed subjects to ignore the measuring to the extent possible during the experiment. The details of the scenes are as follows:

- Going shopping with friends: going shopping by foot and turning around the inside of the store.
- Cooking with friends: going to pick up groceries, cutting and cooking in a standing posture.

- Playing a board game with friends: sitting around a large desk and playing a board game.
- Doing group work: using a white board or sitting on a nearby chair.
- Having a meal with friends: eating a meal in a sitting posture, no restriction on meal content.
- Relaxed talk with friends: sitting in a relaxed state on a couch and chat.

5   Evaluation of Laugh Detection Using Deep Learning

Twenty hours were measured in total during the experiment, consisting of scenes related to the six scenarios, for twenty minutes each and repeated ten times. Duration of laughers for each measurement is reported in Table 1.

Table 1. The duration of laughing time (20 min/ 1 test)

Total laugh time (sec)						
Experiment no.	Shopping	Cooking	Game	Group work	Eating	Talking
1	46.0	84.2	291.9	137.8	43.7	182.1
2	71.2	104.5	137.9	41.7	42.9	48.9
3	87.9	17.2	226.7	30.4	32.8	79.2
4	17.7	52.5	103.7	37.9	22.4	69.2
5	42.6	24.7	85.9	99.2	32.6	148.4
6	58.4	60.2	128.1	174.5	38.6	89.3
7	57.2	42	301.9	164.9	42.6	50.6
8	43.2	65.6	131.4	86.4	21.7	286.5
9	46.7	56.3	85.1	55.7	32.9	255.6
10	37.3	78.4	92.2	88.3	44.3	68.3

The aggregate laughing time in all measurements was 5,228 s, and the average time for one laughing episode was about 1.7 s. As in the pilot experiment, learning data was prepared to evaluate the laughter detection capability of deep learning. When processing results from this experiment, as pressure change accompanying body movement is measured on many occasions, two parameters are involved in deep learning, namely the transition in pressure value and the transition in inclination in the longitudinal direction of the body. Results point to an upward trend due to the passage of time and a change in pressure triggered by a change in posture including standing or sitting. Therefore, before learning, pressure data was preprocessed according to the procedure displayed in Fig. 6 and then normalized to a [0, 1] range. In step one, noise was eliminated by calculating the moving average per one second. In step two, processing was performed so that the average of the measured values before and after the increase in the inclination change at an interval of a second or more became the same. In step three, the moving average at every ten seconds was subtracted, and the rising trend was eliminated. In step four, the pressure increases that were not relevant to laugh detection were tagged as outliers and those in the top 1% of measurement results every twenty minutes were excluded using the Smirnov Grubbs test and the rest of the data was normalized to a $[0, 1]$ range. In addition, the measured inclination could shift within a $[-180, 180]$ degrees range, to shift to a $[0, 360]$ degrees range and was then normalized to a $[0, 1]$ range. An example of raw measurement data and a part of processed data are shown in Fig. 7. The top row shows the transition in pressure value, while the bottom row shows the transition in gradient value, and the shaded region indicates laughter.

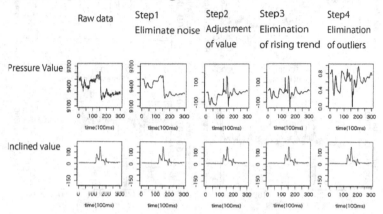

Fig. 6. Steps of data processing

5.1   Creating Learning Data

Five-second data in a fifty-dimensional vector extracted every 0.1 s from the twenty minutes data during the experiment is used for learning as one sample. Those in which the mid value of the vector is included in the laugh are regarded as correct answers, and those for which no determination could be made as incorrect answers. In preliminary experiments, it was found that extremely short laughter was difficult to detect, so laughter that lasted under 0.8 s, which is half the average laughter duration was tagged as incorrect and not considered as laughter, and learning was performed. Measurement data from nine samples out of the six scenes repeated ten times in this experiment was used as learning data. Learning was conducted as 80% of the data set was used as training data and 20% as test data. We used data from one measurement across six scenes as verification data and evaluated whether laughter could be detected from twenty minutes data samples.

5.2   Evaluation of the Learning Method

With deep learning in preliminary experiments, learning was performed by randomly extracting a number of incorrect answers equal to the number of correct answers included in the learning data. However, in this experiment, there

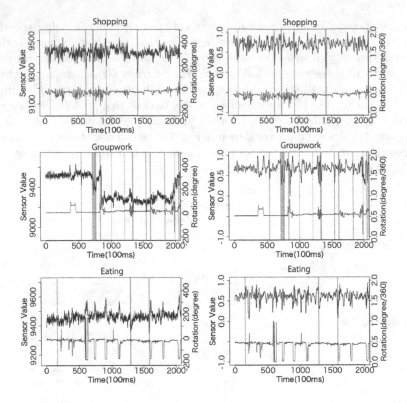

Fig. 7. Example of raw measurement data (left) and a part of processed data (right)

are variations in the motion included in the incorrect answer data. Therefore, we examine the required number and variations of incorrect answer data when extracting the incorrect data set.

5.3 Study on the Number of Learning Datapoints

The number of correct answer datapoints included in the learning data was 44,564. It is worth first mentioning that learning was conducted by randomly extracting a number of datapoints tied to incorrect answers consistent with the number of datapoints tied to correct answers. The accuracy of the classification for the verification data, after learning for 3,000 epochs and showing signs of near convergence, is reported in Table 2.

Table 2. Classification result of verification data

Accuracy (%)	Recall (%)	Precision (%)
83.3	76.6	21.2

Subsequently, a number of incorrect answers datapoints four times larger than that of correct answer datapoints was randomly extracted and learned. The number of correct answers datapoints was 44,564, and the number of incorrect answers datapoints was 178,256. The accuracy of the classification result for the verification data after learning for 3,000 epochs where signs of near convergence were observed is reported in Table 3.

Table 3. Classification result of verification data increasing incorrect answer data set

Accuracy (%)	Recall (%)	Precision (%)
91.6	59.4	34.3

Increasing the number of datapoints tied to incorrect answers to be learned from improved correct answer and relevance rate. As a result, it is considered that variations in incorrect answers were learned to some extent compared with the previous iteration. However, although the recall rate decreased, it appeared to stem from an ability to learn from datapoints tied to correct answers, which are difficult to distinguish from datapoints tied to incorrect answers. In addition, as there were many erroneous detections, it appeared that the learning across correct and incorrect answers was insufficient, and hence an improvement of the learning method was necessary. We also attempted learning by doubling the number of datapoints tied to incorrect answers and going through eight times more learning, but the accuracy was low. It appears to be because if the number of data points tied to incorrect answers is too low, variations of incorrect answers cannot be learned, and conversely if there is an excess of incorrect answers, the learning accuracy will be high to an extent. Therefore, we concluded that the adequate number of data points tied to incorrect answers is at four times that of datapoints tied to correct answers.

5.4   Study on the Extraction Method for Learning Data

From preliminary experiments, we found that some of the correct and incorrect answers are difficult to distinguish. In the preliminary experiments, a short laugh was regarded as incorrect, so some of the incorrect answers actually include laughter. For that reason, we excluded some of the datapoints tied to incorrect answers containing laughter. Subsequently, learning with arbitrarily extracted data with incorrect answers that is difficult to distinguish and learning with data in which correct answers are limited to those that can readily be distinguished are performed, and the accuracy is compared. "Learning by arbitrarily extracting incorrect answer data" extracts incorrect answer data by using the deviation from the average of the measured values every twenty minutes. When laughter occurs, the pressure value drops sharply, so the deviation from the mean tends to be larger for correct answer data. Therefore, half of the incorrect answer data was extracted from one measurement in descending order in terms of deviation from the average value, and the remaining half was extracted randomly. By contrast, when learning by arbitrarily extracting incorrect answer data, values larger than the deviation from average and when laughing had continued for more than a second were chosen as the correct answers. This serves to clarify the characteristics of correct answer data by restraining the set of correct answers to those that can be readily distinguished. Incorrect answer data was randomly extracted. It appeared that learning was near convergence on these learnings after 1,500 epochs. Table 4 reports the accuracy of classification results for the verification data at the time of learning. It is understood that accuracy is high when arbitrarily selecting correct answer data.

Moreover, the relevance rate became low when incorrect answer data was extracted arbitrarily. By using arbitrary extraction of incorrect answer data when learning, we expected to distinguish incorrect answers from laughter with a high accuracy rate. However, the conformity rate decreased, and it appeared difficult to find a difference in the current data set. When learning with arbitrarily extracted correct answers, one consideration is that the accuracy rate improved because correct answers that are difficult to distinguish from incorrect ones were removed.

Table 4. Classification result of verification data using arbitrary selected data set

	Accuracy (%)	Recall (%)	Precision (%)
Extracted incorrect answer data arbitrarily	90.7	60.7	27.7
Extracted correct answer data arbitrarily	91.2	70.2	34.6

5.5   Evaluation of Learning Result

There is a possibility that laughter linked to a modest pressure change could not be detected because the correct answer data set was skewed toward large pressure changes. Therefore, we use this model to analyze the correct and incorrect answers for one laugh, not the detection accuracy for each datapoint of the classification result. As it is known that a slight deviation occurs in detection results in the preliminary experiment and that short laughs cannot be detected, we assume that laughter that can be identified within 0.5 s before and after the laughing section can be detected. In addition, laughter lasting less than a second was labelled as incorrect answer. A part of the corrected classification results is shown in Fig. 8.

5.6   Discussion

Out of the 250 laughs included in the six scenes in the verification data, we were able to detect 75.6% of laughter out of 189 occurrences. By contrast, the number of false positives was 34.1%, 86 out of 252 occurrences. Regarding laughter episodes that could not be detected, duration was short, and often with a low divergence from average. This is thought to be due to narrowing down the correct answers to those that can readily be distinguished. However, as laughter causing large stomach moves can be detected, it can be considered that rough laughter caused by entertainment can generally be detected. As can be seen in the figure below, many erroneous detections occur during meals and shopping. It is difficult to distinguish between noise due to walking and laughter in data on shopping. In this learning we estimate the movement of the upper body from the inclination of the android device, but there is a possibility that considering only the inclination is insufficient to distinguish between noise and laughter during walking. It is a consideration that erroneous detection during a meal stems from unsatisfactory learning of body inclination. Regarding board games and meals, subjects are in both cases in a forward leaning posture, but the measured inclination is forward and backward. This is thought to be due to the height of the desk in the measurement environment. As shown in the figure below, as the desk is tilted, the body is straight, and as the pressure value increases, the android device also tilts forward. When the desk is low, the posture bends back and as the pressure value increases, the android device tilts backward. In the meal scene, the inclination in the backward direction was measured only once in the learning data. Therefore, it can be considered that the characteristics of pressure change due to the forward leaning posture cannot be learned satisfactorily, leading to erroneous detection.

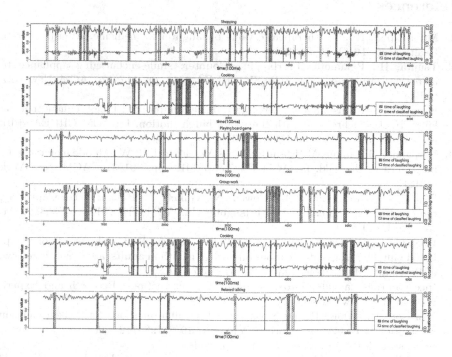

Fig. 8. Part of laugh classification result of 6 scenes

6   Conclusion

In this study, we presented a wearable pressure measurement system using a textile sensor and conducted an experiment setting the stage for a situation where laughter occurs. We then tried to detect laughter by deep learning. As a result, it was shown that laughter could be detected approximately in measurement data linked to various movements in daily life. However, the existence of conditions conducive to erroneous detections, such as having a meal or walking, was also confirmed. To properly implement a life log of laughter in the future, erroneous detection must be reduced by improving the measurement method for inclination and strengthening the learning data. By raising the accuracy of laughter detection, we may be in a position to clarify the relationship between the occurrence of laughter, health, and well-being. Moreover, if the daily amount of laughter could be assessed objectively, one may expect it to be used toward a quantitative index of QOL, and it may also be regarded as a trigger to contemplate the self-reflection of life.

Acknowledgement. This work was supported by JSPS KAKENHI Grant Number 15H01765.

References

1. Mora-Ripoll, R.: The therapeutic value of laughter in medicine. Altern. Therap. Health Med. **16**(6), 56–64 (2010)
2. Tsujita, H., Rekimoto, J.: HappinessCounter: smile-encouraging appliance to increase positive mood. In: ACM SIGCHI EA 2011, pp. 117–126. ACM, New York (2011)
3. Fukushima, S., Hashimoto, Y., Nozawa, T., Kajimoto, H.: Laugh enhancer using laugh track synchronized with the user's laugh motion. In: ACM CHI EA 2010, pp. 3613–3618. ACM, New York (2010)
4. Hernandez, J., Hoque, M.(Ehsan)., Drevo, W., Picard, R. W.: Moode meter: counting smiles in the wild. In: ACM UbiComp 2012, pp. 301–310. ACM, New York (2012)
5. Ryokai, K., Duran Lopez, E., Howell, N., Gillick, J., Bamman, D.: Capturing, representing, and interacting with laughter. In: ACM CHI 2018, No. 358. ACM, New York (2018)
6. Bressington, D., Yu, C., Wong, W., Ng, T.C., Chien, W.T.: The effects of group-based Laughter Yoga interventions on mental health in adults: a systematic review. J. Psychiatr. Ment. Health Nurs. **25**, 517–527 (2018)
7. Incorporation Laughter into Human Avatar Interactions: Research and Experiments. http://www.ilhaire.eu/
8. Morrison, D., Wang, R., De Silva, L.C.: Ensemble methods for spoken emotion recognition in call-centres. Speech Commun. **49**(2), 98–112 (2007)
9. Smile scan. http://www.oss.omron.co.jp/smilescan/
10. Laugh Measurement System via diaphragm. http://www.digitalact.co.jp/warai/device.html (Japanese)

11. Ikeda, M., Itamura, H., Ikenobu, K., Motoshita, S.: Examination of objective classification method of "laugh" by "three point measuring system" of face, throat and belly. In: Japan Society for Laughter and Humour Studies, vol. 19, pp. 75–85 (2012). (Japanese)
12. Shimasaki, A., Ueoka, R.: Laugh log: e-textile bellyband interface for laugh logging. In: ACM CHI EA 2017, pp. 2084–2089. ACM, New York (2017)

Feedback Control to Target Joints Angle in Middle Finger PIP and MP Joint Using Functional Electrical Stimulation

Kyosuke Watanabe, Makoto Oka, and Hirohiko Mori[✉]

Tokyo City University, 1-28-1 Tamazutsumi, Setagaya-ku, Tokyo, Japan
{g1881852, moka, hmori}@tcu.ac.jp

Abstract. In our dairy life, we often have opportunities to give others some tips of finger movements. If we can control the joints angle of each finger to the target joints angle by functional electrical stimulation, it is possible to give others some tips of finger movements. However, controlling the detail movements of fingers by functional electrical stimulation has not realized so far, because the structures of the musculoskeletal system involved in finger movement is very complicated. In this paper, we proposed a controller to control the PIP joint (the second joint of the finger) and MP joint (the third joint of the finger) in the middle finger to the arbitrary target joints angles by giving the electrical stimuli to the flexor digitorum muscle and the extensor digitorum muscle. Based on the knowledge about the relationships of the PIP/MP joints and the muscles, in our controller, the amounts to the flexor digitorum muscle and extensor digitorum muscle comparing with the current joint angles. First, we investigated we can control the PIP and MP joint to the given static target angles. As the result, it was possible to control both of PIP and MP joint to the arbitrary target. We also adopted this controller to control the joints to the target angles which change with time dynamically. Among these trials, we sometimes succeeded to track the changing target angles with time accurately but sometimes failed, in spite of performing the same tasks.

Keywords: Functional electrical stimulation · Surface electrodes · Musculoskeletal system · Motor skill support

1 Introduction

In our dairy life, we often have opportunities to give some tips of body motions or movements to others. Among such situations, we often teach the movement of fingers, such as how to use chopsticks and how to use a pencil. When we teach body motions to others, it is thought that teaching by practicing targeted action directly is more effective than teaching only by explicit knowledge such as words and documents. Teaching by practicing body motion contains tacit knowledge, and it has large amount of knowledge compared to explicit knowledge [1]. However it is difficult to teach implicit knowledge, and so, we sometimes teach it by moving the other's body by some external powers or stimuli, such as touching the other's body directly.

© Springer Nature Switzerland AG 2019
S. Yamamoto and H. Mori (Eds.): HCII 2019, LNCS 11570, pp. 440–454, 2019.
https://doi.org/10.1007/978-3-030-22649-7_35

Roughly speaking, there are two ways to make fingers move by external stimuli. One is operating fingers by an exoskeleton assist mechanism attached to the back of the hand [2], and the other is by causing muscle contraction giving electrical stimulation to the muscles involved in the finger movement. The latter method is called a functional electrical stimulation.

The method by the exoskeleton assist mechanism, make it possible to perform more detailed finger movements than the one by functional electrical stimulation. However, it is hard for people learned by the exoskeleton assist to reproduce the contraction of the muscles of the target movement because the muscles are not driven voluntarily. In this method, furthermore, the device sometimes interfere the motion because it is relatively large. On the other hand, it is suggested that functional electrical stimulation promote the acquisition of target movement because movements of the joints are caused by the muscle contracting in the same manner of the voluntary movements [3]. In addition, the device can be smaller than the one of the exoskeleton assist mechanism.

Though, therefore, we believe the functional electrical stimulation method is more appropriate for teaching finger motions, only the binary control of flexing and extending the finger is possible now by functional electrical stimulation and controlling the detail movements of fingers has not realized so far because the structures of the musculoskeletal system involved in finger movement is very complicated. The motions of the fingers are determined by the joints angle of each finger. So, if we can control the joints angle of each finger to the target joints angle, it is possible to produce the target shape or movement of the hand.

In this paper, we, first, propose a controlling way of bending the finger joints to static target angle, and then, also propose the controlling way of the finger joints tracking the angles changing dynamically in time series. In these controllers, we applied a feedback control considering two aspects: how the contraction of each muscle is involved in each action of finger joints, and the time delay between the electrical stimulation and the finger joints movement.

2 Related Work

2.1 Control of Finger Movement by Functional Electrical Stimulation

Tamaki et al. [4] put 14 surface electrodes on the forearm, totally gave 147 types of stimuli (7×7 pattern of electrical stimulation paths and three levels of electrical stimulation strength), and achieved in total 16 joints flexion or extension movements, which were the independent bending movement of 5 joints and the bending movement of 11 joints linked with other joint movements, However, only the binary control of flexing and extending fingers can be done, and detailed control such as following up to an arbitrary target joints angle has not been realized.

2.2   Follow-Up Control to the Target Joint Angle in 2° of Freedom of the Wrist Joint

Watanabe et al. [5] proposed a method which enabled the wrist joint to control to the target angles in 2° of freedom. In this method, the controller is combined with neural network and PID control and calculate the amount of electrical stimuli to the four muscles involved in the movements of the wrist in the forearm.

This method, however, cannot be applied to the follow-up control of the finger joints angles, because the fingers have multi-joint structures. Each joint of the finger cannot be controlled independently, and the movement is affected not only by the contraction of the muscles but also by the state of other fingers joints. Therefore, it can be considered that the parameter of PID control must be changed depending on the state of other joints and the contraction state of the muscles and, to control the fingers, the relationship of the multi-joint structure must be taken into consideration.

3   Musculoskeletal System Related to Middle Finger Joint and Target Movement of This Work

In this paper, we try to control the PIP joint and the MP joint (see Fig. 1) of the middle finger, and so, the stimuli are given to the flexor digitorum muscle and extensor digitorum muscle (see Fig. 2) because these muscles are involved in the movements of the selected joints.

3.1   Musculoskeletal System Related to Middle Finger Joint

The muscles involved in flexion/extension of the middle finger PIP/MP joint are finger flexor digitorum muscle, extensor digitorum muscle, interosseous muscle, and lumbricalis muscle. Finger flexor digitorum muscle and extensor digitorum muscle are extrinsic muscles located on the forearm. Interosseous muscle and lumbricalis muscle are intrinsic muscles located in the hands. It is known that, while the contraction of flexor digitorum muscle causes flexion of PIP/MP joint, it is largely involved in the flexion of the PIP joint. It is also known that the contraction of extensor digitorum muscle causes extension of PIP/MP joint, and it is largely involved in the extension of the MP joint [7]. Though the intrinsic muscle play an important role of the flexion of the MP joint and the extension of the PIP joint and DIP joint, the surface electrodes attached on the fingers will interfere the finger movements. In this paper, therefore, we only give the electric stimuli to the extrinsic muscles.

3.2   Target Movement of This Work

The movements of human fingers joints are caused by the coordinated contraction of the extrinsic muscles and intrinsic muscles. Aswe, as mentioned above, decided to give the stimuli only to the external muscles in this paper, possible movements are limited. Figure 3 shows the PIP/MP joint motions that human can perform, and Table 1 shows the movements that can be performed only by the contraction of the external muscles.

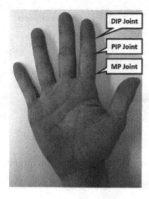

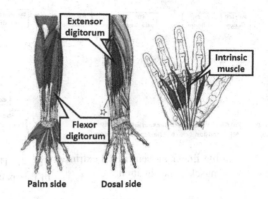

Fig. 1. Name of finger joint

Fig. 2. Muscles related to middle finger joints movement [6]

Considering Table 1 and Fig. 3, possible movements are the flexion of both PIP joint and MP joints, and the flexion of PIP joint flexion only by the contraction of the extrinsic muscles and it is impossible to cause the movement of the extension of PIP joint and the flexion of MP joint without the intrinsic muscles.

As an initial state in this paper, therefore, the finger is extended but relaxed and the electric stimuli are given as follows: The electrical stimulation is given mainly to the flexor digitorum muscle to approach the given target angles of the PIP and the MP from the initial state (see <1> in Fig. 4).

- When the MP joint approaches the target angle, the electric stimulation is also given to the extensor digitorum muscle to cause the cooperative contraction between the flexor digitorum muscle and the extensor digitorum muscle angle (see <2> in Fig. 4)
- Through above processes, PIP and MP joint approach the target angle (see <3> in Fig. 4)

Table 1. Feasible finger joints movements by coordination of extrinsic muscles

	MP flexion	MP extension
PIP flexion	Able	Able
PIP extension	Disable	Able

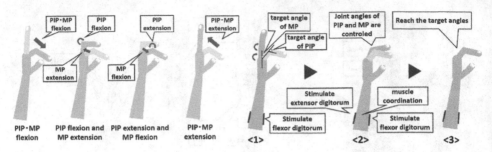

Fig. 3. Feasible finger movement by extrinsic and intrinsic muscles coordination

Fig. 4. The target middle finger joint movement in this paper.

4   Proposal of the Control Method

4.1   Electrical Stimulation Generation

The electrical stimulation used in this paper is a rectangular wave with a frequency of 40 Hz, a pulse width of 0.2 ms, and pulse height from 0 mA to 33 mA. Amount of the electrical stimulation is continuously controlled by the PC.

4.2   Measurement of Joints Angle

To obtain the current status of the fingers as the feedback, we need to measure the joint angles of PIP and MP. There are many ways to measure the finger joint angle, such as using a camera [8], using an optical fiber [9], using an inertial sensor [10], and so on. Using cameras, the occlusion among fingers will cause the failure of the accurate measurement. In this paper, we adopted the inertial sensors to measure the joints angle to avoid the occlusion problems. Figure 5 shows the device attached on the hand. The six-axis inertial sensors, MPU-6050, are attached on the middle phalanx, the proximal phalanx, and the metacarpal bone of the middle finger. Euler angles are obtained from the acceleration and angular acceleration of each sensor using the sensor fusion by the extended Kalman filter. The PIP joint angle can be calculated from difference of the roll angles between the sensor on the middle phalanx and the sensor on the proximal phalanx, and the MP joint angle can be done from the difference between the sensor on the proximal phalanx and the sensor on the metacarpal bone.

4.3   The Controller

In this paper, based on the following two proposals, the amount of electrical stimulation to flexor digitorum muscle and the extensor digitorum muscle are determined by the formulas (1) and (2).

1. The amount of stimulation to each muscle at time t is determined depending on the amount of stimulation given at time t−1
2. Taking into account the time delay of the muscle response, the amount of stimulations are decreased based on the differential terms, when the joints starts to move

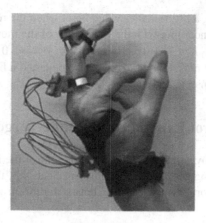

Fig. 5. A state in which a joints angle measurement device is attached

$$S_{f,t} = S_{f,t-1} + (\theta_{PIP,d} - \theta_{PIP,t})K_{f,1}$$
$$+ \{(\theta_{PIP,d} - \theta_{PIP,t}) - (\theta_{PIP,d} - \theta_{PIP,t-1})\}K_{f,2} \tag{1}$$

$$S_{e,t} = S_{e,t-1} + (\theta_{MP,d} - \theta_{MP,t})K_{e,1}$$
$$+ \{(\theta_{MP,d} - \theta_{MP,t}) - (\theta_{MP,d} - \theta_{MP,t-1})\}K_{e,2} \tag{2}$$

Here, $S_{f,t}$ and $S_{e,t}$ indicate the amount of electrical stimulations to the flexor digitorum muscle and extensor digitorum muscle at time t, $\theta_{PIP,d}$, $\theta_{MP,d}$ are the target angles of PIP/MP joint, and $\theta_{PIP,t}$, $\theta_{MP,t}$ are the angles of PIP/MP joint at time t. $K_{f,1}$, $K_{f,2}$, $K_{e,1}$ and $K_{e,2}$ are the control parameters. As the contraction of the flexor digitorum muscle mainly affect the PIP joint movement, and the contraction of the extensor digitorum muscle mainly affect the MP joint movement, the amounts of electrical stimuli to the both muscle are determined based on the target joint angles and the measured joint angles at time t.

Though the amount of the stimuli were determined statically, in Watanabe et al. [4], based on the accumulated error between the current and the target angles ignoring the total amount, the amount of stimulation to each muscle at time t should not be determined independently from the one given at time t−1. Therefore, we considered that we would be able to obtain the correct feedbacks by determined the amount of stimuli at time t, only based on the error between the joints angle at time t/t−1, and the target angle at time t/t−1.

We also modified the last part of the each equations considering the time delay of the response of the muscles after the stimuli.

If the stimulation amount is decreased only after moving beyond the target joints angle, the oscillations of repeating flexion and extension must occur. This differential term must function as gradual decreasing the stimuli considering the time delay of the muscle response.

The control parameters are adjusted according to the response of each joints of each subject to the electrical stimulation. Based on the reference values of $K_{f,1} = 4.0 \times 10^{-5}$

and $K_{e,1} = -1.5 \times 10^{-4}$, a little smaller value is set when the response is bad. $K_{f,2}$ and $K_{e,2}$ is the parameters concerning with the time delay of the muscle response. Based on the reference values of $K_{f,2} = 1.0 \times 10^{-1}$ and $K_{e,2} = -5.0 \times 10^{-1}$, a little larger values were set when the muscle time response is good, and a little smaller values were set when the time response is bad.

5   Feedback Control Experiment to Static Target Angles

In this experiment, we investigate whether we can control the PIP and MP joint to the given target angles. Using the feedback control in Sect. 4.3, the electric stimuli were given to the flexor digitorum muscle, the extensor digitorum muscle.

5.1   Subject

The subjects were three healthy male, and the stimuli were given to the left hand which is the non-dominant hand. The subjects were given an instructions about the experiment and got their consent before the experiment.

5.2   Experimental Procedures and Experimental Conditions

First, the surface electrodes were attached near the motor point [11] of the flexor digitorum muscle and extensor digitorum muscle, confirming the sufficient flexion and extension occurred. Next, we determined the maximum stimuli amounts so as to cause the maximal flexion and extension without hard pain. After that, a feedback control experiment to the set target joint angle was carried out. The subject was asked to sit on a chair, to get his elbow on the desk and set the palm on the upper side. Here, we adjusted his posture to keep the abduction/adduction angle of shoulder and the lateral/medial rotation angle of shoulder joint 0°. We also adjusted his posture to keep the angle between desk plane and line that arm about 45°. The initial posture of the finger joints was set in extended state with no force and relaxed posture (see Fig. 6). After that, feedback control experiments on PIP/MP target joint angle under four conditions shown in Table 2. were conducted. In order to avoid the influence of muscle fatigue, the next trial was carried out after 1 min rest.

5.3   Result

The result of subject A is shown in Fig. 7. We also obtained the similar results for subject B. Looking at Fig. 7(a), (b), (e) and (f), we found it was possible to control the joints angle very accurately under all conditions for two of the three subjects.

Table 3 shows joints angles after 10 s from the start of stimulation in the two subjects A and B who were able to control accurately. The average error of each joint angle was 1.75°, and the maximum error was 6.10° in the MP joint of subject B in condition 4 and it can be said they were very small.

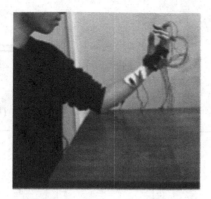

Fig. 6. Posture during experiment

Table 2. Experimental condition and target joints angle under each condition

	Target PIP joint angle [degree]	Target MP joint angle [degree]
Condition 1	45	30
Condition 2	60	30
Condition 3	90	30
Condition 4	75	45

5.4 Discussion

The experimental results indicate that we can control the PIP and MP joints to arbitrarily given joints angle by giving the electric stimuli to the flexor digitorum muscle and extensor digitorum muscle, because the joint angles after 10 s were very precisely controlled under all four conditions.

The PIP target angle were different among Condition 1, Condition 2, and Condition 3, while the MP joint target angles were constant at 30°. In case of being given only to the flexor digitorum muscle, if flexion angle of the PIP joint is tried to make larger, the one of MP joint also become larger. However, the results shows that we can succeed to control only the PIP joint angle suppressing the flexion of the MP joint. It can be said our controller can give the appropriate amounts of stimuli causing the cooperative contraction between the flexor digitorum muscle and the extensor digitorum muscle.

On the other hand, the PIP target angle in Condition 3 is larger than in Condition 4, while the MP target angle is smaller. If we tries to give the larger flexion of PIP, the MP angle also become larger only by giving stimuli to the flexor digitorum muscle. However, the results indicate that we can also succeed to make the larger flexion of PIP suppressing the flexion of the MP. This can be said we can control the amount causing the cooperative contraction between the flexor digitorum muscle and the extensor digitorum muscle.

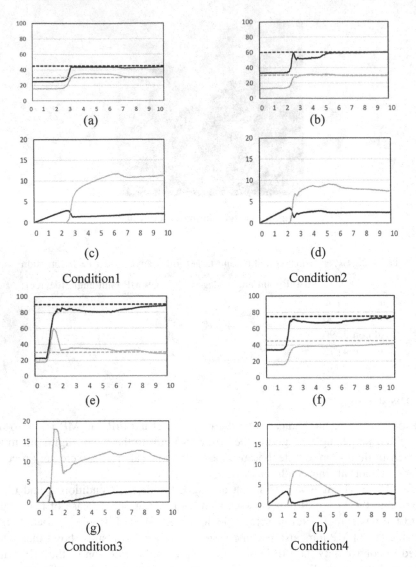

Fig. 7. Experimental result of Subject A (a), (b), (e) and (f) show changes in joint angle (vertical axis: joint angle [degree], horizontal axis: elapsed time from stimulation start [s], solid black line: PIP joint angle, solid gray line: MP joint angle, black dot line: PIP target joint angle, gray dot line: MP target joint angle). (c), (d), (g), and (h) are the amounts of electric stimulus given to each target muscle (vertical axis: electrical stimulation amount [mA], horizontal axis: elapsed time from stimulation start [s] black line: amount of electrical stimulation to flexor digitorum muscle, gray line: amount of electrical stimulation to extensor digitorum muscle).

Here, we consider the effectiveness of the controller proposed in this paper. From the results of Condition 1 (see Fig. 7(a), (c)), Condition 2 (see Fig. 7(b), (d)) and Condition 4 (see Fig. 7(f), (h)), the effectiveness of the differential term in the proposed controller can be shown. Looking at changes in the joints angle and changes in the amount of electrical stimulation in Condition 1, Condition 2, and Condition 4 in time series, even if the joint angle does not reaches the target angle under each condition, the stimuli to the flexor digitorum muscle were decreased and the ones to the extension digitorum muscle were increased when the joints started to move. This is because of the derivative term of the equations and it can be said that this makes it possible to suppress the reputations of the complete flexion and complete extension.

From the results of Condition 1 (see Fig. 7(a), (c)), Condition 2 (see Fig. 7(b), (d)) and Condition 3 (see Fig. 7(e), (g)), it can be said that it is possible to control finger joints by taking into account of their degrees of influences of each muscle on each joint movements. Looking at changes in the joints angle and change in the electrical stimulation in Condition 1, Condition 2, and Condition 3 in time series, both muscles were stimulated after the PIP and MP joints approaches the target angles.

At this time, it was confirmed that the PIP joint angle increases or maintains the current state, and the MP joint angle maintaining or decreasing according to the amount of electrical stimulation given to each target muscle. In making PIP flex, the amount to the flexor digitorum muscle are generally increased and the one to the extensor digitorum muscle are reduced. On the other hand, to try to extend MP, the opposite is done. To try to achieve both goals simultaneously, the amounts to each muscles are offset each other. Therefore, we determine the amount of stimulation to the flexor digitorum muscle to approach the target of the PIP and the one to the extensor digitorum muscle to control MP joint angle. This makes the controller to determine appropriate amounts to achieve both goals simultaneously.

Table 3. The middle finger PIP/MP joint angle 10 s after stimulation of subject A/B

	Subject A		Subject B	
	PIP [degree]	MP [degree]	PIP [degree]	MP [degree]
Condition 1	43.67	30.78	41.12	28.80
Condition 2	60.00	29.28	59.73	29.56
Condition 3	88.34	28.07	92.44	33.33
Condition 4	74.62	41.57	74.85	38.90

6 Tracking Control Experiment to Dynamically Change Target Angles in Time

In the experiment in Sect. 5, we attempted only whether the finger joints can approach to the targets and ignore how to approach to them in time series. As our final goal is to build a system to teach the finger movements to others, the movement process changing with time also important. In this experiment, we attempted to control finger joints to approach to the targets which change with time.

6.1 Subject

We involved the subject, in this experiment, who was healthy male and had the highest control accuracy in feedback control experiment, and performed the tracking control on the left hand joint, which is the non-dominant hand. The subject was given an explanation of the contents of the experiment and got their consent before the experiment.

6.2 Experimental Procedures and Experimental Conditions

The experimental procedures are the same as described in Sect. 5.3. Table 4 shows PIP/MP target angle at each time after starting stimulation. Figure 8 shows the time series graph of the target joint angles.

Table 4. Experimental conditions

Elapsed time since stimulation started [s]	0	8	13	18	23
Target PIP joint angle [degree]		45	45	60	75	90
Target MP joint angle [degree]		30	30	30	30	30

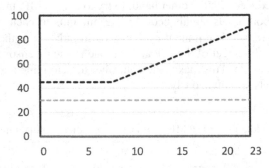

Fig. 8. The time series graph of the target joints angle. vertical axis: joint angle [degree], horizontal axis: elapsed time from stimulation start [s], black dot line: PIP target joint angle, gray dot line: MP target joint angle.

7 Result

Among several trials, we sometimes succeeded to track the changing target angles with time accurately but sometimes failed, in spite of performing the same tasks. Fig. 8 shows the typical results of both. Here, we call the successful "trial A", and the error trial "trial B". In trial A (see Fig. 9(a)), it can be said that both of PIP and MP joints accurately and smoothly track the target joint angle trajectory without large oscillation and time delay. On the other hand, in trial B (see Fig. 9(b)), after 10 to 12 s (see <1>, <2>, <3> in Fig. 9(b)) and 16 to 17 s (see <4> in Fig. 9(b)) sudden and large flexion of the PIP joint occurred. Looking at the results in more detail, we can observe that the accurate tracking can be done while the target angle is constant. After 8 s when the target angle start to increase, three oscillations were observed (see <1>, <2>, <3> in Fig. 9(b)) in trial B. Just after occurring the first oscillation (see <1> in Fig. 9(b)), the amount of stimuli to the flexor digitorum muscle is slightly reduced by the effect of the differential term of the controller (see <1> in Fig. 9(d)). Consequently, the PIP joint angle decreases, and then the amount of stimuli to the flexor digitorum muscle is increased again by the effect of the differential term. It can be considered, therefore, too much influence of the differential term may cause the oscillation of the joints angle.

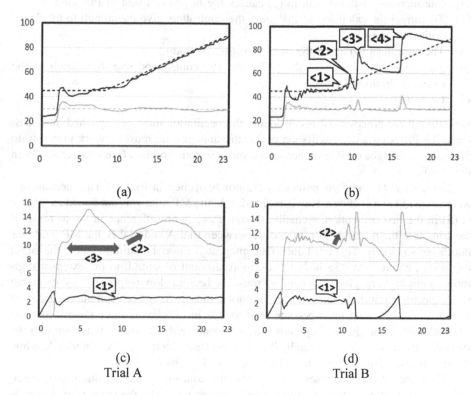

(a)   (b)

(c)   (d)
Trial A   Trial B

Fig. 9. Results of follow-up control experiments on target joint angle trajectory which change with time. The upper line shows the change in joint angle (vertical axis: joint angle [degree], horizontal axis: elapsed time from stimulation start [s], black solid line: PIP joint angle, gray solid line: MP joint angle, black dot line: PIP target joint angle, gray dot line: MP target joint angle). The lower row shows the amount of electrical stimulation given to each target muscle (vertical axis: electrical stimulation amount [mA], horizontal axis: elapsed time [s] from stimulation start, black solid line: the amount of electrical stimulation to the flexor digitorum muscle, gray solid line: the amount of electrical stimulation extensor digitorum muscle), left column shows trial A, right row shows trial B.

8 Discussion

We at first, consider why the oscillation occurred after changing the target angles in trial B. The mechanisms we considered are as follows:

(1) When the PIP target angle starts to change, the controller increases the amount of stimuli to the flexor digitorum muscle (see <1> in Fig. 9(d), <2> in Fig. 9(c)).
(2) As a result, since the MP joint angle also increases, the amount of stimuli to the extensor digitorum muscle are increased.
(3) The increase of the stimuli in (2) causes the large extension of PIP joint.
(4) To correct the extension of PIP joint, the controllers give the stimuli to the flexor digitorum muscle.
(5) The stimuli in (4) cause the flexion of the MP joint.
(6) To correct the flexion of the MP joint, the controllers give the stimuli to the extensor digitorum muscle.
(7) Go to (2).

Repeating these processes, it is considered the oscillation must be happened in trial B. Once the PIP joint angle oscillation occur, the antagonistic muscles work inversely to fill the error, and the oscillation becomes a more serious problem (see <1>, <2>, <3> in Fig. 9(b)).

Here, why the same phenomena were not happened in trial A? The mechanisms were same as (1)–(4) above. However, in trial A, the MP joint was not flexed so largely at (5) in the first oscillation. Actually, though there is no difference in the increase of the stimuli to the flexor digitorum muscle between trial A and trial B, the MP joint was not flexed so largely. This must due to the integrated amount of stimuli before the target angle start change. At <3> in Fig. 9(c), more amount of stimuli to the extensor digitorum muscle were given. Generally, muscles become low-responsive by exposing much electric stimuli. As the extensor digitorum muscle have been stimulated at <3> in Fig. 9(c), the MP joint must become hard to flex in (5) above, and consequently, the controller does not give so large amount of stimuli to the extensor digitorum muscle. Actually, the amount is increased by 0.56 [mA/s] (see <2> in Fig. 9(c)) in trial A, while the one in trial B is by 1.63 [mA/s] (see <2> in Fig. 9(d)).

When we adopt a feedback control, like the controlling way in this paper, based only the error between the target angle and the current angle, the amount of stimuli is increased in a ramp function shape in order to correct the error between the target angle and the measured angle. As a result, the total amount becomes larger than the appropriate amount to reach the target. It is known that the muscle activity does not change essentially until the end of the flexion when a person performs voluntarily [11]. Therefore, the joint angle should be determined not only by the amount of the stimuli but also by the relationship between the amount and the stimulated time, such as how long the stimulation have lasted. It is considered that the lack of this approach must cause the oscillations.

To achieve the goal the combination of feedforward and feedback control are also necessary in the follow-up control by functional electrical stimulation. In the feedforward control, the appropriate amount of stimulation to each muscle should be calculated to achieve the target joint angle trajectory from the current state using a machine learning method such as neural network, in the feedback control the amount of stimuli should be adjusted to the given amount calculated from feedforward control compared to the current status. When a person performs spontaneous physical exercise, it is known that as time delay of about 0.2 s occurs for the vision or somatosensory, he/she calculates the exercise requirements for the target in advance in the brain as the feedforward control [12]. If we can build a feedforward controller where the time until the joints angle starts to change and the joint angle trajectory until reaching the final target are taken into account, we may control movements of the finger joints with time by considering the relationships among the amount of the stimuli, duration of the stimulation, and the joint angle.

9 Conclusion

In this paper, we proposed a way to control the PIP/MP joint in the middle finger to the arbitrary target joints angles by giving the electrical stimuli to the flexor digitorum muscle and the extensor digitorum muscle. Based on the knowledge about the relationships of the PIP/MP joints and the muscles, in our controller, the amounts to the flexor digitorum muscle and extensor digitorum muscle comparing with the current joint angles. As the result, it was possible to control both of PIP and MP joint to the arbitrary target. We also adopted this controller to control the joints to the target angles which change with time dynamically. Among these trials, we sometimes succeeded to track the changing target angles with time accurately but sometimes failed, in spite of performing the same tasks.

10 Future Work

In order to realize control to the target joint angle which changes with time, we will adopt a machine learning method that calculates the amount of stimulation necessary to reach desired joints angle changing with time and consider a new method that adjust the amount of stimuli from the error between the target joint angle and the measured joint angle.

Acknowledgements. This work has been supported by Shotoku Science Foundation.

References

1. Osaki, M.: Comprehending tacit knowledge. Humaniti. Nat. Sci. Pap. **127**, 21–39 (2009). Tokyo Keizai University
2. Zhou, Ma., Pinhas, B., Jerome, D.: Hand rehabilitation learning system with an exoskeleton robotic glove. IEEE Trans. Neural Syst. Rehabil. Eng. **24**(12), 1323–1332 (2016)
3. Hoshimiya, N., Naito, A., Yajima, M., Handa, Y.: Multichannel FES system for the restoration of motor functions in high spinal cord injury patients: a respiration-controlled system for multijoint upper extremity. IEEE Trans. Biomed. Eng. **36**(7), 754–760 (1989)

4. Tamaki, E., Miyaki, T., Rekimoto, J., Sasabe, T.: PossessedHand: techniques for controlling human hands using electrical muscles stimuli. In: CHI 2011 Proceedings of the SIGCHI Conference on Human Factors in Computing Systems, pp. 543–552(2011)

5. Watanabe, T., Iibuchi, K., Kurosawa, K., Hoshimiya, N.: A method of multichannel pid control of two-degree-of-freedom wrist joint movements by functional electrical stimulation. Syst. Comput. Japan **34**(5), 25–36 (2003)

6. Kinniku-Guide. http://www.musculature.biz/40/43/post_163/

7. Ueba, Y.: Hand it's function and dissection (revised fifth edition). KINPODO (2010)

8. Jože, G., Grega, J., Matevž, P., Sašo, T., Jaka, S.: An analysis of the precision and reliability of the Leap Motion sensor and its suitability for static and dynamic tracking. Sensors **14**(2), 3701–3720 (2014)

9. Eric, F., Danilo, Y.M., Murilo, F.M.S., Carlos, K. S.: Development of a glove-based optical fiber sensor for applications in human-robot interaction. In: 2013 8th ACM/IEEE International Conference on Human-Robot Interaction (HRI), pp. 123–124 (2013)

10. Christopher, H., Katrin, W., Mathias, W.: Whole hand modeling using 8 wearable sensors: biomechanics for hand pose prediction. In: AH 2013 Proceedings of the 4th Augmented Human International Conference, pp. 21–28 (2013)

11. Hasue, M.: Orthopedic Nerve Disease Handbook. NANKODO (1983)

12. Donald, A.N., Shimada, T., Arima, K.: Kinesiology of the Musculoskeletal System Foundations for Rehabilitation, 2nd edn. Ishiyaku Publishers, Inc., p. 310 (2012)

13. Osu, R.: Motor control and learning – From the viewpoint of rehabilitation. Jpn. J. Cogn. Neurosci. **7**(3), 217–222 (2005)

Preliminary Investigation of Mechanical Impedance Characteristics During Lane Change Maneuver

Ryutaro Yasui$^{(\boxtimes)}$, Kohei Yamaguchi, Takafumi Asao,
Kentaro Kotani, and Satoshi Suzuki

Department of Mechanical Engineering, Kansai University, Osaka, Japan
{k683789,k534972,asao,kotani,ssuzuki}@kansai-u.ac.jp

Abstract. Driving support systems have been actively developed. These systems use itself vehicle and surrounding environmental information. There is few research about that system using driver's physiological information. However, it is discomfort for drivers because electrodes are needed to attach to drivers. Therefore, we focused on mechanical impedance derived from driver's arm, which are inertia, viscosity, and stiffness. The impedance can be estimated from steering wheel angle, angular velocity, angular acceleration, and torque around a steering wheel shaft where drivers always grip. In this paper, driving simulator experiments were conducted to investigate dynamic characteristics of the impedance in a situation of single lane change without a steering support system, and the time-varying impedance were estimated by using Kalman filter. As results, moment of inertia did not change so much. On the other hand, viscosity and stiffness decreased while steering the wheel.

Keywords: Mechanical impedance · Kalman filter · Lane change

1 Introduction

Driver assistance system (DAS) partially cover driving tasks of cognition, judgement and operation instead of human [1]. Though the DAS becomes widely spreading to us, a problem is a conflict between human and system intention. Therefore, a support by the system should not be bothersome, and its timing is appropriate for human [2]. Existing DAS uses surrounding and vehicle information [3]. The surrounding information is dynamic information of other vehicles and pedestrians and road alignments acquired by some sensors. The vehicle information is, for example, position, speed, and direction of its own vehicle. Not only surrounding and vehicle information but driver information that is physiological information of driver, is necessary to dissolve the conflict between the system and human. If human's driving intention can be estimated from the driver information, it is applicable to haptic-shared-control [4] which is one of a DAS having a mechanism of reaction force to the driver via a steering wheel or pedals. Existing studies estimated driver's steering intentions using their electroencephalogram [5] and eye direction [6]. Drivers are required body constraint and mental stress to obtain the

© Springer Nature Switzerland AG 2019
S. Yamamoto and H. Mori (Eds.): HCII 2019, LNCS 11570, pp. 455–465, 2019.
https://doi.org/10.1007/978-3-030-22649-7_36

physiological information, it is necessary for the system that can collect driver information with low constraint of humans and estimate driver's intention.

Characteristics of human's movement can be expressed by mechanical impedance which is inertia, viscosity and stiffness [7]. In order to begin to move an arm fast, humans rise their arm viscoelasticity by contracting their muscles [8]. In a steering situation, drivers make their arm muscles firm or soft according to vehicle speed and curvature of road [8]. Tanaka et al. estimated human's arm mechanical impedance mechanically equivalent around a steering shaft at a static condition and proposed steering control system using the impedance [9]. In this method it is feasible with existing electronics power steering system, since only steering wheel angle and torque are measured to estimate the impedance, and not constrain driver just griping a wheel. If the impedance in a dynamic situation can be obtained, it is possible to support the drivers in various driving situations.

The objective of this study is to estimate driver's mechanical impedance dynamically unless any constraint like physiological measurement, and develop a steering control system. In this paper, driving simulator (DS) experiments were conducted to investigate dynamic characteristics of mechanical impedance during single lane change situation without DAS.

2 Dynamics and Impedance Identification

2.1 Mechanical Model of Human-Steering System

The equation of motion of a steering system is expressed as

$$M_s\ddot{\theta} + B_s\dot{\theta} = \tau_h + \tau \tag{1}$$

where M_s and B_s are moment of inertia and rotational viscosity due to structural properties around a steering shaft, respectively. The θ is steering wheel angle. The τ_h and τ are operational torque by human and external torque, respectively.

It is hypothesize that a driver controls steering by impedance control [10] as used in robotics, equation of motion of a human-steering system is expressed as

$$M\ddot{\theta} + B\dot{\theta} + K(\theta - \theta_v) = \tau \tag{2}$$

where M, B, and K are target moment of inertia, viscosity, and stiffness for impedance control, respectively. The θ_v is a target steering wheel angle by human control, so-called virtual trajectory. It is ill-posed problem to solve Eq. (2) for the impedance M, B, and K, since θ_v is unknown. To resolve this problem, perturbation method was adopted.

If small displacement $\Delta\theta$ is occurred by small perturbation torque $\Delta\tau$ within a short duration, Eq. (2) becomes

$$M(\ddot{\theta} + \Delta\ddot{\theta}) + B(\dot{\theta} + \Delta\dot{\theta}) + K(\theta + \Delta\theta - \theta_v) = \tau + \Delta\tau \tag{3}$$

By subtracting Eq. (2) from Eq. (3), following equation not including θ_v is obtained.

$$M\Delta\ddot{\theta} + B\Delta\dot{\theta} + K\Delta\theta = \Delta\tau \qquad (4)$$

The $\Delta\ddot{\theta}$, $\Delta\dot{\theta}$, $\Delta\theta$, and $\Delta\tau$ can be obtained by applying a high-frequency-pass filter to $\Delta\ddot{\theta}$, $\Delta\dot{\theta}$, $\Delta\theta$ and $\Delta\tau$, respectively.

2.2 Dynamic Identification of Impedance

In order to identify mechanical impedance, state space model in discrete time system was constructed.

$$x[i+1] = x[i] + v[i] \qquad (5)$$

$$y[i] = \boldsymbol{\theta}^T[i]x[i] + w[i] \qquad (6)$$

where i denotes i-th sample, and system output y is $\Delta\tau$. The vectors x and θ are defined as following equations, respectively. The v and w are system noise vector and observation noise, respectively.

$$x[i] = [M[i] \quad B[i] \quad K[i]]^T \qquad (7)$$

$$\boldsymbol{\theta}[i] = [\Delta\ddot{\theta}[i] \quad \Delta\dot{\theta}[i] \quad \Delta\theta[i]]^T \qquad (8)$$

In order to identify time-varying impedance x, Kalman Filter was constructed. Estimated x is updated by following equations.

$$M[i] = R[i-1] + L \qquad (9)$$

$$k[i] = \frac{M[i]\boldsymbol{\theta}[i]}{\sigma_v^2 + \boldsymbol{\theta}^T[i]M[i]\boldsymbol{\theta}[i]} \qquad (10)$$

$$x[i] = x[i-1] + k[i](y[i] - \boldsymbol{\theta}^T[i]x[i-1]) \qquad (11)$$

$$R[i] = (I - k[i]\boldsymbol{\theta}^T[i])M[i] \qquad (12)$$

3 Lane Change Experiment

Driving simulator (DS) experiments were conducted to investigate impedance characteristics during single lane change without a steering assistance system.

3.1 Apparatus

An outline of the DS is shown in Fig. 1. A steering wheel shaft was connected to a direct drive motor (SGMCS-14C3C41, Yasukawa Electric) to create perturbation and reaction torque. A motor-driver (SGDV-2R8A01B, Yasukawa Electric) was connected to a Windows PC via a DA board (PEX-361216, Interface) and a counter board (PCI-6205C, Interface). The torque and wheel angle and torque were measured at 1 [kHz] by a self-made C++ language program.

A display (LCD-M4K431XDB, IO Data) in front of a driving seat showed an experimental scene created by Unity. Vehicle behavior according to participants' steering operation was calculated by using CarSim (Mechanical Simulation). Figure 2 shows experimental appearance.

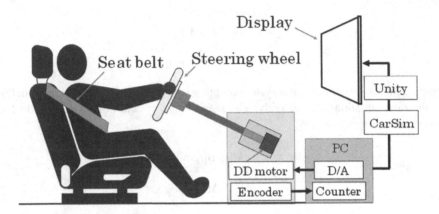

Fig. 1. Outline of driving simulator used in experiments.

Fig. 2. Experiment appearance.

3.2 Experimental Conditions

Course of Lane Change. Figure 3 shows an experimental single-lane-change course [11] used in this experiments. Red traffic cones as red squares in Fig. 3 were placed to set course dimensions as shown in Fig. 3. One set of single-lane-change course was repeated by 200 m interval.

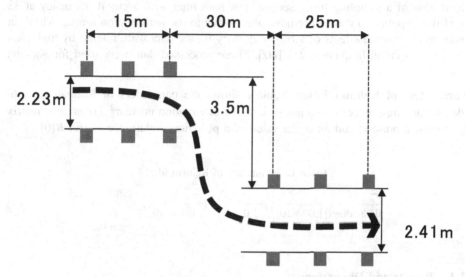

Fig. 3. Dimensions of single-lane-change course. (Color figure online)

Reaction and Perturbation Torques. Reaction torque τ_c to participants' steering operation was generated by impedance control as the steering system shows a following characteristic.

$$M_s\ddot{\theta} + B_d\dot{\theta} + K_d\theta = \tau_h + \tau_p \tag{13}$$

where B_d and K_d are target impedance for control, and τ_p is a perturbation torque. The τ in Eq. (1) is $\tau_c + \tau_p$. From Eqs. (1) and (13), the reaction torque τ_c is to be

$$\tau_c = (B_s - B_d)\dot{\theta} - K_d\theta \tag{14}$$

In this experiment, B_d and K_d were set to 0.5 [Nm s/rad] and 2.0 [Nm/rad], respectively. The structural impedance M_s and B_s were 0.0456 [kgm^2] and 0.2486 [Nm s/rad] identified by other preliminary experiments, respectively.

The perturbation torque τ_p was +1.0 [Nm] or −1.0 [Nm] created as maximum length sequence by a primitive polynomial $f(x) = x^7 + x + 1$. The perturbation torque was changed for each 30 [ms] according to created sequence.

Procedures. Participants sat on the seat and adjusted its position and backrest angle, then fasten four point seat belt. They were asked to grip the steering wheel at 10 and 2 o'clock, and not to re-grip the wheel during a lane change trial. They drove the DS in several sets of single-lane-change for practices. After the practices, they drove 5 test trials. Vehicle speed was set to constant 80 [km/h], therefore participants were not to need to step gas and brake pedals.

Signal Processing. At first, recorded data were interpolated for each 1 [ms] because of fluctuation of a sampling time. Second, low-pass filter with a cutoff frequency at 33 [Hz] were applied to them in remove aliases due to the perturbation torque. Third, in order to remove the effects of virtual trajectory θ_v, the data were filtered by high-pass filter with a cutoff frequency at 1 [Hz]. These processed data were used for Kalman filter.

Parameters of Kalman Filter. Table 1 shows the parameters of Kalman filter to identify the impedance, which are variance of observation noise σ_v^2, covariance matrix L of system noise v, and an initial value of a posteriori covariance matrix $R[0]$.

Table 1. Parameters of Kalman filter

σ_v^2	L	$R[0]$
0.98	diag($[1.0 \times 10^{-15}, 1.0 \times 10^{-5}, 1.0 \times 10^{-3}]$)	γI, $\gamma = 0.1$

3.3 Results and Discussions

Figures 4, 5, 6, 7 and 8 show measured data of 5 trials for each subject. The graphs are torque, steering wheel angle, steering wheel angular velocity, and steering wheel angular acceleration in order from the top for each figure. Time of 0 [s] at horizontal axes express start time of steering for the lane change.

Figures 9, 10, 11, 12 and 13 show estimated impedance with the steering wheel angle of 5 trials for each participant. The graphs show the steering wheel angle, estimated moment of inertia, viscosity, and stiffness in order from the top. The inertia not change so much, the range is from 0.04 to 0.08 [kgm^2] for all participants. In previous research, it has been reported that the inertia are in the range of 0.05 to 0.07 [kgm^2] when static holding of a steering wheel with both hands [12]. Therefore, the estimated inertia in Figs. 9, 10, 11, 12 and 13 seems valid.

The viscosity in Figs. 9, 10, 11, 12 and 13 tend to decrease around the start time of steering. Moreover, the viscosity while steering are decreasing or keep lower. It is thought that participants softened their arm muscles since the impedance is to be a resistance to movement. After the half of steering, the viscosity tend to increase gradually. The participants had been raising their muscle viscosity in order to maintain the wheel angle at 0 [deg] to run straight. The stiffness in Figs. 4, 5, 6, 7 and 8 tend to change as similar to the viscosity.

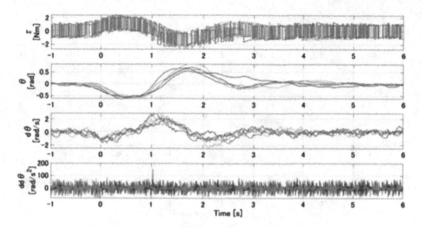

Fig. 4. Measured data for participant A.

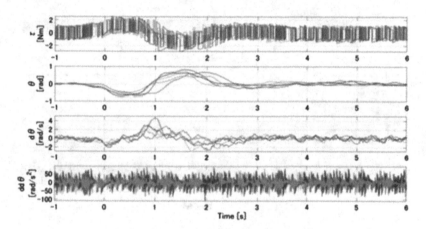

Fig. 5. Measured data for participant B.

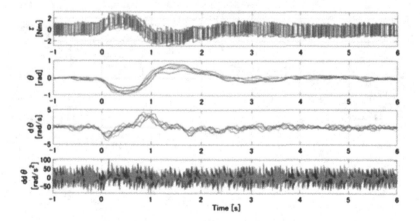

Fig. 6. Measured data for participant C.

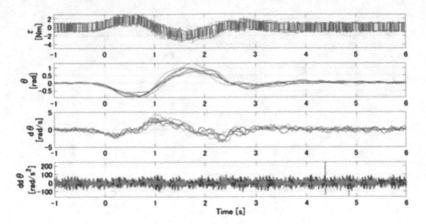

Fig. 7. Measured data for participant D.

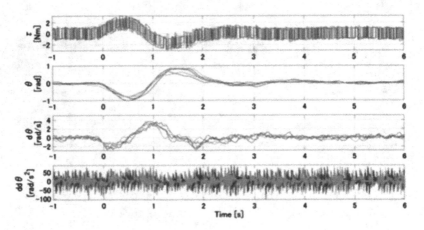

Fig. 8. Measured data for participant E.

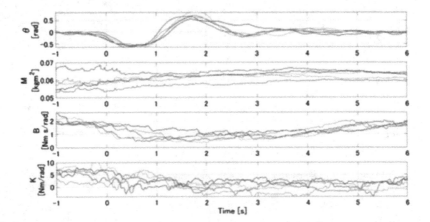

Fig. 9. Estimated impedance for subject A.

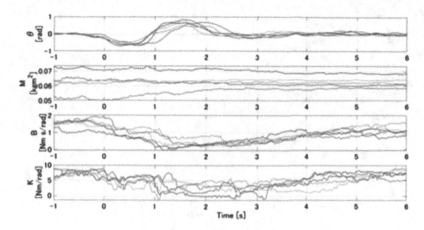

Fig. 10. Estimated impedance for subject B.

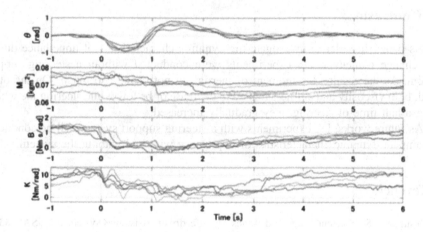

Fig. 11. Estimated impedance for subject C.

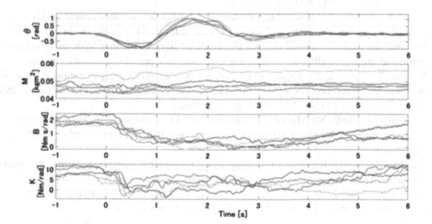

Fig. 12. Estimated impedance for subject D.

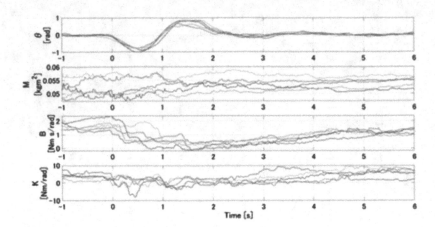

Fig. 13. Estimated impedance for subject E.

4   Conclusions

In this paper, in order to investigate the dynamic characteristics of impedance during lane-change maneuver, DS experiments were conducted without a steering support system. As the results, the moment of inertia did not change so much. On the other hand, both viscosity and stiffness tended to decrease or be low while steering the wheel. After a half time of steering, they gradually increased.

As future works, DS experiments with a steering support system will be conducted to compare dynamic characteristics of impedance with and without the system.

References

1. Tsugawa, S.: Current status and issues on safe driver assistance systems. J. JSAE **63**(2), 12–18 (2009). (in Japanease)
2. Inagaki, T.: Human understand machine, machine understand human. In: Proceedings of Translog, pp. 34–37 (2007). (in Japanease)
3. Asao, T., Suzuki, S., Kotani, K.: Dynamic identification of mechanical impedance for estimating steering intention. In: Proceedings of SSI. pp. 34–37 (2012). (in Japanease)
4. Raksincharoensak, P.: Shared control in advanced driver assistance systems based on risk predictive driving intelligence model, readout, 46(Ext.), pp. 26–31 (2016). (in Japanease)
5. Ikenishi, T., Kamada, T., Nagai, M.: Classification of driver steering intention at the vehicle running based on brain-computer interface using electroencephalogram. Trans. JSME Series C **74**(741), 1347–1354 (2008). (in Japanease)
6. Kamisaka, T., Noda, M., Mekada, Y., Deguchi, D., Ide, I., Murase, H.: Prediction of driving behavior using driver's gaze information. Tech. Rep. IEICE **111**(47), 105–110 (2011). (in Japanease)
7. Tanaka, T., et al.: Analysis of human hand impedance properties during the steering operation. Trans. SICE **42**(12), 1353–1359 (2006). (in Japanease)
8. Tanaka, T., Yamada, N., Suetomi, T., Tsuji, T.: Steering control system using human arm impedance properties. J. JSAE **64**(12), 30–35 (2010). (in Japanease)

9. Deng, M., Gomi, H.: Robust estimation of human multijoint arm viscoelasticity during movement. Trans. SICE **39**(6), 537–543 (2003). (in Japanease)
10. Yoshikawa, T.: Fundamental Theory in Robot Control, Korona, Tokyo (1988). (in Japanease)
11. ISO3888-1, Passenger cars – Test track for a severe lane-change manoeuvre – Part 1: Double lane-change (1999)
12. Hada, M., Yamada, D., Tsuji, T.: Equivalent inertia of human-machine systems under constraint environments. Trans. SICE, 156–163 (2006). (in Japanease)

Medicine, Healthcare and Quality of Life Applications

A New Motion-Based Tool for Occupation and Monitoring of Residents in Nursing Homes

Déborah Alexandra Foloppe[1,2(✉)] [ID], Paul Richard[1], Philippe Allain[2], and Alphonse Calenda[3]

[1] LARIS, EA 7315, UNIV Angers, Angers, France
deborah.foloppe@univ-angers.fr
[2] LPPL, EA 4638, UNIV Angers, Angers, France
[3] GEIHP, EA 3142, UNIV Angers, Angers, France

Abstract. Population ageing bring new challenges in healthcare and has raised issues concerning innovative solutions to optimize the management of elderly. As recommended, new interactive tools must be accessible to users, acceptable, easy to use, motivating and useful for both residents and staff. Virtual Reality is a good candidate to fulfill these specifications. Based on our expertise in Human Computer Interaction and Neuropsychology of ageing, we are developing a platform to offer interactive activities adapted to very-old and dependent people living in nursing homes. It is based on the use of a low-cost markerless RGB-D sensor (AstraTM, Orbbec) to track user body motion. Implemented activities were designed to involve various cognitive abilities, such as sorting game, search game, ball game. In addition, a module records several biomechanical data and generates reports for caregivers. This paper aims to discuss the special needs of research context and to present the designed interaction platform.

Keywords: Application software · Health monitoring · Dependent aged resident · RGB-D sensor · Physical activity

1 Introduction

Ageing becomes the highest priority for the public health policy for France, like in many countries in the world. Over the past decades, healthcare has experienced many changes. France has created specialized nursing home establishments for dependent elderly people. In this context, innovative solutions based on new technologies are proposed. For example, Virtual Reality (VR) techniques have been proposed to support traditional care. VR "is a scientific and technical domain that uses computer science and behavioral interfaces to simulate in a virtual world the behavior of 3D entities, which interact in real time with each other and with one or more users in pseudo-natural immersion via sensorimotor channels" [1]. Indeed, VR makes it possible to expose users to multisensory (often audio-visual only) situations which are controlled.

This paper introduces a new motion-based tool for occupation and monitoring of residents in nursing homes. In the next Sect. 2 (Research Context), we introduce the context of this work. More precisely, this section describes the health status of residents (Sect. 2.1), explains the difficulties to implement adapted activity programs (Sect. 2.2),

© Springer Nature Switzerland AG 2019
S. Yamamoto and H. Mori (Eds.): HCII 2019, LNCS 11570, pp. 469–481, 2019.
https://doi.org/10.1007/978-3-030-22649-7_37

proposes to implement therapeutic activities in order to support health management (Sect. 2.3) and focuses on the interest on and full-body interaction with virtual environments. The following Sect. 3 (System Description) describes needs and specifications at the basis of our work (Sect. 3.1). Then, we present the software (Sect. 3.2) and hardware (Sect. 3.3) used to develop our VR-based system. Furthermore, we describe the application functioning (Sect. 3.4) and expose the different functional modules (Sect. 3.5). Finally, this paper ends with a conclusion and proposes tracks for future work.

2   Research Context

2.1   Older and Highly Dependent Residents

Today, nursing homes must manage a growing number of residents, who enter in these institutions older [2, 3] and more dependent [4]. In French specialized nursing homes, about 54% of the residents are confined to their bed or chair and/or show a severe global cognitive deficit. Moderately dependent people account for 37% of the residents hey show intact or relatively intact cognitive abilities, but they need help to perform Activities of Daily Living (ADL, 17%), or they need help with transfer but move autonomously once they are standing (20%). They all often need help with washing and dressing and cooking. Fully independent or quasi-independent people account for 9% of the residents, but have about 6 pathologies (average per resident) [3, 5]. Overall, at least one-third of residents in the French nursing homes has an Alzheimer's disease or a related dementia [3, 6].

Even nursing homes are first and foremost places to live, the residents' health status calls for vigilance regarding the risks of death, life-threatening illness or a permanent functional deficit [7–12]. Thus, some institutions implement strengthening muscle exercises and balance and fall prevention workshops.

2.2   Difficulties to Implement Adapted Activity Programs

To maintain the quality of life as high as possible is an important goal of health care, especially in incurable pathologies. In very old and dependent people, the stress is made on social participation. The most popular activities in nursing homes are singing, memory game, cooking, board game, cultural outing and walk, intergenerational event, computer workshop, as well as soft gymnastics. Digitally-enabled activities are also taking off, notably thanks to Wii™ and Kinect™, which have democratized video games in the 2010s by making them more accessible and trans generational. Consoles which designed games for young as well as for the elderly were among the most appreciated new technologies in nursing homes.

The management of dependence proposes to cure diseases, to rehabilitate the individual health (e.g., psychotherapy, exercise programs), to modify task procedures, or to adapt the environment (e.g., prostheses, care programs). Various non-pharmacological approaches are proposed, preferentially focusing cognition, motor skills, mood, or social life. Non-pharmacological programs could maintain or improve functioning [13–17] and reduce the subjective burden of caregiving [16, 18]. Unfortunately, despite their benefit, activities for institutionalized people are still underdeveloped. In practice, the management of dependence in elderly relies mainly on the contribution of external help, from families, associations and professional caregivers. In nursing homes, it relies almost exclusively on the professional caregivers who do, in the place of the residents, the activities in which the latter have lost their autonomy. Cooking or gardening proposed to elderly institutionalized people are usually animations, focusing on pleasure, not on residents' empowerment. These animations are not like therapeutic activities. In France, nearly half of nursing homes do not have procedures to prevent the decline of autonomy in ADL of their residents, and only 37% propose educational programs (i.e., information on diseases, medications, warning signs, non-drug therapies). Moreover, more than one-third of residents has indicated that they did not want or could not participate in the occupational activities [19]. Listening to the radio or watching television is the main activity for 49% of residents, while participating in group activities and participating in personal activities are the main activity for 25% and 28% of residents respectively. The most dependent are resting (38% of them) or "bored, look out the window…" (37% of them). A low level of activity has also been described in American studies. Thus, according to Harper Ice [20], 65% of people "do nothing" [21, see also 22–24]. Yet, healthcare institutions are constantly seeking to improve their services, so they can meet residents' needs, without increasing the burden on professional caregivers.

In this context, the research has investigated the underlying causes of this low level of activity in nursing home residents. According literature, the proposed activities can be experienced as frustrating and uninteresting if they do not match individual skills [23, 25]. In addition, when activities are not relevant and meaningful, residents report preferring to watch television or do nothing rather than attend activity sessions [25]. According to data from a French survey [19], half of nursing home managers have difficulty in organizing activities that are adapted to the individual preferences and to the reduced abilities of residents. Consequently, diversification of supply and attention to individual skills, needs and interests in the selection of activities is essential to foster residents' participation and strengthen their self-esteem, enjoyment and/or success [25–27]. Finally, the lack of activity in residents finds explanations in budgetary and human tensions which have been frequently identified [e.g., 28–30]. As a result, it is common to notice understaffed services and precarious employment (e.g., contracting, short-term, part-time). However, such organizational solutions affect the continuity of care and reduces opportunities for residents to benefit from the exercises. Professional caregivers lack of time and, sometimes, they also lack of materials and training, to incorporate, into their daily routine with residents, activities likely to maintain the residents functioning [31]. Consequently, medical and social management of elderly people may benefit from less using service providers to quickly execute the ADL for residents (e.g., dressing, toileting), and promoting therapeutic ADL achieved by residents as independently as possible with the adapted assistance of professional caregivers.

2.3   Improvement Levers: Strengthening Evaluation

Another interest of the therapeutic activity is the associated assessments of patients. In the French nursing home, a geriatric assessment is performed at the entrance of residents to assess their level autonomy and their need for assistances in seventeen basic and instrumental activities. This assessment is used to calculate the fees of managements and treatment in institutions and to calculate the eligibility for public subsidies and reimbursement of costs. In addition, a complementary geriatric assessment is recommended to evaluate sight and hearing, physical health (risk of falling, nutritional status, functional autonomy, depression, and global cognitive deficit. The purpose of this comprehensive assessment is to guide the design of a medical-social project which appropriated to each resident. Such standardized and archived assessments also improve quality of care in nursing homes. Indeed, objective standardized measures can compensate for the usual communication difficulties of residents [32, 33]. In addition, data archiving plays a crucial role in the continuity of care in this sector affected by turnover [34]. Finally, follow-up assessment can be used to measure the impact of an intervention. According to a French survey aiming to assess the quality of services in nursing homes [35], 90% of respondents considered that the different capacities and limits of the resident are regularly evaluated and more than 96% of respondents considered offering a personalized support, based on expectations and the needs collected directly from the resident. Moreover, in the same study, only 30% of responding institutions acknowledged that they did not perform an initial analysis of the resident's needs and 40% did not update data about the residents' needs. Some institutions also acknowledged that they did not have a procedure to evaluate their management of cognitive impairment (25%) or their management of mood and behavior disorders (31%). These data suggest that health professionals are satisfied with an appraising health status of residents, when the opportunity arises, without formal protocol nor quantitative scoring. The underused of a comprehensive assessment may be due to its time-cost and/or can a minor interest of the details of these many tests for their practice.

2.4   Interest of Virtual Reality and Full-Body Interaction

To enable this sector to cope with the constantly changing demands of healthcare and to benefit from it, the interest of new technologies is explored. Especially, VR techniques have been proposed to support traditional care. VR makes it possible to expose users to multisensory situations that are controlled. The scenario and tasks can be imaginary or realistic, but credible. The user is placed as the main actor of the simulation, which evolves according to her actions, made using interaction devices. Interactions with VR solicit various sensorial modalities (e.g., depending on the system: by means of his voice, her gestures). One of the many advantages of VR is that the patients do not need to be in a clinical setting as they can perform the exercises in their own home through tele rehabilitation systems. In addition, patient exercises can be recorded and the data can be used to evaluate patient rehabilitation performance [36, 37]. Another key point is that VR therapy is capable of motivating patients to a larger extent and thereby stimulating new motor and sensory abilities. VR systems can be classified in two categories, immersive systems which simulate a virtual environment, making the user feel that he is present in the virtual environment itself, and non-immersive systems, generally based on large 3D projected screens. While immersive VR systems involve complex interaction devices and head-mounted displays, non-immersive systems use simpler setup and low-cost interaction devices such as computer mice, joysticks, or gamepad [38–41]. A more recent approach is based on mobile devices, chosen because of its accessibility, cost and ease. For example, a study by Luis et al. [42] have used Unity 3D game engine along with Samsung Galaxy S7 and Samsung Gear VR.

Several studies focusing on upper limb motor functions have been done on immersive VR. For example, Cameirao et al. [43] have immersed fourteen participants with acute stroke in a VR rehabilitation gaming system. The interventions include hitting, grasping, and placing virtual objects. Stewart et al. [44] have used a desktop computer and 3D shutter glasses to provide a three-dimensional view of stimuli, and they have obtained successful results with movement and performance improvement. The VR games are also used to focus on arm and hand movement. Both studies have shown participants 'improved functional ability after experiencing the treatment and this benefits their performance in ADL.

Non-immersive VR is gaining popularity as a technique to improve functioning in both motor and cognitive rehabilitation program. A study by Saposnik et al. [45] have compared the safety and efficacy of VR with recreational therapy on motor recovery. The Nintendo Wii gaming system was used. The result has shown that a motor rehabilitation is most effective when the exercise is intensive and specific, regardless of the type of exercise or task done. Thus, simple exercises can be as good as immersive VR based-rehabilitation. In another study, Cai et al. [46] have proposed a stimulation based assistance through iterative learning platform which applies electrical stimulation to two arm muscles. VR applied to health is a growing domain of interest [47, 48]. Body interaction is especially explored because it is known to facilitate user's involvement in the tasks. In addition, pseudo-natural interaction allows dependent people to interact with the system without lengthy preliminary training.

3 System Description

3.1 Needs and Specifications

Elderly living in nursing homes are not stimulated enough, because of staff's time constraints and lack of adapted materials. As a result, the VR system must be a motivating, useful and rewarding mediation tool for both residents and staff. In addition, it must be quick to set up and without requiring long preconfiguration and complex tuning. Finally, it must be inexpensive. In addition, residents of nursing homes have very diverse profiles and have little opportunity to carry out activities adapted to their abilities. Therefore, it is crucial to develop solutions likely to engage both motor components and cognitive components. Moreover, proposed activities must be accessible, meaningful, and enjoyable.

Therapists use to work on short sessions, during which they must evaluate and/or train residents. In addition, the technical part of care must be reduced as much as possible to favor the relational and educational aspects. Therefore, the system must be easy to use. It must propose to quickly launch of activities (e.g., exercise user's settings). Advanced options have been identified, such as exercise program's user's configuration. In addition, resident's data visualization may be useful.

Access to the detailed raw data of residents is not necessary. However, short reports of needs and warning messages when the system detects abnormal data can be useful for staff, especially managers. Variations in resident's data could help testing the effectiveness of interventions and hence guide strategic planning and resource allocation.

A last element of constraint was to obtain a final cost of the system as small as possible for the institutions and to preserve our financial independence to remain free in the solutions of perpetuation of the project (licensing). Several tools – such as commercial solutions, middleware, libraries – could help us to develop our solution, but they are too expensive for a successful business model between nursing homes and academic research and development.

3.2 Development Tools

The software was developed under Unity3D (LTS 2017). The modeling was carried out using Autodesk® 3ds Max® (2019). The platform proposes to perform several activities, each configurable and achievable by means of a depth camera (Astra Pro™, Orbbec). The scripts were written in C # language.

3.3 Hardware

The 3D cameras from Astra series are manufactured by Orbbec in Shenzhen, China. They make it possible to follow the movements of the body of users in a 3D space. Their 3D cameras are small and inexpensive devices ($150 for Astra Pro™). They are compatible with the most popular operating systems and not require a high-performance PC. On Windows, a processor x86@1.8 GHz and 4 GB of RAM are enough. In addition, this sensor works well in most lighting conditions, from a lit environment to darkness. However, intense daylight is known to limit the performance of infrared sensors [49]. Contrary to systems like OptiTrack™, a camera from Astraseries does not require any marker on users. It includes an infrared (IR) camera associated with a coded pattern projector and an RGB camera.

The depth sensor has a 58.4° horizontal and 45.5° vertical field of view. Based on the structured light technique, it provides a 16-bit image with a resolution of 640×480 pixels (at 30FPS). The color camera captures a field of $66.1° \times 40.2°$ and can provide a 16-bit image, $1280 \times 720@30$fps. According to Orbbec tests [50], the sensor accuracy at about 1 m is ± 1–3 mm. Orbbec provides a basic SDK based on OpenNI [51]. The middleware for Astra Pro™ allows to follow up to 8 bodies placed at 60 cm to 8 m from the device, with an optimal detection between 60 cm and 5 m (2.5 m and 3 m according to our own tests). The data can then be sampled at $60° \times 49.5° \times 73°$ in height, width and depth respectively.

3.4   Application Functioning

Figure 1 presents the interaction between the different proposed functionalities.

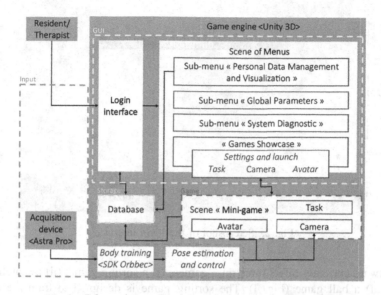

Fig. 1. Schematic representation of the system architecture.

Login Interface. When the software launches, a dialog box displays, asking to enter a username and password and to accept the conditions of use. The dialog box also gives an access for registration (see Fig. 2). The first created account is a therapist-type account because it is not associated with any other user. To create a patient-type account, the user has to associate his account with a registered therapist. The main Scene of Menus is only available after logging in (see Fig. 1).

Scene of Menus. The main Scene of Menus provides access to the Personal Data Management module, the System Diagnostic module and it launches on the Games Showcase module.

Personal Data Management. The personal data management module allows each patient to delete his account and associated data. A part is also dedicated to the addition of personal data such as the age, the level of autonomy (GIR) or the level of activity of the resident. It is also possible to consult the performance data measured during the game (see also "Analysis module").

System Diagnostic. The diagnostic sub-menu allows you to check if the Astra^{TM} acquisition device is working properly. Camera returns are displayed as well as different statistics are displayed. In case of malfunction, warning messages are displayed.

Games Showcase. The Games Showcase sub-menu is generated at its launch, based on a simple XML file in which store different data, such as the game's name as used in scripts, the game's name as displayed for users, the description of the game.

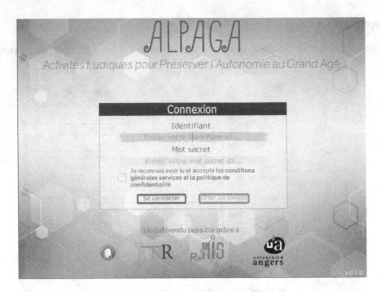

Fig. 2. Screenshot of the login interface.

Our software currently offers three mini-games: (i) a sorting game; (ii) a search-object game; (iii) a ball game (Fig. 3). The sorting game is designed to train the aerobic abilities of the upper limbs and, depending on the settings, the lateral, as well as the cognitive abilities related to categorization. In a virtual bathroom, a colored, light or dark garment is instantiated at the center of the screen. The patient must then touch the laundry basket associated with it. When it's done, another garment is instantiated. The number of clothing categories, the categories, and the positions of the corresponding baskets are configurable. In addition, this activity can be broken down into other scenes and categories of objects of everyday life to propose other levels of difficulty. In the bathroom environment, categorization is based on perceptual color criteria. In the kitchen, the categorization is based on criteria for locating items to be stored in a tempered closet or in the refrigerator. The object-finder game is more about cognitive stimulation. It takes place in a handyman's workshop. An object is instantiated at the center of the screen. The patient must then find and touch the object in the scene. Another mode of the game proposed to search for a pair associated with the presented object. When the patient has pointed at an object in the virtual environment, another object is instantiated. This activity can be broken down into other scenes and categories of objects of everyday life. The ball game is inspired by soccer of handball. It is designed to stimulate lower limbs and balance skills. The scene is located by the sea, on a soccer field or in a meadow. In the center of the upper part of the screen is displayed a soccer goal, and a ball is instantiated at the bottom center of the screen. The patient must shoot in the ball to score a goal.

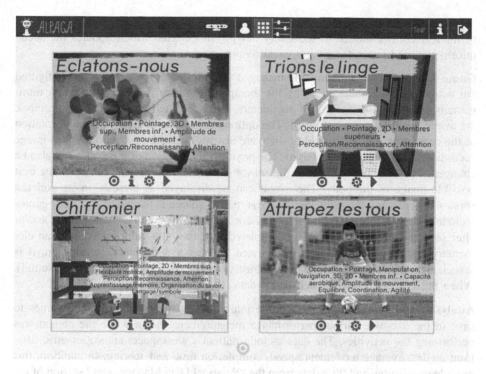

Fig. 3. Scene of Menus displaying the showcase of the proposed mini-games.

3.5 Functional Modules

Apart from the graphic part, the system has 3 functional modules: (i) a game module that offers various fun and customizable activities; (ii) an interaction system, which allows the capture and tracking of the user's body and harvesting information such as the orientation of the joints; (iii) a data analysis module.

Interaction Module. User can control an avatar (humanoid or virtual body points) to interact in the game. The interaction module is composed of the Astra Pro™ opto-electronic device that captures the RGB-D data about the environment. This data is sent to the motion tracking module, which extracts information such as the position and orientation of the user's body joints. The data extraction module is used to generate an artificial skeleton used to animate the virtual avatar instantiated in the scene and to interact with the environment.

The interaction module makes it possible to project the 3D information on the screen and in the 3D virtual space. Of course, different interaction techniques are proposed depending on the mini-game considered. Basically, the techniques are based on the distance between one or more points of interest from the avatar and objects of interest from the virtual environment (e.g., between foot and ball, between the hand and a laundry basket). The selection is made when the user holds her hand over the object for a certain duration, defined in the Global Parameters sub-menu (Fig. 1). In some mini-games, such as soccer, the interaction module manages dynamic objects subject to physical laws (gravity), which can be moved by the user. Collisions of virtual objects of interest are transmitted to the Unity 3D physics engine which updates the scene information and generates the graphical output.

Game Module. The game module manages the mini-games which are preconfigured but which can be parameterized by the therapist accompanying the resident. A mini-game is defined by several sets of parameters, those relating to the angle of the camera, the avatar, and the mini-game itself. The options for changing the position and rotation of the camera as well as its field of view are always available to obtain the best image according to the display device used. The position and rotation of the avatar can also be changed. Thus, the user can move the sensor (rotation and distance) to obtain the best possible image of the body. The avatar can be displayed as a mesh, in its skeleton version, or only as a set of interactive areas (e.g., a sphere at the hand). All mini-games include a stop parameter option: activities can stop after a certain amount of time and/or after several basic tasks have been completed. For the mini-games described, an elementary task corresponds to an instantiated and processed object. In addition, it is associated with a set of measures (e.g., objects found) and triggers effects (e.g., sound). When the stop condition is reached, the data is saved in the database.

Analysis Module. The analysis module intervenes at the end of the mini-games to save in the database various performance measurements taken while the patient was performing the activities. The data include patient's workspace, anthropometric data, joint angles, average movement speed, completion time and scoring. In addition, this module can display and filter data from the "Personal Data Management" section of the scene of Menus.

4   Conclusion

To support men and women institutionalized in long-term care is a challenge that is both ethical and technical. Professional caregivers work daily to make each residents' day better. In this project, a participative method was used to design the system. Developments also strives to maintain our financial independence. The next step is to assess acceptability, accessibility and interest of our system. Nonetheless, perfect our health care system will stay difficult, without placing old-age as a public priority, and without helping institutions to promote the social and therapeutic roles of caregivers.

Acknowledgments. This research received a financial support from the grant n° ANR-11-IDFI-0033, obtained from IDEFI by the Réseau des Écoles de Management et d'Ingénierie de la Santé (www.idefi-remis.fr), a network of schools in health management and engineering.

I am immensely grateful to the specialist in psychomotricity for sharing her wisdom with us during this research. I am also grateful La Retraite, a nursing home in Angers, France, for its collaboration. I thank Paul Richard for his contribution (primary translator).

References

1. Arnaldi, B., Fuchs, P., Tisseau, J.: In: Fuchs, P., Moreau, G. and Guitton, P. (ed.) Virtual Reality: Concepts and Technologies, pp. 3–10. Taylor and Francis, London (2003)
2. Holup, A.A., Hyer, K., Meng, H., Volicer, L.: Profile of nursing home residents admitted directly from home. J. Am. Med. Dir. Assoc. **18**, 131–137 (2017)
3. Muller, M.: 728 000 résidents en établissements d'hébergement pour personnes âgées en 2015 (2017)
4. Doupe, M., et al.: Profiling the multidimensional needs of new nursing home residents: evidence to support planning. J. Am. Med. Dir. Assoc. **13**(487), e9–487.e17 (2012)
5. Makdessi, Y., Pradines, N.: En EHPAD, les résidents les plus dépendants souffrent davantage de pathologies aiguës - Données brutes. In: Études et Résultats (2016)
6. Iliffe, S., et al.: EVIDEM-EoL: quality of care at the end of life. In: Changing practice in dementia care in the community: developing and testing evidence-based interventions, from timely diagnosis to end of life (EVIDEM), pp. 107–138. NIHR Journals Library, Southampton, UK (2015)
7. HAS: Retour d'expérience sur les événements indésirables graves associés à des soins (EIGS) – Rapport annuel d'activité 2017, Saint-Denis-La Plaine, France (2018)
8. Teigné, D., Lucas, M., Leclère, B., Moret, L., Terrien, N.: Panorama des domaines de risques associés aux soins en EHPAD. Geriatr. Psychol. Neuropsychiatr. Vieil. **15**, 117–126 (2017)
9. Terroso, M., Rosa, N., Torres Marques, A., Simoes, R.: Physical consequences of falls in the elderly: a literature review from 1995 to 2010. Eur. Rev. Aging Phys. Act. **11**, 51–59 (2014)
10. Stevens, J.A., Corso, P.S., Finkelstein, E.A., Miller, T.R.: The costs of fatal and non-fatal falls among older adults. Inj. Prev. **12**, 290–295 (2006)
11. Aranda-Gallardo, M., et al.: Characteristics, consequences and prevention of falls in institutionalised older adults in the province of Malaga (Spain): a prospective, cohort, multicentre study. BMJ Open **8**, e020039 (2018)
12. Pin, S., Spini, D.: Impact of falling on social participation and social support trajectories in a middle-aged and elderly European sample. SSM - Popul. Heal. **2**, 382–389 (2016)
13. Grönstedt, H., et al.: Effects of individually tailored physical and daily activities in nursing home residents on activities of daily living, physical performance and physical activity level: a randomized controlled trial. Gerontology **59**, 220–229 (2013)
14. Gillespie, L.D., et al.: Interventions for preventing falls in older people living in the community. Cochrane Database Syst. Rev. (2012)
15. Rusted, J., Sheppard, L.: Action-based memory in Alzheimer's disease: a longitudinal look at tea making. Neurocase **8**, 111–126 (2002)
16. Lamotte, G., Shah, R.C., Lazarov, O., Corcos, D.M.: Exercise training for persons with alzheimer's disease and caregivers: a review of dyadic exercise interventions. J. Mot. Behav. **49**, 365–377 (2017)
17. Tennstedt, S.L., Unverzagt, F.W.: The ACTIVE study. J. Aging Health **25**, 3S–20S (2013)
18. Orgeta, V., Miranda-Castillo, C.: Does physical activity reduce burden in carers of people with dementia? a literature review. Int. J. Geriatr. Psychiatry **29**, 771–783 (2014)
19. Groult, S., Chazal, J.: La vie sociale des résidents en EHPA dans «La vie en établissement d'hébergement pour personnes âgées du point de vue des résidents et de leurs proches». Dossiers Solidar. santé. **18**, 52–59 (2011)
20. Harper Ice, G.: Daily life in a nursing home. J. Aging Stud. **16**, 345–359 (2002)
21. Egerton, T., Brauer, S.G.: Temporal characteristics of habitual physical activity periods among older adults. J. Phys. Act. Health **6**, 644–650 (2009)

22. Bates-Jensen, B.M., et al.: The minimum data set bedfast quality indicator: differences among nursing homes. Nurs. Res. **53**, 260–272 (2004)
23. Benjamin, K., Edwards, N., Ploeg, J., Legault, F.: Barriers to physical activity and restorative care for residents in long-term care: a review of the literature. J. Aging Phys. Act. **22**, 154–165 (2014)
24. De Souto Barreto, P., Demougeot, L., Vellas, B., Rolland, Y.: How much exercise are older adults living in nursing homes doing in daily life? A cross-sectional study. J. Sports Sci. **33**, 116–124 (2015)
25. Tak, S.H., Kedia, S., Tongumpun, T.M., Hong, S.H.: Activity engagement: perspectives from nursing home residents with dementia. Educ. Gerontol. **41**, 182–192 (2015)
26. Cherney, C., Yee-Melichar, D.: Nursing Home Federal Requirements: Guidelines to Surveyors and Survey Protocols (8th Ed.) By James E. Allen. Educ. Gerontol. **41**, 683–684 (2015)
27. Buettner, L., Kolanowski, A.: Practice guidelines for recreation therapy in the care of people with dementia (CE). Geriatr. Nurs. (Minneap) **24**, 18–25 (2003)
28. Bazin, M., Muller, M.: Le personnel et les difficultés de recrutement dans les Ehpad. Études et Résultats, 1067 (2018)
29. Hentic-Giliberto, M., Stephan, S.: Les impacts du vieillissement de la population française sur les systèmes sanitaires et médico-sociaux: une analyse des revues académiques et professionnelles depuis la loi ASV. Manag. Avenir Santé **4**, 99 (2018)
30. Bonne, B.: Rapport d'information n° 341, Paris, FR (2018)
31. Resnick, B., et al.: Barriers and benefits to implementing a restorative care intervention in nursing homes. J. Am. Med. Dir. Assoc. **9**, 102–108 (2008)
32. Jennings, A.A., Linehan, M., Foley, T.: The knowledge and attitudes of general practitioners to the assessment and management of pain in people with dementia. BMC Fam. Pract. **19**, 166 (2018)
33. Bryan, K., Axelrod, L., Maxim, J., Bell, L., Jordan, L.: Working with older people with communication difficulties: an evaluation of care worker training. Aging Ment. Health **6**, 248–254 (2002)
34. Castle, N.G., Engberg, J.: Staff turnover and quality of care in nursing homes. Med. Care **43**, 616–626 (2005)
35. CREAI d'Aquitaine: Enquête qualité régionale EQARS-EHPAD - Rapport de synthèse, Bordeaux, France (2014)
36. Cordella, F., Di Corato, F., Zollo, L., Siciliano, B., van der Smagt, P.: Patient performance evaluation using Kinect and Monte Carlo-based finger tracking. In: 2012 4th IEEE RAS & EMBS International Conference on Biomedical Robotics and Biomechatronics (BioRob), pp. 1967–1972. IEEE (2012)
37. Burdea, G.C.: Virtual rehabilitation: benefits and challenges. Methods Inf. Med. **42**, 519–523 (2003)
38. Henderson, A., Korner-Bitensky, N., Levin, M.: Virtual reality in stroke rehabilitation: a systematic review of its effectiveness for upper limb motor recovery. Top. Stroke Rehabil. **14**, 52–61 (2007)
39. Holden, M.K.: Virtual environment for motor rehabilitation: review. Cyberpsychol. Behav. **8**, 187–211 (2005)
40. Sanchez-Vives, M.V., Slater, M.: From presence to consciousness through virtual reality. Nat. Rev. Neurosci. **6**, 332–339 (2005)
41. Smith, C.M., Read, J.E., Bennie, C., Hale, L.A., Milosavljevic, S.: Can non-immersive virtual reality improve physical outcomes of rehabilitation? Phys. Ther. Rev. **17**, 1–15 (2012)

42. Luis, M.A.V.S., Atienza, R.O., Luis, A.M.S.: Immersive virtual reality as a supplement in the rehabilitation program of post-stroke patients. In: 2016 10th International Conference on Next Generation Mobile Applications, Security and Technologies (NGMAST), pp. 47–52. IEEE (2016)
43. Cameirao, M.S., Bermudez i Badia, S., Oller, E.D., Verschure, P.F.M.J.: Using a multi-task adaptive VR system for upper limb rehabilitation in the acute phase of stroke. In: 2008 IEEE Symposium on Virtual Rehabilitation, pp. 2–7. IEEE (2008)
44. Stewart, J.C., et al.: Intervention to enhance skilled arm and hand movements after stroke: a feasibility study using a new virtual reality system. J. Neuroeng. Rehabil. **4**, 21 (2007)
45. Saposnik, G., et al.: Efficacy and safety of non-immersive virtual reality exercising in stroke rehabilitation (EVREST): a randomised, multicentre, single-blind, controlled trial. Lancet Neurol. **15**, 1019–1027 (2016)
46. Cai, Z., et al.: Design & control of a 3D stroke rehabilitation platform. In: 2011 IEEE International Conference on Rehabilation Robotics, pp. 1–6 (2011)
47. Arip, E.S.M., Ismail, W., Nordin, M.J., Radman, A.: Virtual reality rehabilitation for stroke patients: recent review and research issues. In: AIP Conference Proceedings, p. 050007 (2017)
48. Webster, D., Celik, O.: Systematic review of Kinect applications in elderly care and stroke rehabilitation. J. Neuroeng. Rehabil. **11**, 108 (2014)
49. Vit, A., Shani, G.: Comparing RGB-D sensors for close range outdoor agricultural phenotyping. Sensors **18**, 4413 (2018)
50. Orbbec: 关于 - 让所有终端都能看懂世界. http://www.orbbec.com.cn/sys/cate/16.html
51. Pintor, A.B.: A Rigid 3D registration framework of women body RGB-D images (2016)

Extraction of New Guideline Items from the View Point of ELSI (Ethics, Legal, Social Issues) for Service Utilized AI–Focus on Healthcare Area

Shin'ichi Fukuzumi[1], Mariko Jinno[2], Kasumi Inagaki[2],
Haruka Maeda[3(✉)], Takuya Mizukami[3(✉)], and Osamu Sakura[3(✉)]

[1] RIKEN, Tokyo, Japan
Shin-ichi.fukuzumi@riken.jp
[2] NEC Corporation, Tokyo, Japan
[3] University of Tokyo, Tokyo, Japan

Abstract. The purpose of this study is to extract new guideline items about Artificial Intelligence (AI) development by analyzing ELSI (Ethics, Legal, Social Issues) focuses on service utilized AI from the view point of service provider and service user. Use case (sample service) in healthcare area is considered and interview related to this service is carried out. From the result of the interview and analysis, five guideline items modified from original AI development guideline and seven new guideline items are extracted. After that, questionnaire tests about these services were carried out for 268 IT company employees. From the results, validation of the new guideline items was verified.

Keywords: Artificial Intelligence (AI) · ELSI · Service · Human-centered

1 Introduction

In Technology of Artificial Intelligence (AI) develops rapidly, in future, AI is considered to be able to move and judge autonomously and to instruct and suggest to society and human. Interaction methods between human and AI/robot also becomes to change [1]. When such a thing becomes the reality, for society and human, to accept instruct and suggest by AI which is to be possible to realize, it is necessary to clarify and to solve ethical, legal and social issues (ELSI) which will occur in the future [2, 3].

One of the reasons of these occurrences are considered that conventional experience and user experience don't work [4]. There are many development guideline about new technology like AI [5, 6], however, guideline in the view point of users or services like Human-centered design [7] has not been appeared yet. Recently, standardization about ergonomics interaction with robot intelligence and autonomous systems (RIAS) are discussed and prepared by ISO [8]. But they shows the concept of interaction, so, details will be published future.

The purpose of this study is to extract new guideline items about AI development by analyzing ELSI (Ethics, Legal, Social Issues) focuses on service utilized AI from the view point of service provider and service user.

S. Yamamoto and H. Mori (Eds.): HCII 2019, LNCS 11570, pp. 482–491, 2019.
https://doi.org/10.1007/978-3-030-22649-7_38

This time, service which AI was buried in is proposed, and to generalize new guideline items from extracted ELSI issues is tried.

To consider these issues, we have to pay attention who are users of AI.

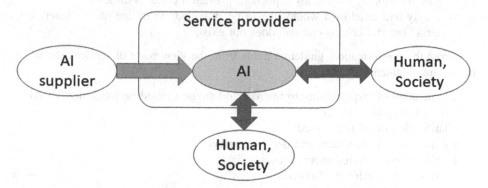

Fig. 1. Relationship among AI, AI supplier and uses [9]

This Fig. 1 shows the relationship among AI, AI supplier and uses (human, society). In detail, these relationships could be described as follows:

- Society/users receive some service by interacting AI directly
- Society/users interact AI intensively or not
- Society/users receive some service from AI without their intension
- Society/users interact with organizations or service provider includes AI

If we discuss intelligent system like AI (includes robot with intelligence), we have to consider all situation described above.

2   Pre Investigation/Interview

Before extracting ELSI issues in AI, interview about issues during cooperation with business section was carried out to five managers in AI research teams who considering business plan of AI technology. Results are listed as follows:

- Property rights/area
  - AI researchers/engineers cannot collect data freely
  - AI researchers/engineers cannot install camera without blind spot
  - It is difficult to judge justification of monitoring in shopping center
  - Police investigation cannot be used GPS data
- Handling of data
  - AI researchers/engineers can use privacy data if they can show merit to data provider (effect, value)
  - AI researchers/engineers can use privacy data if they can promise providers' safety

- It is unpleasant feeling not to know how data are treated
- It is not allowed that data connect to individuals
- About system solution
  - Can AI diagnose or not. If can, is the result able to trust?
  - The monitoring from many aspects to prevent a crime is difficult
  - Safety and relief/trust would like to be provided. There are many "safety criteria" but "relief/trust criteria" does not exist.

From these information, guideline items from the view point of services shown in below are obtained

- Clarification of responsibility to instruct and suggest based on judgement of AI
- Transparency as a service
- Clarification of AI being used
- Clarification of judgement and decision maker
- Clarification of merit/demerit to users
- Clarification of relief/trust criteria

3 Service Proposal

In this research, we focused on healthcare domain where it is thought that there may be many ELSI problems when applied AI. Table 1 shows the type of assumption users, their feature and assumption services.

Table 1. The type of assumption users for medical AI service.

User type	Characteristics	Service
1. Unawareness * health	Not necessary to go to a hospital	Service to let you feel it to be uneasy
II. Unawareness * sick	Not notice one's disease (if notice, will go to a hospital)	Automatic diagnosis + alert
III. Awareness * health IV. Awareness * sick (not go to a hospital)	Not want to go to a hospital (busy, too far, troublesome, not want to accept one's disease)	Go to a hospital: let mind it. A school and a company cope to go to a hospital.

In this, as III and IV are able to realize as services, use case and service will be proposed by focusing to these types, especially type IV.

We considered a service which suggests them to go to hospital when their physical condition is not so good. As a result, new service are proposed as follows:

(1) Information related to physical condition are drawn up automatically at convenience store which target users usually use, and their information are distributed to their home or municipality.

(2) Information related to physical condition of employees are drawn up automatically at entrance gate of office or first log-in every morning, suggest to go to healthcare center in the office or inform to their bosses.

In these two services, about (1), consideration as a service is not enough, for example, a problem about information management and persons or organizations who invests this service. On the other hand, about (2), business impact which are extraction of negative factor to business which employees whose physical condition are not good continue to work and immediate formation change could be clarified. So, this service was concluded to be targeted for investment by company. From this, the service are dealt with as a use case (Fig. 2).

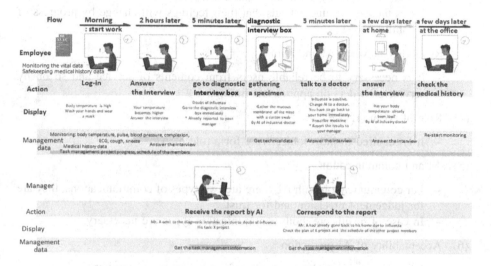

Fig. 2. Service blue print related to employee's healthcare by AI

4   Service Evaluation About ELSI

About this service, interview was carried out to five employees seem to be use this service for extracting ELSI. Their characteristics are as follows:

Gender: four male and one female

Type of job: four engineers related to AI (one manager) and one clerical

All of them don't want to go to the hospital and they don't have any medical history that they want to conceal.

This time, we proposed a sample service of auto-diagnosis in healthcare area. To assume this service to office worker, there may be a lot of ELSI. To extract these issues, brain storming in our research team consists of designer, social science researcher and human factors researcher and interview related to this service is carried out.

From the result of the interview and analysis, five guideline items modified from original AI development guideline and seven new guideline items are extracted. Total eleven guideline items are listed below.

(1) Consider diversity of use case

- It is important for developers to notice that there are problems which judgment is divided by users.
- Problems which judgment is divided by users should be clustered by expert for providing service.

(2) Permeation of comprehensive for AI

- In case that it is difficult to understand service image, e.g. AI is used for a diagnosis, opinions may be changed when service will be pervasive.
- Even though service using AI includes a hesitation, feeling for the service may be changed by continuous and used.
- Users themselves understands that their feelings will change by progress of reliability to AI.

(3) Reliability between AI and human

- It is necessary to be reliable users from contents of service and so on by service providers on appropriate timing.

(4) Role of AI in service

- It is required to judge objectively for a role of AI

(5) AI and communication

- For communication with AI, there are two types of communications, they are for judgement precision and for trust
- In case of healthcare, both communication types are necessary.

(6) Acceptability of AI prediction

- It is likely to occur loathsomeness for labeling by AI prediction.
- Loathsomeness may occur by relationship between users and AI

(7) Self authority

- In related to disclose for personal users data, they can decide their contents and the range of disclosure by themselves.

(8) Cooperation in service

- Smooth cooperation and data sharing shall be required among AIs which have same theme and purpose

(9) Privacy

- There is little feeling of resistance to deposit their own data to administrative.
- There are some items which do not want to be known, they are, privacy related to personal data and related to be sick and physical condition.

(10) Ethics

  – There are ethical index and items which needs agreement for usage of primary data and forecasting data (analysis results).

(11) User support

  – An escape or help are necessary in case of feel inconvenience when user personal data was collected really.
  – User interface/Human interface which users are easy to communicate with AI shall be prepared

(12) Accountability

  – Intention to collect personal data is necessary to be clear and reasonable.
  – Merit to be collected personal data by AI is necessary to be able to imagine.
  – It is necessary to clarify remaining data.
  – It is necessary to clarify the necessity to remain data
  – Procedure of informed consent and agreement are mandatory
  – Even if this procedure are carried out, sometimes usage except agreement is doubted.

In these, acceptability is one of important elements to consider ergonomics of AI. Acceptability is influenced by social/society needs based on culture, ethics, religion, and so on. If we can extend human centered design (HCD) concept to social/society, it is useful to deal with not only acceptability of robot to social/society but also ergonomics of AI.

5 Verification of the Guideline

To verify the reliability of the new guideline, questionnaire about ELSI points according to service and contents of each guideline was carried out to 268 employees in an IT company. Parts of questionnaire are as follows (Table 2):

Table 2. Questionnaire list for evaluating validity of guideline items

No.	Question items
1.	What do you feel about diagnosis interview by AI?
2.	What do you think about the instruction from AI that you should go to the diagnosis interview box due to the doubt of influenza?
3.	What do you think that AI reports your condition about doubt of influenza to your manager?
4.	What do you think that doctor changes from AI to human during your medical examination?
5.	What do you think that AI reports the result of your medical examination to your manager automatically?
6.	What do you think about monitoring your vital data (heart rate, body temperature, etc.) by AI?

The results are shown in Table 3, 4, 5, 6, 7 and 8.

Table 3. Results for question No. 3.

What do you feel about diagnosis interview by AI? (multiple answers allowed)

MA	Number of answer	Ratio (%)	Related guideline number
Sense of incongruity for Interviewed by AI	24	9.0	
Won't answer to interview by AI during the work	41	15.3	
If not so many items, will answer the interview by AI	211	78.7	(1), (8)
It's happy to suggest disorder of my physical condition that I don't notice	179	66.8	(4)
It seems good that I can answer to AI easily	68	25.4	
Others	28	10.4	

Table 4. Results for question No. 4.

What do you think about the instruction from AI that you should go to the diagnosis interview box due to the doubt of influenza? (multiple answers allowed)

MA	Number of answer	Ratio (%)	Related guideline number
Sense of incongruity for Interviewed by AI	26	9.7	
It seems good that I can recognize the doubt of influenza at my desk	132	49.3	
It seems good that I can receive suitable instruction by AI objectively	146	54.5	(4)
I will go to the medical box according to the AI direction in consideration of the influence on rotation	181	67.5	(6), (7)
I will not go to the medical box against the instruction of AI if it is doubt degree	26	9.7	
I will not go to the medical box because the medical examination of AI seems not to be reliable.	14	5.2	
I will not go to the medical box because there is net compelling force in the instruction by AI	17	6.3	
Others	33	12.3	

Table 5. Results for question No. 5.

What do you think that AI reports your condition about doubt of influenza to your manager? (multiple answers allowed)

MA	Number of answer	Ratio (%)	Related guideline number
It seems better that AI reports the condition to manager than myself	102	38.1	
I would like to decide whether report to manager or not if it is doubt degree	72	26.9	
If influenza, I allow AI to report my condition to my manager, However, do not report without permission if the disease that does not want to be known around	185	69.0	(9), (10)
Others	23	8.6	

Table 6. Results for question No. 6.

What do you think that doctor changes from AI to human during your medical examination? (multipie answers allowed)

MA	Number of answer	Ratio (%)	Related guideline number
It seems reliable to talk to human doctor though only AI is anxious	183	68.3	(3), (5)
Human doctor is better than AI because it is difficult to communicate with AI	39	14.6	
Human doctor is better because the results of medical examination by AI is not reliable	21	7.8	
AI doctor is better because accuracy of the medical examination seems higher than human doctor	19	7.1	
AI doctor is better because not influenced by the affinity	23	8.6	
I would like human doctor to have a responsibility of the result of the medical examination	119	44.4	
Others	42	15.7	

Analyzing these tables, the items obtained 50% or more are related to all guideline items extracted in Sect. 4 (except No. 11). And about No. 11, as this item is related to usability, it is mandatory requirement for using service.

From these results, the guideline items extract in Sect. 4 seems to be valid.

Table 7. Results for question No. 7.

What do you think that AI reports the result of your medical examination to your manager automatically? (multiple answers allowed)

MA	Number of answer	Ratio (%)	Related guideline number
It seems better to report AI to manager	98	36.6	
I would like to decide whether report of the result of the medical examination to manager or not	78	29.1	
If influenza, I allow AI to report my condition to my manager. However, do not report without permission if the disease that does not want to be known around	178	66.4	(9), (10)
Others	28	10.4	

Table 8. Results for question No. 8.

What do you think about monitoring your vital data (heart rate body temperature, etc) by AI? (multiple answers allowed)

MA	Number of answer	Ratio (%)	Related guideline number
No problem	83	31.0	
There is no sense of incongruity because items are similar to periodical health	157	58.6	(2)
It is uncomfortable to monitor vital data constantly because it is not a periodical health examination	69	25.7	
I would not like to check my health by organization even though a periodical health examination	14	5.2	
It is not good that vital data may be checked by manager and human resource division	72	26.9	
I would like to choose monitoring items before collecting data	102	38.1	
It is necessary to be known monitoring items, usage and user of these data before collecting	180	67.2	(12)
Others	30	11.2	

6 Conclusion

This research shows the AI related guideline from the view point of user and service. They are different from any guideline from the view point of development. This time, target service is only healthcare area and our proposed service. To the future, we will apply this guideline to the other service area and enlarge application area.

References

1. Kosinski, M., Wang, Y.: Deep neural networks are more accurate than humans at detecting sexual orientation from facial images. J. Pers. Soc. Psychol. **114**(2), 246–257 (2018). ISO9241-210: Human-centred design for interactive systems (2010)
2. https://www.theguardian.com/technology/2016/mar/24/tay-microsofts-ai-chatbot-gets-a-crash-course-in-racism-from-twitter. Accessed 27 Feb 2019
3. https://www.nytimes.com/2018/03/19/technology/uber-driverless-fatality.html. 27 Feb 2019
4. Roto, V., Law, E., Vermeeren, A., Hoonhout, J. (ed.): Use experience white paper - bringing clarity to the concept of user experience. In: Result From Dagstuhl Seminar on Demarcating User Experience, 15–18 September 2010, pp. 1–12 (20100
5. IEEE: Global initiative for Ethical Considerations in Artificial Intelligence and Autonomous Systems (2018)
6. Ministry of internal affairs and communications in Japan: AI development guideline (2018) (in Japanese)
7. ISO; fDIS9241-210: Ergonomics of human–system interaction—Part 210: Human-centred design for interactive systems (2019)
8. ISO: PDTR9241-810: Ergonomics—Ergonomics of human-system interaction—Part 810: Human-system issues of robotic, intelligent and autonomous systems (2019)
9. Fukuzumi, S., et al.: Extraction of new guideline items from the view point of ELSI (Ethics, Legal, Social Issues) for service utilized AI – focus on healthcare area. In: 32nd Domestic Conference on Japanese Society for Artificial Intelligence, 3H1-OS-25a-04 (2018). (in Japanese)

Development of a Promotion System for Home-Based Squat Training for Elderly People

Yuki Hirasawa[1], Takuya Ishioka[2], Naka Gotoda[3], Kosuke Hirata[1,4], and Ryota Akagi[1(✉)]

[1] Shibaura Institute of Technology, 307 Fukasaku, Minuma-ku, Saitama-shi, Saitama 337-8570, Japan
rakagi12@shibaura-it.ac.jp
[2] Kagawa University, 2217-20 Hayashi-cho, Takamatsu-shi, Kagawa 761-0396, Japan
[3] Kagawa University, 1-1 Saiwai-cho, Takamatsu-shi, Kagawa 760-8521, Japan
[4] Japan Society for the Promotion of Science, 5-3-1 Kojimachi, Chiyoda-ku, Tokyo 102-0083, Japan

Abstract. The mass and strength of skeletal muscles decrease with increasing age, especially those of the knee extensor muscles. For elderly people, the decrease in force-generation capability of the knee extensor muscles reduces their ability to perform activities of daily life. Hence, the maintenance and/or improvement of knee extensor muscle strength is very important for elderly individuals. Home-based squat training without any special equipment or venue is considered to be useful for preventing age-related decreases in strength of the knee extensor muscles. The current study was designed to develop an administration system for elderly people to routinely perform body mass-based squat training at home. The characteristics of the new system are the use of onomatopoeia to allow participants to self-check their movements during squat training, and the provision of feedback functions for maintaining motivation towards the training. We performed an experiment to test the validity of our vision using a pilot version of the administration system. However, clear effectiveness of our proposed system was not proven. In this experiment, we used onomatopoeia for only one position, despite the fact that onomatopoeia are useful for evaluating and focusing upon differences in movements involving multiple joints. Hence, it is reasonable to assume that the full benefit of onomatopoeia was not realized with the current experimental design. Judging from the current results, our plan related to this system requires further refinements.

Keywords: Video annotation · Onomatopoeia deformation · Advice feedback · Muscle mass and strength

1 Introduction

It is well known that the mass and strength of skeletal muscles decrease with increasing age, especially those of the knee extensor muscles (Candow and Chilibeck 2005; Kubo et al. 2007; Overend et al. 1992). For elderly people, the decrease in force-generation capability of the knee extensor muscles reduces their ability to perform activities of

© Springer Nature Switzerland AG 2019
S. Yamamoto and H. Mori (Eds.): HCII 2019, LNCS 11570, pp. 492–501, 2019.
https://doi.org/10.1007/978-3-030-22649-7_39

daily life, such as walking (Kim et al. 2000) and standing up from a chair (Hughes et al. 1996). Hence, the maintenance and/or improvement of knee extensor muscle strength is important for elderly individuals.

Resistance training is effective for preventing this age-related decrease in muscle strength. For example, many people may consider going to a training gym to routinely perform resistance training, because of the availability of special equipment and professional trainers. However, this is not convenient or practical for everybody. In addition, for people without the appropriate knowledge of resistance training methods, it can be dangerous to perform resistance training using such equipment. Taken together, resistance training at a training gym is not a universal solution, especially for elderly people.

There is a possibility that squat training improves the strength of the knee extensor muscles. Here, we investigated the effectiveness of promoting body mass squat training at home and without special equipment, in order to reduce injury risks, while facilitating continuation of the training. Our previous study (Ema et al. 2017) identified two problems with such resistance training: (1) Elderly people cannot easily check their own movements during squat training, and (2) It is difficult for elderly people to maintain their motivation towards home-based squat training. In order to address these problems, the current study aimed to develop a new promotion system for home-based squat training that includes automated feedback and support.

Performing squat training with correct form is important for reducing the risk of injury and maximizing the training effect. Hence, a system that enables users to objectively confirm their training motion is thus desirable. A smartphone or tablet can easily be used to capture moving images while performing the home-based squat training. Moreover, if an objective evaluation of the motion during exercise is automatically generated, based on the moving images, users can check their own motion. In addition, users should be able to easily interpret the evaluation of the motion. One possible approach to help with users' comprehension is to use onomatopoeia. Onomatopoeia are words whose sound is imitative of a sound made by or associated with its referent, such as "bang", "bow-wow", etc. In the new system, we incorporated onomatopoeia in a video of squat training recorded using a smartphone and/or a tablet camera. Moreover, we tried to maintain the motivation for users to train, because training interruption can induce a decrease in muscle strength among elderly individuals. The current study thus aimed to develop an administration system for elderly individuals to routinely perform body mass-based squat training at home.

2 System Summary

2.1 Sensors

A method for monitoring the speed of body movements in training is required, because the relationship between the speed and comprehension of onomatopoeia is a significant point on the feedback video. In order to obtain the speed data, we designed a wearable device incorporating 3-axis magnetic accelerometers and gravity sensors, to evaluate joint position, angle, angular velocity and acceleration. We also considered affordability and ease-of-use in the device and interface design, as follows: (1) the sensor and the video environment are easy to obtain; (2) the price of the sensor and the video system are low; (3) the sensors are small enough to affix to the hip and knee joints; (4) the video system can be easily installed; and (5) manipulation of the sensors and the video can be managed by elderly individuals. We used hook-and-loop fastener tape for the sensors, to make them easily attachable and detachable, and adopted video capture equipment such as a smartphone on a tripod or a webcam for visual monitoring.

2.2   Onomatopoeia

Based on the sensor data, our system generates a visual transformation in which the shape or size of a relatable image, i.e., the characters of onomatopoeia, changes as a training hint, assisting comprehension of the correct or required movement. First, because our system is used for squat exercises, we selected the word "Gu" as the onomatopoeia because this word can enable Japanese users to instinctively evaluate the degree of their effort. The displayed character size and shape transform according to the joint angle and its change, respectively. For example, if a joint is flexed rapidly, a large and thin letter is displayed, and vice versa. Additionally, the color of the character changes based on the presence or absence of motion. A red character is used during squatting, and a green character when standing. These visual effects were intended to help users understand their body posture and movement speed. Furthermore, by imparting onomatopoeia to each of the joints involved in the physical exercise, users can obtain information about each joint motion and can understand the overall motion of their bodies. Therefore, the onomatopoeia transformation can express differences in the movements of plural joints by using different sizes, speeds and angles.

As shown in Fig. 1, the user's squatting motion and characters of onomatopoeia for each joint are simultaneously displayed on the screen of a smartphone or tablet with our web application installed. Users are able to check their overall motion from the squat animation displayed on the left side. The web application has a zoom function that enables users to easily distinguish the precise differences between joint motions based on the changes in character size and shape of onomatopoeia. By selecting a specific body part, an enlarged view of interest is displayed in the right side of the display. The degree of magnification can be adjusted using a slide bar.

2.3   Feedback

In addition to the combined use of animation and onomatopoeia, a real time feedback function was designed to help users visualize their efforts to train. As shown in Fig. 2, users record an animation with a smartphone or tablet. The video data are automatically transmitted to a cloud and onomatopoeia are added to the training motion of the animation data. After finishing the training session, the user can start a web application to confirm their motions with onomatopoeia. If they performed the squat exercise accurately, the character size of the onomatopoeia changes smoothly (Fig. 3(b)). The onomatopoeia shown in Fig. 3(a) indicates an inaccurate form during squat exercise. As shown in the conceptual diagram (Fig. 4), we can compare the two animations

Fig. 1. Screen of the web application installed in a tablet/smartphone

displayed on the web application: one is a sample animation of the experienced instructor, and the other is the users' animation during the squat exercise.

A second feedback function indicates the improvement of muscle strength. Users perform muscle strength testing every month using a dynamometer (CON-TREX MJ, PHYSIOMED, Germany) and the results are stored in the proposed system and shown as a graph. This function is designed to maintain and/or increase motivation regarding the continuation of home-based squat training among elderly users.

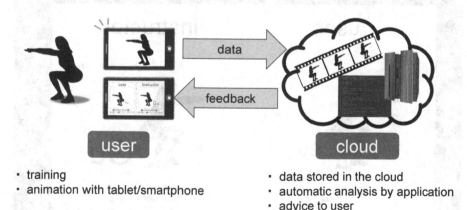

· training
· animation with tablet/smartphone

· data stored in the cloud
· automatic analysis by application
· advice to user

Fig. 2. Flow of the administration system

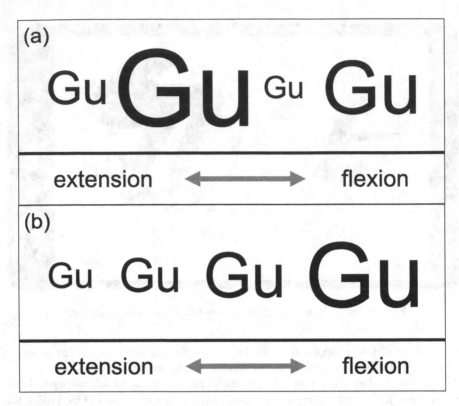

Fig. 3. Specific examples onomatopoeia of inaccurate form (a) and accurate form (b) during squat exercise

Fig. 4. Conceptual diagram of the two animations displayed on the web application

3 Pre-study

In the pre-study, we first verified the operation of the web application. The participant was a young male. To quantify the joint position and angular velocity during squatting, the sensor devices were attached to the greater trochanter, knee joint cleft and lateral malleolus. The participant performed several squat repetitions, and we recorded the motion.

The web application identified the sensors as the center of rotation of each joint, and detected the position and angular velocity of the sensors. Thus, we confirmed that the squat motion can be quantified appropriately by using the web application, and that an animation with onomatopoeia based on the device data of devices could be generated.

4 Experiment

4.1 Participants

Eight young men participated in the study (age: 23 ± 1 year; body height: 172.3 ± 5.8 cm; body mass: 65.3 ± 9.1 kg; mean $\pm$ standard deviation). The participants were divided randomly into two groups in order to evaluate the usefulness of the feedback function with onomatopoeia for improvement of squat motion. In both groups, the squat motion was recorded from a sagittal plane. In Group A, the participants were able to check their own motion using the feedback function, which displays the squat animation superimposed by numerical data of joint position and angular velocity (Fig. 5). In Group B, the squat animation with onomatopoeia, intended to help the user instinctively understand their joint position and angular velocity, was used as an alternate feedback function (Fig. 6). The character size of the onomatopoeia represented the joint angle and angular velocity. Specifically, the font size was small when the knee joint was extended, and increased in size with knee flexion. In addition, to indicate a standing position, the character color changed with hip position. When the device attached to greater trochanter was in the initial highest position (i.e., standing), the character became orange (Fig. 7). In other positions, the character was red (Fig. 8). The participants in this experiment had received no direct instruction on squat training from an athletic trainer, but they had some information about squat form.

4.2 Protocol

In order to evaluate the improvement of squat motion, all participants performed squat exercise four times for two days. Considering the difference in knee extensor strength between young and elderly individuals (Overend et al. 1992; Kubo et al. 2007), a 20 kg barbell was used as a load in this experiment. As in the pre-study, the sensor devices were attached to the greater trochanter, knee joint cleft and lateral malleolus. Before the squat training on the second day, the participants viewed their own motion from the first day using the feedback function. They then established a learning objective for the second day by comparing their own squat animations with numerical data (Group A) or

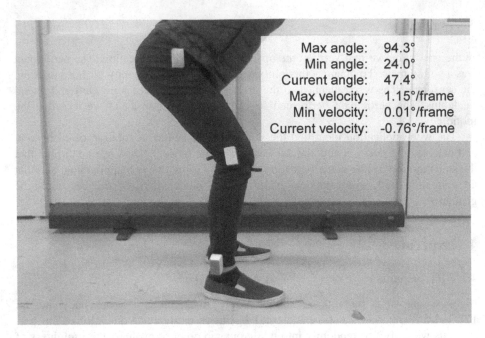

Fig. 5. Feedback by the animation and numerical data in Group A

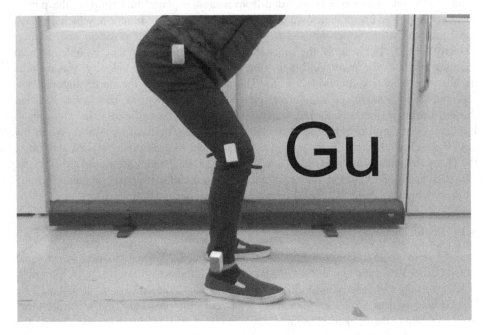

Fig. 6. Feedback by the animation and onomatopoeia in Group B

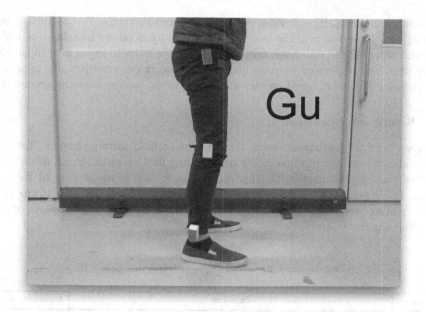

Fig. 7. Onomatopoeia at the standing position

Fig. 8. Onomatopoeia at large knee flexion angle

onomatopoeia (Group B) with those of the experienced instructor. For instance, if they felt that their hip position at the lowest point of the squat on the first day was higher than the posture of the instructor, they set an objective to try to lower their hips. After the training, we interviewed the participants as to what extent were they able to achieve their learning objective, based on viewing their training motion from the second day.

4.3   Results and Discussion

In Group A, three participants were able to achieve their learning targets (Table 1). They indicated that the position of the waist during the downward phase of the squat exercise was easy to understand. This seemed to be due to the display of the joint angles. In contrast, it was difficult for the members of Group A to perform squat exercises at a constant speed because of the time-course changes in the displays of joint angle and angular velocity.

Table 1. Learning objectives of Group A and Group B

Group A	Objective	Accomplishment
Subject A	To flex the knees while paying attention to the maximum knee joint angles	×
Subject B	To flex the knees while paying attention to the maximum knee joint angles	O
Subject C	To smoothly flex and extend the knees	O
Subject D	To keep the position relationship between the knees and the toes	O

Group B	Objective	Accomplishment
Subject E	To smoothly change the size of onomatopoeia	O
Subject F	To perform squat exercise at a regular speed	×
Subject G	To shorten the duration of the standing position	O
Subject H	To smoothly flex and extend the knees	×

In Group B, two participants were able to achieve their learning targets (Table 1). It was easy for the participants of Group B to instinctively understand the differences in motion during squat exercise between the downward and upward phases, because of the displayed onomatopoeia. However, two participants could not achieve their learning objectives. In this experiment, we displayed onomatopoeia in only one position. As described above, however, the use of onomatopoeia is effective for expressing differences in movements of plural joints. In other words, the full benefit of onomatopoeia may have been difficult to realize using the current experimental design. We thus could not demonstrate a clear difference in the usefulness of the system between Groups A and B.

5   Conclusion

We proposed a new administration system for elderly individuals to routinely perform body mass-based squat training at home. The characteristics of this system are to include onomatopoeia and real time or long-term feedback functions. Judging from the results of our experiment, however, our plan requires further refinements.

Acknowledgements. This study was partly supported by JSPS KAKENHI (Grant Number: JP17KK0174).

Conflict of Interest. The authors declare that this research was conducted in the absence of any commercial or financial relationships that could be construed as a potential conflict of interest.

References

Candow, D.G., Chilibeck, P.D.: Differences in size, strength, and power of upper and lower body muscle groups in young and older men. J. Gerontol. A Biol. Sci. Med. **60**, 148–156 (2005)

Ema, R., Ohki, S., Takayama, H., Kobayashi, Y., Akagi, R.: Effect of calf-raise training on rapid force production and balance ability in elderly men. J. Appl. Physiol. **123**, 424–433 (2017)

Fujino, Y., Kikkawa, M., Sagisaka, Y.: A collection of onomatopoeias in Japanese sports. In: Oriental COCOSDA International Cordinating Committee on Speech Datavases and Speech I/O System Assessment, pp. 160–164 (2003)

Hughes, M.A., Myers, B.S., Schenkman, M.L.: The role of strength in rising from a chair in the functionally impaired elderly. J. Biomech. **29**, 1509–1513 (1996)

Kim, J.D., et al.: Relationship between reduction of hip joint and thigh muscle and walking ability in elderly people. Jpn. J. Phys. Fitness Sports Med. **49**, 589–596 (2000). [In Japanese]

Kubo, K., Ishida, Y., Komuro, T., Tsunoda, N., Kanehisa, H., Fukunaga, T.: Age-related differences in the force generation capabilities and tendon extensibilities of knee extensors and plantar flexors in men. J. Gerontol. A Biol. Sci. Med. **62**, 1252–1258 (2007)

Overend, T.J., Cunningham, D.A., Kramer, J.F., Lefcoe, M.S., Paterson, D.H.: Knee extensor and knee flexor strength: cross-sectional area ratios in young and elderly men. J. Gerontol. **47**, M204–M210 (1992)

Designing Doctor–Patient–Machine System of Systems for Personalized Medicine

Tetsuya Maeshiro[1(✉)], Yuri Ozawa[2], and Midori Maeshiro[3]

[1] Faculty of Library, Information and Media Studies, University of Tsukuba,
Tsukuba 305-8550, Japan
`maeshiro@slis.tsukuba.ac.jp`
[2] Ozawa Clinic, Tokyo, Japan
[3] School of Music, Federal University of Rio de Janeiro, Rio de Janeiro, Brazil

Abstract. This paper presents a description of doctor–patient–machine as system of systems to design an integrated system for personalized medicine, the "haute-couture" medicine. We use the hypernetwork model that enables analyses of dynamic aspects of the system integrating the specifications of relationships described in the system. Multiple types of relationships can coexist in the same representation.

Keywords: Relationality · Description model ·
Quantitative relationship · Multiple viewpoints

1   Introduction

This paper discusses the necessary properties of the model to describe Doctor–Patient–Machine system of systems, the attributes of the functional interactions amond doctors, patients and machines, and the design of functional interactions of such system of sytems.

The primary objective of the doctor–patient–machine modeling is to establish the analytical and prediction framework of the well being and health care of the patient, which is a person. More specifically, two functions are necessary. The first one is the curing mechanism when some disease emerges and intervene with control if some deviation occurs, and the second one is the mechanism to maintain the present status within a predefined range of deviations.

This paper introduces two concepts, which are the dynamism of the structure reflecting the time sequence or changes in the time domain, and the blackbox element whose internal mechanism is unknown but its existence is certain or can be assumed. The dynamic structure requires the description of addition and deletion of elements of the system. This paper discusses the incorporation of the dynamism related to the time-domain aspect and the blackbox elements into the systems model.

© Springer Nature Switzerland AG 2019
S. Yamamoto and H. Mori (Eds.): HCII 2019, LNCS 11570, pp. 502–513, 2019.
https://doi.org/10.1007/978-3-030-22649-7_40

The presence of machine learning related techniques in clinical treatment environment is increasing with the advance of machine learning techniques, particularly after the development of the deep learning algorithm [1]. The use of machines in clinical environment will increase in the future and this direction is irreversible. Although the use of machines in today's conditions is limited to assist doctors, the patients will also be exposed to the machines present in the medical examination room in future. In this paper, the machine denotes an algorithm or an application embedded in a physical computing machine. A more accurate expression would be a software system, usually based on machine learning algorithms, that provide any kind of medical information that is useful for either doctor or patient in order to reach decisions related to the treatment of the patient.

2   Representation of Doctor–Patient–Machine System of Systems

Today, direct and concurrent interaction between doctor and machine during medical consultation is rare. Figure 1(A) illustrates the current stage of interactions in medical examination rooms, which is gradually changing to interaction shown in Fig. 1(B). The links indicate the interactions between the connected elements. In Fig. 1(B), the machine is basically hidden from the patient, and naturally the interactions between the doctor and the machine are also masked from the patient. The next stage will be the interaction structure shown in Fig. 1(C), where the machine interacts with both doctor and patient, indicated as links α and β. The interactions α and β are basically different. More advanced case will be Fig. 1(D), where the doctor and patient possess his own machine, possibly functioning constantly and not just during the medical consultation.

A typical conventional research project and system is IBM Watson [2], primarily targeting oncological treatments, mainly to suggest anticancer drugs. Other projects are similar. Conventional projects in machine assisted diagnoses and healthcare [3] rely on published trials and test results to match with the patient's current conditions for selecting treatment strategies. However, this is simply a larger scale version of the treatment details described in treatment guidelines recommended by medical councils and societies. Although this method can be interpreted to be a "personalized" if the genomic data are used because genomic data is personal, no life background and history of the patient is considered. Therefore, conventional personalized medicine is only partially personalized, and the crucial defect is that the life history of the patient has equivalent or more importance than patient's physical conditions when defining treatment strategy.

The interactions represented by links in Fig. 1 are different from conventional concept of interactions, which denote some kind of information or "matters" that are exchanged by the related entities. In this paper, the interaction denotes any kind of functional relationships necessary to implement the exchange of "matters" between the entities, besides the non-measureble "matters" and functional

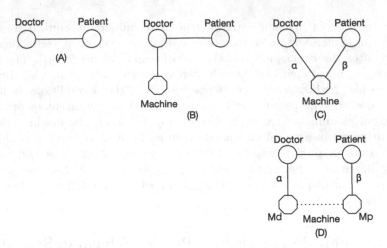

Fig. 1. Change of doctor–patient–machine interaction structure

elements necessary for functional relationship between the entities. Furthermore, we also differentiate the combination of binary interactions from N-ary interactions. This is another difference from conventional studies, partially due to the limited description capability of employed models, where any interaction is decomposed into a set of binary interactions.

Figure 2 illustrates the description of the integrated system of two systems, which are the doctor (human) described as a system and the machine described as a system. The thin circles represent the physical boundary (shape) of each system. Multiple viewpoints exist to describe and understand the integrated system. Figure 2 is an illustrative example of one of possible facets. It should be noted that the relationships between the human and the machine is directly connected to the components of the two systems (human and machine), and the set of these relationships constitute the integrated system of a given facet. Depending on the viewpoint, the thin circles become meaningless, as the integrated system is the result of often complex relationships between human and machine systems. The physical boundary is completely different from the boundary defined by functions, if such boundary can be defined.

The interactions α and β of Fig. 1(C) are different, as the doctor and patient not only requires different kinds of information, but even for the same data, information presentation or visualization are different for the doctor and the patient, as these two have different basic knowledge. In the more advanced case described in Fig. 1(D), the machine interacting with the doctor and the machine interacting with the patient can communicate directly without the intermediation of either doctor or patient. This type of communication is completely different from previous communications (Fig. 1), because although the machine communicates with human in Fig. 1(B) and (C), the communication of the machine is always with a human. On the other hand, the communication in Fig. 1(D) is more precisely an information exchange and functional interactions among machines without involving humans in the process. Therefore, all limitations imposed by human intervention is cleared, which is basically the (1) size limit, (2) speed limit and (3) functional merger. The first two are simple. The data size becomes limited by the storage capacity of the machines involved in the communication, so the primary data of images and structures that have considerable data size can be exchanged. In medical examinations, multiple images or structural data are generated, so the data size is high. The speed limit is similar, as the amount of transmitted data per unit time is order of magnitudes faster in computer only communication, limited only by the data transmission speed and read and write speed limit of storage devices. The third limitation is particular to computer-computer communication, currently impossible if human is involved. It is technically possible for the machines to provide a kind of API (application programming interface) to enable access of internal functionalities to allowed parties. In a illustrative situation, a patient with his machine (M_p in Fig. 1(D)) in a examination room is connected with the doctor's machine (M_d in Fig. 1(D)), and these two machine exploit the functionality of the other machine for necessary tasks. The doctor's machine (M_d) can provide functions to visualize the patient's test results and analyses of prognostics. On the other hand, the patient's machine (M_p) may offer mainly access means to patient's past data. Other functions are possible, and the point is that the machines constitute an temporary integrated system of machines M_d and M_p.

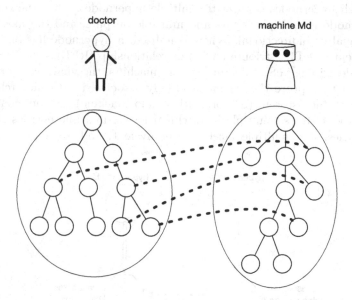

Fig. 2. Description of functional relationship between doctor and machine. System of systems (SoS) of doctor and machine represented with their components illustrating interactions and functional relationships between doctor and machine. The graph representations inside thin circles denote the representations with activated rulesets. The description is similar for patient and machine SoS.

The hypernetwork model [4] is used to describe the SoS of doctor, patient and machine (Fig. 1). Each hypernode is a collection of rulesets, which is a superimposed representation of multiple descriptions that the hypernode is used to describe. One description is activated at a time, invoked by the activated rulesets of other hypernodes. Therefore, the selection of the activated ruleset is governed by the ruleset of the hypernode that is connected with direction to the hypernode.

Figure 4 illustrates the basic mechanism of description activation or visualization of a given perspective. Suppose the hypernode A is connected to the hypernode B. This is the simplest case, two hypernodes and unidirectional connection from one hypernode to the other hypernode. The hypernodes A and B are instances in the pool of hypernodes, and are not directly visualized, as multiple perspectives are superimposed and meaningless for direct interpretations. In Fig. 4, the hypernodes A and B contain N_A and N_B rulesets, respectively. Following the rule activation pattern defined in the hypernode A, suppose the ruleset A_X is activated among N_A rulesets. Note that only one ruleset is activated at a time. Then if the destination hypernode of the activated ruleset A_X is the hypernode B, the role of the hypernode B is also specified in the ruleset A_X. Another possible description is the ruleset ID to be activated in the hypernode B directly specified in the ruleset A_X.

The visualized hypernodes A and B (Fig. 3) are actually the rulesets A_X and B_Y activated from the sets of rulesets in hypernodes A and B. In more realistic descriptions, multiple hypernodes connect to both hypernodes A and B, and both hypernodes connect to multiple hypernodes. Thus the connection of a hypernode is multiple inputs and multiple outputs, and the link is either unidirectional or bidirectional. When visualized, a hypernode has one of three roles: concept (CPT), attribute (ATT) or relationship (REL).

When describing SoS of doctor–patient–machine, the viewpoint (or facet or perspective) to capture the system is closely associated with hierarchical levels defined in each system (doctor, patient and machine) and boundaries that separates the systems. multiple hierarchical levels, multiple entities separated by boundaries, and multiple facets are equivalent, and are represented with

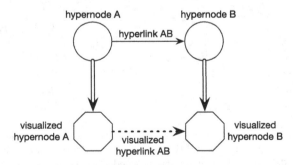

Fig. 3. The ruleset Ax is activated from the set of rulesets in hypernode A, which defines the activated ruleset By in hypernode B

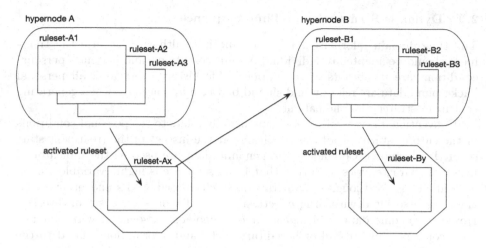

Fig. 4. The ruleset Ax is activated from the set of rulesets in hypernode A, which defines the activated ruleset By in hypernode B

relationships in hypernetwork model. They are functionally equivalent, differing in interpretation defined by the viewpoint. In the case of hierarchy, phenomena associated with each hierarchical level is treated as an independent phenomenon and consequently interpreted as a different viewpoint to represent the target system. In the case of boundaries, the association is more indirect, where the entities that the boundary separates correspond to the perspectives. The boundaries function as relationships among involved entities. The sequenced activation of rulesets defines the viewpoint.

2.1 Unknown Elements

When describing the doctor–patient model with attached machines, the health related aspects are mainly treated. The problem is the existence of many unknown elements that constitute a system of the doctor and patient. The number of unknowns are particularly large for elements directly related to the disease in question. Therefore, in the SoS in Figs. 1(C) and (D), not every elements of doctor and patient are elucidated, thus no accurate representation is possible. Naturally the machine is completely describable, as it is designed by human. We represent the unknown elements as blackbox elements that presumably exist. The following cases of unknown are possible: (1) unknown existence and unknown relationship existence; (2) known or existence possible, but unknown relationship with other elements; (3) known or existence possible, relationship with other elements known or existence possible. The term "existence possible" means that the existence can be assumed based on a hypothesis, but the existence is not certain or confirmed. The relationship with other elements denotes any kind of interaction or functional interdependence among the element and other relevent elements.

2.2 Dynamic Structure and Time Sequence

The time domain information is important in health-care because the treatment should be adapted to individual patient conditions, and patient's personal conditions are the results of the patient's life history. Therefore, all personal background data are relevant and should be taken into account when generating treatment strategy for the patient.

Conventional personalized medicine usually refers to the personal conditions of the current status, or of the conditions at the instant of the treatment start or of the diagnosis. Commonly the genomic data are used as the indicator of personal characteristics. It is true that DNA sequence is highly variable among individuals, and although only a fraction is elucidated, SNPs and other variations are associated with drug effectiveness and likeliness of onset of diseases. However, genome data is biological, and phenomena associated with genomic data contains only natural or hereditary facts, and information related to the current conditions of the patient are absent. Medical treatment of patients, on the other hand, involves social aspects, such as family composition, social status, job, daily activity patterns, food preferences, body activity patterns, among others. These aspects should be considered when determining treatment strategy, which results in personalized treatment. Perhaps these aspects have higher weight than genome related biological aspects when elaborating treatment strategy, although no sufficient foundation is available.

The personalized medicine investigated in this paper is fundamentally different from conventional concepts and topics discussed in conventional research which have narrow meaning limited to biological data.

Then the life history of the patient should be modeled, which implies that a model with description capability of the time domain structural change is necessary.

Figure 5 is a conceptual illustration, where the time axis is added to the N-dimensional space to represent system structures. Basically the ΔT between adjacent times is a constant value, although not a requisite. The structures of adjacent times $N - 1$, N and $N + 1$ are visualized independently, but these are internally described independent of the value of ΔT.

Elements belonging to two structures of adjacent time instances are related based on relationships among them. Basically, two types of representation are possible when time domain description is used. One is to connect individual hypernodes and links with relationship hypernodes, and the other one is to introduce a single REL hypernode with details of differences as ATT hypernodes connected to this REL hypernode. Both represent the differences between two structures as a relationship, differing on the description detail level. To simplify the description, the time domain differences are described only between the adjacent structures, although the differences can be described by introducing REL hypernode that connects structures of arbitrary time instances. Figure 6 illustrates the description of relationships between two structures of adjacent times, where the differences are represented by REL hypernodes that connect to the relevant hypernodes in either or both structures of time $T[N]$ and $T[N + 1]$.

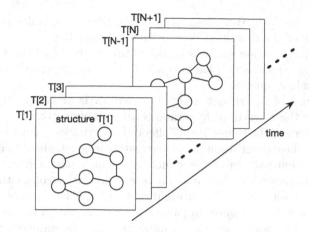

Fig. 5. Sequence of structures on time domain. "structure $T[1]$" denotes the structure at the instant $T[1]$, and so on.

The primary role of gray hypernodes is REL, as they define the relationships between the hypernodes and links that are different in two structures.

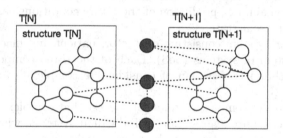

Fig. 6. Describing relationship between structures of adjacent times.

The integrated system is represented according to the perspective to visualize the system, which is closely related to the function of the interest. The system is not a simple collection of entities, as the hypernodes connected by links, but it is a representation that combines the elements.

2.3 Wave Propagation Analysis

The structural properties of the represented SoS is analyzed using the wave propagation patterns. The main purpose of the wave propagation analysis is the prediction of phenomena associated with the health status of the patient. The method is basically to inject a fictional pulse to multiple elements in the description, and to analyze the propagation pattern over the whole system. The analysis is possible in two directions, one for structural analysis with fixed time, and the other one form time domain analysis, where the pulse propagates on time dimension of the described system with adjacent times.

The wave propagation analysis explores this property of the hypernetwork model, that the ruleset activation is controlled by the hypernode that connects to the hypernode in question.

The sequence of the ruleset activation pattern is analogous to wave propagation, where the rulesets of hypernodes are subsequently activated, and the activation pattern of the rulesets of all affected hypernodes defines the avtivation pattern of the whole description. If the avtivation is constrained to a single time, then the activation pattern of the structure is elucidated. On the other hand, when the propagation on time domain is enabled, it becomes the prediction when the ruleset activation is in future direction, and the retrospective analysis for past direction. In any wave propagation analysis, only a fraction of hypernodes in the pool is usually activated, implying that the number of hypernodes of visualized network is smaller than the number of hypernodes in the pool.

The time sequence description is particularly useful to predict the future prognosis, and to analyze the influences of changes in elements of the components of the system.

Two immediate applications of the system representations are: (i) analysis of the structure, by investigating the consequences/influences of the changes in system components (change, addition and deleteion); and (ii) prediction, particularly on time domain, i.e., prediction of the future conditions based on the past history and the present state.

The integrated system consisting of doctor, patient and machine (Fig. 1) is treated as a system of systems (SoS). Each of the three components (doctor, patient and machine) is a system of considerable complexity and can also be interpreted as a SoS.

Various failures of complex systems [5] suggest that complex systems cannot be represented as a pure aggregation of individual systems, where the interactions among component systems can be represented as a couple of relationships. Furthermore, it is assumed that functional boundaries can be clearly described. If these assumptions were valid, incidents of failures of complex systems should be minial, which is false. One method is to try to extract the interactions among component systems as simple as possible, Similar method is to design the integrated system (SoS) to contain only simple functional interactions among the component systems. However, both methods are ignoring the reality, where such extraction or design is not possible in real world. This is particularly true for the doctor-patient-machine SoS discussed in this paper.

Physical boundaries among the three entities, doctor, patient and machine, is easily characterized. However, the most important point is whether a boundary can be defined in the representation from the functional perspective, which is necessary for the wave propagation analysis. Our ongoing project on the description of doctor-patient-machine SoS suggests that any represenation of the functional aspect of arbitrary two entities, for instance doctor and machine, patient and machine or doctor and patient, requires the description of elements that belong to different hierarchical levels in both entities (Fig. 2). The hierarchical level refers to the conventional hierarchical levels in structural representations.

An important role of the machine M_d is to assist doctors (Fig. 1) to diagnose and to build treatment plan. These actions involve numerous decision makings by the doctors. Similarly, patients are also requested to make decisions regarding his own treatment. The decision making by doctors involve imaginations and predictions under insufficient information. The ability of this prediction differentiates the skill of experiment and novice doctors. On the other hand, no such differences exist among patients. The primary role of the machine M_d assisting doctors is to provide analytical results that can be deduced from data stored in the machine, which is information based on past data. For the prediction by skilled doctors, all relevant information is valuable.

For the prediction by skilled doctors, all relevant information is valuable. The prediction of future progress of patient conditions by machines are the results of calculations using past data and machine learning techniques, which are the replications of past accumulated cases.

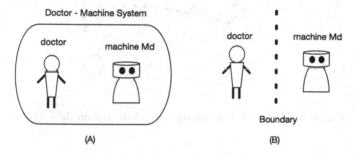

Fig. 7. System representation of integrated human (doctor) and machine, each of which is also described as systems. The boundary between human and machine is also represented.

Following the line of our previous works [4], we assume that the component systems cannot be extracted separately, implying that the boundary among the components cannot be defined.

Figure 8 illustrates the possibility to change the level of description details of human-machine SoS. The top description represents the most abstract level, and the bottom one a more detailed. Adequate level of details can be chosen for purposes. Each representation denotes a different viewpoint, impossible using conventional models.

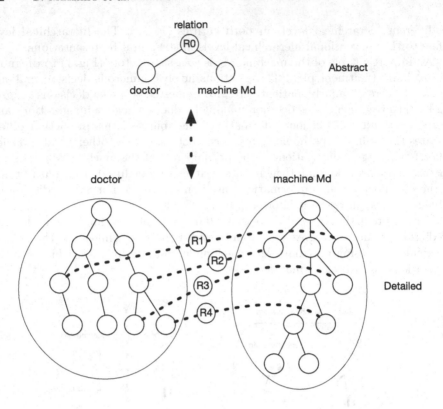

Fig. 8. Abstract level of descriptions of doctor-machine SoS.

3   Conclusions

The time domain is a requisite element when representing doctor patient machine as an integrated system. The conventional health care aid systems focus on the patient conditions that are measureble with medical exams, and the individual factors often mean gene level factors, also measureble with medical exams. However, no personal life history is considered, which plays an important role in planning personalized treatment strategy for the patient.

This paper presented the framework that enables the description of previously ignored aspects of patient's personal data. Analyses are also possible using the gramework, and are particularly useful to estimate the future changes and to detect influences of changes in elements of the system.

Acknowledgments. This research was supported by the JSPS KAKENHI Grant Numbers 24500307 (T.M.) and 15K00458 (T.M.).

References

1. Hinton, G.E.: Learning multiple layers of representation. Trends Cogn. Sci. **111**, 428–434 (2007)
2. Malin, J.L.: Envisioning watson as a rapid-learning system for oncology. J. Oncol. Pract. **9**, 155–157 (2013)
3. Chen, Y., Argentinis, E., Weber, G.: IBM Watson: how cognitive computing can be applied to big data challenges in life sciences research. Clin. Ther. **38**, 688–701 (2016)
4. Maeshiro, T.: Framework based on relationship to describe non-hierarchical, boundaryless and multi-perspective phenomena. SICE J. Control Measur. Syst. Integr. **11**, 381–389 (2019)
5. Clearfield, C., Tilcsik, A.: Meltdown: Why Our Systems Fail and What We Can Do About It. Atlantic Books (2018)

Relationship Between Rage Tendency and Body Conditions

Tetsuya Maeshiro[1(✉)] and Miharu Ino[2]

[1] Faculty of Library, Information and Media Studies, University of Tsukuba,
Tsukuba 305-8550, Japan
maeshiro@slis.tsukuba.ac.jp
[2] Department of Informatics, University of Tsukuba, Tsukuba 305-8550, Japan

Abstract. This paper analyzes the relationship between the easiness to get raged and physical conditions associated with recall process of past memories. We tested if the easiness to get raged can be detected using measurement of physical conditions in such situations. The results indicate that it is possible, particularly for females.

Keywords: Rage · Anger · Body conditions

1 Introduction

This paper investigates the body conditions particular to persons that are easier to get raged and those who are not. Here we denote rage as violent anger or angry fury, stronger than the anger, often accompanied by physical aggressions. Statistics indicate that rage incidents are increasing. The familiar term "road rage" denotes aggressive driving and maneuvers against other cars while driving a car. A different statics in Japan indicates that elementary school students' violent acts have increased about fourfold in ten years from 2008 to 2017.

This work investigates extreme anger, and anger constitutes one of six basic emotional states. Estimation of emotional states, particularly of the six basic emotional states, has been investigated since the beginning of psychology [1]. Particularly the study to elucidate the relationship of the basic emotional states with autononomic nervous system has been active. As one of six basic emotional states, several studies on anger have been published. However, no study treated more extreme cases of anger or blowups, and no studies on relationship with physical conditions have been published. This paper analyzes the influences of rage on body conditions, namely ECG (electro cardiogram), EEG (electro encephalogram) and EDA (electro dermal activity).

There seems to be a correlation between the personality related to aggression and cardiovascular reactivity. Izawa et al. reported the result of survey with twenty undergraduate students [2], where the aggression was related with the increase of the systolic blood pressure and diastolic blood pressure at the time of provocation, rise in systolic blood pressure at rest after provocation, and association between reduction of systolic blood pressure and diastolic blood pressure.

© Springer Nature Switzerland AG 2019
S. Yamamoto and H. Mori (Eds.): HCII 2019, LNCS 11570, pp. 514–522, 2019.
https://doi.org/10.1007/978-3-030-22649-7_41

Klimecki et al. conducted a subject experiment using an unequal economic game to anger the subjects [3]. Three subjects played the game, consisting of one participant and two experimental collaborators. The actions of two cooperators were determined in advance, instructed to take only the actions that benefit themselves and harm the participant. Initially, most participants were equally distributing profits to the two cooperators, but when one collaborator began provocative acts, some participants took "revenge actions" to provoke the collaborators. Brain activities were measured by using fMRI to analyze the "revenge" factor in contributors. They found that the participant was feeling anger, and the dorsal prefrontal cortex, denoted the ceremonial command tower, which plays a role in cognition, motivation and judgment, was active. The temporal lobes of the brain and the amygdala also were active.

There is a study on the relationship between anger and brain activity and physical condition [4]. It was reported that the brain activity of the left forehead became dominant and the heart beat rate increased. This study classified methods to induce anger in the experiment, (1) natural situation, (2) recall of personal events, (3) induction by facial expressions, (4) image guidance, (5) insults, and (6) provocations.

The details of these methods are as follows.

1. Instruct experiment collaborators to take harassing behaviors to participants, such as taking abusive attitude towards subjects.
2. Listen the upsetting events beforehand from the participants. Read out these events to the participants, forcing them to remember the event.
3. Experiment collaborators create facial expressions of intended emotion, inducing these emotions to the participants.
4. Present photos of the International Affective Picture System (IAPS) to evoke various emotions.
5. Instruct the experiment collaborators to write insulting comments to the text preliminarily written by the subject. Then let the subject read the comment to evoke anger.
6. Provoke directly the participants, by instructing the experiment collaborators to answer sentences like "I cannot hear" even if the participants say in loud voice.

There is a study on autonomic nerve responses during psychological stress and palmar perspiration [5]. This study investigated the amount of perspiration in healthy subjects' palms at normal and mental stress (mental arrhythmias, bicycle exercise) load, and analyzed autonomic nerve responses (blood pressure, electrocardiogram) and sweating of the palm. Quantitative analysis indicated that the heart rate, the systolic blood pressure and the diastolic blood pressure, and the sweating amount of the palm significantly increased under the mental load.

Some studies have used personalized recall to induce anger, and reported relationships with autonomous nervous systems [6–11]. However, these studies focused on the activity patterns of autonomous nervous systems when participants were in anger state, and no study investigated the relationships with past experiences.

2   Methods

This paper tested the following hypothesis.

1. The changing behavior of body conditions depends on the existence of raging experiences by the participant.
2. The changing behavior of body conditions also depends on gender.

Experiment was conducted with two groups of participants, each consisting of five males and five females, totaling twenty participants. The difference of the two groups is if they had raging experience in the past or not.

Therefore, the participants whether belonged to Group-A with raging experiences or Group-B without raging experiences. Obviously the raging experiences were participants' personal experiences, and the judgment of that experience as raging or not is also personal. On the other hand, there are no methods to verify the existence of rage in participant's life except direct interview with sincere answer. However, since there are no definitive methods to verify each participant's claims, we used this classification. Although the interpretation of the experience and its classification as raging or not is personal and not standardized, at least the integrity inside the person is assured. The point is whether a person interpreted the experience as raging or not. It is difficult to control the evaluation criteria if the experience is raging among all participants. Furthermore, the experience is personal, and "virtual" experience is more realistic to the participant than reading or listening descriptions of raging situations, as the participants confront images when recalling past experiences.

The experiment was conducted in the following sequence.

1. Rest for two minutes
2. Remember happy moments for eight minutes
3. Rest for two minutes
4. Remember raging (Group-A) or unpleasant (Group-B) moments for eight minutes
5. Questionnaire

The experiment aims to measure the physical conditions when participants are in raged condition. Therefore, the ideal experiment would be to put literally the participants in raged conditions. However, since the raging experiences involve breaking or throwing things and physical violences, we took an indirect approach to force the participants to recall their experiences, emulating their experiences internally. We assume that emotional aspects can be reconstructed without body movements, at least partially. This method is similar to "recall of personal events" described before, the second method introduced in [4]. The participants explain details of incidents that made them angry before the experiments, and the experiment collaborator reads out the content. However, we asked the participants to remember their experiences and did not request their explanations, because the experience was painful for the participants and may cause extreme emotion and unpleasantness.

The body conditions were measured during the whole experiment, from the beginning to the end. ECG, EEG and EDA were measured using Bitalino(r)evolution. The two rest stages (stages 1 and 3) are used as the control condition to be compared with stages recalling happy moments (stage 2) and raging or unpleasant moments (stage 4).

The physical condition values were analyzed using relative values based on the control condition (rest stage), as the individual variability of these values were high. Additionally, the relative value between happy and raging was also calculated.

Thus the following relative values were calculated: (i) rage minus rest; (ii) happy minus rest; (iii) rage minus happy. These conditions were analyzed between the Group-A and -B, and the gender difference was also analyzed.

Figure 1 is an example of physical conditions measurement.

3 Results and Discussions

We analyzed the results of the whole participant groups and separately based on gender to the two hypotheses, as the both Group-A and B consists of equal number of male and female participants. In both EDA and ECG measurements, we analyzed the relative values, since the absolute values of both measurements are highly participant dependent, and direct comparison of absolute values among participants is of little value. Therefore, the following three relative values were calculated: (1) relative value of happy moments, which is the difference between the happy moments and resting stages; (2) relative value of raging moments, which is the difference between the raging moments and resting stages; and (3) difference between raging and happy moments. The first two values are the values relative to the control condition.

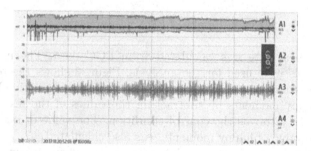

Fig. 1. Example of a measurement result with Bitalino(r)evolution

We found that the EDA and ECG are possible indicators to classify persons that are likely to get raged or not, as there were differences with significance in these measurements. Specifically, the participants of Group-A and Group-B showed different body condition changing behavior.

Figure 2 shows the results of EDA measurements. Since EDA values are strongly person-dependent, we calculated relative EDA values of raging and happy moments by subtracting the values of the resting condition values, using the latter as the control condition. The value of raging moments relative to the value of happy moments was also calculated.

Figure 2 indicates that the Group-A and -B have different relative value changing patterns, as the Group-A showed positive relative values in all three analytical conditions, i.e., happy minus resting stage, raging minus resting stage and raging minus happy stage. On the other hand, the Group-B showed negative relative value in raging minus resting stage and raging minus happy stage, and negligible difference in happy minus resting stage. Group-A has higher EDA values in all cases, suggesting that persons with raging experiences show stronger EDA variations, or more direct expressions.

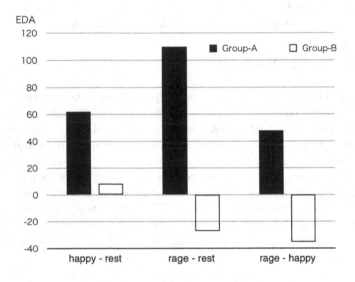

Fig. 2. Results of EDA measurements

The heart beat rate was calculated from ECG data. The maximum and the average rates were used for the analysis. Figure 3 shows the results of HR measurements. Analogous to EDA analysis, we calculated relative HR values of raging and happy moments by subtracting the values of the resting condition values, using the latter as the control condition. The value of raging moments relative to the value of happy moments was also calculated.

Both Group-A and -B showed increase of HR when rise in emotion was observed, with slightly higher values of happy images than raging moments, although very small and this difference had no statistical significance. The mean HR and maximum HR values showed similar value changing patterns among the happy, raging and resting conditions, where the HR value of both happy and raging moments were higher than the resting condition, which is in accordance with other studies. Moreover, the Group-A showed equivalent HR values between raging and happy moments. However, both mean and maximum HR of happy moments were higher than raging moments in Group-B participants, suggesting that the image of happy moments was clearer than raging moments, since the Group-B consists of participants without extreme anger experience, and it is possible that their anger or irritating memories were not so strong, resulting in not so high HR.

When measured with HR, Fig. 3 suggests that the strength of happy moments is high, as both mean and maximum HR were approximately identical in Group-A, as the raging memories of the participants of Group-A were strong. Surely the raging moments consist of possibly negative emotions, which is opposite to happy moments that consist of positive emotions. However, the strength of the influence on HR is identical.

Only the maximum HR of rage minus control condition had statistical significance, and there was no significance in average HR values.

3.1   Gender Differences

Significant differences were observed between male and female participants, as the body condition changes were different. Figure 4 shows the relative values of EDA of male and female participants. The changing pattern is different for Group-A and -B of male and female. For Group-A male participants, the value of raging moments was the highest, followed by happy and resting stages, as in all three relative value conditions (happy−rest, rage−rest, and rage−happy) the values are positive. On the other hand, the value of rage−happy condition is negative for Group-B male participants. Furthermore, the values of happy−rest and rage−rest of Group-A are higher than those of Group-B.

On the other hand, EDA of female participants showed different relative value changes than male participants. Similar to male participants, all three values were positive (happy−rest, rage−rest, rage−happy) for Group-A, but all negative for Group-B, suggesting the opposite mechanism that affect the EDA. Moreover, EDA during raging moments was higher than happy moments in Group-A, but happy moments was higher in Group-B.

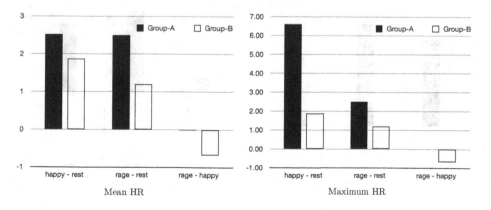

Fig. 3. Results of HR measurements. Mean HR and maximum HR.

The changes were more evident in females, as there was statistical significance. On the other hand, no changes with statistical significance were observed in male participants.

Figure 5 shows the difference of HR response for male and female participants. Both male and female participants had different value change patterns from the genderless measurement results shown in Fig. 3. This discrepancy is normal, as the average, which is the genderless group analysis in this case, is different of components (male and female groups) that constitute the whole group [12]. In both male and female cases, the happy and raging moments result in higher HR than the resting condition for Group-A. The difference, however, appears in comparison between raging and happy moments, where the raging results in higher mean HR for males, and lower for females. The HR values of Group-B are also different for males and females. The mean HR of raging moments is lower than the resting and happy moments for males of Group-B. On the other hand, raging moments result in a slightly higher average HR for females of Group-B. Since Fig. 5 is the mean HR, we also analyzed the peak HR, which reflects instantaneous response and thus clearer influence can be observed.

Figure 6 shows the difference of maximum HR for male and female participants. Similar to the mean HR case (Fig. 5), both male and female participants had different value change patterns from the genderless measurement results.

Both male and female participants had different value change patterns of HR (Figs. 5 and 6) from the genderless measurement results shown in Fig. 3. The male participants of Group-A had high maximum HR for raging moments, followed by happy moments. On the other hand, less similarity was observed between male and female participants of Group-B. The maximum HR of the resting condition of female participants was the highest, and raging moments resulted in the lowest HR. This lower HR of raging moments than happy moments was also observed in male Group-B participants.

Table 1 summarizes the factors with statistical significances.

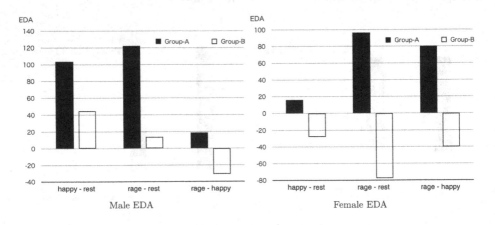

Fig. 4. Results of EDA measurements. Male and female subjects.

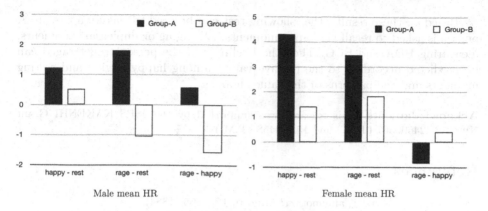

Fig. 5. Mean HR values. Male and female subjects.

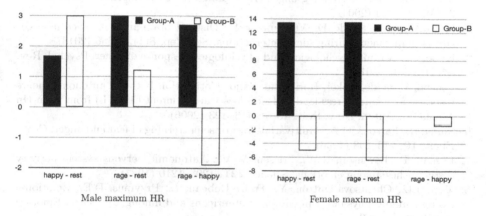

Fig. 6. Maximum HR values. Male and female subjects.

Table 1. Statistical significances of measured features

	Group-A and -B	Male	Female
EDA	Yes	No	Yes
Happy minus rest (max HR)	No	No	Yes
Raging minus rest (max HR)	No	No	Yes

4   Conclusions

The present study aims to clarify the rage and physical conditions. The results indicate that the physical conditions change differently for persons with raging experiences and those without. The experiments presented in this paper is useful to detect in advance if the person is likely to get raged or not.

We found that the EDA and ECG are possible indicators to classify persons that are likely to get raged or not, particularly for females.

Based on these results, the following test can be used to classify a person. A person is asked to recall (1) happy moments, (2) raging or unpleasant moments, measuring EDA and ECG. Then the likeliness of the person to get raged can be predicted according to the relative values among happy, raging and resting moments and the patterns of the value changes.

Acknowledgments. This research was supported by the JSPS KAKENHI Grant Numbers 24500307 (T.M.) and 15K00458 (T.M.).

References

1. James, W.: What is an emotion? Mind **9**, 188–205 (1884)
2. Izawa, Nagano, Ida, Kodama, Nomura: Relationship between hostility and cardiovascular reactivity during anger (In Japanese). Psychophysiol. Psychophysiol. **22**(3), 215–224 (2004)
3. Klimecki, O.M., Sande, D., Vuilleumier, P.: Distinct brain areas involved in anger versus punishment during social interactions. Sci. Rep. **8**(1), 10556 (2018)
4. Kubo, Ga, Kawai: Psychological and physiological response of anger. Psychol. Rev. **57**(1), 27–44 (2014)
5. Umeno, Hamade, Yokoi, Hori, Ono, Saijo: Correlation between autonomic nerve response at mental stress load and skin loss water content (TEWL) from palm (In Japanese). Auton. Nerv. Syst. **43**(5), 416–423 (2006)
6. Sinha, R., Parsons, O.A.: Multivariate response patterning of fear and anger. Cogn. Emot. **10**, 173–198 (1996)
7. Ekman, P., Levenson, R.W., Friesen, W.V.: Autonomic nervous system activity distinguishes among emotions. Science **221**, 1208–1210 (1983)
8. Tsai, J.L., Chentsova-Dutton, Y., Freire-Bebeau, L., Przymus, D.E.: Emotional expression and physiology in european americans and hmong americans. Emotion **2**, 380–397 (2002)
9. Foster, P.S., Webster, D.G.: Emotional memories: the relationship between age of memory and the corresponding psychophysiological responses. Int. J. Psychophysiol. **41**, 11–18 (2001)
10. Schwartz, G.E., Weinberger, D.A., Singer, J.A.: Cardiovascular differentiation of happiness, sadness, anger, and fear following imagery and exercise. Psychos. Med. **43**, 343–364 (1981)
11. Davidson, R.J., Schwartz, G.E.: Patterns of cerebral lateralization during cardiac biofeedback versus the self-regulation of emotion: sex differences. Psychophysiology **13**, 62–68 (1976)
12. Rose, T.: The End of Average. HarperOne, San Francisco (2017)

A Study on Design Process Model Based on User Experience - Development for the Concept of Service for Vision-Impaired People

Fuko Oura[✉], Takeo Ainoya, and Keiko Kasamatsu

Tokyo Metropolitan University, 6-6 Asahigaoka, Hino, Tokyo, Japan
fu.a7te@gmail.com

Abstract. In recent years, the elderly population is increasing in Japan, and the population with disabilities has also a tendency to increase. In addition, due to changes in social conditions, changes in values and diversification of living standards have occurred among elderly and disabled people. The importance of considering diversity is emphasized in also various efforts for improves QOL (quality of life). Among such social backgrounds, the role of the design field is to improve the lives of people with diverse needs through designing goods and services or a system. The important point of view for such designing (especially when targeting users with diverse needs) include What kind of process or method do you set for develop service and a system. In this paper, we focus on methods of designing services targeting users with diverse needs such as elderly people and disabled people, and discuss methods and processes. We propose a co-creative type of approach based on the concept of user experience and participatory design. In addition, we aim to gain insight for practicing co-creative design approach, through Case verification by service development of wearable devices for vision-impaired people.

Keywords: Design process · Co-creation · User experience · Vision-impaired people

1 Introduction

In recent years, the elderly population is increasing in Japan, and the population with disabilities has also a tendency to increase. In addition, due to changes in social conditions, changes in values and diversification of living standards have occurred among elderly and disabled people [1]. The importance of considering diversity is emphasized in also various efforts for improves QOL (quality of life).

In this paper, we focused on the process of designing services for visually impaired people towards users with diverse needs. It was aimed at gaining insight to conduct the proposal process through its proposal of the design process and through case verification.

S. Yamamoto and H. Mori (Eds.): HCII 2019, LNCS 11570, pp. 523–533, 2019.
https://doi.org/10.1007/978-3-030-22649-7_42

2 The Positioning of This Research

2.1 Design Approaches Emphasized the Users' Point of View

In order to consider various needs of the elderly and the visually impaired, the characteristics of the design approach of existing user viewpoint are arranged. We conducted a literature survey on the peripheral concepts of participatory design (Participatory design) and UX (User eXperience) design.

2.2 Mapping on Design Approaches

Based on the survey, we mapped it as shown in the Fig. 1. The vertical axis shows the direction of information and knowledge as the character of the design approach. The horizontal axis shows whether it is co-creative or optimized as the purpose of the design approach [2]. We also mapped prior studies on participatory design processes for elderly or disabled people [3–8] (see Fig. 1).

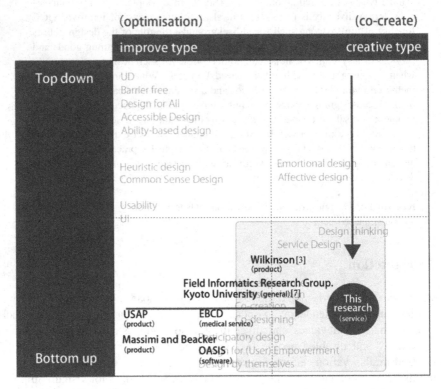

Fig. 1. Mapping on design approaches emphasized the users' point of view and the positioning of this research.

Previous design approaches for elderly people or handicapped people are actively being carried out particularly in the improvement type part.

In other word, such design Is mostly on the purpose of improvement of the existing system, or the design for the determined environment to some extent. However, people, goods, and services have come to have various providing forms.

Design for elderly people or handicapped people is now required to design aiming to create value combining user's needs and seeds, not only improvement of existing system. Therefore, we aimed at co-creative design for service concept development by incorporating the user participation phase into the design process.

The purpose of this paper is to propose a design process model that focuses on the creation of more value than existing prior research, for the design method of services targeting users with diverse needs such as elderly people and disabled people. Furthermore, we verified the proposed method and obtain insight to work on practicing co-creative design through the case at the concept development phase of the process.

3   Process Proposal

We propose the user experience-based co-creative design process as a design process model for service concept development for users with diverse needs such as elderly people or handicapped people (see Fig. 2).

Fig. 2. The user experience-based co-creative design process.

The goal of the proposed design process is that designed solution improves users' experience. Four phases including participatory sessions is incorporated in the process. The four phases are "collecting the experience and the context by the users' participation", "collecting the requirements through users' participant", "idea generation by users' participation" and "evaluate the designs by users' experience".

4   Case Verification

4.1   Case Overview

In this verification, we focused on four phases including participatory sessions in the process, and verified based on a case of design projects that the author participated in. The case studied was the development of the service concept of the wearable device for vision-impaired people (see Fig. 3). The wearable device to be designed is a glasses type support device for vision-impaired people, and it was a prototype model developed by OTONGLASS Co., Ltd. It had the function of scanning the character information in front of me and converting it to audio information. In this case of the design project, it was aimed at verifying whether or not the function of reading letters can be used successfully in the use situation in daily life and concept design of a new service utilizing data collected in the future through wearable devices.

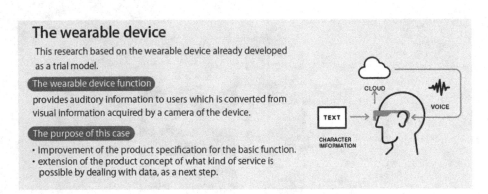

Fig. 3.   Device targeted as a case, and object of design project.

4.2   Case Implementation Details

Four participatory sessions were conducted with the actually participation of the user, "Behavior observations to function verification", "Focus group interview for collecting users' opinion", "Depth interview for extracting Insight from a medical perspective", "Workshop for idea generation to provide new services" (see Fig. 4). We gathered insights toward the application of the proposed process from the implementation results.

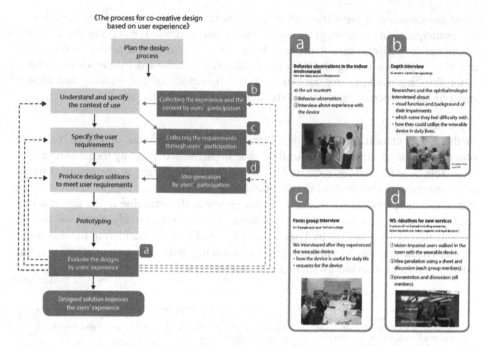

Fig. 4. The user experience-based co creative design process.

Behavior Observations to Function Verification

Object

The purpose was to clarify the specification requirement when using the main function of "converting character information in front of eyes to voice" while walking in space.

Participants

The total number of participants was 3, including 2 low-vision people and 1 blind person. The blind person was participating with accompanying guide dog.

Implementation Environment

This session was conducted in the 21st Century Museum of Contemporary Art, Kanazawa (in Japan).

Procedure

First of all, three participants were gathered in the meeting room, and an interview was conducted on grasp of the current situation and experiences of utilizing character information in order to grasp individual characteristics. After the Interview, the participants were guided to the start point of the preset route, and the participants wore the smart glass. Participants walked along the route with helpers and designers respectively. Since there was not much character information arranged in the museum, this time we posted the text all over the place. Participants were asked to walk while reading the bulletin using a device. Designers actively asked the participants to grasp the situation and reaction concerning the use of the device. We tried to find out mainly about the intention of the action and how they perceive. Designers actively interviewed the participants in order to grasp the situation and reaction concerning the use. We attempted to get information mainly about the intention of the action or how they perceive. Behavior during walking, conversation was recorded by the video camera. After finishing walking, we looked back on the details of the walking and shared concrete experience or opinions on the functions of the device were done.

Implementation Result

In the phase <Evaluation of Design Plan by User's Experience of Use>, "behavior observation for specification verification" was implemented by using the prototype. We were able to gather information on how users react when using in the assumed usage environment and what parts of the experience are bottleneck (see Fig. 5). Even with the use of the same device, the perceived experience was different due to the difference in user characteristics, so they indicated a different reaction respectively. From this fact, in <Evaluation of Design Plan by User's Experience of Use>, Considering the difference in user characteristics, it is necessary to experiencing and evaluating as many users as possible in order to avoid evaluating only some users.

Persona: Female in her fourties, Low Vision
She works at the cultural center and goes out almost every day, including work and riverside and department stores.
The main transportation are walking, buses, taxis. She usually use white canes.

Place	in front of posting on the corridor wall	at any time during walking corridor, information area	in front of flyers / posters in Information area	Open space Information Plaza
Behavior	Scan the characters posted on the wall again and again	Follow the guidance of a helper to approach the position of the letter	Scan the characters of various leaflets and compare them	Scan in various directions
Thought	She turns to the place where the letter exists and scan it, but she can not scan the whole sentence quite well	It tends to overlook the existence of surrounding text information.	If the device can read letters of various designs, the range of information that can be picked up will widen	Because she do not know the position of character information, she tried to scan various directions for the time being.
Requirement	If there is a difference in the way the left and right appear, they hope they can adjust according to how you see it.	They want to know where the character information is	It is better to increase recognizable fonts, character sets, and color schemes.	They want to know that character information is in sight when walking, or to know the direction in which information is present.
Affective	It is a bit tough for me to read it again and again. It may be subtle if the sentence can not be read accurately.	It is somewhat difficult to use while walking that you can not read without letters in front of you.	Sorry a limited range of recognizable characters is limited. I am happy to understand even words alone.	It seems not to work well if you do not know the position of character information. Even if it is read aloud, I do not know what information I picked up.
Actual behavior				

Fig. 5. Example of created scene map.

Depth Interview for Extracting Insight from a Medical Perspective
Object
In order to grasp the characteristics of the each user's view and the needs obtained from their context, we conducted a depth interview with the vision-impaired user and the ophthalmologist.

Participants
Participants were several people with visual impairment, and each interview was conducted individually. An ophthalmologist at a university hospital participated as an interviewer. Every participant with visual impairment was a low vision and was a patient in charge of an ophthalmologist who participated as an interviewer.

Implementation Environment
Since the interview included questions concerning visual functions and diseases of vision-impaired participants, it was carried out at the examination room of the university hospital for consideration to the patient.

Procedure
First of all, an ophthalmologist interviewed on the basis of the medical record about the visual function of the user and the background of vision disorder. Next, the investigators (1) interviewed about how to view normally, and scenes troubled in daily life, (2) interviewed about what kind of scene they could use wearable devices while experience the device.

Implementation Result
In the phase <Collecting the experience and the context by users' participation>, "Depth interview for extracting Insight from a medical perspective" was implemented. By Intervention by people who have some knowledge of the characteristics and lives of vision-impaired people, such as ophthalmologists and helpers, it has made it possible to draw more fulfilling information from vision-impaired people.

Focus Group Interview for Collecting Users' Opinion
Object
The purpose was to obtain hints to lead to design through collecting needs in daily life or finding common experiences and requirements for vision-impaired people.

Participants
The participant group was about 5 to 10 people each time. Most of the participants were those who never experienced the wearable devices before. We conducted focus group interviews with multiple groups using community of visually impaired people in the community and community of patient of ophthalmic unit.

Implementation Environment
Depending on the condition, it was conducted at the ophthalmology in the participant community area or conference space of public facilities etc.

Procedure
We first gave a lecture on the overview and usage of the wearable device, and then asked them to experience the device. The experience was mainly reading text information in the room where the focus group was done, reading books, documents, pastry and other character information around the body. While experiencing the devices, discussed how existing functions could be utilized in their lives, and what they hope to be able to do for each problem in daily life.

Implementation Result
In the phase <Collecting the requirements through users' participation>, "Focus group interview for collecting users' opinion" was implemented. Through the participation of many users, we were able to extract the user's request which the designer alone can not know.

On the other hand, in the focus group interview, there was a great possibility that the amount of information and contents obtained by the facilitator's command were different.

Workshop for Idea Generation to Provide New Services

Object
To create ideas based on the viewpoints of the parties and to consider ideas from the legal and technological viewpoints.

Participants
Participants were 27 persons including five vision-impaired persons, five helpers, five designers, five engineers, five legal designers and two supporters. Each group consisted of a total of five people, one helper, one designer, one engineer, one legal designer, and one supporter. this session was conducted at once with all 5 groups.

Implementation Environment
Walking was carried out in the Yokohama city. Opening session and idea generation were carried out at Fabrication laboratory in Yokohama.

Procedure
The designer made a preliminary walk on each corresponding route before the workshop in order to confirm the route to walk in each group.
⟨opening session⟩
Introduction Presentations were given on the development objectives of the wearable device and current issues. After that, participants were divided into groups, and wearable devices were distributed one by one to each group.
⟨walking in the city⟩
Each group walked a different route determined with wearing the wearable device. Each Route was about one hour route including train movement. Meanwhile, participants were free to communicate.

⟨idea generation⟩
After walking around the town, each group repeated a two or three sets of "Sharing ideas in groups" → "filling in sheets individually" while looking back on the walk experience in the group. Finally, ideas that got favorable comment among each group was shared and all participants discussed about these ideas.

Implementation Result
<idea generation by users' participation>, "Workshop for idea generation to provide new services" was implemented and a total of 116 ideas were generated (see Fig. 6). Three kinds of ideas were obtained by roughly classifying them. One is the idea close to improved thought. The second is the idea generated as an acceptable solution based on a relatively common need but not an improved one. In addition, co-creative ideas created by the interaction between the user and other participants were obtained through the walking experiences, respectively.

5 Result

Through the implementation of the case study, seven points to consider in the implementation of the participatory design process were extracted.

Common Experience and Individual Experience
Understanding whether the needs are based on common experiences or based on individual experiences will be one of the judgmental factors for considering at what level to put it in the design plan.

Participant Group Size
Whether to emphasize the volume of the group size or to emphasize the individual context by reducing the group size needs to be planned according to the aim of each phase.

Total Participation or Singly Participation
There are a limited number of cases where users can participate continuously in the design process over a long period of time.

It is a point to consider when planning whether to recruit participants from time to time and make opportunities with more diverse participants at any time.

Involvement of Persons with Expertise
By Intervention by people who have some knowledge of the characteristics and lives of vision-impaired people, it has made it possible to draw more fulfilling information from vision-impaired people. Experts with engineering knowledge also contribute greatly to the development and evaluation of design.

User Motivation
To show whether or not the target design affects the lives of participants themselves and whether the design can possibly influence in the future is one of the key points for enhancing the will to participate.

Utilization and Devising of Tools According to User's Situation
Utilization and ingenuity of tools for actively discussions and sharing information
should be set according to the user's situation, and designers need to make efforts to
prepare the environment which users can easily talk.

Resource Issues for Implementation
In participatory designs, resources are often restricted in terms of location, time, money
and the like. The point is the know-how for executing participatory design in constraints and presenting the possibility of risk reduction and quality improvement as a
result by implementation.

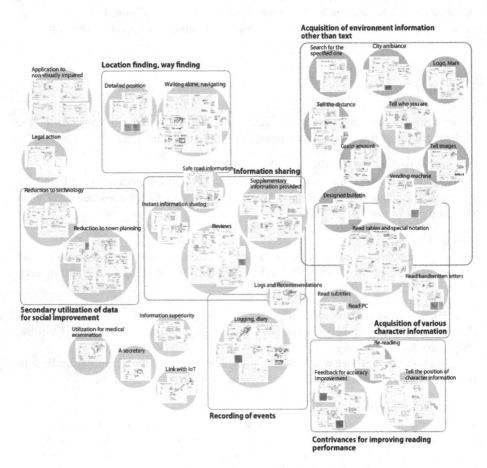

Fig. 6. Created ideas at the workshop.

6 Discussion

One of the limitations of this research is focusing on the phase of information dissemination and collection, mainly against the proposed process in the case study, and the convergence of information and the verification of the integration phase are not sufficiently verified. The future study is to show applicability in other cases, and to make a design process model that can be utilized at the actual design site.

References

1. Ministry of Internal Affairs and Communications of Japan HP. http://www.soumu.go.jp/main_sosiki/joho_tsusin/policyreports/japanese/papers/h12/html/C1000030.html
2. Ueda, K., et al.: Emergent synthesis methodologies for manufacturing. Ann. CIRP **50**(2), 535 (2001)
3. Wilkinson, C.R., De Angeli, A.: Applying user centered and participatory design approaches to commercial product development. Des. Stud. **35**(6), 614–631 (2014)
4. Lindsay, S., Jackson, D., Schofield, G., Olivier, P.: Engaging older people using participatory design. In: Proceedings of the CHI 2012, p. 1199. ACM Press, New York (2012)
5. Demirbilek, O., Demirkan, H.: Universal product design involving elderly users: a participatory design model. Appl. Ergon. **35**(4), 361–370 (2004)
6. Robert, G.: Partcipatory action research: using experience-based co-design (EBCD) to improve healthcare services. In: Ziebland, S., Calabrese, J., Coulter, A., Locock, L. (eds.) Understanding and Using Experiences of Health and Illness. Oxford University Press, Oxford (2013)
7. Ishida, T.: Field Informatics: Kyoto University Field Informatics Research Group. Springer, Berlin (2012). https://doi.org/10.1007/978-3-642-29006-0
8. Massimi, M., Baecher, R.: Participatory design process with older users michael. In: the 9th ACM Conference on Creativity and Cognition, pp. 114–123. ACM Press, New York (2006)

How to Overcome Barriers
for the Implementation of New Information
Technologies in Intensive Care Medicine

Akira-Sebastian Poncette[2,3], Christian Meske[1,2],
Lina Mosch[3], and Felix Balzer[2,3(✉)]

[1] Freie Universität Berlin, Garystr. 21, 14195 Berlin, Germany
[2] Einstein Center Digital Future, Wilhelmstraße 67, 10117 Berlin, Germany
felix.balzer@charite.de
[3] Department of Anesthesiology and Intensive Care Medicine,
Charité – Universitätsmedizin Berlin (corporate member
of Freie Universität Berlin, Humboldt-Universität zu Berlin,
and Berlin Institute of Health), Berlin, Germany

Abstract. In highly technical environments, as for instance, the intensive care unit (ICU) in hospitals, developments in digital health are promising for bringing benefits for both the patient and hospital by increasing patient safety and reducing healthcare expenses. However, the digital transformation of ICUs remains slow, and healthcare organisations hesitate to implement new technologies. With this qualitative study, we have aimed to identify potential barriers to the implementation of new information technology in the ICU. Data collection was conducted through ethnography in form of field research. In subsequent focus groups, the Consolidated Framework for Implementation Research (CFIR) was utilised to assess and evaluate the implementation process. For the outer setting, the complex and time-consuming privacy and legal issues were identified; for the inner setting, the ICU as a stressful environment with high patient turnover and staff fluctuation leading to a negative implementation climate was described. Engagement from the ICU staff in regard to embracing the possibilities of digital innovation was found to be limited, and the usage of the new technology was hindered by low perceived usability. To the best of our knowledge, this is the first evaluation of barriers for the implementation of digital health technologies in the ICU. Identified barriers underline that for a digital transformation, not only technological advancements are necessary. End-user involvement and contribution for the conceptualisation and training in digital literacy are more needed than ever before.

Keywords: Healthcare · Hospital · Patient monitoring · IT adoption ·
Implementation barriers · Intensive care medicine · User-centered design ·
Digital literacy

A. S. Poncette, L. Mosch, F. Balzer—Department of Anesthesiology and Intensive Care Medicine, Charité – Universitätsmedizin Berlin.

S. Yamamoto and H. Mori (Eds.): HCII 2019, LNCS 11570, pp. 534–546, 2019.
https://doi.org/10.1007/978-3-030-22649-7_43

1   Introduction

1.1   Digital Transformation of the ICU

"Digital transformation of health services encompasses the instrumented effort to meaningfully introduce new digital information and communication technologies and corresponding new processes and stakeholder behaviour into the health sector" [1]. In intensive care medicine, technology always has played an essential role. Monitoring of patients' vital parameters, replacing organ functions through machines (respirator, extracorporeal membrane oxygenation, dialysis) and documenting patients' health status in the patient data management systems (PDMS) are essential parts of the intensive care unit (ICU).

Developments in the field of information and communication technologies and their application in healthcare are promising further improvement of patients' health. In intensive care medicine telemedicine and digital health are mirrored in remote patient monitoring with mobile devices such as tablets or even in entire tele-intensive care units (tele-ICUs), where intensive care is performed by non-specialised healthcare personnel who are supervised and supported by a remote intensivist physician through modern digital communication technologies and high speed data transmission [2]. These developments promise a benefit for both the patient and hospital [3, 4]. Generally speaking, expectations for the digital transformation of ICUs include the increase of patient safety through highly sensitive, specific and at the same time less invasive measurement of vital parameters [2]. Improved visualization of monitoring parameters and clinical decision support systems on an as-needed basis have been found to reduce reaction time (e.g. time to diagnosis) of ICU staff [5, 6]. And with the Internet of Things (IoT), digitalisation in healthcare will become pervasive.

However, the digital transformation of intensive care medicine remains slow and healthcare organisations hesitate to introduce new technologies [7, 8]. So, what are the reasons for this hesitancy and the lagging implementation of digital health into healthcare organisations? What keeps hospitals and healthcare providers from introducing new digital tools? Identifying barriers that impede the implementation of digital health technologies on the ICU is a key aspect if we want to advance the effective and meaningful digital transformation of intensive care medicine.

1.2   Barriers to Implementation

Barriers to implementation of digital health applications into healthcare systems can be clustered in (1) poor usability, (2) limited knowledge and awareness and (3) lack of resources [10–14]:

Poor Usability. Healthcare technologies have always been lagging behind in terms of usability and user-friendly design [9, 15, 16]. This provokes adverse effects like the emergence of additional work, relative disapproval of technologies and also increases the probability of medical errors [9, 10]. Poor usability often results from high complexity of technologies associated with non-existent interoperability [11]. Unfortunately, this characterizes many digital health technologies and contributes to implementation failure [12].

Limited Knowledge and Awareness. A study by Moeckli et al. found that the lack of healthcare professionals' understanding of technologies implemented in a tele-ICU was a major barrier to implementation, as was the lack of demand for respective innovations [13]. Moreover, missing the advantages of digital health technologies over conservative practices poses a barrier to implementation [14].

Lack of Resources. Further main barriers to digital health implementation are a shortage of dedicated resources. For example, financial investments and protected time for staff members are seldom approved when installing a novel technology [11].

The limited engagement of those responsible for driving health innovations in authorities (leadership engagement) is designated to hinder the successful completion of the implementation [15, 16].

1.3   Research Goal

With this qualitative study, we aimed to identify barriers to the implementation of novel technology, focusing on the particularities of the intensive care setting and to discuss strategies to overcome these. Developed strategies may inspire future research, product development and healthcare provision for a more rapid and sustainable move towards digital transformation in healthcare.

2   Methods

2.1   Setting

We conducted this study at an intensive care unit of a large German university hospital between February 2016 and December 2018 shortly after the implementation of the Vital Sync™ Virtual Patient Monitoring Platform 2.4 developed by Medtronic plc as a remote patient monitoring using tablet computers. Participants of the study included the ICU staff team (nurses, physicians, respiratory therapists) as well as coordinators of the ICU (senior physician, nursing management). Prior to the study, all participants gave their consent to participate, and the local ethics committee provided ethical approval for this study (EA1/031/18).

2.2   Research Team and Study Design

The research team consisted of a physician with background in anesthesiology, intensive care medicine, geriatrics and digital health (AP), a senior medical student with a focus on digital health (LM), a professor of digital health, who is a computer scientist and anesthesiologist (FB), and a professor of information systems and digital transformation (CM). We chose an exploratory qualitative research approach using ethnography, a field research with subsequent focus groups was conducted as previously described [17].

2.3 Data Collection and Analysis

For optimal ethnographic research conditions, we chose to immerse with the ICU staff in a four weeks field study. This way, we aimed to observe ICU routine and interaction with the ICU staff. After the field study, regular visits during the whole study period followed. Field notes were subsequently discussed and summarised in focus groups with the authors and the head of the ICU staff. First conclusions were iteratively challenged by the interdisciplinary research team. For data analysis, the Consolidated Framework for Implementation Research (CFIR) was used [12, 15]. The CFIR is a well-used framework that was chosen to provide the possibility to holistically evaluate the implementation process of a digital health technology [11–13]. Additionally, login frequencies of ICU staff were retrieved from the tablet computers.

2.4 Technical Setup

Implementation of the Vital Sync™ was conducted on a ten bed Post Anesthesia Care Unit (PACU), an ICU mainly for postoperative patients that need a short term (24 h) intensive care treatment and monitoring. The primary patient monitoring device used at the time of the study was the Philips IntelliVue patient monitoring system (MX800 software version M.00.03; MMS X2 software version H.15.41-M.00.04). All parameters including the electrocardiogram (ECG), blood pressure, temperature, or ventilator parameters of mechanically ventilated patients were displayed through the Philips IntelliVue patient monitoring system on stationary touchscreen displays at the bedside and on a monitor at the central nurse station.

The Vital Sync™ Virtual Patient Monitoring Platform was used as secondary monitoring and received vital parameters (1 Hz) from five out of a total of ten ICU beds. Transmitted vital parameters included peripheral capillary oxygen saturation (SpO_2), pulse rate (PR), end-tidal carbon dioxide level ($etCO_2$) and respiratory rate (RR), and were retrievable from six tablet computers (two large iPads, two iPad minis, two Microsoft Surfaces) and one stationary monitor at the central nurse station. In addition, the integrated pulmonary index (IPI), a respiratory score, was automatically calculated from the above-mentioned parameters and displayed on all devices [18]. These five parameters were retrievable after logging into an iPad (six-digit code) or a Surface (username and password) and further logging into a Vital Sync™ website (iPad) or software (Surface) with another username and password. The Vital Sync™ software was web-based and with the specific URL retrievable from any computer connected to the hospital's intranet. The installation of the new system did not interfere with the ICU routine.

2.5 Software

When a new patient arrives on the ICU, the patient is virtually added to the Vital Sync™ Monitoring Software at the bedside in a 7 step process as described on the product homepage [19]. All four vital parameters, SpO_2 = peripheral capillary oxygen saturation, PR = pulse rate, RR = respiratory rate, $EtCO_2$ = end-tidal carbon dioxide and the IPI (=Integrated Pulmonary Index) score are displayed in the patient-specific view. At the bottom of the display, the CO_2 Waveform is displayed (see Fig. 1).

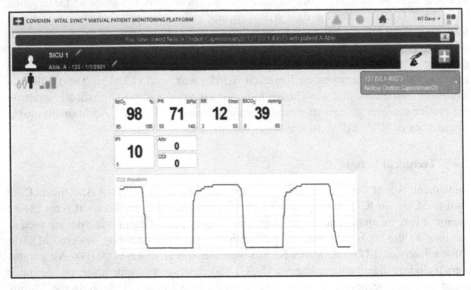

Fig. 1. Screenshot of the patient view of the Vital Sync™ Virtual Patient Monitoring Platform 2.4; all four vital parameters (SpO_2 = peripheral capillary oxygen saturation, PR = pulse rate, RR = respiratory rate, $EtCO_2$ = end-tidal carbon dioxide) and the IPI (= Integrated Pulmonary Index) score are displayed [19]

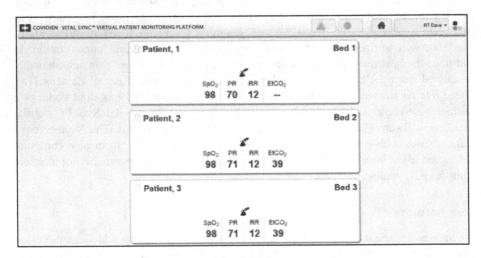

Fig. 2. Screenshot of the patient tile view of the Vital Sync™ Virtual Patient Monitoring Platform 2.4; all four vital parameters (SpO_2, PR, RR, $EtCO_2$) [19]

When the home button on the top right is pressed, the patient tile view (all patients of the ward) is shown. In this view, a configurable selection of numeric parameters (i.e. SpO_2, $etCO_2$, PR, and RR) without waveforms of all connected patients is presented (see Fig. 2).

2.6 Installation and ICU Staff Training

The on-site setup of the devices was finished in May 2018. Usage of the system began in the same month after instruction into the device of the ICU staff (physician, nurses and respiratory therapists) over a period of one month. Additionally, two workshops were offered to explain further technical backgrounds and for hands-on training with the new technology. ICU staff training was continued on an as-needed basis.

2.7 Mapping of CFIR Domains to Study-Specific Areas

The Consolidated Framework for Implementation Research provides a guideline for the assessment and evaluation of an implementation process and helped us to contextualise the given data. We mapped the CFIR domains to the respective study-specific areas (see Table 1). The special characteristics of our study setting comprised the PACU with its high patient turnover personnel (from external and internal staff pools) and patients, a multidisciplinary team (physicians, nurses, respiratory therapists using Vital Sync™) that was responsible for several ICUs [15].

Table 1. Mapping of CFIR domains to study-specific areas [11, 15]

CFIR domain	Study-specific areas
Intervention characteristics	Remote patient monitoring system with integrated CDSS
Outer setting	Federal and state entities, university hospital
Inner setting (structural characteristics, networks & communications, culture, implementation climate)	PACU (ICU), multidisciplinary team of several ICUs, high patient and personnel fluctuation
Characteristics of individuals	ICU staff: nurses, physicians, respiratory therapists
Process	Implementation of a remote patient monitoring system on an ICU

3 Results

3.1 Usage

Random visits to the installation site indicated that up to this point, the Vital Sync™ was hardly ever used by the ICU staff. This was confirmed by review of the login details of the devices. In consequence, intensified ICU staff training was conducted from May to December 2018, which made no considerable improvements.

3.2 Barriers

As barriers to implementation of the Vital Sync™, all aspects that hindered or delayed the installation and usage of Vital Sync™ were considered (see Fig. 3).

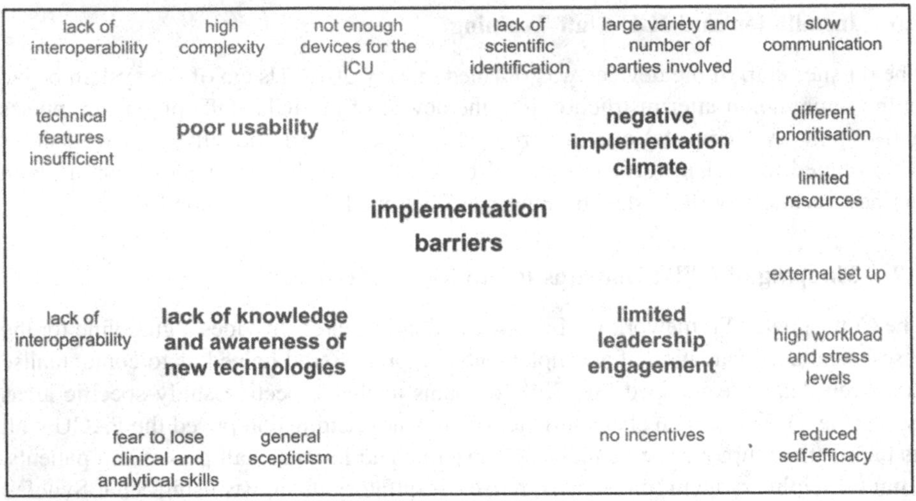

lack of interoperability	high complexity	not enough devices for the ICU	lack of scientific identification	large variety and number of parties involved	slow communication
technical features insufficient	**poor usability**			**negative implementation climate**	different prioritisation
		implementation barriers			limited resources
					external set up
lack of interoperability	**lack of knowledge and awareness of new technologies**			**limited leadership engagement**	high workload and stress levels
	fear to lose clinical and analytical skills	general scepticism		no incentives	reduced self-efficacy

Fig. 3. Identified barriers to implementation of Vital Sync™, a remote patient monitoring device for intensive care medicine

Negative Implementation Climate. A challenge for the implementation of Vital Sync™ was the variety and number of parties involved in the project. Along with slow communication channels (email), time-consuming processes for complicated privacy and legal issues and having different project prioritisation between parties (e.g. ICU project leader of Vital Sync™ versus legal department of hospital) led to delays of installation of more than 6 months.

Negative implementation climate was further influenced by limited available resources such as digital infrastructure (non-existent interoperability of Vital Sync™ with other devices such as a respirator) and lack of time for staff training due to high workload. Because the research team and the intervention itself have been set up and planned mainly without the involvement of internal ICU staff, the ICU personnel was lacking scientific and academic identification with the Vital Sync™ system. Another characteristic of the ICU was the high fluctuation of both ICU personnel and patients which along with missing communication led to a non-usage of the remote patient monitoring system.

Limited Leadership Engagement. The Vital Sync™ implementation was lacking a general leadership engagement and motivation from ICU and implementation stakeholders to promote the usage of Vital Sync™. This limited leadership engagement was due to the fact that the implementation project was developed externally and responsibilities about leadership in the ICU team and implementation team not clearly defined. High workloads and stress levels were the main reasons for the limited leadership engagement regarding Vital Sync™ implementation.

Lack of Knowledge and Awareness of Digital Health Technologies Among ICU Staff. A key factor that hindered the implementation of the Vital Sync™ software was ICU staffs' limited knowledge and awareness of digital health technologies and their potential. We observed a general skepticism towards new digital technologies among the ICU staff, related to the fear to lose clinical and analytical skills when applying digital health. This also contributed to the fact that the relative priority of the project was different among responsible stakeholders (leader of the research team, senior physician on ICU, head of nursing department), impeding the implementation process.

Perceived Limited Usability. The implemented remote patient monitoring system (Vital Sync™) was perceived as hard to set up and complicated to use. The main reason users stated this was the confusing design of the application and the perceived high complexity of features (e.g. Clinical Decision Support System - IPI). Another point of criticism was the lack of interoperability with other devices, e.g. the respiratory machine or blood pressure.

Also, not all patient beds were equipped with Vital Sync™ and not every staff member could get a personal mobile device. In total only 6 tablets were available for a team of one respiratory therapist, three physicians and up to six nurses per shift. Devices had to be returned to the docking station after usage and were not individualised. Furthermore, only four vital parameters were displayed on the remote monitor, which was considered insufficient by healthcare professionals on the ICU.

4   Discussion

4.1   Summary

As part of the installation of the Vital Sync™ Virtual Patient Monitoring, we conducted this study at an ICU through means of ethnography and focus groups. The results show multilayered implementation barriers in all domains of the CFIR. For the outer setting, the complex and time-consuming privacy issues were identified, whereas, for the inner setting, the ICU as a generally stressful environment with a high patient and staff fluctuation lead to a negative implementation climate. Regarding the characteristics of the individuals, engagement from the ICU staff in regard to embracing the possibilities of digital innovation was lacking. And the process itself was hindered by limited perceived usability. In Fig. 4, strategies to overcome these perceived barriers to implementation are proposed by applying the CFIR as a structure.

4.2   Implementation Climate

Leadership involvement and identification with the proposed new technology has found to be vital for a successful implementation. This also applies to the involvement of the end-users (ICU staff) in the conceptualisation, development and implementation of the new technology, which may even be more challenging in rural hospitals

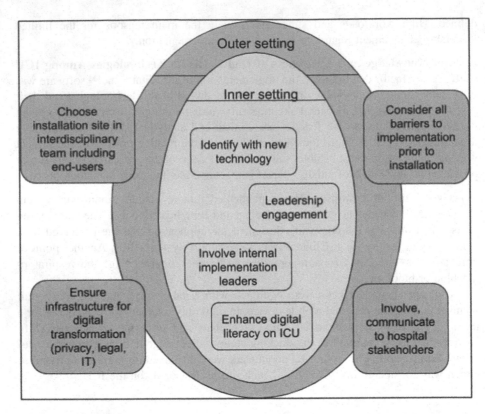

Fig. 4. Strategies to overcome perceived barriers to implementation of a remote patient monitoring device on ICU (divided into outer and inner setting according to the modified CFIR)

compared to the university environment. To overcome this barrier, a formally selected internal implementation leader should be announced, get protected time and made familiar with the responsibilities and roles within the team [11]. If the ICU staff are highly interested in implementing new technology, choosing the right system in an interdisciplinary approach is highly recommended. Since communication over email is known to be slow and potentially induce misunderstandings [24], few but effective meetings in person with an agenda and predetermined roles for all participants might be more sufficient.

In a university hospital environment, early identification of general barriers to the implementation of new technology (e.g. malfunctioning technical infrastructure) may support its application in the single departments and hospital wards. The primary challenge in this context relates to privacy and legal aspects of digital transformation. Although from May 2018, security and privacy requirements for personal health data are set in the General Data Protection Regulation (GDPR), expertise and guidance in regard to digital health applications especially in hospitals are still lacking [2]. In addition, digital transformation comes with an ever-rising number of interconnected and intersectoral health systems. This needs an information technology infrastructure, which is in many healthcare institutions (especially in rural areas) still to be established [25].

Regarding the intensive care unit (in this case the PACU) as the installation and implementation site, careful considerations of possible barriers to implementation have to be taken into account in an interdisciplinary team. In the conceptualization phase, all factors of the installation site have to be rated as a potential barrier or not. In our case, high fluctuations of ICU staff (from external and internal pools) and patients resulted in high workloads for individual staff members. This led to insufficient training with the proposed technology. Another ICU, with less turn-over of patients and staff may have been a better place for the implementation.

4.3 Involvement of Leadership Engagement in Implementation

As one of the inner settings of the CFIR, leadership engagement is rated as supportive in all stages of the development and implementation of new technology in an existing environment - e.g. the ICU [12]. In our study, we can confirm that the insufficient involvement of key stakeholders in the implementation of novel technology lead to delayed and unsuccessful implementation. On the one side, key stakeholders of university hospitals are challenged by several tasks such as patient care, research, education and management of staff or procurement at the same time [20]. Pressure can come from application deadlines for a research grant on the one day and an urgent therapy for a critically ill patient on the other. In addition, stress levels in the intensive care environment are generally high through critically ill patients, high turnover of patients, fluctuations of ICU staff, ongoing noise through alarms, and high distraction rates with no fluent workflow [21]. Thus, the priority of the implementation of new technology may be rated as low from day to day. On the other side, prioritization often goes along with interest and motivation in a specific topic. In this multifaceted dilemma, the 'I don't have time' mentality in university hospitals hence may possibly rather be understood as 'I am not interested enough to prioritize this'. From a person, who is not interested in a specific topic, less support can be expected [21].

The full support and involvement of key stakeholders is an essential element for a successful implementation of new technology in ICU. Key stakeholders should motivate and empower ICU staff, inform and communicate about the expected outcomes and goals of the project, solve problems that may occur, and communicate with the outer setting. Strategies to involve key stakeholders might include the following:

- Find out the *motivations* and *interests* of the key stakeholders
- *Involve* key stakeholders *early* in the conceptualization phase
- Make key stakeholders *identify* with the proposed project
- Explain new technology taking into account their *motivations and interests*
- *Inspire* key stakeholders of the proposed new technology; show its *advantages* over the current system
- Explain key stakeholder *roles and responsibilities*

4.4 Enhancing Digital Literacy of Healthcare Providers

Digital Health does not only achieve a translation from analog to digital processes, but also induces new processes. This is not only limited to the increasing human-computer interaction, but also refers to the fact that in the future humans will have to trust other sources of information that guide clinical decision making, as for instance artificial intelligence systems or remotely located specialists (tele-ICU). Thus, new responsibilities or roles in an ICU structure may change due to digital technology. When addressing digital transformation, it is therefore important to include all end-users. Ensuring the wide-spread digitisation in ICU (e.g. through implementing patient data management systems) and enabling digitalisation in ICU (e.g. through the intramural communication with mobile devices such as tablets and smartphones), only has an impact when healthcare providers are trained to use digital technologies (digital literacy) and their feedback used to jointly create user-centered solutions for patient care. For digital transformation, this final step is crucial. To enhance digital literacy as well as to foster innovation in healthcare, we encourage hospitals to offer trainings in digital health to their staff through expert workshops, simulations or e-learning, also to get them acquainted with current developments in digital health. Another method en vogue is the hackathon concept. A hackathon is a competition event where teams battle against each other usually over 48 h for the best solution to a specific problem. Conducting a healthcare hackathon inside a hospital has an enormous innovation potential just by bringing healthcare providers together with developers and IT designers [22, 23].

4.5 Embrace Usability and Advantage of New Digital Health Solutions

Although the electronic health records (EHR) have been implemented in the US healthcare system over nine years ago, EHR usability (referring to the efficient, effective and safe use of technology) is still not fully optimised for clinical use [26]. Insufficient usability of EHR even reduces patient safety [27]. Usability issues are not only limited to EHR but concern all medical devices. With digital transformation, we want to take advantage of digitalization, including the intuitive use of software and hardware, embracing usability to harmonise human-computer interaction. In a stressful environment as the ICU [20], stress should not be induced through the use of digital applications. Rather, digital applications should calm and focus the user for an efficient, effective and safe work. In usability research various low-cost methods are available [28]. One technique for example includes the user to think-aloud when using the new system. This is a simple and cost-effective way to discover potential usability issues. The key to optimal usability of digital systems and the basis of a usability test are the early involvement of users in the design process and acknowledging their feedback.

5 Conclusion

The successful implementation of novel technologies in an ICU setting requires a thorough assessment of the possible barriers in different settings and a diligent planning of how to overcome those. However, for digital transformation, not only technological advancements are necessary. The early involvement and continuous training of the end-user are more needed than ever before.

References

1. Bourek, A., Bourekeu, W.: Expert Panel on effective ways of investing in Health (EXPH) 37
2. Poncette, A.S., et al.: Clinical requirements of future patient monitoring in the intensive care unit: qualitative study. JMIR Med. Inform. 7(2), e13064 (2019). https://doi.org/10.2196/13064
3. Noah, B., et al.: Impact of remote patient monitoring on clinical outcomes: an updated meta-analysis of randomized controlled trials. npj Digital Med. 1, 20172 (2018). https://doi.org/10.1038/s41746-017-0002-4
4. Kumar, S., Merchant, S., Reynolds, R.: Tele-ICU: efficacy and cost-effectiveness of remotely managing critical Care. Perspect. Health Inf. Manag. 10, 1f (2013)
5. Michard, F.: Hemodynamic monitoring in the era of digital health. Ann. Intensive Care 6, 15 (2016). https://doi.org/10.1186/s13613-016-0119-7
6. Gozal, D., Weissbrod, R., Ronen, M.: A pilot evaluation of the Integrated Pulmonary Index (IPI) in patients undergoing procedural sedation: a two-phase observational evaluation. JCAO 2, 2 (2018)
7. De Georgia, M.A., Kaffashi, F., Jacono, F.J., Loparo, K.A.: Information technology in critical care: review of monitoring and data acquisition systems for patient care and research. Sci. World J. 2015 (2015). https://doi.org/10.1155/2015/727694
8. Hüsers, J., et al.: Innovative power of health care organisations affects IT adoption: a bi-national health IT benchmark comparing Austria and Germany. J. Med. Syst. 41, 33 (2017). https://doi.org/10.1007/s10916-016-0671-6
9. Campbell, E.M., Sittig, D.F., Ash, J.S., Guappone, K.P., Dykstra, R.H.: Types of unintended consequences related to computerized provider order entry. J. Am. Med. Inf. Assoc. 13, 547–556 (2006). https://doi.org/10.1197/jamia.M2042
10. Fairbanks, R.J., Caplan, S.: Poor interface design and lack of usability testing facilitate medical error. Joint Comm. J. Qual. Saf. 30, 579–584 (2004). https://doi.org/10.1016/S1549-3741(04)30068-7
11. Anderson, J.G., Vagnoni, E.: Social, ethical and legal barriers to E-health. Int. J. Med. Inf. 480–483 (2007). https://doi.org/10.1016/j.ijmedinf.2006.09.016
12. Ross, J., Stevenson, F., Lau, R., Murray, E.: Factors that influence the implementation of e-health: a systematic review of systematic reviews (an update). Implementation Sci. 11 (2016). https://doi.org/10.1186/s13012-016-0510-7
13. Moeckli, J., Cram, P., Cunningham, C., Reisinger, H.S.: Staff acceptance of a telemedicine intensive care unit program: a qualitative study. J. Crit. Care 28, 890–901 (2013). https://doi.org/10.1016/j.jcrc.2013.05.008
14. Nohl-Deryk, P., Brinkmann, J.K., Gerlach, F.M., Schreyögg, J., Achelrod, D.: Barriers to digitalisation of healthcare in Germany: a survey of experts. Gesundheitswesen (2018). https://doi.org/10.1055/s-0043-121010

15. Damschroder, L.J., Aron, D.C., Keith, R.E., Kirsh, S.R., Alexander, J.A., Lowery, J.C.: Fostering implementation of health services research findings into practice: a consolidated framework for advancing implementation science. Implementation Sci. **4**, 50 (2009). https://doi.org/10.1186/1748-5908-4-50

16. Stolee, P., Steeves, B., Glenny, C., Filsinger, S.: The use of electronic health information systems in home care: facilitators and barriers. Home Healthc. Nurse J. Home Care Hospice Prof. **28**, 167–181 (2010). https://doi.org/10.1097/01.NHH.0000369769.32246.92

17. Charlesworth, M., Foëx, B.A.: Qualitative research in critical care: has its time finally come? J. Intensive Care Soc. **17**, 146–153 (2016). https://doi.org/10.1177/1751143715609955

18. Ronen, M., Weissbrod, R., Overdyk, F.J., Ajizian, S.: Smart respiratory monitoring: clinical development and validation of the IPI^{TM} (Integrated Pulmonary Index) algorithm. J. Clin. Monit. Comput. **31**, 435–442 (2017). https://doi.org/10.1007/s10877-016-9851-7

19. Vital Sync^{TM} Virtual Patient Monitoring Platform 2. Medtronic. https://www.medtronic.com/covidien/en-us/products/health-informatics-and-monitoring/vital-sync-virtual-patient-monitoring-platform-2-6.html

20. Lindfors, S., Boman, J., Alexanderson, K.: Strategies used to handle stress by academic physicians at a university hospital. Work **43**, 183–193 (2012). https://doi.org/10.3233/WOR-2012-1364

21. Kumar, A., Pore, P., Gupta, S., Wani, A.O.: Level of stress and its determinants among Intensive Care Unit staff. Indian J. Occup. Environ. Med. **20**, 129–132 (2016). https://doi.org/10.4103/0019-5278.203137

22. Angelidis, P., et al.: The hackathon model to spur innovation around global mHealth. J. Med. Eng. Technol. **40**, 392–399 (2016). https://doi.org/10.1080/03091902.2016.1213903

23. Olson, K.R., et al.: Health hackathons: theatre or substance? A survey assessment of outcomes from healthcare-focused hackathons in three countries. BMJ Innov. **3**, 37–44 (2017). https://doi.org/10.1136/bmjinnov-2016-000147

24. Byron, K.: Carrying too heavy a load? The communication and miscommunication of emotion by email. Acad. Manag. Rev. **33**(2), 309–327 (2008). https://doi.org/10.5465/amr.2008.31193163

25. Kooti, F., Aiello, L.M., Grbovic, M., Lerman, K., Mantrach, A.: Evolution of conversations in the age of email overload. In: Proceedings of the 24th International Conference on World Wide Web, WWW 2015, pp. 603–613. Republic and Canton of Geneva, Switzerland. International World Wide Web Conferences Steering Committee (2015). https://doi.org/10.1145/2736277.2741130

26. Nohl-Deryk, P., Brinkmann, J.K., Gerlach, F.M., Schreyögg, J., Achelrod, D.: Barriers to Digitalisation of Healthcare in Germany: A Survey of Experts. Gesundheitswesen (Bundesverband Der Arzte Des Offentlichen Gesundheitsdienstes (Germany)), 4 January 2018. https://doi.org/10.1055/s-0043-121010

27. Howe, J.L., Adams, K.T., Hettinger, A.Z., Ratwani, R.M.: Electronic health record usability issues and potential contribution to patient harm. JAMA **319**(12), 1276–1278 (2018). https://doi.org/10.1001/jama.2018.1171

28. Ratwani, R.M., Hodgkins, M., Bates, D.W.: Improving electronic health record usability and safety requires transparency. JAMA **320**(24), 2533–2534 (2018). https://doi.org/10.1001/jama.2018.14079

29. Peischl, B., Ferk, M., Holzinger, A.: The fine art of user-centered software development. Softw. Qual. J. **23**, 509–536 (2015). https://doi.org/10.1007/s11219-014-9239-1

Development of a Interface Which Was Customized for People with Disabilities Using 3D Printers

Yudai Sato[1]([✉]), Takeo Ainoya[1], Ryuta Motegi[2], and Keiko Kasamatsu[2]

[1] serBOTinQ, Tokyo Metropolitan University, 6-6 Asahigaoka, Hino-shi, Tokyo, Japan
yudaisato141@gmail.com
[2] Tokyo Metropolitan University, 6-6 Asahigaoka, Hino-shi, Tokyo, Japan

Abstract. The UI (User Interface) usable by handicapped people has used a combination of ready-made products in the past. However, combining ready-made items alone is not sufficient for ease of use, and not only the yaw and row of the operating angle but also the angle of the pitch must be considered. In this research, we design the interface design of the Boccia robot project, temporarily prototype an interface capable of analyzing and manipulating UX (User experience) and UI for people with disabilities by mockup using 3D printers, and using CAD production and 3D printers Proof and modify the actual prototype outputted and produced it. Through four steps, we made interface of Boccia robot by repeating the process of CAD data production, 3D printing, verification from evidence investigation through idea sketch. It became clear that the technical and knowledge necessary for implementation and the need for structural thinking are also necessary.

Keywords: 3D printer · Custom interface · Design process

1 Introduction

Conventional interfaces for persons with disabilities have used combinations of off-the-shelf components like wheelchair controllers, for example. However, combining ready-made products alone is not sufficient for ease of use when considering the degree of disability, and not only the yaw and row of the operating angle but also the angle of the pitch is important and must be taken into consideration. However, like the introduction movie of Apple's accessibility page, Apple products can implement technologies that can be customized according to the extent of the obstacle, as well as ophthalmic equipment Oton Glass that extends the ability to read letters for visually impaired people, As well as the interface of Microsoft's Xbox Adaptive Controller announced in 2018, a customizable interface has been announced depending on the degree of disability, and the importance of interfaces specialized for persons with disabilities is being recognized globally.

© Springer Nature Switzerland AG 2019
S. Yamamoto and H. Mori (Eds.): HCII 2019, LNCS 11570, pp. 547–555, 2019.
https://doi.org/10.1007/978-3-030-22649-7_44

We analyzed UX and UI for disable people using mockup using 3D printer as a theme of interface design of Boccia robot project, rapid prototype interface that can be operated with idea sketch, outputted by CAD production, 3D printer Proof by actual prototype, made with modifications made.

The project members are two students specializing in product design in charge of design review, one student specializing in car design, one student specializing in motion graphics, and one product designer in charge of design direction We made a total of five people in total, two other students specializing in robotics who was in charge of the moving parts when building the implementation model.

2 Design Process

2.1 Step 0

The design process of this project, like the development of Apple's ipod, observes users from the comparison with competitors, finds problems and repeats the process of design creation, prototyping, verification, so that unprecedented music We adopted the design thinking that produced the player. By thinking of design thinking (see Fig. 1), I thought that I could answer social needs more accurately than before. In this research, we focused on three processes of creation centered on idea sketches, 3D CAD, trial production with 3D print, and verification with printed prototype.

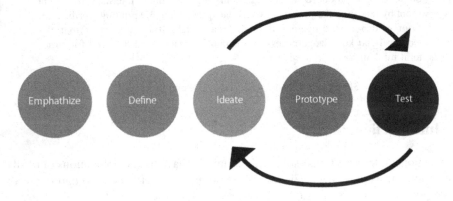

Fig. 1. Design thinking process

2.2 Step 1

When entering the design work, the disposition can be pushed in any scene during the competition Button arrangement, the size of the button, easy operation that can be intuitively operated even in a tense situation, if it becomes an obstacle to the competition However, it was not so small that it was difficult to operate, but on condition that moderate size feeling which is easy to operate was drawn, I drew a number of idea sketches (see Fig. 2) and verified.

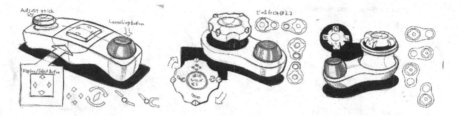

Fig. 2. Idea sketches

Three ideas which seems to be highly likely to finish beautifully in a short time easily in the 3D skills of 3D CAD production within the member and the 3D print are selected while matching the conditions described earlier from the idea sketch, Combining CAD data, making actual size prototypes with 3D printers, and combining buttons, joysticks, rotary selectors as an operation system.

Project participants actually operated and verified the prototype of the three proposals, and as a result there is a need to revalidate the size of the buttons and the spacing between the buttons, and the rotary selector is more disabled than the joystick, It was hard to use for the result (see Figs. 3 and 4). In addition, as a result of the verification, it was found that the operation method and the operation environment are different depending on the extent and kind of the obstacle, so it was decided to produce three kinds of interfaces, the operation with the wrist, the operation with the chin, the operation with the finger.

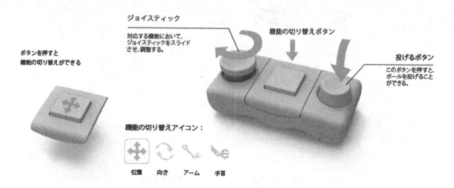

Fig. 3. A prototype combining a joystick and a button

2.3 Step 2

In Step 2, prior to entering the idea sketch verification, based on the previous result, measurement of the width of each hand of each person to check the size and interval of the button, interface mounting position when operating with chin, between buttons Was confirmed.

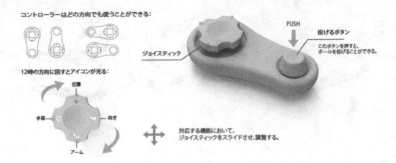

Fig. 4. A prototype combining a rotary selector

Drawing multiple idea sketches (see Fig. 5) reflecting the survey result, 3D printing with type of wrist operation, type operated with chin, type operated with fingers, 3D printing (see Fig. 6) with variable interface and manipulation with chin even by hand, I verified again (see Fig. 7).

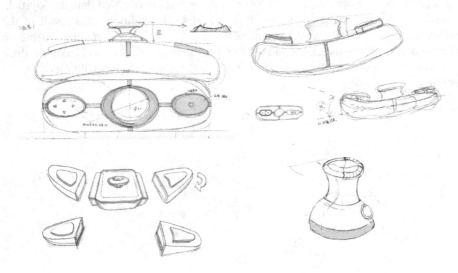

Fig. 5. Idea sketches of step 2

As a verification item, it is confirmed whether reliable operation with arm, chin and finger is confirmed. For two proposals of arm manipulation and jaw manipulation type, it is necessary to revalidate the height of the button with respect to the angle of the button and the finger operation type. Also, the variable interface is technically challenging when implementing it, and it was postponed in this project.

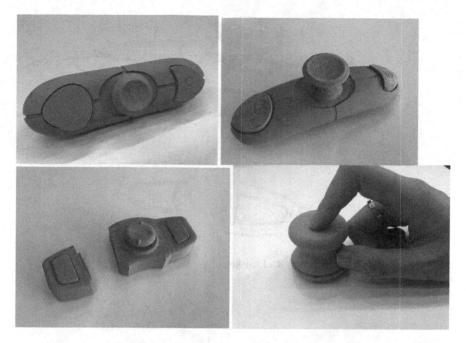

Fig. 6. 3D print model of step 2

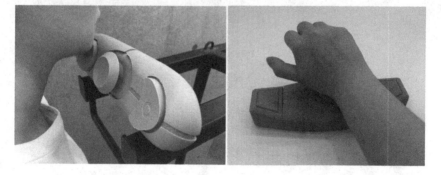

Fig. 7. Validation of 3D model

2.4   Step 3

We verified the angle and height of the button which was newly verified in the secondary verification, and verified the design that considers not only usability but also the sports feeling as a parasport tool.

First of all, the definition of sports sense is derived from the discussion, and the sports feeling is defined as having a meaningful form in everything, even in the extreme state when operating, like F1 steering, for example, and carried out an idea sketch (see Fig. 8). 3D prints of ideas (see Figs. 9, 10 and 11) selected as clean shapes that are

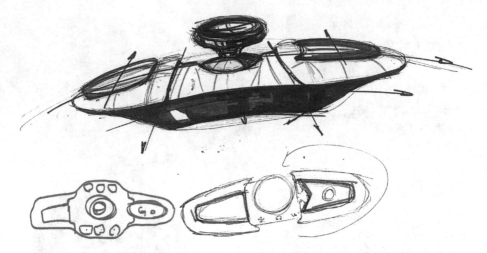

Fig. 8. Ideasketchs of step 3

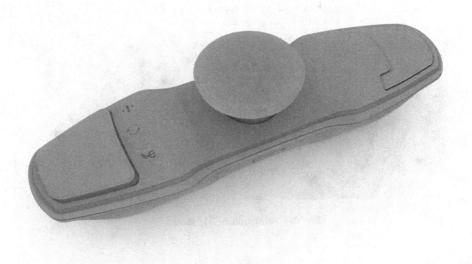

Fig. 9. Rendering of arm manipulation type

consistent with the above conditions while conforming to the above conditions are out of a plurality of sheets, among which the arm model type mounting model was produced this time. When building a mounting model (see Fig. 12), a student specializing in robotics built a mounting part, and the designer designed the housing part so that the

Fig. 10. Renderings of chin and finger manipulation type model

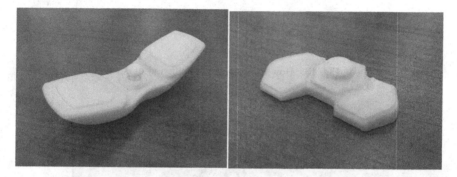

Fig. 11. 3D print models of chin and finger manipulation type model

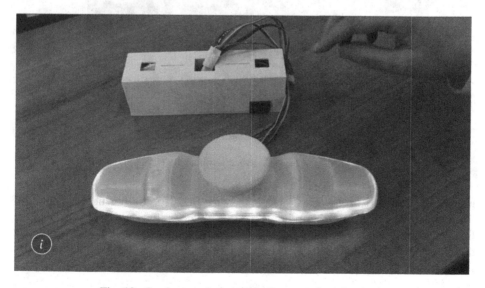

Fig. 12. Implementation model of arm manipulation type

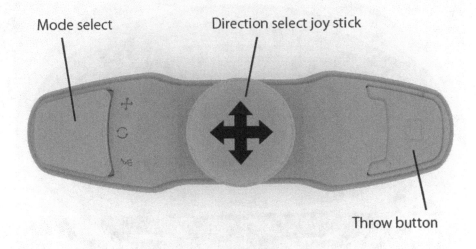

Fig. 13. How to use arm manipulation type

Fig. 14. Boccia robot

mounting part enters.In the operation method (see Fig. 13), the function switching of the movable part of the Botcher robot is made with the button on the left side, and the light of a different color is lit up according to the switching mode. You can handle the direction of the machine with the joystick in the middle, and throw the ball from Bocchiarobot (see Fig. 14) with the button on the right.

3 Discussion

From the evidence survey through the idea sketch, we have made interface of Boccia robot project by repeating CAD data production, 3D printing, verification process. Although it is a nice aspect of this process to actually touch and validate the 3D printed model, it takes time to produce CAD data and output it with a 3D printer, the point that it requires technology and knowledge for implementation, It also became clear that structural thinking is also required.

However, if these problems are overcome, we think that it is a very effective process that can accurately answer social needs for design and interface development.

References

1. Brown, T.: Change By Design. ISBN 978-0061766084 (2006)
2. Andoh, M.: User Experience Design Textbook. ISBN 978-4-621-30037-4 (2016)
3. Sato, T., Kameyama, H.: Application to the P2M of Agile development Lean product development and Design thinking (2012)
4. Apple Homepage. https://www.apple.com/jp/accessibility/. Accessed 9 Mar 2019
5. Oton Glass Homepage. https://otonglass.jp. Accessed 9 Mar 2019
6. Microsoft Homepage. https://www.microsoft.com/en-us/p/xbox-adaptive-controller/8nsdbhz1n 3d8. Accessed 9 Mar 2019
7. Fujitsu Homepage. http://www.fujitsu.com/jp/group/fri/column/opinion/201404/2014-4-4. html. Accessed 9 Mar 2019

Development of Boccia Robot
and Its Throwing Support Interface

Ryotaro Suzuki$^{(\boxtimes)}$, Rintaro Onishi, Keiko Kasamatsu, Yoshiki Shimomura,
Osamu Nitta, Ryuta Motegi, Shin Tsuchiya, Nami Shida,
and Naoyuki Takesue$^{(\boxtimes)}$

Tokyo Metropolitan University, Tokyo, Japan
ntakesue@tmu.ac.jp

Abstract. Boccia is one of sports designed for the disabled. In boccia, to propel balls to the target, throwing, rolling, kicking and using tools such as a ramp are permitted. Therefore, a wide range of people with or without disabilities can participate in the game. However, at present, boccia games are classified according to the degree of disability. It is difficult that people with severe disability and people without disability participate in the same game together. Therefore, in this study, we propose "RoBoccia", boccia using robotic throwing device that is shared by players and is connectable with various interfaces. We provided the robotic throwing device and an operational interface to operate it. In addition, we developed a throwing support interface using laser pointers to present the estimated lobbing and rolling distances to the operator intuitively. Finally, we verified the usefulness of the developed robot by carrying out the field experiments.

Keywords: Boccia · Sport robot · Throwing · Operational interface

1 Introduction

Boccia, one of the official sports in the Paralympic sports, is paid a lot of attention to because of coming Olympic/Paralympic 2020 [1]. Boccia is a sport created in Europe and designed for people with severe cerebral palsy and people with other severe functional disability [2]. The rule is similar to curling and petanque. The players are divided into two teams (red and blue) and throw or roll their colored balls as close as possible to a target ball. When the end comes, the closest team to the target ball scores.

As a feature of boccia, some throwing methods and assistance of helpers are allowed according to the degree of disability of player. If a player can throw balls by hands even with disability of lower limbs, the player can participate in the game by using a movement aid such as a wheelchair. He or she can also receive assistance of handling balls by a helper during the game as necessary. If it is difficult for a player to use hands, the player can join the game with a helper and kick the ball with feet. In case where it is difficult to use both hands and

© Springer Nature Switzerland AG 2019
S. Yamamoto and H. Mori (Eds.): HCII 2019, LNCS 11570, pp. 556–567, 2019.
https://doi.org/10.1007/978-3-030-22649-7_45

Fig. 1. Concept chart of "RoBoccia", boccia using robotic throwing device that is shared by players and is connectable with various interfaces (Color figure online)

feet, the player can participate in the game by using a ramp. In the case of using a ramp, the player manipulates the ramp by giving instructions to the helper, and rolls the ball with a tool called a head pointer attached to the head. In this way, boccia is a sport that a wide range of disabled people can participate in. In addition, it is attracting attention as a universal sport that not only people with disabilities but also elderly people and children can participate.

On the other hand, boccia games are classified and performed, because of the difference in throwing ability depending on the degree of disability. For example, in throwing with a foot or a ramp, it is impossible to lob balls. As a result, the range of strategies in the game is limited. In addition, it is difficult for the helper to perfectly manipulate the ramp according to the intention of the player. As an effort that a person with disabilities participate in sports, "Cybathlon" has been held [3]. Cybathlon is a sports event where athletes use equipments to which state-of-the-art technology such as robot wheelchairs and powered prosthesis is applied. Also, information and communication technology (ICT) and simulation technology are applied to boccia [4,5]. As project based learning in university, throwing and assisting devices in boccia and bocce, which is said to be the sport that became the origin of the boccia, have been designed [6–8]. However, we cannot find a device that provides enough performance of throwing and rolling to play boccia games so far.

Therefore, in this study, we propose "RoBoccia", boccia using robotic throwing device that is shared by the players and is connectable with various interfaces such as a joystick, a trackball, a foot pedal, a mouth interface and so on, as illustrated in Fig. 1. We developed a throwing robot that acts as an motor organ extending the throwing ability of the player, and that can selectively lob and roll a ball within a court of about 10 m [9,10]. In addition, by providing various operational interfaces for this robot, it is possible to correspond to a wide range of physical conditions. Furthermore, we developed a throwing support interface that presents the estimated lobbing and rolling distances to the operator with

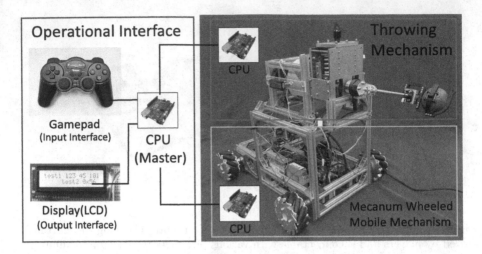

Fig. 2. The developed boccia robot

the laser pointers that are mounted on the robot [11]. By this boccia robot, it is expected that everyone enjoy playing boccia without the classification.

2   Development of Boccia Robot

An overview of the boccia robot developed in this research is shown in Fig. 2. The robot is mainly composed of a throwing mechanism, a mobile mechanism, and an interface unit including controllers. The outline explanation is described in the following section.

2.1   Throwing Mechanism

The developed throwing mechanism is shown in Fig. 3. In this mechanism, a stepping motor with gear and an arm are connected via a clutch. The axis of the arm has an eccentric cam with compression coil springs. After applying an electric power to the clutch, during the rotation of the arm to the initial angle, the eccentric cam compresses the springs. When disconnecting the clutch by turning off, the potential energy stored in the springs is instantaneously released and the arm is swung. The potential energy of the springs can be changed by setting the initial angle of the arm, α, which determines the initial velocity of the ball.

In addition, a hand mechanism shown in Fig. 4 grips the ball by the finger of the one link mechanism with the tension springs before throwing the ball. After the clutch in the throwing mechanism is disconnected, the arm accelerates and the centrifugal force acting on the ball increases. At the certain angle of the arm, the finger comes off and the ball is released from the hand. The angle of

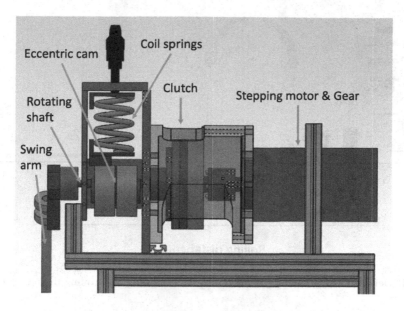

Fig. 3. Throwing mechanism

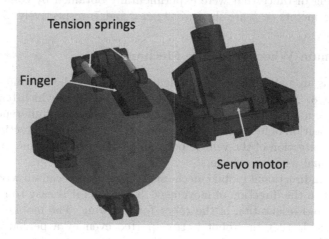

Fig. 4. Hand mechanism

the hand (wrist), β, can be changed by the servo motor shown in Fig. 4, which determines the release timing of the ball or the throwing angle.

In this robot, throwing distance is determined by two parameters of the arm initial angle α and the wrist angle β as described above. Here, the throwing distance is defined as the lobbing distance which is the distance to the landing point of the ball and the rolling distance which is the distance to the stopping point of it. The definition of two throwing parameters α, β, the lobbing distance L and the rolling distance R are illustrated in Fig. 5. Also, the lobbing distance

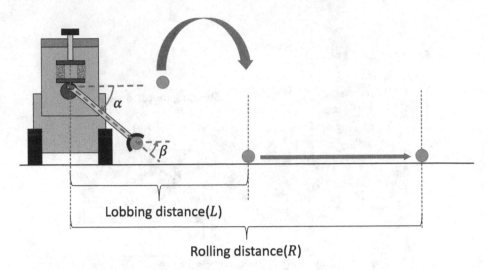

Fig. 5. Definition of throwing parameters α, β & lobbing and rolling distances L, R

and the rolling distance that were experimentally obtained by combinations of throwing parameters α, β are shown in Figs. 6 and 7, respectively.

2.2   Mecanum Wheeled Mobile Mechanism

The robot has an omnidirectional mobile mechanism by the mecanum wheels as shown in Fig. 8. The mecanum wheel is a special wheel in which barrel-shaped free rollers are mounted at an angle of 45° on the wheel circumference. By controlling the rotation of four motors, it is possible to move in all directions without changing the direction of the vehicle body in addition to the same movement as the conventional wheeled vehicle.

In the omnidirectional mobile mechanism using the mecanum wheel, there is no constraint in the direction of movement. Therefore, it is easy to finely adjust the position and orientation of the robot for throwing. The mobile mechanism makes it possible that the robot is transported even by a person with severe disabilities. Furthermore, it also allows the robot to act autonomously in the future.

3   Operational Interface of Boccia Robot

The operational interface has a role of mediator between the operator and the boccia robot. As shown in Fig. 2, the throwing mechanism, the mobile mechanism and the interface unit in the boccia robot each have micro-controllers (Arduino). The micro-controllers communicate sensor information and operational command via I²C. The controller of the operational interface acts as the

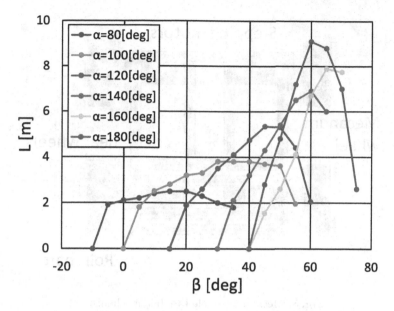

Fig. 6. Lobbing distance depending on α, β

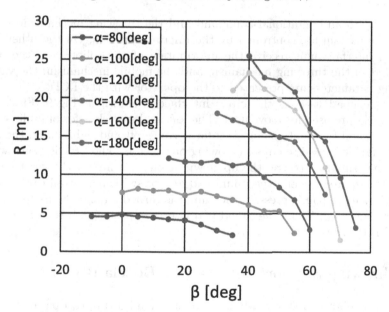

Fig. 7. Rolling distance depending on α, β

master and the others as the slaves. A gamepad (game controller) is implemented as an input interface and a liquid crystal display (LCD) as an output interface. When the operator operates the gamepad, the input to gamepad is

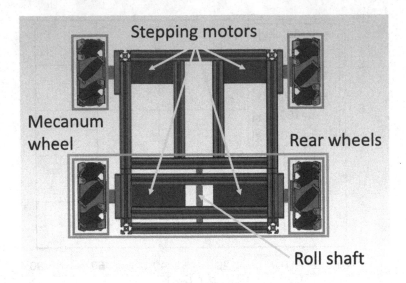

Fig. 8. Mecanum wheeled mobile mechanism

converted into an operational command and the throwing mechanism and the mobile mechanism are controlled by the micro-controllers. On the other hand, when an interface unit receive the information of the robot from the micro-controllers of the throwing mechanism and the mobile mechanism, the value of throwing parameters are presented to the operator with the LCD.

The gamepad used as the input interface is shown in Fig. 9. Firstly, the analog sticks are used for movement. The left analog stick is for omnidirectional movement, and the right analog stick for turning left and right. Next, the arrow pad on left side is used to adjust throwing parameters. The left/right arrow pads are for the arm angle α, and the up/down arrow pads are for the wrist angle β. Lastly, the square pad and the round pad are for switching on/off of the clutch. When the square pad is pressed, the clutch is turned on and the motor and the arm are connected. When the round pad is pressed, the clutch is turned off and the ball is thrown.

4   Throwing Support Interface of Boccia Robot

The boccia robot can throw a ball variously by adjusting two parameters, the arm initial angle α and the wrist angle β. However, it is difficult for the beginner to select the parameters and estimate the throwing trajectory. Therefore, we developed a throwing support system that presents what kind of throwing will be performed according to the set parameters. In this system, the lobbing and rolling distances are presented by projecting the laser pointers to the expected landing point of lob and the expected stopping point of roll based on the calculation from the parameters.

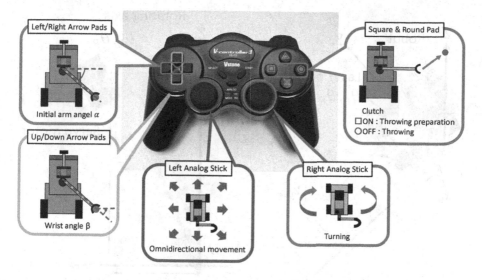

Fig. 9. Input interface of Boccia robot

The arrangement of the throwing support system is shown in Fig. 10. Here, the throwing direction of the ball is along with X-axis. The laser pointer is mounted on the robot at an angle φ as shown on the right side in Fig. 10. Therefore, by controlling the direction of the laser pointer with a servo motor, it is possible to project the laser pointer at an arbitrary point in the throwing direction on X-axis.

The procedure of presentation by laser pointers is described as below. Firstly, the micro-controller of the operational interface receives the values of α and β from the micro-controller of the throwing mechanism. Secondly, the lobbing distance L and the rolling distance R are calculated based on the data previously obtained from experiments. Then, the calculation of the following equations is performed assuming that the angles are $\theta_L = \theta_R = 0$ when the laser pointers point in the direction parallel to X-axis.

$$\theta_L = \arctan \frac{\sqrt{y_{0L}^2 + z_{0L}^2}}{L - x_{0L}} \tag{1}$$

$$\theta_R = \arctan \frac{\sqrt{y_{0R}^2 + z_{0R}^2}}{R - x_{0R}} \tag{2}$$

where, θ_L and θ_R are the angles of servo motors for laser pointers of lobbing and rolling distances, respectively. x_{0*}, y_{0*}, z_{0*} represent the offset position of the laser pointer and servo motor shown in Fig. 10.

Finally, the servo motors for lobbing and rolling distances are commanded to rotate to the calculated angles θ_L and θ_R, respectively, and present the estimated landing and stopping points to the operator by turning on the laser pointers.

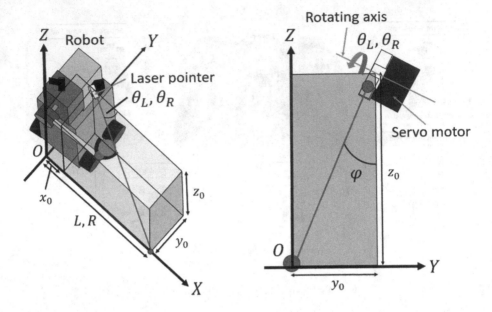

Fig. 10. Arrangement of laser pointers and servo motors

An appearance how the lasers are actually pointed is shown in Fig. 11. Here, the red point represents the lobbing distance, and the green point indicates the rolling distance. The user can intuitively imagine the ball thrown to the target position, because this throwing support interface directly presents throwing distances on the actual court. Also, this system can be used without calibration of coordinates on the court, because the laser pointers are mounted on the robot itself and the coordinates of the robot and laser pointers are fixed.

5 Field Experiments

We conducted the field experiments of the developed boccia robot in the boccia class which was held at Arakawa Campus, Tokyo Metropolitan University. A wide range of people, for example, from beginners to athletes belonging to a Boccia's club team and from young people to senior citizens, participated in this class.

Firstly, we played a game of 6 ends between 3 regular persons in the boccia class (red team) and the robot (blue team) operated by one of the authors as shown in Fig. 12. Three of the red team consist of two persons with disabled leg or foot, who throw balls by hand on their wheelchair, and one healthy person. As a result of the game, the robot team won by 4 red points and 6 blue points. Throughout the game, the robot was rather in the lead. However, there were also scenes where people were in the lead. From this experiment, it was confirmed that the developed boccia robot had sufficient performance to play boccia games because it could play with people who threw by hand in ordinary boccia games.

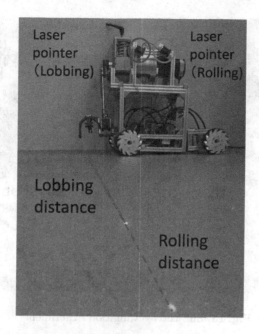

Fig. 11. Throwing support interface that presents lobbing and rolling distances

Fig. 12. Game between Boccia robot and people (Color figure online)

Next, we had people who came to the boccia class use the boccia robot as shown in Fig. 13. Also, we conducted a questionnaire survey. As a result of a questionnaire survey, all of people answered "It's fun to try", but nearly half

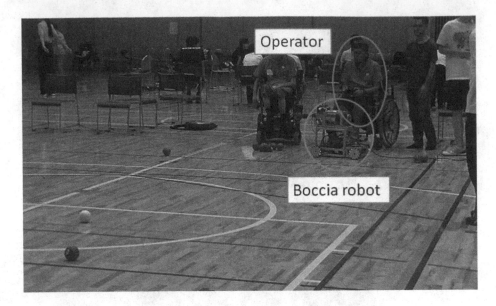

Fig. 13. Subjective evaluation experiments

of people answered "It's difficult to operate." One of the reasons that people answered "It's difficult to operate" is thought to hesitate to adjust the throwing parameters α and β. Although the throwing distance estimated by α and β was presented, the person who operates the robot for the first time did not know how the throwing distance changes by α and β. Based on the field experiments, it was found that an interface that made it easier for the beginners to operate the robot had to be developed.

6   Conclusions

In this study, we developed the boccia robot as a robotic throwing device to introduce in boccia games. In addition, we developed the throwing support system that presents the estimated throwing distance based on the combination of throwing parameters. By this throwing support system, the operator can intuitively imagine the ball thrown and adjust the throwing parameters. Then, it was confirmed by the field experiments that the boccia robot had sufficient performance to play boccia games, and that many people could enjoy it. However, it was found that there was still a problem in operability.

As future works, to make the boccia robot more widely available for people with disabilities we will implement various operational interfaces besides the gamepad. In addition, we will improve the throwing support system and aim to be a robot that users can operate more easily. And then, we will conduct evaluation experiments with various disabled people. In the evaluation experiments, we will improve usability of boccia robot by feedback of their opinions.

References

1. Boccia: Official website of the Paralympic Movement. https://www.paralympic. org/boccia
2. Boccia International Sports Federation (BISFed). http://www.bisfed.com/
3. Cybathlon Official Site. http://www.cybathlon.ethz.ch/
4. Cyber Boccia. https://www.1-10.com/robotics/works/cyber-boccia
5. Ribeiro, J.D., Faria, B.M., Paulo Moreira, A., Reis, L.P.: Realistic boccia game simulator adapted for people with disabilities or motor disorders: architecture and preliminary usability study. In: Rocha, Á., Correia, A.M., Adeli, H., Reis, L.P., Costanzo, S. (eds.) WorldCIST 2017. AISC, vol. 571, pp. 165–176. Springer, Cham (2017). https://doi.org/10.1007/978-3-319-56541-5_18
6. Kaufman, J., McGee, J., Scott, M., McCafferty, P., Dora, E.: Boccia Ball Ramp for Independent Use by Persons in Cerebral Palsy League, Summary report, Ohio University (2010)
7. Erickson, S., Haley, W., Vaughan, T.: Olympic Bocce Ballers, Summary report, California Polytechnic State University, San Luis Obispo (2011)
8. Deschamps, J., Hughes, M., Lynch, T.: Bocce Ball Launcher: An Adaptive Bocce Ball Device, Summary report, California Polytechnic State University, San Luis Obispo (2013)
9. Onishi, R., Kasamatsu, K., Shimomura, Y., Takesue, N.: Development of pitching mechanism in Boccia robot. In: Proceedings JSME Robomech 2018, 2P2-E12 (2018). (in Japanese)
10. Onishi, R., Suzuki, R., Kasamatsu, K., Shimomura, Y., Takesue, N.: Improvement of throwing mechanism in Boccia robot and verification of repeatability. In: Proceedings Annual Conference RSJ 2018, 2H2-04 (2018). (in Japanese)
11. Onishi, R., et al.: Development of pitching support system of Boccia robot and field experiment. In: Proceedings SICE SI 2018, 1D2-17, pp. 972–975 (2018). (in Japanese)

Nursing Care Support System for Caregiver and Older Adults

Madoka Takahara[✉], Kakiha Nakamura, Fanwei Huang, Ivan Tanev, and Katsunori Shimohara

Doshisha University, Kyoto 610-0394, Japan
takahara2012@sil.doshisha.ac.jp

Abstract. In a so-called super aging society such as Japan, a serious problem faced is that of achieving effective and high-quality care support for older adults. This study focusses on the psychological aspect and sleep problems related to this issue. We propose a system for decreasing the burden of care on caregivers. Specifically, we aim to actualize a system that periodically checks the sleeping situation of older adults, gives suggestions or advice when they have difficulty sleeping, and controls the room environment, such as illumination and air conditioning. Thus, this study addresses the following three research issues: A. Learning mechanism of an individual's sleep state, B. Conversation control to enable a care recipient to undertake behavior modifications leading to improvement in sleep, C. Information-sharing mechanism to foster mutual understanding and acceptance between the care recipient, caregiver, and related people. This paper presents our research concept, scheme, and approach, as well as a discussion of their significance based on results of field experiments. Especially, in this paper, we mention about Conversation control system.

Keywords: Nursing care · Sleep · Older adults · Information sharing · Mutual awareness · Mutual understanding

1 Introduction

Given the rapid progression into a super-aging society in Japan, one of the typical problems in a 24-h society is nursing care for older adults during the night. Specifically, caregivers suffer from the burden of providing long-term care because older adults need periodic care for the night. They have to monitor and check older adults' sleeping situation periodically, give suggestions or advice when older adults have difficulty sleeping, and control the room environment, such as illumination and air conditioning. Consequently, caregivers themselves experience sleep problems, which may negatively affect their attitude to older adults. Such a situation seems to drive a vicious circle, and it is obviously worse for both caregivers and care recipient.

A lot of caregivers are middle aged, and they often have to quit their job to care for older adults, as providing care and working are hardly compatible. According to an employment status survey in 2017, about 100,000 workers annually leave their jobs, most of whom are aged 55–59 years. Half of them want to keep working even while

S. Yamamoto and H. Mori (Eds.): HCII 2019, LNCS 11570, pp. 568–577, 2019.
https://doi.org/10.1007/978-3-030-22649-7_46

being caregivers. However, in the present situation, it is difficult for them to provide care for older adults and invest in their regular work [1].

The population of older adults is estimated to keep increasing more and more in the future. Achieving effective and high-quality care support for older adults while reducing the burden for caregivers are pressing concerns in Japan. Special care is due not only for care recipients but also for caregivers; the care stress and irregular daily rhythm experienced by caregivers drain them physically and mentally. Sleep problems among care recipients and caregivers are clearly serious. Caregivers cannot sleep well, because they have to care for older adults all day. Sleep deprivation increases risk of depression, dementia, lifestyle-related diseases, and obesity. In other words, the lack of sleep can cause diseases in many people. Thus, caregivers are at risk of contracting diseases and be new care receivers themselves. Accordingly, the care problem in Japan can be expected to become serious in the future. However, studies on sleep care support system has not emphasized the needs of both care recipients and caregivers in home care.

In this research, we propose a caregiver support system for nursing care of older adults. This system supports the sleep not only care recipients but also caregivers.

2 Caregiver Support System

To reduce caregivers' burden of the long-term care, we propose a caregiver system that automatically executes a caregiver's functionality. It aims not to replace caregivers but to support them by reducing the number of their periodic tasks. Caregivers have conversation skills, know-how, experience, and knowledge of nursing care, which has been cultivated over many years. The system should, therefore, achieve functionality by substituting caregivers' performance through data acquisition and learning mechanisms. Moreover, to foster reliable relationships, mutual understanding, and acceptance among older adults, their family members, and caregivers, it is indispensable for the system to provide them with an information-sharing mechanism on the care recipient's sleep data. Thus, the goal of this research is to improve and resolve the serious sleep problems of both caregivers and older adults.

Figure 1 shows the system configuration of the proposed system. It is composed of a mattress sensor to measure a person's biometric data related to their sleep state, Google Home to that provides suggestions and/or advice, Nature Remo to control home appliances linked with Google Home, and a PC to control these devices and execute the system's functionality.

For the first step of the research, we develop and compare with the deference of effect to the participants in physically and mentally between synthesized voice and human voice of a person who is the participant's relative through Google home.

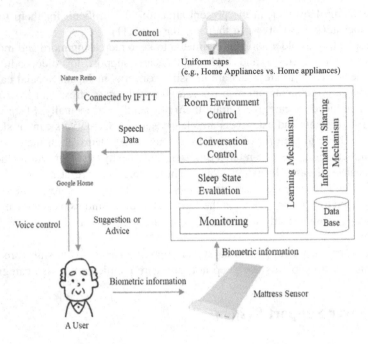

Fig. 1. System configuration.

3 Related Works

Japan is ranked tenth in the world in the number of people suffering from mental diseases. It is also ranked first in number of beds in mental hospitals. The percentage of people who have sleep disorders in worldwide ranges from 9% to 15%; that in Japan is 20%. At present, the economic loss attributed to sleep loan is JPY 35trillion/year in Japan. Further, sleep loan causes depression, obesity, dementia, and other disorders. On average, it takes three weeks (12 h/day) for people to return the sleep loan [1].

Sleep disorders increase the risk of lifestyle-related diseases and depression. This problem has been observed in Japan owing to changes in lifestyle. Meanwhile, the quality and duration of sleep vary greatly with age and are determined by numerous other factors. Previous studies have shown that sleep disorders commonly occur in older adults.

Nishino and his team emphasized how humans spend a significant part of our lives sleeping, which is essential for our physical and psychological well-being. However, sleep can be easily impaired by psychological and physical disorders [2, 3]. Shimamo to and his team suggested that a decline in the quality and total duration of sleep decreases physical activity levels and increases daytime sleepiness as well as the risk of lifestyle-related diseases and depression [4].

Takadama and his team focused on this problem and proposed a concierge-based care support system to provide a comfortable and healthy life for older adults. The system estimated a user's daily sleep stage and stores such personal data as big data, thereby enabling care workers and doctors to design personal care plans for specific users more effectively [5–7].

Takahara et al. proposed an indirect biofeedback mechanism that helps patients keep track of their sleep quality and condition by monitoring a device that displays a virtual plant. They also proposed a mechanism through which the patient, family members, and medical staff can share indirect biofeedback information. An experiment was conducted in a senior care home using five elderly people and two healthy people as subjects, with family members and medical staff participating in the experiment. The experiment attempted to clarify the usefulness of indirect biofeedback in the improvement of a patient's sleep. They also aimed to confirm that patients, their family members, and medical staff could deepen their mutual understanding and mutual acceptance by sharing indirect biofeedback information. Consequently, they may be able to judge whether indirect biofeedback through the virtual plant is useful for improving patients' sleep condition [8].

4 Proposed Method

To develop the proposed system, we addressed the following research issues:

A. Learning mechanism of an individual's sleep state
B. Conversation control to enable a care recipient to undertake behavior modifications leading to sleep improvement
C. Information-sharing mechanism to foster mutual understanding and acceptance between the care recipient, caregivers, and related people

4.1 Learning Mechanism of Sleep State

The proposed system can acquire a care recipient's sleep data, including "sleep score," "heart rate," "body motion," "sleep time," and "nocturnal awakening," through a sleep mattress sensor developed by TANITA. In this study, we incorporate a learning mechanism to extract the regularity of sleep quality from the relationship between the care recipient's physical condition/age/disability/daily activity and the above sleep data using genetic programming (GP).

GP is a systematic method for prompting computers to automatically solve a problem. GP starts from a high-level statement of what needs to be done and creates a computer program to solve the problem without requiring the user to know, specify, or structure the solution in advance [9].

In this research, the characteristics of sleep are notably expressed in an introductory sleep phase for 90 min. We focus on and adopted the introductory sleep phase as an indication of sleep quality evaluation.

4.2 Conversation Control enabling Behavior Modifications Leading to Sleep Improvement

Figure 2 shows the proposed system.

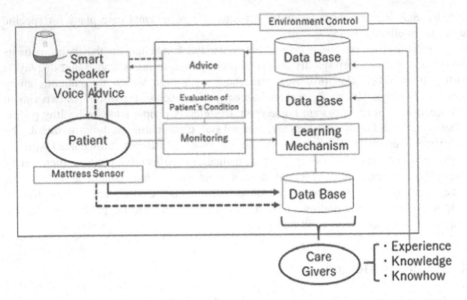

Fig. 2. Structure of the proposed system.

In this research, we aim to solve issues in generating suggestions and/or advice based on the evaluation of a care recipient's sleep state, controlling the conversation with a care recipient in the proposed system, and controlling the room environment, such as illumination and air conditioning. Moreover, utilizing a bedside Google Home is important given that older adults mainly use voice communication.

Based on veteran caregivers' conversation skills and experiences, several basic pieces of advice on such topics as optimal wake-up time, bedtime, and bath time, as well as typical conversation templates, are preset. The lights in the bedroom are controlled depending on the optimal waking and sleep time.

- **Tools in this research**

In this research, we use the following tools for nursing care of older adults.

- Nature Remo

Nature Remo is a smart remote controller that can control every home electronic appliance though Wi-Fi. This can be accessed by Google Home or a mobile phone.

- Google Home

Google Home is a smart speaker. Nature Remo can control every home electronic appliance by voice via Google Home. In the experiment, when the participant asks Google Home about his/her sleep information, Google Home provides feedback of the previous day's sleep information, suggests their ideal wake-up time/bed time, and turns on/off the lights automatically.

- TANITA SL-511

TANITA SL-511 is a sleep mattress sensor that has built-in high-precision body motion detection sensor. It detects the user's body motion, breathing, and heartbeat from under the bed in real time. The system sends the data to a server.

We employ Sleep Score, which is calculated by TANITA algorithm based on data from the mattress sensor. We also develop a learning mechanism based on Sleep Score and other data; feedback of the data is provided as information sharing to care recipients and their supporters via a web application.

4.3 Information-Sharing Mechanism

Information sharing between people is useful for mutual awareness in general, as shown in Fig. 3.

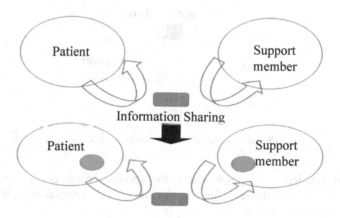

Fig. 3. Visualization of mutual awareness.

For example, a patient's friend comes to see the patient; a staff member learns of this fact; and the patient also knows that the staff member is aware of the fact. Mutual awareness denotes that parties know that they share given information with one another.

However, sometimes medical staff might be in strong position, whereas patients might be in a weak one, in the sense that the patient depends on the medical care given by the staff. Meanwhile, the patient pays for the medical care and services given by the staff. Information that should be shared by others, such as medical staff and family members, is the patient's personal information.

Information sharing between the patient and medical staff should be carefully designed considering the points mentioned above. It might be quite significant for a patient to be aware of being understood and accepted by others through information sharing [8]. Meanwhile, a patient's extremely personal information that cannot be usually seen and known by others may need to be protected. In general, the patient does not want others to know his/her extremely personal information. In addition, direct numerical feedback, displayed as drastic numerical changes, might be perceived as unfamiliar data and give users a negative feeling.

As such, we consider the significance of indirect representation, that is, indirect biofeedback. Information represent as indirect biofeedback and shared by others is the patient's personal information, but it is not too specific or too comprehensive, enabling acceptability on the part of the patient that the personal information is seen and known by others.

Figure 4 shows the model of mutual acceptance that we aimed to create between care recipients and others.

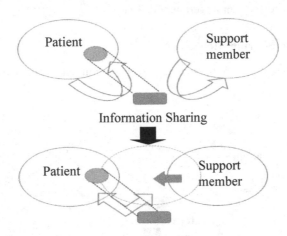

Fig. 4. Visualization of mutual acceptance.

Once the personal information that is too specific or too comprehensive to the patient could be shared, the resulting situation should be expected to be beyond mere mutual awareness, i.e., mutual acceptance [8].

Figure 5 shows a model of information sharing to foster mutual understanding and acceptance not only between care recipients and caregivers but also between them and related people, such as the recipient's family. They can monitor the change in the care recipient's sleep state and then confirm sleep improvement.

The sleep quality of a care recipient is deeply related to his/her relationship with the caregiver. To improve a care recipient's sleep quality, it is necessary for a care recipient and a caregiver to improve their relationship. Thus, in this research, we facilitate the sharing of information of both care recipient and caregiver using a web application. The system shares their information to foster mutual understanding and acceptance.

5   System Structure

The Table 1 shows the contents of speech through Google home.

The contents of synthesized voice speeches are changed from person's speeches a bit with asterisks because of a feeling of strangeness with the speeches by synthesized voice. Fig. 6 shows the system image of this experiment.

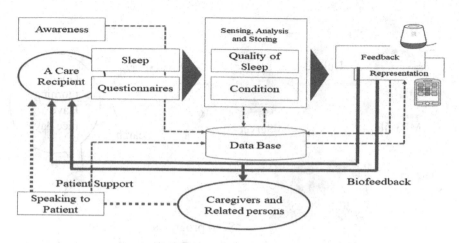

Fig. 5. Visualization of information sharing

Table 1. The contents of speech.

		8:00	10:00	22:00
1 day	Human	Morning! You finished streches?	Good mornig!	How was your day? Good night.
	Synthesized	* Good mornig. Did you finish streches?		
2 day	Human	Good mornig. Umi(dog) is waiting for you	Good morning. It is cold, right? You should wear warm clothes.	Please relax. Good night.
	Synthesized			
3 day	Human	Good morning. Have a nice day!	Good morning! Willyou go to somewhere today?	Please take a rest. Good night.
	Synthesized		* Good morning. Would you go to somewhere today?	
4 day	Human	Good mornig. Today is cold.	Good morning. You should get sunshine.	Would you remember the today's good things! Good night.
	Synthesized			
5 day	Human	Good morning. Good luck with your job.	Mornig. You could sleep well?	Please do not catch a cold. Good night.
	Synthesized		* Good morning. Did you get a good night's rest?	

The PC and Google home are connected via the same Wi-Fi. We construct a server and upload the MP3 files of both synthesized and person's voices.

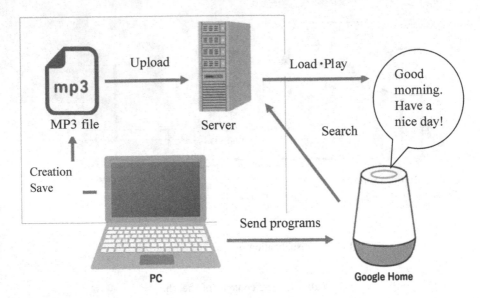

Fig. 6. The system image.

6   Experiment

In order to investigate what and how influence two types of voices through Google home result in to the participant's sleep quality, heart rate and mental situation, we conduct an experiment with 2 participants (1 male, 1 female) in 10 days, each experiment is 5 days after the pre-experiment about one month.

- The participants
  - Female (69 years old), male (72 years old)
  - They are a married couple and they are living in their home.
- Experimental terms
  - 10 days (Synthesized voice experiment: 5days, person'svoice: 5days)
  - The both first days of the experiments are same day of the week.
  - First week: The speeches by synthesized voice,
  - Second week: The speeches by person's voice
- The rules
  The system plays the voice through Google home 3 times a day in their home (mainly at their living room). The contents of the voice are different very day every time.
- Evaluations
  - Subjective evaluation
    Questionnaires before and after the experiments

- Objective evaluation
  Sleep qualities and Heart rates of the participants

7 Conclusion

We have proposed a caregiver support system for nursing care of older adults to decrease the burden of caring for caregivers. This system helps care recipients in the following two aspects. First, the system periodically checks the care recipient's sleeping situation, gives suggestions or advice when they have difficulty sleeping, and controls the room environment, including illumination and air conditioning. Second, the system helps both care recipients and caregivers to be aware of their sleep quality and condition, by monitoring a device that is displayed on a web application. Thus, they can deepen mutual acceptance and understanding.

In future work, we will develop the proposed system. Specifically, the development will focus on the following three research issues: A. Learning mechanism of an individual's sleep state, B. Conversation control to enable a care recipient to undertake behavior modifications leading to sleep improvement, and C. Information-sharing mechanism to foster mutual understanding and acceptance between care recipients, caregivers, and related people.

Further, we will conduct preliminary experiments at a normal home. Afterward, we will perform field experiments with older adults in their own home, with their permission.

Acknowledgement. This study was supported by JSPS KAKENHI Grant Number 18H05725. Moreover, we would like to thank all of the members who supported me during this study. We would especially like to express my sincere gratitude to Orylab Inc., who not only imparted the professional knowledge necessary for this research but also provided full assistance.

References

1. Nishino, S.: The Stanford Method for Ultimate Sound Sleep. Sunmark Publishing (2017)
2. Nishino, S., Taheri, S., Black, J., Nofzinger, E.: The Neurology of Sleep in Relation to Mental Illness, Neurobiology of Mental Illness, pp. 1160–1179. Oxford University Press, New York (2004)
3. Mignot, E., Taheri, S., Nishino, S.: Sleeping with hypothalamus, emerging therapeutic targets for sleep disorders. Nat. Neurosci. **5**, 1071–1075 (2004)
4. Shimamoto, H., Shibata, M.: The relationship between physical activity and sleep: a literature review. Cent. Educ. Lib. Arts Sci. **2**, 75–82 (2014)
5. Takadama, K.: Concierge-based care support system for designing your own lifestyle. In: AAAI Spring Symposium, pp. 69–74 (2014)
6. Harada, T., et al.: Real-time sleep stage estimation from biological data with trigonometric function regression model. In: AAAI Spring Symposium Series, pp. 348–353 (2016)
7. Takadama, K., Tajima, Y.: Sleep monitoring agent for care support and its perspective. IEICE ESS Fundam. Rev. **8**(2), 96–101 (2014)
8. Takahara, M., Huang, F., Tanev, I., Shimohara, K.: Sharing indirect biofeedback information for mutual acceptance. In: Yamamoto, S. (ed.) HIMI 2017. LNCS, vol. 10273, pp. 617–630. Springer, Cham (2017). https://doi.org/10.1007/978-3-319-58521-5_49
9. Huang, F., Takahara, M., Tanev, I., Shimohara, K.: Emergence of collective escaping strategies of various sized teams of empathic caribou agents in the wolf-caribou predator-prey problem. IEEJ Trans. Electron. Inf. Syst. **138**(5), 619–626 (2017)

Author Index

Printed in the United States
By Bookmasters